Joseph Agar Beet

A Commentary on St. Paul's Epistles

to the Ephesians, Philippians, Colossians, and to Philemon

Joseph Agar Beet

A Commentary on St. Paul's Epistles
to the Ephesians, Philippians, Colossians, and to Philemon

ISBN/EAN: 9783337381356

Printed in Europe, USA, Canada, Australia, Japan

Cover: Foto ©Lupo / pixelio.de

More available books at **www.hansebooks.com**

A COMMENTARY

ON

ST. PAUL'S EPISTLES

TO THE

EPHESIANS, PHILIPPIANS, COLOSSIANS,

AND TO PHILEMON.

BY

JOSEPH AGAR BEET.

London:

HODDER AND STOUGHTON,

27, PATERNOSTER ROW.

MDCCCXC.

Printed by Hazell, Watson, & Viney, Ld., London and Aylesbury.

PREFACE.

IN the present volume I have expounded the third group of St. Paul's Epistles, those written during his first imprisonment at Rome. It is well that the four Epistles are expounded in one volume. For they are most closely related in thought and expression, and unitedly present a very definite phase of St. Paul's thought; a marked development of the thought embodied in the great group already annotated. This rich development can be appreciated only by consecutive study of the whole group.

The distinctive features of my earlier volumes dominate this new work. As before, my aim has been not merely to reproduce the sense which the Apostle designed his words to convey, but also to use his letters as a means of reproducing his conception of the Gospel and of Christ, in order thus to reach the actual teaching of Christ and those unseen realities which He came to reveal to men. Consequently, as before, my exposition of the Epistles of Paul is a specific contribution to Systematic Theology. And, since these Epistles contain important evidence of the truth of the doctrines so firmly believed by the Apostle, my exposition of them is also a contribution to the Evidences of Christianity. This accounts for my long and full discussion of the authorship of the Epistles now annotated; and for the frequent indication, throughout the exposition, of words and phrases revealing the hand of Paul. For my method of research required me to prove that the doctrines set forth in these Epistles were actually taught by St. Paul. And it accounts also for the somewhat polemic form of the closing Dissertations in which I have embodied the chief results of our study.

For two classes of readers I have written expressly, for students of the Greek Testament and for intelligent readers of the English Bible. The former will find a careful grammatical exposition of the Greek text of the Epistles; and will catch the reason for many English renderings which to others will seem harsh or even ungrammatical. They will notice that at every point, both in my translation and in my frequent paraphrases and summaries of the language of St. Paul, I have endeavoured to reproduce the exact meaning and emphasis of the Greek words written by him. This frequent and careful reproduction of his meaning will also be of use to many who are unable to verify it by comparison with the original, but who wish to grasp, through the medium of their own language, as accurately and fully as possible the thoughts of the great Apostle.

My chief helpers have been, as before, Meyer and Hofmann among Germans, and Ellicott and Lightfoot among English commentators. To these I may add the very full and able commentary on the Epistle to the Colossians by Kloepper, and a most accurate and acute exposition of the same Epistle, in *The Pulpit Commentary*, by Findlay. So good is this last work that, but for the difference of aim noted above, it would have been needless for me to attempt another exposition. Dr. Maclaren's volume on the same Epistle in *The Expositor's Bible* is most excellent. But as a popular exposition for general readers, rather than for students, its aim differs widely from that of my own work. Of another kind, but also good, are the contributions to *The Cambridge Bible for Schools* by Moule.

On the genuineness of the Epistles now annotated, I am glad to refer to the very able and attractive *Introduction to the New Testament* by Dr. Salmon.

PREFACE.

On the Christian Ministry, about which I have said something in my Dissertation on "Paul's Conception of the Church," I must express my great obligation to the very able Dissertation in Lightfoot's *Philippians*. Although published twenty-two years ago, it seems to me to be still the best work on this important subject. Also of great value are a recent volume on the same subject by Dean Lefroy, and Dr. Hatch's Bampton Lectures on *The Organization of the Early Churches*. I have also read with care Gore's *Ministry of the Christian Church;* but, for reasons given in my Dissertation, I am compelled to reject the most conspicuous conclusions of the author.

To all Christian readers I commend most earnestly a careful study of these profound Epistles. A commentary is but a guide-post pointing to something far better than itself, or at best a companion leading others along a path the writer has himself trodden. That path each one must tread for himself, if he is to gather the flowers which adorn it and to find the hidden treasures to which it leads. These treasures are beyond the price of rubies. And they are within reach of every one who, guided by the Spirit of the Truth, walks in the steps of the Great Teacher.

WESLEYAN COLLEGE, RICHMOND,
27th September, 1890.

CONTENTS.

INTRODUCTION—

Sec. i. RETROSPECT AND PROSPECT.
,, ii. ARE THE EPISTLES GENUINE?
,, iii. TO WHAT EXTENT ARE OUR COPIES AND VERSIONS CORRECT?
,, iv. PHILIPPI, EPHESUS, COLOSSE, AND THE CHURCHES THERE.
,, v. TIME AND PLACE OF WRITING, AND THE OCCASION, OF THE EPISTLES.

EXPOSITION OF THE EPISTLE TO THE PHILIPPIANS—

Sec. 1. Ch. I. 1, 2. A Christian Greeting.
,, 2. Ch. I. 3—11. Praise and Prayer for the Christians at Philippi.
,, 3. Ch. I. 12—18. Paul's bonds, adversaries, and friends.
,, 4. Ch. I. 19—26. Paul's confident hope, in view of life and death.
,, 5. Ch. I. 27—II. 18. Sundry exhortations, supported by the example of Christ.
,, 6. Ch. II. 19—24. About Timothy.
,, 7. Ch. II. 25—30. About Epaphroditus.
,, 8. Ch. III. 1—16. Warnings against bad men; and Paul's contrary example.
,, 9. Ch. III. 17—IV. 1. Worldly-minded church-members, with whom is contrasted the Christian's hope.
,, 10. Ch. IV. 2, 3. About Euodia and Syntyché.
,, 11. Ch. IV. 4—9. Sundry Exhortations.
,, 12. Ch. IV. 10—23. Philippian Liberality. Farewell.
[REVIEW OF THE EPISTLE.]

EXPOSITION OF THE EPISTLE TO THE COLOSSIANS—

Sec. 1. Ch. I. 1, 2. Apostolic Greeting.

DIV. I. PRAISE AND PRAYER. CH. I. 3—14.

Sec. 2. Ch. I. 3—8. Paul thanks God for his readers' faith.
,, 3. Ch. I. 9—14. Paul's prayer for their further development.

DIV. II. THE TRUTH CONCERNING CHRIST. CHS. I. 15—II.

Sec. 4. Ch. I. 15—17. Christ's relation to God, and to the Universe.
,, 5. Ch. I. 18—20. His relation to the Church and to the work of salvation.
,, 6. Ch. I. 21—23. The Colossian Christians in their relation to Christ.
,, 7. Ch. I. 24—II. 3. Paul's relation to the Church, and to the Christians at Colossæ.

DIV. III. WARNING AGAINST ERRORS. CHS. II. 4—III. 4.

Sec. 8. Ch. II. 4—7. Do not forsake the teaching already received.
,, 9. Ch. II. 8—15. Warning against error in the guise of Philosophy and Judaism.
,, 10. Ch. II. 16—III. 4. Warning against various dogmas, Jewish or Gentile, contrary to Christ.

DIV. IV. PRACTICAL APPLICATION. CHS. III. 5—IV. 6.

Sec. 11. Ch. III. 5—11. General Moral Teaching : Negative.
,, 12. Ch. III. 12—17. General Moral Teaching : Positive.
,, 13. Ch. III. 18—IV. 1. Directions to specific classes of persons.
,, 14. Ch. IV. 2—6. Sundry General Directions.

DIV. V. PERSONAL MATTERS. CH. IV. 7—18.

Sec. 15. Ch. IV. 7—9. Tychicus and Onesimus.
,, 16. Ch. IV. 10—18. Sundry Greetings.
   [THE ERRORS AT COLOSSÆ.] [THE GNOSTICS.]
      [REVIEW OF THE EPISTLE.]

EXPOSITION OF THE EPISTLE TO PHILEMON—

Sec. 1. Vv. 1—3. Paul's greeting to Philemon.
,, 2. Vv. 4—7. Paul's joy at Philemon's Christian love.
,, 3. Vv. 8—21. The Request about Onesimus.
,, 4. Vv. 22—25. Conclusion.
      [CHRISTIANITY AND SLAVERY.]

EXPOSITION OF THE EPISTLE TO THE EPHESIANS

Sec. 1. Ch. I. 1, 2. The Greeting.

CONTENTS. xi

DIV. I. DOCTRINE. CHS. I. 3—III.

Sec. 2. Ch. I. 3—14. Praise for God's eternal purpose of mercy to Jews and Gentiles.
,, 3. Ch. I. 15—23. Prayer that the readers may recognise in themselves the great power which raised Christ from the dead.
,, 4. Ch. II. 1—3. Paul and his readers were once dead by reason of their sins.
,, 5. Ch. II. 4—10. But God has made them sharers of the resurrection life of Christ.
,, 6. Ch. II. 11—22. Through Christ both Jews and Gentiles have been brought near to God.
,, 7. Ch. III. 1—13. The Gospel of peace between Jews and Gentiles has been committed to Paul.
,, 8. Ch. III. 14—21. Paul prays that his readers may know Christ and thus attain the consummation designed by God.

DIV. II. MORAL TEACHING. CHS. IV.—VI.

Sec. 9. Ch. IV. 1—16. Unity and Growth of the Church.
,, 10. Ch. IV. 17—24. A total change of life needed.
,, 11. Ch. IV. 25—V. 21. Sundry Precepts.
,, 12. Ch. V. 22—33. Directions to Wives and Husbands;
,, 13. Ch. VI. 1—4. To Children and Parents;
,, 14. Ch. VI. 5—9. To Servants and Masters.
,, 15. Ch. VI. 10—17. The Christian Warfare.
,, 16. Ch. VI. 18—20. A request for prayer.
,, 17. Ch. VI. 21—24. About Tychicus. Farewell.
[REVIEW OF THE EPISTLE.]

DISSERTATIONS—
Diss. i. THESE EPISTLES COMPARED WITH THOSE TO THE ROMANS, CORINTHIANS, AND GALATIANS.
,, ii. PAUL'S CONCEPTION OF THE CHURCH.
,, iii. PAUL'S CONCEPTION OF CHRIST.
,, iv. THE GOSPEL OF PAUL.

TO THE READER.

v. 10*a*, *v.* 10*b*, denote the former, and latter, parts of verse 10.
v. 10f, *v.* 10ff,   ,,   verses 10, 11 ; and verses 10, 11, 12, etc.
O.T. and N.T.   ,,   the Old and New Testaments.
AV. and RV.   ,,   the Authorized, and Revised, English Versions.
LXX. denotes the Septuagint Greek Translation of the Old Testament.
See my *Romans* page xx.
Put-to-shame represents one Greek word.
[Square brackets] enclose references to the Greek Text.
In the Exposition *italic type* is used only for my literal translation of the words of the verse under exposition; and, in the Dissertations, for quotations from the Epistles now annotated. Other quotations from Scripture, and paraphrases, are enclosed in 'single commas.'

INTRODUCTION.

SECTION I.

RETROSPECT AND PROSPECT.

IN former volumes I have endeavoured to expound the Epistles to the Romans, Corinthians, and Galatians. These Epistles we found accepted in the second century throughout the Christian Church without a shadow of doubt as written by the Apostle Paul. And the strong presumption of genuineness thus afforded was raised to absolute certainty by our examination of the contents of the Epistles; especially by comparison, one with another and with the statements of the Book of Acts, of various casual references to matters of fact, and by the harmonious and life-like portrait of the mental and moral character of the writer which we found depicted in clearest lines on the pages of each Epistle. We found that the four Epistles were written within a year, amid the activities and anxieties of Paul's Third Missionary Journey. His movements during that year, we were able, in the light of these Epistles and of the Book of Acts, to trace with considerable accuracy.

At various points in our course we tried to reproduce, in a fragmentary way, Paul's conception of the Gospel he preached and of Christ. This reproduced conception we compared here and there with other writings of the New Testament. Our comparison assured us that the doctrines so firmly held by Paul, or doctrines equivalent, were actually taught by Christ, and that Christ actually claimed the supreme dignity reflected so clearly in the entire teaching and thought of Paul. And the confident belief by Paul and others that Christ rose from the dead, taken in connection with its effect upon the entire subsequent history of mankind and with the fitness of the Gospel to supply our own spiritual need, convinced us of the truth of that which the Apostles so firmly believed, and assured us that Jesus of Nazareth actually rose from the dead and that He is in very truth the Uncreated Son of God.

2. These results we shall in the present volume assume, and make the basis of further theological research. Four other Epistles, each claiming to have been written by Paul, now demand attention. Unfortunately, we have not for them the clear historic light which illumined the circumstances, and enabled us to fix approximately the date, of the Epistles already annotated. And the contents of some of them have, rightly or wrongly, given rise in some minds to doubts about their authorship. The evidence of their genuineness, we shall therefore carefully sift.

If, as I hope to prove, we have good grounds for accepting with confidence these Epistles as from the pen which wrote those already expounded, our study of them will greatly enlarge our view of Paul's conception of the Gospel and of Christ. Thoughts found only in germ in the earlier Epistles, we shall now find fully developed: and we shall find other thoughts not even suggested before, but when once suggested seen to be logically deduced from, or in harmony with, Paul's earlier teaching. We shall thus be able to trace development in the thought of the Apostle. In the earlier Epistles we felt the earnestness of conflict: we shall now find the serene calm of victory. We shall find also the fulness of mature thought. Captivity of body has set the prisoner's spirit free for loftier flights than were possible amid the activities of apostolic toil. The narrow limits of prison walls opened to him a vision farther reaching and more glorious than any he had seen while hasting over sea and land to proclaim the good news of salvation. This profounder teaching will greatly strengthen our hold of the fundamental truths already learnt, will quicken and delight our intelligence, and will raise us, amid the tumult and anxiety of earth, ourselves to share the calm which filled the breast of the imprisoned Apostle.

SECTION II.

ARE THE EPISTLES GENUINE?

1. That each of the Epistles before us was accepted without a shadow of doubt throughout the Christian Church in the latter part of the second century as a genuine work of the Apostle Paul, is

proved by frequent quotations in the extant works of Tertullian, Clement of Alexandria, and Irenæus.

2. So TERTULLIAN, *Prescriptions against Heretics* ch. 36: "the apostolic Churches ... in which their authentic letters are read, uttering the voice and representing the face of each one. Is Achaia near to thee? Thou hast Corinth. If thou art not far from Macedonia, thou hast Philippi, thou hast Thessalonica. If thou art able to go to Asia, thou hast Ephesus. But if thou art near to Italy, thou hast Rome." Here are omitted only Galatia and Colossæ, places far inland and therefore less accessible than those mentioned. Similarly *On the Resurrection of the Flesh* ch. 23: "The Apostle teaches, writing to the Colossians, that *we were once dead, aliens, and enemies of the mind of the Lord, when we were engaged in the worst works;* then, *buried with Christ in Baptism, and risen together in Him through faith of the energy of God who raised Him from the dead. And you, when ye were dead in sins and uncircumcision of your flesh, He hath made alive with Him, all sins being forgiven to you.* And again, *If with Christ ye are dead from the elements of the world, how indeed as if living in the world do ye submit to* another's *judgment?* ... Then, *If ye have risen,* says he, *with Christ, seek those things which are above where Christ is, sitting at the right hand of God. Think about the things which are above, not those which are below.* ... He adds also, *For ye are dead,* i.e. to sins, not to yourselves, *and your life is hidden with Christ in God.* ... When he writes to the Philippians, *If in any way,* he says, *I may attain to the resurrection from the dead: not that already I have obtained or am made perfect. ... But I follow after if I may lay hold of that in which I am laid hold of by Christ.* More fully, *Brethren, I do not reckon myself to have laid hold. But one thing* I do, *forgetting things behind, reaching after things before, I follow after the goal for the prize of blamelessness for which I run.* So *Against Marcion* bk. v. 17 he speaks of "that Epistle sent to the Ephesians, not to the Laodiceans: but Marcion was eager to give it a false title, as though he were a very diligent student of it. But the title is of no importance, since the Apostle wrote as much to all men as to some." He then quotes in chs. 17, 18 a great part of the Epistle, noting here and there Marcion's mutilations. "*Remembering that ye formerly were Gentiles in flesh. Ye were called uncircumcision by that which is called circumcision in the flesh made by hand, that ye were at that time without Christ, alienated from intercourse with Israel, strangers to their covenants and promise, having no hope and without God in the world. ... But now,* says he, *in Christ, ye who were far off, have been made*

near in His blood. . . . How does he prove that women ought to be subject to their husbands? Because *man*, says he, *is head of woman . . . as also Christ is head of the Church*. Similarly also when he says: *He loves his own flesh who loves his wife, as also Christ loves the Church. . . . No one*, says he, *hates his own flesh*, unless indeed Marcion alone, *but nourishes and cherishes it, as also Christ the Church.*" In chs. 19, 20, Tertullian quotes at length the Epistles to the Colossians and Philippians as written by "the Apostle;" and says in ch. 21 that through its shortness the Epistle to Philemon alone escaped mutilation by Marcion.

3. CLEMENT of ALEXANDRIA in the *Pædagogue* bk. i. 6 (p. 311, ed. Migne) quotes almost word for word Ph. iii. 12—15 as written by Paul: and in *Miscellanies* bk. iv. 13 (p. 1300) he quotes Ph. i. 29— ii. 2, i. 7, ii. 20, 21, as written to the Philippians by "the Apostle." So in bk. i. 1 (p. 705) he quotes Col. i. 28 as written by "the Apostle . . . in the Epistle to the Colossians;" and similarly Col. ii. 4, 6, 7, 8 in ch. 11, p. 748f. The Epistle to the Ephesians he quotes very frequently: e.g. *Pædagogue* bk. i. 5, p. 269: "Most clearly, writing to the Ephesians, he (the Apostle) revealed the matter sought for, saying in some such way as this;" quoting almost word for word Eph. iv. 13—15.

So IRENÆUS in bk. v. 13. 3: "And again to the Philippians he (the Apostle) says;" quoting Ph. i. 20, 21. Also in § 4: "the Apostle in the Epistle to the Philippians says;" quoting ch. iii. 10, 11. As contained "in the Epistle to the Colossians" he quotes in bk. iii. 14. 1, Col. iv. 14, and in bk. v. 14. 2, Col. i. 21, 22. In bk. v. 2. 3, of which fortunately we possess the original, Irenæus says, "as the blessed Paul says in the Epistle to the Ephesians, *Because members we are of the body, of His flesh and of His bones*, word for word from Eph. v. 30. Also in ch. xiv. 3: "as the Apostle says to the Ephesians, *In whom we have redemption through His blood, even remission of sins.* And again to the same persons, *Ye*, says he, *who once were far off, have been made near in the blood of Christ.* And again, *Making of no effect enmities, in His flesh, the law of precepts with decrees.* (Eph. i. 7, ii. 13, 15.) But also in every Epistle the Apostle testifies," etc.

The short Epistle to Philemon is not quoted by Clement of Alexandria or by Irenæus. But it is three times quoted word for word by ORIGEN as written by Paul to Philemon: *On Jeremiah*, Homily 19, p. 263; *Series of comments on Matthew*, § 66, p. 884, § 72, p. 889. JEROME in the Introduction to his commentary upon it defends the genuineness of the Epistle to Philemon against objections based on the unimportance of its matter.

4. In the letter sent in A.D. 177 from the Churches of Vienna and Lyons in Gaul and given at length by Eusebius, (*Church Hist.* bk. v. 2,) Phil. ii. 6 is quoted word for word. In the FRAGMENT OF MURATORI are enumerated among " the Epistles of Paul " those to the Ephesians, Philippians, Colossians, and Philemon. JUSTIN MARTYR, in ch. 85 of his *Dialogue with Trypho* and again in ch. 138, calls Christ *first-born of every creature;* referring evidently in each case to Col. i. 15. There is an apparent reference to the same in chs. 84, 100. In ch. 3 of the Epistle of POLYCARP to the Philippians, a work probably genuine, we read of " the wisdom of the blessed and glorious Paul, who when he came among you . . . also when absent wrote to you letters ; " or probably " a letter." In the same Epistle, ch. 1, we read *by grace ye are saved, not of works,* word for word from Eph. ii. 8.

5. The above quotations, with multitudes similar, are complete proof that each of the three longer Epistles was well known by Christians throughout the Roman Empire before the end of the second century, and was accepted without a shadow of doubt as a genuine work of Paul. The quotations from Tertullian prove that they were accepted as in the main genuine before the middle of the century by Marcion, an avowed enemy of the Gospel. Throughout the literature of the early Church, there is no trace of doubt about their authorship.

It is right to say that the so-called Epistle of Barnabas is several times quoted confidently by Clement of Alexandria (e.g. *Misc.* bk. ii. 6, p. 965 Migne, and ch. 20, p. 1060, and bk. v. 10, p. 95) as written by the companion of Paul ; and is quoted by Origen (*Against Celsus* bk. i. 63, *On First Principles* iii. 2. 4) as the Epistle of Barnabas. But it is not referred to by Irenæus : and, though apparently known to Tertullian, nothing is said by him about its authorship. It is reckoned as spurious by Eusebius (*Church History* bk. iii. 25) and by later writers. This case warns us not to accept, as decisive proof of authorship, the testimony of any one writer. The force of the above quotations lies in the unbroken and confident unanimity thus revealed in Churches widely separated.

This unanimous consent is at once a strong presumption of the genuineness of the Epistles before us. We ask whether it is confirmed or contradicted by their contents.

6. We consider first the Epistle to the PHILIPPIANS.

In Acts xxviii. 31 we leave Paul in prison at Rome, after an appeal to Cæsar ; and in Ph. i. 13 we find him in *bonds,* weighing the possibilities (*vv.* 20—23) of *life* and *death,* and sending (ch. iv. 22) greetings from members *of Cæsar's household.* In Ph. i. 1, as in 2 Cor. i. 1, *Timothy,* who was present with Paul (Acts xvii. 14, xviii. 5) at the founding of the Churches of Philippi and Corinth, is associated with him as joint author of the Epistle. The description of Timothy in Ph. ii. 19—22, and his hoped-for mission to Philippi, are in close agreement with 1 Cor. iv. 17. The gift of money from Philippi to Paul at Rome accords completely with the statement in 2 Cor. xi. 8, 9 that when he was in want at Corinth his needs were supplied by money sent from Macedonia, in which province was Philippi; and with the great liberality of another kind of which Paul boasts in 2 Cor. viii. 2. His deep anxiety about the Church at Corinth expressed in 2 Cor. ii. 13 and vii. 5 has its counterpart in the loving care for the Christians at Philippi which breathes in Ph. i. 7, 8, 27, ii. 19, iv. 1. Paul's reference in Ph. iii. 6 to his past life recalls Gal. i. 13. Amid a somewhat changed tone, easily explained by changed surroundings and prospects, the careful student will find innumerable coincidences in theological thought and expression revealing the mind and hand of Paul. Many of these will be noted in our exposition. As examples I may here quote the word *righteousness* as used in Ph. iii. 9 compared with Rom. x. 3, iii. 21, 22; *emptied himself* in Ph. ii. 7 compared with 2 Cor. viii. 9; *the cross of Christ* in Ph. iii. 18 and Gal. vi. 14; the term *children of God* in Ph. ii. 15 compared with Rom. viii. 16, 17, Gal. iii. 26, iv. 6, 7. In Ph. iii. 14 we have a metaphor from the Greek athletic contests, as in 1 Cor. ix. 24—27. In Ph. iii. 17 Paul points to himself as an example: a close coincidence with 1 Cor. xi. 1. Similarly, the boasting in Ph. iii. 5, 6 is in close agreement with 2 Cor. xi. 22—33.

This far-reaching coincidence of thought and expression will be the more significant if the Epistle before us be compared with those which do not bear the name of Paul. It is complete confirmation of the belief of the early Church. So convincing is this combined proof that almost all modern scholars, including many who like Renan and Pfleiderer reject the faith so firmly held by Paul, accept the Epistle to the Philippians as written by the great Apostle.

7. We turn now to the Epistle to the COLOSSIANS. And everywhere in it we meet with words, phrases, thought, and arrangement already familiar, and in great part peculiar to Paul. The greeting recalls at once Ph. i. 1, 2, 2 Cor. i. 1, 2. As in Romans and Galatians, we have first doctrine and argument, then moral teaching. As in Ph. i. 3—11, the letter before us begins with thanks to God for the readers' spiritual life, and passes on to prayer for their further progress. Notice the word *redemption* in Col. i. 14, Rom. iii. 24, 1 Cor. i 30; *reconciled* to God in Col. i. 20, 22, slightly modified from the word in Rom. v. 10, 2 Cor. v. 18—20; Christ the *Image of God* and *Firstborn*

in Col. i. 15 and in 2 Cor. iv. 4, Rom. viii. 29; the *mystery* once *hidden* but now *manifested*, in Col. i. 26, ii. 2, iv. 3 as in Rom. xvi. 25, 26, 1 Cor. ii. 7; *wealth* in a metaphorical sense in Col. i. 27, ii. 2, as in Rom. ii. 4, ix. 23, xi. 12, 33; *the rudiments of the world* in Col. ii. 8, Gal. iv. 3; *buried in Baptism* and *risen-with* Christ in Col. ii. 11, 12, Rom. vi. 4, 5; *puffed up* in Col. ii. 18, 1 Cor. iv. 6, 18, 19, v. 2, viii. 1, xiii. 4; death with Christ a reason for no longer living the old life, Col. ii. 20, Rom. vi. 2; lists of sins in Col. iii. 5, 8, as in Rom, i. 29—31, 1 Cor. vi. 9, 10, Gal. v. 19—21; *the old man* in Col. iii. 9 as in Rom. vi. 6; and everywhere the intensely Pauline phrases *in Christ* and *in the Lord*. Paul's earnest care and prayer in Col. ii. 1 for Christians he has never seen is in close agreement with Rom. i. 9—11; as is his request in Col. iv. 3 for his readers' prayers, with Rom. xv. 30, 31, 2 Cor. i. 11, Ph. i. 19. The metaphor, peculiar to Paul, of the Church as *the body* of Christ, found already in 1 Cor. xii. 12—27, Rom. xii. 4, 5, meets us in Col. i. 18, 24, ii. 19, with a new development viz. Christ the *Head*. The admonition to women in Col. iii. 18 is in close harmony with 1 Cor. xi. 3; as is Col. iii. 15 with Ph. iv. 7. In Col. iv. 7 *Tychicus* is said to *have* been *sent* to Colossae: in Acts xx. 4 he is a companion of Paul in travel, and is called a native of the province of Asia in which Colossae was situated. That *Mark* was (Col. iv. 10) *cousin of Barnabas*, helps to explain Acts xv. 37: an important coincidence. That *Luke*, the reputed author (see my *Corinthians* p. 493) of the Third Gospel, is said in Col. iv. 14 to be a *beloved* friend of Paul, suggests a reason for occasional points of contact between that Gospel and the theology of Paul. The autograph in Col. iv. 18 recalls Gal. vi. 11.

The real significance of the above coincidences can be fairly estimated only by careful and consecutive study of the Epistle itself and by comparison of it with the earlier Epistles of Paul and with other documents not from his pen. For some of these words and phrases are used by other writers. Their value as proofs of common authorship lies in their accumulation in this one short Epistle, and in their relation to the surrounding train of thought.

It is right to say that some good scholars, of whom Pfleiderer is perhaps the best representative, deny that the Epistle to the Colossians is from Paul, on the ground that the errors therein combated were not prevalent till long after his death; that it contains teaching not found in his acknowledged Epistles and in part contradicting them; and that it contains words and phrases not used in his earlier letters. The issue thus raised must be decided by judging whether it is more

easy, accepting the Epistle as genuine, to explain these three grounds
of objection, or, rejecting it as spurious, to account for the coincidences
noted above and the universal and confident reception of the Epistle
in the latter part, and probably in the middle, of the second century.
This alternative we will now consider.

The words and phrases peculiar to this Epistle, when carefully
examined, need cause little surprise. Surely a writer so versatile as
Paul's acknowledged Epistles prove him to have been would not
exhaust his vocabulary in four epistles. Indeed the new topics now
dealt with suggest and require words not used before. And, in spite
of differences, the style is closely akin to that of the Epistle to the
Philippians, and not far removed from that of the earlier Epistles.
It is true that we have in this Epistle elements of teaching not found
in the Epistles already annotated. But, as I shall endeavour to show
in Diss. i., these new elements are legitimate and most valuable
developments of the principles underlying the acknowledged Epistles.
Is it not more likely that such developments would take place in the
mind and thought of Paul than among disciples removed from him
by more than a generation? Indeed the change from active evangelistic labour to the solitude of a prison would naturally suggest, in
a man like Paul, profound investigation of the foundations of his
faith. The wonder would be if such investigation were barren of
results. On the other hand the entire extant literature of the second
century presents nothing comparable for a moment to the solid
advance in Christian thought embodied in this Epistle. To place it
fifty years after the death of Paul, is an utter anachronism. Lastly,
any argument based on the supposed later date of the errors here
combated is most uncertain. For they were, as we shall see in a
special note, an outgrowth of influences at work before the birth of
Christ. And, so far as they can be traced in this Epistle, the errors
at Colossae were very rudimentary. Much more developed is the
Gnosticism of Cerinthus who is said to have been a contemporary of
the Apostle John. We see then that the objections noticed above
have little weight as proofs that the Epistle is not from its professed
writer.

Take now the other side of the alternative. We shall see that
the developments of Paul's teaching contained in this Epistle are of
the utmost value. They are embodied in language which either is
from his pen or is a servile imitation of his style. In this last point
the Epistle before us presents a great contrast to that to the Hebrews.
Could such profound thought and such servile imitation proceed from
any one man? Or, again, can we conceive that such a teacher, a

worthy successor to the Great Apostle and an illustrious exception to the intellectual barrenness of his age, would hide himself and bury his fame under the mask, and in the grave, of a forgery? Or, lastly, can we conceive a forged letter making its way to distant Carthage and to Gaul, and gaining acceptance everywhere, without a shadow of doubt, as a genuine work of Paul? Certainly, these accumulated improbabilities are infinitely greater than any difficulty in supposing that the Gnosticism of the second century existed in germ in the days of Paul and that the teaching of this Epistle is from the pen of the great thinker who expounded so grandly in the Epistle to the Romans the principles of which it is a logical development. We may therefore accept with confidence the Epistle to the Colossians as a genuine work of Paul.

8. The beautiful Epistle to PHILEMON contains nothing inconsistent with its genuineness, and bears everywhere marks of the hand and character of Paul. Among these last must be reckoned the absence of any request for the manumission of Onesimus. Tact so delicate belongs not to a forger. The names sending greeting to Philemon are a valuable coincidence with the same names in the Epistle to the Colossians.

9. The Epistle to the EPHESIANS bears nearly all the marks of genuineness adduced for that to the Colossians, and some others. We have a similar greeting, arrangement, and general style. Notice again the words *redemption* in ch. i. 7; *wealth* in ch. i. 18, ii. 7, iii. 8, 16; *mystery* in ch. i. 9, iii. 3, 4, 9; Christ *the Head* of the Church, *His body* in ch. i. 22, iv. 12, 16; *the old man* in ch. iv. 22; desire for his readers' prayers in ch. vi. 19; and the phrases *in Christ* and *in* the *Lord*. As marked coincidences with the earlier Epistles, we notice also in ch. i. 4, 5, 11 the words *purpose, chosen, predestined*, embodying teaching in complete harmony with Rom. viii. 28, 29, ix. 11; *adoption* in Eph. i. 5, as in Rom. viii. 15, 23, ix. 4, Gal. iv. 5; *sealed with the Spirit*, the *earnest* of our inheritance in Eph. i. 13, 14, iv. 30, as in 2 Cor. i. 22; *surpassing* in Eph. i. 19, ii. 7, iii. 19 as in 2 Cor. iii. 10, ix. 14 and its cognates in 2 Cor. i. 8, iv. 7, 17, xii. 7, etc.; *faith* occupying in Eph. i. 13, 19, ii. 8, iii. 17, iv. 5 its familiar place in the theology of Paul; *the covenants* in Eph. ii. 12, a close parallel with Rom. ix. 4; Jews and Gentiles in common ruin and common salvation in Eph. ii. 3, 11—22, iii. 6, as in Rom. i. 16, iii. 9, x. 12, xv. 8, 9; the Church as a *temple* in Eph. ii. 20—22 as in 1 Cor. iii. 16, vi. 19, 2 Cor. vi. 16; *the grace of God given* to Paul in Eph. iii. 2, 7, 8 as in Rom. xii. 3, xv. 15, 1 Cor. iii. 10; *the less than least of all saints* in Eph. iii. 8, compared with 1 Cor. xv. 9; *edification* in

Eph. iv. 12, 16, 29 as in Rom. xiv. 19, xv. 2, 1 Cor. xiv. 3, 5, 12, 26, 2 Cor. x. 8, xii. 19, xiii. 10; and many others revealing throughout the Epistle the familiar hand of Paul. [Even the anaculothon in Eph. ii. 1 has a close parallel in Rom. v. 12.]

A genuine mark of authorship, and a conspicuous feature of the Epistle to the Ephesians as compared with the others of the same group, is the reappearance and careful treatment of the distinction of Jew and Gentile so conspicuous in the earlier Epistles of Paul as compared with the works of all other N. T. writers. This distinction meets us in the outburst of praise (ch. i. 12, 13) at the beginning of the Epistle. It is silently suggested by the change of pronoun between ch. ii. 1, 2 and v. 3. The inferior position of the Gentiles before their conversion, and their union with Jews as now reconciled to God, are fully expounded in ch. ii. 11—22. And this union is said in ch. iii. 6 to have been a part of the eternal purpose of salvation.

This language reveals a mind long and deeply occupied with the different relations of Jew and Gentile to the Kingdom of God. How large a place this distinction had in the mind of Paul, we learn from Rom. i. 16, ii. 9, 10, 25—29, iii. 1, 9, 1 Cor. i. 22—24, x. 32, Gal. iii. 27, Col. iii. 11. And indisputably it is a mark of early date. For it is impossible to conceive that, after Jerusalem had been taken and the race scattered and after Gentile Christianity had gained a secure and independent position, any writer would lay so much stress on the equality in spiritual privilege of the Gentiles to the Jews. Jewish Christians who still clung to their ancient prerogatives would not place the Gentiles on their own level. A Gentile writer who had witnessed the final dispersion of the Jewish race would consider it but small honour that God has placed the Gentiles on a level with the nation which had murdered the Son of God. Now early date is a strong presumption of genuineness. For it is in the last degree unlikely, while men were living who had known Paul, that the work of some unknown author would have been widely and confidently accepted as his.

Another mark of early date is the enumeration, in Eph. iv. 11, of Church officers as Apostles, Prophets, Evangelists, and Pastors and Teachers. For, as we learn from the tone of the letters attributed with much probability to Ignatius and as we infer from later writers, monarchical episcopacy was firmly established early in the second century. Had there been in the Church an order of bishops distinct from the elders, whom we may here identify with the pastors and teachers, these could not have been passed over here in silence. On the other hand, this enumeration is in complete accord with 1 Cor.

xii. 28. This last passage explains also the phrase *apostles and prophets* in Eph. ii. 20, iii. 5.

Against the unanimous and confident acceptance of the Epistle in the latter part of the second century, supported as it is by these internal marks of genuineness or of early date, the words and phrases and grammatical constructions more or less peculiar to this Epistle have no weight. For they are easily explained. Living thought ever clothes itself in new forms. Taken as a whole, the Epistle is incomparably nearer in diction and modes of thought to the acknowledged Epistles of Paul than is any document other than those which bear his name.

As in the Epistle to the Colossians, so in that to the Ephesians, we shall in Diss i. find new and legitimate and most valuable developments of the principles unfolded in the earlier Epistles. These developments give to each Epistle great and independent worth. In each case they have been put forward as marks of a later hand. But, as we have already seen in the companion Epistle, they reveal the thought and hand of Paul. On the other hand, the argument against the genuineness of the Colossian Epistle based upon the late date of the errors therein combated has no force against the Epistle now before us. For it contains no definite refutation of specific error. Nor can any one say that the style of this latter Epistle is in any way more unlike that of Paul than is the Epistle to the Colossians.

One special argument, however, is brought against the Epistle to the Ephesians by not a few who accept its companion as genuine. The many close coincidences in thought and expression are appealed to in proof that it is a later imitation of the Epistle to the Colossians. These coincidences are indisputable. As important elements common to the two Epistles and peculiar to them, I note Christ *the Head* of the Church, in Col. ii. 18 and Eph. i. 23, in Col. ii. 19 and Eph. iv. 16; *dead through trespasses* but now *made alive* with Christ in Col. ii. 13 and Eph. ii. 5; the inward change described in Col. iii. 9, 10 and Eph. iv. 22—24. Compare also Eph. iv. 32—v. 2 with Col. iii. 12, 13; Eph. v. 3—6 with Col. iii. 5—8; Eph. v. 19 with Col. iii. 16; Eph. v. 22—vi. 9 with Col. iii. 18—iv. 1, a long and close parallel. Since the Epistle to the Colossians has a specific occasion in the definite errors therein refuted, nearly all who reject one of the Epistles as not genuine reject that to the Ephesians. Certainly, the close and sustained similarity proves either that one Epistle is a servile imitation of the other or that they are the twin offspring of one mind.

Our choice between these suppositions depends upon our estimate of the Epistle to the Ephesians as compared with that to the Colossians. That it has a distinctive and dominating and all-important mark of its own, Diss. i. will, I hope, make clear to us. The characteristic feature of the Epistle to the Colossians is its exposition of the Person of Christ: the chief matter of that to the Ephesians is the Church. This is very conspicuous in Eph. v. 22—33 as compared with Col. iii. 18, 19. The question before us turns on our estimate of the Epistle itself and of this independent element in it. It can therefore be answered only by careful study of it. I hope that the exposition before us will convince the reader that in grandeur and worth the Epistle to the Ephesians is unsurpassed by any human composition. Its great and independent value is admitted even by Pfleiderer who denies its genuineness. And its worth proves its genuineness. For we cannot conceive a man capable of the profound thought which breathes throughout this Epistle becoming so servile an imitator even of an Apostle. Independent thought always clothes itself in fitting language of its own.

On the other hand if our judgment be that the Epistle is a worthless imitation, we are at once met by an inexplicable difficulty, viz. the early and unanimous and confident acceptance of it as written by Paul. If the work were from a later hand, is it conceivable that every trace of its origin should have vanished utterly from the memory of the early Church? Certainly this is an historic difficulty which needs to be reckoned with. It is increased by the widespread and uncontradicted tradition which connects with Ephesus the last years of the Apostle John. For he would know whether the Church in which he lived had an Epistle from the hand of his departed colleague. Consequently, if not written by Paul, the Epistle must be a work of the second century. Yet in the middle of the century it was accepted as genuine, even by Marcion an enemy of the Gospel!

Some have suggested that the name of Paul was prefixed by some good man to a work of his own, not to deceive, but in order to call attention to sentiments similar to those of the great Apostle. This suggestion is completely overturned by comparison of evidently spurious documents bearing the names of Apostles. All these are worthless in themselves, never gained general reception, and nearly all were expressly rejected by Church writers. A more marked contrast than that between these wretched parodies and the Epistles before us cannot be conceived. The comparison attests the genuineness of the document so familiar and so precious to all Christians.

Another suggestion is that the Epistles to the Colossians and Ephesians have, one or both, been interpolated, that on the basis of a shorter work actually written by Paul have been erected, probably by one hand, the two documents we now possess. This suggestion will, I hope, be disproved by our study of the text of the Epistles, and by the harmony and order and life we shall find therein. It is also disproved by the complete general agreement of all our early copies. The Epistles attributed to Ignatius were interpolated. For the few existing copies of them reveal different recensions. But it is inconceivable that the original works of the great Apostle, which must have been prized and guarded by the Churches to which they were sent, should pass utterly out of view, and that one single corrupted recension should usurp and retain the place thus vacated.

It is worthy of note that these wild suggestions come only from those who have already persuaded themselves that Christ did not rise from the dead, and that Christianity with its mighty effect upon the world is a result of the preaching of men who were in most serious error touching the nature and teaching of their Master.

In view then of their universal and confident reception throughout the Roman Empire, by friends and enemies, in the latter part of the second century, of their deep and broad and minute agreement with the thought and phraseology of Paul, and of their matchless and independent worth, we may accept without a shadow of doubt each of the Epistles before us as a genuine work of the Apostle Paul.

SECTION III.

TO WHAT EXTENT ARE OUR COPIES AND VERSIONS CORRECT?

1. The Greek text of the Epistle to the Philippians presents, touching the correctness of our copies, no difficulties worthy of mention. Of changes adopted without note by the Revisers, only the following have any practical importance :—

1. Ch. i. 11 : *fruit* for *fruits*.
2. „ „ 14 : *the word of God* for *the word*.
3. „ „ 16, 17 : rearrange the sentence.
4. „ „ „ : *raise up* for *add*.
5. „ „ 23 : *but* instead of *for*.
6. „ „ „ : *for it* instead of *which*.
7. „ ii. 4 : *not looking* for *look not*.
8. „ „ 9 : *the name* for *a name*.
9. „ „ 30 : *hazard* for *not regarding*.

10. Ch. iii. 3: *by the Spirit of God* for *God in the Spirit.*
11. ,, ,, 11: *from the dead* for *of the dead.*
12. ,, ,, 16: omit *rule, let us mind the same thing.*
13. ,, iv. 3: *Yes,* for *and.*
14. ,, ,, 13: *Him* for *Christ.*
15. ,, ,, 23: *your spirit* for *you all.*

All these are accepted without doubt by all recent critical editors, i.e. by Lachmann, Tischendorf, Tregelles, and Westcott and Hort; except that about No. 6 Tregelles expresses in his margin a slight doubt. I think that all may be accepted with perfect confidence. On the other hand, no important reading which the editors agree to accept is overlooked by the Revisers.

The few readings open to doubt and of any importance whatever are noted in the Revisers' Margin. They are as follows:—

1. Ch. ii. 2: *of the same mind* or *of one mind.*
2. ,, ,, 12: omit or insert *as.*
3. ,, ,, 26: add or omit *to see you.*
4. ,, ,, 30: *the Lord* or *Christ.*
5. ,, iii. 13: omit or insert *yet.*

All these are uncertain and unimportant.
No variations worthy of attention are overlooked by the Revisers.

2. The Epistle to the Colossians presents more important variations.
The following list includes all changes adopted without note by the Revisers and worthy of attention here:—

1. Ch. i. 2: omit *and* the *Lord Jesus Christ.*
2. ,, ,, 3: omit *and* before *Father.*
3. ,, ,, 6: after *fruit* insert *and increasing.*
4. ,, ,, 10: *by the knowledge of God* for *in* or *for the knowledge, etc.*
5. ,, ,, 14: omit *through His blood.*
6. ,, ,, 16: twice omit *that are.*
7. ,, ii. 2: omit *and of the Father and.*
8. ,, ,, 11: omit *of the sins* of the flesh.
9. ,, ,, 13: *through* for *in* the trespasses.
10. ,, ,, ,, : *forgiven us* instead of *you.*
11. ,, ,, 20: omit *wherefore.*
12. ,, iii. 5: *the* members for *your* members.
13. ,, ,, 15: *Christ* for *God.*
14. ,, ,, 16: to *God* for to *the Lord.*

15. Ch. iii. 20 : *in* the Lord for *to* the Lord.
16. ,, ,, 22 : *the Lord* for *God.*
17. ,, ,, 24 : omit *for* before *ye serve.*
18. ,, ,, 25 : read *for* instead of *but.*
19. ,, iv. 8 : read *that ye may know our estate.*
20. ,, ,, 18 : omit *amen.*

Of these variations, there is among recent editors some difference about Nos. 2 and 6 : about five more of them, the critical editors since Lachmann have been agreed : all the others are accepted by all editors, from Lachmann to Westcott and Hort. The entire list may, I believe, be accepted with perfect confidence.

The readings noted in the Reviser's margin as open to doubt are :—

1. Ch. i. 7 : *our* or *your.*
2. ,, ,, 12 : *us* or *you.*
3. ,, i. 21 : *has He reconciled* or *ye have been reconciled.*
4. ,, ii. 2 : general disorder.
5. ,, ,, 7 : omit or insert *in it* before *in* or *with thanksgiving.*
6. ,, ,, 18 : *seen* or *not seen.*
7. ,, iii. 4 : *our* or *your* life.
8. ,, ,, 6 : omit or insert *upon the sons of disobedience.*
9. ,, ,, 13 : *the Lord* or *Christ.*
10. ,, ,, 16 : *Christ* or *Lord* or *God.*
11. ,, iv. 15 : *their* or *her.*

In each of these cases the balance of probability seems to me to incline somewhat to the Revisers' preference ; decidedly so in No. 1, a reading of some importance. In No. 4, a most important passage, the complete confusion of the oldest documents renders impossible a reliable decision : but the balance of probability inclines very decidedly to the Revisers' preference. See note in Lightfoot's *Colossians.* In No. 6, the word removed by the Revisers to their margin has been confidently rejected by all critical editors since Lachmann marked it as doubtful. Evidence external and internal seems to me decisive against it. In No. 8, the words noted in the margin as doubtful are supported by a preponderance of ancient documents so great as at first sight to exclude doubt. But they are omitted by the very excellent Vatican MS., and have the appearance of being copied from Eph. v. 6 ; and are for this reason confidently rejected by all critical editors since Lachmann marked them as doubtful. Internal reasons seem to me to favour the genuineness of the words. See note. In No. 11, where the variations have considerable interest, the Revisers' preference seems to me well grounded. The other readings noted in the margin are of little practical importance.

In ch. i. 20, the words *through Him* are omitted in some of the best MSS. and versions, and by Lachmann and Tregelles without note and in the margin of Westcott. This omission might fairly claim a place in the Revisers' margin. No other variation worthy of attention is omitted by them.

On the whole, in the Greek text of the Epistle to the Colossians, the only problems of importance not yet solved for us by Textual Criticism are the various readings in chs. i. 7, ii. 2, iv. 15.

3. In the Epistle to PHILEMON, the only changes worthy of mention accepted without note by the Revisers are those in *vv.* 2, 12, which are also adopted by all recent editors, without note except on *v.* 12 in the margin of Tregelles. It may be received with confidence. The only reading of any importance open to doubt is that noted in the margin of *v.* 6, where perhaps a slight probability inclines towards the Revisers' preference: but certain decision is impossible.

4. In the Epistle to the EPHESIANS, the changes adopted without note by the Revisers and worthy of attention are:—

1.	Ch.	i.	18 : *heart* for *understanding*.
2.	,,	ii.	1 : insert *your* before *trespasses*.
3.	,,	,,	17 : insert *peace* before *to those near*.
4.	,,	,,	19 : insert *ye are* before *fellow-citizens*.
5.	,,	,,	21 : *every building :* instead of *all the building*.
6.	,,	iii.	3 : *was-made-known* for *He made known*.
7.	,,	,,	6 : *the* for *His*.
8.	,,	,,	8 : *to the Gentiles* for *among the Gentiles*.
9.	,,	,,	9 : *stewardship* or *dispensation* for *fellowship*.
10.	,,	,,	,,: omit *through Jesus Christ*.
11.	,,	,,	14 : omit *of our Lord Jesus Christ*.
12.	,,	,,	21 : insert *and* before *in Christ Jesus*.
13.	,,	iv.	6 : *in all* instead of *in you all*.
14.	,,	,,	17 : omit *other* before *Gentiles*.
15.	,,	v.	2 : *you* instead of *us*.
16.	,,	,,	9 : *light* for *Spirit*.
17.	,,	,,	21 : *Christ* for *God*.
18.	,,	,,	23 : *Himself Saviour* for *and He is Saviour*.
19.	,,	,,	27 : omit *it* before *to Himself*.
20.	,,	,,	30 : omit *of His flesh* to end.
21.	,,	vi.	9 : for *your* read *of them and of you*.

22. Ch. vi. 10 : omit *my brethren.*
23. ,, ,, 12 : read *this darkness.*
24. ,, ,, 16 : read *among all* for *upon all.*

All these are accepted without note by all recent editors, except No. 15, a reading of no importance, adopted by all but Lachmann; and No. 20, about which Tregelles, while omitting the words in question, expresses doubt. All may, I think, be accepted with confidence.

The readings noted in the Revisers' margin as open to doubt are :—

1. Ch. i. 1 : insert or omit *at Ephesus.*
2. ,, ,, 15 : omit or insert *love.*
3. ,, ii. 5 : *with Christ* or *in Christ.*
4. ,, iii. 9 : insert or omit *all* before *men.*
5. ,, iv. 9 : omit or insert *first* before *into the lower parts.*
6. ,, ,, 32 : *you* or *us.*
7. ,, v. 2 : *for us* or *for you.*

For Nos. 1 and 2, important and difficult variations, see notes. In No. 3, the oldest and best uncial, viz. the Vatican MS., the accurate Coptic version, and one of the best cursives, support the reading in the margin against all other authorities. But the practical difference is slight. The other marginal readings are unimportant.

No variations worthy of note and of any claim to genuineness are overlooked by the Revisers. In short, the Greek text underlying the four Epistles here annotated may be accepted throughout with full confidence as, within narrow limits, representing correctly the original text of these Epistles.

5. In the renderings of the REVISED VERSION of the Epistle to the PHILIPPIANS, among many improvements I note the following. In ch. i. 13, *the whole prætorian guard* is much more accurate than *all the palace.* The rendering in ch. ii. 6, *counted it not a prize to be on an equality with God* is, in my view, not correct: but in v. 7 the rendering *emptied himself* instead of *made himself of no reputation* is an unspeakable gain, not merely as a more correct reproduction of Paul's thought but as shedding light on the profound mystery of the Incarnation. In ch. iii. 9 *a righteousness of my own* is a most happy rendering, instead of the less accurate *my own righteousness.* *Our citizenship,* in v. 20, is much better than the misleading or almost meaningless word *conversation :* and *the body of our humiliation, of his glory,* in v. 21, corrects a serious misrepresentation. In

2

ch. iv. 3, the rendering *help these women, for they laboured with me in the Gospel*, makes clear Paul's reference to the two women just mentioned by name. *In nothing be anxious* (v. 6) is a good reproduction of Paul's meaning and emphasis, and replaces a rendering very liable to be misunderstood, *be careful for nothing*. Even the change in v. 7 from *through Christ Jesus* to *in Christ Jesus* is not without significance. The rendering *I have learnt the secret* in v. 12 does something to reproduce the sense completely buried under the A. V. *I am instructed*. To these might be added many smaller improvements. And I do not know of anything to set against them.

In the Epistle to the COLOSSIANS, the marked improvements are not so many. But the change at the beginning and end of ch. i. 16 from *by Him were all things created* to *in Him, through Him* is very important as stating more accurately the relation of the Son to the work of creation. The Revisers' rendering of ch. ii. 15, *having put off from Himself* the principalities, reproduces fairly the meaning of Paul's words, and thus calls attention to a difficulty quite concealed by the A. V. *having spoiled etc.* Similarly, in v. 18 *dwelling on the things which he hath seen* is much nearer to Paul's intention than *intruding into etc.* *Severity to the body* in v. 23 is better than *neglecting of the body*: and *not in any value against indulgence of the flesh* is intelligible and fairly correct, whereas the A. V. is unintelligible.

On the other hand, an aggravated form of the blemish mentioned on p. 541 of my *Corinthians* is found in ch. i. 16, where the Revisers have displaced a very correct and idiomatic rendering *for Him* in favour of the meaningless words *unto Him*. They have also failed to make clear the evident reference of ch. iv. 11, viz. that the three men mentioned were the only Jews who had been a comfort to Paul.

In PHILEMON 12, *my very heart* is better than *mine own bowels*. Similarly, in v. 20. In v. 13, *on thy behalf* is more accurate than *in thy stead*.

The absence of any special errors of rendering in the A. V. of the Epistle to the EPHESIANS has left no occasion for improvements worthy of special mention here. But throughout these four Epistles are a multitude of minor changes (e.g. Eph. iv. 29 *speech* instead of *communication*) which, though not individually of great moment, give collectively a much better conception of Paul's meaning than does the earlier Version.

SECTION IV.
PHILIPPI, EPHESUS, COLOSSÆ, AND THE CHURCHES THERE.

1. PHILIPPI was situated some eight miles from Neapolis, now Kavala, on the northern shore of the Ægean Sea, in a level and well-watered and luxuriant plain surrounded by mountains and separated from the sea by a ridge of hills from 1,000 to 1,600 feet high. Over this range of hills and through Philippi passed the Egnatian Way, the great road from Asia Minor to the Adriatic and to Rome.

The city was rebuilt by Philip of Macedon, father of Alexander the Great, on the site of an older town called, from the many streams flowing through the plain, Crenides, or 'Springs of Water.' On the plain of Philippi was fought after the death of Julius Cæsar the famous battle, renewed after twenty days on the same field, in which his murderers, Brutus and Cassius, were crushed by Octavius, who afterwards became the Emperor Augustus, and Mark Antony. To commemorate the battle Augustus afterwards made Philippi a Roman colony, and gave to it the further privileges known as 'the Italic right.' On the Roman colonies, see my *Corinthians* p. 16. By an interesting coincidence, coins of Philippi have been found bearing, as was usual with colonies, Latin inscriptions, in marked contrast to other Macedonian coins with Greek inscriptions.

Philippi was the first European town in which Paul laboured. On his second missionary journey, probably in A.D. 52, (see my *Galatians* p. 193,) he arrived at Troas on the eastern shore of the Ægean Sea. From Troas, Mount Athos on the opposite coast of Macedonia, though distant more than eighty miles, is sometimes seen in the rays of the setting sun. And we can well believe that at Troas Paul's thoughts went out after the mighty continent of Europe, now nearer to him than ever before. No wonder that in a dream a man of Macedonia besought his help. A rapid voyage of two days brought the little band to Neapolis. Thence, at once apparently, they passed on over the ridge to Philippi. That no synagogue is mentioned, suggests that not many Jews lived there. But Paul found some women, Jewesses or proselytes who were accustomed to meet together for prayer by the river-side. He was soon gladdened by the conversion of Lydia, apparently a woman of position, and later by that of the gaoler, and of their households. From this beginning sprang the Church at Philippi.

The reality of the good work thus begun was soon proved. The passing stranger was remembered after his departure by those to whom he had spoken words of life. Not only once but twice, even when he was at Thessalonica, the next city in which he preached, they sent a contribution of money for his support: Ph. iv. 16. Nor was this all. During his eighteen months' sojourn at Corinth, money was sent (2 Cor. xi. 9) to him from Macedonia, doubtless either altogether (cp. Ph. iv. 15) from Philippi or stimulated by the liberality of the Philippians.

Paul's second visit to Philippi was some six years later and along the same route. A fugitive from deadly peril at Ephesus he came to Troas, thinking not of his peril but of Titus whom he hoped to meet there with news about the unfaithful Church at Corinth: 2 Cor. ii. 12, 13. But Titus was not at Troas: and Paul hurried across the Ægean to seek him in Macedonia. Landing at Neapolis he doubtless again pushed on to Philippi. And there or at least in Macedonia the wished-for messenger came, and with good news. In Macedonia Paul laboured for some time, and then went on to Corinth: Acts xx. 2. On the return journey, accompanied by Luke who had been with him on his first visit to Philippi, (as we infer from 'we were' and 'we sailed' in Acts xvi. 12, xx. 6,) Paul spent Easter there, and went on his way, probably for the last time and with dark forebodings, to Jerusalem.

The curtain now falls on this most interesting Church until in some measure it is lifted by the Epistle before us. And with the close of this Epistle it falls again. The letter from Polycarp to the Church at Philippi, quoted on p. 5, says nothing about the state of the Church there except that Valens, a presbyter of it, and his wife, had been guilty of avarice. In subsequent history we hear nothing more. And to-day, amid quiet meadows, a few ruins are all that remain to mark the site of what once was Philippi.

2. Far more important than Philippi was EPHESUS, the splendid capital of the Roman province of Asia.

On the western coast of Asia Minor, some 300 miles due east of Corinth, into a bay partly closed by the island of Samos, the river Cayster flows through a plain about five miles across bounded to the north by low hills and to the south by the somewhat loftier range of mount Prion.[*] To the south of the river, upon and around a double hill called mount Coressus [*] and upon the northern slopes of mount Prion stood Ephesus, a city built, together with others on the same

---

[*] As these mountains are named by Mr. Wood, who was led by his discoveries to transpose the names previously given to them.

coast, in the early dawn of the history of their nation, by Greeks from across the Ægean Sea.

Close outside the city, as we now know, from its earliest days stood a temple to the goddess Artemis. Even Herodotus in the fifth century B.C. speaks of the temple of Ephesus as worthy of note: bk. ii. 148. On or near the same site were successively erected and burnt several temples, of which all were famous but each surpassed in splendour its predecessor. One of these is said to have been burnt, apparently soon after its completion, in B.C. 356, on the day of the birth of Alexander the Great. This was followed, on the same site and a few years afterwards, by the temple standing in all its glory in the days of Paul. Of this temple Pausanias speaks as surpassing all buildings raised by men: bk. iv. 31. 8. And everywhere Ephesus was known as the 'sacristan of the great Artemis:' Acts xix. 35.

From the time of the Persian wars to that of Paul, Ephesus enjoyed great and increasing commercial prosperity. The rich country around supplied to the city abundant produce. And ships from every port filled its market with merchandise, to be exchanged for that borne along the great roads leading from Ephesus to the interior of Asia Minor. So Strabo says, "Owing to its good situation, the city increases day by day, being the greatest emporium on this side the Taurus mountains:" bk. xiv. p. 641. In the bloom of Greek art, Ephesus was famous for its painters and sculptors. And when art had faded, it was widely known as the chosen home of magic. So Clement of Alexandria speaks of "the so-called Ephesian letters," a kind of charm, as being "far famed:" Misc. bk. v. 8, p. 72. The wealth of Ephesus and the luxuriant climate of the Asiatic coast produced also an unbridled self-indulgence for which the city was long notorious.

When the Roman province of Asia was formed, the commercial and religious importance of Ephesus, and the easy access to it from the west, made it the residence of the Roman Governor and the centre of Roman authority.

Such then was Ephesus when visited by Paul. Its temple, ancient and yet in full glory, was a wonder of the world and the veneration of all heathendom. Its quays and markets were crowded by men of every nation, enriching a city already rich. The soft climate invited to every kind of luxury. And over all the majesty of Rome shed the lustre of its mighty presence.

About A.D. 260, Ephesus was plundered and its temple set on fire by barbarian invaders. And from this time the temple passes from our view. It probably shared the fate of others in A.D. 399, when a decree was issued by the Emperors Arcadius and Honorius for the destruction of all temples except such as could be used for churches. So complete was its destruction that until a few years ago no trace remained, nor was the site known, of the building which had been the glory of Ephesus and of Asia. A careful search for it was undertaken in the year 1863, under the auspices of the Trustees of the British Museum, by an English Architect, Mr. J. T. Wood, whose patient and well directed efforts were rewarded in 1869 by discovery of the long lost temple. During the next five years sufficient remains were found not only to place the site beyond doubt but to give a good and reliable idea of the building itself. These discoveries agree in the main with the scanty notices of Vitruvius, *On Architecture* bks. i. 2, iii. 1, iv. 1, and of Pliny, *Natural History* bk. xxxvi. 21. The temple was rectangular, 343 ft by 164 ft, not including the steps which surrounded it on all sides. It consisted of a central chamber, or Cella, containing the famous image of the goddess, with a vestibule in front and a large chamber behind. Around this building were two rows of Ionic fluted columns, about seven feet in diameter at the bottom of the shaft and about fifty-six feet high, supporting the roof of the temple. Pliny says that 36 columns were sculptured. And five drums or parts of drums of columns elaborately sculptured with life size human figures in high relief were found by Mr. Wood and may now be seen at the British Museum. Broken fluted drums in great abundance were brought to light. Portions of the marble pavement of the temple were found ; as also parts of the pavements of two earlier temples on the same site. Also, with other inscriptions in the Theatre and other parts of the city, twenty-six inscriptions were found among the ruins of the temple conferring citizenship upon various foreigners who had rendered service to the Ephesians. A careful reprint and translation of these most interesting records of early Ephesian life, and a full account of the excavations, abundantly illustrated, are given in first-rate style in Wood's *Discoveries at Ephesus*. Also interesting, and not superseded by Mr. Wood's volume, is Falkener's *Ephesus*.

We must now trace Paul's connection with Ephesus. From Acts xvi. 6 we learn that, on his second missionary journey, he was 'hindered by the Holy Spirit from speaking the word in Asia.' This suggests that his purpose was, after passing through Phrygia and Galatia, to carry the Gospel to that important province. And, if so, his eye must have rested on its great metropolis. But God had more pressing work for him to do, viz. to carry the Gospel at once to its future home, the great continent of Europe. On his return journey, as recorded in Acts xviii. 19, Paul paid a flying visit to Ephesus in company with his faithful helpers Aquila and Prisca who remained there, apparently for several years. That no Christians are mentioned, suggests that there was then no Church there. But as usual Paul went to the synagogue of the Jews, by whom he was well received and invited to remain. This he could not do, but promised soon to return.

Some time after Paul's departure, there arrived at Ephesus an eloquent and earnest Alexandrian Jew, Apollos, who eagerly advocated, as he imperfectly understood them, the claims of Jesus. And, while doing so, he learnt from Aquila and Prisca the real significance of the Gospel he endeavoured to proclaim. Shortly afterwards he crossed the Ægean Sea to Achaia, and continued there his earnest work for Christ.

In the spring of A.D. 55, according to the reckoning on p. 193 of my *Galatians*, Paul, fulfilling his promise, again arrived at Ephesus. Since Aquila and Prisca are referred to in 1 Cor. xvi. 19 as with him at Ephesus, we may suppose that they were there to welcome his arrival. He found in the city some twelve disciples of Christ who had received neither Christian Baptism nor the distinctively Christian gift of the Holy Spirit. From his teaching they received the inspiration of a new life. Their Baptism was doubtless an important era in the history of the young Church.

As at Corinth, Paul began his work at Ephesus in the synagogue of the Jews. After three months, opposition arose. But already he had gathered round him a band of faithful men. These he now separated from the synagogue; and found for them a home in the school of Tyrannus, possibly a Greek teacher of philosophy or rhetoric. Here Paul laboured for two years, a longer time than he had before spent in one place; and with great success. From Ephesus as a centre the Gospel became known throughout the whole province. Asiatic superstition was confronted by the most wonderful miracles recorded of Paul. Certain Jews who attempted to use as a charm the name of Jesus were utterly confounded by the evil spirits they tried to exorcise. And many Christians, convicted by the manifested power of God, confessed that they had been secretly practising the magical arts of their former days; and proved their sincerity by bringing out and burning publicly their secret books to the value of some £2000 of our money.

From Ephesus, about Easter of A.D. 58 probably, (see *Galatians* p. 193,) Paul wrote his first extant Epistle to the Corinthians. He was then purposing to start soon for Macedonia and Achaia.

His departure was hastened by the tumult described in Acts xix.
23—41: see p. 511 of my *Corinthians*. I may now add that in the
inscriptions reprinted in Wood's *Ephesus* the birth-day of Artemis is
several times said to be a religious festival, and said to be in the
month of May. We have also frequent mention of silver images,
which would find work for Demetrius and his companions. The
word rendered 'town-clerk' is also frequent as an official title at
Ephesus. And the phrase 'temple-keeper of Artemis' and others
similar are frequently found (cp. Acts xix. 35) as titles of the city.

On his return journey, Paul summoned to Miletus the elders of the
Church at Ephesus, and gave them the address recorded in Acts xx.
18—35. All this reveals the importance of that Church.

Then followed a Jerusalem Paul's arrest and imprisonment, his
voyage to Rome, and his imprisonment there. During that imprisonment, as we shall see, the letter before us was written.

From 1 Tim. i. 3 we learn that Paul had requested Timothy to
remain at Ephesus to deal with church-matters there which needed
special attention. And his words seem to imply that this request
was made when Paul was himself at Ephesus, but starting for Macedonia. A multitude of reasons combine to assure us that this, and
the similar request in Tit. i. 5, were not earlier than Paul's arrest at
Jerusalem. If so, these Epistles, which I cannot but accept as
genuine, prove that after his imprisonment at Rome Paul was set
free and again visited Ephesus. The circumstances of his visit
are altogether unknown. But from the letter to Timothy we learn
that the fears expressed at Miletus were only too well grounded and
that the Church at Ephesus was then beset by many perils. The
charges to Timothy and Titus by no means imply that they were per-
manently settled at Ephesus and in Crete as chief pastors, or bishops.
And of any such office we have no hint in the New Testament. See
Diss. ii. 10. Nor do we know whether the Second Epistle found
Timothy still at Ephesus.

Our last glimpse of the Church at Ephesus in the New Testament
is Rev. ii. 1—7, where as metropolis of Asia it is addressed first
among the seven Churches. From this we learn that, while still
faithful in the main, the Church had lost something of its early
fervour.

Beyond the limits of the New Testament a reliable tradition connects with Ephesus the last years of the Apostle John: see Irenaeus
bk. iii. 3, 4 and Clement of Alexandria *What rich man etc.* § 42.
It was afterwards the seat of an archbishop. Here was held in
A.D. 431 amid much confusion the Third General Council; and, in

A.D. 449, amid still greater confusion, a gathering summoned as a general council but afterwards not acknowledged as such and known ever since as the Robber Synod.

With this tumultuous assembly closes practically the history of Ephesus and of the Church at Ephesus. For long centuries the site of the city has been an utter solitude without inhabitant. But, strange to say, the railway from Smyrna to Aidin has a station little more than a mile from its ruins. Between the city and the railway station is the site of the temple.

The candlestick (Rev. ii. 5) has been removed from its place. And even the splendid metropolis it once illumined has ceased to be counted among the cities of the world. But its name will never die. Throughout the world it is known, chiefly through the labours and letters of a Jewish tentmaker. But that tentmaker was an Apostle of Jesus Christ.

3. We now leave the beautiful coast of the Ægean and the splendid metropolis of the Roman province of Asia, through a gate of which there are still remains, and go inland over the hills to Magnesia and then eastward, some 120 miles in all, almost to the boundary of the province and into what was popularly and indefinitely known as Phrygia. On the banks of the Lycus, a stream flowing into the Mæander and now called the Tchoruk Sù, are ruins which have been, with reasonable certainty, identified as those of COLOSSÆ, some three miles north of Chonos, a modern straggling village on the site of a mediæval town known as Chonai. See Hamilton's *Researches in Asia Minor* vol. i. pages 509–523. Some ten miles lower down the stream, which here flows somewhat north of east, to the south of the stream and on the slopes of the Cadmus range, are important ruins of a racecourse, gymnasium, theatres, and other buildings, which have been identified as those of Laodicea; and six miles away, north by east, with the stream flowing about midway between the two sites, are the still nobler ruins of Hierapolis on the slope of lower hills bounding the valley of the Lycus on the north. The site of Hierapolis is described by Hamilton as one of special beauty. A weird strangeness is cast over the scene by thick incrustations in all grotesque forms deposited by a small stream strongly impregnated with lime which falls into the Lycus near this point. There is also a hot spring of some 100 degrees Fahrenheit. So near are the ruins of the three cities that all may be visited in one day.

COLOSSÆ is mentioned by Herodotus (bk. vii. 30) as a great city through which the army of Xerxes passed on its way to invade

Greece. Xenophon (*Anabasis* bk. i. 2. 6) speaks of it as being, some 80 years later, "populous, prosperous, and great." But the notices of later writers seem to imply that long before Paul's time it had sunk into comparative decay. Lightfoot says, "Without doubt Colossæ was the least important church to which any Epistle of St. Paul was addressed."

LAODICEA, till then an obscure town, had risen into great importance shortly before Paul's day. So Strabo, bk. xii. p. 578. Under the Romans it became the political capital of the surrounding district. HIERAPOLIS seems to have been, owing to the beauty of its position and the medicinal properties of its springs, a favourite health resort.

The rich pastures around were famous for their large flocks of sheep. All three towns were enriched by their trade in dyed wool. For the rich colours of their dyes, Strabo tells us (bk. xii. p. 578) that Laodicea and Colossæ were specially famous; and that (bk. xiii. p. 630) for this they owed much to the mineral waters of Hierapolis. He says also that the country was specially liable to earthquakes. Of one such, which happened apparently shortly before this Epistle was written and which desolated Laodicea, we read in Tacitus, *Annals* bk. xiv. 27. From this, he tells us, Laodicea recovered without help from Rome.

From Josephus (*Antiq.* bk. xii. 3. 4) we learn that Antiochus the Great (B.C. 223—187) transplanted 2,000 Jewish families to Lydia and Phrygia. Doubtless some of these settled in the valley of the Lycus. Cicero says (*For Flaccus* § 28) that large sums of money were sent from Laodicea to the temple at Jerusalem. This reveals the presence of a large Jewish population. It is not unlikely that among the Phrygians (Acts ii. 10) at Jerusalem on the Day of Pentecost were some from these three cities.

About the founding of the Churches in these cities, we know nothing except from this epistle. We learn from Col. ii. 1 that Paul had never visited Colossæ or Laodicea. To these we may add by sure inference the neighbouring city of Hierapolis. He twice passed through Phrygia: Acts xvi. 6, xviii. 23. But his route, so far as we can trace it, would not lead him near the valley of the Lycus.

Indirectly, however, the Churches of the Lycus were probably results of Paul's labour. The Colossians received the Gospel from their fellow-citizen, Epaphras: Col. i. 7, iv. 12. The nearness of the three cities assures us that it would at once spread from one to the others. And the earnest interest of Epaphras embraced them all: Col. iv. 13. It is therefore probable that directly or indirectly he was founder of the three Churches. Now Paul laboured for three years at Ephesus: Acts xx. 31. Through his continued preaching there 'all those inhabiting Asia heard the word of the Lord, both Jews and Greeks:' ch. xix. 10. It is not unlikely that from the lips of Paul, on a visit to the metropolis of the province, Epaphras heard and accepted the Gospel which he afterwards preached in his own city and those around it. Possibly Paul charged him to do this. If so, we can the more easily understand his description of Epaphras in Col. i. 7 as *a faithful minister of Christ on our behalf.*

Whether Paul paid his hoped-for (Philemon 22) visit to Colossæ, we do not know. But if the Pastoral Epistles be genuine, he was set free, and visited Ephesus and Miletus: 1 Tim. i. 3, 2 Tim. iv. 20. And if so, he may have extended his journey to the Churches of the Lycus.

The only later reference in the New Testament to these Churches is the letter preserved in Rev. iii. 14—22. Naturally it was addressed to the most important of the three cities. In *v.* 14, 'the beginning of the creation of God,' we have a thought in close harmony with Col. i. 15, 16.

The subsequent history of these cities and Churches contains little worthy of note. With this Epistle the Church at Colossæ disappears altogether from view, except as here and there the name of its bishop is appended to the decrees of a council. The bishops of the more important sees of Laodicea and Hierapolis were present at the General Councils at Nicæa, Ephesus, and Chalcedon; and, two years before this last, at the Robber Synod at Ephesus. About A.D. 363 was held at Laodicea a provincial council which has left us, in its sixtieth Canon, a list of the books of the New Testament agreeing exactly with our English Bible except that it omits the Book of Revelation, the earliest list so nearly complete. And for some centuries the two sees retained their importance. A thin and scattered population, Turkish with a mixture of Greeks and Armenians, lives around the ruins of these once important cities, and cultivates the soil which still retains its ancient fertility. And, as of old, the country is still occasionally visited by earthquakes.

SECTION V.

TIME AND PLACE OF WRITING, AND THE OCCASION, OF THE EPISTLES.

1. For the first time Paul now writes as a prisoner: Eph. iii. 1, iv. 1, vi. 20, Ph. i. 7, 13, Col. iv. 3, 18, Philemon 10, 13, 22, 23. These frequent references to his bondage reveal the deep mark it had made in his thought and heart, and thus prove that his imprisonment lasted for some time. Now in the Book of Acts no long imprisonment of Paul is recorded earlier than his arrest at Jerusalem. This is a very strong presumption that these Epistles were later than his arrest. And this is the confident judgment of all scholars.

2. After his arrest, Paul remained for more than two years a prisoner at Cæsarea, was then taken to Rome, the journey occupying many months, and remained there in prison for not less than two years: Acts xxiv. 27, xxviii. 30. Whether he was then set free, we have no sure information. This long imprisonment affording abundant leisure for writing letters suggests itself at once as the time when these Epistles of captivity were written. We therefore ask, were they written during the earlier or the later part of it, i.e. from Cæsarea or from Rome? That they were written from Rome, an early and unanimous tradition attests. With such scanty indications as we have, we will now test this tradition.

Cæsar's household in Ph. iv. 22 points very clearly to the imperial palace at Rome. And ch. i. 13, *manifest in the whole prætorium* or *prætorian guard* suggests much more forcibly the pretorian guard at Rome than the narrow limits of the governor's palace at Cæsarea. Against these indications there is nothing to set. It is therefore generally admitted that probably the Epistle to the Philippians was written from Rome during Paul's imprisonment there.

That the Epistle to the Colossians was written at the same time as that to the Ephesians, is made almost certain by the reference in Eph. vi. 21 and Col. iv. 7 to *Tychicus, a beloved brother and faithful minister in the Lord*, as evidently the bearer of each Epistle, taken in connection with the very close similarity of the Epistles in thought, order, and phraseology, a similarity without parallel in the New Testament, and with the proof given in Introd. ii. that both Epistles are from the pen of Paul.

The Epistle to Philemon was apparently (v. 12) taken by *Onesimus*, who is said in Col. iv. 9 to be accompanying Tychicus to Colossæ. Moreover, of six men with Paul who send greeting to the Church at

SEC. 5.] INTRODUCTION. 29

Colossæ, we notice that five send greeting to Philemon. These remarkable coincidences prove conclusively that the short letter to Philemon was written and sent at the same time as those to Ephesus and Colossæ.

We now ask, were the three Epistles written from Cæsarea or from Rome? That they were written from Rome, an early and widespread tradition asserts. Meyer and others argue that they were written from Cæsarea, on the ground that it is more likely that a runaway slave would go to Cæsarea than to Rome which was much further and involved a long sea voyage, that from Rome to Colossæ Tychicus and Onesimus would pass through Ephesus and that if so Paul would have commended Onesimus to the Church there as he does to that at Colossæ, and that Paul's request (Philem. 22) for a *lodging* implying hope of an early journey to Colossæ suggests Cæsarea, from which place, had Paul been set free, he might have travelled through Colossæ to Ephesus and to Rome.

These arguments have no great weight. In all ages longer routes to the metropolis have been more easy than shorter routes from one provincial town to another, and fugitives have ever preferred to hide themselves among the multitudes of a great city. Possibly Onesimus' plan was to leave Tychicus at Ephesus and to pass on without delay to the master he had wronged at Colossæ. Reasons unknown to us may have given Paul hopes of early liberation. And his deep interest in the young Churches on the Lycus, acknowledged in Col. ii. 1, may have prompted him to plan an early visit to them.

On the other side I can adduce only one argument, viz. indications that the three Epistles were written later than that to the Philippians. Although in its tone of triumphant calm and in the absence of serious discussion about Jew and Gentile this last Epistle is closely related to those to Ephesus and Colossæ, it is in teaching and phraseology much more closely related than they are to the earlier Epistles and especially to that to the Romans. Compare Ph. iii. 9, *not having a righteousness of my own, even that which is from law, but that which is through faith of Christ, the righteousness* which is *from God on the condition of faith:* a very close coincidence with Rom. i. 17, iii. 21, 22, x. 3. Also cop are Ph. iii. 4—6 with 2 Cor. xi. 21—30; and note other phrases found only in the earlier Epistles. These coincidences seem to me far to outweigh the arguments adduced by Meyer.

Against this earlier date of the Epistle to the Philippians, but not necessarily against the other Epistles being written at Rome, it has been objected that Ph. iv. 10 implies a long interval between Paul's arrival at Rome and the letter to Philippi, an interval long enough for news of his imprisonment to reach Philippi, for delay there, for the journey and illness of Epaphroditus, for news of his illness to reach Philippi, and for Epaphroditus to know this. But probably, even for all this, a year would suffice. For the journey from Rome to Philippi along splendid Roman roads and across the narrow straits would occupy probably not more than a month and could be made at almost any time of the year. And the illness of Epaphroditus may have been on the eastern side of the straits where it might soon become known at Philippi.

Another objection is based on Ph. i. 20—26, which suggests that a crisis of Paul's trial was near. From this, some have inferred that the letter was written near to the close of his imprisonment. But it is quite possible that in the mismanagement of Nero's rule Paul's trial was delayed after its decision had seemed to be near.

Reviewing the whole case, the balance of evidence seems to me to incline somewhat to the earlier date of the Epistle to the Philippians. And this implies that the other letters were written, not from Caesarea, but from Rome. We may suppose that the letter to Philippi was written within the first year of Paul's imprisonment at Rome and at a time when the decision of his case seemed to be near; that a further delay arose of more than a year; and that towards the close of it, when Paul was again hoping for liberty, Epaphras arrived with news about the Colossians and the Christians of Asia. This is to me much easier than to suppose that, after the remarkable development of thought embodied in the Epistles to the Ephesians and the Colossians, Paul could write the Epistle to the Philippians in which we find no trace of this development. Between the Epistles an interval must be allowed which if not very long was sufficient for a marked growth in the thought of the Apostle. Probably this growth was stimulated by the news brought by Epaphras. In Diss. iii. of my *Corinthians* we have seen that Paul arrived in Rome probably early in A.D. 62. If so, he may have written to the Philippians early in A.D. 63, and the other three letters a year later.

The occasion of the Epistles is involved in what has just been said. Paul is a prisoner in charge of the Pretorian guard at Rome, expecting an early decision of his case, but utterly uncertain whether it will bring him liberty and further work for Christ or sudden death. A messenger arrives with a contribution in money from the Church at Philippi which has already given several proofs of its care for him. Epaphroditus even apologizes for the lateness of the gift, by saying that circumstances had delayed it. On his way to Rome, he had been dangerously ill: and news of this had reached Philippi. The traveller is eager to return, in order to remove, by his own presence among them again, the anxiety thus caused to his fellow-Christians at home. And Paul sends with him, as an abundant recompense for their kindness to him, this beautiful letter in which he pours out his joy and gratitude for this remarkable proof of the Christian character of his beloved children in the faith.

The expected decision is deferred : and Paul lingers in prolonged bondage. But within the narrow walls of his prison he ponders the grandeur of the Eternal Son and the eternal purpose of salvation. During this long delay, probably near to its close, the Apostle is cheered by the arrival of Epaphras, an earnest Christian worker from the far off valley of the Lycus, who has himself planted the Gospel in its three cities and now narrates all this to Paul. The news fills him with joy. But the joy is mixed with anxiety caused by indications that at least in Colossæ serious error is taking root, error which threatens to undo the good work already begun. That the letter was addressed to Colossæ, suggests that there the danger was greatest. That Paul directs the letter to be read also at Laodicea, implies that this neighbouring city was infected. The one slight reference (Col. iv. 13) to Hierapolis suggests that it was the smallest of the three Churches.

Either for other reasons or at Paul's request, Tychicus is going to Asia, his native province, and to Colossæ. Paul writes and sends with him a letter setting forth, in view of the errors there prevalent, the greatness and sufficiency of the Son of God in His relation to the Church and to the Universe. And since on his way Tychicus must pass through Ephesus and must cross the province of Asia, Paul writes, and sends with him, another letter to the Ephesians and to the various Churches of the province.

Before this time, a runaway slave of a Christian at Colossæ called Philemon, who apparently had robbed his master, had come to Rome and come within Paul's influence and by him had been led to Christ. Already the young convert had been helpful to the imprisoned Apostle. But Paul now sends him back to his defrauded master, in company with Tychicus who was going to the same place, and sends with him a third letter begging his friend to receive back as a Christian brother the returning fugitive.

Bearing these documents, familiar now in every land and almost in every home and more precious than diamonds, the strange companions in travel started on their long journey over land and sea, leaving the great Apostle, whose loving and anxious heart and earnest prayers followed their steps, still in bonds at Rome.

In the following exposition, the Epistle to the Philippians is placed first, as being nearest in its teaching and phraseology to the Epistles already annotated. And this seems to me, as I have endeavoured to show, the most likely order of time. The Epistle to the Colossians comes next, as dealing with a specific matter, namely the news brought by Epaphras about the error spreading at Colossæ. Then follows the letter to Philemon, dealing with another specific, but less important, matter. Last of all I have placed the profound Epistle to the Ephesians which treats of no specific matter but sets forth, from its own point of view, the Eternal Purpose of Salvation and its realisation in the One Church of Christ.

EXPOSITION OF THE EPISTLE TO THE PHILIPPIANS.

SECTION I.
A CHRISTIAN GREETING.
CH. I. 1, 2.

Paul and Timothy, servants of Christ Jesus, to all the saints in Christ Jesus who are at Philippi, with the bishops and deacons: ² *grace to you and peace from God our Father and the Lord Jesus Christ.*

1. The absence of any assertion of authority here and in 1 Th. i. 1, 2 Th. i. 1 is explained by the evident and unanimous loyalty to the Apostle of these two Macedonian Churches. This permitted him to place his beloved disciple and himself on the same level as alike doing the work of the one Master: *Paul and Timothy, servants of Christ Jesus.* Cp. Rom. xvi. 21, 1 Cor. xvi. 10, and note under Rom. i. 1. This reminds us that Paul and Timothy were together when the Gospel was first preached at Philippi. For the same reason the name of Silas is added in 1 Th. i. 1, 2 Th. i. 1. The association of Timothy with Paul in other Epistles recalls also the close spiritual relationship recorded in Ph. ii. 19—22, 1 Cor. iv. 17.

Saints: see under Rom. i. 7. This common designation of all Christians, read in the light of the Old Testament, implies that God had claimed for Himself all the professed servants of Christ, thus placing them, in privilege and solemn obligation, on a level with, or rather infinitely above, the *holy* objects of the Old Covenant. *In Christ Jesus:* as in 1 Cor. i. 2. In distinction from the Old Covenant, our consecration to God is brought about through the historic facts of Christ and is consummated by spiritual union with Him. *Who are etc.:* emphatic assertion that *at Philippi* there are *saints in Christ Jesus. All the saints:* so Rom. i. 7, 1 Cor. i. 2, 2 Cor. i. 2; but not Eph. i. 1, Col. i. 2. Totality is very conspicuous in *vv.* 3, 4, 7, 8. Writing to the Philippian Christians as individual saints, Paul thinks of them *all* without exception.

Bishops and deacons: evidently two orders of Church officers. So 1 Tim. iii. 2, 8: cp. Ep. of Clement, ch. 42, in my *Corinthians* App. I. In Acts xx. 28 Paul speaks of the elders of the Church at Ephesus as *bishops;* thus implying, as here, a plurality of bishops in one Church. That the two titles describe one office, is implied in Tit. i. 5, 7. Our word *bishop* is an English form of the Greek word here used, which denotes an overseer. 'Elder' was a Jewish title: cp. Mt. xvi. 21, Num. xi. 16, Ex. iii. 16, 18. *Deacons:* see under Rom. xii. 7. Why Church officers are mentioned in this greeting and in no other from the pen of Paul, is matter of mere conjecture. Something unknown to us brought them to his mind while writing; possibly the part they had taken in the contribution of which this letter is an acknowledgment. [This is not forbidden, though not favoured, by the absence of the article.] Doubtless Paul's reference would be understood by those to whom it was written.

2. Word for word as in Rom. i. 7, 1 Cor. i. 3, 2 Cor. i. 2, Philem. 3. The suitability of these well-chosen words had printed them on the mind of Paul. He desires for his readers *grace* or *favour,* and, resulting from it, *peace,* i.e. inward rest arising from consciousness of safety, *from our Father, God, and* from *Jesus Christ,* the one *Lord* or *Master.*

SECTION II.

PRAISE AND PRAYER FOR THE CHRISTIANS AT PHILIPPI.

Ch. I. 3—11.

I thank my God for all my remembrance of you, ¹*always in every petition of mine on behalf of you all making the petition with joy,* ²*for your fellowship in furtherance of the Gospel from the first day until now;* ³*being confident of this very thing, that He who has begun in you a good work will complete* it *until the Day of Jesus Christ;* ⁴*according as it is right for me to be of this mind on behalf of you all, because I have you in my heart, both in my bonds and in* *the defence and confirmation of the Gospel, all of you being partakers with me of grace.* ⁸*For God is my witness, how I long for you all in the tender mercies of Christ Jesus.*

⁹*And this I pray, that your love yet more and more may abound in knowledge and all discernment,* ¹⁰*so that ye may approve the excellent things, that ye may be sincere and without stumbling to* the *Day of Christ,* ¹¹*being made full* of the *fruit of righteousness, that* which is *through Jesus Christ, for glory and praise of God.*

3. The first person singular shows us that Paul thinks of himself alone as writer of this letter. Accordingly, in ch. ii. 19, Timothy is spoken of merely in the third person. He is associated with Paul only in the superscription. Contrast 1 and 2 Thess., where by the first person plural maintained throughout Paul joins with himself Silvanus and Timothy as sharing his sentiments, thus reminding us that they had recently shared his labours and perils at Thessalonica. On the other hand, this Epistle was evoked by special liberality towards Paul alone.

Paul's entire *remembrance* of the Philippian Christians, i.e. all that he remembers about them, this looked upon as one pleasant memory, is a ground of thanks to God. *My God:* as in Rom. i. 8. The 'good work' wrought in his readers, Paul feels to be a personal gift to himself from *God*, before whom in the solitude of his own spirit he stands: for this work was an answer to his prayers and in part a result of his own labours.

4. A collateral statement showing with what good reason Paul thanks God for his entire remembrance of his readers. So good was this remembrance that every prayer for every one of them was to him always a matter of joy. This joy explains his thanks. And it becomes, even in his prison at Rome, the key-note of the Epistle. So chs. i. 18, 25, ii. 2, 17, 18, 28, 29, iii. 1, iv. 1, 4, 10. *Always . . . every . . . all* justify and expound 'all my remembrance of you.' With this acknowledgment of universal excellence compare the more guarded, yet strong, language of 1 Cor. i. 4—8. *Petition,* or *supplication:* a definite prayer prompted by felt need: so *v.* 19, ch. iv. 6, Rom. x. 1, Lk. i. 13. It suggests urgency.

This unmixed delight aroused in the breast of Paul by his every thought about the Christians at Philippi gives to them a unique place of honour among the Churches of the New Testament. We shall, therefore, eagerly gather together as we pass along all indications of their character and conduct, and shall regret that these are so scanty.

5. This verse is parallel with, and expounds, 'for all my remembrance of you,' stating the special feature in the Philippian Christians which evoked Paul's joy and gratitude. *Fellowship:* a disposition to share with others effort, toil, peril, enjoyment, or material good, either by receiving from them a share of their good or ill, or by giving to them a share of ours. It is a word very common and important with Paul: e.g. Rom. xii. 13, xv. 26, 27, 1 Cor. i. 9, x. 16, 18, 20, 2 Cor. i. 7, vi. 14, viii. 4, 23, ix. 13, xiii. 13. *In furtherance of* (or *for*) *the Gospel:* aim of this co-operation, viz. to spread the good news of salvation. For this end the Philippian Christians worked together, either one with another, or the whole body with Paul and others. For an example of such co-operation, see ch. iv. 3. And their brotherhood was not only universal but had been constant throughout their entire Christian course: *from the first day until now.* Constancy is the great test of personal worth. A fellow-worker always ready to co-operate is beyond price.

That this one excellence is here given as itself a sufficient reason for Paul's unmixed joy and gratitude, reveals its unique importance. And this we can understand. For, that God has committed the spread of the Gospel to the voluntary co-operation of a multitude of workers, gives special value to a virtue which leads a man to work easily with others. And, since all sin and selfishness tend to set man against man, the spirit of brotherhood implies all Christian excellence. It is therefore a sure test of character. For its only source is that 'love' (see *v.* 9) which is a 'fulfilment of the Law.' This spirit of brotherhood prompted the contribution of which this letter is an acknowledgment: cp. ch. iv. 14. And in this matter also the Philippian Christians showed equal constancy: *v.* 15. But whether Paul refers here to this special form of brotherhood, we do not know. Certainly it was not his sole reference.

6. A firm persuasion underlying Paul's gratitude for his readers' co-operation for the spread of the Gospel. *Complete:* bring to perfection, to the goal towards which it tends: Rom. xv. 28, 2 Cor. vii. 1. *Begun, complete:* same contrast in 2 Cor. viii. 6, Gal. iii. 3. The co-operation was *a good work,* but so manifestly incomplete that Paul can speak of it only as a good work *begun.* He traces it, however, to a personal Worker, Whose Name he need not mention. And he is sure that what *He has begun* He *will complete.* Thus the work already done assures Paul that greater things will follow. And the prospect of these greater blessings makes his remembrance of the Philippian Christians so pleasant. This is the real significance of all present spiritual good in ourselves or others. Its incompleteness proclaims that from the same personal Source greater things will come.

The Day of Jesus Christ: as in *v.* 10, ii. 16, 1 Cor. i. 8, v. 5, 2 Cor. i. 14. The frequent use of these simple words in this definite sense shows how definite and important in the minds of the early Christians was the Second Coming of Christ. *Until* the Day of Christ; suggests a further spiritual work during life, like that already begun, to be consummated in the Great Day. This phraseology suggests that Paul did not know certainly that the Return of Christ would be delayed for centuries after the last of his readers had been laid in the grave. But the Day of Christ, not the day of death, must ever be the aim of His servants' forward look. For in that Day, and not till then, will the good work which God is now doing in His people's hearts be completed and manifested. Not for the day of death, which will rend asunder what God has joined, but for the Day of their Lord's return, His servants wait. In that Day He will present to Himself the spotless Church. And towards that consummation tends our present growth in spiritual life.

7. A statement in harmony with, and thus supporting, the confident hope just expressed. *To be of this mind:* to cherish this hope. [The word rendered *mind* is a link connecting this Epistle with that to the Romans, and suggests a common author: cp. Rom. viii. 5, xi. 20, xii. 3, 16, xiv. 6, xv. 5; Ph. ii. 2, 5, iii. 15, 19, iv. 2, 10.] *On-behalf-of you all;* recalls the universal terms in *vv.* 3, 4. *Right:* same word as *righteous* and *just.* That simple justice demands this firm expectation of the final consummation of every one of his readers, implies strong proof of their sincerity and excellence. Similar thought in 2 Th. i. 3, ii. 13: cp. i. 6.

Because etc: ground of the *right* just mentioned. Its ultimate ground is uncovered in the last words of the verse, for which the preceding words prepare the way. It was not Paul's love for his readers that made it right to expect that the work begun in them would be completed, but his loving remembrance that the smile of God which shines on him shines also on them. The Philippian Christians have an abiding and large place in Paul's heart: and this moulds all his thought about them. *My bonds;* implies that Paul was in prison while writing this letter: so *vv.* 13, 14. This clause is to be joined probably to the foregoing. Within the narrow limits of Paul's prison walls, his readers are ever with him. And whenever, either to visitors in his prison or before heathen judges or elsewhere, he defends against attack the truth of the Gospel, or when he endeavours to impart to believers a firmer and fuller knowledge of it, he thinks ever of his beloved converts at Philippi. Thoughts of them dispel in part the gloom of his dungeon, and strengthen his defence of the Gospel. Thus the changing circumstances and occupation of the Apostle throw into relief his constant thought of them. *All of you being etc.:* the aspect in which they are present to him. *Partakers:* cognate to 'fellowship' in *v.* 5 : they were *joint-sharers with him. Grace:* the undeserved favour of God, to which Paul owes whatever he has or is: so 1 Cor. xv. 10. God's smile rests, as he remembers, on every one of his readers. Therefore, while looking forward to the completion in himself of that which the grace of God has begun, Paul feels himself bound by his sense of right to expect a like completion of the work begun in them. Thus his hopes for them are traced to the only sure ground of hope, the undeserved favour of God.

8. This verse supports the new thought introduced in *v.* 7, viz. that Paul has his readers in his heart. *God, my witness:* a genuine trait of Paul, Rom. i. 9, 1 Th. ii. 5. *Long-for:* same word in ch. ii. 26, Rom. i. 11, 1 Th. iii. 6, 2 Tim. i. 4. *You all;* maintains the universality which is so marked a feature of this section. *Tender-mercies:* same word in 2 Cor. vi. 12 ; see note. While Paul bears his readers in his heart, he feels that his love for them is an outflow of the *tender mercies of Christ.* That divine tenderness is the element in which Paul's love breathes and lives. Thus, to *v.* 7, *v.* 8 is a climax.

Such are Paul's first thoughts about his readers. As he turns in thought to them, one feature of their character absorbs his attention, viz. their harmonious co-operation for the spread of the Gospel. This co-operation is universal, and has been constant throughout their course. So sure a mark is it of Christian excellence that it makes every prayer for them a delight, and every remembrance of them thanks to God. The secret of this joy is Paul's firm confidence that what he sees in his readers is but the beginning of a development which will not cease till consummated in the Day of Christ's Return. And this confidence is made obligatory to him by his loving recognition, amid his various hardships and labours, of the evident grace of God shining upon them as well as upon himself. And, while protesting his yearning for them, he remembers that its source and the element in which it moves are not human but divine, that his love is but an outflow of the tender love which fills the breast of Christ.

9. After mentioning for a moment in *v.* 4 his petitions to God for his readers, Paul now adds to his thanks for the good work already begun in them and his hopes for its completion a definite prayer for its progress: *and this I pray.* The matter of this prayer, he de-

scribes as its purpose: he prays *in order that* their *love etc. Love:* the principle which prompts us to do good to our fellows; as always when not further defined. So Rom. xii. 9, xiii. 10, 1 Cor. xiii. It is the distinctive feature of the Christian character. By asking for its increase, Paul assumes its existence. And rightly so. For it is implied (*v.* 5) in 'fellowship,' of which mutual love is always the animating principle. *Knowledge:* more fully 'scientific knowledge,' an orderly and comprehensive acquaintance with something; as in Rom. i. 28, iii. 20, x. 2: a favourite word of Paul, especially in his later Epistles. Its frequency there is a mark of his mature thought, and perhaps of his deepening conviction of the need, in order to escape prevalent dangers, of a fuller knowledge of the Gospel. *Discernment:* perception of qualities. Frequent in classical Greek for perception by the bodily senses. Paul desires for his readers a comprehensive acquaintance with things divine and a faculty of distinguishing right from wrong in the various details of life. The word *all* recalls the number and variety of these details. *Abound:* either itself abundant in quantity or results, as in 2 Cor. i. 5, Rom. iii. 7; or possessing abundance of *knowledge and discernment*, as in 1 Cor. viii. 8, 2 Cor. viii. 7. According to the one interpretation, Paul prays that his readers' love may increase and their increasing love be associated with knowledge: or, that the knowledge which already enriches their love may increase, and thus enrich it still more. The difference here is slight. Perhaps the latter sense is nearer to Paul's thought. For he passes at once in *v.* 10 to the desired result of *knowledge and discernment,* showing that of them he thinks chiefly. *Yet more and more:* further and further in the same direction. This is a courteous acknowledgment that his readers' love is already rich in, and enriched by, knowledge.

10. Further purpose, and then a final purpose, of the enrichment in knowledge. *Approve,* or *prove:* put to the test with good purpose, i.e. to detect the good. *The excellent things:* literally, *the things that differ.* But the good aim already implied in the word rendered *approve,* and the result which Paul expects (in *v.* 10*b*) to follow this proving, imply that the difference referred to is that of superiority. Same words in same sense in Rom. ii. 18. Same purpose in Rom. xii. 2. Only a divinely given comprehension of the great realities and discernment of moral details will enable us to distinguish the comparative excellence of various modes of action. And no gift is of greater practical worth.

That ye may be etc.: i.e. 'seek Christian intelligence in order that it may mould your character.' *Sincere:* unmixed with any foreign matter. So 1 Cor. v. 8, 2 Cor. i. 12, ii. 17, 2 Pet. iii. 1, Wisdom vii. 25. The meaning is well illustrated in Plato's *Phædo* pp. 66*a*, 67*a*.] *Without-cause-of-stumbling:* having nothing against which either themselves or others may strike their foot and fall. Same word in the latter sense in 1 Cor. x. 32, in the former sense in Acts xxiv. 16. Here perhaps in the former sense, causing themselves to stumble. For Paul is referring to the development of his readers' own spiritual life. Everything foreign to the Christian life tends to trip up in the Christian course him who tolerates it. Paul desires for his readers spiritual intelligence in order that they may accurately distinguish moral qualities, in order that thus there may be in them no mixture of impure elements and that they may escape the peril of falling which such foreign elements involve. *The Day of Christ:* as in v. 6. The recurrence of this thought reveals its firm hold of the mind of Paul. *To the Day etc:* ultimate goal of Paul's thoughts about his readers. He desires them to be pure and to be preserved from falling in order that they may be so found in that day. Same words and thought in ch. ii. 16, Eph. iv. 30, 2 Tim. i. 12. The slightly different words in v. 6 note a slightly different thought, viz. the time to which he desires his readers' spiritual development to continue.

11. A collateral element in Paul's prayer, placing beside the foregoing negatives, 'without mixture and without stumbling,' a positive blessing. He desires them not only to stand erect in the Day of Christ but to be then *full of fruit*. *Righteousness:* right doing, conformity with the moral standard, as in Rom. vi. 13, 18, 20. *Fruit of righteousness:* the good results growing naturally, in the moral order of the universe, out of right doing. Same words and similar thoughts in Jas. iii. 18, Prov. xi. 30. This harvest of blessing, only to be had by right doing, Paul desires his readers to have to the *full*. [The difficult accusative καρπόν specifies the remoter object of the desired filling. The Philippian Christians are its immediate object. *The fruit of righteousness* is, as matter of fact, that with which they are to be *made full*. But perhaps the accusative case represents the fruit rather as the extent of the fulness, or as the aim of Paul's prayer. He desires his readers to be made full in the sense, and to the extent, of obtaining the fruit of righteousness. Same construction in Col. i. 9.] The fruit is *through Jesus Christ*. For only through His agency come good works and their good results. They thus show forth the *glory and praise of God*, i.e. His splendour evoking admiration (see under Rom. i. 21) and verbal acknowledgment. And this ultimate result of the blessings

which Paul asks for his readers is also the final aim of his prayer for them. He prays for them the more earnestly and confidently because he knows that the answer to his prayer will reveal the greatness of God and evoke in earth and heaven a louder note of praise to Him. Cp. Rom. xv. 7.

As usual, Paul's first thought about his readers is praise to God for them. But the incompleteness of the good work for which he gives thanks moves him at once to pray that the work begun in them may make progress. So good is the work that Paul needs only to pray that it may advance in the same direction. For in their spirit of brotherhood he recognises that love which is the essence of the Christian character. Especially he prays that, as hitherto so in greater measure, their love may be rich in general Christian intelligence and in the faculty of discerning moral excellence, such excellence being a condition of spiritual purity and safety and of that right doing which will produce a harvest of blessing and thus make the Philippian Christians rich indeed. This harvest of blessing can come only through Christ, and will reveal the splendour of God and thus redound to His praise.

SECTION III.

PAUL'S BONDS, ADVERSARIES, AND FRIENDS.

CH. I. 12—18.

Moreover, I wish you to know, brethren, that the matters touching me have fallen out rather for progress of the Gospel; [13] *so that my bonds have become manifest in Christ in the whole Prætorian and to all the rest,* [14] *and the more part of the brethren having become confident in the Lord through my bonds are more abundantly bold to speak fearlessly the word of God.* [15] *Some indeed even because of envy and strife, but others also because of good will, proclaim Christ.* [16] *These, out of love, knowing that for defence of the Gospel I am set.* [17] *But the others out of a spirit of* faction *announce Christ, not purely, thinking to raise up affliction for my bonds.* [18] *What then? Only that in every way, whether pretence or truth, Christ is announced. And in this I rejoice; yes, and I will rejoice.*

After praise and prayer for his readers, Paul now speaks about himself; i.e. about (*vv.* 12-14) the results of his imprisonment, about (*vv.* 15-17) his enemies and friends, and about (*v.* 18) the joy indirectly caused to him both by friends and enemies

12. *To know:* literally, *to come to know,* to learn. Paul now begins to give information. *I wish you to know:* similar words in 1 Cor. xi. 3; cp. Rom. i. 13, 1 Cor. x. 1, xii. 1, 2 Cor. i. 8, 1 Th. iv. 13. *The matters touching me:* the entire circumstances, doings, and experiences, of Paul. Same words in same sense in Eph. vi. 21, Col. iv. 7. *Progress:* same word in *v.* 25, 1 Tim. iv. 15; Gal. i. 14, Lk. ii. 52, 2 Tim. ii. 16. *The Gospel* makes *progress* (same idea in 2 Th. iii. 1) geographically, when the good news is carried from place to place; numerically, when one after another believes it and confesses Christ; spiritually, when as a 'power of God' it more and more moulds the inner and outer life of men. The word *rather* suggests a comparison or contrast between the expected and actual results of the events or circumstances about which Paul here writes, and thus implies that these events were likely to hinder the Gospel. Notice that the hardships involved in them are, throughout the Epistle, left entirely out of sight. The only point present to Paul's thought is their effect upon the spread of the good news of salvation.

13. A result of 'the things which happened to' Paul, stated as a proof and measure of the progress of the Gospel caused thereby. [ὥστε with the infinitive throws the emphasis on the foregoing statement, and indicates that the words which follow are a result affording proof and measure of this statement. Verses 13 and 14 tell to how great an extent the events and circumstances which threatened to hinder the Gospel have actually helped it forward.] *My bonds;* indicates the nature of the events referred to in *v.* 12 as likely to hinder the Gospel, viz. Paul's imprisonment, and confirms the suggestion in *v.* 7 that this letter was written in prison. Paul will now tell us how his arrest, which for so long time put an end to his active and successful labours, actually helped forward the cause for which he laboured. *Manifest in Christ:* set visibly before the eyes of men in their relation to Christ. Similar thought in 2 Cor. iii. 3: 'ye being made manifest that ye are an epistle of Christ ministered by us.' The real nature of Paul's imprisonment was made public, as occasioned not by crime but by the prisoner's relation to Christ.

The Prætorium: a Latin word denoting something belonging to the Prætor, a title given to the leader of the Roman armies. It denotes sometimes the general's tent. The same word denotes in Mt. xxvii. 27, Mk. xv. 16, Jno. xviii. 28, 33, xix. 9 the residence of a provincial governor. Similarly Acts xxiii. 35, 'Herod's prætorium.'

In a few clear cases, e.g. Tacitus, *Histories* bk. i. 20, it denotes the imperial body-guard, the *Prætorian* regiments, a corps of some 10,000 picked troops instituted by Augustus, and stationed, under Augustus in part, under Tiberius entirely, at Rome. This reference would give good sense here. We can conceive Paul, a prisoner who had appealed to Cæsar, committed to the charge of Prætorian soldiers, one of them always with him; and that thus the Gospel which Paul preached became known throughout the whole Prætorian guard. It has been suggested that the word refers to a great camp of the Prætorians established by Tiberius just outside Rome. But we have no proof that the word is ever so used. It is therefore better to accept here the indisputable reference noted above. See a very good note by Lightfoot.

Inasmuch as the residence of a Roman governor was also called *Prætorium*, the use of this word here is not in itself absolute proof that this Epistle was written from Rome. But it somewhat confirms other indications (especially ch. iv. 22) to this effect.

And to all the others.] Not only within the limits of the imperial body-guard, but to every one around, the nature of Paul's imprisonment became known.

14. A second result, showing further how much the events which happened to Paul have aided the progress of the Gospel. *The more part of the brethren;* reveals a minority, even among Christians, whose confidence in Christ was not increased by Paul's *bonds*. This minority must have included the opponents mentioned in *v.* 15. Possibly it may have included also some timid friends in whom Paul's imprisonment evoked, not faith, but fear. *In the Lord;* must be joined, not to *brethren*, to which it would add no meaning, but to *being-confident* specifying in very emphatic manner the Personal Ground of their increasing confidence. Through Paul's imprisonment most of the Christians around reposed new trust in Christ: for they saw in Paul, as they had never seen before, the presence and power and sufficient grace of Christ. Thus was 'Christ magnified' in Paul's body: *v.* 20. [This use of the Greek dative to denote an instrument is not uncommon: see Rom. xi. 20, xv. 18. To take *my bonds* as the ground of confidence, though grammatically admissible, (see Philem. 21,) gives no intelligible sense. Paul's imprisonment was the occasion, and in this sense the instrument, of trust in Christ, but could not be its ground. Moreover, the ground of this confidence is clearly stated: it is *in Christ.*] *More-abundantly bold;* recognises previous abundant boldness, which is now surpassed. *Fearlessly;* adds definiteness, and thus emphasis, to *more-abundantly bold.* No mixture of fear weakened the courage with which they proclaimed *the word of God*.

Thus in a twofold way did Paul's imprisonment aid the spread of the Gospel it threatened so seriously to hinder. By means of his long confinement, Christ became known throughout the most influential part of the Roman army, and to all the men around the prisoner. And such was his conduct in prison that he became to most of the Christians at Rome a revelation of the universal grace of Christ, and thus led them to put in Him new confidence and, trusting in Him, to give to the winds all fear and with greater courage than before proclaim the message of God.

15. The last words of *v.* 14 remind Paul that not all who 'speak the word of God' are prompted by confidence in Christ evoked by his imprisonment. Among them he distinguishes two classes inspired by different motives. *Because of envy:* moved by vexation at Paul's success: same words in Mt. xxvii. 18, Mk. xv. 10. *Strife:* active opposition, a natural result of *envy*. Same words together in 1 Tim. vi. 4. 'Even ill-will prompted by my success and a resolution to oppose me are motives to some men for preaching Christ. *Good-will:* either something which seems good to us, as in Lk. x. 21; or a wish for the good of others, as here. These senses often coalesce, as in Rom. x. 1. The meaning here is determined and expounded by the word 'love' in *v.* 16. *Proclaim:* as heralds announce the coming of a king. *Proclaim Christ:* as in 1 Cor. i. 23, xv. 12, 2 Cor. i. 19, iv. 5, xi. 4.

The hostility to Paul, revealed in *v.* 15, on the part of some who preached Christ, indicates a conception of the Gospel radically different from his. This suggests that these were Judaizing teachers like those referred to in Gal. i. 7, vi. 12 and like the apparently similar teachers mentioned in 2 Cor. xi. 4, 13, 22. And the suggestion is strongly confirmed by the plain reference to such teachers in Ph. iii. 2, 3.

16, 17. Further description of the two classes who 'preach Christ,' justifying the foregoing account of them; and arranged, like 2 Cor. ii. 15, 16, in inverse order. *Out of love:* the inward source of their preaching. Grammatically we may render either *They who* preach *out of love* do so *knowing that etc.*, or *These* preach *out of love knowing etc.* To a similar alternative interpretation *v.* 17 is open. Since the words *out of love* add definitely to the sense already conveyed by the word 'good-will' in *v.* 15, noting that this good-will is the central Christian virtue of *love*, I prefer, with A.V. and R.V., the latter interpretation [So Heb. vii. 21, xii. 10. The other in

Rom. ii. 7, 8, Gal. iv. 22.] The preaching prompted by 'good-will' springs out of *love*. This can only be love towards Paul, in contrast to the hostility described in v. 17. *Knowing that etc.*: ground of this special manifestation of Christian love. Notice here genuine phraseology of Paul: so Rom. v. 3, vi. 9, xiii. 11, 1 Cor. xv. 58, 2 Cor. i. 7, iv. 14, v. 6, 11. *Defence of the Gospel*: same words in v. 7. For this purpose Paul has been *set* by God in his present position in the Church. These men *know* this. And their Christian love inspires sympathy with the Apostle in his great work, and moves them to preach the Gospel committed to his charge. Consequently, in addition to men of baser motives there are those who 'also because of good-will proclaim Christ.'

17. Another class who 'preach Christ.' They must have been included in, and therefore not more numerous than, the minority (v. 14) whose confidence in Christ was not increased by Paul's imprisonment. Whether they constituted the whole minority, or whether there were in it others of different spirit, we do not know. *Out of* a spirit of *faction*: same words in Rom. ii. 8, where see note. They denote a low and mercenary spirit, ready to do base work for hire or in order to gain selfish and contemptible ends. One such motive is mentioned in Gal. vi. 12. Paul thus traces to their source 'the envy and strife' spoken of in v. 15. He intimates that his opponents were annoyed at his success, because it interfered with their own selfish aims, and that on this account they stirred up conflict against him. *Announce Christ*: bring the news that Christ has come. It is practically equivalent to 'preach Christ,' but leaves out of sight the official position of the herald. These words, which are in part a repetition, are added here to expose the incongruity of *announcing Christ out of party spirit*. *Not purely*: a comment. With this announcement of Christ was mixed a base element. *Thinking to raise up etc.*: exposition of the foregoing. It justifies Paul's charge that the preaching referred to was an outflow of mercenary spirit. *For my bonds*: i.e. for Paul in prison. So Rom. viii. 26, 'helps our weakness.' They thought that what they were doing was making or would make Paul's imprisonment more bitter to him. How this was to be, Paul does not say. But we can easily suppose that these were Jewish Christians who, like the Judaizers in Galatia, insisted on the continued and universal observance of the Jewish law as a condition of the salvation brought by Christ. They knew that the Apostle strongly denounced their teaching as subversive of the Gospel. And they *supposed* that by earnestly preaching Christ and winning converts, and thus gaining influence in the Church, they

would annoy Paul and make him feel more keenly the confinement which limited his effective opposition to them. *Affliction:* usually, external hardship. Here and in 2 Cor. ii. 4 it denotes severe inward sorrow caused by the unworthy conduct of Christians. This implies that to Paul such conduct was hardship as real as actual persecution.

Notice the contrast between the friends who *know,* their action being based on truth and reality, and the opponents who *suppose* but who labour, as *v.* 18 will show, under delusion.

18. *What then?* literally, *for why?* same words in Rom. iii. 3. They support, under the form of a startled question, or seek support for, something foregoing. Paul has just said that even his opponents, speaking with mercenary motives, nevertheless 'announce Christ.' This assertion he will now strengthen. *In every way:* expounded in detail by the following words. *Pretence:* as a cloak concealing the real motive. *In truth:* the apparent corresponding with the real. Paul supports the assertion in *v.* 17 by saying that it *only* amounts to this, that in every variety of mode, some being actually what it seems to be, and some a mask covering most unworthy aims, *Christ is* nevertheless *announced.* The second repetition of this last thought reveals its large place in Paul's thoughts about the various motives of the preachers at Rome. *In this* great fact Paul has present *joy:* and future joy awaits him, for reasons which he proceeds to give. Thus did his opponents fail. They thought, by propagating a Gospel which he condemned, to make his fetters more painful. Their efforts caused him joy, and gave him a hope of still further joy to come.

We have seen that *v.* 15 implies teaching about Christ and the Gospel by Paul's opponents quite different from his own. We naturally ask, How could Paul expect from such teaching good results? In very different language does he speak of opponents in Gal. v. 12, 2 Cor. xi. 15. An answer is not far to seek. Efforts to lead astray Paul's converts could do nothing but harm, and were therefore denounced in strong terms. But the words 'preach Christ' suggest that the activity of the adversaries at Rome was directed chiefly to those outside the Church. Such activity would at least spread the name of Christ, and might open a way for purer teaching. Possibly also, in accordance with the calmer tone which breathes throughout the letters written in prison, Paul's maturer thought may have detected a better side even in teaching which aroused his indignation while engaged in active labour in the face of many enemies. His joy reminds us that very imperfect teaching may be better than no teaching, and warns us not to despise imperfect forms of Christianity. Probably the worst form of it is better than the best non-Christian teaching.

Such are the tidings about himself which Paul sends to his readers. His imprisonment has brought the name of Christ into influential circles which otherwise it could hardly have reached; and the bondage of one preacher has opened the lips of many. It is true that some of these are moved by ill-will. They think by their activity to make the prisoner's chain more galling. But by preaching Christ they are doing good. So completely have they missed their aim that their efforts to trouble Paul have caused him abiding joy.

SECTION IV.

PAUL'S CONFIDENT HOPE, IN VIEW OF LIFE AND DEATH.

CH. I. 19—26.

For I know that to me this will result in salvation through your supplication and the supply of the Spirit of Jesus Christ, ^{20} *according to my eager expectation and hope that in nothing I shall be put to shame, but that with all boldness, as always so now also, Christ will be magnified in my body whether through life or through death.* ^{21} *For to me to live is Christ: and to die, gain.* ^{22} *But if to live in the flesh be my lot, this to me is fruit of work.* ^{23} *And what I shall choose for myself, I do not know. Moreover, I am held fast from the two sides, having my desire for dissolution and to be with Christ: for it is very far better.* ^{24} *But to abide in the flesh is more necessary, because of you.* ^{25} *And, being confident of this, I know that I shall abide, and abide with you all for your progress and joy of faith,* ^{26} *that your ground of exultation may abound in Christ Jesus in me through my presence with you again.*

After describing his outer surroundings of bonds, friends, and enemies, Paul closed § 3 by describing their inward effect upon him, viz. joy now and further joy in the future. This joy marks the transition to § 4 which describes his inner life in its relation to his outward surroundings. In vv. 19, 20 Paul justifies the joy expressed in v. 18, by a confident hope: and in vv. 21—26 he looks at this confidence in its relation to the alternative of life and death which is now before him.

19. A reason, viz. knowledge of the result, justifying Paul's joy that, even by his enemies and as a mask concealing a wish to annoy him, 'Christ is proclaimed.' Not his only reason, but one suiting his course of thought, which now passes from the life around him to the life within. *This:* as in v. 18, that 'Christ is proclaimed' even by enemies and in pretence. *Salvation:* in its usual sense of final deliverance from the spiritual perils of earth into eternal safety; as in v. 28, ch. ii. 12, Rom. i. 16, x. 1, 10, xi. 11, xiii. 11. Paul's joy that Christ is preached is not dimmed by the ill-will which occasioned it: for he knows that this effort to add bitterness to his imprisonment will work out for him spiritual safety and final deliverance. How this is to be, he does not say. But we know that, to the faithful, hardship develops spiritual strength, and thus fits for the battle of life and leads to final victory. In this way tribulation works endurance and hope: Rom. v. 3. Similarly, Paul's thorn in the flesh was designed by God to preserve him from spiritual peril: 2 Cor. xii. 7. Just so, the ill-will of his enemies was a safeguard preserving him for final *salvation*. Consequently, it could in no degree dim his joy that Christ was preached. Indeed his joy was increased by the manifest victory over all evil involved in the spiritual benefit resulting from his enemies' attempt to vex him.

The word *salvation* cannot mean release from imprisonment. For Paul is quite doubtful, as we shall see, whether life or death awaits him: there is no visible connection between his enemies' hostility and his own escape from prison, and no indication that the word is used here in any other than its ordinary sense.

Supplication or *petition:* as in v. 4. His readers' urgent request to God was a means through which Paul expected these good results. He knows that they pray for him, and is sure that God will answer their prayers in the development of his own spiritual life in spite of, and by means of, the hostility of his enemies. Another note of genuineness: cp. Rom. xv. 30, 2 Cor. i. 11, 2 Th. iii. 2. It reveals Paul's high estimate of the value of prayer for others. *Supply,* or *bountiful-supply:* see under 2 Cor. ix. 10. Grammatically, *the Spirit of Jesus Christ* may be either Himself the matter supplied (cp. Gal. iii. 5) or the Author of the supply. The practical difference is very slight. For the Holy Spirit given is Himself the active source of all spiritual good: and He supplies our need by Himself becoming the animating principle of our life. He is therefore both Giver and Gift. But since the Holy Spirit is usually thought of as definitely once for all given to all who believe, it is better to think of Him here as actively supplying Paul's various spiritual needs. Notice two channels through which Paul expects blessings. He knows that his readers at Philippi will pray for him ; and that in answer to their prayer the Spirit of Jesus will by His own presence supply the spiritual needs occasioned by Paul's peculiar circumstances.

20. A personal and appropriate condition on which depends the realisation of the assured expectation just expressed: *according to* etc. *Eager-expectation:* see under Rom. viii. 19. To this, the word *hope* adds the idea of expected benefit. *That in nothing* etc.: negative side of the expectation, as usual placed first. *Put-to-shame:* deserted by God in the hour of trial and thus covered with ridicule by the failure of his hopes. Paul is sure that *in nothing* that awaits him will this happen. Same word in same sense in Rom. v. 5. This objective sense involves also here the subjective sense of fear or ridicule, as in Rom. i. 16. But the trust in God which pervades this page suggests that Paul thinks, not of what he will feel, but of what will happen to him. *In all boldness:* positive side of Paul's expectation. *Christ will be magnified:* in the subjective view of men, to whom Christ will occupy a larger place through that which they see in Paul; cp. Lk. i. 46, Acts x. 46, v. 13 ; also Lev. x. 3. Notice that in this enlargement Paul is represented not as himself magnifying Christ, but only as His body the locality in which *Christ will be magnified*. *Boldness*, or *unreserved speech:* see under 2 Cor. iii. 12. Paul has an assured hope that God will give him grace to speak the whole truth without fear of consequences, and that in his unreserved speech will be revealed the greatness of Christ. An example of this in Acts iv. 13. Thus the realisation of Paul's hope depends upon himself. But even for courage he trusts to God and to the Spirit of Jesus Christ. Already Christ is *always* magnified in Paul. And he has a firm hope that what has been hitherto will be *now also*, even amid his peculiarly trying circumstances. This modest recognition of his own moral excellence is in close harmony with 2 Cor. i. 12.

In my body: special locality of the revelation in Paul of the greatness of Christ. The weakness and suffering and peril of Paul's fettered body will show forth the greatness of Him who is able to fill His servants, even in prison, with confidence and peace and joy. *The body* is specially mentioned as that side of Paul which comes in immediate contact with his hard surroundings and in which is seen manifested the greatness of Christ. The importance here given to *the body* is a note of genuineness. Cp. Rom. vi. 12, viii. 13, xii. 1.

A tremendous alternative overhanging Paul's bodily life cannot be overlooked in this eager glance into the future. In any case, *Christ will be magnified*. But Paul knows not *whether* it will be *through*

4

the continued preservation of his body in *life*, or *through* his *death*.

Such is the failure of the attempt to make Paul's imprisonment more galling. His opponents think to annoy him by preaching a Gospel he does not approve. Their attempt to vex him fills the prisoner with joy. For their preaching, though containing serious error, makes known the name of Christ to some who perhaps otherwise would not hear it. And Paul knows that their hostility is one of the many things working together for his good, giving occasion for Christian patience, and thus strengthening him for the remaining battle of life. That he is unmoved by such annoyance, evokes a sure confidence of final salvation. And this confidence is supported by knowledge that the beloved ones at Philippi pray for him and that the Spirit of Christ will supply his every need. This assurance of final victory rests upon an assurance that in every trial God will give to Paul a courage which will show forth the greatness of Christ, and is not shaken by his uncertainty whether life or death awaits him.

21—26. The just mentioned alternative, 'whether by life or by death,' as it presents itself to the wavering thought and feelings of Paul. *To me;* introduces conspicuously the personal experience of Paul. *To live is Christ;* proves that 'Christ will be magnified . . . by life.' Cp. Col. iii. 4, 'Christ your life;' Gal. ii. 20, 'Christ lives in me.' Christ animates and permeates Paul's entire activity, so that all his words and acts are really said and done by Christ and are therefore an outflow of Christ living in him. Consequently, the personality of Christ is the centre and circumference of the entire life of Paul. If so, in his body the character and greatness of Christ will ever appear. And the various events of life, pleasant and unpleasant, will but show how great Christ is.

To die is gain.] Whatever earthly wealth the Christian loses by death, he gains in the wealth of heaven infinitely more. For all material good is but a scanty and dim outline of the eternal reality. And none except the servants of Christ can speak of death as gain. Others may bravely give up life in a noble cause. They thus endure with worthy aim, so far as they can see, the loss of all things. The Christian martyr suffers no loss, for he knows that death is immediate enrichment.

These last words were not needed to prove that Christ will be magnified in Paul's death. For the martyr's dying courage is part of the life which Christ lives in him. But they strengthen the proof already given. For the greatness of Christ is revealed in every one who calmly looks death in the face for Christ's sake, and declares it to be gain. Such victory reveals the presence of one greater than death. These words are also a contrast suggested by the alternative now before Paul.

22. *To live in flesh;* takes up 'to live' in *v*. 21. The added words are needed, after the implied reference to a life beyond the grave, to show that Paul refers now, not to his real life which is exposed to no uncertainty, but only to life *in* mortal *flesh*. *Work:* immediate result and embodiment of sustained effort. *Fruit of work:* further result developed from work done, according to its own organic laws. *If* Paul continue *to live* on earth, his continued life will be *work* done; and from this work he will gather good *fruit*. Close coincidence in Rom. i. 13.

[Two renderings of this verse, as in R.V. text and margin, are possible. (a) The words *If to live in* the *flesh* may be a complete conditional clause; and *this* is *to me fruit of work* a direct assertion limited by the foregoing condition. In this case we must supply from the general train of thought some such words as *be my lot*. The following words, *and what I shall choose*, will then come naturally as an additional thought. The word *if* will suitably introduce one side of the alternative of life and death which now fills the thought of Paul. And this alternative suggests easily the inserted words *be my lot*. For Paul is now uncertain what his lot will be. Or we may take (b) *If to live in flesh . . . fruit of work* as one conditional clause, and the words *what I shall choose for myself I know not* as the main assertion. That which in (a) is expressly stated, viz. that Paul's life in flesh brings with it fruit of labour, is in (b) only casually implied, the main assertion being that Paul knows not what to choose. The question is whether *this* is *to me fruit of labour* is an independent and direct assertion, or is merely subordinate to the assertion following. The importance of the thought contained in these words favours the former supposition. Moreover, to (b) the word *if* (εἰ) presents a difficulty. For, although it may be used, as Ellicott follows Meyer in saying, in a syllogistic sense as in Col. iii. 1, we have no case in the N.T. of this use where the idea of uncertainty is altogether absent. And here there is no doubt whatever that for Paul *to live* is to work and to have *fruit of* his *work*. Nor have we in the N.T. a case of καί used as (b) would require. On the other hand, the supplied words required by (a) are easily suggested by the terrible alternative before the prisoner awaiting his trial. Paul is sure that in his body Christ will be magnified, but knows not whether this will be by preserved life or by a martyr's death. If he live, his life will be a continued incarnation of Christ. If he die, death will enrich him. These last words seem to give a preference to death. But this, Paul repudiates. To him both death and life are gain. He therefore takes up the alternative of life, and tells its real significance and worth. Instead of saying simply *to live in flesh, this is to me fruit of work*, Paul expresses the uncertainty of his present position by prefixing the word *if*, conveying easily the sense *if* it be my lot *to live in* the *flesh etc.* This exposition gives the chief prominence to the most important words of the sentence, *this is to me fruit of work*, which the other exposition hides in a conditional clause. In spite therefore of the preponderant judgment of both ancient and modern expositors, I venture to give a slight preference to (a). But the practical difference is not great.]

I do not know or *I do not say*. The latter is the meaning everywhere else in the N.T. of the word so rendered. The former is its more common use in classical Greek. And as a reader was accustomed to the one or the other, he would probably interpret Paul's words. The difference is slight. The latter interpretation makes Paul simply silent: the former makes him silent because he has nothing to say.

23. Additional detail about Paul's state of mind in view of the great alternative. *Held fast from the two* sides: whichever way he looks, from that side comes an irresistible influence. 'To live in the flesh' is for Paul a prolonged incarnation of Christ, and brings with it work producing a harvest of blessing. And 'to die is gain.' Yet, in spite of this double and contrary compulsion, Paul has a *desire* in the matter. It is *for dissolution :* literally, *taking-to-pieces.* A cognate word, in the same sense of death, in 2 Tim. iv. 6. Often used in classical Greek in the sense of release or departure. *And to be with Christ:* inseparably connected in Paul's thought with *dissolution.* While saying that a double compulsion from two directions holds him fast, he yet acknowledges that his desire goes in the direction of dissolution and the immediate companionship of Christ which it gives. Over this preference Paul lingers, and supports it by a direct assertion: *for it is very far better.* That he looked upon the state entered at death as a companionship of Christ *very much better* than his present state of fruitful work, implies that in his view the departed servants of Christ are, while waiting for the greater glory of the resurrection, already in intelligent intercourse with Him infinitely closer than the fellowship enjoyed on earth. Notice that Paul's thought about death is not, as with many, mere rest from the hardships of life, but actual intercourse with Christ. A close coincidence with 2 Cor. v. 8, where see note; and thus another mark of common authorship.

24. Paul's wavering thought, drawn in different directions, turns again to the advantage of continuing on earth. *To abide in the flesh:* similar phrase in Rom. vi. 1, xi. 22, 23, Col. i. 23. Although his wearied heart yearns for the fuller fellowship with Christ which death will bring, he recognises the more pressing need that he remain a time longer in the weakness of bodily life. Notice the contrasted comparatives: 'very far better' and *more necessary*. *Because of you:* the beloved Christians at Philippi as representing all those whom Paul's continued life will benefit.

25. Two renderings possible: *and, being confident of this, I know that*, or *and this I confidently know that etc.* The former refers the word *this* to the foregoing, making the necessity of Paul's continuance in the flesh a ground of his assurance that he shall so continue: the latter merely makes a very strong assertion without giving any reason. Paul's habit of giving reasons favours the former rendering. He is quite sure that there is more need for him to remain than to depart; and this assurance convinces him that that which is more needful will be his actual lot. *Abide:* absolutely, continue in his present state. *Abide with you all:* relative continuance, prolonged association with the Christians at Philippi. *Progress and joy of faith:* probably *progress* in the Christian life and the *joy* which always accompanies growth, both progress and joy being derived from *faith*, the unique condition of Christian life.

26. Further aim of Paul's continuance with his readers. It is evidently a purpose of God, who will preserve him. *Ground of exultation:* as in Rom. iv. 2. *May-abound:* that you may have more and more to glory in and boast about. This increase of matter of exultation will be *in Christ:* for He is the element, as well as the ground, of all Christian boasting. So 1 Cor. i. 31. *In me:* Paul liberated from prison would be to the Philippians an occasion of increased exultation, Christ being its element and ground. Similarly in *v.* 20, 'Christ will be magnified *in* my body,' and *v.* 14, 'confident in the Lord through my bonds.' *Through my presence with you again;* expands in detail *in me.* Paul's presence once more at Philippi after his imprisonment will give to the Christians there in his person an increased confidence and exultation in Christ. Thus will his continued life increase his readers' faith in God, and consequently their joy and their spiritual growth.

The ground and worth of the confidence in *v.* 25 we cannot now determine. If, as we have good reason to believe, the pastoral Epistles are genuine, this confidence was justified by the event. And possibly the Holy Spirit may have revealed to Paul, by spiritual insight into the needs of the case, God's purpose to deliver him from the terrible peril of his trial before Nero and to restore him to active work. (Cp. Acts xxvii. 22—26, a close parallel.) But the assured expectation of evil recorded in Acts xx. 25 was, as we learn from 1 Tim. i. 3, not actually realised. And the matter is unimportant. The truth of the Gospel preached by Paul rests upon a broad historical basis, of which his testimony is only one factor, and not upon his personal infallibility.

Section 4 gives us invaluable insight into the inner life of one of the greatest of the early followers of Christ, at a crisis which tests most severely the character of any man, viz. amid health and strength the alternative of life and death. The uncertainty which breathes in every line accords with the statement in Acts xxv. 11, xxvii. 1, that Paul went to Rome to be tried before Nero, a judge whose verdict and sentence no one could foresee. Yet, in this uncertainty, there is in the mind of Paul perfect certainty touching all that is really dear to him. He knows that even the hostility of false brethren is leading him to eternal safety, and as a ground of this confidence knows also that the hope he cherishes cannot be put to shame and that whatever awaits him will serve only to show forth the greatness of Christ. On the other hand, the uncertainty which has left its record even in the trembling phraseology of these verses pertains only to matters about which Paul was indifferent; in view, not of possibilities equally worthless, but of alternative prospects of equal and infinite value. Each side of the alternative has irresistible allurement. Continued life is continued manifestation of Christ in Paul, and work fruitful in a harvest of blessing. His presence on earth is needful for his converts, whose confidence in Christ will be increased by his return to them. But death is immediate enrichment: for it takes him at once to the presence of Christ. Yet the wearied eye and heart of the prisoner turn from the fascinating vision. For the sake of his children in the faith he cheerfully acquiesces in what seems to him to accord both with their need and with God's purpose, and looks forward confidently to restoration to active work for them.

SECTION V.

SUNDRY EXHORTATIONS, SUPPORTED BY THE EXAMPLE OF CHRIST.

CH. I. 27—II. 18.

Only act as citizens worthy of the Gospel of Christ, that, whether I come and see you or be absent, I may hear of your affairs, that ye stand in one spirit, with one soul together contending by your belief of the Gospel, [28] *and not affrighted in anything by the adversaries, which is for them proof of destruction, but of your salvation, and this from God:* [29] *because to you it has been graciously given on behalf of Christ, not only to believe in Him, but also to suffer on His behalf;* [30] *having the same contest, such as ye saw in me and now hear to be in me.*

[1] *If there* be *then any encouragement in Christ, if any consolation of love, if any fellowship of the Spirit, if any tender feelings and compassions,* [2] *make full my joy, that ye may mind the same thing, having the same love, with united souls minding the one thing;* [3] *doing nothing by way of faction nor by way of vainglory, but with lowliness of mind each counting others better than themselves;* [4] *not each of you looking to his own things, but each of you also to the things of others.* [5] *Have this mind in you which was also in Christ Jesus,* [6] *who existing in the form of God, did not count His equality with God* a means of *high-handed self-enrichment,* [7] *but emptied Himself, taking* the *form of a servant, being made in* the *likeness of men:* [8] *and, found in fashion as a man, He humbled Himself, becoming obedient even unto death, death on a cross.* [9] *For which cause also God exalted Him beyond measure, and graciously gave to Him the name which is beyond every name;* [10] *that at the name of Jesus every knee may bow of heavenly ones and earthly ones and those under the earth,* [11] *and every tongue confess that Jesus Christ* is *Lord, to* the *glory of God* the *Father.*

[12] *So then, my beloved ones, according as always ye have obeyed, not as in my presence only, but now much more in my absence, with fear and trembling work out your own salvation.* [13] *For it is God who works in you both to will and to work, for His good pleasure.* [14] *Do all things without murmurings and disputings,* [15] *that ye may become blameless and pure, children of God without blemish, in* the *midst of a generation crooked and perverted, among whom ye are seen as luminaries in* the *world,* [16] *holding forth* the *word of life, that I may have whereof to exult in* the *Day of Christ that not in*

vain I have run, neither have laboured in vain. ¹⁷ *Yes, if even I am being poured out* as a libation *upon the sacrifice and service of your faith, I rejoice, and rejoice with you all:* ¹⁸ *and, the same thing, rejoice ye all, and rejoice with me.*

After speaking in §§ 3, 4 about the things concerning himself, Paul comes now to those immediately concerning his readers. He bids them stand firm in face of their enemies, *vv*. 27—30; exhorts to unity, ch. ii. 1, 2; and to unselfishness, supporting this exhortation by the example of Christ, *vv*. 3—11; points out that on this depends their salvation, *vv*. 12, 13; exhorts them to a spotless life, *vv*. 14—16; and concludes with an expression of joy on their account, *vv*. 17, 18.

27–30. *Only:* as in Gal. ii. 10, iii. 2, v. 13. All that Paul has to say is summed up in this one exhortation. *Act-your-part-as-citizens:* same word in Acts xxiii. 1, from the lips of Paul: a remarkable coincidence. Also 2 Maccabees vi. 1, xi. 25. It represents the Church as a free city, like those of ancient Greece, of which all Christians are citizens. Possibly this word here, and the cognate word in ch. iii. 20, were suggested by the municipal rights which distinguished the citizens of the Roman colony of Philippi from the provincials around: cp. Acts xvi. 20. Citizenship involves privileges and duties. Paul therefore bids his readers act *worthily of the Gospel*, which is both their charter of privileges and their law.

This general exhortation the rest of § 5 expounds in detail.

In order that . . . I may hear that etc.: the first detail in Paul's exhortation, in the form of a purpose which he bids his readers have in view in their behaviour as citizens of the Kingdom of God. He urges them to act worthily in order that he may have the joy of hearing about their worthy conduct. He thus adds to his exhortation a motive, viz. his own attentive interest in them. Cp. ch. ii. 1. *Whether . . . or:* two ways in which, as circumstances may determine, Paul hopes to hear about his readers, viz. either by visiting and seeing them and thus hearing from their own lips, or if absent by the report of others. Even in their midst, he would *hear* about their steadfastness. In this case, hearing would be associated with coming and seeing, in the other case, with absence. The form of the alternative suggests that Paul thinks chiefly of hearing about his readers from a distance. He assumes that his life will be spared. Otherwise, he would neither visit nor hear about them.

That ye stand etc.: the matter Paul wishes to hear about his readers; and consequently the real object of his first exhortation. *Stand:* maintain your position in the Christian life. A word and thought familiar to Paul: ch. iv. 1, Eph. vi. 11—14, Rom. v. 2, xi. 20, etc. It suggests the presence of enemies or dangers threatening to drive them back or cause them to fall. *In one spirit:* one animating principle moving the many members of the Church, this principle looked upon as the element *in* which they maintain their position: either the One Holy Spirit, who is (1 Cor. xii. 9, 11) the one personal inward source of life and harmony to the many servants of Christ; or the inward harmony which He imparts to those in whom He dwells, as suggested by *one soul.* Since this Person and this harmony are cause and effect, the distinction is unimportant, and was perhaps not clearly marked in the writer's mind. Notice that, as in an army, so in the Church, harmony is a condition of steadfastness. The disunited fall.

Now follow two collateral clauses, each noting a condition of the desired steadfastness, viz. mutual help in the conflict, and fearlessness. *Contend:* the Greek original of our word *athlete.* It represents the Christian life as a struggle for a prize, like the athletic contests of Greece. See note under 1 Cor. ix. 27. *Together-contending:* athletes represented as comrades in one struggle, each helping the others. Similar word in Rom. xv. 30, where Paul begs his readers to join with him, by praying for him, in the struggle of his apostolic work. But here he does not expressly mention his own conflict; and on the other hand the words *one spirit, one soul,* place conspicuously before us the desired union of the Philippian Christians one with another. Paul remembers that his readers are engaged in one great struggle, and desires that in it all may act together, as though the many were impelled by the soul of one man, this harmony being a condition of the steadfastness of which he hopes to hear. *Soul:* see under 1 Cor. xv. 53. It is that side of man's immaterial nature which is nearest to the body and directly influenced by it, and through the body by the outer world; and is thus distinguished from the *spirit,* which is that in man nearest to God and directly influenced by the Spirit of God. The soul is therefore the emotional side of man, that which is roused by his surroundings. Paul desires that his readers be moved by one impulse. *The faith* (or *belief*) *of the Gospel:* belief that the good news is true. The Gospel is the object-matter believed. So 2 Th. ii. 13, Col. ii. 12; cp. 'faith of Christ' in Ph. iii. 9.

28—30. A second collateral clause, noting a second condition of steadfastness, with comments upon it. *Affrighted:* as a horse takes fright at a sudden alarm. *In anything:* any adverse circumstances, be they what they may. *Adversaries:* same word in 1 Cor. xvi. 9; and, of one tremendous opponent, in 2 Th. ii. 4. The definite term *the adversaries* shows that the conflict implied in the foregoing words was in part caused by abiding personal enemies, Jews or Gentiles. Samples may be found in 1 Th. ii. 14, Acts xvii. 5, xvi. 19, these last being at Philippi. Paul bids his readers not to be frightened out of their compact rank by any attack of their enemies.

Which is etc.: an encouraging comment on the fearlessness which Paul desires in his readers. *Destruction:* see under ch. iii. 19 and note under Rom. ii. 24. *Proof:* same word in Rom. iii. 25, 2 Cor. viii. 24. The fearlessness of the persecuted will be to their enemies a proof that eternal ruin awaits them. For it will reveal supernatural help given to the persecuted, and thus prove that God is with them, and that consequently their opponents are fighting against God. An example of this in Acts iv. 13, v. 39. *To them* or *for them:* this proof being an objective reality before their eyes, whether they see it or not. *Salvation:* as in *v.* 19. Their own courage, being evidently divinely given, is to them a proof that God is with them and that therefore they are on the way to eternal safety. So is every manifest work of God in us an earnest of final deliverance. *And this from God:* not only actually a proof, but designed by God to be such. Both the courage and the proof therein implied are *from God.* Taken in itself, this last statement might cover *destruction* as well as *salvation,* stating that both elements of the proof are *from God.* But, since the explanation which follows in *v.* 29 refers only to the persecuted, probably to them only refer the last words of *v.* 28.

29. A proof that the courage of the persecuted was designed by God to be to them a proof of their ultimate salvation. *Graciously-given:* or *given-as-a-mark-of-favour* or *grace:* frequent with Paul, found only with him and Luke. A cognate word, frequent with Paul, is found elsewhere only in 1 Pet. iv. 10: see under Rom. i. 11. *On-behalf-of Christ:* in order to advance His pleasure or interests. *To believe in him:* a phrase very common with John, with Paul only Rom. x. 14, Gal. ii. 16. The repeated words *on his behalf* lay great stress on the fact that the sufferings endured by the Philippian Christians were endured in order to help forward the Kingdom of Christ. God had ordained, in His favour towards them, that they should not only accept as true the promises of Christ but *also* undergo suffering in order to advance a work dear to Him. Their

sufferings were, therefore, part of a divine purpose; and consequently the proof involved in them was part of that purpose.

Since the mention here of faith is only casual and is designed chiefly to throw into prominence the sufferings for Christ which follow faith in Him, it is unsafe to base upon these words a definite proof that faith is a gift of God. But, since we should never have believed in Christ had He not first spoken to us, and had not God exerted upon us influences leading us to accept the words of Christ, we may in this guarded sense speak of faith as a gift of God. Similarly, sufferings are gifts of God's favour: for they come upon us by His design and for our good. This seems to me all that can fairly be inferred from this verse. The scantiness in the N.T. of proofs that faith is a gift of God was perhaps occasioned by the danger lest, if it were taught more definitely, we might wait for faith as for some gift not yet bestowed, instead of at once accepting the promises of Christ.

30. A statement collateral and subordinate to that of *v.* 29, giving to the persecuted still further encouragement. *Conflict:* the ordinary word for the athletic contests referred to in *v.* 27. *The same conflict* or *the same sort of conflict as ye saw in me:* close coincidence with Acts xvi. 19—24. The persecutions of Paul's readers arose from the same cause, and therefore belonged to the same category, as his own scourging and imprisonment at Philippi. They might therefore look for similar divine help. And this letter tells them that similar hardships and perils surround him now at Rome. When Paul was before their eyes at Philippi, they *saw* in him a conflict like their own present troubles. And *now* from a distance they *hear* tidings which reveal *in* his person a similar conflict. Yet at Philippi they saw him unmoved by his enemies. And from this letter they hear that he is unmoved now. Thus Paul brings the example of his own courage to inspire his readers.

Turning to the Christians at Philippi, Paul's one thought is that they may act in a manner worthy of the spiritual commonwealth to which they belong and of the good news they have heard. His own deadly peril reminds him that they also are exposed to hardship and peril. He therefore bids them maintain their position in face of their foes; and to this end exhorts them to contend bravely shoulder to shoulder, armed with their belief of the good news; and to be undismayed by their enemies. Their fearlessness will be a proof of the destruction awaiting their foes and of the deliverance awaiting them, and this by God's design. For their persecutions are no mere accident, but are a part of God's great purpose of mercy, He having ordained that they shall not only believe the promises of Christ, but also suffer to advance His kindgom. Their hardships have the same source and the same gracious aid as the hardships at Philippi from which God so wonderfully delivered Paul, and as the hardships now at Rome, in which, while he writes, Christ is daily magnified.

II. 1, 2. Another exhortation arising out of, and in part repeating and developing, the exhortation in ch. i. 27—30. *If there be then:* an appeal based on the conflict just mentioned. *Encouragement:* speech calculated to prompt to action or endurance: same word as 'exhort' in Rom. xii. 1, where see note. *In Christ:* 'if in the spiritual life, of which Christ is Himself the surrounding and lifegiving element, there is anything to move you.' Cp. 1 Cor. i. 10, 2 Cor. x. 1. *Consolation:* kind words to one in sadness, thus distinguished from the word rendered *encouragement*. Such kind words Christian *love* ever prompts. 'If *love* prompts words of comfort to those in sorrow, remember me in prison at Rome and yield to my request.' *Fellowship of the Spirit:* either a sharing with others the gift of the Holy Spirit, or brotherliness prompted by the Spirit. The latter would give to the word *fellowship* the same sense as in ch. i. 5, and is suggested by the Christian harmony so earnestly desired in the words following. It is therefore the more likely interpretation. A close parallel in Rom. xv. 30, where an appeal is supported by reference both to Christ and to the 'love of the Spirit,' i.e. the love with which the Holy Spirit fills the hearts of those in whom He dwells. *Tender-mercies:* as in ch. i. 8. To this word, the word *compassions* adds the idea of pity towards one in distress, viz. Paul at Rome. Thus the 4th plea is related to the 2nd, which recalls the idea of distress: the 3rd is related to the 1st, giving the divine source of the disposition Paul desires. 'If there is anything in Christ moving you to yield to my request, if my sufferings claim the consolation which love is ever ready to give, if the Holy Spirit whom ye have received as the animating principle of a new life is a spirit of brotherhood, if in your hearts sufferings can evoke tenderness and pity,' etc. The earnestness of this fourfold appeal prepares us for a request of the highest importance.

To the word *any* before *tender-mercies* all uncials and many cursive MSS. agree to give a form utterly ungrammatical and unintelligible, a manifest error. The error extends only to one or two letters, and makes no appreciable difference in the meaning of the passage. That an error so evident has passed uncorrected in all the older and many of the later Greek MSS. is certainly remarkable, and proves that even the agreement of the best copies is no absolute guarantee against error. But one trifling slip does nothing whatever to shake our confidence in the general accuracy of our copies. Moreover it reveals the accuracy of the transcribers, an accuracy not less valuable because it is sometimes unthinking.

2. An earnest request, for which the foregoing pleas have prepared the way. *Fill up my joy:* implying that if the readers will yield to Paul's request nothing will be wanting to make him *full of joy.* Cp. 1 Th. iii. 8, 9. We have here again (cp. ch. i. 4) the golden thread of *joy* which runs through and illumines this Epistle. Notice that, although grammatically *fulfil my joy* is the matter of Paul's request, it is really another plea, the actual request being added, in the form of a purpose, in the words following. This first request is an appeal to fill with gladness the heart of the prisoner awaiting his trial at Rome. *That ye may etc.:* the real request, put in rather furtively as the aim the readers are to have in view. They must resolve to *mind the same thing.* By so doing they will fill Paul with joy. *Mind:* as in Rom. viii. 5. *The same thing:* actuated by a like aim; as in ch. iv. 2, Rom. xii. 5, 2 Cor. xiii. 11. This purpose is expounded and developed in two participial clauses. *The same thing,* which Paul desires in his readers, is *love* one to another, *the same love* in each breast. *The one thing:* stronger than *the same thing,* stating that the readers are not only to agree in thought and aim but to agree in one definite aim. That this aim is to be Christ and His Kingdom, Paul leaves them to infer. *With-united-souls:* similar words in ch. i. 27. It is best to connect this word closely with those following, as describing the manner in which they are to *mind the one thing,* thus giving to this clause the chief weight. The harmony is to pervade not only the intelligence but the emotions. Cp. 'from the soul' in Eph. vi. 6, Col. iii. 23. The earnestness of these repeated pleas reveals the infinite importance of Christian unity: and this is confirmed by similar language in Rom. xv. 5, 1 Cor. i. 10, Eph. iv. 3—6, and by the Saviour's prayer in Jno. xvii. 21—23.

3, 4. Two other participial clauses, each warning against a disposition fatal to Christian unity and commending the opposite virtue. *Faction:* as in ch. i. 17. *Vainglory,* or *empty glory:* an appearance without reality. *By way of faction and vainglory:* two distinct paths, along neither of which would Paul have his readers go. He warns them both against a mercenary spirit and against a desire for empty show. In this clause we have no verb. Since the repeated word *by-way-of* suggests actions along a mental line marked out, it is better to supply the word *doing.* It was needless to insert it: for action was clearly implied. *Lowliness-of-mind:* see under Col. iii. 12.

It is suggested by the word 'mind' in *v.* 2. [The Greek article indicates the well-known virtue of humility.] This virtue must be in active exercise when Christians compare *themselves* with *others*.

Looking-at: not making *his own* interest the goal of his forethought. See under 2 Cor. iv. 18. *But also;* rather softens the foregoing absolute prohibition. Paul now requires, not that the interest of others be the only object of our thought, but that it have a place along with our own interest. Similar teaching in 1 Cor. x. 24, 33, xiii. 5. It is therefore another note of common authorship. Whether the above warning against selfishness was prompted by something special at Philippi, we have no means of knowing. The universality of selfishness, imperilling everywhere Christian unity, forbids us to infer from these words such special occasion.

5—11. A new sentence bringing suddenly before us the supreme example of Christ. A close coincidence with Rom. xv. 3, 2 Cor. viii. 9. Since the example of Christ does not bear directly on Christian unity, but is the absolute opposite of every kind of selfishness, which is a universal hindrance to unity, it is best to understand the example of Christ as adduced simply to give the strongest possible support to the words immediately preceding. *Have this mind etc.:* 'cherish *in yourselves* as an object of your thought the thought and disposition *which was in Christ.*' *Also in Christ Jesus:* the mind which was actually in Christ *and* that which Paul desires in his readers being placed side by side.

Notice that although the words which follow refer to the not yet Incarnate Son, (see under *v.* 7,) He is here called *Christ Jesus.* So 2 Cor. viii. 9, 1 Jno. iv. 2. This reveals Paul's intense conviction of the continuous and undivided personality of the Eternal Son and the God-Man. This made it easy to give to the Pre-incarnate Son the name He bore as Man among men; the more so because only through His appearance in human form is the Eternal Son known to men. It is specially easy here because Paul is really adducing the example of the Incarnate Son, tracing however the example of Christ on earth to the purpose of the not yet Incarnate Son contemplating His approaching life on earth. See below.

6 11. The thought of Christ which Paul desires in his readers he expounds in *vv.* 6—8, in its successive stages of self-emptying and self-humiliation until He hangs dead on the cross, this being the lowest point in His descent. Then follows in *vv.* 9—11 His exaltation by the Father, until to the Name of Jesus is paid universal homage, all this being a divine recompense for His self-humiliation

and an inducement to men to follow His example. We have thus a unique and infinite example of unselfishness, crowned by unique honour.

6—8. The voluntary descent of Christ, in its two successive stages. Verses 6, 7 describe His original condition, and His surrender of it at His Incarnation: *v.* 8 describes the condition then assumed, and His action to the moment of death. We thus find the Son in three positions, in His original glory, as man on earth, and dead upon the cross.

Form: that in which essence manifests itself; the sum total of that by which an object is distinguished from other objects and thus made known. Whatever we can see, hear, or touch is the form of a material object: whatever we can grasp with the mind is the form of a mental object. It is to the essence what the outside is to the inside, what the manifestation is to the underlying and unseen reality. It is "the utterance of the inner life" (Trench) of whatever exists. Same word in the N.T. only Mk. xvi. 12; also Dan. v. 6, 9, 10, vii. 28, iv. 33, Isa. xliv. 13, Job iv. 16. Cognate words in Rom. ii. 20, 2 Tim. iii. 5; also Gal. iv. 19, Mt. xvii. 2, Mk. ix. 2, Rom. xii. 2, 2 Cor. iii. 18, Rom. viii. 29, Ph. iii. 10, 21. It is closely related in sense to 'image,' which however suggests the idea of comparison and similarity. *Existing:* a more emphatic word than 'being,' yet common. It recalls the condition and surroundings of existence.

These words refer evidently to the not yet incarnate Son. For they describe His state when He 'emptied Himself' by 'becoming in the likeness of men,' i.e. by His birth as a human child. To this, as we have seen, the words 'Christ Jesus' are no objection. Nor is it an objection that this is an example for men on earth. For the action even of the Father is made in Mt. v. 45—48 an example for men. Moreover the entire action of Christ on earth is an outflow in human form of His divine nature. See under *v.* 11. These words therefore describe the Eternal Son before, and apart from, His incarnation. He was then *in the form of God.* And since, without an intelligent mind to grasp it, *form* would lose its real significance, we must conceive the Son contemplated by the Father and by the bright ones of heaven. They saw in Him an expression corresponding to the essence of God. This implies that the Son was, before His Incarnation, a Person distinct from the Father. And, if so, a divine Person. Otherwise His self-manifestation would be (cp. 2 Tim. iii. 5) a deception, which is inconceivable. Consequently, these words imply equality with God. And this is explicitly assumed in the words following. See Dissertation iii.

The phrase *in the form of God* was chosen doubtless for contrast to 'form of a servant.' This contrast reveals the supreme unselfishness of Christ.

On the Mount the Incarnate Son assumed, in the presence of the chosen Apostles, as He did after His resurrection to the disciples going to Emmaus, a *form*, or mode of self-manifestation, different from that in which they were accustomed to see Him: Mk. ix. 2, xvi. 12. And our bodies, having laid aside their present transitory 'shape,' will share, as their mode of self-presentation, the glorious *form* in which Christ Himself will appear: Ph. iii. 21.

His equality with God: literally *the existing in a manner equal to God.* The Greek article points to a definite thought already before us. And this is found, and found only, in the words *existing in the form of God.* For He who thus existed must have also existed *in a manner equal to God.* These last words tell us the inner reality underlying *the form of God.* And, as we have seen, He whose existence can be thus described must be divine.

In these words Paul's teaching about the nature of the Son finds its culmination. Throughout his Epistles the Son occupies a place infinitely above that of the loftiest creatures. He is here explicitly assumed to be *equal to God*.

This equality Christ *did not count* a means of *high-handed self-enrichment:* or, more literally, *no high-handed self-enriching did He deem the being equal to God.* [The verb underlying the substantive I have rendered *high-handed self-enrichment* means to snatch, to take hold of quickly with a strong hand. With such strong-handed taking, very frequently injustice is associated, yet not always: for the word is used of a man grasping his own sword; and in Jno. vi. 15, Acts viii. 39, 2 Cor. xii. 2 the same word is used without any thought of injustice. But it always denotes taking hold of, or snatching, something not yet in our hands. This is made quite certain by an argument in Chrysostom's Homily (vi. 2) on this passage. The precise word here used is found in non-Christian Greek only, I believe, in Plutarch's *Morals* p. 12a for a violent act of seizure, according to the usual active sense of the termination. For the booty seized, the passive form ἅρπαγμα is common in later Greek. Lightfoot quotes three passages from early Christian writers in which apparently this meaning is given to the word ἁρπαγμός which is used in the passage before us. It is so understood here by him and Ellicott and several early Greek writers. But these two modern commentators suggest no reason why Paul passes by the common phrase ἅρπαγμα ἡγεῖσθαι and uses instead the rare word ἁρπαγμός. The natural explanation is that the word chosen expresses a sense not conveyed by the word passed over. And, if so, the difference of sense must be sought in the different termination. Moreover, Lightfoot's exposition gives to ἁρπάζω the sense of refusing to let go that which one already securely holds, a sense which it never has. The real meaning of the verb is illustrated by one of Lightfoot's own quotations, Eusebius, *Church History* bk. viii. 12, where we have τὸν θάνατον ἅρπαγμα θέμενοι written about men who, casting themselves from high roofs, laid violent hands on death and made it their own. Evidently death was not theirs until they threw themselves down. Lightfoot compares the words εὕρημα and ἕρμαιον. But, like ἅρπαγμα, these words denote always an acquisition, not an ancient possession. And equality with God was to the Eternal Son no acquisition. Consequently it could not be an object to be snatched hold of. Again if, as Lightfoot interprets, the Son did not clutch His equality with God, we must suppose that he allowed it to go from His grasp, that He gave it up. Surely this is inconceivable. The Son gave up 'the form of God,' i.e. the utterance of the inner reality of the divine existence, in order to assume the form of a servant: but, even when He had emptied Himself, He was in very truth essentially equal to God.

The force of this combined objection seems to me irresistible. The exposition before us makes Paul use a rare word which suggests a meaning he did not intend instead of a common word expressing exactly his intended meaning; gives to the root of the word here used a sense it never has, viz. to hold fast something already in one's hand; and implies that the Son of God did not refuse to give up His equality with God.

Meyer and Hofmann, expositors unsurpassed for grammatical accuracy and exegetical tact, give to the word ἁρπαγμός its natural sense, and interpret the passage to mean that the Son did not look upon His divine powers as a means of self-enrichment. They understand this passage to describe the Son contemplating His own divine powers in view of His approaching entrance into the world. He did not look upon his equality with God as a means of laying hold for Himself, after becoming man, of the good things of earth, wealth, enjoyment, power; but, instead of this, laid aside the form of God, i.e. the assertion of His divine powers, and took His lot merely as a man among men. Christ thus presents an infinite contrast to the gods of Homer, who ever used their superhuman powers for their own enjoyment.

This exposition seems to me altogether satisfactory. It accepts the natural grammatical meaning both of the root and the termination of the uncommon Greek word here used. Meyer appropriately compares a similar word used in 1 Tim. vi. 5 to describe persons who looked upon piety as a means of gain. In their thought piety and gain were coincident: to have the one was to have the other. And it agrees most fully with the context. For Christ's refusal to use His divine powers to take for Himself as man material good was the highest conceivable example of seeking not His own things, but the things of others.

The Latin writers generally, Tertullian, Ambrosiaster, Ambrose, Augustine, led astray by the Latin rendering *rapina*, a word denoting *plunder*, explain this passage to mean that Christ did not look upon His equality with God as an act of robbery, in other words, that He deemed Himself to be justly equal to God. This exposition is quite consistent with the following word ἀλλά: see my *Corinthians* p. 124. But it gives to the words *equality with God* the meaning of 'assumption of equality with God,' a meaning in no way suggested by the context; and makes injustice to be the most conspicuous idea of ἁρπαγμός, an idea not belonging to the word. Moreover, it reduces this passage to an exposition of *in the form of God* with no direct bearing upon Christ's self-humiliation as an example of unselfishness, thus leaving unexplained its emphatic position in the sentence.

This exposition is based on the Latin versions, and is almost confined to the Western Church. It thus came into the English Versions, Protestant and Roman Catholic. But it is rejected by almost all modern expositors.

Of Greek commentators, Origen (*On Romans* bk. v. 2, p. 553) expounds the passage to mean 'did not reckon it a great thing for Himself that He was equal to God:' and he is followed by Theodore of Mopsuestia and by Theodoret. But the connection between this exposition and Paul's Greek words is not evident. Chrysostom expounds it to mean that Christ did not look upon His own equality with God as something which He had taken by force, and which since it was acquired by force might be lost by force and must therefore be carefully guarded. Instead of doing this, and conscious that His equality with God was securely His own, Christ 'emptied Himself,' thus laying aside for a time the manifestation of His equality with God. This exposition gives to the word ἁρπαγμός the sense of ἅρπαγμα, and thus fails to explain Paul's substitution of a rare and less suitable word for one common and altogether suitable. And it makes the connection between verses 6 and 7 so distant as to be unrecognisable. On the other hand, it holds fast the true sense of ἁρπάζω, viz. to take hold of something not yet in our grasp. A somewhat similar exposition is found in other Greek writers. Others again quote the words of Paul as an example of the condescension of Christ, without expounding their exact meaning.

Lightfoot says that his own exposition "is the common and indeed almost universal interpretation of the Greek Fathers, who would have the most lively sense of the requirements of the language," and gives a long list of quotations. These quotations support him in rejecting the exposition of the Latin Fathers. But not one of them confirms his own exposition. So far as I know it is not supported by any ancient writer. And inasmuch as the writers he quotes evidently understood ἁρπαγμός in the sense of acquirement or something acquired, and Chrysostom speaks of this as implied in the word, they really contradict the exposition they are quoted to support. On the other hand, I do not know of any ancient writer who holds Meyer's view. We are therefore left, in the interpretation of this difficult passage, without any help from the early Christian writers. See further in the *Expositor*, 3rd series, vol. v. p. 115.

7. Exact opposite of counting His equality with God a means of self-enrichment. *Himself:* emphatic. A grasping hand frequently empties those on whom it is laid. So did the hand of the Eternal Son: but it was upon *Himself* that the violent hand was laid. The two participial clauses following specify with increasing clearness the way in which the Son's self-emptying was manifested.

The likeness of men: close coincidence with Rom. viii. 3, 'in the likeness of the flesh of sin.' It suggests that Christ was not in every respect a man. And this is fully consistent with Paul's frequent description of Him as Man: e.g. Rom. v. 15, 18, 1 Cor. xv. 21, 47, 1 Tim. ii. 5. Since the human race is older than sin, we may think of the essential attributes of manhood without thought of sin, and, using the word in this correct sense, speak of Christ as truly man. On the other hand, the universality of sin justifies our including it now in our conception of mankind. In this sense, Christ was not man, but *in the likeness of men.* For in outward form He was exactly similar to the race which inherited Adam's sin. 'In all things He was made like to His brethren:' Heb. ii. 17. These two modes of viewing our race forbid us to infer from this verse that Christ was not actually man. *Being-made:* literally *having-become:* same word in Rom. i. 3, Gal. iv. 5. By clothing Himself in a humanity like that of other men, the Eternal Son entered a mode of existence new to Him. These words are Paul's counterpart to Jno. i. 14, 'The Word became flesh.'

By entering a mode of existence like that of Adam's children, the Son took the *form of a servant*, or *slave*. For creatures are essentially the property of the Creator, bound to use all creaturely powers to work out His will. This simple exposition forbids us to infer from these words that Christ was ever servant to an earthly master. The Son assumed the obligations of a creature. He who had been recognised by angels as bearing the 'form of God' presented Himself on earth to the eyes of men as one doing the work of another.

In connection with His entrance into human life, and with His assumption of a creature's form, the Son *emptied Himself*. These words involve the whole mystery of the Incarnation. They therefore demand in their exposition the utmost caution and reverence.

The words *emptied Himself* assert that the Son exerted upon Himself an influence which deprived Him, while on earth, of some fulness which He previously had, and made Him in some sense *empty*. And this suggests that this self-emptying was the negative condition of His assumption of a servant's form.

It will help us to understand these words if we first note a broad distinction between certain elements which go to make up, so far as we can understand it, the nature of God.

Love is the essence of God: 1 Jno. iv. 8, 16. Consequently, to lay aside His love, even for a moment, would be not to empty, but to deny and mutilate Himself. For an empty vessel still retains all its essential parts. Nor could the Son (cp. 2 Tim. ii. 13) interrupt the full exercise of His infinite love. Indeed of that love His entire life on earth was a ceaseless outflow. Moreover all the moral attributes of God are involved in His unique attribute of love. To be untrue or unjust would be unloving. Consequently, the essential truth and justice of the Son could not even for a moment become inoperative. These therefore were not in any way laid aside at the Incarnation.

On the other hand, the natural attributes of God stand in a different relation to Him. His power is not necessarily, like His love, always in full exercise. It is active only so far and in such manner as His love and wisdom determine. To refrain from its full exercise is therefore not inconsistent with the nature of God. A limitation even of knowledge does not necessarily contradict infinite love. Yet both power and knowledge increase immensely the practical value of love.

With this distinction in view we turn to the recorded life of the Incarnate Son. We find Him (Lk. ii. 52) growing in knowledge, and yet acknowledging at the close of His life (Mk. xiii. 32) that He did not know the day of His return. Yet strangely mingled with this human ignorance we find in Him divine omniscience: Jno. ii. 25. The Son was guided (Lk. iv. 1) by the Holy Spirit; and in the strength of the Spirit (Lk. iv. 14, Mt. xii. 28) were wrought His miracles. This limited knowledge reveals the presence in the God-Man of a human spirit capable of limitation and increase. And that the indivisible personality of the Eternal Son accepted the limitations of a pure human spirit, and was anointed for work (Acts x. 38) by the power of the Holy Spirit, implies a renunciation for a time and for man's salvation of the full exercise of His divine powers. See under 2 Cor. viii. 9. To this renunciation indisputably refer the words before us. How He who from all eternity knows all things, and by the word of His power upholds all things, could in any sense accept the limitation of human knowledge and become a medium of the operation of the power of the Holy Spirit, is beyond our thought. It is to us inscrutable, because divine. But it is the mystery of divine love.

Notice that although in one sense, as here stated, the Incarnate Son was empty, in another sense even upon earth He was (Jno. i. 14) 'full of truth and grace.' The difference is only verbal. The words of John look upon grace and truth as contents of the Son's divine personality: the words before us assume that they are part of His nature and therefore remain with him even when He had emptied Himself.

We may therefore reverently believe that, in order to save man, the Eternal Son entered a life subject to human limitations; and that in order to do this, while retaining in full exercise the infinite love which is the essence of God and which could not be even for a moment inoperative, the Son deliberately laid aside, by an influence upon Himself which no creature can exert, the full exercise of His divine powers, thus permitting them to become for a time latent. Guided by infinite wisdom and prompted by infinite love, the Eye Omniscient was for a moment closed, and the power which made the world became latent. The possibility of this self-emptying lies deep in the mystery of the Divine Trinity. But it is the most wonderful outshining conceivable of the infinite splendour of divine love.

Every attempt to understand the Great Renunciation must hold fast the real Manhood, the unchangeable Divinity, and the undivided Personality, of the God-Man.

Since the exercise of the Son's divine powers were the utterance of His inner essence, of His equality with God, that which He laid aside was the 'form of God.' But this is not expressly asserted here. On the other hand, we have no hint, and no reason to believe, that He laid down His 'equality with God.' We are merely told that He did not look upon it as a means of seizing for Himself the good things of earth.

8. Further and final descent of the Son, in graphic delineation. Some ancient versions and the Rheims Roman Catholic version punctuate, *being made in the likeness of men and found in fashion as a man: He humbled Himself.* But this extension of the last clause of v. 7 is rather tautological, and gives to the words *He humbled Himself* an unaccountable abruptness: whereas the punctuation of the A.V. and R.V. gives to the whole sentence a more harmonious and majestic flow and to each clause due weight. Paul describes first the not yet incarnate Son, then His descent into humanity, then depicts His condition as a man among men, and His further descent, until He reaches its lowest point and hangs dead upon the cross.

Fashion (in N.T. only 1 Cor. vii. 31) differs from 'form' as any occasional appearance or visible clothing differs from an expression which corresponds to actual inner reality. The 'form of God' is the appropriate self-manifestation of the Son's essence, of 'His equality with God.' The *fashion as a man* was the outward guise of humanity, a visible clothing bearing only a distant relation to the actual nature of the Son. It is practically the same as 'in the likeness of men,' except perhaps that it recalls more conspicuously the outward aspect of Christ as an individual man. In this outward guise, by those who sought Him, the Incarnate Son was *found*. This last word keeps before us, as does the conspicuous repetition of the word 'form,' the self-presentation of the Son both as God and as man.

Humbled Himself: chose for Himself a lowly path. Such was Christ's every step from the manger to the grave. *Becoming obedient:* mode of Christ's self-humiliation. It is related to *He humbled Himself* as is 'taking the form of a servant' to 'He emptied Himself.' Having laid aside the manifestation of His divine powers and become Man, the Son entered also the path of obedience, the normal moral state of man. He thus manifested in the human form of obedience His essential and absolute devotion to the Father. *As far as to death:* the extent of Christ's obedience. [Cp. 2 Tim. ii. 9, Heb. xii. 4.] In the path of obedience He went on till He reached the grave. *Death upon a cross:* a graphic detail marking the extreme limit of the downward path which God marked out for His Son on earth, and which He obediently trod. He refused not to die a criminal's death. This was the lowest step of the lowly path entered when He emptied Himself.

Such is the example by which Paul supports his exhortation that his readers seek not their own things, but also the things of others. It is found in the visible human life of the Son of God, of whom therefore Paul speaks as 'Christ Jesus.' The thoughts which manifested themselves in the Incarnate Son he bids us think in ourselves. And, since these thoughts were earlier than the incarnation, he lays open to us the mind of the pre-existent Son. Contemplating His approaching life on earth, He did not look upon His divine powers as a means of grasping the good things which are to so many men objects of highest ambition and desire; but gave up, for the term of His life on earth, the exercise of these powers, thus leaving His divine personality in a sense empty, accepted the distinctive features of service, and became like men. Nor was this all. A further descent begins where the first ended. We go to seek the self-emptied Son, and we find Him clothed in a guise such as men wear. He treads a lowly path marked out for Him by divine command, until it leads Him to death in its most shameful form. As we gaze at Christ dead upon the cross, and remember the splendour from which He came and the earthly possibilities which were within His reach, and remember also that He left that glory and endured that shame of His own free will and in order to save the lost and to make them sharers of His glory, we see in Him an example of unselfishness the most sublime we can conceive.

9—11. The matchless exaltation which followed the matchless self-humiliation of Christ. *For which cause also God:* the divine recompense for the foregoing. *Him:* emphatic; the divine Author and divine Object of this exaltation placed side by side. *Highly-exalted:* literally *exalted-beyond* measure. *Graciously-given:* same word in ch. i. 29. The name given was a mark of the Father's favour to the Son. *Beyond every name:* corresponding to *exalted-beyond* measure. This *name* comes up to, and goes *beyond*, *every* other. Same thought in Heb. i. 4. As a definite object of thought, it is *the name*. Not necessarily the name Jesus, which is merely that by which He was actually known among men; nor any special articulate sound; but the name which belongs to, and denotes, in heaven and earth, the personality of Him that was born at Bethlehem. For this, not an articulate sound, is the one essential point. The exaltation and name of Christ are a gift of the Father, as in Eph. i. 20—22, Col. ii. 12, 1 Cor. xv. 15, 27.

10, 11. A purpose of God in exalting Christ. *In the name of*

Jesus: so 1 Cor. vi. 11, Eph. v. 20, Col. iii. 17, 1 Pet. iv. 14, Jas. v. 14. A *name* is personality as known and recognised among men, and as distinguished from others. In the recognised personality of Jesus abides the Majesty before which God designs all to bow. *Every knee bow:* graphic delineation of the act of worship. So Eph. iii. 14, Rom. xi. 4, xiv. 11. *Those-in-heaven:* its angelic inhabitants. Same word in Eph. i. 3, 20, ii. 6, iii. 10, vi. 12, 1 Cor. xv. 40, 48, 49. *Those-on-earth:* living men. Same word in ch. iii. 19, 1 Cor. xv. 40, 2 Cor. v. 1. *Those-under-the-earth:* the dead, in contrast to the living. So Homer (*Iliad* bk. ix. 457) speaks of Pluto as "Zeus under the earth." It is unsafe to infer from this term that Paul thinks of universal worship earlier than the resurrection. His threefold division includes angels and men at the moment of writing: and he divides the latter into those now living and those already dead. Without thought of time, looking only at the persons belonging to these three all-inclusive classes, Paul says that God exalted Christ in order that every one of them should bow to Him. Nor is it safe to infer from *every knee* that angels and departed human spirits have bodily form. For these words were naturally prompted by Paul's thoughts about living men: and with these he easily associated angels and the dead. *Acknowledge:* see under Rom. xiv. 11. *Every tongue acknowledge;* completes the picture of worship. The words *every knee bow, every tongue confess* are appropriately taken from Isa. xlv. 23 (quoted in Rom. xiv. 11), where God solemnly announces His purpose of salvation for the Gentiles. And inasmuch as that ancient purpose will be fulfilled in homage paid to Christ, and only thus, the submission to God foretold by Isaiah is legitimately stated here in the form of submission to Christ. *Jesus Christ* is *Lord:* confessed submission to the rule of Christ; so 1 Cor. xii. 3. *For* the *glory of God* the *Father:* manifestation of the Father's greatness, evoking His creatures' admiration, this being here represented as the ultimate purpose for which God exalted Christ. As ever, Paul rises from the Son to the Father. Close coincidence in 1 Cor. xv. 28: cp. Eph. i. 12, 14.

We cannot conceive this worship and praise to be other than genuine. Consequently, all men are embraced in the purpose of salvation which raised Christ from the grave to the throne. But this by no means implies that all men will actually be saved. And, as we shall see under ch. iii. 19, Paul did not expect that all men will eventually be saved. The harmony of the two passages is found in the truth that God has made the fulfilment of His own purpose of mercy contingent on man's submission and faith. Nor

SEC. 5.]   PHILIPPIANS I. 27—II. 18.   73

can we, from the word *those-under-the-earth*, infer a probation in Hades, even for those who did not on earth hear the Gospel. For it is quite possible that the fate of these will be determined by their acceptance or rejection of such light as they had on earth. And, if so, their eternal song will be a designed result of Christ's victory over death. The whole passage is so easily explained by Paul's teaching elsewhere that we cannot fairly infer from it any further teaching about the position or prospects of the dead.

Christianity differs from all other religions in presenting a perfect model of human excellence, suitable alike for all persons in all circumstances, an absolute standard by which every one may and must be measured and judged. To this example appeal is constantly made in the N.T.: 1 Cor. xi. 1, 2 Cor. viii. 9, Rom. xv. 3 ; 1 Pet. ii. 21, 24, 1 Jno. ii. 6. This being so, it might be expected that of the human life of Christ we should have a very full record, that we should be told much about Him in whose steps we are bidden to tread. Such is not the case. If from the Gospels we deduct the miracles and teaching of Christ, there remain only scanty memorials of the Saviour. It is well that this is so. Had we more details, we should imitate these, forgetting perhaps the deep underlying principles of the sacred life. As it is, we are directed chiefly, as in the passage before us, to those elements in Christ apparently furthest above reach of imitation, to His incarnation and His death for our sins. The reason is evident. In these supreme events shone forth in its intensest lustre the inmost heart of the Eternal Son. Consequently, Paul bids us, not to do as Christ did, but to have the mind that was in Him. Notice specially, in the example of Christ here set before us, two elements, unsparing self-abnegation for the good of others and unreserved obedience to God. These led the Son from heaven to earth, and from earth to the grave ; and from the cross and the grave, in a ruined world, to the splendours of the eternal throne and the ceaseless songs of wondering angels and of a ransomed human race. In that path it is ours to tread.

12, 13. Verse 12 is an exhortation based on the foregoing ; *v.* 13 is a reason for it. The one main exhortation is prefaced by several preparatory clauses.

So then etc.: a designed moral consequence of the foregoing. *Beloved-ones:* ch. iv. 1 twice : a mark of the tenderness of this epistle. Cp. Rom. xii. 19, 1 Cor. x. 14, xv. 58, 2 Cor. vii. 1. *Obeyed:* viz. the apostolic authority of Paul. For only thus can we account for the mention of his *presence* and *absence*. Such authority he claims over his children in the Gospel in 1 Cor. iv. 14, 15, 21,

v. 3. He does so in confidence that his commands are the will of God. This mention of obedience recalls the example of Christ in v. 8, and the authority (1 Th. ii. 6) with which Paul might command. They had *always obeyed:* close agreement with ch. i. 5, 'from the first day until now.' This recognition of previous obedience softens somewhat Paul's silent assumption of authority. He only bids them continue to act *according as* they had *always* done. They were *not* to act *as* though their action were prompted by Paul's *presence.* [The word ὡς is omitted in the Vatican MS. and some good versions. But its omission is so easily accounted for that we may with some confidence retain it. It gives the readers' subjective view, in Paul's wish, of their own conduct.] *Now much more:* the *absence* of the teacher's help making their own care more needful. *With fear and trembling:* with anxious care as in a matter serious and difficult: a Pauline phrase; see 1 Cor. ii. 3, 2 Cor. vii. 15, Eph. vi. 5. It suggests the real peril to which Christians are exposed, and especially the great peril of selfishness. *Salvation:* as in ch. i. 19: deliverance from the perils which surround the Christian life. That it is their *own salvation* is good reason why they should *work* it *out* with anxious care, and with even greater care in Paul's absence than when his watchful eye is on them. *Work-out:* literally *be working out:* same word in Rom. v. 3, 2 Cor. iv. 17; 20 times in the Epistles of Paul, 3 times in the rest of the N.T.: it is akin to the word in v. 13. It denotes effective effort, and implies that deliverance day by day is a result of persistent work: cp. Eph. vi. 13. While using all means to strengthen our spiritual life, we are bringing about our present and final deliverance. So sailors have often toiled to save their ship from the rocks and themselves from a watery grave.

13. Encouragement to work out our own salvation. Paul assumes that there is One who works in us, speaks of Him as a definite object of thought, and calls Him *God.* [To this last word he gives great prominence by bringing it to the beginning of the sentence.] *Works:* 1 Cor. xii. 6, 11, Rom. vii. 5, Eph. i. 20, ii. 2, instructive parallels; 17 times with Paul, 3 times in the rest of the N.T. Like the kindred word in v. 12, it is a note of Pauline authorship. The cognate substantive is used in ch. iii. 21. It is the in-working activity of God. *In you:* within your personality, body or spirit: cp. Eph. ii. 2, Col. i. 29; also Eph. i. 20. Even *to will,* the inward determination to act, is a result of God working in us. *And to work:* the inward effort to accomplish the formed purpose. Both the purpose and the energy with which we work it out are here

said to be an inward work of God. His *good-pleasure:* that which seems good in the sight of God, as in Mt. xi. 26, suggesting possibly that it is for the good of others. Same word as *good-will* in ch. i. 15; where however the context makes the idea of benefit to others much more conspicuous than here. *On-behalf-of* His *good-pleasure:* in order to accomplish a purpose pleasing to God. Cp. Eph. i. 5, 9.

This verse by no means implies that these divine influences are irresistible. And indisputably they are resisted. For God's good pleasure is (1 Tim. ii. 4) that all men be saved; whereas not all men are saved. Even to an impenitent man Paul says (Rom. ii. 4), 'God is leading thee to repentance;' although evidently the divine influences were completely thwarted. Yet in all cases these influences are real and of infinite worth. For without them there would be no good in man. But their actual effect depends upon our surrender to them.

We have here a plain statement of prevenient grace, a divine influence in man preceding and producing whatever in him is good, from the earliest desire for salvation to final victory over the last temptation.

Verses 12, 13 present two opposite and yet completely harmonious sides of the Christian life. The latter is the source and ground and motive of the former. All good in man, from the first good desire, is an outworking of a divine purpose and power. Through the Gospel, and the written and unwritten Law, God is ever exerting an influence leading men to repentance and salvation. He does this in order to gratify His own desire to save and bless. The actual result depends upon man's self-surrender to these influences. Other influences would lead him in an opposite direction. Man's only choice is to which of these influences he will yield. On this depends his fate. Consequently, if he rises, he rises entirely by the power of God: if he sinks, it is because he refuses influences which would raise him.

These divine influences ever prompt, and are designed to evoke, human effort. Consequently man's earnest effort is a condition of salvation. But both this effort and its good results are the outworking of the purpose and power of God. A knowledge that our own purposes are from God, and that our efforts are armed with His power, and that our victory will gratify Him, are strong encouragement to put forth all our powers.

The exhortation in *v.* 12 is to Christian perseverance; and thus takes up and completes that in ch. i. 27—30. In *v.* 27 Christian harmony was mentioned casually as a condition of victory, and in ch. ii. 1, 2 it was made matter of direct exhortation. In *vv.* 3, 4 we were warned against selfishness, the great enemy of Christian harmony. And in *vv.* 5—11 this warning and its implied exhortation were supported by the unique example of Christ's self-humiliation for the good of others and His exaltation by God. This supreme example Paul brings, in *vv.* 12, 13, to bear upon his readers. But instead of bidding them to imitate Christ, or rather to cherish a disposition like His, which would be merely a repetition of *v.* 5, he bids them, by obedience, work out their own salvation. He thus implies that the only way of safety is the path of self-humiliation and obedience trodden by Christ: a lesson we all need to learn. Underneath an apparently abrupt transition we find, as so often with Paul, an important lesson. A similar train of thought occurs in 1 Cor. ix. 22—27, where Paul says that his own salvation depends upon his efforts to save others. 'Since the Eternal Son, instead of using His divine powers to obtain for Himself the good things of earth for which so many strive, allowed them to remain latent, and trod the path of self-humiliation and obedience, a path which led Him to infinite glory, thus marking it out as the way of safety, walk ye along the same path, remembering the spiritual perils which surround you, and therefore walk as carefully in my absence as in my presence. Do this remembering that in our own moral efforts God is working out His own good pleasure.'

14—16. After exhortations to courage, unity, unselfishness like that of Christ, and the implied warning that upon obedience depends personal salvation, Paul adds an exhortation touching the manner in which he would have these exhortations obeyed. *All things;* covers and goes beyond the matters already mentioned. *Murmurings:* 1 Cor. x. 10: talk expressing dissatisfaction, especially clandestine talk as grumbling often is. It is most easily understood here of dissatisfaction with the rough lot referred to above, such dissatisfaction being really murmuring against Him who has allotted our earthly position and surroundings. *Doubtings* or *reasonings:* ideas closely allied, that about which we reason being naturally open to doubt while the reasoning continues. Same word in Rom. i. 21, xiv. 1, 1 Cor. iii. 20, 1 Tim. ii. 8, Jas. ii. 4, Lk. ix. 46, 47. Dissatisfaction with our lot arises necessarily from want of faith in Him who with infinite wisdom and love has chosen for us our path and who will soon cover us with the splendour of heaven and fill us with eternal joy. Hence all *murmurings* are an outward expression of inward *doubtings*. And both these are utterly unworthy of children of God.

Therefore, whatever duties and burdens life lays upon them, Paul bids his readers *do all things without murmurings and doubtings*.

15, 16. Aim of the foregoing exhortation: then a statement about the readers' relation to the world: and lastly a further aim touching Paul and his work.

That ye may-become etc.: a designed result of laying aside 'murmurings and doubtings.' *Blameless:* men with whose outward aspect none can find fault. *Pure*, or *mixtureless:* men in whose inward disposition there is no foreign element. Thus *blameless* and *pure* correspond respectively to 'without murmurings' and 'without doubtings.' *Children of God:* Rom. viii. 16, 21, ix. 8: a point of connection between Paul and John, Jno. i. 12, xi. 52, 1 Jno. iii. 1, 2, 10, v. 2. A similar phrase in Rom. viii. 14, 19, ix. 26, 2 Cor. vi. 18, Gal. iii. 26, iv. 6, Heb. ii. 10, xii. 5, Lk. xx. 36, vi. 35, Mt. v. 45. These words here, without any special occasion, reveal the deep root of this thought in the writer's mind, and are thus a mark of authorship. They note a close relation to God. *Spotless:* Eph. i. 4, v. 27, Col. i. 22, Heb. ix. 14, 1 Pet. i. 19, Jude 24, Rev. xiv. 5: without blemish, or anything to cause reproach. Notice three negatives, *blameless, mixtureless, spotless*, emphasising absence of all evil inward or outward. That this absence of evil is represented as a result to be attained by avoiding murmurings and doubtings, suggests that these defects are the last to cling to the Christian; that he who avoids them will escape all evil. And rightly so. For absence of doubt is perfect faith: and absence of murmuring reveals profound inward peace. These words reveal also Paul's high appreciation of the present moral character of his readers. *Generation:* see under Eph. iii. 5. *Crooked:* opposite to 'straight,' as in Luke iii. 5. *Crooked generation:* Acts ii. 40. *Perverse:* twisted in different directions, especially of misshapen or mutilated limbs. So Mt. xvii. 17, Lk. ix. 41: 'generation unbelieving and perverted.' Instead of being upright, they were crooked in character and conduct: instead of being a normal growth, they were deformed cripples. Among such men and in conspicuous contrast to them, Paul desired his readers to be without blemish, thus revealing their divine lineage: *children of God, spotless in the midst etc.* Since the stress evidently rests on the words *spotless in the midst etc.*, describing what sort of *children of God* the Philippians were to be, we cannot infer from these last words that Paul looked upon them as not yet children of God. Consequently, this verse in no way contradicts Gal. iii. 26, iv. 6.

Among whom etc.; keeps up the contrast between Christians and those around them. *Are-seen:* same word in Mt. vi. 5, 16, 18; also rendered *appear* in Mt. i. 20, ii. 7, 13, 19. It is akin to the Greek word for light, and denotes in its simplest form 'to give light:' e.g. Jno. i. 5, v. 35. Similarly, the form here used is found in Mt. xxiv. 27, Rev. xviii. 23. But in a wider sense it is constantly used for the visible manifestation of an object, whether by its own light or by light cast upon it. The participle is the Greek original of our word 'phenomenon.' Amid a perverse generation the spotless children of God are conspicuously seen: and, since (Eph. v. 8) their nature is light, they shine. *Luminaries: light-givers:* same word in Gen. i. 14, 16, Wisdom xiii. 2, Sirach xliii. 7, for the sun and moon. In Rev. xxi. 11 it denotes the brilliance of a precious stone. *Luminaries in the world;* keeps up the contrast noted above. Like stars at night, so shine the children of God in a dark world. The foregoing words described what Paul would have his readers be: those now before us say what they actually are. Whatever be their degree of brightness, they *are seen*. That they are said to be seen *as luminaries in the world,* is a recognition of their lofty position, and an implied exhortation of the most persuasive kind to walk worthy of it.

Word of life: the Gospel, as a channel through which God bestows eternal life, 1 Cor. i. 21, xv. 1: so 'words of eternal life' in Jno. vi. 68; 'words of this life,' Acts v. 20. The singular number here, *word of life,* looks upon the Gospel as one whole.

Holding-forth: as if with outstretched arm: a word not uncommon for one holding to another's lips food and drink. By proclaiming the Gospel we hold out to the lips of famishing ones the bread of eternal life, and reach out a light revealing perils which otherwise would be certain destruction, and revealing also a way of safety. Thus the Gospel is the light of life. The slight change of metaphor from the heavenly bodies shining by their own brightness to men holding out a light to guide others is easily understood. The former conception represents Christians as shining with superhuman brightness and as raised immeasurably above the world: the latter represents them as actively endeavouring to save others. These two clauses explain how the *children of God are seen as luminaries in the world.*

For a ground-of-exultation for-me: further purpose of the exhortation in *v.* 14, viz. joy to Paul himself at his readers' Christian conduct. Similar thought in *v.* 2: cp. Rom. i. 13. *For the day of Christ:* as in ch. i. 6, 10. This third mention so early in the Epistle shows how definite in Paul's thought was that day, and how steadily his thoughts about the future went forth to it as their goal. *That not in vain, etc:* contents of this *ground-of-exultation Run:* 1 Cor. ix. 24, 26, Gal. v. 7. *Run in vain:* Gal. ii. 2, a close coincidence. *I-have-run* suggests the runner's intense effort: *I-have-laboured* suggests the weariness of effort; same word in Jno. iv. 6, same root in 2 Cor. vi. 5, xi. 27, Gal. vi. 17. Paul desires proof, in the light given by his readers to the dark world, that his own strenuous efforts and frequent weariness for them have not been in vain. Such proof will be to him a ground of exultation, i.e. of triumphant confidence in God; just as to his readers will be (ch. i. 26) Paul's own deliverance from prison. And this exultation will reach forward to that Day ever present to Paul's thought when the inward spiritual life began on earth and manifested imperfectly here will receive its full and visible consummation in the light of eternity, and earthly toil receive its abundant recompense.

17, 18. Sudden break in Paul's line of thought, followed by a comment upon the words foregoing. He has just spoken of his strenuous efforts for his readers: he will now speak of his possible death on their behalf.

Poured-out-as-a-libation: technical term for wine poured out upon or beside sacrifices or holy objects: same word in Num. xxviii. 7, iv. 7, Gen. xxxv. 14. *If I am even being poured out:* an extreme possibility. Even if Paul's hopes of release be fallacious, if his present imprisonment be a beginning of the end, if the legal process now going on be God's way of removing him from earth, he nevertheless rejoices. Same word and tense in 2 Tim. iv. 6, a very close parallel, referring to Paul's last imprisonment previous to his execution. *Service:* public and especially sacred ministration. Same word in *v.* 30, 2 Cor. ix. 12: cognate word in Rom. xiii. 6, where see note; and in Phil. ii. 25. *Your faith:* object of this ministration. By leading his readers to faith in Christ, Paul was performing a public and sacred work. And, since this service was rendered to God, their faith was a *sacrifice* presented by Paul. Similar thought in Rom. xv. 16, where in similar language the believing Gentiles are represented as an offering to God. Another note of common anthorship. 'The Gentiles' and their *faith* may be conceived as the 'offering' and *sacrifice* laid upon the altar. Similar sacrificial language in Ph. iv. 18. Whether the words *upon the sacrifice* were suggested by the heathen practice (so apparently in *Iliad* bk. xi. 775) of pouring wine *upon* the slain victim, or are merely used in the frequent and looser sense of something done in connection with or in addition to the sacrifice as in Acts iv. 17, 2 Cor. ix. 6, we cannot now determine. Either thought would explain Paul's language.

The practical meaning is clear. Paul has long been labouring in discharge of a public and sacred duty laid upon him by God, to lead the Gentiles to faith in Christ. He now contemplates the possibility of the sacrifice thus presented to God being consummated by the pouring out of his own life.

I rejoice: not necessarily that Paul's life is being sacrificed, but that he has been permitted, even at so great a cost, to lead his readers to faith. *I rejoice with you all:* 'I share your joy, rejoice that ye are joyful,' i.e. with a joy resulting from faith in Christ. This is the most common use of the compound word so rendered, and gives a good sense. It is therefore needless to render it *congratulate,* as if it meant a verbal expression of sympathy with another's joy. Paul rejoices to see the result of his own self-sacrifice; and his joy is increased by the joy of those for whom he has laboured and suffered. *You all;* recalls the universality so conspicuous in ch. i. 3, 4.

The same thing, rejoice: cherish *the same* joy that I have. Even if Paul's imprisonment be the way to death, he still rejoices at his own success and at his readers' joy. He now bids them to *rejoice* in Christ, and to rejoice that he is joyful. Thus this important section, like §§ 3 and 4, closes on the key-note of joy sounded in ch. i. 4. Similar exhortations in chs. iii. 1, iv. 1.

REVIEW. Paul's hope of release from imprisonment is based in part on the needs of his readers. To them, after speaking about himself, he now turns. All he has to say to them is comprised in one exhortation, viz. to act in the City of God in a way worthy of the Gospel of Christ. This worthy action Paul then expounds in detail. His own conflict reminds him that they also have enemies. Against these he bids them stand firmly. To this end he urges harmony and fearlessness, saying that this last will be to them a proof of their own salvation present and future, and that sufferings are a part of God's good purpose, both for himself and for them. Paul then returns with greater earnestness to the need for unity. The prisoner at Rome pleads for the gratification to himself which his readers' harmony will bring, and begs them to cherish the one great purpose. He warns them against selfishness and vanity, commending humility and care for the good of others. In this he quotes the supreme example of Christ, who contemplating His approaching life on earth did not look upon His divine prerogatives as a means of obtaining for Himself material good, but on entering the world laid aside the full exercise of His divine powers in order to assume human limitations and thus save men, and who on earth trod the humble path of obedience till it led Him to the grave. The force of this example Paul increases by pointing to the honour conferred by God on the Risen Christ and to the universal homage designed for Him. Armed with this example, Paul reminds his readers that upon their earnest effort to imitate Christ depends their final salvation, and encourages them to such effort by saying that their conflict is no trial of human strength, but that in them God is working out His own good purpose. These exhortations he concludes by urging them to lay aside murmuring and doubt, to aim at a spotless character, and, by holding forth to others the word of life, to become lights in a dark world. He closes the section by looking forward to the Day of Christ and the joy He hopes then to have in the result of His present labours. So great is the joy thus in prospect that Paul's present joy of anticipation is not dimmed even by the possibility that his present imprisonment may end in death. Nor does this possibility prevent him from rejoicing in his readers' joy in Christ. He bids them share his joy.

SECTION VI.
ABOUT TIMOTHY.
CH. II. 19—24.

But I hope in the Lord Jesus to send Timothy to you shortly, in order that I also may be of good cheer, knowing your affairs. ^{20} *For I have no one of equal soul who in a genuine way will be anxious about your affairs.* ^{21} *For they all seek their own things, not the things of Jesus Christ.* ^{22} *But the proof of him ye know, that, as a son serves a father, with me he has done service in furtherance of the Gospel.* ^{23} *Him then I hope to send, whenever I see the issue of my affairs, forthwith.* ^{24} *But I trust in the Lord that I myself also will shortly come.*

After general exhortations to the Christians at Philippi, Paul comes now to speak about two of his fellow-workers, each closely related to them; about Timothy in § 6, and in § 7 about Epaphroditus.

19. *But I hope:* Paul's actual and cheerful expectation, in contrast to the possibility (*v.* 17) that his death is near. For the words, *that I also may know*, suggest a hope that he will live till Timothy's return. Probably also the fuller hope expressed in *v.* 24 was already present to Paul's thought and moulding his words. And apparently the mission of Timothy was dependent (see *v.* 23) on Paul's liberation. *Hope in* the *Lord Jesus:* who is able to rescue him from impending death, and whose purpose, as Paul thinks, is so to do. *Also:* in addition to the benefit to the Philippians from Timothy's visit. This purpose reveals Paul's deep interest in his readers. News about them will be encouragement to him. Close coincidence in 1 Th. iii. 6, 2 Th. i. 3.

20—22. Reason for Paul's *wish to send* Timothy, and him specially. *Of-equal-soul:* see under the word *soul* in ch. i. 27. Paul has *no one* in whom care for the Philippians kindles the same emotions as in Timothy. If he had wished to say that Timothy's care was equal to his own, he would need to have indicated this by writing 'no one else.' The comparison is between others and Timothy, not between Timothy and Paul. *In-a-genuine-way:* as a real, born son naturally cares for his father's interests: a cognate word in ch. iv. 3, 2 Cor. viii. 8, 1 Tim. i. 2, Tit. i. 4. *Be-anxious-about:* forethought so intense as to become painful. Same word in ch. iv. 6, 1 Cor. vii. 32, 33, 34, xii. 25, Mt. vi. 25, 27, 28, 31, 34, x. 19, Lk. x. 41. The contradiction with Ph. iv. 6 is only apparent. There is a care for the future which implies doubt, and is therefore utterly unworthy of the Christian: and there is a forethought which may be, and often is, painful, and yet a genuine outflow of intelligent Christian love. A cognate word, and a close coincidence, are found in 2 Cor. xi. 28. The sad statement in v. 20, v. 21 justifies by a universal description of the men around Paul whom he might conceivably send to Philippi. *Their own things:* same words in same sense as in v. 4: a marked contrast to *your affairs.* *The things of Jesus Christ:* the interests of His kingdom, which include the highest well-being of the Philippian Christians.

The reason here given implies that self-seeking unfits a man to be a reliable witness of the spiritual life of others. And correctly so. For all selfishness dims spiritual vision, and thus veils to us spiritual things good or bad. Therefore selfish men cannot bring to Paul a trustworthy report.

To this description of the men surrounding Paul, there is no exception: *they all seek etc.* A remarkable parallel to 1 Cor. i. 12, iii. 1—3, v. 2, vi. 5. As at Corinth, so at Rome, the men referred to were doubtless real though very imperfect Christians. The different language of Col. iv. 10—14 suggests that the men there mentioned were not with Paul when he wrote this Epistle: and this would account for the absence of any greetings to the Philippians from Christians at Rome: an important coincidence. Of men such as those here described, Paul would not wish to speak.

22. Description of Timothy, in contrast to the men just referred to. *The proof of him:* the attestation of his real worth: close parallel in 2 Cor. ii. 9. *Ye know:* a coincidence with Acts xvi. 3, xvii. 14 where we learn that Timothy was with Paul at the founding of the Church at Philippi; and with ch. xx. 4 which says that Timothy accompanied Paul on a journey through Macedonia, in which province Philippi was. *A child:* close coincidence with 1 Cor. iv. 17, where Paul when sending Timothy to Corinth speaks of him as his 'beloved and trustworthy child.' *Father:* coincidence with 1 Cor. iv. 15, where Paul claims to be the *father* of the Corinthian Christians. *With me he has done service,* or *has served:* a slight change of metaphor. While saying that Timothy has served Paul *as a son* serves his *father*, Paul remembers that, from another point of view, Timothy and himself are alike children and servants of another Master. He therefore now speaks of Timothy as joining *with* himself in serving One whom it is needless to name. *In furtherance of the Gospel:* for its spread and triumph: same words in same sense in ch. i. 5; more fully in *v.* 12, 'for the progress of the Gospel.' This was the aim of the service in which, as the Philippians knew, Timothy joined with Paul.

23, 24. Resumption, from *v.* 19, of Paul's purpose to send Timothy, after a digression about his fitness, unique among others unfit, for this mission; followed (*v.* 24) by a hope of himself coming. *Him then etc.:* more fully, *this man then on the one hand I hope to send . . . on the other hand I trust in* the *Lord that myself etc.:* a double hope cherished by Paul. *Hope to send:* resuming *v.* 19. *My affairs:* same phrase as 'your affairs' in *v.* 19; and practically identical with 'the matters touching me' in ch. i. 12. It must refer to some great crisis which would determine Paul's conduct. And this is most easily explained as the issue of the trial before Nero, for which Paul was waiting during his imprisonment at Rome. These words are thus a coincidence with Acts xxviii. 30. *Forthwith:* as soon as Paul's case is decided, he will send Timothy. That he was unwilling to send away his beloved son in the Gospel before the decision, we can well understand.

Trust in the *Lord:* as in ch. i. 14. Paul's hope of coming to Philippi has its root in the Master whom he serves. A fuller exposition of this hope and of its ground is given in ch. i. 25, 26.

REVIEW. After expressing his joy about his readers, a joy which even the possibility of death does not dim, Paul now turns, in hope of prolonged life, to practical matters. He has something to say about two of his helpers. Timothy he hopes soon to send in order that he may bring back news about the Church at Philippi. On such an errand Timothy is the only one he can send: for Paul's other associates are incapacitated, by their selfishness, for correct spiritual vision and a correct estimate of the spiritual state of others. But Timothy, as a genuine son, shares even Paul's anxieties for the Churches; and has proved this, as the Philippians know, by service rendered to Paul, and to God in fellowship with Paul. The sending of Timothy is however for the present hindered by Paul's uncertainty about the issue of his trial. When this is dispelled, he will at once send Timothy. But he cherishes a purpose resting on his Master's power and purpose that he will himself shortly come.

In this section we again meet Timothy, whom Paul has associated with himself as joint author of the Epistle, and whom we have already met in 1 Cor. iv. 17, xvi. 10, 2 Cor. i. 1, 19. And the features of the man are the same. As before he is Paul's child in the faith; and is in sympathy with him so complete that he is both the eye and the lips of the Apostle, his trusted delegate to a distant Church. Again he is joint author of an apostolic letter. Yet the notice of him here is no repetition. For Timothy's fitness to bring Paul spiritual intelligence affords valuable insight into his character and into all Christian character. The casual description of Paul's associates is no small proof of the historic truthfulness of his Epistles.

SECTION VII.

ABOUT EPAPHRODITUS.

CH. II. 25—30

A necessary thing, however, I counted it, to send to you Epaphroditus, my brother and fellow-worker and fellow-soldier, but your apostle and minister of my need: ²⁶ *inasmuch as he was longing for you all, and distressed because ye had heard that he had been sick.* ²⁷ *For indeed he was sick, near to death. Yet God had mercy on him, and not on him only but also on me, lest I should come to have sorrow upon sorrow.* ²⁸ *The more eagerly therefore I have sent him, that seeing him ye may again rejoice, and I be less sorrowful.* ²⁹ *Receive him then in the Lord with all joy, and hold in honour such men.* ³⁰ *Because by reason of the work of Christ he drew near even to death, having hazarded his life in order to supply the lack of your service for me.*

From the hoped-for mission of Timothy in the near future, Paul now passes to that of Epaphroditus, who was evidently the bearer of this letter.

25. *Necessary, however:* although Paul hopes himself soon to come. The ground of this necessity is stated in v. 26. *EPAPHRO-DITUS:* only here and ch. iv. 18, yet evidently a tried and valued associate of Paul. We have here five details about him; three giving his relation to Paul, a fourth his relation to the readers, and the fifth a relation both to the readers and to Paul. *Brother:* so 2 Cor. ii. 13, 'Titus my brother.' *Fellow-worker:* as in Rom. xvi. 3, 9, Ph. iv. 3. *Fellow-soldier:* for Paul's work is also conflict. It suggests peril in which Epaphroditus bravely stood by Paul. But this does not necessarily imply an earlier association with Paul: for they might have been associated at Rome. If so, this title is a courteous recognition of his courage in discharging his commission. Similarly, the word *fellow-worker* may have been prompted by work done recently at Rome. Paul remembers that Epaphroditus is united to himself as a child of the same divine Father, as a companion in the same great work and in conflict against the same enemies. *My, your:* in Greek, consecutive words, placing in conspicuous contrast the relation of Epaphroditus to the Philippians and his relation to Paul. *Apostle:* as in 2 Cor. viii. 23; see under Rom. i. 1: one sent on special business. What Paul's *need* was, we learn from ch. iv. 14—18, viz. his poverty in prison at Rome and the resulting hardship, a need removed by the contribution brought by Epaphroditus. *Minister:* a cognate word in *vv.* 17, 30; the same word in Rom. xiii. 6, xv. 16. Both Paul in fostering the faith of the Philippian Christians and Epaphroditus in bringing to Paul their contribution were performing a sacred and public service, as sacred as the high-priest's ministrations at the altar. Same thought in ch. iv. 18. Epaphroditus was thus a minister of the Philippian Christians: for he was carrying out their instructions and conveying to Paul their gift. He was also a minister of Paul's *need:* for, by discharging the mission entrusted to him by the Church, he removed that need. See under ch. iv. 18.

26. Ground of the necessity to send Epaphroditus. *Longing-for you all;* keeps before us, as do the same words in ch. i. 8, the universal excellence of the Christians at Philippi. *Distressed:* literally *homeless;* a vivid description of a mind in trouble. Epaphroditus earnestly wished to return to the brethren at Philippi in order that their anxiety might be dispelled by seeing him in good health. How they heard of his sickness, and how he knew that they had heard, we do not know. But communication between Rome and the Roman colony of Philippi along the splendid Egnatian road, would be, if not regular, yet frequent.

Notice a genuine trait of excellence. Many are glad for others to know of their sickness or trouble, especially if caused by service done for them. But this good man was sorry that, through their hearing of it, his own trouble had caused trouble to others.

27. Paul's comment on the sickness and recovery of Epaphroditus. *Indeed he was sick;* adds conspicuously to the report heard by the Philippians an attestation that the report was true. *Near to death:* literally, 'as neighbour side by side of death.' *God had mercy on him;* suggests man's helplessness in sickness and God's complete control of sickness and recovery. *Sorrow upon sorrow:* a note of sadness, evoked by memory of the illness of Epaphroditus and of the sorrow and apprehension thus caused to Paul, amid the prevailing joy of this Epistle. Cp. 2 Cor. vi. 10. It implies other sorrow besides that occasioned by the illness of Epaphroditus. *Mercy also upon me;* reveals Paul's felt helplessness under the new sorrow then looming before him. In this helplessness he recognises the restoration of his friend as God's compassion towards himself. Thus one act was, in different ways, kindness to two men equally helpless. Paul's gratitude also teaches that they who share the sorrows of others have in others' joy a special joy of their own.

28. Restatement of the bearing of Epaphroditus' sickness upon his mission by Paul to Philippi. *More-eagerly therefore:* parallel to 'I counted it necessary' in *v.* 25. The comparative suggests tha the illness and recovery of Epaphroditus did but increase Paul's eagerness to send him. That in *v.* 29 Paul bids his readers welcome Epaphroditus, suggests that he was the bearer of this epistle. Same use of the word *I-have-sent* in Col. iv. 8, Eph. vi. 22, Acts xxiii. 30. The above reasons for sending him to Philippi suggest that his going there was not matter of course, as one goes back home after discharging a mission, that he may have had other reasons for his journey to Rome, and that possibly he was not a resident at Philippi. But we learn from *v.* 30 how eagerly he entered into the Philippians' purpose to help Paul. *Again rejoice:* their usual joy being overshadowed by hearing of Epaphroditus' illness, a shadow only to be removed by knowing that he is well. *Less-sorrowful:* another note of sadness: cp. *v.* 27. Even the removal of Paul's sorrow about Epaphroditus would leave him only less sad. This indicates other and abiding sources of sorrow.

29, 30. Recommendation of Epaphroditus. *Receive in the Lord;*

same words in Rom. xvi. 2. Their reception of him must be an outflow of their union with the One Master of him and them. *Every joy:* as in Rom. xv. 13, Jas. i. 2. No sort of joy was to be lacking in their reception of Epaphroditus. *Such men:* this not being a solitary case but one of a class of which all deserve like honour. *The work of Christ:* cp. 1 Cor. xv. 58. What the work was, we learn from the latter part of the verse. Epaphroditus' discharge of his mission was both a sacrifice (ch. iv. 18) to God and *work* done for *Christ. Even to death:* same words as in *v.* 8. Epaphroditus trod in the steps of Christ, even to the edge of the grave. *Hazarded his life:* literally *gambled with his life,* (Ellicott,) making very prominent the apparent recklessness of his conduct and the great risk he ran. *The lack* of *your service for me.* The public and sacred service (*v.* 25) rendered to Paul fell short in one point, viz. the personal presence of the Philippian Christians who would gladly have themselves ministered to his comfort. This one deficiency Epaphroditus endeavoured, even at the risk of life, to supply. Same thought and words in 1 Cor. xvi. 17. He thus did *the work of Christ.* [Notice two genitives dependent on the word *lack*. The service was deficient: hence *lack of service.* It lacked the personal presence of the Christians at Philippi: the *lack of you.*]

The word *death* links together *vv.* 27 and 30 as referring to the same deadly peril. We infer therefore that the sickness which brought Epaphroditus near to death was occasioned by his mission to Rome. He deliberately exposed his life in order to discharge this mission, and thus actually fell into serious illness. This may have been through exposure on the journey or through contagion at Rome. All details are unknown.

We have here a beautiful episode in the story of Paul. The Philippian Christians heard of his imprisonment at Rome, and wished to send him help. But for a time they had no means of doing so. At last Epaphroditus, a Christian whom they well loved, happens to be going to Rome. A contribution is made, and is sent by Epaphroditus. Either on the journey or at Rome, in consequence of exposure needful to bring the money to Paul, and cheerfully endured, the messenger became dangerously ill. And Paul felt deeply that courageous care for him had brought a brother to the gates of death. Epaphroditus recovered. He joined Paul, apparently, not only in peril but in Christian work. But tidings of his illness reached Philippi. This, Epaphroditus knew; and knew that the tidings would fill his brethren with sorrow. He was therefore eager to return, to allay their fears by showing himself well in their midst. This eagerness to return Paul appreciated, and resolved to use his return as an opportunity of sending to his beloved friends at Philippi the letter before us. The joyful reception of Epaphroditus at Philippi, with this precious letter from the imprisoned Apostle, is veiled from our view in the unwritten past.

SECTION VIII.

WARNINGS AGAINST BAD MEN; AND PAUL'S CONTRARY EXAMPLE.

CH. III. 1—16.

As to the rest, my brethren, rejoice in the Lord.
To write the same things to you, to me indeed is *not irksome, and for you* is *safe.* ² *Keep eyes on the dogs: keep eyes on the bad workers: keep eyes on the concision.* ³ *For we are the circumcision, who worship by the* Spirit *of God, and exult in Christ Jesus, and have no confidence in flesh;* ⁴ *although I might have confidence even in flesh. If any other thinks to have confidence in flesh, I yet more:* ⁵ *circumcised the eighth day, of* the *race of Israel,* the *tribe of Benjamin, a Hebrew from Hebrews;* touching the *Law a Pharisee;* ⁶ *touching zeal, persecuting the Church, touching righteousness,* viz. *that in* the *Law, become blameless.* ⁷ *But things which were gain to me, these for the sake of Christ I have counted loss.* ⁸ *Yes indeed, and I count all* to be *loss for the sake of the superiority of the knowledge of Christ Jesus my Lord, for whose sake I have suffered loss of all things: and I count them refuse that I may gain Christ,* ⁹ *and be found in Him, not having a righteousness of my own, that* which comes *from law, but that* which comes *through faith of Christ, the righteousness from God on the* condition of *faith,* ¹⁰ *in order to know Him and the power of His resurrection and* the *partnership of His sufferings, being* day by day *conformed to His death,* ¹¹ *if in any way I may attain to the resurrection from the dead.* ¹² *Not that I have already obtained or am already made perfect: but I press on if I may also lay hold of that for which I have also been laid hold of by Christ Jesus.* ¹³ *Brethren, not yet do I reckon myself to have laid hold: one thing, however,* I reckon, *forgetting the things behind and stretching forward to the things before* ¹⁴ *I press on towards* the *goal for the prize of the high calling of God in Christ Jesus.*

¹⁵ *So many then as are perfect, let us be of this mind. And if in*

anything ye are otherwise minded, also this will God reveal to you. ¹⁶ *Only whereto we have attained, let us walk by the same.*

1a. An exhortation covering all that Paul has left unsaid: *as to the rest.* Same words in ch. iv. 8, Heb. x. 13. *Rejoice in:* as in ch. i. 18, iv. 10, Col. i. 24. The *Master*, Christ, is the surrounding, pervading, life-giving element *in* which Paul bids his readers *rejoice.* This joy is an outflow of that with which Christ Himself is full: and it becomes ours by inward spiritual contact with Him as servants doing His work. In proportion to our loyalty to Him is our *joy in the Lord.*

1b. Abrupt introduction of a new topic. For the short foregoing exhortation to 'rejoice in the Lord' could not conceivably be *irksome* to Paul, i.e. something to which he would go with reluctance, nor specially *safe* for his readers. We must therefore suppose that from some cause unknown to us, possibly interruption, a new topic was unexpectedly introduced into the Epistle when apparently approaching its close. And the three times repeated warning which at once follows in *v.* 2 and which might easily be distasteful to the writer suggests irresistibly that to it refers the word *safe*. If so, to this warning refer also the words *to write the same things.* This implies that on this subject Paul has already written to the Philippian Christians. But in this Epistle there is as yet no warning against any one. Even the reference to Paul's opponents at Rome is not put in the form of a warning to the Christians at Philippi. He has said nothing of which these words can be called a repetition. Indeed this would be true even if they referred to the foregoing exhortation: for he has not before urged his readers even to 'rejoice in the Lord.' The only approach to this is ch. ii. 18. Nor is it likely that the repetition refers to earlier oral teaching. For this would make the word *write* emphatic: whereas the Greek emphasis is on *the same things.* The absence of other explanation suggests that the repetition refers to some warning in an earlier letter to the Philippians now lost. Against this suggestion there is no objection. For it is hardly possible that all the letters which Paul wrote are preserved to us. There is clear mention in 1 Cor. v. 9 (see note) of a lost letter to the Corinthians. Polycarp, in his *Epistle to the Philippians*, says that Paul 'when absent wrote letters to you.' But this is not a conclusive proof: for the plural form *letters* is often used for a single written communication, e.g. 1 Maccabees x. 3, 7, xii. 5, 19; and this may have been Polycarp's meaning. That Paul refers here to an earlier and lost letter, is the easiest explanation of his words,

In such letter he may have warned the Christians at Philippi against Jewish enemies. And certainly his own experience in many places justified the warning: see Acts xiii. 45, xiv. 2, 5, 19, xvii. 5, 13. To this danger he refers in 1 Th. ii. 15, Rom. xv. 31. And he remembers it while writing this Epistle. To mention it again, is not, he tells us, a duty from which he recoils: and to do so may guard his readers from real danger.

2. *Keep-eyes-on:* pay attention to. Same word in Col. iv. 17, 1 Cor. i. 26, x. 18, etc. It denotes the simple act of looking, ocular or mental. *Dogs:* a term of contempt, frequent with Gentiles and Jews. To the latter, dogs, feeding as they do in Eastern cities on all sorts of refuse, were an incarnation of degraded ceremonial impurity. So Mt. xv. 26, Rev. xxii. 15; cp. Mt. vii. 6: also Isa. lvi. 10, 11. This common term expressing Jewish contempt for Gentiles, Paul here applies to Jews, (see below,) indicating that the men referred to were outside and beneath the Covenant of God. *Workmen:* same word in 2 Cor. xi. 13, 'guileful *workmen*,' 2 Tim. ii. 15, Mt. ix. 37, 38, x. 10, xx. 1, 2, Lk. xiii. 27 etc. They were active and laborious: but their aims and methods were *bad*. *The concision:* a contemptuous modification of the word rendered 'circumcision.' Its cognate verb describes in 1 Kgs. xviii. 28 the self-mutilations of the prophets of Baal: similarly Lev. xxi. 5. It thus places the circumcision of these Jews beside the mutilations of the heathen. A close parallel in Gal. v. 12. The article before each substantive indicates a definite class of men. The essential harmony, amid total difference, of the terms used suggests that they present only different aspects of the same men. And this is confirmed by the order of the words, which passes from the general to the specific. This warning receives great emphasis from the repetition of the verb, *beware*. Three times, under three different aspects, Paul warns his readers of the same danger. The compactness of these words suggests that possibly they are an exact repetition of words already written by Paul. Certainly they embody a warning already given. The word *concision* proves that *v.* 2 refers to Jews. Upon these Paul flings back the term of contempt so freely cast by them at Gentiles as men outside the Covenant of God and as compared with themselves no better than unclean animals. He admits their laborious effort, but calls it bad. And the bodily rite in which they trust, he places on a level with heathen mutilation. That they were not members of the Church at Philippi, we infer with certainty from the universal commendation in ch. i. 3—5. Yet the earnestness of the warning assures us that the danger was real and near. Paul's

parody of the word 'circumcision' suggests that he refers roughly and generally to the Jewish race as a whole, or rather to the mass of it which rejected Christ. But his warning would include any Jews like those at Corinth (see my *Corinthians* p. 477) who under guise of a false profession had crept into the Church (cp. Gal. ii. 4) in order to overturn it. Indeed the strong words in 2 Cor. xi. 13—15 against men of this class is an important coincidence with this verse. But, inasmuch as in Ph. iii. 5, 6 we have no reference to professed Christians like that in 2 Cor. xi. 23, probably Paul refers here chiefly to non-Christian Jews.

The anti-Christian Jews, Paul justly calls *the concision:* for every outward form of religion destitute of inward devotion is practically the same as heathen ritual. While boasting of the ancient and divine rite, they were really trampling under foot the purpose for which it was given. The rite so desecrated could not be called 'circumcision,' but required a meaner name.

3. A contrast, justifying the term 'concision.' *We:* emphatic. To Paul and his readers belongs *the* title *circumcision.* Consequently, the only term left for the men here referred to is that just given them. *The circumcision:* the circumcised persons, as in Eph. ii. 11, Rom. iii. 30, iv. 9, xv. 8, Gal. ii. 9. *Who worship etc.;* describes *the* real *circumcision. Worship:* same word in Rom. i. 9, 25, 2 Tim. i. 3 etc. It is used only of service rendered to God; frequently of the service of the temple, as in Heb. xiii. 10. Consequently it is needless to mention here the object of worship. Notice that *circumcision* involves worship: for Israel was set apart to be a worshipping people. *By the Spirit of God:* who prompts and guides this worship. [Cp. Rom. viii. 13, 14.] *And exult in Christ Jesus:* cp. Rom. v. 11. See under Rom. ii. 17. Like all the circumcised, Paul and his readers are accustomed to boast: but the encompassing element of their boasting is the living personality of Christ. *And have no confidence etc.:* third point in the description of the true circumcision. *Confidence* is implied in *exult:* for all exultation rests on some foundation, and therefore involves trust in some object personal or impersonal. These men based their hopes on something in their own bodies. For to them circumcision, not being accompanied by a spiritual change, was a mere outward rite. Paul describes the Christian life as a service of God, prompted and guided by the Spirit of God; as a joyous confidence resting in Christ as its element; and negatively as not resting on anything belonging merely to outward bodily life.

Since many of Paul's readers were Gentiles, and yet all are evidently included in this description, the circumcision here referred to must be spiritual only ; as in Rom. ii. 29, Col. ii. 11. The ancient rite was a mark of the covenant with God. But all who have the characteristics here given are included in the New Covenant, and are therefore, but in greater degree, in the position formerly occupied by the circumcision. And, if so, nothing but the contemptuous term used by Paul remains to those who trust for the favour of God to the outward rite.

4—6. A boast which Paul has, but refuses to use. By showing us a confidence he might cherish, Paul adds force to 'no confidence in the flesh.' As himself the chief object of Jewish hostility to Christianity, Paul passes easily from the general statement in *v.* 3, 'we are etc.,' to the details in *vv.* 4—6 which refer to himself only. The emphatic word *I* recalls Paul's unique position as compared both with enemies and friends. *Although etc.:* literally *although myself having confidence even in flesh:* contrasted statement subordinate to the foregoing. Paul has a confidence : for his condition is one in which he might trust. And the confidence in which he might indulge reaches down *even* to the *flesh*. *If any one etc.:* an independent statement of the foregoing. *Thinks* or *thinks-well;* denotes approval of a course of action or thought, as in Mt. iii. 9, Lk. 1. 3 : 'if to any one it seems good to trust in the flesh.' *I more:* 'I have more to trust in than he.' Similar language in 2 Cor. xi. 21. Paul thinks fit to play for a moment the part of his opponents that he may show how much better he can play it than they. Then follow in detail the grounds on which he might rest a confidence in the flesh.

5, 6. *Circumcised the eighth day :* and therefore not a proselyte. Notice the accurate observance of the letter of the Law. *From the race of Israel:* and therefore not a son of a proselyte, or an Edomite. *Tribe of Benjamin:* nearer specification of his relation to the sacred race. Paul knows his own tribe. Moreover Benjamin not only gave to Israel its first king, whose name Paul bore, but was faithful to the House of David when the ten tribes revolted. *Hebrew:* 2 Cor. xi. 22. In Acts vi. 1 it denotes a Hebrew-speaking Jew in contrast to the Hellenists who spoke Greek, thus marking a distinction within the Jewish nation. And elsewhere in the N. T. it has reference to language. Probably so here. Although born at Tarsus, Paul clung to the ancient language and customs of his nation. He did so by parental training : for his parents also were *Hebrews*. A close coincidence with Acts xxiii. 6, where Paul calls himself a son of Pharisees. For, more than other Jews, Pharisees clung to everything which distinguished Israel from the rest of mankind.

After noting, in ascending scale, four points of honour in his pedigree, as Jews boasted, Paul now gives three points bearing upon his personal character and conduct. The similar phrases *touching law, touching zeal, touching righteousness*, mark the transition. *Pharisee:* important coincidence with Acts. xxiii. 6, xxvi. 5. *Touching law:* looked at from the point of view of the general principle embodied in the law given at Sinai, and in the Books of Moses. This principle, viz. that the favour of God is to be obtained by obedience to authoritative prescriptions of conduct, found in the Pharisees its strictest exponents and adherents. And Paul was *a Pharisee*. If, again, we take *zeal* as our standard of measurement, we find proof of his earnest advocacy of Judaism in that he was *persecuting the Church*. Important coincidence with Gal. i. 13, 14: cp. 1 Tim. i. 13. *Righteousness:* the condition of a man who enjoys the judge's approval: see under Rom. i. 17. In order to distinguish his meaning here from 'Righteousness through Faith,' Paul adds the specifying words, *that in law*. He is speaking of such righteousness as may be found in obedience to prescriptions of conduct. From this point of view, Paul had *become blameless*, i.e. he had reached a position in which no fault could be found with him. He had done all that could be done to obtain the favour of God by obedience to law.

Of the seven points of boasting, the first four pertain evidently to bodily descent; and thus abundantly justify Paul's declaration that he has a confidence even in the flesh. These points are supplemented by three others not bearing so directly on the same. But the continued series suggests a continued train of thought. And doubtless Paul felt that the obedience to law by which he sought formerly the favour of God was only outward and bodily, and that even the zeal which prompted his persecution of the Church had its ultimate source in motives pertaining to the present bodily life. Notice that each point in the series was one which Paul's opponents would admit to be a valid ground of boasting.

An interesting coincidence with *vv.* 4—6 is found in 2 Cor. xi. 21—27. But there Paul is speaking to Jews who were also (*v.* 22) professed 'ministers of Christ.' Here, without any reference to Christianity, he speaks simply of Jews. This suggests that the men against whom Paul here warns his readers were, at least for the more part, not Christians even in name.

7. Paul's solemn renunciation of his own Jewish boasting, in emphatic contrast to the foregoing, and followed in *v.* 8 by a still wider renunciation. It is an exposition of 'no confidence in flesh'

in v. 3, after the contrast in v. 4 and its exposition in detail in vv. 5, 6.

Things-which: literally *what sort of things*, noting a whole class, to which belong the above details. *Gains to me:* each item being, from Paul's then point of view, an enrichment to him. *I-have-counted:* a calculation made and completed in the past, and the abiding estimate now remaining. *For the sake of Christ,* or *because of Christ:* expounded in v. 8. *Loss:* either the *gains* themselves written off as lost; or the things formerly looked upon as making him richer now looked upon as making him poorer, i.e. as doing him harm. The former exposition is all that the words demand, and all that is implied in the word 'suffered-loss' in v. 8. We therefore cannot give to the word *loss* the second and fuller sense. The whole class of various things which Paul once looked upon as *gains*, he has now written of as one *loss*.

8. *Yes, indeed:* an abrupt breaking off, making the reassertion more forceful. *I count:* the reckoning represented in v. 7 as already made, now represented as going on day by day. *All-things:* wider than 'what sort of things' in v. 7. *My Lord:* in harmony with 'my God' in ch. i. 3 and Rom. i. 8. Paul has come to know *Christ Jesus* as his own *Master;* and has found this *knowledge* to surpass all other good. Indeed it has revealed to him the worthlessness of all merely earthly gains. And, influenced by this superior knowledge, he now reckons to be *loss all things* he once prized.

For whose sake etc.: an emphatic and categorical statement of the loss involved in Paul's reckoning. The things mentioned above were once wealth to him: they are now worthless. Consequently, where before he was rich, he is now poor. Moreover, the things thus lost were those he most prized. Therefore, in losing them he *suffered the loss of all things.* This loss was occasioned by the person and work of Christ, *for whose sake* it was cheerfully endured. Notice the emphatic repetitions: *I have counted, I count, I count; loss, loss, suffered-loss; for Christ's sake, for the sake of the superiority of the knowledge of Christ, for whose sake.* [More definite than πάντα is τὰ πάντα, including all forms of material good.] In proportion as we know Christ does earthly wealth cease to be an enrichment to us. We look upon it only as an instrument of serving Christ. Therefore, like Paul we may say that because of Christ we have lost all things. Of this complete, inward, subjective loss, all objective loss for Christ's sake is a partial and easy realisation in outward form, easy in proportion to our knowledge of Christ.

And I count them *refuse:* added as an explanatory parallel to

I have suffered, keeping before us Paul's subjective estimate of the change which has taken place in him. *Refuse:* anything thrown away, either excrement rejected by the body, or the leavings of a feast incapable of giving further nourishment or pleasure. Such does Paul reckon the Jewish prerogatives in which once he boasted. And this reckoning has been to him practically the *loss of all things*.

9—11. Purpose of the reckoning described in *vv.* 7, 8, i.e. the greater gain for which Paul cheerfully submitted to the 'loss of all things.' It is therefore practically an exposition of 'for the sake of Christ,' and 'for the sake of the superiority of the knowledge of Christ.' *Gain Christ:* 'make Him my own and thus obtain infinite enrichment.' For all that Christ has and is belongs to His servants: and having Him they have all they need. The word *gain* is a marked contrast to the things which to Paul were once gain but which he now counts to be loss. *Be found in Him:* second item in Paul's purpose. He desires so to gain Christ that He will be to him the home and bulwark of his soul and the pervading element of his spiritual life. The word *found* suggests a recognition by others of Paul's inward union with Christ. In the searching scrutiny which will make known whatever is now hidden, Paul will *be found* safe in Christ. *Righteousness:* as in Rom. i. 17; see note. *A righteousness of my own:* very close coincidence with Rom. x. 3. As Paul never forgot, an unchanging law of the Kingdom of God makes spiritual blessing conditional on agreement with a divinely erected standard. Consequently, to be in Christ, implies *righteousness*. The only question is the kind of righteousness and the source from which it is derived. The righteousness through which Paul hopes to gain Christ is not *a righteousness of* his *own*, i.e. an agreement with a divine standard resulting from his own effort and which therefore he can claim as *my own*. Such would be the righteousness which the Jews were ever, though vainly, seeking to derive from the Law by careful observance of its prescriptions. *From law:* as in Gal. iii. 21; a close parallel. [The absence of the Greek article suggests the abstract principle 'Do this and live,' a principle which received historical and literary embodiment in the Law of Moses.] Cp. Ph. iii. 6, Gal. iii. 11, 18, 23, iv. 4, 5, 21, v. 4, 18, 23, vi. 13. It is practically the same as 'from works of law' in Gal. ii. 16 three times. *Through faith of Christ:* belief of the words of Christ, as in Rom. iii. 22, Gal. ii. 16. *From God:* source of this righteousness. By proclaiming that He receives into His favour all who believe the Gospel, God gives righteousness to all who believe. And this *righteousness* received *from God* is in absolute contrast to all righteousness of their own, i.e. derived from their own obedience, for which the Jews were ever striving. Same contrast in Rom. x. 3. *On-the-condition-of faith:* literally *on faith:* same words in Acts iii. 16. They represent faith as the condition *on* which, whereas just above it is the channel *through* which, *righteousness* comes forth *from God*.

The unexpected occurrence here of the word *righteousness* in this peculiar sense, the emphatic repetition of the word *faith*, and the coincidence in phraseology and thought with Rom. iii. 22, Gal. ii. 16, iii. 21, are very clear indications of Pauline authorship.

10. The slight change of phrase, *in order to know Him*, indicates that this is not a third item of Paul's aim in addition to those in *v.* 9, but is rather a further purpose to be attained by gaining Christ and being found in Him. *To know Him:* as though Paul's present knowledge were so defective as to be unworthy of the name. This fuller knowledge of Christ is yearned for also in Eph. i. 17, iii. 19, iv. 13. It is obtained only by (*v.* 9) gaining Him for our own and by abiding in Him. These words expound 'for the sake of the excellence of the knowledge of Christ' in *v.* 8; as 'that I may gain Christ' in *v.* 8 expounds 'for the sake of Christ' in *v.* 7. *And the power etc.;* expounds what is involved in *to know Christ. The power of His resurrection:* the power of God which raised Christ from the dead. For His resurrection is emphatically a manifestation of divine power: and in this manifested power lay its practical worth: cp. 2 Cor. xiii. 4, Rom. i. 4. From *v.* 11 we learn that the ultimate goal of Paul's desire is to 'attain to the resurrection from the dead.' To experience that resurrection is to *know the power* which raised Christ. For the one resurrection is a result of the other. Had not Christ risen, there had been no faith in Him, no Gospel, no Christianity, and therefore no resurrection to eternal life. Moreover, our present spiritual life is a victory over sin gained for us and in us by the power of God which raised Christ. It will be consummated in a bodily resurrection like His. That power in its full manifestation, Paul desires to know. A very close and important parallel is found in Eph. i. 19, 20. The intimate connection between the resurrection of Christ, the believer's present victory over sin and moral elevation, and His final victory over the grave, a connection ever present to Paul's thought, at once suggests the above exposition, and makes needless any other.

Fellowship of His sufferings: partnership with Christ in His sufferings: cp. 1 Cor. i. 9, x. 16. They who for Christ's sake, and in order to save men, endure hardship, are sharing His sufferings for the world's salvation. For their sufferings, like His, are caused by man's sin, are endured in loyalty to God and love to mankind, and are working out God's purpose of mercy. Close coincidence in Col. i. 24, 2 Cor. i. 5. This companionship of suffering, Paul desires to know. And wisely. For we know Christ only so far as we share His loyalty to God and love to men. And if we share these, the circumstances of life will often lead us to endure hardship in order to save those whom Christ has taught us to love. Of such partnership with Christ, the annals of the Church are full. Happy they on whom rests most heavily this yoke of Christ.

The resurrection is placed before the *sufferings* of Christ because Paul's thought went out first to the glory which should follow. He then remembered that to this goal there is only one path; and in view of the goal desires to tread that path.

Being-conformed etc.: way in which this knowledge of the fellowship of Christ's sufferings is to be obtained, a path Paul is already treading. Every step towards a martyr's grave was making him more like Christ who died on the cross. This clause gives definiteness to the foregoing one, and shows that Paul has in view both the death of Christ and the deadly peril which overshadows him while he writes.

11. The ultimate goal of Paul's desire. *The resurrection* or *resurrection-out-of:* a strong term, used in the N.T. only here. *From the dead:* more definite than 'resurrection of the dead,' and found only in Lk. xx. 35, Acts iv. 2, 1 Pet. i. 3. It suggests removal from among the dead, and is used only of Christ and His servants. Although the lost (Jno. v. 29) will rise, resurrection will not separate them from the dead. Paul desired to *attain to* the uprising forth from the midst of the dead, the 'resurrection of life.' This will be the Christian's final triumph over his last foe; 1 Cor. xv. 26. And it implies victory over all enemies who now bar his path. For whatever tends to overturn his faith tends to rob him of his glorious consummation. A close parallel in Lk. xx. 35. This phrase, peculiar to the blessed dead, by no means asserts or implies that they will rise before the unsaved. And Christ asserts that the two resurrections, 'of life' and 'of judgment,' will take place in the same 'hour.' *If in any way:* as in Rom. i. 10, xi. 14, Acts xxvii. 12; noting a purpose which Paul desires to achieve *in any way*, and therefore at any cost. It suggests difficulty, and earnest desire prepared to encounter any difficulty.

REVIEW OF 7—11. Paul has declared that, in contrast to the Jews, he has no confidence in the flesh; and has shown the significance of this assertion by specifying several matters pertaining to bodily life in which conceivably he might have confidence.

He now tells us that he has renounced, and continues to renounce, all these matters of boasting; and describes the greater gain which has allured him to this renunciation. Things once prized as gains, he has written off as loss; and this because of Christ and because of the greater gain of knowing Him. This renunciation has been to him the loss of all things; so valuable to him once were the gains he has renounced. They are to him now only the refuse which we haste to cast away. Paul desires to make Christ his own, thus gaining real enrichment; and to have Him for his home and refuge. To this end he needs the approval of the great Judge, which he can obtain not by anything in himself but only by the divinely-given righteousness promised to those who believe. He desires to win Christ and to be found in Him, in order thus to know Him, and especially to know by experience the mighty power which raised Christ from the dead. The only way to this experience of the power which wrought in Christ is by partnership in the sufferings which reached their culmination in the cross. And these Paul is eager to share. His ultimate aim is to attain the glory of those who in the Great Day will rise from and cast off the dust of death and thus enter into immortal life.

In these verses Paul contemplates the great change which had turned the entire current of his life. It was no new and loftier view of morality or even a more enthusiastic love for his fellows; but a new aim in life, and this aim a new relation to Christ and a deeper knowledge of Him, the ultimate aim being a share in the resurrection of the just.

12—14. The chief feature of the spiritual life described in *vv.* 7—11 is the aim, manifold and yet one, therein so emphatically and repeatedly set forth. In *vv.* 12—14 this aim is placed in still clearer light, thus receiving even greater prominence as an all-controlling element of Paul's inner life.

12. *Not that:* as in 2 Cor. i. 24. It guards from misinterpretation the foregoing assertion, by saying that this lofty aim does not imply actual attainment. *Obtained:* literally *received* or *taken*. The object received is not mentioned, attention being for the moment limited to the act of reception. But the word *press-on* suggests that Paul has already in view the prize mentioned in *v.* 14. This prize can be no other than the full blessedness of the Kingdom of Christ. And, for this, Paul must wait till the 'resurrection from the dead.' Notice the accurate use of the Greek tenses. The aorist, *I-have-*

obtained, denotes the mere act of reception: the perfect, *am-made-perfect* denotes its abiding result. The denial *not already attained* covers Paul's past life to the moment of writing. He has not yet received the prize he has in view. Lightfoot's exposition, 'not as though by my conversion I did at once attain,' puts into the Greek aorist a meaning quite foreign to it and belonging only to the English preterite: see *The Expositor,* 1st series, vol. xi. p. 375.] *Already . . . already:* emphatic denial of present attainment. A close parallel in 1 Cor. iv. 8. *Made-perfect:* same word from the lips of Paul in Acts xx. 24; Heb. ii. 10, ix. 9, xi. 40, xii. 23, etc. A cognate adjective, rendered 'perfect,' in Ph. iii. 15, and 1 Cor. ii. 6 where see note. These words denote a development which has reached its goal. Consequently, the exact sense in each case will vary according to the goal the writer has for the moment in view. They suggest here that the prize Paul seeks is to be obtained by personal maturity. Since it is given in the Great Day (cp. 2 Tim. iv. 8) Paul probably means here that it is not yet so secure to him as to be no longer an object of earnest effort.

I-press-on: literally *pursue,* i.e. follow quickly with a view to take hold of. Same word in Rom. ix. 30, 31, xii. 13, 14. *Lay-hold:* stronger form of the word rendered *obtain.* The words may be compared as *take* and *take-hold. Of that for which:* or with equal grammatical correctness *inasmuch as.* The former rendering would assert that Christ has taken hold of Paul with a definite aim, and that Paul presses forward in order to achieve that aim, i.e. to lay hold of that for which Christ has laid hold of him. The second exposition would leave unmentioned, as in *v.* 12*a,* the object Paul desires to grasp, stating only that Christ has laid hold of him and giving this as a reason for his own earnest effort. Between these renderings (RV. text and RV. margin) we cannot decide. And the practical difference is slight. Paul knows that Christ has laid His hand on him. This must be with a definite purpose, a purpose to be attained by Paul's own effort. To accomplish this purpose is the object of his strenuous endeavour.

13, 14. An affectionate repetition and development of *v.* 12. *Reckon:* a favourite word of Paul: close parallel in 2 Cor. xi. 5. *I . . . myself:* each word emphatic, a vivid description of self-estimation. Cp. Jno. v. 30, 31. *Not-yet:* connected grammatically with *reckon.* But in Paul's thought *reckon to have laid hold* forms one idea. He has not yet reached the point at which he can soberly calculate that he has achieved the aim of life.

One thing, however, I do: the last two words being supplied from the sentence following which describes what Paul is doing. *Forgetting etc.:* as a racer thinks not of the ground already passed, but only of that still before him. *The things behind:* the earlier stages of his Christian course. For the Jewish delusions in *vv.* 5, 6 were no part of his marked-out path. *Stretching forward to etc.:* like a racer with hands reaching out eagerly towards the goal: a graphic delineation. *The things behind . . . the things before:* a conspicuous contrast which cannot be reproduced in English. *I-press-on;* takes up the same word in *v.* 12. *The goal:* the end of the course already in view and directing and quickening the racer's rapid steps. *The prize:* in N.T. only here and in 1 Cor. ix. 24: same word in Ep. of Clement ch. v.; see my *Corinthians* p. 521. The context shows that Paul refers to the garland given to successful athletes at the Greek festivals. See my *Corinthians* p. 157. While forgetting the ground already trodden and pressing eagerly towards the goal, the racer was really pressing on towards the garland he hoped to win. *The . . . calling of God:* as in Rom. xi. 29; see under Rom. viii. 28. It is the Gospel looked upon as a voice of God summoning men to Himself. *High calling:* belonging to a realm infinitely above everything on earth: cp. Heb. iii. 1. The Gospel has its source in heaven, and calls men up to the place whence it comes. Of this divine and heavenly summons, given to all who hear the Gospel, the voice on the way to Damascus was a particular case. It bids us contend for a prize. Hence *the prize of the high calling.* Paul remembers that God has called him to contend for a glorious prize, and that to enable him to win it Christ has laid His hand upon him. He therefore presses forward with the goal in view, to grasp the prize. *In Christ Jesus;* asserts either that the *high calling* was given *in* connection with *Christ,* or that Paul's eager effort for the prize had Christ for its encompassing and pervading and animating element. The latter exposition, giving as it does to these concluding words a much richer significance, is probably correct. A similar ambiguity in 2 Cor. xii. 10.

Paul's chief thought in *vv.* 7—11 about his spiritual life was a purpose to win and to know Christ, that thus he may obtain a place in the resurrection of the just. In *vv.* 12—14, this purpose is made more definite by a repeated and emphatic assertion that Paul has not yet attained the object he so earnestly desires; and is then developed into actual and intense effort. This effort is clothed in Paul's favourite metaphor of the Athletic Festivals of Greece. He is a racer pressing forward along the course, forgetting the ground already trodden and eagerly straining every nerve to reach the goal and thus obtain the prize.

This metaphor presents an invaluable picture, and an essential condition, of healthy Christian life; viz. incessant and strenuous effort and sustained progress. The goal is the resurrection of the just. We can reach it only by pursuing now the path marked out for us by God. Consequently, every moral victory is a step towards the prize which will be given in that Day.

15, 16. Practical application of the foregoing. That Paul here implicitly claims perfection, after disclaiming it in *v.* 12, proves that the word was not to him a technical term for one definite stage of the Christian life. The context shows that the perfection denied in *v.* 12 was such as would make needless further effort and progress. That assumed here is doubtless the Christian maturity mentioned in 1 Cor. ii. 6, xiv. 20, Heb. v. 14, and there contrasted with spiritual infancy. It implies a firm grasp of the Gospel and a full surrender of our heart and life to its transforming power. Possibly Paul has here in view some who claimed to be *perfect* or *full-grown*. Instead of denying their claim, he shows the obligation it involves. They who call themselves men in Christ are bound to contend as athletes for the great prize. Similar thought and expression in 1 Cor. viii. 1. *Of this mind:* viz. pressing on towards the prize. Since Paul, whom all would admit to be a mature Christian, disclaimed absolute perfection and was striving with all his might for something he had not yet attained, he bids his readers, so many as suppose themselves to be mature Christians, to make the same self-estimate and the same resolute effort.

In anything otherwise minded: some detail not in harmony with the *mind* of Paul. That it is only a mere detail, is implied in the absence of censure and in the hope immediately expressed. 'If in any matter you do not share my self-estimate and earnest effort, *even this* error God will dissipate by heavenly light.' *Reveal:* as in 1 Cor. ii. 10, Gal. i. 16; see under Rom. i. 17. It denotes always the Hand of God lifting a veil and thus imparting to men by light from heaven actual knowledge, ordinary or extraordinary. Paul bids his readers imitate his own self-estimate and earnest effort, and expresses an assured hope that if they do so, and if in any detail they fall below the example just set before them, even this error will be removed by God.

16. Concluding exhortation, in the form of a limitation to the foregoing. 'Let us count as nothing our present attainments and press forward: *only* in so doing let us pursue the direction in which *we have attained* our present position.' A similar thought underlies the argument in Gal. iii. 3, where Paul exposes the folly of turning aside from the path in which his readers have obtained spiritual life. That argument and this exhortation assume, not that the readers are infallible, but that they have made indisputable progress. Of this, their own moral sense was to them an infallible witness. They know that they have come out of darkness into light. Paul expresses his own determination, and encourages his readers, to go forward; and warns that their progress be in the direction which their past experience has proved to be right. So will all real progress mental and spiritual be along the lines of whatever progress we have already made. But we must be sure that our progress is real. Of this, neither Paul nor his readers had any doubt. *Walk:* same word in Rom. iv. 12, Gal. v. 25, vi. 16, Acts xxi. 24; describing, as here, a spiritual path.

Such are Paul's safe words to his readers. Around them are enemies, unworthy of the name of men, yet busy, and boasting in the Covenant of God. Their professed loyalty to that Covenant is unreal. Its true sons are Paul and his readers, Jews and Gentiles. For the worship of the true Israelites is prompted by the Spirit of God: and their boast is in Christ and not in anything pertaining to mere bodily life. Yet in whatever the Jews boast, Paul might boast still more. For, whatever they claim, he has. But to him all such trust, and indeed all reliance upon earthly good, have vanished at the magic name of Christ. Paul's one aim now is to win Christ as his spiritual home and refuge, that thus he may know Him; and by knowing Him obtain a place in the resurrection of the just. Yet this lofty aim does not imply attainment. Paul has not reached the goal on which his eye is fixed. But day by day he is pressing forward. And his strenuous effort after spiritual progress he holds before his readers as a pattern for all who claim to be men in Christ. If in any detail, of thought or action, they cannot as yet embrace this all-controlling purpose, Paul confidently hopes that new light from heaven will enable them to do so. But whatever else they do, their effort and progress must be along the path which already has led them from sin to God.

SECTION IX.

WORLDLY-MINDED CHURCH-MEMBERS, WITH WHOM IS CONTRASTED THE CHRISTIAN'S HOPE.

CH. III. 17—IV. 1.

Be joint-imitators of me, brethren, and mark those who thus walk, according as ye have us for *an example.* [18] *For many walk of whom I often said to you, and now say even weeping,* that they are *the enemies of the cross of Christ:* [19] *whose end* is *destruction, whose God* is *the belly, and* their *glory* is *in their shame, who mind the earthly things.* [20] *For our citizenship is in heaven, whence also we wait for a Saviour,* the *Lord Jesus Christ,* [21] *who will refashion the body of our humiliation conformed to the body of His glory, according to the working whereby He is able even to subject to Himself all things.*

[1] *So then, my brethren, beloved and longed for, my joy and crown, in this way stand in the Lord, beloved ones.*

Exhortation to imitate Paul, *v.* 17: opposite conduct of some church-members, *vv.* 18, 19: with which is contrasted the Christian's hope, *vv.* 20, 21: concluding exhortation to steadfastness, *v.* 1.

17. *Joint-imitators of me, become ye:* join with others in imitating Paul. The chief word here differs only one syllable from that in I Cor. iv. 16, xi. 1, where Paul speaks of himself as an example. [So always when a genitive follows the word *imitators:* cp. I Th. i. 6, ii. 14.] This is simpler than the exposition 'join with me in imitating Christ:' for there is no reference in the context to the example of Christ; whereas in *v.* 17*b* Paul speaks expressly of himself and others as patterns to the Philippians.

Mark: to look with a purpose, especially with a view to avoid, imitate, or obtain. Compare and contrast the same word in Rom. xvi. 17. Same word as *look-at* in ch. ii. 4, and 2 Cor. iv. 18. The word *walk* takes up the similar, though not the same word in *v.* 16. *Who walk thus:* viz. imitating Paul. *According as ye have etc.:* a fact with which the above exhortations are in agreement. [This exposition gives to καθώς its full force as introducing a harmony. Had it introduced merely an exposition of οὕτως, ὡς would probably have been used, as in Eph. v. 28, 33.] *Us:* in contrast to *me,* including Paul and those who *walk* as he does. Such persons are an enrichment to the Philippian Christians: *ye have a pattern.*

Same word and sense in 1 Th. i. 7, 2 Th. iii. 9, where as here many men are one pattern; and in 1 Tim. iv. 12, Tit. ii. 7: same word in slightly different sense in Rom. v. 14, vi. 17, 1 Cor. x. 6.

While exhorting his readers in *vv.* 15, 16 Paul placed himself among their number: 'let us be of this mind ... we have attained.' Conscious that he is himself doing what he exhorts, he now bids them to imitate him; and in so saying remembers that others are setting the same example. Upon these disciples who follow the steps of their teacher, Paul advises his readers to fix their attention, making use of the pattern they possess. He thus teaches the value of study of Christian character.

Notice that the example of Paul did not supersede the need and value of the example of others who imitate him. For a less example under our immediate observation is sometimes more effective than a greater one at a distance. And various good men present varieties of excellence suitable for imitation in various positions of life.

18. Reason for the foregoing exhortation; viz. that *many* pursue an opposite path. These were apparently church-members. For the hostility and sensuality and worldliness of pagans was so familiar to Paul that it would hardly move him to tears. The neutral word *walk* (see under 1 Cor. iii. 3) simply places beside the walk of those who imitate Paul the outward life of these unworthy men. The path in which they walk is left to be inferred from what follows. *Many* and *often:* notes of importance. *I have often said:* probably when present at Philippi, where Paul must have been twice and possibly oftener, during his third missionary journey. It may also have included written warnings. The singular number, *I said*, suggests special warnings from Paul himself. *Even weeping;* reveals the terrible position of the men referred to and the damage they were doing. *The enemies of the cross;* implies that the death *of Christ* holds a unique place as a chief means of the advancement of His Kingdom. And this can be explained only by Paul's teaching in Rom. iii. 24—26 that our salvation comes, by the grace of God, through the death of Christ making the justification of believers consistent with the justice of God. To resist the cross of Christ, is to resist the tremendous earnestness of God meeting a tremendous need of man, and the infinite love, there manifested. We wait to know more about the men guilty of sin so great.

19. Further description of 'the enemies of the cross.' *Whose end:* as in 2 Cor. xi. 15, where see note. *Destruction:* utter ruin: see note under Rom. ii. 24, and especially *The Expositor*, 4th series, vol. i. p. 24. That ruin is here said to be *the end* of these men, implies clearly that Paul believed in the possibility of final ruin. For if all men will at last be saved, destruction cannot be their *end*. In that case the end of all men would be eternal life. The plain words before us prove that such universal salvation was altogether alien to the thought of Paul. For the universal purpose of salvation, see under ch. ii. 11. *Whose . . . whose:* stately repetition. *The belly:* not 'their belly.' The seat of appetite for food is looked upon in the abstract as one definite idea; and is thus in some sense personified; so 1 Cor. vi. 13. This gives great force to the terrible charge *whose God is the belly*. A similar, though slightly different thought in Rom. xvi. 18. The appetite for food and the desire for pleasant food, with all the self-indulgence of which this appetite is a representative, are the supreme power which these men obey. The lower element of their nature controls the whole of it. The absence of the word *whose* before *glory in their shame* joins these words to the foregoing as together forming a second item in the description. *Glory:* that which evokes admiration: see under Rom. i. 21. That which evokes from their fellows admiration of them, and to which they look for admiration, is found *in* that which is *their* disgrace and ought to cover them with *shame*. To them, their degradation is their ornament. *The earthly things:* good or ill, these looked upon as a complex yet definite idea: hence the plural, and the definite article. *Who mind:* as in *v.* 15, ii. 2, 5, Rom. viii. 5, etc.: a word frequent in this Epistle. The things of earth, i.e. material good and ill, are the objects of their mental activity. Exact contrast in Col. iii. 1; 'mind the things above.'

About these enemies of the cross, Paul's first thought is the ruin which awaits them. He then mentions the most conspicuous feature of their character, viz. that desires common to animals are the supreme object of their worship, the lower thus ruling the higher. Closely connected with this terrible inversion, we find that that which gains for them admiration with their fellows is really their disgrace. All this Paul traces to its ultimate source, viz. concentration of their thought on things pertaining to the material world. This preference of the lower for the higher is inevitably degrading. Hence comes the supremacy of bodily appetites, and the distorted vision which mistakes a disgrace for an ornament. The result is ruin. Since Christ died in order to raise us above the dominion of the perishing world in which our bodies live, they who surrender their mental powers to contemplation of earthly things and their nature to the control of its lowest elements, by so doing declare war against 'the cross of Christ,'

This fearful description of men who must have been church-members is in sad agreement with 2 Cor. xii. 21. It is thus a note of genuineness. But we have no hint that these were members of the Church at Philippi. And this is contradicted by ch. i. 4 and the general tone of the Epistle. Nor do we know whether or not they were at Rome, where Paul was writing.

20. This verse supports the condemnation implied in the last words of v. 19 by pointing to the city *in heaven* whose rights of citizenship are despised by those who fix their thoughts on 'earthly things.' *City* or *commonwealth:* the city looked upon as the home of municipal life and rights. Same word in 2 Macc. xii. 7: 'root up the whole city of the men of Joppa, so that the *municipality* of Joppa shall cease to be.' Practically the sense would be the same if we gave to the word the meaning *citizenship* or *rights-of-citizens*, which it sometimes has. For where the city is there are the citizen rights. *Our* city: viz. of Paul and those who imitate him; as in v. 17, 'us a pattern.' Cp. Clement of Alex. *Miscellanies* bk. iv. 26: "For the Stoics say that heaven is properly a city, but the things on earth no longer cities; said to be such, but not so actually ... the Elysian plains are the *municipalities* of just men." *Is*, or better *exists, in heaven*, in complete contrast to 'the earthly things' of v. 19. Our commonwealth is *in heaven:* same thought in 2 Cor. v. 1, Gal. iv. 26, where see notes. It is in heaven because there Christ is, in whom dwells the power which in the new earth and heaven will create the glorified home of His servants now on earth. *Whence: out of* heaven, from within the veil which now hides from our view the unseen world. *We-wait-for:* a strong word used in the same connection in Rom. viii. 19, 23, 25, 1 Cor. i. 7, Gal. v. 5, Heb. ix. 28: cp. 1 Th. i. 10. *Also we wait etc.:* in addition to already having a city in heaven. *Saviour:* Eph. v. 23. Also 2 Tim. i. 10, Tit. i. 4, ii. 13, iii. 6, Acts xiii. 23 in a sermon by Paul, referring to Christ; 1 Tim. i. 1, ii. 3, iv. 10, Tit. i. 3, ii. 10, iii. 4, referring to God. Our home in which we have municipal rights exists in heaven: and we are eagerly waiting for One from heaven who will rescue us from the perils and hardships around.

21. The deliverance which the expected Saviour will work, and the standard with which it will correspond. *Fashion-anew:* give to it an altered shape and guise. Same word in 1 Cor. iv. 6, 2 Cor. xi. 13, 14, 15. This use of a word denoting only a change of shape suggests the continuity of the present and future bodies. Cp. Rom. viii. 12, 'raise your mortal bodies.' And this continuity must be, in a way inconceivable to us, real. But it does not imply, any more

than does the continuity of our bodies on earth, identity of material atoms. Niagara remains the same while every drop of water is ever changing. It is rather a continued relation to the human spirit of its material clothing. A description of the change is given in 1 Cor. xv. 35—53. *Our body*, not bodies: as in Rom. vi. 12; see note under Rom. i. 21. *The body of*, i.e. standing in relation to, *our humiliation*. On earth the servants of Christ are exposed to weakness, sickness, reproach, hardship, and peril. This their lowly estate, so inconsistent with their real rank, is determined by the constitution of their material clothing, which is therefore *the body of their humiliation*. But when Christ comes out of the unseen world He will *refashion* it. The body of Christ is the visible, material, human manifestation of His divine splendour: *the body of His glory*. *Conformed:* sharing the form of: akin to the word *form* in ch. ii. 6. It is stronger than the word rendered *fashion-anew*, denoting such change of the mode of self-presentation as implies a share of the inward constitution of the body of Christ. When Christ appears, the changed bodies of His servants will become so like His body, which belongs to His essential splendour, as to share its mode o presenting itself to those who behold it.

According to the working etc.: a measure with which will correspond the coming change. This phrase is a marked feature of this group of Epistles: Col. i. 29, Eph. i. 19, iii. 7, iv. 16, cp. Col. ii. 12, Ph. ii. 13. *Working:* literally *inworking* or *activity*, an inward putting forth of power. It is the Greek original of our word *energy*. Literally rendered, Paul's words are *according to the energy*, or *the inworking, of His being able*, i.e. of His ability, *to subject to Himself etc. All things:* all the various objects in the universe, persons and things, these looked upon as a definite object of thought. *To subject to Himself all things:* 1 Cor. xv. 27, 28. It suggests that not yet do all things bow to Christ. But Christ has the abiding power to bend to His will all the component parts of the universe. The conformation of our bodies to His body will correspond with the activity of this abiding power. And this power confirms greatly our faith that He will remove from our bodies those mortal elements hostile to us and insubordinate to Him. These words also suggest that the victory to be gained in our bodies is part of a greater victory which will embrace and rescue *all things*. Thus, as ever, Paul rises from the particular to the general, from the partial to the universal.

Christ's ability to subject all things to Himself does not contradict the sad indication in *v.* 19 that some will be finally lost. For the putting forth of His power is determined by His infinite wisdom, which passes our thought.

Notice here a clear proof of the divinity of Christ. The resurrection will be His work, a work in harmony with His infinite power.

IV. 1. *So-then:* as in ch. ii. 12. It introduces a desired practical result of § 9, and completes the exhortation begun in ch. iii. 19. *My brethren:* recalling ch. iii. 17. *Longed-for:* natural result of being *loved.* Notice the warm affection of this double description, an affection prompted both by the unique excellence of the Philippians and by their love for Paul. *My joy:* understood only by those who have children in the faith. Paul's converts at Philippi were its living embodiment. *And crown:* as in 1 Cor. ix. 25: the garland given to successful athletes. Close parallel in a letter to another Macedonian Church: 1 Th. ii. 19. These converts of Paul were themselves to be his joyous reward. For they were a divinely-given result, and therefore a reward, of his labours. Moreover, since only in the light of the Great Day shall we see the full result of our labours on earth and be able to estimate the worth of a soul saved or lost, Paul speaks in 1 Th. ii. 19 of the crown as given at the coming of Christ. *In-this-way stand:* as do Paul and those whom in ch. ii. 17 he held up as a pattern. *Stand:* as in Rom. v. 2, etc.; maintain your spiritual position in spite of burdens which would press you down and of enemies who would put you to flight. *In the Lord:* 1 Th. iii. 8: the personality of the Master whom they serve being the only firm standing ground of the Christian life. *Beloved:* intensifying this loving appeal.

In § 8, after a warning against Jewish opponents, Paul pointed to his own religious life, and especially to his eagerness for progress, as a pattern for his readers. In § 9, he bids them observe and follow the men who imitate this pattern. This exhortation he justifies by pointing to sensual men who while bearing the name of Christ yet live for the present world. In contrast to these he describes the hope of a glorious resurrection cherished by himself and others, a hope prompted and measured by the omnipotence of Christ. In this hope and this example Paul bids his much-loved readers stand.

This appeal to the expectation of a bodily resurrection, in an exhortation to walk worthy of Christ, reveals the moral and spiritual power of the Christian's hope of future glory. This hope takes hold of eternity, and thus saves us from drifting with the current around.

SECTION X.

ABOUT EUODIA AND SYNTYCHE.

CH. IV. 2, 3.

Euodia I exhort, and Syntyche I exhort, to be of the same mind in the Lord. ³ *Yes, I request thee also, true yoke-fellow, assist them; women who in the Gospel joined with me in my struggle, with Clement also and the rest of my fellow-workers whose names are in the Book of Life.*

A new matter abruptly introduced. *Euodia, Syntyche:* names of women, both found on inscriptions. Grammatically they might also perhaps be names of men. But no such men's names are found elsewhere: and women are expressly referred to in v. 3, where the reference must be to these two persons. This mention by name suggests that they held a prominent place in the Church, and that the conduct which evoked this appeal was serious and notorious. Whether, like Phœbé (Rom. xvi. 1) they were deaconesses, we do not know. They recall to us Lydia and the women who used to meet for prayer at Philippi when Paul first went there: Acts xvi. 13, 14. The exact repetition of the appeal suggests that it was needed by both women, and equally. *The same mind:* as in ch. ii. 2. It implies that they were conspicuously of different mind, i.e. that they had openly quarrelled. *In* the *Lord:* the encompassing element of the hoped-for reconciliation. It is to be no mere human agreement, but a concord flowing from contact with the one Master.

3. *Yoke-fellow:* e.g. oxen under one yoke; often used in Greek for a wife and for persons in any way joined together. *True*, or *genuine:* as in 1 Tim. i. 2, Tit. i. 4; cognate word in Ph. ii. 20: one who is actually what his name describes. Either the man referred to here was indicated orally by Paul to Epaphroditus, or there was some one at Philippi who would be at once recognised as intended by this term. In other words, this phrase needs a key which has not come down to us. The *yoke-fellow* may be Epaphroditus himself, whom in ch. ii. 25 Paul calls his fellow-worker and fellow-soldier, and who occupied a unique position as messenger from Philippi and bearer of this letter. If so, these words pay honour to him as one worthy to be called a sharer of the Apostle's toil. But this reference, not being itself evident, would need to be explained to Epaphroditus. It has also been suggested as early as the time of

Chrysostom that *yoke-fellow* is a proper name, and that Paul added the word *true* to assert that the man was worthy of his name. [Notice its emphatic position before the substantive qualified.] This suggestion is supported by the proper names around, Euodia, Syntyché, Clement. If such a name existed in the Philippian Church, the reference would be caught at once: and the epithet *true* would be understood. The name, which we may write *Synzygus*, is not found elsewhere. But many Greek proper names occur only once: and we cannot suppose that all are preserved. A suggestion of Ellicott, that Paul refers to the chief of the bishops at Philippi, is most unlikely. For we have no hint, except possibly at Jerusalem, of any one raised so completely above his fellow-presbyters as to be accosted by Paul with this title. The only explanations, therefore, are the two noted above, the one implying a private indication of Paul's meaning, the other implying the existence at Philippi of a man bearing a name not found elsewhere. Neither of these explanations is unlikely. But, between them, our data do not enable us to decide.

Assist them: 'join with them in grappling with the difficulty caused by their quarrel:' same word in Lk. v. 7. The pronoun *them* is feminine, referring evidently to the two ladies mentioned above. Paul wishes this true partner in his own toil to render help towards their reconciliation. *Women who etc.:* a description of the past services of these ladies, in support of this request for help. [αἵτινες introduces a class of persons to which these women belong, this involving a reason for helping them.] *Joined-with me in my struggle:* literally, 'joined with me in an athletic contest:' same word in ch. i. 27. Paul's gratitude remembers the severity of the struggle in which they came to his aid. This gave them a claim to help from his friends. *In the Gospel:* 1 Th. iii. 2, Rom. i. 9: cp. 'fellowship for the Gospel' in ch. i. 5. They joined with Paul in his efforts to spread the Gospel, efforts severe like those of athletes. The hardship involved in evangelical effort at Philippi, we learn from 1 Th. ii. 2. And not only with Paul but *also with* another whom he mentions by name, *Clement*, did these ladies co-operate. Nay more. So eagerly did they join in every good work that they associated themselves with Paul's other *fellow-workers:* cp. ch. ii. 25. This proves that their co-operation was not, as is often the case, prompted by personal friendship. They were ready to assist all sorts of Christian workers. Yet these excellent ladies had quarrelled. Possibly, as so often in all ages, their eagerness in Christian work led them in different and opposite directions, and thus caused collision. And now, along with the record of their excellence, this blemish stands against them on the imperishable page of Holy Scripture.

That Clement is mentioned by name, implies that in some special way these ladies were associated with him. Probably his name recalled some incident giving them a further claim to help. That Paul speaks here of help *in the Gospel*, suggests that Clement was a preacher of the Gospel. All else is unknown.

Origen in his *Comm. on John* vol. vi. 36 identifies this *Clement* with the author of the extant *Epistle of Clement:* see my *Corinthians* App. i. But the commonness of the name and the total absence of connecting links forbids the inference.

The Book of Life: as in Rev. iii. 5, xiii. 8, xvii. 8, xx. 12, 15, xxi. 27; cp. Lk. x. 20. In Ex. xxxii. 32, 33 we have a 'book' of God, a register of His servants: similarly Ps. lxix. 28 'Book of Life' or 'living ones ... written with the righteous.' Possibly the N.T. use of the word may have been immediately derived from Dan. xii. 1, where we have a register of those who will rise to eternal life. While mentioning only one of his fellow-workers, Paul remembers that other names unmentioned by him are securely recorded among the heirs of salvation.

These verses give an interesting glimpse into early church life. We have the struggle involved in preaching the Gospel, Paul's various helpers in this work, and the two ladies who rendered assistance to him and to his brave comrades. Then steps in human imperfection. The ladies quarrel: and their quarrel comes to the ears of the prisoner at Rome. It is so serious as to demand mention in his letter to the Church. But the mention is only a recognition of their excellence, an exhortation to unity, and a request for help in the work of reconciliation.

SECTION XI.

SUNDRY EXHORTATIONS.

CH. IV. 4—9.

Rejoice in the *Lord always: again, I will say, rejoice.* ⁵ *Let your equity be known to all men. The Lord is near.* ⁶ *In nothing be anxious; but in everything, by prayer and by supplication, with thanksgiving, let your requests be made known to God.* ⁷ *And the peace of God, which surpasses all thought, will guard your hearts and your thoughts, in Christ Jesus.*

⁸ *As to the rest, brethren, whatever things are true, whatever things honourable, whatever things righteous, whatever things pure, whatever things lovely, whatever things of good report, if there be any excellence and if any praise, take account of these things;* ⁹ *what things also ye have learnt and accepted, and heard and seen in me, these things do. And the God of peace will be with you.*

A series of exhortations, without grammatical links: cp. Rom. xii. 9—18.

4. *Rejoice in* the *Lord:* as in ch. iii. 1. It takes up, after the interposed matters of §§ 8—10, the thread then suddenly dropped. *Always:* the new feature in this verse. Constancy is a distinguishing mark, and a measure, of Christian joy. *To rejoice in* the *Lord always*, is to rejoice when all earthly joy is withdrawn; and when the light of earth shines most brightly, even then to find our highest joy in the Master's smile. A noble example in Hab. iii. 17, 18. All other joy is subject to change. But they whose joy is an outflow of union with a Master in heaven walk in the light of a sun which never sets. And their joy is a safeguard against the perils both of earthly joy and earthly sorrow. *Again I will say:* emphatic repetition, revealing the importance, in Paul's view, of Christian joy. Of such joy, he is himself, as every page of this Epistle testifies, an illustrious example.

5. *Equity:* a disposition which does not press to the full the claims of absolute justice; but, tempering these claims by a generous reasonableness, is satisfied sometimes with less than is due. It is discussed at length in bk v. 10 of the *Nic. Ethics* of Aristotle, who explains it as being akin to justice but better than justice. It is eminently a Christian virtue: and the disposition which presses our claims to the full extent allowed by justice is eminently non-Christian. Paul bids us so to act that *all men* may see and know our generous reasonableness. Therefore we must treat all men with equity.

The Lord is *near:* at His second coming. For the 'Day of Christ' was ever in Paul's thought: ch. i. 6, 10, ii. 16. And he has just referred to His expected return. Probably had Paul known that long ages would elapse before the return of Christ, he would not have used these words. But it is unsafe to infer from them that he confidently expected to survive His coming. The greatness and the certainty of that event, for which we to-day like Paul centuries ago wait eagerly as the consummation of all our hopes, occupied his entire field of view; and obscured completely the secondary question of time. If Christ be coming, to bring in by His presence the eternal day, then to our thought in all ages *the Lord* is *near*.

The nearness of the coming of Christ is a strong dissuasive from the grasping spirit which made needful the foregoing exhortation. They who look for His appearing will not demand, from dying men around them, the last farthing they owe. Cp. 1 Cor. vii. 29, Jas. v. 7.

6. *Anxious:* not the forethought which enables us to guard against coming troubles, but the useless and painful care which merely brings the sorrows of to-morrow to spoil the pleasures of to-day. See under ch. ii. 20. *In nothing:* absolute prohibition of all anxiety of every kind. Same prohibition from the lips of Christ in Mt. vi. 25—34. See under 1 Cor. vii. 32. This anxiety arises from the common delusion that our happiness and well-being depend upon the possession of material good. It injures our body; and, by filling the mind with earthly care, blocks out the elevating influence of heavenly things; and exposes us to the terrible temptation of seeking in forbidden paths relief from present distress. This peremptory command, so difficult to obey, assures us that all anxiety is needless.

But in everything: exact positive counterpart of the foregoing negative exhortation. It is virtually Paul's remedy for anxiety. *Prayer and supplication:* same words together in Eph. vi. 18, 1 Tim. ii. 1, v. 5, Ps. vi. 10, Dan. ix. 21, 23. The word *prayer* is used only in reference to God, and denotes every kind of verbal approach to God. *Supplication,* or *petition:* earnest request for some special good, whether from God or from man. See ch. i. 4. Paul bids us go in every difficulty to God in prayer and beg from Him the help we need. *With thanksgiving:* same connection in Col. iv. 2, 1 Th. v. 18, 1 Tim. ii. 1. Thanks should be an element in our every approach to God, and be associated with every petition. Thus will memory of benefits and answers to prayer already received aid our prayers by stimulating a confident hope of good things to come. *Requests:* things asked for. Same word, and the cognate verb twice, in 1 Jno. v. 15. *Made-known to God:* i.e. we must put our wants into words, as though He needed to have them made known to Him. Thus God puts Himself by our side as our friend that we may have the relief of pouring into His ears our tale of sorrow. By so doing, we grasp the consolatory truth that God knows our need.

Notice Paul's remedy for anxiety. In every difficulty we must tell our case to God. We must put it in the form of request for help. This request must be mingled with thanks for the innumerable mercies already received. In the light of these mercies, of God's promise to answer prayer, and of His loving sympathy, anxiety cannot live.

7. *And the peace of God will guard etc.:* blessed result which will follow the use of this remedy. It is not a prayer but a prophecy. *Peace:* inward rest arising from absence of disturbing causes within or around us, a happy consciousness of absolute safety. So Rom. i 7; where see note. *Peace of God:* not 'with God' as in Rom. v. 1. Rather compare Jno. xiv. 27, 'My peace I give to you.' The words *of God* distinguish this *peace* from all other by pointing to its divine source and nature. Cp. 'righteousness of God' in contrast to 'their own righteousness' in Rom. x. 3. It is the profound calm of omnipotence which fills the breast of God and which nothing can disturb, which He gives to, and by His presence and power works in, His servants. It shuts out all anxiety, which is always a result of felt helplessness. As the Giver of this peace, He is called in v. 9 'the God of peace.' *All thought:* literally *all mind:* same word in Rom. i. 28, vii. 23, 25. It is the mental faculty which looks through outward appearances to the underlying realities. This peace, because divine, goes further than man's *mind* can follow or comprehend. It *passes* the *thought* not only of those around but of those to whom it is given, who wonder at their own peace in the midst of sorrow or peril and acknowledge it to be a gift and work of God. Same thought and a cognate word in Eph. iii. 20, 'beyond all things which we ask or think.' It is true that whatever comes from God surpasses human thought. But the peace of God is here expressly said to do so because it is found, not only in heaven where we expect it, but amid the anxieties and unrest of earth. And the unexpected contrast between storms around and peace within evokes surprise.

Shall guard: shall keep with military power; either from injury, as here and 1 Pet. i. 5, or from escape as in Gal. iii. 23, 2 Cor. xi. 32. Since anxiety exposes us to spiritual peril, the peace of God, by excluding anxiety, guards from peril. Breathed into us by infinite power, it is itself almighty: and, filling our hearts, it will guard us on every side from all evil. Just so the Roman garrisons in frontier towns guarded them from attacks of enemies, and enabled the inhabitants to carry on in peace their daily work. *Our hearts:* those inmost chambers whence come thoughts and actions. See under Rom. i. 21. *Thoughts:* the products of mental activity. Same word in 2 Cor. xi. 3. *The peace of God will guard the hearts* of His people so that sin shall not invade them, *and* their *thoughts* so that doubt and fear shall not trouble them. *In Christ Jesus:* His divine personality being a bulwark sheltering them from evil. This implies that the peace of God is definitely a Christian grace.

Thus Paul guarantees the effect of the remedy he proposes. He bids us take to God in prayer, with gratitude for past mercies, whatever now causes anxiety. And he assures us that if we do so we shall have, instead of anxiety, a peace which is God's work and gift; and that this peace will be itself a protection guarding our hearts from the entrance of evil and guarding our thoughts from taking a wrong direction. This divine safety is ours in Christ Himself the home and refuge and bulwark of our spiritual life.

8, 9. Concluding exhortations; to meditation in *v.* 8, to action in *v.* 9*a*: followed in *v.* 9*b* by a promise. *As to the rest:* same words and sense in ch. iii. 1, introducing words which cover all that Paul has left unsaid. *So many things as;* suggests number and variety in each of the following classes. Notice the stately six-fold repetition. *True:* words, acts, and disposition corresponding with reality, especially with the eternal realities, with which our thought and conduct must ever be in harmony, as opposed both to falsehood and to error. It includes, but is much wider than, truthfulness. Cp. Eph. iv. 21, v. 9, 1 Jno. i. 6. *Honourable:* deserving and gaining respect. It suggests the dignity which pertains to conduct worthy of Christ. Only, in N. T., here and 1 Tim. ii. 2, iii. 4, 8, 11, Tit. ii. 2, 7. *Righteous:* agreeing with the authoritative standard of human conduct; as in ch. i. 7, Eph. vi. 1. *Pure:* unstained by evil of any kind, as in 2 Cor. vi. 6, vii. 11, 1 Pet. iii. 2, 1 Jno. iii. 3. *Lovely:* only here in N. T.; Sirach iv. 7, xx. 13. It denotes the attractive sweetness of Christian excellence. *Of-good-report:* cognate word in 2 Cor. vi. 8: whatever sounds well when spoken of. *If any etc.:* an hypothesis which every one admits to be true, and which if true supports this exhortation. If there be such qualities, as undoubtedly there are, their existence makes them worthy of attention. *Excellence*, or *virtue:* common in classic Greek for excellence of any kind, moral, mental, bodily, or merely material; this looked upon as giving worth to its subject. In N. T., only 1 Pet. ii. 7, 2 Pet. i. 3, 5. Possibly the reason of its rarity is that the N. T. writers look upon human excellence, not as inhering in man and giving him worth, but as wrought in him by the indwelling Spirit of God. *Praise:* outward verbal recognition of *excellence*, which is inward and essential. It corresponds with *of-good-report*. *Excellence* covers the five preceding details. 'If there be any intrinsic human excellence, and if it have among men any recognition of its worth.' *Take-account-of:* reckon them up, so as to estimate and appreciate their worth: same favourite word in ch. iii. 13. Paul bids his readers calculate the worth of various kinds of moral excellence. And, feeling how many and various are its elements, he goes into detail and bids them contemplate actions, words, and dispositions which correspond with reality; and which therefore claim and gain respect; those which agree with the eternal standard of right; and are unstained by pollution; those which possess the charm of moral beauty; and which when mentioned secure for themselves name and fame among men.

Verse 8 is Paul's commendation of the science of Ethics. Only by careful meditation can we distinguish and appreciate moral worth. This is the real value of Christian biography. It sets before us in a variety of forms the various elements of Christian excellence. And this value is not destroyed, although the worth of a particular memoir is lessened, by occasional overstatement. Even if the portrait be overdrawn, it sets before us a model worthy of imitation.

9. To the exhortation to ponder the foregoing virtues, Paul now adds an exhortation to practise them; and supports this last by his readers' previous acceptance of his moral teaching and by his own example. Not only are these virtues worthy of 'being taken account of' but the Philippian Christians *have also* already *learnt* them *and have accepted* them as good. *Learnt:* intellectual apprehension. *Accepted:* moral approval, as in 1 Cor. xv. 1, etc. Probably these virtues were learnt from the lips of Paul. But it was not needful to say this. From whomsoever learnt, they had been understood and approved. *Heard:* not to be joined to the foregoing, to which it would add nothing, but to the words following. 'Not only *have ye learnt and accepted* these virtues but *ye have also heard and seen* them exemplified *in me,*' viz. in Paul's verbal intercourse with them and in the life he had lived before their eyes. Happy they who can speak thus to their pupils. Such can with authority say *do these things.* Thus by the lessons already learnt and approved, Paul urges his readers to practise the virtues he has just bidden them to ponder.

To the above exhortation, as in *v.* 7, Paul adds a promise: *and God shall etc.* Where God is, there is peace, viz. 'the peace of God.' He is therefore *the God of peace.* So Rom. xv. 33, 1 Cor. xiv. 33. *With you:* as in Rom. xv. 33. The Giver of peace *will ever be with* those who keep His commands,

Paul cannot conclude his letter without again and more emphatically bidding his readers to rejoice. And in their joy he bids them, in view of the near approach of the Great Judge, to treat all men not merely with strict justice but with reasonable fairness. He bids them dismiss all anxiety; and, in order so to do, to take to God all causes of anxiety, mingling their prayers with thanks for past mercies. All that now remains is covered by two exhortations and a promise. Paul bids his readers ponder the various forms of moral excellence. But in so saying he remembers that they have already learnt and approved the virtues he bids them ponder. And he reminds them that they have seen these excellences exemplified in himself. He exhorts them to practise what they have learnt and seen; and assures them that in so doing the Author of peace will Himself be their companion.

SECTION XII.

PHILIPPIAN LIBERALITY. FAREWELL.

CH. IV. 10—23.

I rejoice in the Lord greatly that now at length ye have revived your thought on my behalf; for which also ye were taking thought, but ye were without opportunity. ¹¹ *Not that I speak in respect of want. For I have learnt in whatever circumstances I am to be content.* ¹² *I both know how to be abased and I know how to abound. In everything and in all things I have been initiated into the mystery both to be filled with food and to be hungry, both to abound and to be in want.* ¹³ *For all things I have strength in Him who gives me power.* ¹⁴ *Nevertheless ye did well that ye had fellowship with me in my affliction.* ¹⁵ *Moreover, yourselves also know, Philippians, that in the beginning of the Gospel when I went out from Macedonia no church had fellowship with me for the matter of giving and receiving except ye only.* ¹⁶ *Because even in Thessalonica both once and twice ye sent for my need.* ¹⁷ *Not that I seek for the gift, but I seek for the fruit which is increasing for your account.* ¹⁸ *But I have got all things, and I abound; I am full, having received from Epaphroditus the things from you, an odour of a sweet perfume, a sacrifice acceptable, well-pleasing to God.* ¹⁹ *And my God will supply every need of yours, according to His wealth, in glory, in Christ Jesus.* ²⁰ *To God, our Father, be the glory for the ages of the ages. Amen.*

[21] *Greet every saint in Christ Jesus. There greet you the brethren with me.* [22] *There greet you all the saints, especially they of Cæsar's household.*
[23] *The grace of our Lord Jesus Christ be with your spirit.*

This section contains the specific occasion of the Epistle, viz. the gift brought to Paul at Rome from Philippi by Epaphroditus, added almost as a postscript to the far more important matters mentioned above.

10. *I rejoice*, literally *rejoiced:* when the gift arrived from Philippi. Paul himself does what in v. 4 he bid his readers do. This keeps up the tone of joy which runs through the Epistle : so ch. i. 4, 18, 25, ii. 2, 17, 18, 28, 29, iii. 1, iv. 1, 4, 10. *In the Lord:* as in ch. iii. 1. The joy occasioned by the gift from Philippi was no mere human emotion, but was distinctly Christian, i.e. prompted by union with the Master. *Greatly:* calling marked attention to a cause of special joy; cp. Mt. ii. 10. *Now at length;* suggests delay. But not reproach: for the delay is at once and satisfactorily explained. *Revived*, or *burst-forth-again:* as a branch puts forth new shoots. So did the Philippians produce, by this gift to Paul, a new development of spiritual life. *Thought* or *thinking:* same word as in ch. i. 7, ii. 2 : mental activity for the good of Paul. This was the specific matter of the new development: *touching your thought on my behalf.*

For which: viz. the well-being of Paul, represented as the mental basis or aim of their thought. Not only had their Christian life burst forth now into a new practical development of care for Paul, but even before this their minds were at work in the same direction: *ye were also taking thought. Ye-were-without-opportunity:* apparently, without means to send a contribution. The opportunity was afterwards found in the journey of Epaphroditus, whether it was undertaken expressly to carry the gift or for some other purpose. In the former case, the circumstances which made the journey possible were the opportunity; in the latter, the journey itself. Possibly poverty may have been the hindrance; and better circumstances the subsequent opportunity. But an approaching journey of Epaphroditus to Rome for other reasons is the easiest explanation.

Thus Paul mentions the delay, and apologises for it. The new shoot reveals continuous life, latent before, but now assuming visible form. The gift was somewhat late. But its lateness was caused not by want of loving care but by lack of means to carry thought into action. At last the means had been found: and the consequent outburst of pent-up love had filled Paul with joy.

This delay implies that, when the relief from Philippi arrived, Paul had been a long time in want. For the news had reached Philippi, and after some delay a gift had been sent to Rome. It is difficult to suppose that this time of want includes the two years (Acts xxiv. 27) at Cæsarea. And, if not, Paul must have been many months at Rome when he wrote this Epistle. This is therefore an indication of its date. See Introd. v.

11. *Not that:* introducing, as in ch. iii. 12, a safeguard against misinterpretation. *By way of want:* as though his words were prompted by deep need. The expression of joy in *v.* 10 might seem to be the voice of a starving man whose distress had been unexpectedly relieved. That this is the explanation of his glowing words, Paul denies.

For I have etc.: proof of this denial. *Content:* or literally *self-sufficient*. The cognate substantive occurs in 2 Cor. ix. 8, 1 Tim. vi. 6: a simpler word, in 2 Cor. xii. 9, where we have the same thought in another form. The syllable *self-* states not the source, but the inwardness, of this sufficiency, in contrast to external possessions. Its divine source is stated in *v.* 13. Aristotle, *Nicom. Ethics* bk. i. 7, defines the *self-sufficient* to be that which 'even by itself alone makes life worthy of choice and needing nothing.' This definition we may accept. That is *self-sufficient* which has in itself whatever is needful for its highest well-being, and is therefore independent of everything external to itself. Christian contentment is not a narrowing down of our desires to our poor possessions, but a consciousness of infinite wealth in Christ, in whose hands are all things already working for His servants moment by moment their highest good. He who has this consciousness is independent of his environment. His sufficiency is in himself. *In whatever circumstances I am:* including the dungeon in which Paul wrote these words, and in which before the arrival of Epaphroditus he had been in actual want. Paul's contentment was not natural but acquired. *I-have-learnt;* suggests gradual acquirement by the toilsome effort of the learner. But the task has been accomplished. *I:* very emphatic. In this school each must learn personally and for himself.

12, 13. Exposition in detail of Paul's self-sufficiency. Having 'learnt,' he says *I know*. The lesson learnt, he then unfolds. *To-be-abased:* same word in 2 Cor. xi. 7, where it is the exact opposite of being exalted; so Lk. xiv. 11. It includes every kind of going down, whether into poverty, or dishonour, or prison, or sickness, or the grave. This downward path Paul knows how to tread so as not to slip, so to descend that every step down be spiritual elevation. This knowledge many have not. Consequently adversity produces in them gloom and repining and fear and resentment and rebellion, thus doing them serious spiritual harm. E.g. many have lost their confidence in God and their spiritual life through commercial disaster. But the real cause of this ruin is not adversity which is powerless to injure those who understand its source and purpose, but want of knowledge. He who has found in Christ the full supply of all his need can take these perilous steps with safety. *I-know-also;* adds to the foregoing, with stately repetition, its necessary complement. *To-abound:* to have more than we need. It is a counterpart, not to *abase*, which would require as counterpart 'exalted,' but to the special kind of abasement which Paul had been enduring, viz. poverty. Many who passed unscathed through adversity are ruined by prosperity. For they are satisfied with material good. This ruin is caused by their not knowing how to rise in wealth, fame, power, and yet remain 'lowly in heart.' But Paul had learnt even this difficult lesson. Consequently, he was beyond reach of injury from either the ups or downs of life. He was independent of the uncertainties of the world around; and therefore 'self-sufficient.'

Verse 12*b* is a fuller exposition of *v.* 12*a*; as is *v.* 12*a* of *v.* 11*b*. *In everything and in all things:* things around looked at individually and collectively. 'In whatever position I am, and in whatever combination of circumstances.' *Initiated-into-the-mystery:* cognate to the Greek original of our word *mystery*. See note under 1 Cor. iii. 4. The use of this word here sheds light upon the cognate word already found in 1 Cor. ii. 7, iv. 1, Rom. xvi. 25, by suggesting that Paul refers, not to a mere secret, but definitely to teaching known only, like the Eleusinian mysteries, to the initiated. It thus embodies a development of Paul's earlier teaching. Paul is telling us how he came to *know how to be abased etc.* He had been led into the secret chamber of God and had there learnt that which is known only by those whose eyes and ears God opens. Notice the gradation: *I have learnt, I know, I have been initiated into the mystery. Both ... and, both ... and;* suggests the completeness and the unity of the secret Paul has learnt. *To-be-filled-with-food:* i.e. satisfied. Same word in Mt. xv. 33, 37 etc. It suggests that in prison Paul had been in want of food. *Hungry:* exact opposite of the foregoing. This contrast is a specific case under the more general contrast in *v.* 12*a*. It is followed by a restatement of the more general contrast. *To-abound:* to have more than we need.

To-fall-short or *to-be-in-want:* to have less than we need. Same word in same sense in 2 Cor. xi. 9 etc.

13. Triumphant summing up of the practical result of what Paul has learnt. He knows: therefore he is strong. *All-things:* very emphatic: it includes abasement, hunger, abundance. *Strength:* spiritual muscle and force. In the Christian struggle Paul was like a man in robust bodily health and strength. *For all things* within the horizon of duty and desire, he has unlimited strength. *In Him who gives me power:* Christ, in whom Paul lives and acts, and whose power (2 Cor. xii. 9) rests upon him. He is to Paul not merely the bulwark protecting him on every side by its own strength, but an all-pervading and life-giving personal element breathing into him His own omnipotence. From this inward union with Christ is derived the strength which fits Paul for all things he has to do. The strong man helps the weak by bearing his burden for him. Christ helps us by breathing into us a strength which makes our burdens light.

The word *Christ*, (A.V.) appears in the margin of the Sinai and Clermont MSS. and in nearly all the later Greek copies. This suggests the origin of a large class of various readings, viz. that they were explanatory glosses, afterwards incorporated into the text.

This great assertion must not be diluted. Whatever lies within the horizon of duty and necessity and desire, Paul can do. To him as to God there is no question of can or cannot. In Christ Paul is morally omnipotent. But, just as God's inability to lie (Heb. vi. 18) does not in the least degree limit His infinite power, (for lying is contrary to the divine nature and therefore outside the horizon of divine action,) so Paul is strong only for that which Christ would have Him do. All else is outside Christ, the sphere of his strength. But within the limits of the personality of Christ lay Paul's whole action, thought, and life. Consequently, this limit was no limit to him. And he felt himself endowed with infinite strength. To him therefore the burdens of life were light; and its toil was easy.

These words embody an important secret into which Paul had been initiated, and which enabled him to sink or to rise without spiritual injury. He knows how to be abased because he knows that underneath him are the Everlasting Arms: he can therefore go down into the depth without fear and without damage. He can rise without danger: for he knows that God who raises him will guard His servant from the perils of exaltation. He is therefore safe. Neither height nor depth can separate him from the love of God in Christ Jesus.

Notice the four steps in this great climax. Paul has learnt: therefore he knows: he has learnt the secret: consequently he can do all things.

14. *Nevertheless etc.*: a corrective on another side to the corrective introduced in v. 11. Although it would be an error to suppose that Paul's joy was prompted by his deep need, he by no means valued lightly the gift which supplied that need. He says that his readers *did nobly*. *My affliction*: Paul's hardship at Rome, which was relieved by the contribution from Philippi. This involved monetary loss, and therefore some degree of hardship, to the Christians there. They cheerfully submitted to this hardship, and thus *became partners* (see under chs. i. 4, iii. 10) *with* Paul *in* his *affliction*. In so doing they *did well*.

15, 16. Additional facts, known to the readers and casting light upon the fact just mentioned. *Also yourselves know*: as well as Paul. He thus supports the foregoing statement, not by new information, but by an appeal to knowledge shared by himself and his readers. *Philippians;* gives definiteness to this appeal by naming the persons appealed to. *In the beginning of the Gospel*: thrust prominently forward, contrasting conspicuously with the gift just acknowledged the liberality of days long past. These words are explained at once by those following. They take us back to the time when Paul first preached in Europe; and remind the Philippians that their present action was only continuance in a path entered at the beginning of their Christian course. We find the same words in the Ep. of Clement, ch. 47 (see my *Corinthians* p. 528) referring to the time when Paul wrote 1 Corinthians. *When I went out from Macedonia;* grammatically may refer to an event contemporary with, or following, Paul's departure from Macedonia. [See Winer's *Grammar* § 40, 5a.]

From Acts xvii. 15 we learn that some Macedonian Christians, apparently from Beroea, went with Paul out of Macedonia to Athens. The words before us imply that then or soon afterwards the Philippian Christians sent money to Paul. Whether this was the gift mentioned in 2 Cor. xi. 9, we do not know. If, hearing that Paul had gone to Corinth, they sent to him there a deputation with a gift, this would explain both Ph. iv. 15 and 2 Cor. xi. 9. For it would be a gift in the beginning of the Gospel after Paul had left Macedonia. Or, less probably, the gift from Philippi may have reached Paul as he was leaving Beroea for Athens. In any case, the contribution here mentioned is an important coincidence with 2 Cor. xi. 9: for this passage proves that Paul did not refuse gifts from friends at a distance. *Had-fellowship:* simpler form of the word in *v.* 14. They became partners with Paul. *For an account of giving and receiving:* purpose of this partnership; similarly ch. i. 5, 'fellowship for the Gospel.' They entered into partnership with Paul in order to have with him dealings about *giving and receiving*, i.e. about transferring money from one to the other. Paul leaves his readers to remember that the *giving* was on their part, and the *receiving* on his; merely saying that both sides of the transaction were present to their mind and purpose. This explains abundantly the words here used, without involving the idea of spiritual recompense as in Rom. xv. 27. *Except ye alone:* an example splendid in its solitariness. Not only did their spiritual life at once take this form : but the example thus set was at first not even imitated by others.

16. *Because even etc.:* a definite fact confirming the foregoing negative statement. *Even in Thessalonica:* in addition to, and earlier than, what they did when Paul 'went forth from Macedonia.' A close coincidence with Acts xvii. 1, which tells us that *Thessalonica* was the first city at which Paul lingered after leaving Philippi. During the few weeks (Acts xvii. 2) spent there, the Philippian Christians sent *twice* to supply his *need:* a wonderful proof of the influence upon them of his preaching. Truly their liberality dated from 'the beginning of the Gospel.' *Once and twice;* lingers over the repetition of this kindness. This second contribution in so short a time is very significant. Others would have thought that one gift was all that could be expected from them. But even a second present did not exhaust the liberality of the Philippian Christians. For, apparently, they sent to him another shortly afterwards to Corinth. *My need:* as in ch. ii. 25, Paul's poverty (cp. 2 Cor. xi. 8) owing probably to his inability to maintain himself (2 Th. iii. 8) while preaching at Corinth.

17. *Not that;* introduces a corrective to *vv.* 15, 16, as do the same words in *v.* 11 a similar corrective to *v.* 10. Each corrective supplements the other. Paul's joy about the gift from Philippi (*v.* 10) was not prompted by his deep need. And his appreciation of it (*vv.* 15, 16) was prompted, not by eagerness for money, but by eagerness for his readers' spiritual profit. *The gift:* whatever from time to time, as circumstances determine, their liberality might prompt; this looked upon as a definite object of thought. *I seek for the gift:* an abiding state of mind which Paul disavows. *But I seek for:* stately repetition. *Fruit:* as in Rom. i. 13: the reward of the Philippians' liberality; this looked upon as its organic outworking according to the laws of the Christian life. Day by day, as one act of liberality follows another, this reward is *increasing*. *For your account;* recalls the same words in *v*. 15, 'for account of giving and receiving.' While the Philippian Christians entered into partnership with Paul in order to have dealings with him in a matter of giving and receiving, a harvest of reward was growing which was reckoned to their credit. These last words, and Paul's constant reference of reward and punishment to the Great Day, indicate that to this he refers here: so ch. i. 6, 10.

18. An added statement containing another reason why Paul does not desire a gift; viz. that his wants are completely supplied. *I have all:* or better, *I have to the full all things. And abound:* not only supply but overflow. *I-am-filled-full:* of all material good. Notice the climax: *I have all, I abound, I am filled full. Having received etc.:* means by which his needs have been fully supplied. This clear assertion that Epaphroditus had brought to Paul a gift from Philippi explains ch. ii. 25, 30.

An odour etc.: a comment on the gift from Philippi, revealing its real significance. *Odour of perfume:* Eph. v. 2; Gen. viii. 21, Ex. xxix. 18, Lev. i. 9, 13, 17, etc.: a frequent O. T. phrase picturing the acceptableness of sacrifice to God. *Sacrifice:* as in Rom. xii. 1. *Acceptable, well-pleasing:* a climax. Same words in Acts x. 35; Rom. xii. 1, 2, xiv. 18, 2 Cor. v. 9. Since all these phrases are frequently followed by the word *to-God*, it probably refers to all of them. *To God* a fragrant *perfume* goes up and a *sacrifice* is offered which is *acceptable* and *well-pleasing* to Him. Apparently the gift from Philippi was only kindness to a prisoner in poverty at Rome. But whatever is done to the servant is done for the Master: and whatever is done for Christ brings abundant recompense. This gift is therefore a seed producing already a harvest of blessing for its generous donors; and a sacrifice laid on the altar of God. The sacrifice is fragrant to the mind of God: it is a gift He will receive and be pleased with.

19. Verse 18 has brought the gift from Philippi into the presence of God. This reminds Paul of the recompense which will follow it. *My God:* as in ch. i. 3. The recompense will follow because the prisoner at Rome stands in a personal relation to God. *Supply*, or *fill:* same words as 'filled-full' in *v*. 18, which it recalls. *Will-supply:* a definite promise, as in *vv*. 7. 9. *Every need:* of body and spirit; every necessity and every yearning of their whole nature. *Need of yours:* corresponding to 'my need' in *v*. 16. *His riches:* a favourite conception of Paul; Rom. ii. 4, ix. 23, xi. 33, Eph. i. 7,

18, ii. 7, iii. 8, 16. It is here a picture of God's ability to supply our need, as a rich man can remove the present want of the poor man: cp. Eph. iii. 20. *According to His riches:* measure of the promised supply. This will not only come out of the wealth of God but will correspond with its infinite abundance. Consequently, *every need* will be supplied. *In glory:* locality or surrounding element of this supply. Same words in similar sense in 2 Cor. iii. 7, 8, (9,) 11. It is the splendour which will surround the final reward and triumph; as in Col. iii. 4, i. 27, Rom. v. 2, ii. 7, 10. Amid the brightness of the great day, every need and every yearning will be gratified. *In Christ:* in virtue of our inward union with Him. The abundant supply will be *in glory*, as its visible clothing evoking admiration; and *in Christ*, as its encompassing, all-pervading source and element. Cp. same words at end of v. 7.

This great promise makes even the half-conscious yearnings of our nature to be themselves a prophecy of future blessing. For their complete satisfaction in the glory of heaven is pledged by the wealth of God.

20. Outburst of praise evoked by the promise in v. 19; and marking the close of the topic introduced in v. 10. *To God, our Father:* literally *God and our Father;* i.e. God who is *also* our Father. See note under Gal. i. 5. As ever, Paul's song of praise is directed to the *Father*. In these words he acquiesces in the eternal recognition of the grandeur of God manifested in His mercy to men. This recognition he seals by a final *Amen.*

VERSES 10—20 preserve for us one of the most beautiful incidents in the story of Paul or of the early Church. From them we learn that his imprisonment at Rome was aggravated by poverty, that he was not only in prison but in want. All this reached the ears and moved the hearts of the Christians at Philippi. But either from straitened circumstances or more probably from lack of a messenger they were for a time unable to render the help they were eager to give. At length an opportunity occurred. Epaphroditus offered to take their contribution to Rome. On the way he fell dangerously ill. Indeed he risked his life in order to discharge his mission of mercy. But the gift from Philippi arrived safely at Rome, and supplied at once and fully the prisoner's need. Paul was filled with joy. But his was not the joy of a starving man suddenly relieved. His happiness was not dependent on the kindness of far-off friends. For he had learnt the secret of the Christian's poverty and suffering. To him the presence and smile of God were an all-sufficient supply of every need and a source of infinite strength. The prisoner's joy is distinctively Christian. He knows that this gift is seed from which already an abundant harvest is growing up for the donor's enrichment. Being prompted by loyalty to Christ, it is a sacrifice laid upon the altar of God, an acceptable sacrifice filling His courts with pleasant perfume. And it will be repaid, as will everything done for God, by a full supply of every need in the splendour of heaven.

Paul remembers that this was not the first gift from Philippi. Very soon after he founded the Church there the brethren sent him money while preaching the Gospel in the city of Thessalonica; and that not once but twice. And apparently shortly afterwards they again sent him money to Corinth. Consequently, their action now is but continuance in a path entered at the commencement of their Christian course. It is only another outflow of that spirit of brotherhood which, as Paul said in ch. i. 5, they had manifested from the beginning. In monetary help they set the first example; an example which others were somewhat slow to follow. Nay more. We learn from 2 Cor. viii. 1 that in the great collection for the poor Christians at Jerusalem the Churches of Macedonia were very conspicuous. Our thoughts go at once to the acknowledged liberality of the Church at Philippi, the earliest of the Macedonian Churches founded by Paul. And we cannot doubt that they who set the first example in Macedonia of Christian giving were equally prominent in the contribution for Jerusalem. Indeed the liberality of Macedonia must have been in great part an imitation of the example set by the Church at Philippi. If so, then as so often since, men who were eager to contribute money for the need of a beloved teacher were also ready to do so for unknown, but suffering, Christians in a far-off land. Thus 2 Cor. viii. 1 is an important coincidence with Ph. iv. 16.

It is worthy of note that the Church marked by this constancy of liberality, not only presented nothing needing from Paul even a word of rebuke, but affords the noblest of the many pictures of early Christian Churches reflected in his Epistles. In the apostolic age the Church at Philippi stands supreme in its spotless beauty. And to the generosity of that Church we owe this letter, written to acknowledge it, and all the untold blessings it has conveyed to thousands of the servants of Christ. Little thought the faithful ones at Philippi that the gift they so readily sent to relieve the Apostle's distress would enrich the Church of Christ in all ages with a priceless treasure. Never was there a more wonderful proof that they who do good do better than they think.

21, 22. Salutation. To the Church collectively is committed a greeting for every member of it: *greet ye every saint*. We may expound either *every saint in Christ Jesus,* noting their relation to Christ as in ch. i. 1; or *greet in Christ Jesus every saint,* noting a definitely Christian greeting. Since the word *saint* is already sufficiently definite, this latter exposition which would give spiritual emphasis to the greeting is somewhat the more likely. So 1 Cor. xvi. 19, and probably Rom. xvi. 22.

Why, writing to a Church so much beloved, in which there must have been so many persons well known to him, Paul does not add greetings to individuals, we do not know. Possibly, where all (ch. i. 4; but compare Rom. i. 8 and contrast Rom. xvi. 3—15) were so good, Paul was unwilling to give special prominence to any; or preferred to give them less prominence by sending personal greeting orally by Epaphroditus.

The brethren with me: those more closely associated with Paul in prison, and thus distinguished from *all the saints,* i.e. the church-members at Rome. Same words in similar, though perhaps slightly different, sense in Gal. i. 2. These companions are called *brethren,* although (ch. ii. 20) they do not fully share the Apostle's spirit. *Cæsar's household,* or *house:* either the emperor's palace, or its inmates of all kinds from his relatives and state officials down to the humblest slaves. Between these meanings the difference is very slight. So Diogenes Laertius (*Lives of Philosophers* bk. v. 5. 3) says that Demetrius was *of* Conon's *house.* Paul's words assert that even in the home of Nero, perhaps the most corrupt spot on earth, were Christians. The servants of the palace were very numerous and various; and even the lowest of them would naturally, among others of the same class, be proud of his position. Possibly this special salutation was occasioned by the closer contact of the members of the imperial household with the prisoner of the Prætorian Guard.

23. Paul's farewell, almost word for word as in Gal. vi. 18.

REVIEW OF THE EPISTLE. The prisoner at Rome, over whose head hangs the sword of a capricious tyrant and whose imprisonment had been aggravated by poverty, writes to the Christians at Philippi to acknowledge a gift which has completely supplied his need.

To beloved brethren, Paul has no need to assert his official position, and simply places himself beside Timothy as a servant of Christ. But the officers of the Church have, for reasons unknown to us but probably creditable to them, the unique honour of definite mention in the opening salutation. After the salutation, Paul's first thought is thanks to God for the universal excellence of the Christians at Philippi, which makes prayer for them a delight and encourages a just and loving confidence of their final salvation. These thanks are followed by prayer for their growth in knowledge and in usefulness.

The anxiety of the Philippian Christians calls for news about the imprisoned Apostle, about his circumstances and his feelings. His apparent misfortunes have, by inspiring confidence in the Christians at Rome helped forward the preaching of the Gospel. This gives Paul abiding joy. And this joy is not destroyed by the fact that some preach Christ out of ill-will to the Apostle. Their hostility pains him the less because he knows that it is working for him spiritual good, and is therefore helping his eternal salvation. This reference to Paul's inner thought becomes a reflection on the page on which he writes of his utter uncertainty of life and death, and of the profound and equal calm with which he views each side of this tremendous alternative.

From himself Paul now turns again to his readers. One thing only he begs from them, that they play their part as citizens of the Kingdom of God in a way worthy of Christ. This will require from them persevering courage and united effort in face of their enemies. On unity the Apostle lays special emphasis; and warns against the subtle forms of selfishness so fatal to it. As a supreme example of unselfishness, he points to the incarnation and death, and subsequent exaltation, of the Son of God. He also warns his readers that upon their conduct depends their salvation, and begs them so to act as to be lights in a dark world and an eternal joy to himself. To him, every sacrifice for them is an abiding joy.

Paul then commends Timothy, his proved and faithful son in the Gospel, whom he hopes soon to send; and Epaphroditus who at the risk of his life had discharged the mission entrusted to him and had thus rendered to the Apostle eminent service. He bids the Philippian Christians receive back with due honour their faithful messenger.

With this commendation Paul was closing his letter But, for his readers' safety, he adds a warning, viz. against Jewish opponents and Jewish self-confidence. In such confidence Paul might himself indulge : but his knowledge of Christ has made it impossible. He has no present attainments in which to rest; but is eagerly pressing forward to a goal still beyond him. He bids all who claim to be men in Christ to imitate his example. A sadder warning follows. Some church-members, by their worldly and sensual spirit, prove themselves to be enemies of Christ. This unworthy spirit Paul rebukes by pointing to the expected Saviour and the complete change which His coming will bring.

Next follows a word of kindly expostulation with two excellent ladies whose quarrel was the more serious because of their Christian activity. Then come charming words of spiritual exhortation and of wise counsel.

Lastly, Paul speaks at some length about the gift which prompted this letter. The gift filled him with joy; not because of the poverty it relieved—for Paul has learnt a secret which makes him superior to the burdens of life—but because of the harvest of blessing which already it is producing for his readers, and because it is an acceptable sacrifice to God, who will supply in the glory of heaven the givers' every need. A few words of general greeting close the Epistle.

In the pages of the Epistle to the Philippians we see reflected the most attractive picture in the New Testament of Christian life and a Christian Church. Scarcely a word of reproof disturbs the joyous outflow of Paul's warm affection. And this affection finds equal response in the abiding and loving care of the Philippian Christians for Paul. Among the Apostolic Churches they hold indisputably the place of honour. And to thousands of men and women tossed about by the uncertainties and anxieties of life, this letter, written in a dungeon at Rome under the shadow of the gallows yet everywhere vocal with exuberant joy, has been the light of life. As our gladdened eyes turn from that far-shining light to rest for a moment on the broad and silent pastures where once was the busy Roman colony of Philippi, we see fulfilled an ancient prophecy: THE GRASS WITHERETH, THE FLOWER FADETH; BUT THE WORD OF OUR GOD SHALL STAND FOR EVER.

EXPOSITION OF THE EPISTLE TO THE COLOSSIANS.

SECTION I.
APOSTOLIC GREETING.
CH. I. 1, 2.

Paul, an apostle of Christ Jesus through the *will of God, and Timothy* our *brother, to the saints and faithful brethren in Christ at Colossæ.* ² *Grace to you and peace from God, our Father.*

Verse 1 is the same as 2 Cor. i. 1. Whether *Timothy*, who is not mentioned in the twin letter to Ephesus, is mentioned here because of some special relation to Colossæ, we do not know. But the scantiness of our information leaves this quite possible. He may or may not have been Paul's penman. The same word denotes *faithful* or *trustworthy* in 2 Cor. i. 18, etc., and *believing* in ch. vi. 15; senses quite distinct but closely allied. Between them here, it is most difficult to decide. Since faith is implied in the word *brethren*, and again in the phrase *in Christ*, and since this Epistle is a warning against serious error, we may perhaps find in this word a recognition that the *brethren at Colossæ* are *trustworthy*. It is not certain whether *in Christ* refers to the word *saints* as well as to *faithful brethren*. Perhaps only to this latter phrase. For it needs further definition as noting a distinctively Christian brotherhood, more than does the word *saints* which outside the Aaronic priesthood belongs only to Christians.

2. The benediction is only *from God our Father.* For this no special reason can be given. Paul thinks only, when wishing his readers *grace* and *peace*, of the divine *Father from* whom such blessing comes; not, as usual, of the Son also, the joint source with the Father of all good.

Writing to the Colossian Christians whom he has never seen,

Paul remembers that by the will of God he has the position and responsibility of an Apostle. He joins with himself, as approving the letter he is writing, his brother Timothy; and addresses his readers as men claimed by God to be specially His own and as brethren in Christ worthy of confidence. He desires for them the smile of God and the peace which only that smile can give.

DIVISION I.
PRAISE AND PRAYER.
CHAPTER I. 3—14.

SECTION II.
PAUL THANKS GOD FOR HIS READERS' FAITH.
CH. I. 3—8.

We give thanks to God, the *Father of our Lord Jesus Christ, always about you, when praying;* ⁴*having heard of your faith in Christ Jesus and of the love which ye have towards all the saints,* ⁵*because of the hope laid up for you in the heavens, whereof ye heard before in the word of the truth of the Gospel,* ⁶*which is present among you, according as also in all the world it is, bearing fruit and increasing, according as also among you, from the day when ye heard and understood the grace of God in truth;* ⁷*according as ye learnt from Epaphras our beloved fellow-servant, who is a faithful minister of Christ on our behalf,* ⁸*who also declared to us your love in* the *Spirit.*

3. As to the Philippians, so here Paul begins with praise for God's work in his readers and with prayer for its further development. *We-give-thanks:* so 1 Thess. i. 2, 2 Th. i. 3; where however the plural is explained by the close relation of Silvanus and Timothy to the Thessalonican Christians. Here, possibly, the plural is used, in contrast to Ph. i. 3, because Paul's more distant connection with the Church at Colossæ permits him to fall back on somewhat official phraseology. *God,* the *Father of our Lord Jesus Christ:* same words as in Rom. xv. 6, 2 Cor. i. 3, except that here

Paul omits the copula 'and' which there formally joins together the titles *God* and *Father of etc.* He to whom Paul gives thanks is *God*, the divine Person whom Christ used to address, and to speak of, as His *Father*. *Give thanks . . . always about you :* better than *always when praying about you :* for it is more likely that Paul would say that his thanks were ceaseless, than that his prayers were ceaseless, for his readers. *When praying :* i.e. in his regular devotions. He is always thanking God about the Christians at Colossæ: and the specific time and manner of this perpetual thanksgiving is his approach to God in prayer.

4. Special occasion and matter of these thanks. When Paul heard of his readers' *faith* and *love* he began, and continues, to thank God on their behalf. *Faith in Christ:* Eph. i. 15, 1 Tim. iii. 13, 2 Tim. i. 13, iii. 15; not elsewhere in the N. T. It must not be separated from Paul's frequent phrase *in Christ;* and notes that the personal object of our faith is also its encompassing element. Faith saves because Christ is the element in which it dwells and rests. *Love which ye have :* for love is an enrichment to those who possess it. *Faith* takes inward hold of *Christ : love* reaches out *towards all the saints.* The universal scope of Christian love is a mark of its genuineness.

5a. Real significance of this faith and love; and therefore the ultimate reason of Paul's thanks: *because of the hope etc.* All Christian hope is a germ developing into the glory of heaven: it is the dawn of the eternal day. And this is its real worth. In his readers' faith and love Paul saw a foretaste of eternal blessedness: and this prompted his thanks on their behalf. Similarly, in Phil. i. 6 he looks forward to the completion of the work already begun. The simplicity of this exposition renders needless all attempts, necessarily forced, to represent this *hope* as in any way the cause or reason of the faith and love. Verse 3 is Paul's thanksgiving: *v.* 4, its immediate occasion: and *v.* 5, its ultimate *cause* or ground. See a good paper by Findlay in *The Expositor*, 1st series, vol. x., p. 74.

The infinite objective reality underlying the Christian *hope* gives even to the subjective hope itself an objective reality; and prompts us to think and speak of it as such. Now this objective reality is *in heaven*, far away from us and above reach of the uncertainties of earth. It is therefore a *hope laid up in heaven*. For, where our treasure is, there is our heart and our hope. Thus a hope cherished in the breast of men on earth is guarded from disappointment by the security of heaven. Similar thought in Ph iii. 21. Notice here in close relation faith, love, hope: so in the same order, 1 Th. i. 3; a close parallel: also 1 Cor. xiii. 13, Gal. v. 5, 6.

5b, 6. Objective source of this hope, viz. the Gospel preached at Colossæ and throughout the world. *Heard-before;* makes conspicuous the fact that the subjective hope in the heart was preceded by an objective proclamation. *The truth of the Gospel:* Gal. ii. 5: the reality underlying the good news brought by Christ. See under Rom. i. 18. *The word of the truth etc.:* the announcement of this reality. The announcement preceded and caused the Christian hope at Colossæ.

Which Gospel *is present among you:* or, more fully, 'which has reached you and is now present with you.' This suggests the good fortune of the Colossians in that the Gospel had reached them; and the reality of the Gospel which like an overshadowing presence is now among them. *According as also in all the world it is:* a larger fact in harmony with that just stated. Paul carries out his readers' thought from the valley of the Lycus where they had heard the Gospel to *the* wide *world* throughout which *also* the same Gospel *is*, or *exists*, i.e. is heard and believed and gains victories. *All the world:* an hyperbole similar to that in Rom. i. 8. Within Paul's mental horizon, which was very large, the Gospel was everywhere preached. *Bearing-fruit and increasing:* further information about the universal Gospel. *Fruit:* results produced by the organic outworking of its own vitality, viz. the many and various benefits of the Christian life. Same word in Rom. vii. 4, 5, Mk. iv. 20, 28: cp. Ph. i. 11, 22, iv. 17. *Increasing:* as the good news is carried from place to place and its converts multiply, the Gospel itself becomes a larger thing. So Acts vi. 7, xii. 24, xix. 20. Thus it *bears fruit* in the blessings it conveys, and *increases* in the increase of its adherents.

According as also among you: another fact added to, and in harmony with, the foregoing. That the Gospel is preached at Colossæ, is part of a larger fact, viz. that it is preached throughout the world. Paul now adds that its good effects throughout the world are reproduced also at Colossæ. He reduplicates the comparison because the second member of it, viz. the general statement, goes beyond the foregoing particular statement, and therefore needs to be supplemented by the second comparison. These last words are a courteous recognition of the genuineness and extent of the work at Colossæ. The Gospel produced there the good effects it produced elsewhere. This Paul strengthens by saying that the fruitbearing and increase began at once and continue to the present: *from the day when* etc. In the Gospel the Colossians *heard the grace of God,* i.e. the favour to our race which prompted the gift of Christ. And the word needed to be, and was, *understood,* i.e. apprehended by careful thought. *In truth:* so Jno. iv. 23, 24. Correspondence with reality was the surrounding element of their hearing and mental comprehension. While hearing the Gospel and grasping its contents they were dealing not with delusion but with reality.

7, 8. *Ye learnt from Epaphras:* an historical detail in harmony with, and expounding, the general statement in *v.* 5. Like Paul, (Ph. iv. 11,) the Colossian Christians had acquired gradually and with effort their understanding of the grace of God: *ye learnt.* Their teacher's name is given: *Epaphras. Fellow-servant:* with Paul in the service of Christ: same word in ch. iv. 7, Rev. xix. 10, Mt. xviii. 28. The plural number assumed in *v.* 3 is retained: *our . . . us . . . our.* Paul recognises Epaphras as, along with himself, Timothy, and others, doing the work of the one Master.

Who is etc.: a commendation of Epaphras. *Minister:* see under Rom. xii. 7. The added words *of Christ* (cp. 2 Cor. xi. 23) make us certain that the word *minister* is used, not in an official sense as in Ph. i. 1, but in the more general sense of one who does free and honourable work for another. In this work he was *faithful* or *trustworthy:* Eph. vi. 21, 1 Cor. iv. 2. *On our behalf:* emphatic. The difficulty of this reading confirms its genuineness as attested by the best copies. Paul probably means that his interest in the Colossian Christians was so great that the service rendered to Christ by Epaphras in caring for them was rendered also to himself, and that this interest was shared by his companions. Possibly Epaphras may have been urged by Paul to care for the Christians at Colossæ: but this is not necessarily implied in his words.

Who also declared etc.: another fact. It implies that Epaphras had come to Rome and there told Paul the story of the Colossian Church. Consequently, from Epaphras the Colossians heard the good news of the grace of God and Paul heard the good news of the work of God at Colossæ. *Your love;* implies faith, which therefore is not here mentioned. *In* the Holy *Spirit:* the animating principle of all Christian life. Cp. Rom. xiv. 17, 'joy in the Holy Spirit.'

We are here introduced to another of the noble band of Christian workers who surrounded the great Apostle; of whom we have already met Timothy, Titus, and Epaphroditus. Since *EPAPHRAS* was apparently (ch. iv. 12) a Colossian and yet founded the Church at Colossæ, we may suppose that on a journey perhaps to Ephesus, the capital of the province, he heard the Gospel preached by Paul; that he carried back to his own city the good news he had himself embraced and thus became founder of the Church there. Evidently, he had come to Rome; and was remaining there when Tychicus started with this letter. Even in Rome his deep interest in the spiritual welfare and progress of the Christians at Colossæ moved him to ceaseless and very earnest prayer on their behalf. The intelligence of his prayer (see ch. iv. 12) proves him to have been a man of highest worth. Well might Paul call him a *beloved fellow-servant* and a *faithful minister of Christ*. In Philem. 23, for reasons unknown to us he is called a 'fellow-prisoner' of Paul.

Paul's letter to the Colossians begins with an expression of his constant thanks to God on their behalf, prompted by tidings he has heard about their faith and love. This evokes his thanks because it is a sure indication of better things to come. It therefore inspires a hope not dependent for its realisation upon the uncertainties of earth but resting on the security of heaven. These hopes the Colossians owe to the Gospel which has reached their city. Paul reminds them that the same Gospel is preached throughout the world; and that everywhere it is bearing fruit and extending its influence. He is glad to recognise that the same good results have followed the preaching of it at Colossæ from its first proclamation to the present day. This Gospel they had heard from the lips of Epaphras, a fellow-worker of Paul and a minister of Christ: and also from Epaphras Paul had heard the good news about the Church at Colossæ.

The distinctive feature of this thanksgiving is Paul's mention of the universal proclamation of the Gospel throughout the world, and of its universal fruit-bearing and growth. He thus raises his readers' thoughts above their own Church and city to the great world and the Church Universal: a transition of thought always beneficial in the highest degree. Possibly this reference to the proclamation and success of the Gospel throughout the world was suggested by the strange doctrines which it is the chief business of this letter to correct and which were a local perversion of the one Gospel. This local perversion Paul wishes to discuss in the light of the universal Gospel everywhere preached and everywhere successful.

SECTION III.
PAUL'S PRAYER FOR HIS READERS' FURTHER DEVELOPMENT.

CH. I. 9—14.

For this cause also we, from the day we heard it, cease not praying on your behalf, and asking that ye may be filled with *the knowledge of His will in all spiritual wisdom and understanding,* ¹⁰ *so as to walk worthily of the Lord for all pleasing, in every good work bearing fruit and increasing by the understanding of God,* ¹¹ *with all power being made powerful according to the might of His glory for all endurance and long-suffering with joy,* ¹² *giving thanks to the Father who has made you meet for* your *share of the lot of the saints in the light,* ¹³ *who has rescued us from the rule of the darkness and translated us into the kingdom of the Son of His love.* ¹⁴ *In whom we have redemption, the forgiveness of sins.*

9. Result on the writer's side of the fact stated in *v.* 8: *because of this also we etc.* These words place Paul and Timothy, as a third party, in contrast to Epaphras and especially to the Colossian Christians. *From the day we heard:* same phrase in *v.* 6. As soon as the Colossians heard the word of grace, it began to bear continual fruit in them: as soon as Paul heard of their Christian love, he began and continued to pray unceasingly for their further development. *Do not cease praying on your behalf:* cp. Eph. i. 16, 'I do not cease giving thanks on your behalf.' *Praying:* general term for approach to God, as in *v.* 3, where the specific form of prayer is thanksgiving. Here the specific form is immediately added: *and asking that ye may be filled.* Same words together, *praying and asking,* in Mk. xi. 24. *Asking:* more fully *asking as a favour to myself. That ye may be filled:* immediate matter and purpose of Paul's request: further purpose in *v.* 10*a*, with collateral details in *vv.* 10*b*, 11, 12. *Filled:* so that every part of their being be permeated, and thus controlled and elevated, by an intelligent comprehension of the will of God. *Knowledge:* full and complete knowledge, as in Ph. i. 9. *His will:* embracing God's purpose of mercy towards us and the path in which He would have us walk. [The accusative case after *filled,* as in Ph. i. 11, where see note. I specifies the kind and extent of the fulness which Paul has in view.] *Wisdom and understanding:* found together in 1 Cor. i. 19, from the LXX. where the words are often associated; and their cognate adjectives in Mt. xi. 25. *Wisdom:* acquaintance with first principles, these being looked upon by the Jews as a guide in action: see note under 1 Cor. ii. 5. *Understanding:* the faculty of putting together, and reading the significance of, facts and phenomena around. *Spiritual:* wrought by the Holy Spirit: for to Him most frequently does the word *spirit* refer. But the distinction is not important. For the spirit in man is that highest element of his nature on which the Holy Spirit directly operates. Same word in 1 Cor. ii. 13, where see note; ch. iii. 1, xv. 44. It distinguishes the wisdom and understanding wrought in us by the Holy Spirit from that mentioned in 1 Cor. i. 19, 20, ii. 5, 6, 13, iii. 19, 2 Cor. i. 12, Jas. iii. 15. *All wisdom and understanding:* embracing every element given to man of acquaintance with the great realities behind and beneath and above the visible world around, and a faculty of interpreting phenomena of every kind. All this is looked upon here as the surrounding element *in* which was to be realised the fulness of knowledge which Paul desired for his readers. He prays that amid such wisdom and understanding they may be made full with a fulness embracing intelligent acquaintance with the will of God. A similar prayer, including the word here rendered *knowledge*, is found in each of the letters written by Paul during his first imprisonment at Rome: Ph. i. 9, Eph. i. 17, Philem. 6. It may almost be called the key-note of this group of epistles.

10a. Further purpose to be attained by this fulness of knowledge: viz. to take such steps in life as are *worthy of the Lord*, i.e. of the great Master. *Walk worthily of:* so Eph. iv. 1, 1 Th. ii. 12; cp. Ph. i. 27, Rom. xvi. 2. The grandeur of the Master claims corresponding conduct in His servants. How wide is this claim, we shall learn from *vv.* 10*b*, 11, 12, which expound in detail *v.* 10*a*. *For all pleasing:* i.e. in order to please Him in *all* things, making His pleasure our constant aim. So 1 Cor. vii. 32. This aim is the only one worthy of the Master whom we serve. And it will mark out for us a worthy path. Thus Paul desires for his readers knowledge not merely for its own sake but that it may produce in them a worthy Christian life. So Ph. i. 9-11; an important parallel.

10b. The first of three participial clauses describing further the worthy walk which Paul desires for his readers. *Bearing-fruit and increasing;* recalls the same words in *v.* 6. To those who receive it the Gospel communicates its own vitality, and fruitfulness, and growth. As it bears fruit in them so they bear fruit *in every good work*, i.e. in beneficence of every kind. These last two words occur together in 1 Tim. v. 10, 2 Tim. ii. 21, iii. 17, Tit. i. 16, iii. 1; 1 Tim. ii. 10, Rom. ii. 7, 2 Cor. ix. 8, Eph. ii. 10, Ph. i. 6, 2 Th. ii. 17. The visible outgrowth of the Christian's inner life is found *in* good deeds. As before, *fruitbearing* and spiritual *growth* go together. Just as the Gospel by producing good results itself comes to occupy a larger place on the world's great stage, so all good we do to others increases our own spiritual stature. *Knowledge of God:* as in *v.* 9, which it recalls. Just as there Paul desired for his readers full and complete knowledge of God in order that they may walk worthy of Christ their Master, so now, while speaking of the growth he desires to accompany this worthy walk, he mentions the full knowledge of God as the means by which this growth is to be wrought. This quick repetition of the same thought, viz. knowledge as a means of something beyond itself, gives to this thought great emphasis. This emphasis, and the close connection between fruitbearing and growth suggested by the repetition of these words together, with the indisputable fact that fruitbearing as much as growth is a result of knowledge of God, suggests that the instrumental clause *by the full knowledge* of God embraces both *fruitbearing* and *growth.* (Cp. Jno. xv. 7.) If so, the balance of the sentence suggests that the early clause *in every good work* has in some measure the same compass. In other words, Paul desires his readers to be filled with knowledge of the will of God, producing in them a walk worthy of their Master, and along with this a fruitbearing and growth showing itself in every good work and produced by knowledge of God. Just as in *v.* 6 we have a comparison of the work at Colossæ with that throughout the world, and this turned back upon itself by a further comparison of the work throughout the world with that at Colossæ, so here after tracing Christian knowledge to its practical result in Christian conduct Paul traces back Christian beneficence and growth to the instrumentality of specific Christian knowledge.

11. Second detail which Paul desires may accompany his readers' worthy walk, viz. spiritual *power* producing *endurance. Power:* ability to overcome obstacles and to do work. *Being made powerful:* day by day receiving power, like the same tense of a cognate word in Eph. vi. 10, a very close parallel, and Ph. iv. 13. *With all power:* every kind of ability, this looked upon as an objective ornament for the Christian work and fight. Similarly, Eph. iii. 16. *His glory:* the manifested grandeur of God, evoking His creature's admiration. See under Rom. i. 21. With this divine grandeur is associated infinite *might,* i.e. the power of a ruler. And this *might* is the measure of the *power* with which Paul desires his readers to

be made strong: *according to the might etc.* For whatever there is in God He communicates, according to their need and their faith, to His servants.

All endurance: maintenance of our position under all burdens which would press us down and in face of all foes who would drive us back; as in Rom. ii. 7, etc. *Longsuffering:* a holding back of emotion, whether anger as in Rom. ii, 4, Eph. iv. 2, or fear as is implied here by the connection with *endurance.* Paul desires that in spite of *all* obstacles his readers hold on their way and preserve a serene Christian spirit. *With joy:* a desired accompaniment of this endurance and longsuffering. So completely are the Colossian Christians to maintain their position and their serenity in spite of hardships that these are not even to dim their *joy.* This last word adds immense force to those foregoing as a note of absolute victory. The note is clearly sounded in 1 Th. i. 6. But this complete victory is possible only by the inbreathing of power in divine measure.

Grammatically, the words *with joy* might be joined to *v.* 12. And this would preserve in some measure the symmetry of the three participial clauses, giving to each participle a foregoing prepositional specification: *in every good work, in all power, with joy.* The practical difference is very slight. For in any case the *endurance and longsuffering* are associated *with joy.* But these last words would add very little to 'giving thanks:' (for all thanksgiving is joyful:) whereas joined to *endurance* they are a note of triumph. [This is somewhat confirmed by the word μετά which joins together dissimilar or at least distinct objects; and therefore more naturally connects *joy* with *endurance* than with 'thanksgiving.']

12. Third participial detail collateral with, and expounding, the 'worthy walk' of *v.* 10*a.* This must be accompanied not only by fruitbearing and growth, and by divinely-given strength producing joyful endurance, but also by *thanksgiving.* This last is very conspicuous with Paul: ch. ii. 7, iii. 17, iv. 2, Eph. v. 4, 20, Ph. iv. 6. It is cognate to, and was perhaps suggested by the word rendered joy in *v.* 11. The 'endurance and longsuffering' are to be accompanied by 'joy:' and this is to assume the form of expressed gratitude to God. Whether He is here spoken of as *Father* of the Firstborn Son or of us His human brethren, the close relation between Christ and us leaves us unable to determine; and makes the distinction unimportant.

The word *lot* or *allotment,* and the word *saints* which never throws off its O. T. reference and which has here its usual N. T. sense of church-members, these looked upon as claimed by God to be specially

His own, recall the division of Canaan among the sacred people. Similarly Acts xxvi. 18, 'a lot among the sanctified:' a close coincidence, from the lips of Paul. Cp. Num. xxxiii. 54, where the *lot* is the instrument of allotment: and ch. xxxii. 19, Josh. xvii. 6, where it is an allotted portion of the land. And Dt. x. 9, 'For this cause the Levites have no share and *lot* among their brethren: the Lord Himself is his *lot*.' *The lot of the saints* seems to include the whole portion of spiritual blessing allotted to the human family of God. *The share of the lot:* that part of this general allotment of blessing which falls to each *of the saints*. The word *share* reminds us that in this allotment many joined, and that the Colossians were now sharers with the ancient people of God. *Made-meet:* same word in 2 Cor. iii. 6, 'meet or sufficient to be ministers of the New Covenant.' It implies that for this participation some fitness is needed and that this fitness God has given to the Colossian Christians. This can be no other than the righteousness of faith: for righteousness is ever the condition of spiritual blessing, and it can be obtained only by faith. This divinely-given fitness is abundant and constant reason for *thanksgiving*. The O. T. colouring of these words recalls Eph. ii. 12, 13. It somewhat favours the reading *you* found in the two best Greek copies, as against *us* which is read by most other authorities. For the word *you* would contrast the Colossians who were Gentiles with Paul and others who were Jews. Cp. Eph. ii. 1 and 3; 12 and 14. This internal confirmation of our two best witnesses perhaps slightly outweighs abundant documentary evidence on the other side.

In the light: locality or environment, probably, of *the lot of the saints*. Similarly in *v.* 13 'the darkness' has a semi-local sense. *Light* is a characteristic of everything pertaining to the inheritance of the saints. Their eternal home will be a world of light, as God is light and dwells in light: Rev. xxi. 24, 1 Jno. i. 5, 1 Tim. vi. 16. And the glory of that splendour will illumine their path on earth: 2 Cor. iv. 6, Eph. v. 8. Since the lot of the saints is both a future enjoyment (a 'laid-up hope') and a present possession, the words *in the light* must have the same double reference. The sons of God are already heirs (a word cognate with *lot*) and therefore *in the light:* and the light in which they walk is an earnest of their share of the allotment of blessing which belongs to the consecrated people of God.

[*In the light* can hardly be the instrument by which (cp. 2 Cor. iv. 4 'the light of the Gospel') God *made* them *meet* for the inheritance. For its distance from the verb would require this to be very definitely indicated. But the Greek preposition here only notes the light as a surrounding element. Moreover, the contrast with 'out of darkness' in *v.* 13 suggests very strongly that the light is an environment of that for which God has made His people meet.]

13. Further statement of what God has done, expounding *v.* 12 and giving further reason for thanks to God. *The darkness:* the objective realm of evil, looked upon as causing ignorance and gloom and as possessing power and thus exercising *authority* or rule over its victims : so Lk. xxii. 53 ; and Eph. vi. 12, 'this darkness.' It is practically 'the authority of the air' in Eph. ii. 2 ; the rule of moral and spiritual night. These words imply that under this rule all men once lay bound. *Out of* this *rule of darkness* God had *rescued* the Colossian Christians: i.e. by His kindness and power He had brought them out into the light. *Translated:* removed from one place to another : same word in Lk. xvi. 4, Acts xiii. 22, 1 Cor. xiii. 2. *The Son of His love :* who belongs to the love of God as its eternal personal object. The phrase fixes our attention on the relation of the Son to this unique attribute of the Father. *The kingdom of etc. :* the realm over which Christ will reign for ever : Eph. v. 5, Jno. xviii. 36. This kingdom will have its full realisation in the final glory. But already its citizens are being enrolled. And enrolment brings at once a foretaste of the blessings of the rule of Christ. Notice the complete change which God has wrought. Once these Colossians were in bondage under the rule of darkness, a rule shutting out the many blessings of the light. From that realm of darkness God has rescued them and brought them into another realm over which reigns the eternal Son, the divine Object of divine love. By this rescue and this transfer God made these Gentiles meet to share the lot of His holy people. For such benefit, well might Paul wish his readers to give thanks to God.

14. Our relation, in this kingdom, to the King. This verse is a transition from the foregoing thanksgiving to the great matter of this Epistle, viz. the dignity and work of Christ. *In whom . . . redemption :* as in Rom. iii. 24. This last word suggests or asserts that our rescue was costly. In the parallel passage, Eph. i. 7, the cost is stated : 'through His blood.' Since surrender to the rule of sin is the due penalty of sin, rescue from the power of sin implies *forgiveness of sins:* same words in Eph. i. 7, Acts xiii. 38, xxvi. 18, Lk. i. 77, iii. 3, Mk. i. 4, Mt. xxvi. 28, Lk. xxiv. 47, Acts ii. 38, v. 31, x. 43. It is practically the same as justification : for the justified are guilty. And we are (Rom. iii. 24) 'justified through the redemption which is in Christ.' *In whom we have etc.:* objectively through His death and subjectively by inward union with Christ, a union which makes us sharers of all He has and is.

Notice the assurance of personal salvation implied in *we have
. . forgiveness of sins.* For our *sins* and *the forgiveness of* them
are essentially personal matters. This assurance, Paul assumes
that his readers share.

The introduction to the Epistle is now complete. Paul has
thanked God for the Christian life at Colossæ as he has heard of
it from the founder of the Church there, Epaphras. To praise he
has added prayer for his readers, full development in knowledge of
the will of God, this leading to a life worthy of the Master whom
they serve, viz. to fruitbearing and to growth, to joyful endurance
and gratitude to God. This prayer has been on the lips of Paul
from the time he first heard about the work at Colossæ. Abundant
reason for gratitude, he finds in the fact that God has made these
Gentiles sharers in the inheritance promised to the sons of Abraham,
an inheritance in the realm of eternal light; or, to state the same
benefit in other words, He has rescued them from the realm of
darkness and made them citizens of the kingdom of the beloved
Son of God. To this royal Son they already stand in closest relation. For in Him is their liberation: because in Him they have forgiveness of sins.

This gratitude for mercies already received brings us into the
presence of the Son of God. To expound His essential grandeur
and His work, as a corrective to prevalent error, is the chief aim of
this Epistle.

DIVISION II.

THE TRUTH CONCERNING CHRIST.

CHAPTER I. 15—II. 3.

SECTION IV.

CHRIST'S RELATION TO GOD, AND TO THE UNIVERSE.

CH. I. 15—17.

Who is the *image of the Invisible God, firstborn before every
creature.* ^{16} *Because in Him were all things created, in the heavens
and upon the earth, the things visible and the things invisible,*

whether thrones, or lordships, or principalities, or authorities: all things have been created through Him and for Him. ¹⁷ *And Himself is before all things: and in Him all things stand together.*

WITH stately words Paul now begins his exposition of the nature and work of the Son of God; and pursues this august topic, in its various relations, to ch. ii. 3, where it finds a suitable conclusion. The purpose of this exposition, as stated in ch. ii. 4, is to guard the Colossian Christians against persuasive errors. Naturally these errors must have moulded the exposition designed to combat them. We shall therefore seek for indications of their nature in the features peculiar, among the Epistles of Paul, to the important teaching now before us. Fortunately for us and for the Church in all ages, Paul meets these errors, not by direct attack which would have been intelligible only to those acquainted with the errors attacked, but by positive truth instructive to all men in all ages. This method gives to the epistle before us abiding and universal value. It is, moreover, an example to us. Error can be effectively met only by statement and proof of corresponding and opposite truth.

Paul states first the Son's relation to God, *v.* 15*a*; then His relation to the created universe, *vv.* 15*b*—17; then His relation to the Church, *vv.* 18—20; and especially to the Colossian Christians, *vv.* 21—23; lastly Paul's relation to these last in Christ.

15a. *Who is:* solemn assertion touching the abiding nature, relations, and state, of the God-Man. *Image:* a similitude derived from an original, and presenting it more or less accurately and fully to those who behold the similitude. So Mt. xxii. 20, a stamp on a coin; Rev. xiii. 14, a statue. *Who is image of God:* word for word as in 2 Cor. iv. 4, where see note. Cp. 1 Cor. xi. 7, Col. iii. 10, Gen. i. 26. Here, however, we have the added word *invisible* God, shedding light upon the significance of the phrase *image of God* as a manifestation of an unseen person. These words assert that the glorified Son sets forth, to those who behold Him, the nature and grandeur of the Eternal Father. The *image* includes the glorified manhood in which the Eternal Son presents in created and visible form the mental and moral nature of God. Men knew the Father because they had seen the Incarnate Son: Jno. xiv. 9. The possibility and fitness of this mode of presenting the divine nature flow from man's original creation (Gen. i. 26) according to the *image* and likeness of God. And the emphatic word *is*, which asserts an abiding reality, and the following assertion about the creation of the universe, suggest that the words *image of God* describe also an eternal relation of the Son to the Father. The same is suggested in Heb. i. 3, 'outshining of His glory and expression of His substance:' a close and important parallel. Probably, whatever the Son became by His incarnation was but a manifestation in human form of His essential nature and His eternal relation to the Father; these being an eternal archetype of His human nature. They are also the archetype of man as originally created, and in some sense (1 Cor. xi. 7, Jas. iii. 9) of man as he now is; and of the future glorified humanity of the servants of Christ. If so, the revelation of God to man in time has its root in eternity and in God, i.e. in the existence within the Godhead of a person other than the Father, derived from Him, and sharing His divine nature.

God is *invisible*, as being beyond reach of human sight: 1 Tim. vi. 16. And the context of the word *invisible* in 1 Tim. i. 17 suggests very strongly that He is essentially invisible to all His creatures. (Jno. i. 18, 1 Jno. iv. 12, 'God, no one has ever seen,' may or may not deny that others besides men have seen God.) If the words *image of God* describe an eternal relation of the Son to the Father, the word *invisible* must refer, as apparently does 1 Tim. i. 17, to the eternal essence of God. Just as only through the Son came the creatures into being, even the earliest and the highest of them, so probably only through the Son is the Father known even to the highest of His creatures. Thus the word *image* is correlative to *visible*. The essentially invisible Father has in the Son an eternal organ of self-manifestation, an eternal counterpart and supplement to His own invisible nature. His manifestation began when time began, by the earliest act of creation. And each later act of the Son, before His Incarnation, His Incarnation itself, the acts of the incarnate Son, and of the glorified Son, is a further manifestation of the Father. If so, touching the entire nature and relations of the God-Man, Paul's words are in their fullest extent true: He *is* the *Image of God*.

The word *image* suggests the existence of others outside the Godhead. For there can be no manifestation without persons capable of apprehending it. In this sense the Son became the image of God when the earliest intelligent being contemplated Him But what then became actual fact existed in Him potentially in eternity. This first indication of the existence of creatures prepares a way for further reference to them in *v.* 15*b*, and for the explicit mention of them in *v.* 16.

15b. Further description of the Son's relation to the Father, and to the entire created universe, which here finds definite mention;

and a further step in Paul's transition from the invisible Creator, through the Son, to His creatures. *Firstborn:* same word in v. 18, Rom. viii. 29, Heb. i. 6, Rev. i. 5, Lk. ii. 7, referring to Christ; also Heb. xi. 28, xii. 23, Ex. xiii. 2, 15, Num. xviii. 15, etc. It denotes *earliest-born,* in contrast to others 'later-born,' or not *born* but created. The earliest creatures are spoken of by Clement of Alex. and others as 'first-created.' The syllable *-born* describes evidently, without further limitation, the Son's relation to the Father; in close harmony with the word similar in meaning, though different in form, rendered *only-begotten* in Jno. i. 14, 18, iii. 16, 1 Jno. iv. 9. The syllable *first* needs further specification; and finds it in the following words *every creature.*

Creature or *creation:* same word in Rom. viii. 19, where see note; i. 25, viii. 39. [The practical difference between the renderings *all creation* (Lightfoot and R.V.) and *every creature* (Meyer and Ellicott) is very slight. The former looks upon the created universe as one whole; the latter as consisting of various created objects. The latter rendering is preferable. For in v. 16 Paul distributes created objects into categories, thus suggesting that he thinks of them singly. And this is the more usual significance of the phrase here used: e.g. 1 Pet. ii. 13, Col. i. 28, Ph. i. 4, ii. 10, 11, iv. 19, 21, Eph. i. 21, ii. 21, iii. 15, iv. 14, etc. A genitive after πρῶτος, specifying the later objects with which the *first* is compared, is found also in Jno. i. 15, 30, xv. 18. This use of the genitive after a superlative to denote comparison forbids us to infer that the *firstborn* is Himself a *creature.* So Thucydides (bk. i. 1) speaks of the Peloponnesian War as the 'most worthy of mention of those which had happened before it.'] Paul says simply that in relation to every created object the Son is *firstborn.* Moreover, that in v. 16 even the blessed ones of heaven are included in *every creature,* whereas the Son is first-*born,* suggests that His mode of derivation from the Father is essentially different from theirs. Otherwise the transition cannot be explained. (This transition is a close harmony with Jno. i. 14, 18.) And this suggestion is confirmed by the statement in vv. 16, 17 that through the Son were all things created and that He is before all things.

16a. A great fact, justifying the foregoing title of the Son. He is rightly called 'firstborn before every creature' *because in Him were created all things. Created:* akin, in Greek as in English, to 'creature' in v. 15, which it recalls and expounds. The Hebrew word rendered *create* (e.g. Gen. i. 1, 21, ii. 3, 4, v. 1, 2) is predicated only of God; except that in Jos. xvii. 15, 18, Ezek. xxiii. 47 another grammatical form of the same word has its apparently original sense of 'cut,' and in Ezek. xxi. 24 (AV. v. 19) the same form denotes human workmanship. This restriction of its use to the work of God suggests that to *create* is to make as only God can make; not necessarily to make out of nothing, (cp. Wisdom xi. 18, 'created the world out of a shapeless mass,') but at least to bring into existence new forms. In Gen. i. 1, 21, 27, v. 1, 2, vi. 7 this Hebrew word is poorly represented in the LXX. by a Greek word meaning only 'to make.' But in Dt. iv. 32, Ps. li. 12, lxxxix. 13, 48, Isa. xxii. 11, xlv. 8, etc. we find the word used here. In classic Greek the same word denotes frequently the origin of a town or colony or institution; the idea of origin always being present. In the N. T. the verb is found only in Col. i. 16, iii. 10, Eph. ii. 10, 15, iii. 9, iv. 24, Rom. i. 25, 1 Cor. xi. 9, 1 Tim. iv. 3, Rev. iv. 11, x. 6; in each case describing the work of God. So in the LXX. and the Apocrypha. This constant use of the word, the exposition immediately following, and the cognate word 'creature' in *v.* 15 to which this word evidently refers, fix beyond doubt its meaning here. Paul asserts of the Son that *in Him all things* originally sprang into being. *All things:* the entire universe rational and irrational, animated and inanimate, consisting of various parts but looked upon here as one definite whole. Certain of its component parts are at once enumerated. The words *in Him,* so frequent with Paul and especially in this group of epistles to describe the relation of the incarnate Son to His servants on earth and to their salvation, assert here that the Eternal Son bears to the creation of the universe the same relation. (Verse 17 asserts this touching the abiding state of the universe.) The personality of the Eternal Son is the encompassing, pervading, life-giving element in which sprang into being and assumed its various natural forms whatever exists. In His bosom the world began to be. In Him was from eternity its possibility: and in Him the possible became actual. A close coincidence in Rev. iii. 14, 'the beginning of the creation of God.'

In the heavens and upon the earth: further specification in detail of the *all things created in Him,* dividing created objects according to their locality and thus revealing the wide compass of Paul's assertion. A more accurate specification in Rev. x. 6: 'the heaven and the things in it,' etc. Here *the heavens etc.* are looked upon not as themselves created objects but as mere notes of locality. Perhaps this mode of speech was prompted by Paul's thought being directed, as we learn from the words following, not so much to the material universe as to its inhabitants. He does not find it needful to mention here and in Eph. i. 10 the 'things under the earth,' Ph. ii. 10. For the dead were once alive and are therefore covered by the foregoing assertion. *The things visible and the things invisible:* another very conspicuous division of *all things;* suggested by, but not exactly coincident with, the foregoing division. *The visible* includes all persons and things within reach of the human eye : *the invisible* includes, most simply understood, all objects beyond its reach.

Whether thrones or lordships etc.: further details included in *all things*. It is not an exhaustive division as was the last, *visible and invisible*, but a mere enumeration of possible examples belonging apparently or chiefly to *the invisible things*. The list recalls Eph. i. 21, 'principality and authority and power and lordship;' 1 Pet. iii. 22, 'angels and authorities and powers.' The words *principality* and *authority* are found, in singular or plural, and in the same order, in ch. ii. 10, 15, Eph. i. 21, iii. 10, vi. 12, 1 Cor. xv. 24, Tit. iii. 1, Lk. xii. 11, xx. 20; the last three places referring expressly to earthly rulers. These cannot be excluded from the universal assertion of this verse. And in Rom. xiii. 1 Paul teaches that even political power has its ultimate origin in God. But the other quotations refer evidently to superhuman persons in the unseen world. And this evident reference of the other passages quoted above, together with the word *invisible* immediately foregoing, leaves no doubt that to these chiefly Paul refers here. And, if so, these various titles designate various successive ranks of angels. That there are bad angels bearing these titles, and therefore presumably of different rank, Eph. vi. 12 asserts. And, if there are superhuman enemies, there must be also successive ranks of superhuman servants of God. In this verse, however, the existence of angelic powers is not absolutely assumed. Paul merely says that if there be such, be they what they may, they were created in the Son of God.

The distinction between these various titles, and their order in rank, cannot be determined with any approach to certainty. From the titles themselves very little can be inferred. The word *thrones* suggests a position of conspicuous and secure dignity, like that of the twenty-four elders (Rev. iv. 4) sitting on thrones around the throne of God. This is better than the suggestion that they combine to form by their own persons the throne of God, as themselves the bearers of the divine Majesty. *Lordships:* last word in the list of Eph. i. 21; found also in 2 Pet. ii. 10, Jude 8. It is akin to the word 'lord,' and to the word 'rule' in Rom. vi. 9, 14, vii. 1, xiv. 9; and suggests an authority to which others bow as servants. The word rendered *principality* denotes sometimes *beginning* as in

Jno. i. 1, Ph. iv. 15; and sometimes the position of a ruler or officer. A cognate word is rendered 'ruler' in 1 Cor. ii. 6, 8, Eph. ii. 2, Rom. xiii. 3, and frequently in the Gospels and the Book of Acts. This last word designates in Dan. x. 13, 20, 21, xii. 1 certain angel-princes, or angels of superior rank, standing severally in special relation to the kingdoms of Persia, Greece, Israel. The word used in Col. i. 16 is the first syllable of 'archangel.' And Michael, 'one of the chief princes' in Dan. x. 13, is in Jude 9 (cp. 1 Th. iv. 16) called an archangel. The word *authority* (cp. 'authority of darkness' in v. 13, 'authority of the air' in Eph. ii. 2; Mk. vi. 7, Jno. xvii. 2) suggests angelic powers exercising sway over certain portions of the material or immaterial universe. The frequent connection of *principality* and *authority* in this order (1 Cor. xv. 24, Eph. i. 21, iii. 10, vi. 12, Col. ii. 10, 15, Tit. iii. 1, Lk. xii. 11, xx. 20) suggests that this was their order of rank. But it is impossible to define the relation of this pair to the *thrones* and *lordships*. All these titles are twice mentioned together by Origen in his work *On First Principles* (bk. i. 5. 3, 6. 2) as of angelic powers. But he refers evidently to the passage before us, and contributes nothing to its elucidation. Nor is reliable evidence beyond the above scanty inferences from the words themselves to be derived from Jewish literature. All we know is that Paul believed that there are successive ranks of angelic powers, and declares here that all these, whatever they may be, were created in the Son.

16b. An emphatic repetition, and development, and summing up after exposition in detail, of the opening words of v. 16. *All things:* word for word as in v. 16a. *Through Him:* by His instrumentality or agency; see under Rom. i. 5. It describes constantly Christ's relation to man's salvation: Rom. v. 1, 2, 11, 2 Cor. v. 18. The same relation, Paul here asserts, the Eternal Son bears to the creation of the universe. Similarly, both to redemption and creation He bears the relation described by the phrase 'in Christ:' v. 16a. That these two phrases alike describe His relation both to the Church and to the universe, makes very conspicuous the identity of His relation to these two distinct and different objects. A close coincidence in 1 Cor. viii. 6: 'through whom are all things, and we through Him.' A still closer coincidence in Heb. i. 2, Jno. i. 3. [Διά with the genitive is used even where the agent is also the first cause: so Gal. i. 1, Rom. xi. 36, where God is said to be the Agent of the resurrection of Christ, and of all things. But the use of the same preposition constantly to describe the Son's relation to the work of creation and also to man's redemption, of both which the

Father is expressly and frequently (e.g. *v.* 20) said to be the First Cause, suggests very strongly that the preposition was deliberately chosen because the Son is only the Agent, and the Father is the First Cause, of the created universe. This different relation of the Father and the Son is asserted, or clearly implied, in 1 Cor. viii. 6. Thus the preposition before us describes the Son's relation to the entire activity of God.]

And for Him: to please and exalt the Son, and to work out His purposes. The Agent of creation is also its aim. Close, coincidence in Heb. ii. 10. That Christ is only its mediate aim, we infer with certainty from the entire New Testament. The Father's eternal purpose is the ultimate source, and His approbation is the ultimate aim, of whatever good exists and takes place. And, just as the Son is the divine channel through which the Father's purpose passes into actuality, so only through the Son and through His exaltation does creation attain its goal in God. So 1 Cor. viii. 6, xv. 28, Eph. i. 14. In this real sense *all things* are *for Him.*

The word *created* marks the close of Paul's discussion of the creation of all things by the Son. [The Greek perfect, *have-been-created*, calls attention to the abiding result of the act of creation, thus differing from the aorist in *v.* 16*a* which simply notes an event. 'By His agency and to work out His pleasure all things were created in the past and exist now in the abiding present.']

17. A statement reasserting and supplementing the truth embodied in 'first-begotten' in *v.* 15; just as *v.* 16 expounds and supplements 'every creature.' The Son is the Firstborn because He is earlier than all. *He is:* or *Himself exists.* It calls attention to an unchanging existence earlier than every other existing object. Similar words in Jno. viii. 58, Ex. iii. 14. *Before:* in time rather than in rank. For this is the sense of the word 'Firstborn:' and the clear reference of *v.* 16 to *v.* 15 prepares us for another reference here to the same verse. *Consist:* literally stand together as united parts of one whole. It is cognate to the Greek original of our word *system*. *In Him:* as in *v.* 16 'in Him were created.' Just as in the bosom of the Eternal Son all things sprang into being, so in Him as their encompassing element all things find their bond of union and their orderly arrangement into one whole. Similar thought in Heb. i. 3: 'bearing all things by the word of His power.' The word here rendered *consist* is frequent in Plato and Aristotle to denote the orderly arrangement of the various parts of the material universe.

That the universe was created through the agency of the Son of God, is stated by Paul expressly and indisputably only here. The plain and emphatic assertions of *vv.* 16, 17, are therefore an invaluable addition to his other teaching. A close coincidence is found in the broad statement in 1 Cor. viii. 6. But the absence there of reference to the universe forbids us to build upon this passage a sure inference. The full statement in Col. i. 16, 17, given without proof evidently because proof was needless, implies, however, that this teaching had an assured place in Paul's thought. We have similar teaching in Heb. i. 2, a document allied to, though in many points different from, the Epistles of Paul; and very conspicuously in Jno. i. 3. All this proves that the early followers of Christ believed that their Master was Creator of the world.

This belief is an important and almost inevitable corollary from the whole teaching of Paul. The Son is ever said to be the channel through which flows forth from the Father into actuality His purpose of salvation. This salvation will rescue man from a corruption which has infected his entire surroundings. Frequently the forces of nature seem to be hostile to us. In reality they work together for our good. And the coming glorification of the sons of God will one day rescue from the corruption which now enslaves it (Rom. viii. 21) the entire created universe. This present and coming victory is pledged to us in the great truth that He who became Man to save man is also the Creator of man and of whatever exists.

It is worthy of note that all the great religions give an account of the beginning of the world. And naturally so: for man's highest spiritual interests are involved in the question of his origin. Hence Gen. i. is a necessary prologue to the story of the Old Covenant. And its real worth is derived from the historic fact that He who made heaven and earth became the God of Abraham. That their God was the Creator of the world, was a great bulwark of Israel's faith. Similarly, the teaching of Col. i. 16, 17 derives its whole value from that of *vv.* 18-20; as does Jno. i. 3 from the subsequent story of the incarnate Son. For knowledge of the God who made us would be useless had He not come near to save us. It is now the firm ground of our faith. He who made us and the universe, and He only, is able to save us from forces around which seem ready to overwhelm us.

From ch. ii. 4 we learn that the earlier part of this Epistle was written to guard its readers against seductive error prevalent at Colossæ. This suggests at once that the verses before us, which are the most distinguishing feature of the Epistle, refer to the same error. We notice also in ch. ii. 18 a warning against 'worship of angels,' a practice implying undue estimate of their place and importance. This suggests a reason why the successive ranks of angels are selected in *v.* 16 as examples of 'the invisible things' created through the Son; viz. that they had been placed in undue rivalry to the unique honour belonging to Him. All this confirms our inference that Paul has here in view the errors at Colossæ. What these errors were, we shall, at the close of our exposition, endeavour to gather from the notices scattered throughout the Epistle.

That for the more part Paul meets these errors not directly but by stating contrary truth, makes it difficult for us to determine exactly what they were. But it increases immensely the value of the Epistle by making it an assertion of great principles which bear with equal force upon the ever-varying errors of each successive age. Had Paul merely overturned the errors he had in view, his letter would have had practical value only for those among whom these errors were prevalent. But the great principles here asserted can be understood and appreciated by all men in all ages.

In Prov. viii. 22-31 the wisdom of God is associated with the work of creation. And certainly the wisdom of God is divine and eternal. But although in Prov. viii. it is personified, we have there no language which implies that it is an actual Person distinct from the Father. But here the Son, in whom all things were created and through whom (*v.* 20) God reconciles men to Himself, is indisputably a Person and one distinct from the Father. For *v.* 16 is much more than an assertion that all things were made by God. And He by whose agency all things were made is identified by Paul with Him who was afterwards known as Jesus Christ. This teaching implies that with the Father from eternity and personally distinct from Him is another Person. The eternity of the Son implies His divinity. And this is confirmed by the word 'created' which is restricted in O. T. and N. T. to God and is here predicated of the Son. Thus the passage before us is an important contribution to our proof that Christ is divine. See further in Diss. iii.

SECTION V.

CHRIST'S RELATION TO THE CHURCH AND TO THE WORK OF SALVATION.

CH. I. 18—20.

And Himself is the Head of the Body, i.e. *of the Church; who is the* Beginning, *the* Firstborn from the dead ones, *in order that He may become in all things Himself first.* [19] *Because in Him* He was *well-pleased that all the fulness should dwell;* [20] *and through Him to reconcile all things to Himself, having made peace through the blood of His cross, through Him, whether the things upon the earth or the things in the heavens.*

18. *And Himself is:* exact and stately repetition of the opening words of *v.* 17. He through whom all things were created and in whom all find their bond of union *is also the Head of the Body,* i.e. *of the Church.* That this last short explanation is sufficient, shows how familiar to Paul was the thought that the Church is the Body of Christ. This important metaphor we have already found in 1 Cor. xii. 12-27, Rom. xii. 4, 5. The new point here is that of this body Christ is *the Head:* so ch. ii. 19, Eph. i. 22, iv. 15. Accordingly, in the earlier epistles this metaphor sets forth chiefly the relation of Christians one to another: here it sets forth, in harmony with the scope of the epistle which is to expound the dignity of Christ, their relation to Him. The Son of God is not only a Spirit animating, and directing from within, each member and uniting them into one body, but also Himself the Head of the Body, i.e. a part of it, yet occupying a unique and supreme position and from that position directing the whole Body. And this relation is vital. Some other members may be removed and the body live still: separation from the head involves instant death. Perhaps we may say that as divine Christ is the animating and invisible spirit of the Body: as human and yet superhuman and possessing a visible and glorified body He is its Head.

Notice here and in *v.* 24 the word *Church* in a sense more august than we have hitherto met, viz. as denoting definitely and unmistakably the entire family of God: so Eph. i. 22, iii. 10, 21, v. 23—32. Inasmuch as Christ designs His people on earth to be joined in outward and visible fellowship, the word *Church* here denotes probably, not the simple totality of those who are inwardly joined to Christ, but the company of His professed followers with the implied exception of those whose profession is an empty pretence and therefore valueless. For the common local use of the word links with it indissolubly the ideas of outward confession and visible unity. And, in spite of the many ecclesiastical divisions of Christians, there is between all the professed and real servants of Christ a bond of union, recognised in some small degree even by the world around. The true significance of membership in a sectional Church is that by entering it we become members of the universal company of the professed followers of Christ.

Who is etc.: solemn assertions, expounding further Christ's relation to His body. The *Beginning:* earliest in time, as in Gen. xlix. 3, Dt. xxi. 17 where the same word is linked with *firstborn*. Very frequently the earliest is the cause of all that follow. So is Christ. Similarly, Rev. iii. 14, 'the beginning of the creation of God:' for Christ is the Agent and in a real sense the Archetype of the whole creation. Here the reference of the word *beginning* is not stated: but it is suggested by the new topic introduced by this verse, viz. Christ's relation to the Church, and is placed beyond doubt by the words following. He is the beginning of the New Creation because He is *Firstborn from the dead*. For resurrection is the gate through which we shall enter the fully-developed kingdom of God: and His resurrection made ours possible. By Himself rising He opened a path along which we shall enter the glory in which He already is. And by rising *from* among *the dead* through (2 Cor. xiii. 4) the power of the Father, the God-Man entered a new mode of life and in some sense a new world; and may therefore be said to have been *born from the dead*. Since He was the first to pass through death, He *is* the *firstborn from the dead*. The word *firstborn*, recalling *v.* 15, emphasises the similar relation of Christ to the Universe and to the Church. But in *v.* 15 it was followed by mention of the later-created, 'every creature:' here it is followed by mention of those from whose midst the Resurrection-Birth brought Christ, *from the dead*.

That He may (or *might*) *become:* purpose of Christ's rising first. *In all things Himself first* or *holding-the-first-place*. Already the Son is first in time and rank, as being earlier than every creature and as being agent, and bond of union, of the entire universe. That this priority may be universal, i.e. that it might extend to the Church, Christ rose from the dead before any of His servants: and He did so by the deliberate purpose of God. *Become;* notes the historical development of Christ, in contrast to that which *He is*, i.e. to His abiding state, as described in *vv.* 15, 17, 18. The emphatic words *in all things* keep before us the sameness of Christ's relation to the Church and to the Universe.

19, 20. A statement which explains the foregoing purpose by tracing it to its *cause* in the thought of God, and specifies two purposes of God touching His Son, one relating to His Incarnation and the other to the ultimate aim of His death in the restoration of harmony between God and the universe.

In Him: Christ, who is thrust prominently forward to the beginning of the sentence. He *was-well-pleased:* same word as in

Gal. i. 15, 1 Cor. i. 21. This good pleasure cannot be that of the Son: for in *v.* 20 the Son is distinguished, as the Agent or Instrument, from Him whose good pleasure it is to reconcile through Christ all things to Himself: cp. 2 Cor. v. 18. It must therefore be either the Father as in AV. and RV.; or the *fulness* personified, as suggested by Ellicott. This suggestion, however, which implies a rather startling personification, has no support in the context or in the Epistles of Paul: whereas the constant presence of God in the entire thought of Paul as the ultimate source of all good makes the other exposition quite easy. [The change of subject between the verbs *well-pleased* and *dwell* is in complete harmony with the spirit of the Greek language even in the use of the word *well-pleased.*] Paul had no need to say whose good-pleasure it was that the fulness should dwell in Christ. *Fulness:* a word all-important in these epistles: found in ii. 9, Eph. i. 10, 23, iii. 19, iv. 13, Rom. xi. 12, 25, 1 Cor. x. 26, Gal. iv. 4. It denotes a result of the action described by the verb 'fill' or 'fulfil;' and takes all shades of meaning belonging to this verb. Since both the vessel filled and the matter filled into it are direct objects of the verb 'fill,' the word *fulness* may denote (1) a filled vessel, (2) that with which it is made full, as evidently in 1 Cor. x. 26, or (3) the increment by which a partly filled vessel is made quite full, as in Mt. ix. 16. Or, since the verb denotes the accomplishment of a purpose or promise or command, the word *fulness* may denote (4) that in which such accomplishment is attained, as in Rom. xiii. 10, 'love is a *fulness* (or *fulfilment*) of the Law.' The absence here of any defining genitive (contrast ch. ii. 9 '*all the fulness* of the Godhead) implies that the word *fulness* itself conveys a definite thought present to the mind of Paul. And this can only be, in sense (2), the fulness of God, the totality of that with which God is Himself full, of the dispositions and powers which make up, in our thought, the personality of God. These, being infinite, leave no lack or defect in God. They are also a necessary development of our conception of God, thus approaching sense (4); or rather showing its close connection with the simpler meanings of the word. *The fulness* of God is the totality of attributes with which He is essentially full and which go to make up our conception of God. And this is the meaning of the less definite phrase here. The Father *was pleased that all* this divine *fulness should dwell* (or more accurately *make-its-home*) *in Him* who has been just described as the 'firstborn from the dead.'

The past tense *He-was-well-pleased* suggests [as does the aorist κατοικῆσαι] that Paul refers, not to that which the Son is unchangeably from eternity—although we may reverently say (cp. Jno. v. 26) that even in this sense these words are true—but to what He became in time; and, if so, to the incarnation in which the Eternal Son became the God-Man. In that divine-human Person, the entire circle of the attributes of God took up its abode. This is in complete harmony with the complementary truth in Ph. ii. 7, 'He emptied Himself.' For even on earth the Word (Jno. i. 14) was 'full of grace and truth;' and (v. 16) 'from His *fulness* we all have received.' All that belongs to the essence of God was present in Jesus. But the Son deliberately and definitely laid aside for a time in order to become a sharer of our weakness the actual exercise of the outer and lower circle of His divine attributes. It was the essential and unchangeable possession of these attributes which made possible, and gave worth to, this temporary surrender of the exercise and enjoyment of them. But nothing was surrendered even for a moment which was needful to the further purpose stated in v. 20. *All* the fulness; recalls 'in all things.' *Because* the Father had resolved that in Christ should *dwell all the fulness* of the divine attributes, He resolved further that even in the order of resurrection He should have the first place.

20. Second element in the Father's good pleasure. He was pleased (1) that in Christ should all the fulness dwell, *and* (2) *through Him to reconcile etc. Reconcile:* slightly stronger form, found in N. T. only in v. 22, Eph. ii. 16, of the word in Rom. v. 10, 11, 1 Cor. vii. 11, 2 Cor. v. 18, 19, 20; meaning possibly to restore a lost friendship. See under Rom. v. 1. *Through Him:* i.e. Christ, who is ever the Agent, as the Father is the Author, of this reconciliation; so Rom. v. 1, 11, 2 Cor. v. 18. *All things:* same words and same compass as in v. 16. God's purpose is to bring into harmony with Himself all things rational and irrational. *To Himself:* literally *into Himself:* a stronger term than that in Rom. v. 10, 2 Cor. v. 18, 19, 20, Eph. ii. 16, and suggesting close fellowship with God resulting from reconciliation.

Having-made-peace etc.: method of the reconciliation. *Peace:* primarily 'peace with God,' Rom. v. 1: but this brings with it 'the peace of God,' Ph. iv. 7. It is the blessed and abiding result of the act of reconciliation. *Through the blood of His cross:* graphic exposition of *through Him*. God resolved to *make peace* between Himself and man by means of *the blood* shed on *the cross* of Christ. Similarly, though less vividly, Eph. ii. 16, Ph. iii. 18, Gal. vi. 14, 1 Cor. i. 17, 18. *The cross* of Christ is used in this theological sense, in the N. T., only by Paul. It is therefore a mark of genuineness.

About the genuineness of the words *through Him*, documentary evidence is equally divided. But their apparent needlessness might occasion their omission; whereas, if not genuine, it is not easy to explain their insertion. This gives a slight balance of probability in their favour. They are an emphatic resumption of the same words at the beginning of the verse.

Whether the things upon the earth etc.: exposition of the words *all things,* showing that they include not only all objects on earth but those in heaven; and thus indicating that the peace resulting from the death of Christ is designed to leave no discord *upon the earth or in the heavens.* *The earth* is put first because it chiefly and manifestly needs reconciliation. In *v.* 16 *the heavens* were put first, because the angelic powers were created before the inhabitants of the earth.

These words do not prove absolutely that there is disharmony in heaven. For they admit a negative interpretation, viz. that the death of Christ is designed to leave no discord in the entire universe. But they suggest it. And we may conceive that, the entire universe being essentially one and each part contributing to the good of the whole, the blight caused by sin in one part might be an element of discord to the whole. Paul declares that, whatever discord has thus been caused, the death of Christ was designed to remove it.

Although this purpose embraces everything and everyone in heaven and earth, it is unsafe to infer from it that all men now living on earth will eventually be saved. For, although God's purpose cannot fail as a whole but must receive worthy accomplishment, He has thought fit to make its fulfilment in individuals dependent on themselves, thus leaving it abundantly possible that they who now trample under foot the blood of Christ may be finally cast out both from earth and heaven and thus excluded from this universal harmony. Certainly this purpose is not sufficient to disprove the plain contrary assertion in Ph. iii. 19. See under Ph. ii. 10, 11.

Section 5 reveals the importance of section 4. To the material world around and the angelic world above us, it links the work of redemption as wrought by the same exalted Person and as an accomplishment of one great purpose as wide as creation. Paul thus raises his readers at Colossæ out of the narrow valley of the Lycus where they had lately found personal salvation to a platform from which they can survey the entire universe of God to its utmost bound and the successive ages of the past to the moment when the earliest creature began to be.

This width of view is a conspicuous and invaluable feature of these

Epistles as compared with the earlier ones. Paul has reminded his readers (*v.* 6, so *v.* 23) that the Gospel preached to them was preached also throughout the world. He has led out their thoughts (*v.* 16) to the entire visible universe and to the invisible universe beyond it, to the beginning of the world and of whatever began to be, and (*v.* 17) to the abiding constitution of the manifold realm of creation. In Rom. v. 12—19 Paul traced up sin and death to the first father of the race, and taught that the purpose of salvation was coextensive with the race. He here declares that the same purpose embraces not only earth but heaven. He thus makes the cross of Christ the centre of the universe, and links with it the creation of the earliest and loftiest archangel.

SECTION VI.

THE COLOSSIAN CHRISTIANS IN THEIR RELATION TO CHRIST.

CH. I. 21—23.

And you, formerly alienated as ye were and enemies by your *mind in* your *wicked works, yet now He has reconciled* ^{22} *in the body of His flesh, through death, to present you holy and spotless and unimpeachable before Him ;* ^{23} *if at least ye continue in the faith foundationed and firm and not moving away from the hope of the Gospel which ye heard, the* Gospel *preached in all creation under heaven, of which I Paul became a minister.*

21, 22. *And you :* the Christians at Colossæ now conspicuously brought within the scope and operation of the all-embracing purpose of reconciliation. *Alienated as ye were :* calling conspicuous attention to a fact. It describes their state when this purpose found, and laid hold of, them: cp. Eph. ii. 1, 5, 11. *Alienated-ones,* literally *made-to-be-strangers :* a word frequently used to describe men deprived of the rights of citizens: same word in Eph. ii. 12, iv. 18 ; frequent in the LXX., e.g. Ezek. xiv. 5, 7, Ps. lxix. 9 ; and in classic Greek.

Enemies : either hostile to God, or men who have to reckon with God as hostile to them. Which of these meanings Paul intends here, we can determine only by his general conception of the Gospel. We saw under Rom. v. 1 that the justice of God, which as we learnt from Rom. iii. 26 forbade Him to justify believers except through the death of Christ, makes Him in this sense hostile to those who refuse salvation from sin. Thus an obstacle to peace between God and sinners is found in the justice of God. Now Paul declares in Rom. iii. 24—26, expressly and plainly, that God gave Christ to die in order to remove this obstacle to peace. This last doctrine is, in Rom. v. 10, embodied in the words 'being enemies, we were reconciled to God through the death of His Son,' words almost the same as those now before us. Similarly, in Eph. ii. 12, 16 men *'formerly* . . . *alienated* from the commonwealth of Israel,' Christ came to 'reconcile . . . to God through the cross, having slain the enmity thereby.' On the other hand, only once (Rom. viii. 7) does Paul speak of sin under the aspect of hostility to God. (Jas. iv. 4 admits, and perhaps suggests the sense that they who choose the friendship of the world are thereby placed among those who will have to reckon with God as their enemy.) And Paul never speaks of the cross of Christ as the instrument by which God moves the sinner to lay down his hostility. We are therefore compelled to interpret the words 'reconciled . . . through death' in *v.* 22 as meaning that by the death of Christ God removed the obstacle to peace between God and man which lay in His own justice, and thus brought us out of a position in which we had to reckon with God as an enemy into one in which we look upon Him as a friend. This interpretation of the word 'reconciled' in *v.* 22 fixes in the main the meaning of *enemies* in *v.* 21. We shall find that it will harmonize with the context; and may therefore accept it with confidence. Possibly, however, Paul chose the word *enemies* the more readily because, as matter of fact, sinners are actually hostile to God. Had not Christ died, this double hostility would have been irreconcilable.

Your mind: either the faculty of mental discrimination or the operation of that faculty; senses closely allied. [The Greek dative merely states that this enmity has something to do with the readers' minds, leaving the exact relation to be inferred from the context. The simplest expositions are (1) that the mind was the seat of the enmity, as in Eph. iv. 18 where the same word and case mean 'darkened in their mind;' or (2) that the mind was the instrument by means of which the enmity was brought about, as the Greek dative is used in Gal. ii, 13, Eph. ii. 1, 5, 'dead by means of your trespasses.' This latter sense is required by our exposition of *enemies.* For their entire personality was exposed to the hostility of God. Consequently, further specification of the locality of the enmity was needless. On the other hand, we are eager to know by

what means they became enemies of God. Exposition 2 tells us
that it was by the perverted activity of their intelligence which
mistook evil for good; and which thus, instead of leading them to
God, led them into the ranks of His foes. *In your wicked works:*
immoral locality of this enmity. Same thought in Eph. ii. 2. Led
astray by their own wicked thought they wandered among wicked
actions, and thus became exposed to the just anger of God.

Whether Paul intended to say that the alienation as well as the
enmity were caused *by* his readers' perverted *mind* and had its
locality *in* their *wicked works*, we cannot determine with certainty.
But, as matter of fact, the alienation and the enmity had the same
instrumental cause and the same ideal locality. And the absence
here (contrast Eph. ii. 12, iv. 18) of any further specification of the
word *alienated* suggests that Paul intended to say this.

Before stating how the divine purpose just mentioned has been
accomplished in his readers, Paul describes in *v.* 21 their former
spiritual state. Not only were they aliens destitute of the rights
of sons or even of citizens but they were found in the ranks of the
enemies of God. And this separation and hostility were brought
about by their mistaken mode of thought revealing itself in evil
actions.

22. The change wrought by God, and its further purpose. *But
now:* see under Eph. ii. 13. It throws the present reconciliation
somewhat into contrast with the former alienation and enmity. *He
has reconciled:* has brought out of a position in which they had to
reckon with God as an enemy into one in which they can look upon
Him as a friend. Same word in *v.* 20. As before, the Reconciler
is the Father. *The body of His flesh:* the organized structure of
flesh and blood, and therefore weak and mortal, in which Christ
lived on earth. Same phrase in ch. ii. 11, describing the bodies of
the baptized. Contrast Ph. iii. 21: 'the body of His glory.' This
body, when nailed to the cross, is here thought of as the sacred
locality *in* which the Father reconciled us to Himself. Cp. 2 Cor.
v. 19: 'God was, in Christ, reconciling the world to Himself;'
1 Pet. ii. 24, 'Himself bore our sins in His body.' *Through death:*
the precise means of the reconciliation which took place *in the body
of His flesh.*

In order to present etc.: ultimate purpose of the reconciliation.
Cp. Eph. v. 27. *Present:* as in Eph. v. 27, 2 Cor. iv. 14, xi. 2,
Col. i. 28. *Holy:* subjectively holy, i.e. all our powers actually
devoted to the service of Christ. This is the aim of the objective
holiness which God's claim stamps on all objects claimed by Him.

It is therefore the sense intended wherever holiness is represented as a purpose of God. *Spotless:* as in Ph. ii. 15. It is the negative side of holiness. Whatever is unreservedly devoted to God, is spotless; and that only. *Unimpeachable:* as in 1 Cor. i. 8. *Before Him:* either God, as the same words mean in Eph. i. 4; or as in 2 Cor. v. 10 'before the judgment-seat of Christ.' Since Paul is speaking here chiefly about Christ, to Him probably these words refer. The Father has reconciled us to Himself in order that in the great day He may set us before the searching gaze of Christ our Judge in all the sacredness symbolised in outline in the sacred objects of the Old Covenant, without any blemish being detected by the eye of the Judge, or any charge being brought against us by any accuser. Close parallel in Eph. v. 27; except that there the saved are represented as given by the Son to Himself to be His own, whereas here they are placed by the Father before the Son as if for His inspection.

23. A condition on which depends the accomplishment of the foregoing purpose of God, the condition being so described as to invite fulfilment. *Continue in faith*, or *in your faith:* persevere in believing the Gospel. Similar phrase in Rom. xi. 22, 23, vi. 1. [The particle εἴγε lays great stress upon the condition as absolutely essential to, and certainly followed by, the accomplishment of the divine purpose contingent on it. The present indicative, which might be rendered *if-ye-are-continuing*, suggests inquiry whether we are still retaining our faith or *are-being-moved-away from* it. Contrast Gal. i. 6. But Paul's words give no hint whether his readers were or were not so continuing. They simply state that upon this continuance all depends.]

Foundationed: i.e. *placed-upon-a-foundation:* see under Eph. iii. 17. *Firm:* result of being *on a foundation:* same word in 1 Cor. vii. 37, xv. 58. *And-not-moved-away:* negative counterpart to *foundationed and firm.* [The present passive describes the process of removal as now going on.]

Since the good things promised in the Gospel are contingent on continuance in faith, to surrender faith is to *be moved away from the hope* evoked by, and thus belonging to, *the Gospel.* For both *hope* and the blessings hoped for vanish when faith fails.

Which ye heard; recalls the first preaching of the Gospel at Colossæ. Similar thought in *v.* 5. *In all creation:* literally, *in every creature:* same words as *every creature* in *v.* 15. Surrounded by, and within hearing of, all rational creatures the good news has been proclaimed. *Under the heaven:* a strong hyperbole. Everywhere under the arching firmament the good news has been announced. This is in harmony with the many proofs that this epistle was written near to the end of Paul's life. It testifies how widespread was the preaching of the Gospel. And we can well believe that, just as without any apostolic messenger the good news of salvation had reached Rome, so it had reached all the chief cities of the empire.

The emphatic repetition of a thought already expressed in *v.* 6, viz. the universality of the Gospel, suggests that this thought bears upon the special circumstances of the Colossian Christians. And this we can easily understand. They were in danger (ch. ii. 4) of *being moved away from* their *faith* and *hope* by erroneous teaching. Now such teaching is always local. Only the truth is universal. Paul therefore lifts his readers above their immediate surroundings and reminds them that the Gospel which has given them a new hope has been also proclaimed with the same result all over the world.

Of which Gospel *I Paul:* the writer's relation to this universal Gospel. *I Paul:* as in 2 Cor. x. 1, Gal. v. 2, Eph. iii. 1, 1 Th. ii. 18, Philem. 19. It brings the personality of the heroic Apostle to bear on the matter in hand. To forsake the Gospel, is to forsake him. *Of which* Gospel . . . *a minister:* not as now a technical term for a Christian pastor, but in its ordinary sense of one who renders free and honourable service. Paul is a minister of God, of the New Covenant, of the Church, and of the Gospel: for he does the work of God, makes known the terms of the Covenant, seeks to promote the interests of the Church, and spreads the good news of salvation. So 2 Cor. vi. 4, iii. 6, Col. i. 25, Eph. iii. 7. See note under Rom. xii. 8. The same word is found in its technical sense of *deacon* in Ph. i. 1.

In *v.* 5 Paul thanked God for the blessings awaiting his readers in heaven and already an object of their hope, a hope prompted by the Gospel they had heard. And now, when raising the question whether they are continuing in their early faith and are resting firmly on its sure foundation, he reminds them that upon such continuance depends the accomplishment of God's purpose for their eternal salvation, and that therefore to allow themselves to be carried away from that foundation is to allow themselves to be separated from the bright hope which illumines their path, from the Gospel preached throughout the world, and from the founder of the Churches of Asia Minor and of Greece.

Thus has § 6 brought the eternal purpose of God to bear upon the readers of this Epistle; and has linked them, through the Gospel they had heard, with Paul, its writer. This reference to Paul forms a stepping-stone to § 7.

SECTION VII.

PAUL'S RELATION TO THE CHURCH, AND TO THE COLOSSIAN CHRISTIANS.

CH. I. 24—II. 3.

Now I rejoice in my *sufferings on your behalf, and I fill up the shortcomings of the afflictions of Christ in my flesh on behalf of His body, which is the Church ;* ²⁵ *of which I became a minister according to the stewardship of God which was given to me for you, to fulfil the word of God,* ²⁶ *the mystery which lay hidden from the ages and from the generations—but now it has been manifested to His saints, to* ²⁷ *whom God thought fit to make known what is the wealth of the glory of this mystery among the Gentiles, which is Christ in you, the hope of glory;* ²⁸ *whom we announce, admonishing every man and teaching every man in all wisdom, that we may present every man mature in Christ;* ²⁹ *for which thing I also labour, contending according to His working which works in me with power.*

¹ *For I wish you to know how great a struggle I have on behalf of you and of those in Laodicea, and as many as have not seen my face in* the *flesh,* ² *that their hearts may be encouraged, they being knit together in love and for all wealth of the full assurance of the understanding, for knowledge of the mystery of God, even Christ,* ³ *in whom are all the treasures of wisdom and knowledge hidden.*

After describing Christ's relation to the Father, to the created universe, to the Church, and to the readers of this Epistle, Paul mentioned, in the closing words of § 6, himself and his relation to the Gospel. These closing words are the key-note of § 7. Paul tells us in *vv.* 24—29 his office and work in the universal Church; and in ch. ii. 1—3 his special interest in the Churches of Colossæ and Laodicea.

24. *Now:* 'now that I have become a minister of the Gospel. *My sufferings on your behalf,* or *for your benefit:* the hardships to which Paul exposed himself by preaching the Gospel to the Gentiles. They were a foreseen result of his preaching: and, had he not exposed himself to them, Asia Minor and Colossæ would probably still have been in darkness. Similar thought in Eph. iii. 1, 13; and, from a slightly different point of view, in 2 Cor. i. 6. *Amid* these *sufferings,* and with a joy evidently prompted by them, Paul says *I rejoice.* A similar joy in Ph. ii. 17. A somewhat different but kindred joy in Rom. v. 3. Its great Example: Heb. xii. 2. Doubtless

Paul's joy was prompted by the foreseen results of the work which exposed him to these sufferings. *And I fill up etc.:* an added statement which reveals the import and dignity of these sufferings. *Afflictions of Christ:* a phrase not found elsewhere; whereas we often read of *the afflictions* of His servants. By using it Paul associates His sufferings with theirs. *The short-comings of etc.;* implies that *the afflictions of Christ* were not in themselves sufficient to attain their end. What they fell short, Paul's sufferings *fill up. In my flesh:* the locality of these supplementary sufferings, viz. Paul's body, this being described as *flesh,* i.e. consisting of material liable to suffering and death. *On behalf of His body:* fuller counterpart to *on your behalf.* Paul explains *His body* by reasserting the great metaphor in *v.* 18: *which is the Church.* Notice the contrast between Paul's fragile *flesh,* which by its constitution is weak and liable to decay, and Christ's *Body,* which will survive the destruction of all flesh and share the eternal life and royalty of Christ.

In what sense are these strange words true? In this sense. When Christ breathed His last upon the cross, all the sufferings needful for the complete establishment of the Kingdom of God had not yet been endured. For the full realisation of the purposes of God it was needful, not only that Christ should die for the sins of the world, but that the Gospel should be preached to all nations. This involved, owing to the wickedness of men, hardship to the preachers. This hardship Paul willingly endured in order to save men. Consequently, just as the life on earth of the servants of Christ is in some sense an extension of His incarnation, (for in them He lives, Gal. ii. 20,) so the sufferings of Paul were in a similar sense a continuation and completion of the sufferings of Christ. This is in close harmony with, and further emphasises, Paul's constant teaching that Christ's servants share all that Christ has and is and does: 1 Cor. 1, 9, Ph. iii. 10, Rom. viii. 17. But it by no means suggests that Paul's sufferings were in any sense propitiatory or that Christ's sufferings were not so. For the one point in common here mentioned and made conspicuous by repetition is suffering *on behalf of* another. Propitiation for sin is here entirely out of view.

Notice the infinite dignity here given to sufferings endured for the spread of the Gospel. These, Christ condescends to join with His own mysterious agony on the cross as endured for the benefit of the Church which He recognises as His own body. *In* such sacred *sufferings* well might Paul *rejoice.* Notice again, as in *v.* 18 in conjunction with the same metaphor, *the Church* Universal.

25. Paul's relation to the Church. This explains his sufferings on

its behalf. He 'became (v. 23) a minister of the Gospel' as one appointed to do the free and honourable service of proclaiming it: he *became a minister of* the Church as one appointed to labour for its advancement. Same phrase in Rom. xvi. 1; used, not as here in a general sense, but in the technical sense of 'deaconess.' *Stewardship of God:* position of one entrusted by God with wealth for distribution to others: so Tit. i. 7, 1 Cor. iv. 1, ix. 17; cp. 1 Tim. iii. 15. A close parallel in Eph. iii. 2: see also under Eph. i. 10. *For you:* persons for whose benefit this stewardship had been entrusted to Paul. It is, therefore, parallel to 'on your behalf' in v. 24. And it is true of the Christians at Colossæ in the same sense as is Rom. i. 6 of those at Rome. The stewardship given to Paul embraced both Rome and Colossæ. That Paul calls himself a *minister of* the Church, is in harmony with (*according to*) the fact that a *stewardship* of the spiritual wealth *of God* has been *given* to him for his readers. *To fulfil the word of God:* to achieve the full aim of the Gospel, by proclaiming everywhere to Jew and Gentile salvation through faith in Christ, and by leading men to accept it. So Rom. xv. 19: 'fulfil the Gospel.' This fulfilment is here said to be the aim of the stewardship entrusted to Paul. Prophecy and law (Mt. i. 22, Rom. xiii. 8) are fulfilled by their realisation in the foretold event and in actual obedience.

26. Further exposition of 'the word of God.' *The mystery hidden:* favourite thought of Paul; 1 Cor. ii. 7, Rom. xvi. 25, Eph. iii. 4, 5. It is God's eternal purpose to save men through Christ without reference to nationality on the one condition of faith, in the manner described in the Gospel. This purpose is a *mystery*, i.e. a secret known only by those to whom God reveals it by His Spirit. See my *Corinthians* p. 60. It was formed (1 Cor. ii. 7) 'before the ages.' But, inasmuch as it was revealed only (Rom. i. 17) in the Gospel, it lay *hid from the ages*, i.e. from the beginning of the successive periods of human history until the Gospel was proclaimed by Christ; *and from the generations*, i.e. from the successive sets of men living at one time. This last word, in Ph. ii. 15, Eph. iii. 5, Lk. xi. 50, 51. The contrast of *but now manifested* suggests that *from* is chiefly a note of time, as in Mt. xiii. 35. It is the more suitable here because the hidden secret was, during those early ages, away *from* the knowledge of men.

But now it has been manifested: a break in the grammatical structure of the sentence, noting very conspicuously a break in the agelong silence. *Manifested:* set conspicuously before the eyes of men. Same word and same connection in Rom. xvi. 26: see under

Rom. i. 19. *To His saints:* to Christians generally, according to constant N. T. use: so *vv.* 2, 12, iii. 12, Ph. iv. 21, 22. In one sense the secret has been set before the eyes of all to whom the Gospel is preached. But inasmuch as none can see it except those whom God saves from spiritual blindness and thus claims to be His own, Paul says that it was *manifested to His saints.* Since the manifested secret is (*v.* 17) that Christ is in the Colossian Christians who were Gentiles, possibly these *saints* were primarily the Jews who first believed in Christ and thus became His people. To them was revealed the new and great truth that believing Gentiles were to share with them the blessings of the New Covenant. A recognition of this truth is recorded in Acts xi. 18.

27. Further statement expounding 'the mystery manifested to His saints.' *God thought-fit,* or *it was the will of God:* cp. Eph. i. 5, 9, 11. The insertion of this word detains us for a moment to look at the secret now manifested when it was only a determined purpose in the mind of God. *Make-known;* includes the subjective appropriation of 'the mystery manifested to,' i.e. set conspicuously before, 'the saints.' *What is:* of what kind, and how much. *The riches etc.:* the abundance, making its possessors rich, of the splendour which belongs to this great secret: same phrase in Eph. i. 18, iii. 16. Cp. Col. ii. 2, Eph. i. 7, ii. 7, iii. 8, Rom. xi. 33. The spiritual wealth in Christ is a favourite conception of Paul. The frequency of the word *glory* to describe the splendour of the final consummation suggests that this is its meaning here. And this is confirmed by the same word at the end of the verse. Cp. ch. iii. 4, 2 Cor. iii. 7—11, Rom. v. 2. God was minded to make known how abundant is the splendour with which in the great day those initiated on earth into the Gospel secret will be enriched. *Among the Gentiles,* or *in the Gentiles:* same Greek preposition again in the same verse, *in* or *among you:* and, with similar compass, in Gal. iii. 5. It includes both senses. As matter of fact, the abundance of glory is both *among the Gentiles* as a spiritual possession of the whole community, and *within* them as a spiritual possession enjoyed in the inner life of each one. But this full latitude of meaning cannot be expressed by any one English word. The Gentiles taken as a whole and taken individually are the personal locality of the abundance of glory with which *this mystery* will enrich those who know it. Similar words and connection in Eph. i. 18. The great secret was Paul's Gospel, viz. that by faith and in proportion to their faith God receives into His favour, moulds into the inward image of Christ, and will some day cover with splendour, all who believe the good

news announced by Christ. This implies that even Gentiles will be thus received and glorified. And to a Jew, e.g. to Paul, this inclusion of the Gentiles in the coming glory was the most conspicuous feature of the Gospel revelation. To him this was the secret hidden during ages, but now manifested.

Which is; may refer grammatically either to *the wealth of the glory of the mystery,* throwing emphasis on the abundance of the splendour, or specifically to *this mystery.* This latter reference is suggested by the conspicuous repetition of the word mystery in *vv.* 26, 27. Moreover, *Christ in you* is not the abundance of the mystery, but the mystery itself. *In* or *within you* is better than *among you.* For we are ever taught that Christ dwells in the hearts of His people: so Eph. iii. 17, Rom. viii. 10. The word *you* includes the Gentile Christians to whom Paul writes. *Hope of glory:* expectation of the splendour of heaven, as in Rom. v. 1; cp. Tit. i. 2. The felt presence of Christ in our hearts (cp. 1 Jno. iii. 24) assures us that we are in the way of life leading to endless *glory.* Thus *Christ in us* and *the hope of glory* go together; and therefore may be spoken of as equivalent. So 1 Tim. i. 1, 'Christ Jesus our hope;' cp. Col. iii. 3. This presence of Christ in us, Himself a pledge of our eternal splendour, is a *mystery,* i.e. a secret which cannot be conveyed by human words, known only by actual experience and therefore known only by those whom God takes by the hand, leads into His own secret chamber, and teaches as only God can teach. And it will enrich the initiated with the abundant splendour of heaven. All this was for long ages a hidden purpose of God. But He had been pleased to make it known in Paul's day. 'It had been manifested to His saints.'

28. In *v.* 25 Paul rose from himself and his stewardship to the Gospel of God, the great mystery kept secret during long ages but now revealed. This led him to its great matter, viz. Christ. He now returns to the chief thought of § 7, himself and his work. *We:* very emphatic, suggesting perhaps others who acted otherwise. Paul and his companions *announce* Christ. Same word in Ph. i. 17, 18; 1 Cor. ii. 1, ix. 14, xi. 26. *Admonish:* 1 Cor. iv. 14, x. 11, Rom. xv. 14. It includes all kinds of friendly discipline and training, as of a father, brother, or companion; especially reproof with a view to improvement. *Teaching;* is mere impartation of knowledge: cp. ch. iii. 16, Mt. xxviii. 20. *Wisdom:* see under 1 Cor. ii. 5. *In all wisdom:* Col. i. 9, iii. 16, Eph. i. 8. A wisdom in which no element was lacking was the instrument of Paul's teaching. It was from God: 1 Cor. xii. 8, Eph. i. 8, Jas. i. 5, iii. 17. So 2 Cor. i. 12, 'not in fleshly wisdom;' and 1 Cor. i. 17, 'not in wisdom of word.' Against these Paul sets in 1 Cor. ii. 6 a higher wisdom. Armed with it, he teaches every man who comes within his reach. The basis of this varied training is Christ: *whom we announce.*

That we may etc.: practical aim of Paul's teaching. It should be the one aim of all religious teachers. *Present:* as in v. 22. It is Paul's appropriation of God's purpose there stated. Cp. 2 Cor. xi. 2. God reconciled to Himself the Colossian Christians that in the great day He might set them faultless before Christ the Judge: for the same end Paul corrects and teaches all within his reach. *Mature* or *full-grown:* in contrast to 'babes in Christ.' Cp. 1 Cor. iii. 1, Eph. iv. 13, 14. See under 1 Cor. ii. 6. *In Christ:* the encompassing element of this full growth. The emphatic repetition, *every man . . . every man . . . every man,* makes conspicuous the universality of Paul's aim. Every one he meets is to him a possibility of another fully-developed trophy presented in the final triumph. Consequently, *every man* is an object for the discipline and teaching needful to make this possibility actual.

29. After stating in v. 28 his aim in announcing Christ, Paul now records the earnestness with which he pursues it, and the divine source of this earnestness *For which thing:* 'that we may present' etc. Not only does Paul announce Christ, but *also* does this with an earnestness which involves weariness: *I also labour.* Same word and thought in Ph. ii. 16, Gal. iv. 11, 1 Cor. xv. 10. *Contend,* i.e. in the athletic festivals: same word in 1 Cor. ix. 25, where see note, and in Col. iv. 12. It amplifies and explains *I-labour.* So intense are Paul's efforts to save men that he compares them to the intense bodily struggles of a Greek athlete contending for a prize against an equally earnest antagonist. Such *struggle* was *labour* of the severest kind. Same words together in 1 Tim. iv. 10. The word *contend* suggests opponents. And not only is the Christian life itself (Eph. vi. 12) a conflict with spiritual foes, but Paul had in his evangelical efforts actual human opponents: e.g. Col. ii. 4, 2 Cor. x. 10. But of such there is no hint here or in ch. ii. 1. Our thoughts are concentrated on the earnestness of Paul's efforts to save men. And this earnestness sufficiently accounts for the word here used. So ch. iv. 12, where there is no thought of opponents.

According to the working: same words in Ph. iii. 21; see note. Underlying Paul's activity, stimulating and directing it, was a corresponding divine activity. *His working:* probably Christ's, who has just been mentioned. But the distinction is unimportant. The inward activity is from the Father through the Son. *The working which works:* emphatic repetition; so Eph. i. 19. *In me:* so Ph. ii. 13, Eph. iii. 20, ii. 2. *In power:* or less accurately *with power*, i.e. clothed with ability to produce results. And this inward working of Christ evokes, as its appropriate outworking, intense effort of Paul himself like the struggle of an athlete: *according to His working* etc. Thus Paul's proclamation of Christ becomes *labour*.

Notice here as in 2 Cor. x. 7—11 the ease with which Paul passes from 'we' to *I*, and conversely. He remembers his companions and says *whom we announce:* he remembers his own personal and in some sense solitary effort, and says *I labour, works in me*.

II. 1. *For I wish* etc.; supports the foregoing assertion by a proof case, viz. Paul's inward struggle for his readers' good. *Struggle*, or *conflict:* the substantive from which is derived the verb rendered 'contend' in the last verse. It is the Greek original of our word *agony;* and is the technical term for the Greek athletic contests. The verb and substantive are together also in 1 Tim. vi. 12, 2 Tim. iv. 7. From the aim stated in *v.* 2 we learn that this struggle was practically the same as that of Epaphras mentioned in ch. iv. 12, 'agonizing on your behalf in his prayers that ye may stand mature and fully assured.' *On your behalf:* i.e. for your benefit: cp. ch. i. 24, 'sufferings on your behalf.' *Laodicea:* see Intro. iv. 3. Grammatically, the words *have not seen my flesh* might or might not include Colossæ as well as Laodicea. But these words seem to give a reason for Paul's anxiety. And the reason must be valid for both Churches. Moreover, they were so near that if Paul had visited one he would almost certainly have visited the other. We therefore infer with confidence that Paul had never been in the valley of the Lycus. But he knew that there were Christians there. And so anxious was he for their good, while unable directly to help them, that his thoughts about them became a spiritual conflict. Naturally he says *I wish you to know* this: same words in 1 Cor. xi. 3; similar words in ch. x. 1, xii. 1, etc. *In flesh;* gives greater definiteness to the bodily presence involved in *seen my face*. Cp. Eph. ii. 11, 'the Gentiles in flesh.'

2. Aim of Paul's struggles on his readers' behalf. It determines the nature of the struggle. *Encouraged:* same word as *exhort* in Rom. xii. 1, and very common with Paul: cp. Rom. i. 12. It denotes speech designed to rouse men to courage, endurance, or action. *Hearts be encouraged:* same words in ch. iv. 8, Eph. vi. 22, 2 Th. ii. 17. Paul wishes the encouragement to reach the inmost centre of their emotions and the inmost source of their actions. *Their:* not 'your.' It suggests that this inward struggle is not specially for the Christians at Colossæ but for all whom Paul has not seen. *Knit-together:* same word in v. 19, Eph. iv. 16. It denotes the harmonious fitting together of various parts into one whole, each part supplementing the others and helping the whole. *In love:* mutual Christian love, as in 1 Cor. xiii., where see note. It is the encompassing element and bond of this union: cp. Col. iii. 14. *Ye-being* (or better *having-been*) knit together: this loving union one with another being the means by which their *hearts* are to receive *encouragement*. To the encompassing element of this union, viz. *in love*, Paul adds its aim : *and for all wealth etc.* Cp. i. 27. This aim is collateral with that already expressed, *that their hearts etc.* It is another purpose which Paul has in view in his earnest struggle for his readers. The unity which is to bring them encouragement is designed also to lead *to the full assurance of the understanding*, and indeed *to a knowledge of the mystery of God. Full assurance:* same word in 1 Th. i. 5, Heb. vi. 11, x. 22. The cognate verb in Col. iv. 12, Rom. iv. 21, xiv. 5, Lk. i. 1. It is a certainty which fills us. *Understanding:* as in ch. i. 9. *The full assurance* results from the faculty of interpreting the various objects presented to the mind. Such assurance Paul desires his readers to have in an abundance which will make them rich; and as a condition of it desires for them the unity of mutual love. More fully stated, the aim of this unity is *for knowledge of the mystery of God.* These last words keep before us, and by keeping so long before us greatly emphasise, the thought embodied in the word *mystery* in ch. i. 26, 27.

On the various readings here, see Introd. iii. 2. The last words of v. 2 may be rendered either *the God of Christ* or *of God, even of Christ*, or *the mystery of God, even Christ.* This last exposition is at once suggested by ch. i. 27 where 'Christ in you' is Himself 'the mystery.' And it is confirmed by the context; and by the aim of the whole Epistle, which is to set forth the mysterious grandeur of the Son of God. To know Christ, i.e. to comprehend the purpose of His incarnation with an acquaintance derived from personal contact with Him, is to know the mystery of God, i.e. the purpose kept secret during long ages and now revealed, viz. that without respect of nationality God will receive into His favour and cover with eternal glory those who believe the Gospel. The above exposition is confirmed by the word 'hidden' in v. 3, which recalls the same word in ch. i. 26. *Knowledge*, or *full-knowledge:* same word in ch. i. 9, 10: cp. Eph. i. 17, 'in knowledge of Him.'

3. Statement about Christ, proving that He is 'the mystery of

God.' *In whom:* i.e. in Christ, immediately preceding. To refer it to the more distant word 'mystery,' would be an impossible leap over the word 'Christ' and over the important implied assertion that He is 'the mystery of God.' And it would make the word *hidden* almost meaningless: for all mysteries are hidden. Whereas as expounded above the word *hidden* justifies the assumed equivalence of 'Christ' and 'the mystery of God.'

Wisdom: such acquaintance with the great realities as enables a man to choose the best steps in life. See my *Corinthians* p. 47. *Knowledge:* acquaintance with things seen or unseen, great or small. The nearness of the nobler word *wisdom*, which occupies part of the ground usually covered by the word *knowledge*, limits somewhat this last word to matters which have come under our immediate observation. The two words are together in Rom. xi. 33, Eccl. i. 16, 17, 18, ii. 21, 26, ix. 10; in all which places except the last *wisdom* comes first. The word rendered *treasure* denotes in Mt. ii. 11, xii. 35 the place where valuables are kept for safety; in Mt. vi. 19, 20, 21, the valuables themselves. Here it has the latter sense: for Christ is Himself the personal locality of the laid-up wealth. *All the treasures:* all the many forms of spiritual wealth with which wisdom and knowledge enrich their possessors, and which are all to be found in Christ. It is parallel with, and expounds, 'all wealth of the full assurance of the understanding.' Compare Plato, *Philebus* p. 15e, 'having found some treasure of wisdom;' Xenophon, *Memoirs* bk. iv. 2, 9, 'not treasures of silver and gold rather than of wisdom.' In Christ this wealth of wisdom lies out of sight: *hidden.* The idea of concealment, frequently associated with the word treasure, does not necessarily belong to it. For laid-up wealth is not always out of sight. But the 'mystery of God' is essentially *hidden:* close parallel in 1 Cor. ii. 7, 'God's wisdom, in a mystery, the hidden' wisdom. Fully to know Christ, is to know the hidden truths of priceless worth which none know except they whom God leads into His secret chamber and whose eyes He opens to see this inner light. They who know this are indeed rich. But this knowledge is possible only to those whom Christian love knits together in a union which fills their hearts with encouragement; and only to those who are themselves in Christ and thus know and possess, in measure, whatever is in Him: *in whom are all the treasures . . . hidden.*

Such is Paul's earnest and agonizing desire for His readers. His tender sympathy longs to cheer their hearts. But for real encouragement there must be loving union among themselves. Such union will open the channels of the inner life, and will enrich them with an assured comprehension of the great realities known only to those who know Christ. In other words, for those whom he has never seen Paul desires the same blessings as for those to whom he has personally preached Christ.

SECTION 7 describes Paul's relation to the Gospel which has saved his readers. The preaching of the Gospel brings upon him hardship. But this hardship gives him joy: for he remembers its sacred relation to the sufferings of Christ, and its sacred purpose, viz. to benefit the body of Christ. It is inseparably involved in the work, committed to him by God, of making known the great secret, precious and glorious beyond description and hidden during long ages, that Christ dwells in men on earth, a pledge of future glory. This secret Paul proclaims to all within his reach, endeavouring thus to save every one. Hence his strenuous effort for the good not only of those whom he personally teaches but of those Christians who have never seen his face. For all men everywhere, he desires a full knowledge of the profound mystery of God which lies hidden in Christ.

DIVISION II., embracing Chs. i. 15—ii. 3, is Paul's fullest delineation of the Person and Work of the Son of God. He notes first Christ's relation to the Father, as an Image of the Invisible One; and as born, whereas all others were created. He then notes His similar relation to the created universe, to the universal Church, and to the Church at Colossæ; viz. as the Agent through whom all things came into being. Consequently, He is earlier than the brightest in heaven, and holds together in His grasp the entire universe. Similarly, He was the first to pass triumphantly through death. As wide as the universe is the purpose of redemption: for its aim is to reconcile to God all things in heaven and earth. And the Gospel which has brought salvation to Colossæ has done so in all the world. Thus throughout DIV. II. we hear again the note of universality already sounded (ch. i. 6) in DIV. I. All this reminds Paul of the grandeur of the truth which in his own day God had made known to men, a truth hidden during long ages. God had given to men, not truth only, but the living presence in their hearts of Him who made the world, Himself a pledge in them of future blessedness. Remembrance of this moves Paul to strenuous effort to make Christ known everywhere. He has warned his readers that their share in the blessings hidden yet revealed in Christ depends upon their continuance in the word they have already received. How needful was this warning we shall learn from DIV. III.

Notice here (ch. i. 18, 24) the important metaphor of the body of Christ, and the Gospel described (ch. i. 26, 27, ii. 2) as a mystery; aspects of truth already conspicuous in 1 Cor. xii. 12—27 and in 1 Cor. ii. 7, Rom. xvi. 25, and peculiar to Paul.

DIVISION III.
WARNING AGAINST ERRORS.
CH. II. 4—III. 4.

SECTION VIII.
DO NOT FORSAKE THE TEACHING ALREADY RECEIVED.
CH. II. 4—7.

This I say in order that no one may delude you with persuasive speech. ⁵ *For, if indeed in the flesh I am absent, yet in the spirit I am with you, rejoicing and beholding your order and the firmness of your faith in Christ.* ⁶ *As then ye have received Christ Jesus the Lord, walk in Him,* ⁷ *rooted and being built up in Him and being established by* your *faith, according as ye were taught, abounding in thanksgiving.* (Or *abounding in it with thanksgiving.*)

4. Hitherto, although in ch. i. 9 we have the occasion of Paul's praise and prayer for his readers, viz. the good news about them brought by Epaphras, and although v. 23 has suggested a danger of their 'being moved away' from the safe anchorage of their hope, we have had no mention yet of any specific aim of this Epistle. Now for the first time we have a clearly stated and definite aim, viz. to guard the Colossian Christians from erroneous teaching. *I say this:* not merely v. 3; for as we have seen this was added to explain and justify the words preceding. Moreover, v. 5 bears directly on v. 1: and the words 'mystery of God' in v. 2 take up similar words in ch. i. 26. Thus the words *I say this* recall the entire teaching of Div. II., of which indeed ch. ii. 3 is but a compact summing up. In other words, Paul's invaluable exposition of the nature and work of the Son of God was given, not merely to instruct and edify, but

as a safeguard against persuasive error. A good example for us. The only real safeguard against the manifold religious errors is an intelligent and comprehensive knowledge of the central doctrines of the Gospel. Such expositions of truth have abiding worth even when the errors they were designed to combat have passed utterly away. Paul's method of defence makes all the difference between the living epistle before us and the obsolete *Refutation* of Irenæus.

Delude you: 'reason you away from the line.' It is a modification of Paul's favourite word *reckon* in Rom. ii. 3, 26, etc.; and denotes perverse reckoning. With *persuasive-speech:* cp. Rom. xvi. 18, 'by means of smooth-speech and fine-speech deceive the hearts of the innocent;' 1 Cor. ii. 4, 'persuasive words of wisdom.' This persuasiveness does not in itself imply error. The error lies in the word *delude*. What specific delusion Paul has in view, we must learn from the specific warnings following.

5. *For if etc.;* explains the interest in the readers which prompted the foregoing warning, and thus tacitly and very kindly supports it. *Flesh . . . spirit:* favourite contrast of Paul. It is practically the same as 'body' and 'spirit' in 1 Cor. v. 3. While the weak and mortal *flesh* of Paul lingered in prison at Rome, the eye of his *spirit* was fixed on the Christians at Colossæ. *Rejoicing and beholding:* as though the narrative of Epaphras at once gave Paul joy; and led him to contemplate with abiding interest his readers' military regularity and solidity. *Order:* same word and sense in 1 Cor. xiv. 40; cognate word in ch. xv. 23: a not uncommon military term. *Firmness:* or better, *firm-front*. It denotes something made firm. *Of your faith in Christ:* 'the solid front which your faith enables you to present.' Cp. Acts xvi. 5: 'made firm by faith.' The Christians at Colossæ held their position as good soldiers: and their faith in Christ enabled them to present to every enemy an immoveable line of battle. The military tone of this verse suggests that looseness in faith exposes Christians to disastrous overthrow. The phrase rendered *faith in Christ* is not found elsewhere in the N. T.: but we have 'faith towards God' in 1 Th. i. 8, Philem. 5; and a similar phrase 'believe in God' or 'in Christ' in Rom. x. 14, Ph. i. 29, 1 Pet. i. 8, 21, and frequently in the Fourth Gospel.

The truthfulness of Paul compels us to accept these words as complete proof that the Christians at Colossæ had not yet been actually led away by the delusion against which he now warns them. If so, this verse is not only a courteous, but a necessary, recognition, in view of the warnings which follow, of their loyal adherence to the truth.

6. An exhortation, based on v. 5, and followed in v. 7 by collateral details of manner. *Received:* same word in Jno. i. 11, 'His own people received Him not.' Frequently used by Paul in reference to the Gospel he received from Christ: 1 Cor. xi. 23, xv. 1, 3, Gal. i. 9, 12. They who welcome the good news of salvation thereby receive Christ Himself to be their Lord and their life. *As then,* or *inasmuch then as,* ye received etc.: practical application of v. 5. That they have *received Christ* and have thus obtained spiritual solidity, is good reason why they should *walk in Him:* cp. ch. iv. 5, 'walk in wisdom;' Eph. v. 2, 'in love.' 'Let the personality of Christ be the encompassing and guiding and controlling element of every step in life.' Cp. Gal. v. 25: 'If we live by the Spirit, by the Spirit let us also walk.' A good beginning is reason for continuing in the same path.

7. Collateral details about the walk in life which Paul desires for his readers. *Rooted,* same word and form in Eph. iii. 18. It suggests stability and nourishment and life derived from inward contact with Christ: *in Him. Built-up:* same composite word in Eph. ii. 20, 1 Cor. iii. 10, 12, 14, Jude 20. It calls attention to the foundation *on* which the building rises. This second metaphor adds the idea of stability derived from the mutual cohesion of various component parts. [Notice a conspicuous change of tenses. The Greek perfect *rooted* denotes an abiding result of a past event: the present *being-built-up* describes a process now going on. Our 'walk in Him' is a present result of our having first taken root in Christ; and continues only so long as we retain our hold of Him. And, while we walk in Him, our spiritual life, which derives stability from union with our fellow-Christians, makes progress day by day like the rising walls of a building.] Each metaphor supplements the other. The former suggests organic life, and nourishment: the latter suggests strength derived from union of various parts. The words *in Him* forsake the metaphor of a *building,* in order to recall the foregoing exhortation, 'walk in Him,' and to keep before us the inwardness of that union with Christ from which the members of His Church derive cohesion and stability. A condition and accompaniment of our walk in Christ is that we retain our inward grasp of Him and that by compact union with our fellows the Christian life makes daily progress in us. *Being-made-firm by faith:* another collateral detail supporting the foregoing metaphor by singling out and stating in plain language its chief element, viz. immoveable firmness, and by pointing to the channel through which spiritual firmness comes, viz. *faith.*

[The dative of instrument, as in ch. i. 10, is more likely here than that of limitation. For we need to know the channel through which comes the firmness implied in *built-up* rather than the particular element of our spiritual life in which that firmness is to be found: for evidently the whole man is made firm in Christ.] They who rest on the promises of God are themselves immoveable. These last words recall 'the firmness of your faith' in *v.* 5.

According as ye were taught: the directive rule of their *faith*: cp. ch. i. 7, 'according as ye learnt from Epaphras.' The teaching which already has brought them out of darkness into light is to be the guide of their present faith. Similar argument in Gal. iii. 3. *Thanksgiving* is to be associated with *faith;* as in Ph. iv. 6 with prayer. And so abundant are the reasons for gratitude that Paul prescribes for his readers an overflow of thanks: *abounding with thanksgiving:* cp. Ph. iv. 6.

Paul reminds the Christians at Colossæ that they have already accepted Christ as their Lord, and bids them now walk in Him they have received. In other words, he urges that their outward life correspond with the beginning of their Christian profession. There must be continued inward grasp of Christ, firm cohesion with their fellows and progress, and the solidity which faith gives; all this on the lines laid down by those who have led them to Christ, and mingled with thanks to God.

As yet we have learnt nothing about the specific danger which prompted Paul's warning, except that it is one against which the foregoing exposition of the dignity of Christ will shield his readers, and one which threatens to lead them away from the path which at their conversion they entered. We wait for more definite information about the specific and plausible error Paul has in view.

SECTION IX.

WARNING AGAINST ERROR IN THE GUISE OF PHILOSOPHY AND JUDAISM.

CH. II. 8—15.

Take heed lest there will be any one making plunder of you through philosophy and empty deception, according to the tradition of men, according to the rudiments of the world, and not according to Christ. ⁹*Because in Him dwells all the fulness of the Godhead bodily.*

[10] *And in Him ye are made full; who is the Head of all principality and authority;* [11] *in whom ye were also circumcised with a circumcision not made with hands, in the putting off of the body of the flesh, in the circumcision of Christ,* [12] *having been buried with Him in Baptism: wherein* (or *in whom*) *also ye were raised with* Him *through belief of the working of God who raised Him from the dead.* [13] *And you, being dead by* your *trespasses and the uncircumcision of your flesh, He has made you alive with Him, having forgiven us all the trespasses,* [14] *having blotted out the handwriting against us with the dogmas, which was contrary to us: and He has taken it out of the midst, having nailed it to the cross;* [15] *having stripped off from Himself the principalities and the authorities, He made a show* of them *openly, having led them in triumph in it.*

8. Specific danger against which Paul warns his readers. *Take-heed* or *see-to-it:* same word as *behold* in *v.* 5. It denotes simply an act of sight: 'have your eyes open lest' etc. *Making-plunder-of:* or literally *lead-away-plunder.* Paul fears lest his readers be themselves led away by an enemy as spoil. For error enslaves both body and soul. This exposition is suggested by the use in one or two places of this rare Greek word, and of similar words. It is a compound of the word used in 2 Cor. xi. 8; where Churches are said to have been *plundered* by Paul who received their contribution to do work for others.

Through philosophy etc.: means by which Paul feared that his readers might be led captive. *Philosophy:* literally *love-of-wisdom:* a common Greek word. Diogenes Laertius tells us (*Lives of Philosophers* Introd. 12) that Pythagoras was the first to call himself a philosopher or lover of wisdom, on the ground that 'no one is wise except God.' In this sense, the word is one of the noblest in human language, denoting man's effort to understand that which is best worth knowing. In a somewhat similar sense, it is used by Philo to describe the religious teaching of the Jews: e.g. vol. i. 613, 'they who philosophize according to Moses.' And Josephus speaks (*Antiq.* bk. xviii. 1. 1, 2) of the schools of thought embodied in the Jewish sects, Pharisees, Sadducees, Essenes, as philosophies. This last use helps us to understand how a word with an origin so good came to have, as here, a sense evidently bad. Under the guise of professed love of wisdom, men attached themselves to schools putting forth their own explanations of the phenomena of life, explanations for the more part artificial and baseless. Of such baseless philosophies we have abundant and various examples in the many

Gnostic systems prevalent in the second century, strange mixtures of the Gospel with earlier Jewish and Gentile teaching. See note on THE GNOSTICS at the end of this Exposition. These were called *philosophy*: and we shall see that to something of this sort probably Paul refers here. *Deceit:* the teachers of this philosophy being either deceivers or themselves deceived. *Empty:* a hollow form of error.

That both words are under one article, suggests that *philosophy* and *error* are two sides of one instrument of seduction. It claimed to be a search for wisdom : actually it was a hollow deception. A close parallel in 1 Tim. vi. 20, 'the profane empty-voices and oppositions of knowledge falsely so named.' For the precise nature of this teaching we must seek in the warnings which follow and in the foregoing exposition of truth which Paul tells us was written as a safeguard against this persuasive error.

According to . . . *according to* . . . *not according to:* description, positive and negative, of the path along which the captives were led. *Tradition of men:* same words in Mk. vii. 8 ; cp. *vv.* 3, 5, 9, 13 : a close and instructive parallel. Cp. Gal. i. 14 ; and contrast 1 Cor. xi. 2, 2 Th. ii. 15, iii. 6. They who are led away by this philosophy go along a path marked out by no higher authority than that *of men*, from whom it has been handed down. All teaching is apt to become mere *tradition*. For it is easier to learn to repeat results than to understand the processes by which they have been attained and the proofs on which they rest ; easier to accept as decisive a master's *ipse dixit* than to follow his reasoning. False teaching is specially liable to become a tradition. For it has no basis of truth. A conspicuous example of tradition is found in the Talmud which consists almost entirely of assertions of celebrated Jewish teachers ; the greater part having no ground whatever except the teacher's authority. See Barclay's selections in English from the *Talmud*. Similarly the Gnostics handed down secret doctrines professedly received from one or other of the Apostles.

The rudiments of the world: same words and sense in Gal. iv. 3, where see note : the rudimentary teaching derived from the material world. In some sense both Greek philosophy and O. T. ritual were on their better side rudimentary forms of teaching preparatory to the Gospel. And with all false teaching are associated such rudimentary elements of truth. Otherwise the falsehood would not live. In Gal. iv. 3 we learn that this rudimentary teaching brings men 'under bondage.' Similarly, they who seek to lead captive the Colossian Christians would lead them along a path marked out by the traditions of men and by the rudimentary teaching of the material world. Of these two delineations of this wrong path, possibly *the traditions of men* recall rather Jewish teaching; and *the rudiments of the world* that of Gentiles. *And not according to Christ:* not taking for their guide the nature and purposes of Christ. Cp. Rom. xv. 5. And this agrees with Paul's exposition in DIV. II. of the nature and work of Christ, as a safeguard against prevalent error; and especially with the last words of this exposition, 'Christ, in whom are all the treasures of wisdom and knowledge.'

9. A great truth proving, as *v.* 8 assumes, that every path 'not according to Christ' leads astray. That which in ch. i. 19 was a divine purpose is here stated to be an abiding reality: *in Him dwells. All the fulness:* as in ch. i. 19, but now defined by the words *of the Godhead,* or *Deity.* It denotes all that distinguishes God from the highest of His creatures; all the attributes and powers of which God is full, and in which our conception of God finds its realisation. These have an abiding home in the God-Man, and are 'His fulness:' cp. Jno. i. 14. The overflow of this fulness fills us. And because the Eternal Son wears a human body, *in Him* this *fulness dwells bodily:* i.e. in bodily form and manner. We may perhaps reverently say that in the Eternal Son dwelt from eternity the fulness of the Deity. At the Incarnation, the same fulness, dwelling unchangeably in Him, assumed bodily form. And in the glorified humanity of Christ this bodily form continues, as henceforth the abiding dwelling-place of all the perfections of God. The Son assumed bodily form in order that this fulness might fill us, supplying all our need and enabling us to attain the true aim of our being. Now, inasmuch as in Christ dwells this fulness, His nature ought to be the norm of our action. For His fulness is our hope. Consequently, every path which is 'not according to Christ' leads away from the goal of our life.

10. *And we are etc.:* one step farther, viz. from Christ to His people. *Ye are in Him:* as your refuge and bulwark and home. Consequently, since He is full, *in Him ye are made-full* or *made-complete:* same word as in ch. i. 9, 25. It denotes a filling up of an outline of any kind. The outline here is sketched by the needs and aim of our being. They who are in Christ, and so far as they are in Him, find in Him their need supplied and their goal attained. In them remain no unfilled chasms. They have therefore no need to seek anything away from Christ.

All principality and authority: same words in same order in ch. i. 16, and apparently in the same sense, viz. different ranks of angelic powers. Their mention here, after the earlier mention there, suggests very strongly that they had something to do with the error prevalent at Colossæ. And this is confirmed by the same words again in *v.* 15 and by the mention of angels in *v.* 18. See further in the note under ch. iii. 4. Paul here says that, whatever angelic powers have rule or authority over men, of all such Christ *is the Head*. This implies that He is not only their Ruler but stands to them in the relation of the head to the various members of a living body, viz. the living and controlling source of their power and action. Consequently, any trust in angels which leads away from Christ springs from ignorance of their relation to Him.

Notice that the angels, who are here said to be vitally united to Christ as their Head were also created by Him. In other words, their continued life depends upon their abiding union with Him from whom they first received it: and they use their powers under the direction of Him from whom these powers were derived. Doubtless it was to prepare the way for this important harmony, and thus to overturn an error which practically set the angels against Christ, that Paul taught in ch. i. 16 that 'through Him' even the angels 'were created;' a statement nowhere found from his pen except in this Epistle written to dispel this special error.

Notice also that Christ bears to the Church (ch. i. 18) and to the angels the same relation of Head: another important harmony. Both men and angels spring from Him: and of both angels and redeemed mankind He is the Head.

11, 12a. Another important truth added to those foregoing. *Not-made-with-hands:* i.e. superhuman. It emphasises the absence of human agency. Contrast Eph. ii. 11. The same two words, here contrasted, are placed conspicuously side by side in Mk. xiv. 58. This superhuman circumcision has Christ for its encompassing element, being wrought in virtue of inward union with Him: *in whom ye were also circumcised.*

The laying-aside: as we take off and put away clothes. The cognate verb in ch. iii. 9, where the readers are said to have themselves laid aside 'the old man:' a similar verb in 2 Cor. v. 4. Also the opposite verb in Col. iii. 10, 'put on the new man;' and again in *v.* 12. *The body of the flesh:* the human body looked upon in its material constitution, in view of the truth ever present to the mind of Paul (e.g. Rom. vi. 12) that through the needs and desires arising from the constitution of our body sin rules all those whom Christ has not saved. For in fallen man the flesh, although in itself good, has come under the domination of sin and has become a weapon with which sin enslaves its victims. Hence apart from Christ, man's flesh is (Rom. viii. 3) 'flesh of sin' and his body (ch. vi. 6) a 'body of sin.' Circumcision is only the outward removal, by human hands, of a small part of that body which to so many is an instrument by which sin holds them captive. But the servants of Christ have stripped off from themselves and laid aside their entire body of flesh, inasmuch as they have been completely rescued from its deadly dominion. Henceforth they stand in a new relation to their own bodies: these are no longer the throne of sin but the temple of God. *In the laying aside of the body of the flesh:* the environment in which took place the circumcision *not made with hands.* While the one was done the other was done. Or, practically, the two clauses describe under two aspects the same inward experience. The two figures are linked together by the next clause: *in the circumcision of Christ,* the better circumcision which has Christ for its source and distinguishing mark.

Having-been-buried with Him in your *Baptism:* another description of this inward and spiritual circumcision, specifying also its time and outward instrumentality. A close parallel with Rom. vi. 4: a parallel the more remarkable because in the N. T. this mode of thought is found only with Paul, and is extremely rare even with later Christian writers. Already, in Rom. vi. 3—11, Gal. ii. 20, vi. 14, we have been taught that, like Christ and in Christ, we are to be dead to sin, i.e. completely separated from it as the dead are separated from the world in which they once lived, by means of that death upon the cross by which Christ Himself was separated from the penalty and curse and power of sin under which for our sakes He once groaned; and that consequently Baptism, the visible gate through which the convert from heathenism entered the company of the professed followers of Christ, is designed to be the funeral service of the old life announcing publicly that life has ceased and separating the dead man completely from the land in which he lived. In this sense the Colossian Christians were *buried* in the grave of Christ; and this burial took place *in* their *Baptism.*

Although this burial is evidently metaphorical, we have no hint that *Baptism* refers to anything except the outward rite. Indeed the metaphor needs the outward rite as its basis and explanation. And in Rom. vi. 3, so similar in thought and expression, 'baptized for Christ' refers indisputably to the rite, of which Paul goes on to explain the inward significance.

The sudden and conspicuous introduction of a new topic, *circumcised . . . circumcision . . . circumcision,* in this warning against error suggests irresistibly that, as in Galatia (Gal. v. 2, 3) so in Colossæ, the false teachers insisted on circumcision as a condition of salvation. This reveals a Jewish element in the error here combated. (In v. 16 this suggestion is placed beyond doubt.) Paul declares that circumcision by the hands of men is needless for the servants of Christ because they have already undergone a more complete circumcision, that in the Baptism by which they were outwardly and formally joined to Christ their whole body, not a mere fragment of it, looked upon as a body of sin, its real earlier condition, was buried in the grave of Christ. Consequently, they have actually experienced that circumcision of the heart of which Moses and the Prophets (Dt. xxx. 6, Ezek. xliv. 9) so frequently spoke as the real condition of spiritual blessing.

12b. *Wherein also:* or *in whom also.* Grammatically, each rendering is equally admissible: and the context affords no sure ground of decision. On the one hand, 'Baptism' is the nearest antecedent: and *raised with* Him evidently supplements 'buried with Him,' recalling forcibly the ancient mode of the rite (see under Rom. vi. 4) and the baptismal water under which the convert sank and from which he rose. Paul may wish to say that in their Baptism his readers were not only buried, but also raised, with Christ. On the other hand, Christ in His relation to His people is the chief thought of the whole sentence: 'in Him dwells' and 'in Him ye are,' vv. 9, 10; 'who is the Head,' v. 10; and 'in whom also ye were circumcised,' v. 11, where the first three words are the same as in v. 12b. Paul may wish to say, still thinking of the dignity of Christ, that in Him we have been not only circumcised with a superhuman circumcision but *also raised together with* Christ *through faith.* It cannot be objected that our resurrection is not with Him but in Him. It is both *in* Him, resulting from inward union with Him, and *with* Him, introducing us to a life enjoyed by fellowship with Him. So expressly Eph. ii. 6, 'raised together with Him ... in Christ Jesus.' This latter exposition is slightly favoured by the added words *through faith.* For to say that in Baptism they were raised through faith is somewhat clumsy: whereas the words 'buried with Him in Baptism' would be evenly balanced by the addition, *in Him* ye *were also raised through faith.* But confident decision is impossible; and unimportant. For each exposition embodies a truth. The command of Christ made Baptism, to those not yet baptized, whether Jews or heathens, a condition of His favour; and therefore the only ordinary way to the new life which flows from His death, burial, and resurrection. In this correct sense, in their Baptism the Colossian Christians had risen with Christ. On the other hand, their resurrection was in Christ as well as with Christ. For it both resulted from inward contact with Him and placed them by His side.

Through faith: the constant condition of salvation in all its aspects; Ph. iii. 9, Eph. ii. 8, iii. 12, 17, Rom. iii. 22, etc. *Working:* see under Ph. iii. 21. It was the active power of God raising Christ from the dead. A close and important parallel in Eph. i. 19. *Faith* or *belief of the working etc.:* belief that the activity *of God raised Him from the dead.* According to a common Greek construction, the genitive specifies the object of faith, and in this case the object-matter. So Ph. i. 27, 2 Th. ii. 13. Similarly, in Ph. iii. 9, Eph. iii. 12, Rom. iii. 22, 26, it specifies the personal object of faith. These words assert that saving faith (like that of Abraham, Rom. iv. 21) rests upon the recognised power of God.

The phrase *raised together with* Christ is found also in ch. iii. 1, Eph. ii. 6. In this last place the readers are said to be also 'seated with Christ in the heavenly places.' Similarly, believers are crucified, dead, and buried, with Christ: *v.* 20, Rom. vi. 6, 11, 4. This remarkable teaching is both very familiar to Paul and peculiar to him. It demands our best attention.

Under Rom. vi. 6 we have learnt that we are dead and crucified with Christ in the sense that we have shared with Him the results of His own death, that through His death upon the cross we have escaped completely, as He escaped, from the penalty and burden and dominion of sin. The day will come when we shall share to the full the results of His resurrection and ascension: for, ourselves risen from the dead, we shall sit with Him upon His throne in endless life. In that day we shall say, I am risen with Christ and through Christ and in Christ. For we shall share His throne, this being a result of His resurrection and ascension, and of our inward union with Him, a union begun on earth. For, had He not risen, we should not have believed in Him, and should not rise with Him. Now, when a future event is absolutely certain, we sometimes speak of it as present or past. For the future seems inadequate to express such certainty. Just so, as Paul looked forward with perfect confidence to the day when he will sit with Christ in glory, and remembered that no hostile power could prevent that glory, he felt that it was already his. And when, looking back to the cross and to the empty grave of Christ, he remembered that all the glory awaiting him was a result of His death and resurrection, and felt in his own heart and life the presence and power of the Risen

One bearing him forward to the great consummation, the intervals between Christ's resurrection and his own conversion and between his present life on earth and the realisation of his hopes in the great day seemed to vanish from his view; and he felt himself to be already risen and enthroned with Christ. This anticipatory language is the more easy because a certainty touching the future is to a large extent an actual present influence upon us. Our confident hope becomes a mental platform on which we stand and from which we view all things. The heir to vast estates looks upon them as already his own; and takes them into all his plans for life. In this sense Paul was already risen with Christ. In his Baptism he had been laid in His grave: for it was a formal declaration that in Christ his old life of bondage had ceased. And through a faith grasping the infinite power which raised Christ from the grave Paul was himself made a sharer of the immortal life to which His resurrection and ascension had introduced the humanity of Christ, already a sharer virtually of that victory over death which will soon, as it seemed to him, be his in outward bodily reality.

Notice that faith is the link between Christ's resurrection and our own. Our assurance that the power of God is able to raise the dead enables us to believe that God actually raised Christ. A result of this faith will be that the same power will raise us. And a foretaste of that final resurrection we have in the new life which the power of God has already breathed into us, and which reveals itself day by day in victory over sin and communion with the spiritual world. In Eph. i. 19, 20, this relation between the resurrection of Christ and our present spiritual life is further expounded.

13. Another statement, in a somewhat different, yet related, form, of the great change described as 'risen with' Christ. *And you:* in addition to Christ whom 'God raised from the dead.' It emphasises by repetition this second resurrection. Same words in ch. i. 21, where they add, to God's purpose to reconcile all things to Himself in Christ, the actual reconciliation of the readers of this Epistle; similarly Eph. ii. 1. In ch. i. 21 Gentile Christians were contrasted with Jewish Christians. But the word 'ye-were-raised' in ch. ii. 12, which certainly includes Gentiles, forbids such contrast here. At the same time these introductory words raise into great prominence the Colossian Christians to whom Paul now writes; and the words *uncircumcision of your flesh* remind us that they were Gentiles. *By trespasses:* the instrument with which these *dead ones* were slain. Same words and sense in Eph. ii. 1.

In what sense these men were formerly *dead,* must be determined by Paul's general system of thought. Since they were manifestly living, their death could not be that of the body. Since it was caused by trespasses, and was connected with *uncircumcision,* it could not be inherited depravity resulting from Adam's 'one trespass:' Rom. v. 18. Moreover, the *dead ones* have been *made-alive* in close connection with the resurrection of Christ, and their *trespasses* have been *forgiven.* Now we remember that (Rom. vi. 23) the wages of sin is death. This death can only be utter ruin of body and soul. It will be consummated (2 Th. i. 9, Mt. x. 28) in the day of judgment. But inasmuch as sinners are already beyond reach of salvation except by the power of Him who raises the dead, and are separated from the Source of Life, a separation producing moral corruption, Paul correctly and frequently speaks of them as already *dead.* See under Rom. vii. 9, Eph. ii. 1, 1 Tim. v. 6: also Jno. v. 24, 25, a most important coincidence enabling us to trace the teaching of Paul to the lips of Christ; 1 Jno. iii. 14, Rev. xx. 14. Just as a dead and a sleeping child differ chiefly in that, whereas the latter will wake up to life, activity, growth, and manhood, nothing awaits the former except corruption and worms, a difference which all human power fails utterly to bridge, so and in infinitely greater degree differ those whom God *has,* and those whom He has not, *made alive together with Christ:* cp. Jno. v. 25. Such was the awful former position of the Colossian Christians. They had committed trespasses: and these trespasses were bars shutting them up in the doom and gloom of eternal corruption.

Uncircumcision: joint cause with *trespasses* of this death. Or rather it places their death by reason of trespasses in its relation to their outward separation from the ancient people of God. Similar thought in Eph. ii. 11, 12. The uncircumcised bodies of the Colossians once bore witness to their separation from the God of Abraham and from the chosen nation of the Old Covenant. By commanding circumcision God had claimed for His own the human body. The heathen live in ignorance or rejection of this claim and are thus outside the Covenant. The words *uncircumcision of your flesh* came the more easily to Paul's pen because, in the heathen, with absence of the seal of the Covenant was associated moral bondage to the rule of the bodily life.

Such was the terrible position of those to whom Paul now writes. They had again and again fallen into sin, and were as their bodies bore witness outside the Covenant of God. Consequently, they were separated from the only life worthy of the name, and were under the dominion of eternal corruption, a dominion from which no earthly power could save them.

Has-made-alive: has removed all that is involved in the word *death*. By reuniting them to Himself, the source of life, God breathed into them new vital power, a power opening to them a prospect of endless development and activity, a spiritual development already begun. *You together with Him:* a very emphatic mode of asserting that God has so joined us to Christ that the act by which He gave life to the sacred corpse in the grave gave immortal life also to us. This is really equivalent to the statement in *v.* 12, 'ye were raised together with Him.' But this statement now before us looks at the inward spiritual life received by believers, when they believe, in consequence of the life then breathed into the Saviour's lifeless body. Verse 12 looked at their removal from the realm of spiritual death and restoration to the land of the living resulting from Christ's uprising from the sleep of death. Both expressions are again together in Eph. ii. 5, 6. The words before us are the more suitable here because the new life thus received is derived each moment from vital inward contact with the Risen Lord.

All the trespasses: suggesting many sins, and an all-embracing pardon. *Having-forgiven etc.:* a condition involved in this new life. Since surrender to death is the just and inevitable punishment of sin, restoration to life implies forgiveness; and necessarily follows it. Just so, to a man doomed to die, pardon is life. *Forgiven:* literally *bestowed-favour-upon:* same word in Rom. viii. 32, Phil. i. 29, ii. 9; and in the same sense in Col. iii. 13, 2 Cor. ii. 7, 10, xii. 13. By the change from *you* to *us,* Paul puts himself among those whose *trespasses* are *forgiven.*

14. This forgiveness is now traced to *the cross* of Christ, the means by which was removed the obstacle to forgiveness which lay in the written law. It is added in the form of a second participial clause, which passes, according to the frequent habit of Paul in matters of great importance, into direct assertion. *Blotted-out,* literally *washed-out:* a common word for complete removal of writing. The defective nature of ancient ink made it easy. Same word and sense in Rev. iii. 5, Acts iii. 19, Ps. lxix. 29, Dt. ix. 14; and, in a similar sense, in Rev. vii. 17, xxi. 4. *The handwriting:* a later Greek word, usually in the sense of a written obligation; so Tobit v. 3, ix. 5. In this sense it passed without change into Latin.

Dogma: an exact reproduction in English of the Greek word here used. It denotes something which 'seems good,' e.g. an opinion which commends itself as true or a course of action which commends itself as wise. It is frequently used for the expressed judgments of the Greek philosophers, for a joint resolution touching some united action, and for the decrees of an authority which claims to determine the conduct of others. So in Lk. ii. 1, 'there went out a *decree* from Cæsar Augustus;' Acts xvii. 7. The decisions of the conference at Jerusalem (Acts xv. 23—29) are in ch. xvi. 4 called *dogmas*. Similarly Ignatius *To the Magnesians* (ch. 13) speaks of 'the *decrees* of the Lord and of the Apostles.' In this verse *the dogmas* must be the various commands, ritual or moral, of the Law of Moses, looked upon simply as the decrees of an authority claiming to direct and control man's conduct. For *the handwriting against us* can be no other than the Law of Moses which Paul speaks of in 2 Cor. iii. 6 as 'the letter which kills.' And this condemnatory document is the chief feature of the Old Covenant. The connection between *the handwriting* and *the dogmas* is not determined by the grammatical construction; but is left to be inferred. Perhaps it is easiest to understand it as *the handwriting* written with *the dogmas*, as in Gal. vi. 11 we have an 'epistle written with (large) letters.' But, however we render these words, their meaning is clear. The Law was made up of dogmas, i.e. of commands claiming simply obedience. And these decrees gave to the Law its power *against us:* for we had broken them; and they cried out for punishment.

Which was contrary to us: a very conspicuous repetition, given as an express assertion, of the words *against us*. This remarkable emphasis indicates Paul's chief thought in this verse, a thought ever present to his mind, viz. the condemnation pronounced by the Law, and the barrier thus erected between man and God. Similarly, in Rom. vii. 3 the law of marriage condemns a married woman to bondage while her (bad) husband lives. Such a law seemed to be against her best interests.

Usually, the word rendered *handwriting* denotes something written by the person whom the writing binds. It is not so here. Man is bound by a law written not by himself but by God. But this does not in the least degree make Paul's language inappropriate. The essential point is obligation resting upon a written document. By whom written is immaterial. Indeed it is the national law not made by us which gives its binding force to the bond we have ourselves signed. Another point is that the document consists of decrees claiming obedience.

The word *dogmas* proves that the *handwriting* was the Law of Sinai, which consisted entirely of written decrees. For the law written on the heart, (Rom. ii. 15,) although marking out certain actions as forbidden, would hardly be thus described. The change in v. 13 from 'you' to 'us' made it easy for Paul to write of the Law of Moses as hostile: for doubtless, as a Pharisee, he had often quailed under its condemnation. And in this condemnation even the heathen were included. For we read in Rom. iii. 19 that the Law was given to Israel to make the whole world silent and guilty before God. The Law of Sinai proves that all men are under the anger of God. For it awakens the law written within, and through that inner law pronounces sentence even upon those who have never heard of the God of Israel.

The mention of forgiveness recalls to Paul's thoughts the tremendous sentence written in unmistakable characters in the commands of the ancient Law. He remembers that in former times this written law had seemed to be his worst enemy. And even now forgiveness can come only by *blotting out* its terrible *decrees*.

And He has taken it away out of the midst: a restatement, in the form of direct assertion, of what is already implied in *blotted-out*. The writing completely erased is here described as an obstacle removed. [The Greek perfect suggests the abiding result of the removal of the great barrier blocking the way to forgiveness.] Having *nailed it to the cross:* means by which the obstacle was removed. The person holding the bond has driven a nail through it and fastened it to the cross of Christ, thus making it invalid. This is a very graphic way of saying that the obstacle to forgiveness which lay in the Law, i.e. in the justice of God of which the Law is an embodiment, was removed by means of the death of Christ. Practically, the nails which fastened to the cross the hands and feet of Jesus, and thus slew Him, pierced and rendered invalid the Law which pronounced our just condemnation.

15. Perhaps the most obscure verse in the New Testament. Its obscurity arises from our ignorance of the precise nature of the error here combated.

[The verb ἐκδύω denotes 'to take off clothes.' The very rare verb ἀπεκδύομαι adds the idea of laying aside the stripped off clothing. An accusative following these verbs may denote either the person unclothed or the clothing taken off: for both person and clothes are direct objects of the act of unclothing. The middle voice denotes most simply removal of one's own clothing. In this sense it occurs in ch. iii. 9; and the corresponding abstract substantive in ch. ii. 11. But the middle voice of all sorts of Greek verbs denotes not infrequently merely an action for the benefit of the actor. This would allow us to take *the principalities etc.* as the persons unclothed. And this is done by the Vulgate, which renders *expolians princip. etc.* But we cannot think that Paul would use in this more remote sense, without any indication of his meaning, a word so commonly used in, and therefore naturally suggesting, the simple meaning of laying aside one's own clothes.

The principalities and the authorities may be either the clothing laid aside, or may belong only to the next verb *made-a-show-of* as its direct object, the clothing laid aside not being specified. This seems to have been the favourite exposition of the Latin Fathers, who suppose that the clothing laid aside was the human flesh of Christ. Their rendering would be, 'having stripped Himself' of His own body by death, 'He made a show of the principalities,' etc. This exposition has found its way into the MSS. FG, which read 'having laid aside the flesh, He made a show' etc. Probably the word *flesh* was an explanatory note which was afterwards copied into the text: a frequent source of error in the text of the N. T. To this exposition it is an objection that, by putting the object before the verb it gives to the angelic powers a prominence not easily explained. On the other hand, the Greek Fathers generally accept the other interpretation, viz. that *the principalities etc.* were themselves the garment laid aside and the object of the public *show*. This interpretation agrees so well with the grammatical structure of the verse that we may, with most modern commentators, accept it.]

Two questions remain. *The principalities and the authorities* are undoubtedly successive ranks of angels. Are they good or bad? And did God or Christ strip them off from Himself?

In *v.* 10 and ch. i. 16, where the same words are found in the same order, they certainly denote good angels, as does the word 'angel' when not otherwise defined. But, that here the angelic powers are said to have been stripped off and laid aside, suggested to the Greek Fathers that Paul refers to hostile, and therefore bad, angels. This is the plain reference of the same words in Eph. vi. 12; where, however, the meaning is made quite clear by the foregoing mention of 'the devil' and of strenuous conflict, and by the absence of any mention of good angels. But to the Colossians Paul says nothing about hostile angels: in *v.* 10 he uses the words before us of good angels: and in *v.* 18 we have, based upon this verse, a dissuasion from 'worshipping of angels,' such worship being inconceivable except as rendered to holy beings. Again, *the principalities etc.* are here looked upon as a robe which must have been previously worn, or it could not have been laid aside. In what sense could evil spirits be thus conceived? Only by supposing that in their attack on the Incarnate Son they clung to Him like a deadly robe, and that in repelling their attack He stripped them off from Himself. But I do not know that enemies attacking are ever so described: and of such desperate struggle with evil powers we have as yet in this place no hint. Another serious objection is that this exposition involves a change of subject of which we have no indication. Certainly in *v*. 13 it is the Father who has made us alive together with Christ and forgiven us all trespasses. In *v*. 14 there is no hint of change of subject. For it is in perfect harmony with Paul's thought to say that the Father blotted out the handwriting against us and nailed it to the cross. Indeed God is said in Rom. iii. 25, 26 to have given Christ to die in order to reconcile the justification of believers with His own justice. If *v*. 15 refers to Christ repelling an attack of evil spirits, we have a most important change of actor in the scene before us which could hardly have been made in perfect silence. An exposition surrounded by such difficulties can be accepted only after all others have failed.

Is there any sense in which until the death of Christ and no longer the angels of heaven were, or might be spoken of as, a robe of God? There is. In Gal. iii. 19 we read that the Law was 'ordained by the agency of angels:' see my note. The whole argument in Heb. i., ii., especially ii. 2 'the word spoken by the agency of angels,' implies that they were the medium through which the revelations of the Old Covenant were given. If so, we may speak of these bright messengers as the robe in which God revealed Himself to men during long ages. Only under the veil of angelic forms and through angel lips did they see His face and hear His voice. Even at the Incarnation (Lk. ii. 9) God approached man in the same mysterious garb. But in Christ the veil was laid aside. Through the lips of the Incarnate Son God spoke to man face to face and revealed His unveiled glory. He thus stripped off and laid aside the garb He had previously worn. This action of God is a strong reason why the Colossian Christians should not (*v*. 18) 'worship angels.' To do so, is to cling to a superseded mode of Divine revelation. The prevalence of this error suggested this mention of angelic powers. In Christ the Law as a means of salvation has passed away, having been nailed (*v*. 14) to His cross: therefore none may now (*v*. 16) pronounce sentence against others on legal grounds. And in Christ God has (*v*. 15) laid aside the visible mediation of angels: consequently, no one (*v*. 18) may any longer worship them.

Openly: i.e. without reserve, telling the whole truth. Same word in 2 Cor. iii. 12. By laying aside the mediation of angels, God revealed the whole truth about them and their relation to Himself and to men. They are seen to be our helpers not our lords. *Having-led-them* etc.: an exposition of the foregoing, describing the manner of this unreserved and public *show* of the discarded angelic robe. *Led-in-triumph:* same word as in 2 Cor. ii. 14, where see note. If *the principalities* etc. were enemies, this word would naturally suggest a train of captives led along as in a Roman triumph and revealing by their number the greatness of the victory. And it must be admitted that this natural connection of thought favours the exposition of the Greek Fathers noticed and rejected above. But the serious objections to it, stated above, outweigh this support. Moreover apparently the word denoted originally the peaceful Greek processions in honour of Dionysius: and this made more easy its use by Paul when thinking only of a public procession and not of the military victory implied in a Roman triumph.

How did God, in Christ or in His cross, lead the angels, good or bad, in triumphal procession and thus make them a public *show?* Perhaps in two ways. The changed position of angels in the New Covenant as compared with the Old was itself a conspicuous manifestation by God of their subordination to the Son. It made plain to all men that they were no longer His medium of revelation to man. Again, their occasional appearance around the person of Christ is another public mark of their changed position. They are now manifestly subordinate to the Son as His servants: e.g. Mt. iv. 11, Lk. xxii. 43, Mt. xxviii. 5; xxiv. 31, xxvi. 53. In the N. T. angelic mediation as a means of revelation to man is almost laid aside; and angels appear only to pay homage to the Son or to help His servants; in other words, as swelling the train of Christ the Conqueror. The incompleteness of this explanation is perhaps due to our ignorance of the exact nature of the error this Epistle was designed to overturn.

The last words of *v.* 15 may be rendered with equal right *in Him* or *in it.* The former rendering is better. For it was in the entire personality of Christ rather than in His 'cross' and death that God revealed the subordinate position of angels. And this suits the scope of § 9, of which Christ and His relation to us are the chief feature. In Him was manifested to men the victory of God involved in the establishment of the New Covenant.

The exposition implied in the Vulgate is maintained by Meyer: that of the Greek Fathers by Ellicott and Lightfoot. The exposition

I have adopted differs little from that of Alford, and from that advocated by Findlay in a very able paper in *The Expositor*, 1st series, vol. x. p. 403 and in *the Pulpit Commentary*. Mr. Findlay has done good service by calling attention to the original connection of the Greek word rendered *triumph* with the Dionysiac processions.

In SECTION 9 the warning already given in § 8 becomes much more definite. The error warned against is called philosophy, i.e. an attempt to reach the realities underlying the phenomena around; and is further described as empty deception. Its source is mere human tradition : and what good it possesses belongs only to the rudimentary teaching common to the whole human race. In contrast to it, Paul points to Christ as the norm of Christian belief and practice. In Him dwells all completeness; a completeness shared by all who dwell in Him. To Him bow the hierarchy of heaven. And even the blessings of the Old Covenant belong to His servants by their union with Him in Baptism. So closely are they joined to Him that they have lain in His grave, and already share His resurrection life. This life implies, as its condition, forgiveness of sins. And this forgiveness is traced to the death of Christ, by which was removed the barrier to forgiveness based upon the ancient Law or rather upon the eternal justice of God of which that law was a literary embodiment. In the Old Covenant God revealed Himself to men in the garb of angelic agency. But in these better days that garb has been laid aside : and those bright spirits, who in former times appeared as the highest powers on earth, bearers of the might of God, appear now merely as swelling the train of One Greater than themselves.

Notice in this warning, as marked features of the error combated, philosophy and tradition, angelic powers and circumcision. This suggests that the error contained both theosophic and Jewish elements. And this suggestion will be confirmed in § 10.

We notice also that, to guard against this error, Paul relies wholly on a setting forth of the Christian's relation to Christ. This explains the full exposition in DIV. II., before the error is mentioned, of the Person and Work of Christ.

SECTION X.

WARNING AGAINST VARIOUS DOGMAS, JEWISH OR GENTILE, CONTRARY TO CHRIST.

CH. II. 16—III. 4.

*Let not any one then judge you in eating or in drinking, or in a matter of a feast or of a new moon or of a sabbath, *[17]* which things are a shadow of those to come, but the body is Christ's. *[18]* Let no one rob you of your prize, desiring to do it in lowliness of mind and worshipping of angels, investigating things which he has seen, vainly puffed up by the mind of his flesh, *[19]* and not holding fast the Head, from whom all the body, through the joints and bands receiving supply and being knit together, increases with the increase of God.*
[20] *If ye died with Christ from the rudiments of the world, why as though living in the world are ye placed under dogmas? *[21]* 'Handle not, nor taste, nor touch,' *[22]* (all which things are to perish in the using up of them,) according to the commandments and teachings of men: *[23]* things which have indeed a repute of wisdom in will-worship and lowliness of mind and unsparing treatment of the body, not in any value against indulgence of the flesh.*
[1] *If then ye have been raised together with Christ, seek the things above, where Christ is, sitting at the right hand of God: *[2]* mind the things above, not those upon the earth. *[3]* For ye are dead, and your life lies hidden with Christ in God. *[4]* When Christ shall be manifested, your life, then also ye with Him will be manifested in glory.*

This section falls into three clearly marked divisions, each comprising four verses. Ch. ii. 16—19 specifies the errors referred to in the more general warning of § 9, distinguishing their Jewish (*vv.* 16, 17) and theosophic (*vv.* 18, 19) elements: ch. ii. 20—23 brings to bear against them one factor of the positive teaching in § 9, viz. our death with Christ: and ch. iii. 1—4 brings to bear upon them another factor, viz. our resurrection with Christ.

16. Practical application of the foregoing, especially of *v.* 14. 'Since God has nailed to the cross of Christ, and thus made invalid, the written obligation of the Old Covenant with its decrees, do not submit to any one's award of praise or blame on the ground of its prohibitions or prescriptions: for these have passed away.'

Eating . . . drinking: same words in Rom. xiv. 17, and similar

thought; cp. *v.* 13, 'let us no longer judge one another.' They
might refer, as they do associated together in Rom. xiv. 21, to meat
and wine offered in sacrifice to idols. But, that this is not Paul's
main reference here, is proved by *v.* 16*b*, which mentions distinctively
Levitical ordinances, by the mention in *v.* 11 of circumcision, which
involves obedience to the whole Law of Moses, and the mention
in *v.* 14 of a written obligation. The word *eating* refers therefore
chiefly to the Levitical prohibition of unclean animals as food. The
word *drinking* suggests that the would-be judges extended to themselves the Mosaic prohibition of wine to Nazarites (Num. vi. 3) and
(Lev. x. 9) to priests while officiating at the altar. In other words,
they not only maintained the abiding obligation of the Law but also
claimed to belong to the narrower circle of Nazarites, and possibly
wished to force into it the entire Church of Christ. Paul's protest
against this judgment is in close accord with Rom. xiv. 13, 14. And
it is a complete abrogation of the Law of Moses, of which a conspicuous feature was distinction of meats.

Feast . . . new-moon . . . sabbath : same words in same order
in Ezek. xlv. 17, Hosea ii. 11 ; in the inverse order in 1 Chr. xxiii.
31, 2 Chr. ii. 4, xxxi. 3. *Feast:* a yearly festival, as in Acts xviii.
21, Mt. xxvi. 5, xxvii. 15, Lev. xxiii. 4, etc. *New-moon :* same word
in Num. xxviii. 11—15 : it refers to the special sacrifices at the
beginning of each month. *Sabbath :* the weekly day of rest. This
is the ordinary meaning of the word ; and is determined here by the
ascending scale of frequency, annual, monthly, weekly. These three
terms include all the sacred seasons of the Jewish year.

17. *A shadow :* an intangible outline caused by, and revealing
the approach of, a solid reality. Important coincidence of language
and thought in Heb. viii. 5, x. 1. Indeed this verse contains the
germ of very much in that Epistle. *The things to come;* or *about to
be :* either the New Covenant or the eternal glory. There is no
grammatical objection to the former : for the future must be measured, as in Rom. v. 14, from the point of view of the *shadow* or
type. And the Jewish restrictions and sacred seasons suggest at
once by contrast our present service of Christ. On the other hand,
since the *shadow* was still existing, though fading, when Paul wrote,
the words *things to come* seem to point forward to the far future.
So Heb. viii. 5 : 'shadow of the heavenly things.' Indeed the distinction is unimportant. For Christian life on earth receives its real
worth from the glory awaiting the children of God. Just so the day-
dawn is of worth chiefly as herald of the day. The prescriptions of
the Old Covenant were outlines both of the Gospel and the spiritual

life which it at once imparts and of the eternal temple and service and sabbath. Even the old restrictions of food have their counterpart in a loyalty to Christ which controls our food and all the little details of life: e.g. 1 Cor. viii. 13. *The body*, i.e. the solid and tangible reality, (*of the things to come,*) is *Christ's*, i.e. belongs to Him, so that he who has Christ has the reality whose approach was dimly foreshadowed by the Old Covenant. Cp. Josephus, *Jewish Wars* bk. ii. 2. 5, 'asking a *shadow* of royalty when he had seized the substance (or *body*) of it.' In Heb. x. 1, the contrast is between a mere outline cast by a shadow and a complete picture or 'image.' Possibly here the choice of the word *body* was prompted by the use Paul had made of it in Col. ii. 17.

Verse 17 supports *v*. 16. Since Christ is ours, with all He has and is, we have the reality dimly outlined in the ancient ordinances. Consequently, the ancient ritual, once of value as an outline of things to come, is now worthless. Thus, as throughout this Epistle, Christ is Himself a sufficient safeguard against all error.

The warning in *v*. 16 proves how far Paul was from placing the Lord's Day in the same category as the Jewish Sabbath. And this warning is not altogether needless now. For it is possible to degrade into a mere prescribed rite this precious and abiding gift of Christ to His Church. That this warning does not in any way contradict the divine authority and abiding validity and infinite value of the Lord's Day, I have in my note under Gal. iv. 11 endeavoured to show.

18. Another warning. Whether it refers to another class of false teachers or to another element in the teaching combated in *vv*. 16, 17, Paul's words do not indicate. *Rob-of-the-prize :* by giving as an umpire an unfavourable judgment. This one word is a compound of that rendered *prize* in 1 Cor. ix. 24, Ph. iii. 14. And the prize is in each case the same, viz. eternal life, the reward of victory in the good fight of faith: 1 Tim. vi. 12. In *v*. 16 some one is supposed to be pronouncing sentence on the ground of eating and drinking. Here some one is supposed to be setting up himself as umpire in the Christian race and judging the prize in a spirit hostile to Paul's readers. [Notice the present imperative in *vv*. 16 and 18. It suggests that what the false teachers are already saying practically amounts to a hostile judgment.] Paul warns his readers not to submit to the judgment of the one or the other. And his words imply that such submission will rob them of the hope which is to them the light of life.

Lowliness-of-mind : same word in Ph. ii. 3. Whether it was real or only professed, Paul does not say. In either case his warning remains the same. *Worship:* the outward form of religious adoration: same word in Acts xxvi. 5, Jas. i. 26, 27. This outward adoration, these men paid to *the angels. Wishing* to do so *in* (or *with*) *lowliness of mind etc.:* description of the profession and outward action of the would-be umpire. (For the lowliness of mind must in some way have made itself known.) We may conceive him pretending to be unworthy immediately to approach God or the Son of God, and therefore in his humility directing his worship towards the created spirits who from heaven minister to the needs of men on earth. Paul says that what such men actually *wish* is to deprive his readers of the prize for which they are running the Christian race.

[The object-matter of this *wish* must be inferred from the long word foregoing. Evidently the would-be umpire wished to give a hostile decision. So 2 Pet. iii. 5, 'this lies hidden from them, they wishing it to be hidden.' The Greek phrase here, θέλων ἐν, is found in the LXX. as a rendering of a Hebrew phrase denoting 'to take delight in.' But in this sense it never took root in the Greek language; and therefore is not likely to be so used here. Moreover, a man's own delight in these things would do no harm to Paul's readers unless he tried to force his own religious tastes upon them. But, however we understand the grammatical structure, practically the sense is the same. Paul feared that by this professed humility and this worshipping of angels his readers might be beguiled, and thus robbed of their prize.]

Investigating etc.: another detail collateral with *in lowliness etc.* Probably it refers specially to *worshipping of angels*, and traces this worship to its professed origin and foundation, viz. visions of angels. The word rendered *investigate* denotes originally *to step into* something, especially with a view to take possession of it. It is also used of mental entrance into a subject with a view to examine and thus take mental possession of it. So 2 Maccabees ii. 30, 'to *investigate* and to make discourse about all things and to be much occupied with the details, is fitting for the author of the story.' *Things which he has seen:* professed visions of the unseen world. Like so many teachers of strange doctrines in all ages, these men professed to *have seen* something unseen by others. These supposed visions then became matters of investigation, i.e. of comparison and inference; and thus became the foundation of a system of teaching and of religious rites.

Vainly: either without reason or without result: senses closely allied. Same word in Rom. xiii. 4, 1 Cor. xv. 2, Gal. iii. 4, iv. 11.

Grammatically it may be joined to the words foregoing or to those following. For the order of the original is, *things which he has seen, investigating vainly puffed up by etc.* The word *in-vain* is best understood as Paul's verdict about the uselessness of this investigation of these fancied visions. For it is needless to say that self-inflation is *vain.* 'He talks about *things which he has seen* and makes his own visions a matter of laborious inquiry: a useless inquiry.' Paul declares that this useless inquiry is the only foundation of his worship of angels and of his pretended humility.

Puffed-up: same word in 1 Cor. iv. 6, 18, 19, v. 2, viii. 1, xiii. 4; and not elsewhere in N. T. Notice that here only the false teachers are said to be *puffed up,* and of these Paul speaks in the third person: but at Corinth the same charge is brought against the whole Church. *The mind of his flesh:* not exactly the same as, but similar to, 'the mind of the flesh' in Rom. viii. 6. *His flesh:* that portion of flesh and blood, with all its belongings physical and psychological, which is owned by one person. It is the bodily side of his nature. *Mind:* the inward eye which looks through phenomena to the reality underlying them: same word in Ph. iv. 7, Rom. i. 28, vii. 23, 25, etc. Here the bodily nature is said to have a mind. And rightly. For the bodily appetites ever tend to dominate the intelligence, and to make it their slave. And since each mind thus dominated has a development of its own, both *mind* and *flesh* are here individualized: *the mind of his flesh.* Now the animating principle of the flesh is selfishness: for our bodies care for nothing except their own protection and maintenance and indulgence. Consequently, the mind of our flesh always begets an inflated self-estimate, which is a form of selfishness. This accounts for the supposed visions: for the selfish man is ever ready to believe anything which flatters his own vanity; and few things do this more than belief that he has personal and unusual intercourse with the unseen world. This man pretends to investigate his wonderful revelations; and on the ground of them pays outward adoration to angels. And, blinded by his own vanity, he attributes his desire to worship angels to a humility which dares not approach God Himself. Paul warns his readers that these empty products of self-esteem will, if accepted, rob the Christian of the prize he has in view; and that this is their real aim.

Such is perhaps the easiest explanation of this very obscure verse. Doubtless the obscurity is caused by our ignorance of details well known to the readers. Paul says plainly that worship of angels was part of the teaching of these false guides. And we can easily believe that they claimed to have seen visions of angels, and made these visions a matter of serious though empty examination. If so, the word *in-vain* would reveal in a moment the unreality of these boasted researches. And Paul's explanation of them as a product of a self-estimate inflated by a sensual mind was probably verified by personal knowledge of the men who put forward these lordly claims.

The sense of this verse is completely changed by the corrected reading *which he has seen*. See Introd. iii. Lightfoot, moved by the difficulty of the passage, suggests that error may have crept into all our copies, and proposes a reading of which no trace whatever is found in any ancient MS., version, or quotation. A better suggestion in the same direction is made by Westcott and Hort; and may be rendered *treading empty air*. But that the true reading should have utterly vanished from the almost innumerable witnesses to the original text of the Epistle, is in the last degree unlikely. Even the erroneous insertion of the negative shows that the suggested reading was unthought of in the early Church. Its complete obliteration is much more difficult to accept than is the exposition given above. See a very good paper by Findlay in *The Expositor* 1st series, vol. xi. p. 385.

The express mention of angels here sheds light upon the mention of them in *v.* 15 where they are said to be led by God in triumphal procession, in *v.* 10 where Christ is said to be their Head, and in ch. i. 16, where He is said to be their Creator.

Worship of angels was a conspicuous feature of the Gnostic sects so prevalent in so many strange varieties throughout the second century and traceable in their early origin almost or quite to the days of the apostles. So Irenæus (*On Heresies* bk. i. 31. 2) speaks of the Cainites as appealing to angels, "O angel, I use thy work: O authority," (same word as in Col. ii. 10, 15,) "I perform thy operation." And Theodoret in his note on this passage says that a synod at Laodicea (in A.D. 364) forbade prayer to angels. This prohibition reveals how deeply the practice here condemned had taken root in the immediate neighbourhood of Colossæ. And this worship of angels implies as its basis supposed visions of the unseen world. See further in the note at the close of the Epistle.

19. Further description of the false teachers, tracing their error, negatively, to their failure to grasp, or to retain hold of, Him from whom as the Head flows to the various members of the body nourishment and stability and growth. *The Head:* as in *v.* 10 and ch. i. 18: the one highest member, itself a part of the body yet directing all the other members, which live only so long as they are united to each other and to the Head. The would-be seducer does *not hold fast the Head*, i.e. he has no firm union with Christ, the one great reality, and therefore investigates unreal visions and betakes himself to angel worship.

From whom etc.: reason for holding fast the Head, a reason which explains the aberrations of those who fail to do so. *The joints:* Eph. iv. 16: the various points of contact of the various parts of the body. *Ligaments:* the bands which hold together the bones which form the joint. In this technical sense of *ligaments* the word is used by the Greek medical writers. *The joints and ligaments* comprise the whole mechanism by which the various parts of the body become one whole. *Receiving supply:* see under 2 Cor. ix. 10. The supply in this case must be nourishment. We need not assume that Paul means that nourishment flows through the joints and ligatures. Probably his one thought was that without the bodily union of which these were the means the various members of the body would receive no nourishment. *And knit-together:* same word as in *v.* 2. *The increase of God:* i.e. wrought by God, 1 Cor. iii. 7: cp. 'peace of God' in Ph. iv. 7. Paul here asserts that the entire body of Christ, consisting of various members, all receiving from Him nourishment and compactness, so long as they are closely fitted and joined each to the others, grows with a growth which God works and gives. Hence the need for holding fast the Head: for, separate from Him, there is neither nourishment nor compactness nor growth. Through want of this union with Christ, the false teacher is given up to his own vagaries. Close coincidence of words and thought in Eph. iv. 16.

Verses 16—19 contain the specific warning of the Epistle. We note in it two distinct elements. Paul warns first against those who would maintain as still binding, and even extend, the prescriptions of the ancient law: and then against those who, relying upon fancied intercourse with the unseen, would set up a worship of their own invention. To this second error Paul gives great attention, unveiling its source in blind conceit fostered by sensuality. But against each error his real safeguard is a knowledge of Christ in His relation to His Church. They who know Christ have the reality dimly foreshadowed in the Old Covenant, and therefore will not wish to re-establish it. And He is the Head of the Church, His body, consisting of various members each receiving from Christ, in virtue of its close union with Him and with the other members, nourishment and compactness and growth. They who know this will not be led astray by empty fancies even about the bright ones of heaven.

20—23. These verses bring to bear against the errors mentioned or alluded to in *vv.* 16—19 the teaching in § 9 that through the death of Christ His servants have been placed beyond the domain of the ordinances of the written Law.

If ye died: not doubt, but logical sequence. For death is plainly asserted in ch. iii. 3. It brings to bear against all restrictions of food the teaching of *vv.* 11, 12: for baptism and resurrection imply death, and death is essentially a separation from the life previously lived. *Died with Christ:* same words in Rom. vi. 8; and practically the same in 2 Tim. ii. 11, Gal. ii. 20. *The rudiments* of *the world:* as in *v.* 8, which it recalls and in some measure explains. These rudiments of religious education belong to the bondage of spiritual childhood: Gal. iv. 3. Under them Christ was Himself in bondage when for our sakes He took (Ph. ii. 7) the form of a slave and was made (Heb. ii. 17) in all things like us, and became (Gal. iv. 5) under law and (ch. iii. 13) under the burden and curse of our sins. From this subjection Christ was set free by His own death. That death we have shared: for through His death our old life of bondage has come to an end. In this sense we are (ch. iii. 3) *dead with Christ,* and thus removed *from the elements of the world.* Same thought, but not so fully expressed, in Gal. vi. 14: 'crucified to the world.' Paul asks *why,* if all this be so, his readers are *submitting-to-dogmas as* though they were still *living* their old life *in the world. Allow-yourselves-to-be-dogmatized:* the passive form of a verb derived from the word *dogma.* The active form is found n Esth. iii. 9, 2 Macc. x. 8, and means to issue an authoritative command. The passive form here used does not, however, imply that the Christians at Colossæ were actually submitting to this spiritual tyranny; and therefore does not necessarily imply blame. But it implies that efforts were being made to place them under the bondage of dogmas. Paul's question reveals how inconsistent with their relation to Christ and His death is such bondage. To try to maintain it, is to try to keep in prison one whom death has set free. By showing this, Paul practically exhorts his readers not to bare the neck to the yoke which others would impose. Notice the contrast *died . . . from the . . . world* and *living in* the *world:* cp. Rom. vi. 2. This verse is a practical application of *v.* 14. For the decrees which the false teachers would reimpose have been nailed to the cross of Christ and thus made invalid.

21. Various prohibitory dogmas which the false teachers sought to impose. This correct meaning of these words was observed so early as Tertullian: *Against Marcion* bk. v. 19. But it was overlooked by some of the Latin Fathers. What the prohibited things were, Paul did not find it needful to say. His readers knew well. The word *taste* evidently refers to the eating and drinking of *v.* 16. And to the same refer most probably the words *handle* and *touch*. This inference is strongly confirmed by *v.* 22: for food and drink are, and most things are not, destroyed in their use. Of the three words, the first seems to be somewhat stronger than the third, which seems to denote always a mere touch, whereas the first is sometimes used in the sense of 'take hold of.' Hence the RV. reverses the order of the AV. The words are in an ascending scale of stringency. Of this, that, and the other, these teachers say, 'Do not take it, do not even taste it, do not so much as touch it.'

22a. *All which things:* those forbidden by the dogmatizers. *Are for destruction by the using:* they exist in order to be used up and thus destroyed. This proves that the forbidden things were articles of food. For all such are by their nature perishing; and attain the aim of their existence by being consumed. Cp. 1 Tim. iv. 3, 'to abstain from articles of food, which God created to be partaken of.' Also 1 Cor. vi. 13, 'food for the belly, and the belly for the food:' i.e. each is designed for the other, and both will pass away. And 2 Pet. ii. 12, 'born to be caught and destroyed.' The argument here is that, since these articles of food were created in order to be eaten, to forbid them is to bring back the state of childhood (cp. Gal. iv. 3) in which for a time certain things were not allowed to be put to their natural use.

22b. These words have evidently no connection with those immediately foregoing. Consequently, *v.* 22*a* must be a parenthetic comment on the prohibitions of *v.* 21; and *v.* 22*b* must be joined to 'dogmatized' in *v.* 20, as a further description of the ordinances which the false teachers sought to impose. *Commandments:* verbal prohibitions, resting on doctrinal grounds or *teachings*. All were of human origin. This clause recalls a similar rebuke of empty forms of religion in Isa. xxix. 13, which in the Lxx. reads, 'teaching *commands* of men and *teachings*.' It was quoted by Christ in Mt. xv. 9 as a warning to some who 'transgress the commandments of God because of' their 'tradition.' This similar use of O. T. words suggests whether Paul had heard of the discourse of Christ there recorded.

We saw under *v.* 16 that the mention of 'drink' proves that the false teachers not only maintained but exaggerated the Mosaic prohibitions. Such exaggerations were evidently *commandments and teachings of men*. And the divine commands of the Law of Moses became mere human precepts when they were asserted to be still binding after they had been revoked by Christ. The perpetual obligation of the Law was therefore a demand resting only on human authority. Consequently, all the prohibitions suggested in *v.* 16 come under this description, and under the warning in *v.* 8.

23. Paul's final and solemn judgment about the mere human and traditional teaching which forms the basis of the dogmas which some would impose on the Christians at Colossæ. They are *things* (or better *a class of things*) *having indeed a repute of wisdom*. In other words, these 'commands and doctrines' belong to a larger category to which as a whole the following words apply. *Repute* (literally *word*) *of wisdom:* a verbal utterance of wisdom, i.e. either called wise or claiming to be wise; senses closely allied. This recalls 'philosophy,' i.e. 'love of wisdom' in *v.* 8, by which Paul feared that his readers might be despoiled. *Self-imposed-worship:* evidently the 'worship of angels' in *v.* 18, this looked upon as a fiction of man's invention. It keeps before us, as in *vv.* 8, 22, the human origin of that which Paul here condemns. *Lowliness-of-mind:* again recalling *v.* 18 where, as here, a professed inward state of mind is joined with outward forms of religion. *Unsparing treatment of* one's *body:* harsh refusal to it of that which rightly or wrongly it desires. It seems to be a description of the prohibitions in *v.* 21. And these three things, self-imposed worship, apparent humility, ascetic self-denial, are represented as an encompassing element, perhaps as an auriole of glory, of the false teaching Paul here combats: *in self-imposed-worship etc.* This composite surrounding gained for it the *repute of* wisdom. [Paul's language suggests that it was an empty repute: μέν solitary.]

This apparent glory was no mark of real worth: *not in any honour*. The precise meaning of these words is very obscure. Perhaps Paul wishes to say that this unsparing treatment, this refusal of all pleasant things, was no *honour* to the body, i.e. no recognition of its true dignity. For all asceticism is contempt of the body. From the *body*, the organized unity belonging to each one, Paul now turns to *the flesh*, the material constitution which human bodies have in common, which creates common needs, likes, and dislikes, and thus exerts a common influence on the spirit within. *Indulgence* (or *satiety*) *of the flesh:* a supply to the full of these needs and desires, good or bad. The word rendered *against* is in itself neutral; and may refer, as the context determines, to something gratifying, or checking gratification of the flesh. Perhaps the latter here. And, if so, we may join these words closely to the word *honour*. Thus understood, the verse means that these human prescriptions, though possessing a repute of wisdom, as being apparently fitted to show men a way to the attainment of their highest good, are not associated with any real honour to the body in the way of guarding it from the self-indulgence which so often covers it with shame.

Verses 20—23 prove that our relation to Christ renders, or ought to render, impossible submission to the empty dogmatism of *vv.* 16—19. And from it we may glean something about the nature of this dogmatism. We have what seem to be some of the very words of these spiritual autocrats; words forbidding by mere human authority the eating of food destined by the Creator to be eaten. We are reminded that their worship of angels was a fiction of their own fancy; and that their hard treatment of their own bodies was not accompanied by any real honour to the body as the temple of God, and was not of any use to enable men to resist the temptations to self-indulgence prompted by the constitution of the body. Yet, as so often in the history of the world, this homage to citizens of the unseen world, this refusal of the luxuries and comforts of life, and the apparent humility of which these seem to be an outward expression, gained for these teachers credit for rare wisdom, i.e. for acquaintance with things unknown to the multitude. All this surrounded with an illusive auriole of glory the spiritual tyranny with which these apparently wise ones sought to dictate, by their own arbitrary will, restrictions to those foolish enough to submit to them. But to those who are Christ's such submission is impossible. For by His death they have themselves died, and have thus escaped from all spiritual bondage.

III. 1—4. The new life into which, by their union with Christ in His resurrection and ascension, Christians have already entered, a life utterly inconsistent with bondage to human dogmas. Thus, after bringing to bear upon the errors of ch. ii. 16—19, in *vv.* 20—23, the believer's union with Christ in His death, Paul now brings to bear on the same the believer's union with Christ in His resurrection and ascension.

If then ye have been raised together with Christ: more glorious counterpart of ch. ii. 20, which it recalls. It takes up a statement in ch. ii. 12 and makes it a basis of exhortation. Through the resurrection of Christ we have been made citizens of the world to which He has gone and sharers of its wealth and glory. That this resurrection with Christ includes not only new spiritual life but also a place with Christ in glory, is made clear by the exhortation which follows. *The things above:* the blessings of heaven. These are the reward of faithful service on earth, and are within reach of present human effort and are its noblest aim. Indeed every effort to please Christ and to advance His kingdom may be looked upon as an effort to gain the things at His right hand: for these are an inevitable and known result of such effort. Cp. Rom. ii. 7, 'seek glory and honour and incorruption.' *Where Christ is:* cp. Rev. xxii. 12, 'My reward is with Me.' Christ and the reward are together. Paul's assertion is then further developed. Among the things above *Christ is;* more accurately defined, He is *at the right hand of God:* and He is there, not worshipping or standing, but *sitting* in majesty. Same teaching in Rom. viii. 34, Eph. i. 20, Heb. i. 3, 13, viii. 1, x. 12, xii. 2, 1 Pet. iii. 22, Mt. xxvi. 64 etc. These passages reveal a thought familiar in the early Church.

2. *Mind the things above:* literally *the things above, make these the objects of your thought.* The repetition of *the things above* keeps conspicuously before us the new and lofty element just introduced. *Not the things on the earth:* cp. Ph. iii. 19, 'who mind the earthly things.' This antithesis to *the things above* recalls the low aims of the false teachers. For their whole thought was, in spite of their religiousness, after the passing things of earth.

3. Reason for the foregoing exhortation, viz. that the life which Paul's readers once lived on earth has ceased: consequently they can no longer 'mind the things on the earth.' *Ye-are-dead* or *ye-have-died:* in the death implied in the burial of ch. ii. 12 and hypothetically stated in *v.* 20. Christians are not merely 'dead to the world,' i.e. separated by the death of Christ from its control, but dead absolutely; i.e. their former life which was entirely earthly has come absolutely to an end. So complete is the change that Paul can describe it only by saying that they are *dead.* And the dead care nothing for things pertaining only to the world they have left. So, if Christians are true to their profession, will they no longer care for things merely belonging to earth.

And your life: like Christ they still live, though dead: so Rev. i. 18, 'living and was dead;' 2 Cor. v. 15, 'all died . . . they who live.' For they share already the immortal life of the Risen One. And this is their only life. For all they have and are and do is an outflow of it. On earth they are living a life which in its essence belongs to heaven and which will develop into eternal life. *Lies-hidden:* beyond human sight and beyond reach of accident and death. *With Christ:* for they are dead, buried, and risen with Him. Whatever Christ has and is, they share. *In God:* the surrounding and life-giving element of the new life, and its impenetrable bulwark. As Christ is (Jno. xvii. 21) in the Father, so are Christians *with Christ in God.* And, in the arms of omnipotence, their life, though apparently exposed to deadly peril, is absolutely and for ever safe.

This Christian life, hidden as to its root and essence beyond reach of human intelligence and human attack, is also incomprehensible in its manifestations. For these are an outflow of its hidden essence. Thus are men on earth living a life hidden from the children of earth, a life absolutely safe, a participation of Christ's life in heaven. For by union with Christ in His death on the cross their old life has ceased; and by union with the Risen One they have entered a life altogether new.

4. This life cannot be for ever hidden. Like all hidden things, it must be manifested: Mk. iv. 22. *When Christ etc:* or *whenever Christ be manifested:* suggesting uncertainty about the time of an event which itself is absolutely certain. *Manifested:* set publicly before the eyes of all men in the great day. So will all men themselves be manifested: 2 Cor. v. 10. The same word is used of Christ's self-presentation to men in His earthly life: Jno. xxi. 1, 14. To describe His appearance in judgment, the word 'revelation' is also used: 1 Cor. i. 7, 2 Th. i. 7, 1 Pet. i. 7, 13. For in that day manifestation and revelation (see under Rom. i. 19) will coincide: i.e. Christ will be set before the eyes of all; and all will actually see Him.

Christ is *our life:* for we shall live (Jno. xiv. 19) because He lives and because (Gal. ii. 20, Jno. xvii. 23) He lives in us and we in Him. Consequently, where Christ is, there is our hidden life: and when Christ is manifested to the eyes of all men, then shall we also be manifested, sharing the splendour of His manifestation. *With Him:* a frequent phrase, making conspicuous the truth that we shall be all that Christ has and is. *In glory:* surrounded with a splendour which will excite the admiration of all: so 2 Cor. iii. 7, 8, 9, 11, Ph. iv. 19, 1 Tim. iii. 16. At present the real dignity of the sons of God is hidden from the eyes of men and indeed from their own eyes, as Christ is hidden from mortal sight. In that day Christ in His essential grandeur will appear and with Him will appear also the grandeur with which He will adorn His servants. Cp. Ph. iii. 21, 'conformed to the body of His glory,' and Rom. viii. 19, 21, 'revelation of the sons of God . . . glory of the children of God.'

The believer's death and his pursuit only of things in heaven will in nowise unfit him for life on earth, or lessen his interest in things around. For the things of earth reach forward in their influence into the world to come. For instance, the movements of political life and the course of war have again and again helped or hindered the progress of the Gospel. Consequently, the Christian man whose eyes are open to the many spiritual issues at stake will watch these movements with deepest interest. Even the details and drudgery of common life receive thus importance and dignity. On the other hand, the new light in which he views all things will save him from the degrading tyranny which the uncertainties of earth exercise over those whom Christ has not made free.

Notice that in the phrases '*dead*' and '*risen* with Christ' we have an ideal Christian life which is ours objectively in Christ; and which it is our privilege to make subjectively our own by faith. Hence Paul sometimes speaks as though his readers were already actually dead with Christ: at other times he urges them to appropriate the inward experience thus described. Contrast Col. iii. 5 with *v.* 3 and Gal. v. 24. This apparent contradiction is easily understood, and is spiritually helpful. To speak of believers as already dead with Christ, helps our faith: to urge them to put to death their members on the earth, warns us that the ideal needs to be made actual.

DIVISION III. reveals the specific occasion of the Epistle, viz. errors, or possibly one composite error, which some unknown persons were actively pressing on the Christians at Colossæ. Before mentioning this great danger, Paul armed his readers in DIV. II. with a complete protection against it, viz. a full exposition of the nature and work of Christ. He begins DIV. III. by saying in § 8 that he has written this exposition in order to guard them from seductive and perverse reasoning; and then goes on to recognise the solid front which faith enables them to present to all opponents, and to beg them, as already they have laid hold of Christ, to make Him the surrounding element, the nutritious soil, and the firm foundation, of their life and movement.

In § 9 Paul's warning becomes more definite. The false teaching professes to be philosophy; but is really empty deception. It is such as we might expect from its outward source, viz. mere human tradition, and from its inward principle, viz. the rudiments of religion common to all mankind. And it does not take for its directive principle the one true norm, viz. the Person and Work of Christ. This norm, Paul further expounds, keeping in view the errors at Colossæ and thus to some extent indicating their nature. From

§ 10 we shall learn that the seducers worship angels. And in § 9 Paul says that Christ, in whom the whole nature of God finds perfect embodiment in human form and in whom His people find their full development, is Himself Lord of the successive ranks of angels. From § 10 we shall also learn that the false teachers sought to enforce the restrictions and ordinances of the Jewish Law. And Paul teaches in § 9 that in Christ His people have received the fulness of which circumcision was but an outline, and that, just as it is needless to circumcise a corpse, so they who have been spiritually laid in the grave of Christ need no circumcision. Moreover, if dead with Christ, they are also by faith sharers of His resurrection. By forgiving their sins, God raised them from the dead. He did this by nailing to the cross of Christ and thus making invalid the Law which condemned them. Thus, what the ministrations of angels could not do, God did without their aid. So conspicuously subordinate is their position in this culmination of the work of salvation, as contrasted with their more prominent place in the Old Covenant, that God may be said, by placing them in this subordinate position, to have used them simply to swell the triumphant train of the real Conqueror. Thus without exact mention of the errors he is combating, Paul has virtually overturned them by expounding more fully the relation of Christ to the work of salvation.

In § 10, the errors indicated in general language in § 9 are stated without reserve. The false teachers not only maintain the abiding validity of the Law, which God had made invalid by nailing it to the cross of Christ, but add to its stringency. And other teachers, or more probably the same, amid professions of humility as unworthy directly to approach God, pretending to receive instruction from visions of the inhabitants of the unseen world, bow in worship to angels. From this it is evident that the errors which Paul combats comprise two elements, Jewish and theosophic. The former he rebuts by asserting that the Law is only an unsubstantial outline, of which the solid reality belongs to Christ. The latter element he condemns as worthless by pointing to its real source, viz. an inflated self-estimate, offspring of a mind dominated by the needs and pleasures of the bodily life, a delusion possible only to those who have no hold of Christ and who do not know that from Him is derived, by the mutual contact and close cohesion of the members of His Body, spiritual nourishment, firmness, and growth. The entire mass of restriction and ritual, resting as it does simply upon mere human assertion and pertaining only at best to the rudiments of religion common to the whole world, is for us completely set aside by the cross of Christ, which has for ever separated us from the things in which once we lived. It is far below the feet of those who are already sharers of the immortal life of the Risen Saviour and already citizens of the world in which He reigns. Our one aim now is to seek, even while we tread the soil of earth, the infinite and abiding wealth of heaven. Our thoughts and hearts go forward to that day when the inner life, hidden now not only from the world, but in great part even from us who live it, will by the appearance of Christ be manifested in the splendour of the eternal glory.

Notice how in DIV. III. Paul has led us down into, and completely out of, the mist and gloom of error. Before we entered the dark valley, he had already fixed our gaze upon the Son of God, Creator of the world, crucified that He might reconcile us to God, and risen from the dead. In § 8 he warned us that danger was near. In § 9 the outlines of the enemy became discernible. In § 10 he came fully into view: and we seemed in Paul's argument to enter into deadly conflict with him. In that conflict, death came to our rescue, even the death of Christ upon the cross. We lay dead with Him. Then burst upon us like the light of Easter morn the bright vision of ch. iii. We saw Christ not only risen from the grave, but seated at the right hand of God. In the brightness of that vision we forgot that our bodies are still doomed to corruption and worms. These had vanished from our view. And we felt ourselves to be already where Christ is; and that henceforth the only matters worthy of our thought and effort are the realities which abide with Christ in God.

Notice how throughout DIV. III. Paul points to Christ. With Him we go down into the grave. In death we are with Him. And His presence guides us up to the light of day. As throughout this Epistle, so especially in this Division, the Son of God is All and in all.

DIVISION IV.
PRACTICAL APPLICATION.
Ch. III. 5—IV. 6.

SECTION XI.
GENERAL MORAL TEACHING: NEGATIVE.
Ch. III. 5—11.

Put to death then the bodily members which are upon the earth— fornication, uncleanness, passion, evil desire, and the covetousness, which is idolatry; [6] *because of which things comes the anger of God upon the sons of disobedience.* [7] *Among whom ye also walked once, when ye lived in these things.* [8] *But now, also ye, put away all things, anger, fury, badness, railing, shameful talking, out of your mouth:* [9] *lie not one to another; having put off the old man with his actions,* [10] *and having put on the new man which is being renewed for knowledge according to the image of Him that created him.* [11] *Where there is not Greek and Jew, circumcision and uncircumcision, barbarian, Scythian, bond, free; but Christ is all things and in all.*

In the light of the glory of the Risen Lord, which shone upon us in ch. iii. 1—4, the errors prevalent at Colossæ have utterly vanished. In the rest of the Epistle, no trace of them remains. But Paul remembers that his readers are still men on earth, exposed to the temptations incident to human life. Therefore, as he comes down from this Mount of Transfiguration, he uses the brightness of the vision as a moral influence deterring from sin, and prompting every kind of excellence. In other words, the vision of Christ in ch. iii. 1—4 is a transition from the specific errors treated in Div. III. to the principles of general morality taught in Div. IV. In § 11 we have negative moral teaching, i.e. a warning against various forms of sin; in § 12, positive moral teaching, i.e. incentives to various kinds of excellence; in § 13, precepts for various classes of persons; and in § 14 sundry general exhortations.

5. Practical application of the foregoing: *put-to-death then.* Cp. Rom. viii. 13, 'putting to death the actions of the body.' [In contrast to Rom. viii. 13, the Greek aorist here bids that the putting to

death be at once completed so that henceforth the bodily members be not dying but dead. Similarly 2 Cor. vii. 7, 'let us cleanse ourselves,' so that henceforth we be clean.] *The members which are upon the earth:* hands, feet, lips, eyes, etc., according to Paul's constant use of the word and his frequent reference to the immoral influence of the body. This implies that the word *death* is metaphorical. And it recalls the very strong metaphor of Mt. v. 29, 30, especially 'one of thy *members* perish.' The body exerts on the unsaved, through its various parts and their various functions, an active and immoral influence. Its members may therefore be represented as a living and hostile power. Not that matter or the body is essentially bad: for they are good creatures of God. But man's body has fallen under the dominion of sin, and has thus become a fetter with which sin binds the spirit within. This hostile power, Paul bids us kill, so that the bodily senses shall no longer, clamouring for indulgence, shape our actions or even our desires. He means that we surrender ourselves to the saving influence which comes to us through the cross of Christ and appropriate by faith the deliverance from the rule of the bodily life which Christ has gained for us by His death. Thus are the members of our body, which once enslaved us, nailed to His cross and thus rendered powerless for evil. And, since this deliverance comes by our own self-surrender and faith, we may be said, as here, ourselves to *put to death the members* of our bodies. Thus (2 Cor. vii. 1) we cleanse ourselves from all pollution of flesh and spirit. *Upon the earth;* recalls the same words in *v.* 2, thus bringing them to bear on this exhortation. Our bodies and all that pertains to them belong to the earth. Therefore, to allow them to rule us, whom God has raised to heaven, is to bow to the dominion of a world which God has placed far beneath our feet.

Fornication, uncleanness: as in Gal. v. 19. *Passion:* an inward emotion aroused by some external object; in this case by an impure object prompting inchastity. Same word in Rom. i. 26. *Desire:* good or bad; see under Gal. v. 17. It therefore needs to be further specified as *evil desire.* It is a wider term than *passion,* and describes a mind going out after some external object. These four terms descend from the specific to the general: intercourse with harlots, any form of outward inchastity, the inward emotion from which inchastity springs, any bad desire. *Covetousness,* literally *having more:* desire for more than our share. The definite article raises this sin into special prominence: and this is increased by the comment which follows. *Which* (or better *which sort of thing*) *is idolatry:* it belongs to a class of things all which are idolatry. Covetousness is worship of material good. And it presupposes that our well-being depends upon having the good things of earth, and that therefore created objects around are arbiters of our happiness. To suppose this, is to put the creature in the place of the Creator, and to put man under the dominion of the accidents of life. Thus (1 Tim. vi. 10) 'love of money is a root of all the evils.' That this apparently casual assertion is repeated in Eph. v. 5, reveals its firm hold of the thought of Paul. This double warning is the more needful because the great evil of covetousness is not at once apparent. Both covetousness and sensuality are exact contraries, in different directions, to seeking the things at God's right hand.

Notice here, as in Rom. i. 29—31, 1 Cor. vi. 9, Gal. v. 20, a catalogue of sins. This marked feature of Paul's writings reveals a familiar student of fallen human nature. Also that, after bidding us put to death the members of our body, Paul mentions first sins directly connected with the body.

This list of sins is placed in grammatical apposition to *the members which are upon the earth* as something which we must *put to death.* Practically it is an explanation of the foregoing metaphor. Paul really wishes us to kill the various sins which once used our bodily powers as instruments of evil. This simple explanation accounts fully for the arrangement of the verse. Paul does not say that these sins are members of our bodies, nor does he ever use such a metaphor. But, looking upon the bodies of the unsaved as organs of sin, as animated by a power hostile to us, he bids us put them to death; and then explains his meaning by saying that what he wishes us to kill is sin in its various forms. Thus this verse is a natural development of the teaching of Rom. vi. 12—19.

6. Solemn assertion of the inseparable connection of sin and punishment. A frequent conclusion to Paul's lists of sins: Eph. v. 6, Gal. v. 21, 1 Cor. vi. 10. He was accustomed thus to guard from abuse the doctrine of Justification through Faith. This solemn assertion greatly strengthens the foregoing exhortation. *Anger of God:* Rom. i. 18, v. 9: His determination to punish. It *comes* 'in the day of anger and of revelation of the righteous judgment of God,' Rom. ii. 5. The certainty of future punishment makes it to Paul's thought a present reality, as though retribution were already on the way: cp. 1 Th. i. 10. It *comes* down from heaven *upon* the wicked. *Disobedience:* same word in Rom. xi. 30, 32, Eph. ii. 2, v. 6, Heb. iv. 6, 11. It is practical unbelief. *Sons of disobedience:* Eph. ii. 2, v. 6: as though the abstract principle were the source of their immoral nature. In each sinner the abstract principle of unbelief has given birth to a child. Similarly Jno. xvii. 12, 'son of destruction;' 1 Jno. iii. 10, 'children of the devil;' Eph. v. 8, 'children of light;' Lk. xx. 36, 'sons of the resurrection.' It is a Hebrew phrase: 1 Sam. ii. 12, 'sons of Belial;' xx. 31, 'a son of death is he.' The phrase suggests how completely disobedience is a part of the nature of sinners.

On the correct reading of this verse see Introd. iii. 2.

7. If in *v.* 6 we omit 'upon the sons of disobedience,' we must render here *in which things ye walked:* cp. Eph. ii. 2, 2 Cor. iv. 2, Rom. vi. 4. This would imply that when the Colossians *lived in these things* they *walked in* them. Now, when used of sinners, the word *live* can mean only the outward manner of life. Touching the inner reality, their state is not life, but death. In this sense none but believers can be said to live and to have vital surroundings: e.g. Gal. ii. 20, 'live in faith.' And, if the word *live* means here only the outward manner of life, it is practically the same as the word *walk*. Consequently, if we omit the doubtful words in *v.* 6, the latter part of *v.* 7 becomes an empty tautology. This confirms the testimony of almost all the ancient documents that these words are genuine; and suggests that this is one more of the many cases in which the Vatican MS. omits genuine words.

If we accept these words as genuine, we must render *among whom also ye walked*. Cp. Eph. ii. 3, 'among whom also we had our manner of life formerly in the desires of our flesh.' They travelled in company with other sons of disobedience. All walked along the same broad way. *Lived in these things:* close parallel in Rom. vi. 2, 'live in it,' i.e. in sin. Somewhat different is Col. ii. 20, 'living in the world.' Formerly Paul's readers lived in the sins mentioned above: they then went along a path trodden by those whose character is derived from, and determined by, the principle of rebellion against God. This justifies the exhortation of *v.* 5, and prepares a way for that of *v.* 8.

8, 9a. *But now:* Paul's frequent contrast of past and present: so ch. i. 22, 26, Eph. ii. 13, Rom. vi. 22, vii. 6. It introduces here, in contrast to the readers' past life just described, a repetition in plain language of the metaphorical exhortation of *v.* 5. *Put-away:* as in Eph. iv. 22, 25, Rom. xiii. 12. *Also ye;* joins the Colossian Christians in present duty with all believers, just as the same words in *v.* 7 joined them with 'the sons of disobedience.' *All things:* including the list in *v.* 5, the further list now added, and every kind of sin. It gives to Paul's prohibition the widest universality.

Anger: a disposition which prompts to inflict pain or injury : see under Rom. i. 18. *Fury:* a bursting forth of this disposition. Same words in same order in Rom. ii. 8, describing God's determination to punish sin. Converse order in Eph. iv. 31. That they are here classed among sins, reminds us how easily anger oversteps the line and becomes evil. *Badness:* general worthlessness, in contrast to excellence : same word in Rom. i. 29, 1 Cor. v. 8, xiv. 20, Eph. iv. 31. *Railing:* the Greek original of our own word *blasphemy.* It denotes any hurtful or evil speaking against God or against man. See under Rom. ii. 24, iii. 8. *Shameful speaking:* foul-mouthed language of any kind. These two forms of improper speech are closely associated. For language hurtful to our neighbour easily becomes coarse abuse. And both are a frequent expression of *anger* and *fury. Out of your mouth;* adds to the prohibition graphic definiteness. 'Put out of your mouth, as unworthy to be in it, every form of bad speech.' To take these words merely as describing the bodily organ of speech, (cp. Eph. iv. 29,) would make them almost meaningless. *Lie not:* another kind of prohibited language. *One to another;* recalls their close mutual relation, as (Eph. iv. 25) 'members one of another.' This separate prohibition of falsehood reminds us of its unique wickedness : cp. Rev. xxi. 8.

9b, 10. Reasons, negative and positive, supporting the prohibitions of vv. 8, 9a. *Put-off:* as one takes off and lays aside clothing. Same word in ch. ii. 15, where see note. *The old man:* same words in Rom. vi. 6. So complete is the change that the man himself as he formerly was is spoken of as an *old* garment laid aside, as though personality itself were changed. So 2 Cor. v. 17, 'the old things have gone by.' *Actions:* same word as in Rom. viii. 13, xii. 4. The various activities of the old life are supposed to have been laid aside together with their one personal source : *the old man with his actions.*

Put-on: as one puts on clothes or weapons, the exact counterpart of *put-off.* Same word in Mt. vi. 25, Cor. v. 3 ; and in Rom. xiii. 12, 14, Gal. iii. 27, where we have close parallels. *The new man:* in marked contrast to *the old man.* So complete is the change, and so distinct from ourselves is the new life, that Paul speaks of it as a new personality put on as we put on clothing. This implies an inner and neutral and unchangeable personality which puts off and on, and another personality with moral qualities which is *put off* and *on. New:* recent in time : same word in 1 Cor. v. 7, Mt. ix. 17, etc. ; a cognate word in Eph. iv. 23. It recalls the shortness of time since the change. The word rendered *renewed* comes from another root found in Eph. ii. 15, iv. 24, 2 Cor. iii. 6, v. 17, and denoting that which is new in quality.

Which-is-being-renewed: a gradual renovation day by day of the new character which has once for all been *put on*. The old character, now put off, was day by day undergoing corruption: Eph. iv. 22. Thus the new life is represented as one definite assumption of a character which henceforth is gradually progressing. The word *renewed* does not necessarily mean restoration to a former state. For 'the New Covenant' is by no means a restoration of the Old Covenant to its original form: and the 'New Earth and Heaven' will differ greatly from the present ones. But it involves the removal of all defects. The renewal will not be complete until every trace of the damage done by sin is erased.

Knowledge, or *full-knowledge:* same word as in ch. i. 9, 10, ii. 2. It notes the direction and aim of this renewal, as designed to bring us *into full-knowledge*. As the Christian life progresses we know more and more of that which is best worth knowing. *Image:* an outward manifestation of the inward reality of God. It is the nature of God as set before the eyes of men. *Him that created:* the Father, as always; Rom. i 25, Eph. iii. 9. This is confirmed by Col. i. 16, where Christ is not the Author, but the Agent, of creation. *According to* the *image etc.;* recalls at once the same words in Gen. i. 26, 27. Cp. Jas. iii. 9. The story of creation teaches that the Creator is Himself the Archetype of His intelligent creatures. Now the Creator knows perfectly whatever He has made. And Paul says that this divine knowledge is a pattern of the knowledge which this renewal aims to impart to men: *for knowledge according to* the *image of Him that created him:* viz. *the new man*, the chief matter of this verse. Consequently, the word *created* must refer to the moral re-creation. This use of a word originally used of the old creation implies that the old and new are analogous. So are all God's works in harmony one with another, and in proportion to the similarity of their occasion. Whether the words *according to the image* etc. be joined to *knowledge* or to *being-renewed*, is unimportant and was perhaps not definite to the writer's mind. For *knowledge* is an aim of the renewal, and the Creator is its pattern: therefore the knowledge aimed at must be a human counterpart of the Creator's infinite knowledge. As the renewal makes progress, we shall in greater measure share God's knowledge of all that He has made and done. In other words, spiritual growth is growth in intelligence.

This mention of knowledge as an aim of renewal is in close

harmony with ch. i. 9, 28, ii. 2, and with the general scope of this Epistle.

[Grammatically, the aorist participles *having-put-off* and *having-put-on* denote only actions preceding, in act or thought, the laying aside of sin to which in v. 8 Paul exhorts; and do not say whether the putting off be something still to be done and therefore a part of the exhortation, or something already done and therefore a reason for it. Each of these expositions is in harmony with Paul's thought elsewhere: cp. Gal. iii. 27 for the latter, and Rom. xiii. 14 for the former. The practical difference is very slight. Perhaps it is best to understand Paul to mean that by joining the company of the followers of Christ the Christians at Colossæ had already formally stripped off from themselves and laid aside their former life and character and had put on a new life; and that he appeals to this profession as a reason for now laying aside all sin. Similar appeal in Rom. vi. 2. This latter exposition may be embodied in translation by rendering, *inasmuch as ye have put off etc.*

11. A comment on the new life just described as a new man undergoing further renewal. *Where there is* etc.: the new life looked upon as a locality in which the old distinctions are no longer found. Paul cannot repress a thought very familiar to him, the great distinctions of *Greek and Jew*, of *bond* and *free;* and these distinctions overshadowed and set aside by *Christ.* Close parallels in Gal. iii. 28, 1 Cor. xii. 13. The similarities and differences of these unexpected allusions to the same human distinctions as set aside in Christ reveal the hand not of a copyist but of one original author. *Greek and Jew:* in this order only here; contrast even 1 Cor. i. 22. These words embrace all mankind from the point of view of Jewish nationality: the words *circumcision and uncircumcision* do so from the point of view of Jewish ritual. The preposition *and* puts, in each pair, the two counterparts in conspicuous contrast and combination. *Barbarian, Scythian:* no longer an inclusive description. The word *Greek,* which to a Jew included usually all nations other than his own, seemed to Paul not sufficiently inclusive. He therefore adds the word *Barbarian,* a frequent and all-inclusive contrast to *Greek:* and to make his description still more specific he mentions by name one of the most barbarous of the barbarian nations. Cp. Josephus, *Against Apion* bk. ii. 38, "The Scythians differ little from wild beasts." As not containing an inclusive description of mankind, these two last words are added without a connecting conjunction. And in the same loose way the words *bond, free,* are added, the reader being left to observe that they

include the whole race. As in 1 Cor. xii. 13, Gal. iii. 27, Paul declares that in the new life these wide distinctions do not exist.

But Christ etc.: a positive truth, of which v. 11a is but a negative counterpart. *All things in all* persons: see under 1 Cor. xv. 28, where 'God is all things in all.' To have *Christ,* is to have *all things:* for He is Himself all that His servants need. *And in all* His servants, as Himself all things to them, *Christ is.* In the slave Christ is, as his liberty; in the Scythian, as his civilisation and culture. And since Christ includes in Himself the whole world of man's need, and dwells in all His servants, all human distinctions, which are but embodiments of human defects, have in the new life passed utterly away. National and social barriers there cannot be where Christ is.

In Div. III. Paul dealt with the specific matter of this Epistle, viz. certain errors prevalent at Colossæ, errors derogatory to the dignity of Christ. For his refutation of these errors, he prepared a way in Div. II. by expounding the nature and work of the Eternal Son. In Div. IV. this refutation of specific doctrinal error is followed by the general principles of Christian morality. And this moral teaching is directly based upon the specific and exalted Christian doctrine with which Div. III. concludes. For with Paul morality is always based upon doctrine: and doctrine is always brought to bear upon morality.

First comes, in § 11, negative moral teaching. And every line reveals the peculiar thought of Paul. The various members of the body, taken as a whole, are in his thought almost identical with various sins, of which he gives a list beginning with sins specially related to the body. All these, the members of the body metaphorically, the specific sins actually, Paul bids his readers kill. He calls special attention to the worship of material good implied in the everywhere-prevalent greed for wealth; and then points to the anger of God which will fall upon those whose character is moulded by rejection of His word. After a direct exhortation to cast away everything of this sort, Paul continues his list by mentioning sins of inward passion and of its outward expression in word, noting specially among sins of the tongue the unique sin of falsehood. He strengthens his exhortation by an ideal picture of conversion which he describes as a laying aside of the old personality and its various activities as one lays aside an old garment, and as a putting on of a new personality marked by progressive renovation tending towards perfect knowledge—like that by which the Creator knows all that He has made. This ideal Christian life, Paul cannot mention without remembering the national, theocratic, and social barriers which separate men, but which are completely broken down by Christ, who dwells in all His people as the full supply of all their need.

SECTION XII.
GENERAL MORAL TEACHING: POSITIVE.
CH. III. 12—17.

Put on then, as chosen ones of God, holy and beloved, a heart of compassion, kindness, lowliness of mind, meekness, longsuffering; ¹³ *forbearing one another, and forgiving each other if any one against any have complaint. According as the Lord forgave you, so also do ye.* ¹⁴ *And upon all this put on love, which is the bond of maturity.* ¹⁵ *And let the peace of Christ rule in your hearts, for which also ye were called in one body: and be thankful.* ¹⁶ *Let the word of Christ dwell in you richly; in all wisdom teaching and instructing yourselves with psalms, hymns, spiritual songs; with grace singing to God in your hearts.* ¹⁷ *And whatever ye do in word or deed,* do all things in the name of the Lord Jesus, *giving thanks to God, the Father, through Him.*

12. Practical consequence of *v.* 10. Just as the negative participial clause, 'having put off' etc., is introduced as a reason for the foregoing exhortation to put away all sins, of which a list is given, so now the positive participial clause, 'having put on the new man' etc., is made the ground of an exhortation to put on all Christian virtues. In each case the ideal Christian life already accepted is made the foundation of an appeal to realize that ideal in the practical details of Christian character. If so, *v.* 11 is a mental parenthesis. Paul interrupts for a moment his line of thought to give expression to other thoughts deeply interwoven into the tissue of his mind and ever ready, when occasion is given, to come to the surface.

Chosen ones of God: same words in Rom. viii. 33; see my *Romans,* p. 277. These were men whom, in the sense there expounded, God had selected from the rest of mankind to be specially His own. *Holy:* men whom, through the death of Christ and the preached Gospel, God has claimed to stand in peculiar relation to Himself. See under Rom. i. 8. The words *holy and beloved* take up and develop ideas already suggested by *chosen ones of God.*

Because chosen by Him before the foundation of the world, they are now sacred persons devoted to His service: and they cannot forget that the divine choice sprang from the love of God which now embraces them. These titles are inserted as a motive for putting on all Christian virtues.

Heart: same word as in 2 Cor. vi. 12, where see note. *Heart of compassion;* suggests that compassion, i.e. kindness towards the needy and helpless, is fitting to man, having its seat in his natural constitution. *Kindness:* as in 1 Cor. xiii. 4. It is that which makes intercourse with others pleasant. *Lowliness-of-mind:* Ph. ii. 3: a mind which does not form lofty plans for its own aggrandisement. Cp. Mt. xi. 29. *Meekness:* see under 1 Cor. iv. 21 : absence of self-assertion. *Long-suffering:* see under 1 Cor. xiii. 4. It is a mind which does not quickly yield to unfavourable influences. Notice here a list of virtues following a list of sins; a close coincidence with Gal. v. 22. Paul reminds his readers that they are God's chosen ones, separated from others to be specially His, and objects of His special love ; and bids them, in view of this their relation to God, to clothe themselves with compassion for the helpless and kindness toward all, with a lowly estimate of themselves, avoiding self-assertion, and refraining from anger.

13. A participial clause expounding the last word of *v.* 12 by showing what 'long-suffering' sometimes involves, and supporting it by the example of Christ. *Forbearing :* to refrain from laying our hands on others in order either to free ourselves from annoyance or to vindicate our rights. Compare a cognate word in Rom. iii. 25. It gives definiteness to the word 'long-suffering' by suggesting a probable occasion for it, viz. the unpleasant action of others. *Forgiving each other;* adds still further definiteness by suggesting a special kind of *forbearance,* viz. towards those who have done us wrong. *Each other:* literally *yourselves:* as though the whole Church were one person, as it is actually the one Body of Christ, so that forbearance towards a fellow-Christian is forbearance towards ourselves. Same word and idea in *v.* 16. Since the whole Church has one interest, each member gains by every good act to another. Indeed, only when forbearance is a benefit to the whole, is it really good. And only to such forgiveness do Paul's words refer. *Forgiving:* same word as ch. ii. 13, 2 Cor. xii. 13, ii. 7, 10, 1 Cor. ii. 12, Rom. viii. 32 : it is forgiveness looked upon as an act of grace or favour.

According as etc. : Christ's forgiveness to us the model, and therefore the motive, of our forgiveness of others. Notice that Paul assumes, as in ch. ii. 13, that his readers know that they are forgiven. This forgiveness is here attributed probably to *the Lord*, i.e. to Christ: in Eph. iv. 32, a close parallel to 'God in Christ.' The distinction is unimportant; for 'the Father judges no one, but has committed all judgment to the Son:' Jno. v. 22. Consequently, the Father's forgiveness is through the Son: or, leaving out of sight the ultimate source of forgiveness in the Father, we may think only, as here, of its immediate source in the Son. *So also do ye:* i.e. forgiving each other. The whole verse is a participial clause expounding 'longsuffering' in *v*. 12.

14. Grand completion of the list of Christian virtues. *Upon all these:* as an outer garment over all the underclothing. *Love:* to our fellows, as always when not otherwise defined: see under 1 Cor. xiii. 1, 3. Literally *the love*, the article making this virtue conspicuous, like 'the covetousness' in *v*. 5. *Bond:* same word in ch. ii. 19, iv. 3, Acts viii. 23. *Love* is a virtue which binds into one harmonious whole the various virtues mentioned above. *Maturity* or *perfection:* cognate to the word in 1 Cor. ii. 6, where see note. Perhaps it is best to understand this uniting bond as being an essential element of Christian *maturity*. Already from 1 Cor. xiii we have learnt that where love is there are all the virtues mentioned in *v*. 12. Love may therefore be called an overgarment enclosing all others, as a bond uniting them into one whole. And, since love is an infallible measure of Christian manhood, it may be called a *bond of maturity*.

The practical and positive exhortation of §12 retains the metaphor of clothing assumed in *vv*. 9, 10. Paul prefaces the exhortation by referring to God's eternal choice of the objects of salvation, to the sacredness of their position, and to the love with which God regards them. 'The new man,' which like a garment his readers are bidden to put on, is one of many colours, comprising many virtues, especially that of mutual forbearance and forgiveness, the latter being represented as kindness to ourselves, made binding upon us by the forgiveness we have received from Christ. These various virtues must be bound into one harmonious whole by the all-encompassing virtue of love, a uniting bond never absent from Christian manhood.

15. *The peace of Christ:* cp. Jno. xiv. 27. Practically the same as 'the peace of God' in Ph. iv. 7: a close parallel. This profound rest of spirit, like all else in the Kingdom of God, is from the Father through the Son; and is therefore *the peace* of God and *of Christ*. *Rule:* literally *award-the-prize:* same word in Wisdom x. 12, and cognate to the word *prize* in 1 Cor. ix. 24, Ph. iii. 14. In later

Greek it is frequently used in the sense of *rule*: for a conspicuous part of a ruler's work is to pronounce decision in matters open to question. This general sense of *rule* or *arbitrate* is all that we can attach to the word here: for nothing in the context suggests a definite prize to be awarded. In all details of life the inward rest which Christ gives is to be the principle determining what we are to be and to do. *In your hearts*: the home and throne and ward of the peace of God: Ph. iv. 7. *To which ye were also called*: the peace of Christ enjoyed by all who believe is an integral part of the purpose for which the Gospel call is proclaimed to men. *In one body*: the Church, as in ch. i. 18, 24. This is the locality in which is to be enjoyed the peace to which God has summoned us. This reminds us that the profound inward rest which Christ gives is a sure source of harmony with our fellow-Christians, and is impossible without such harmony. *Be thankful*: cp. Ph. iv. 7. Gratitude to God is a fertile source of *peace*. Acknowledgment of what He has done for us removes all fear that He will forsake us in the future.

Notice two sides of the Christian life. Paul bids us put on all Christian virtues in our dealings with others; and desires that divinely-given peace be the ruling principle within us, nourishing, and itself nourished by, gratitude to God.

16. *The word of Christ*: the Gospel proclaimed by Christ. So 2 Th. iii. 1, 'the word of the Lord;' and Jno. v. 24, 'My word.' *Dwell*: same word in Rom. viii. 11, 2 Cor. vi. 16, 2 Tim. i. 5, 14. *In you*: i.e. either *within* or *among*. Which of these was in the writer's thought, must be determined by the context. Probably the latter chiefly: for the word *teaching* shows that Paul thinks of *the word of Christ* as spoken by one to others. But, as the spoken word must come from the speaker's heart, the former sense, which is also suggested by the Greek word rendered *dwell*, is not altogether absent. *Richly*; suggests abundance and enrichment. Paul desires the spoken word of Christ to have a permanent and abundant place in the Church at Colossae, and in the lips and thoughts of its members, thus making them truly rich.

In all wisdom: to be joined probably to the words following as specifying the manner of *teaching*, rather than to those foregoing which have already a modal adverb, *richly*. *Teaching, admonishing*: as in ch. i. 28. Teaching is here put first, because the phrase *word of Christ* suggests first the actual impartation of knowledge. *Yourselves*: same word in *v.* 13. It describes a reflex action of the Church upon itself, building up itself by teaching the word of Christ. That this self-edification may be effective, the teaching must be *in all wisdom.* So ch. i. 28; cp. iv. 5: contrast 2 Cor. i. 12. It must be accompanied, as its surrounding element, by knowledge of that which is best worth knowing, and by all sorts of such knowledge. *Psalms:* as in 1 Cor. xiv. 15, sacred poems like those of the Book of *Psalms*. *Hymns:* an English form of the not uncommon Greek word here used, which denotes apparently a short poetical composition in praise to God. *Songs:* literally *odes:* apparently a wider term denoting any kind of poetry to be sung. Hence it was needful to add the word *spiritual:* i.e. prompted and permeated by the Spirit of God. The three Greek words are fairly represented by their English equivalents; the *psalms* recalling the sacred songs of the Old Testament, the *hymns* any song of praise to God, and the *spiritual songs* including any song prompted by the Holy Spirit.

With grace singing: a second participial clause, expounding the cognate word *song* in the foregoing clause. *With grace:* literally *in grace:* cp. 2 Cor. i. 12, 'in the grace of God.' We are to sing in the sunshine of the smile and favour of God, our songs prompted by His smile. *In your hearts:* the melody of the lips coming from, and filling, the heart. *To God:* the Object and Auditor of these songs. And whatever goes up to God must first fill the heart.

In all ages, songs of praise to God have been an important element of worship. So Philo, vol. ii. 484: "Then some one rising up sings a hymn made in honour of God, either himself having made it new or an old hymn of the poets of former days, . . . all others listening except when it is needful to sing the responses: then all, both men and women, sing." Cp. p. 485, where we have a long account of Jewish sacred singing. Of Christian song, even Pliny, in his letter to the Emperor Trajan, bears witness: "They were wont on a certain day to sing a hymn to Christ as God." Paul speaks here of sacred song as a means of Christian instruction. And in all ages popular songs, sacred and secular, have been the most effective teachers.

17. An all-embracing exhortation concluding the general moral teaching. *Whatever,* or literally *everything whatever;* looks upon the entirety of man's conduct as one whole. This is then distinguished into *word* and *deed,* the two great factors of human life. And these are summed up, and the idea of entirety is again expressed, the repetition giving it great emphasis, in the word *all-things.* The *name of* the *Lord Jesus:* the outward expression of the sovereignty of Christ. Paul bids us do all things as His professed servants. It is practically the same as 2 Th. i. 12, 'that the name of the Lord Jesus may be glorified in you.' *Giving thanks to God:* as an accompaniment of their entire activity. A close coincidence in

thought and expression with ch. ii. 7, iv. 2, Eph. v. 4, 20, 1 Th. v. 18. Abiding gratitude is a constant mark of the thought of Paul. *To God*, the *Father:* of Christ as of us. So closely related are these two aspects of the fatherhood of God, that we cannot determine which of them held the first place in Paul's thought here. Gratitude reminds us that God is our Father. And the foregoing mention of Christ reminds us that He is also the Father of Christ.

After, in § 11, bidding his readers lay aside every form of sin as unworthy of those who have stripped off as an old garment their former self and have put on a new self which is daily growing in likeness to God, Paul now proceeds to urge them in detail to put on the virtues belonging to this new life. Thus a negative warning is followed by a description of positive Christian excellence. And rightly: for mere negations never satisfy. He prepares a way for this positive exhortation by pointing to the choice of God which has consecrated all Christians to His service and selected them as objects of His special love. They must therefore act to each other with kindness and forbearance, even where injury has been received. As the crown of all virtues, giving to them unity and ripeness, there must be Christian love. And Paul prays that in their hearts may reign as an arbiter, pronouncing judgment in every doubtful point, the peace which Christ gives. He also desires that in the Church at Colossæ the good word spoken by Christ may ever be abundantly re-echoed in words of instruction and in sacred song. This outline of Christian excellence, necessarily scanty, yet rich, is concluded by an exhortation touching everything in life, viz. that it be done by them as bearers of the one Name which is above every name; with thanks to God, presented through the Master whose name they bear.

The prominence here given to gentleness and forbearance prompted by the love of God and by the example of Christ is worthy of special attention. Mere uprightness, although absolutely essential, can never reveal the full beauty of the Christian character.

SECTION XIII.

DIRECTIONS TO SPECIFIC CLASSES OF PERSONS.

CH. III. 18—IV. 1.

Wives, be in subjection to your *husbands as is fitting in* the *Lord.*
[19] *Husbands, love your wives, and be not bitter towards them.*
[20] *Children, obey* your *parents in all things: for this is well-pleasing*

SEC. 13.] COLOSSIANS III. 18—IV. 1. 223

in the *Lord.* [21] *Fathers, provoke not your children, that they be not discouraged.*
[22] *Servants, obey in all things* your *lords according to flesh, not with eye-service as men-pleasers, but in singleness of heart, fearing the Lord.* [23] *Whatever ye do, work from the heart, as for the Lord and not for men;* [24] *knowing that from* the *Lord ye shall receive the recompense of the inheritance. The Lord Christ, ye serve.* [25] *For he that acts unjustly will receive the injustice he has done: and there is no respect of persons.* [1] *Masters, the just thing and equality render to* your *servants, knowing that ye have a Master in heaven.*

After putting before his readers in § 12 virtues appropriate to, and binding upon, all Christians alike, Paul remembers that many of his readers bear one to another special relations, involving special and mutual obligations. Of these mutual relations of certain classes of his readers, he now speaks: viz. of wives and husbands in *vv.* 18, 19; of children and fathers, in *vv.* 20, 21; of servants and masters, in *vv.* 22—iv. 1. In each pair of relations, the subordinate member is put first as being under a more conspicuous obligation.

18, 19. Literally, *Women, be in subjection to the men:* for the Greek language has no distinctive terms corresponding to our words *wife, husband.* But the reference to married persons is unmistakable. *Be-in-subjection:* not worse in quality but lower in position. Same word in Lk. ii. 51, 1 Cor. xv. 28, the divine pattern of subordination; and in Tit. ii. 5, 9, 1 Cor. xiv. 34, Rom. xiii. 1, 5, etc. It suggests arrangement and order. *Fitting in* the *Lord:* such subordination being an appropriate acceptance on their part of the position given by Christ to women. A fuller account of this suitability is given in Eph. v. 22—24.

Literally, as above, *Men, love the women. Bitter:* contrasted in Jas. iii. 11 with 'sweet.' Cognate word in Rev. viii. 11, x. 9, 10. Similar words in all languages denote acute unpleasantness of word, demeanour, or thought. The stronger party, having nothing to fear from the weaker, is frequently in danger of acting or speaking harshly. To refrain from such harshness, even towards those we love, is sometimes, amid the irritations of life, no easy task. But it is binding upon the Christian.

20, 21. *Obey:* literally, 'listen from below,' i.e. listen to, and obey, their commands. The wife must place herself in a lower position as compared with her husband: children must pay attention to their parents' bidding. *In all things;* cannot include sinful commands: for even a parent's command cannot excuse sin, although it may mitigate the blame attaching to the child. Sometimes, but very seldom, a command evidently unwise is not binding on a child. But such cases are abnormal and do not come within the horizon of Paul's thought. The universality here asserted embraces the entire activity of the child in all ordinary cases. A sinful command lays no obligation upon wife, child, or servant. This exception reveals the imperfection of all verbal precepts. They must be interpreted, not always according to the letter, but in the light of the inborn moral sense. This is specially true of positive commands. *Well-pleasing:* without any limitation as to the person pleased. (So Tit. ii. 9.) Obedience is beautiful in itself and therefore pleasant to God and man. *In* the *Lord:* as in *v.* 18. The child's obedience to his parents must have Christ for its encompassing and permeating element. See further under Eph. vi. 1.

Then follows the corresponding obligation to *the fathers*. These only are mentioned, as being the chief depositaries of parental authority. *Provoke:* conduct calculated to arouse either action or emotion. In the former and in a good sense, in 2 Cor. ix. 2: here in the latter and in a bad sense. Paul forbids irritating commands or action. Close parallel with the injunction in *v.* 19. It notes in each case a frequent fault of the stronger party. *That they be not discouraged:* motive for the foregoing. Irritating commands cause little ones to lose heart: and than this nothing is more fatal to their moral development.

Such are the duties involved in the tender relations of life. Wives must take a lower place, and children must listen to their parents' commands. And in each case this must be in the Lord, i.e. as part of their service of Christ. Such conduct befits the wife's actual position, and is beautiful in the child. It is, to both wives and children, the real place of honour. But they to whom this submission is due are themselves bound by corresponding obligations. They must pay the debt of love; and must refrain from making their superior strength a means of gratifying a vexatious spirit, and thus causing pain.

22. From relations implying social equality, Paul now passes to a most important social relation implying inferiority; a relation already treated casually but forcibly in 1 Cor. vii. 21*f*. *Servants,* or *slaves:* see under Rom. i. 1. *Obey:* a duty binding alike on children and slaves. *In all things:* same words and compass and limitation as in *v.* 20. *Lords:* ordinary Greek term for *masters*. Cp. Gal. iv. 1, 1 Pet. iii. 6. It is the exact correlative to *servants*. The one works at the bidding and for the profit of the other. See under Rom. i. 1.

This common use of the word *lord* gives definiteness to it when applied to Christ. He is the Master whose word we obey and whose work we are doing. See especially ch. iv. 1. *Lords according to flesh:* their domain being determined and limited by the outward bodily life. Same phrase in Rom. ix. 3, 5, 1 Cor. x. 18. This limitation suggests that there is another department of the slave's life not controlled by an earthly master.

Not with etc.: description, negative and positive, of the kind of service to be rendered. *Eye-service:* found only here and Eph. vi. 6. It is work done only to please the master's eye. All such servants look upon themselves *as men-pleasers*. To please men, is their aim: and therefore naturally their work is only such as falls within the range of human observation. Such merely external service is utterly unworthy of the Christian. For it brings him down to the level of those whose well-being depends on the smile of their fellows. A close parallel from the pen of Paul in Gal. i. 10. *Singleness of heart:* exact opposite of *eye-service*, which is a hollow deception and does not come from the *heart*. *Fearing the Lord:* i.e. Christ, *the* One *Master*. Where true reverence of the Master is, there is *singleness of heart:* for His eye searches the heart. Where the all-seeing Master is forgotten, we seek as our highest good the favour of men: and our service sinks down to the external forms which alone lie open to the eye of man. Thus fear of the Supreme Lord saves even the slave from degrading bondage to man.

23. Another exhortation, without connecting particle, expounding and supporting the exhortation of v. 22. *Whatever ye do*, or *be doing:* emphatic assertion of a universal obligation. *From* the *heart:* literally *from* the *soul*, i.e. the seat of life. Same phrase in Eph. vi. 6, Mk. xii. 30, Dt. vi. 5. That which we *work* with our hands must not be mechanical but must flow from the animating principle within. *As for the Lord:* the worker's view of his own work, in contrast to a lower view of the same, 'as men-pleasers.' Our *work* must be done to please *the* One *Master*, *and not men*, each of whom is but one among many. [The negative οὐκ, where we might expect μή, embeds in an exhortation a virtual assertion. 'The work ye do is not for men.']

24. *Knowing that etc.:* a favourite phrase of Paul, e.g. Rom. v. 3, 1 Cor. xv. 58. It introduces a reason for the foregoing, based on known reality. *From* the *Lord ye shall receive:* counterpart to 'for the Lord.' *The inheritance:* eternal life, looked upon as awaiting the slave in virtue of his filial relation to God. So Rom. viii. 17. And inasmuch as the blessings of eternal life are in proportion

(2 Cor. v. 10) to the faithfulness of his service of Christ, they are spoken of as *the recompense of the inheritance.* This will come *from the* one *Master. Knowing* this, and doing all our work for Him, we do it ' from the heart.' *Ye-serve* or *serve-ye the Lord Christ:* either an emphatic reassertion of an objective truth underlying *vv.* 22—24, or an exhortation to make this truth subjectively the principle of our own life. The former exposition tells the slave his privilege: the latter bids him claim it; cp. 1 Cor. vii. 23. As *v.* 24*a* is a statement of known fact, perhaps the former exposition is better: but the practical difference is slight.

25. *He that acts-unjustly;* seems to refer specially to unjust masters, although it would include slaves. The same word in Philem. 18 refers to a slave's dishonesty. But that Paul refers here to the master's injustice, is made likely by the fact that this assertion of just recompense is given to support the foregoing assertion that Christian slaves are servants of Christ: *for he that etc.* That they are such, is more easily understood if they remember that even their master, at whose caprice they sometimes seem to be, *will* himself *receive* exact retribution for whatever *injustice he has done.* A very close coincidence of thought and phrase in 2 Cor. v. 10. This chief reference to the master is also supported by the word *respect-of-persons:* same word in same connection in Rom. ii. 11. For the master has very much more of the outward aspect which might seem to claim exemption from just retribution than has the slave. Moreover, a reference to masters is a convenient stepping stone to ch. iv. 1, where we learn that even slaves have claims upon their masters' justice.

IV. 1. The corresponding duties of *masters*, already suggested in ch. iii. 25. *The just-thing;* recognises rights between master and slave. Similarly, in Mt. xviii. 23-34 we have commercial transactions between a master and his slaves. The specific application to the slave of the essential principles of justice, Paul leaves to the master's own sense of right. *The equality:* a word frequent in Greek for even-handed justice, almost in the sense of our word *equity.* And this is probably its meaning here. Not only *the just thing,* viz. that which law demands, but *also equity,* that even-handed dealing which can never be absolutely prescribed by law. It has been suggested that Paul here bids masters treat their slaves as equally with themselves members of the family of God: so Philem. 16. But this would need a more definite indication than we have here, whereas the exposition adopted above is suggested naturally by the foregoing word *just.* We may therefore accept it as the more likely. *Knowing that etc.:* cp. ch. iii. 24. The action of the master, as of the slave, must rest upon the same basis of intelligent apprehension of objective reality. As in ch. iii. 22, so here, we have a contrast between *the* many *lords* and the One *Lord.* This must influence both slaves and masters.

The longer space given to slaves than to masters is easily accounted for by their greater number in the Church. The fuller treatment of the case of slaves as compared with that of the relations mentioned in ch. iii. 18—21 is explained by the greater difficulty of the subject. Possibly it was suggested to Paul by the conversion and return of Onesimus, a runaway slave. But, apart from this, the immense importance of the bearing of Christianity upon the position and duty of slaves justifies abundantly this careful treatment of the subject.

It is easy to apply to the relation of employers and hired servants, domestic and commercial, Paul's teaching about a relation which has now happily in this country passed away. For morality rests, not upon exact prescription, but upon broad principles. The worth of specific prescriptions is in the principles they involve. This gives to moral teaching a practical application far wider than the actual words used. Modern masters and workpeople who think only of the money each can make from the other sin against both spirit and letter of the teaching of this section.

Paul has now dealt specifically with the more conspicuous and important social relations, and has shown how the Gospel bears upon each. Those in subordinate relations must accept their position as a part of their relation to Christ; as must those who occupy superior positions. Even slaves must remember that their hard lot is in a real sense sacred. In that lot they are serving, not men, but Christ. Moreover, their service is not vain. As recompense, they will receive in the kingdom of God the inheritance which belongs to His sons. Paul bids them live up to this glorious position, to look upon themselves as servants of Christ, and to render to Him with joyful hearts such service as His piercing eye will approve. On the other hand, masters must remember that they owe to their slaves not merely what the law demands but even-handed fairness.

SECTION XIV.

SUNDRY GENERAL DIRECTIONS.

Ch. IV. 2—6.

Continually devote yourselves to prayer, watching therein with thanksgiving; ³ *at the same time praying also about us, that God may open to us a door of the word, to speak the mystery of Christ, because of which also I am bound;* ⁴ *in order that I may make it manifest, as I must needs speak.*

⁵ *Walk in wisdom towards those outside, buying up the opportunity.*

⁶ *Let your word be always with grace, seasoned with salt, to know how ye must needs answer each one.*

Continuously-devote-yourselves to prayer, or *persevere in prayer:* same words and sense in Rom. xii. 12, Acts i. 14. They suggest a continuance which requires effort. *Watching:* same word in 1 Cor. xvi. 13. It is the opposite of sleep: Mt. xxvi. 40, 1 Th. v. 6, 10. In our persistent prayers, our spiritual faculties must be in active exercise. We must, while we pray, be keenly alive to our own needs and dangers and to the promises of God. *With* (or *in*) *thanksgiving:* appropriate accompaniment, or surrounding element, of these watchful prayers. Close coincidence with ch. iii. 17, 15, ii. 7. Ceaseless prayer combined with ceaseless praise was the atmosphere of Paul's spiritual life.

3, 4. Beside prayer in general, to which in *v.* 2 Paul exhorts, he now places specific prayer for himself and his companions: *at the same time praying also about us.* He includes doubtless Timothy and other companions who share Paul's toil and need. *That God may open etc.:* precise object for which Paul would have his readers pray. *A door of the word:* a door for the Gospel to go through, i.e. an opportunity of preaching it. Cp. Acts xiv. 27. Such opportunity has already been given to Paul at Ephesus and Corinth: 1 Cor. xvi. 9, 2 Cor. ii. 12. He desires it now. His request implies that the events of life, on which such opportunities depend, are under the control of *God.*

To speak etc.: purpose of the desired opportunity. It expounds the *door of the word. The mystery of Christ:* as in Eph. iii. 4; cp. Col. i. 27, ii. 2. It is the secret which pertains to Christ and lies hidden in Him, a secret known only to those to whom God reveals it. That this secret has been committed to Paul and that therefore he is able to *speak the mystery of Christ*, makes him eager for an opportunity of doing so. *Because of which I am also bound,* or *lie bound:* the hostility of the Jews, which caused his arrest, having been aroused by his faithful proclamation of salvation for all men. Paul remembers the price he has paid for the privilege of preaching the Gospel. *Make-manifest:* set publicly and conspicuously before the eyes of men: see under Rom. i. 19. It is the correlative of *mystery:* ch. i. 26, Rom. xvi. 25. Another slightly different correlative is 'reveal:' Eph. iii. 5, Rom. xvi. 25. Paul desired so *to speak* as to set before all men the Gospel in which lies hidden, ready to be revealed to those who receive the word in faith, the great secrets which to know is eternal life. For this end he desires *that God may open for* him *a door of the word.*

As I must needs speak: not obligation but absolute necessity. Same word in same sense in *v.* 6, and in Eph. vi. 20, Rom. i. 27, viii. 26, 1 Cor. viii. 2. The needs of the world and the grandeur of the Gospel were to Paul an imperative necessity leaving him no choice but compelling him as if by main force to preach the word wherever he could and at all cost. This felt necessity forces from him now this cry for the help of his readers' prayers.

Notice here a marked characteristic of Paul, viz. constant desire for the prayers of Christians. So Rom. xv. 30, 2 Cor. i. 11, 2 Th. iii. 1, Eph. vi. 19. This desire is the strongest possible proof of his confidence in the power of prayer.

The open door for which Paul begs his readers to pray must have included the opening of his prison door: for in prison he could not preach the Gospel as the world's need demanded. But the progress of the Gospel, not personal liberty, was the real object of his desire. Indeed, personal liberty was to him of value chiefly as a means of preaching the word.

5. Preaching the word reminds Paul of those outside the Church, and of the influence upon them of everything done by members of the Church. *In wisdom :* as in ch. i. 28, iii. 16. *Those outside:* as in 1 Cor. v. 12. In our various relations to these, we must choose our steps in the light of knowledge of the eternal realities. *The opportunity* or *season:* the fit time for action: same word in Gal. iv. 10, vi. 9, 10. Paul thinks either of life as an opportunity of advancing the Kingdom of God, or of any opportunity which may from time to time arise. Since life is made up of opportunities, and from these derives its worth, the practical difference between these expositions is hardly perceptible. *Buy-up:* same word as *redeem* in Gal. iii. 13,

iv. 5. By using well an opportunity we make it our abiding enrichment: and the effort required in doing so is the price paid for the enrichment. The greatness and value of the possibilities of life, he opportunities it affords for influencing the unsaved, and the difficulty of seizing them as they pass, demand that every step be taken with wisdom.

This verse closely resembles Eph. v. 15, 16.

6. *Your word:* especially to 'those outside,' as is suggested by the end of the verse. *With grace:* same words as in ch. iii. 16. But here apparently we have the frequent classic sense of *gracefulness.* Same word in this sense in Eccl. x. 12, 'The words of a wise man's mouth are grace;' and Ps. xlv. 2, 'Grace is poured in thy lips.' The discourse of Christians should ever be clothed with moral attractiveness. (The common associations of the word *grace* remind us that this attractiveness is by the undeserved favour of God.) *Seasoned,* i.e. made pleasant to the taste, *with salt:* same words together in Mk. ix. 50, Lk. xiv. 34. To the idea of attractiveness to the eye suggested by the word *grace,* these words add that of piquancy to the intellectual taste. *To know how etc.:* further account of the discourse Paul desires in his readers. *To answer each one:* either objecting, or asking information. *Must needs answer:* to Paul's thought a good answer is an absolute necessity. He desires his readers *to know how* to give an answer which in *each* case will meet this necessity. The same necessity rests upon all who advocate the Gospel among those who professedly reject it. Cp. 1 Pet. iii. 15.

DIVISION IV. shows how the doctrinal teaching of Christ bears on morals and quickens into beauty even the common and little things of life. Christ requires from His servants a complete separation from all evil, and bids them put on a new life marked especially by kindness and forbearance. The Gospel, which places all men on one spiritual level as children of God, does not obliterate social distinctions; but makes each of them an opportunity of serving Christ. Even the great Apostle begs for his readers' prayers that he may have opportunity to speak the word as it needs to be spoken. And he remembers that in their words to others they need wisdom and the ornament of a Christian spirit.

DIVISION V.
PERSONAL MATTERS.
CH. IV. 7—18.

SECTION XV.
TYCHICUS AND ONESIMUS.
CH. IV. 7—9.

All the matters referring to me, Tychicus will make known to you, a beloved brother and faithful minister and fellow-servant in the Lord; ⁸*whom I have sent to you for this very thing, that ye may know the things about us and that he may encourage your hearts,* ⁹*with Onesimus our faithful and beloved brother, who is one of you. All the things here, they will make known to you.*

7. *The matters referring to me:* same words in same sense in Ph. i. 12. All matters personal to Paul, Tychicus will tell the Colossian Christians. It is therefore needless for Paul to say more about his condition or surroundings. *Minister:* see under Rom. xii. 8. The same word denotes the office of a *deacon* in Ph. i. 1, 1 Tim. iii. 8, 12; and possibly Rom. xvi. 1. But its various uses make it unlikely that standing here alone it has this technical sense. This would require further specification, as in Rom. xvi. 1. Nor is it probable that the word alone would bear the sense of 'minister of the Gospel' or 'of Christ;' as in ch. i. 7, 23, 25. It is easiest to suppose that *Tychicus* was Paul's minister or assistant; according to the simplest meaning of the word, e.g. Mt. xx. 26, xxiii. 11, and the corresponding verb in Philem. 13, Rom. xv. 25, Heb. vi. 10. In this sense Mark was 'useful' to Paul 'for ministry': 2 Tim. iv. 11. That Tychicus belonged to a band of helpers surrounding Paul, is made likely by the fact that Paul sent him, as here stated, to Colossæ, also (Eph. vi. 22, 2 Tim. iv. 12) to Ephesus twice; and had thoughts of sending him (Tit. iii. 12) on another mission. An important coincidence with all this occurs in Acts xx. 4, where Tychicus is one of a small band of companions travelling with Paul. In this last passage he is said to be a native of Asia, of which Roman province Ephesus was the capital: another important coincidence. The above references are our only sources of information about Tychicus. But he was *a beloved brother and trustworthy helper.* While speak-

ing of him thus, Paul remembers that both himself and Tychicus are servants of one divine Master; and therefore calls him a *fellow-servant:* same word in ch. i. 7. Similar transition of thought in Ph. ii. 22. *In the Lord:* embracing probably the entire description of Tychicus: same words in Ph. i. 14, Eph. iv. 1, vi. 21. The one Master was the surrounding element of the whole brotherhood, of the assistance to Paul, and of the joint service.

8. *Whom I have sent:* so Paul frequently sent to various Churches his trusted helpers: 1 Cor. iv. 17, 2 Cor. ix. 3, Ph. ii. 19, 23, 25, 28, 1 Th. iii. 2, 5. In this mission, the matters referring to himself were Paul's first thought: *v.* 8. But, remembering that others share his perils and toils and the interest and affection of the Christians at Colossæ, he passes from the singular in *v.* 7, 'touching me,' to the plural here: *that ye may know the things concerning us. Encourage your hearts:* as in ch. ii. 2. Thus Tychicus had a double errand, to take information about Paul and his companions and to cheer and stimulate the Colossian Christians.

9. *Onesimus:* only here and Philem. 10. This passing mention of him receives light from, and casts light upon, the Epistle to Philemon. See Introd. v. *Faithful* or *trustworthy:* specially suitable as a commendation of a runaway slave. *One of you;* implies that in some way Onesimus came from Colossæ, either as a native or as a former inhabitant. *All the things here;* marks the completion of the matter opened by similar words at the beginning of *v.* 7.

The mention of Tychicus in *v.* 7 and of Onesimus in *v.* 9 links this Epistle closely with those to the Ephesians and to Philemon. The references to Tychicus here and in Eph. vi. 22 are valuable comments on the character of a good man about whom we know very little. Thus this casual insertion of these two names both helps us to reproduce in thought the surroundings of the Apostle, and affords some confirmation of the genuineness of the Epistles which bear his name and of the historic truthfulness of the Book of Acts.

SECTION XVI.
SUNDRY GREETINGS.
CH. IV. 10—18.

There *greets you Aristarchus, my fellow-prisoner; and Mark the cousin of Barnabas, about whom ye have received commands, if he* come to you receive him; ¹¹ and Jesus who is called Justus. Of those who are of the circumcision, these only are fellow-workers for the kingdom of God, men who have become a help to me.

¹² There greets you Epaphras, who is one of you, a servant of Christ Jesus, always wrestling on your behalf in his prayers, that ye may stand mature and fully assured in every will of God. ¹³ For I bear him witness that he has much labour on behalf of you and of those in Laodicea and those in Hierapolis.

¹⁴ There greets you Luke, the beloved physician; and Demas.

¹⁵ Greet ye the brethren in Laodicea, and Nymphas and the Church in their house. ¹⁶ And when the letter has been read among you, cause that it be read also in the Church of the Laodiceans, and that ye read the letter from Laodicea. ¹⁷ And say to Archippus, Take heed to the ministry which thou hast received in the Lord, that thou fulfil it.

¹⁸ The greeting of me Paul by my own hand. Remember my bonds. Grace be with you.

10. 11a. *Aristarchus:* another companion of Paul, a Macedonian from Thessalonica. He was with Paul in the tumult at Ephesus, and on the return journey from Corinth through Macedonia to Jerusalem, and on his voyage as prisoner to Rome: Acts xix. 29, xx. 4, xxvii. 2. He sends a greeting to Philemon: Philem. 24. He is here called a *fellow-prisoner*, a title given in Philem. 23 to Epaphras, while Aristarchus is called only a fellow-worker. Similarly in Rom. xvi. 7 two kinsmen of Paul are called his fellow-prisoners. The word thus used means accurately a prisoner of war. (Cp. Ph. ii. 25, 'fellow-worker and fellow-soldier.') Its precise significance here would be explained by Tychicus: but it is unknown to us. The transference of the title from Aristarchus to Epaphras is specially puzzling, the more so as the letters seem to have been written at the same time. Whether these men voluntarily shared in turn the discomfort of Paul's prison, or through loyalty to him were themselves actually imprisoned, we have no means of knowing. But in any case this term is a title of high honour. Little did these faithful friends of Paul dream that their imprisonment, of whatever kind it was, would be to them on the imperishable page of Holy Scripture a title of honour as wide as the world and more lasting than time. This cursory mention of Aristarchus reminds us of the great multitude, not thus recorded, whose record is with God.

Mark: Philem. 24: another link connecting the Epistles. Evidently the same man as in 2 Tim. iv. 11, where he has a commendation similar to that in *v*. 11. There is no reason to doubt that he was the man referred to by Peter (1 Ep. v. 13) as 'Mark, my son.' Apparently he was 'John, surnamed Mark' in Acts xii. 12, 25, xv. 37, who in *v*. 39 is called, as here, simply *Mark*. The mother of this last had a house at Jerusalem to which Peter went when released from prison : Acts xii. 12. And the Mark here mentioned was (*v*. 11) a joy to Paul. This identification is confirmed by the explanation it affords of Barnabas' strong wish to keep him as his companion after he had once proved faithless : Acts xv. 37—39. For in that case they were cousins. And the references to Mark here and in 2 Tim. iv. 11 are pleasant proofs how completely the timid one had regained the friendship and approval of Paul.

Eusebius (*Church History* bk. ii. 15) says that the Mark to whom Peter refers was the author of the Second Gospel ; and (bk. iii. 39) quotes Papias, a writer of the second century, to the same effect. Similarly Irenæus (bk. iii. 10. 6) quotes the beginning and end of the Second Gospel as written by 'Mark, the interpreter and follower of Peter.' Eusebius says also (bk. ii. 16) that he founded the Church at Alexandria.

Cousin: the constant sense, except in very late Greek where it has the sense of *nephew*, of the common Greek word here used. So in Num. xxxvi. 11 (LXX.) it is used as a rendering of 'their uncle's sons.' And Eusebius (*Ch. Hist.* iii. 11) speaks of Simeon, second bishop of Jerusalem, as said to be *cousin* of Christ, on the ground that his father Clopas was brother to Joseph. *Barnabas :* the last mention in the N. T. of this valued friend of Paul.

About whom : i.e. Mark, the chief person in Paul's thought now. *Received commands :* already conveyed, as is implied in the past tense. Whether by messenger, or by a lost letter, we do not know. The plural number, *commands*, in view of the frequent use of the word in the singular, e.g. Eph. vi. 2, Rom. vii. 8—13, suggests that Paul's will was conveyed in more ways than one. Notice the apostolic authority implied in this word. The tenour of these commands is evidently given in the words following. *If he come to you ;* suggests that Mark had been sent on a mission, and that Paul was uncertain whether in discharging it he would visit Colossæ. Very similar injunction in 1 Cor. xvi. 10, 'if Timothy come, see that' etc. *Receive him :* welcome him in whatever aspect he presents himself, whether as Paul's delegate or simply as a brother Christian. Same word in same sense in 2 Cor. vii. 15, xi. 16, Gal. iv. 14.

Jesus : the Greek form of the Hebrew name Joshua, and used for the ancient leader in the LXX. constantly, and in Acts vii. 45, Heb.

iv. 8. The same name is also found in the genealogy of Christ: Lk. iii. 29. Its use here as a designation of an obscure Jewish Christian proves that the Eternal Son bore on earth, not merely a human name, but a name given to ordinary men. *Justus:* a Latin name meaning *just* or *righteous*, and common as a Jewish surname. It is the name given by Eusebius (*Ch. Hist.* iii. 35) to the third bishop of Jerusalem, a Jew. Same name in Acts i. 23, undoubtedly of a Jew; and in ch. xviii. 7 of a proselyte.

11b. The words *who are of* the *circumcision* are joined by AV. and RV. to the foregoing. This punctuation makes the words following an absolute assertion, and excludes even Epaphras from the number of Paul's helpers. But this is plainly contradicted by *v.* 12 and ch. i. 7. The words above must therefore be joined to those following, as nominative absolute, limiting the assertion therein contained. Evidently, Paul means that these three men were Jews, and were the only Jews who, by joining with him in work for the Kingdom of God, had been a comfort to him. This meaning is best reproduced by rendering *Of those who are of* the *circumcision, these only etc.* *Of* the *circumcision:* same phrase in Rom. iv. 12, Gal. ii. 12, Tit. i. 10, Acts x. 45, xi. 2. It describes their origin by pointing to the visible sign of the Covenant which of old God made with their race. *These only;* reminds us of the wide-spread hostility of the Jews to Paul. Cp. Tit. i. 10. *Fellow-workers:* as in Ph. ii. 25, iv. 3: cp. 2 Cor. viii. 23, '*fellow-worker for you.*' They laboured together, each with each and all with Paul, *for* the advancement of *the Kingdom of God;* i.e. for the eternal kingdom, over which God will reign for ever, and of which His servants, rescued from the grave to die no more, will be citizens, every citizen sharing its glory and blessedness. For that kingdom Paul and his companions toiled, by drawing men to Christ and thus making them even on earth citizens of this heavenly kingdom, and by teaching each citizen to labour for the same object. They were thus *fellow-workers,* co-operating harmoniously. Since the work of God needs the co-operation of many workers, a chief Christian excellence is that spirit of harmony which enables one to work well with others. It is the willing subordination of the individual to the general good. Absence of this spirit of brotherhood has frequently hindered the usefulness of able men. *Men who etc.:* a larger class to which these three, and of Jews these *only,* belonged; viz. those *who were,* or *became,* a *comfort* or encouragement to Paul.

Such were Paul's three Jewish friends at Rome: Aristarchus from Thessalonica, in some way a sharer of his imprisonment; Mark from Jerusalem, himself once a deserter and a cause of contention between Paul and his old friend Barnabas, but now a valued helper; and a brother unknown to us but bearing the sacred name. All these joined with Paul in his toil for the Kingdom of God; and each was to the Apostle, amid the hardships of that toil, a joy in sorrow and a stimulus to exertion. Mark was soon to leave him, and would possibly visit Colossæ. But about him Paul had already sent directions that he receive a worthy welcome.

12. Another greeting, from *Epaphras*, the founder of the Church at Colossæ: see under ch. i. 7. *Who* is one *of you:* same words and sense as in *v.* 9. Like Onesimus, Epaphras came from Colossæ either as a native or as a former inhabitant. *Servant of Jesus Christ:* a title of highest honour, though shared by all Christians. For the faithfulness of our service of Christ is the measure of our spiritual stature. *Always etc.:* further description of Epaphras. *Wrestling:* same word as *contend* in ch. i. 29. *Wrestle in prayers:* same words in Rom. xv. 30. The effort of Epaphras' prayers was like the intense effort of a Greek athlete contending for a prize. The appropriateness of this phrase is felt by all to whom prayer is a reality. And to Epaphras this intense effort was ceaseless: *always wrestling*. He thus exemplified the exhortation in *v.* 2.

Stand: maintain our position and erectness in spite of enemies or burdens threatening to drive us back or crush us. So Eph. vi. 11, 13, 14, Rom. v. 2, xi. 20, etc. That the Colossian Christians might thus maintain their position in spite of the snares of false doctrine and the hostility of open enemies, was the definite purpose of the earnest prayers of Epaphras. *Mature* or *full-grown:* as in 2 Cor. ii. 6, where see note. *Fully-assured:* same word and sense as in Rom. iv. 21, xiv. 5. A cognate word in Col. ii. 2, Heb. vi. 11, x. 22. While praying that the Christians at Colossæ may firmly hold their own, Epaphras remembered that only full-grown men in Christ can do this, and that of this Christian maturity assured faith in Christ is an essential condition. *In every will of God:* in everything God desires us to do and to be, this looked upon as the spiritual locality of Christian firmness, maturity, and confidence. Epaphras prayed that his converts might know without doubt whatever God would have them do and be, that every element of His will might be realised in their spiritual growth, and that thus they might maintain their spiritual position.

13. Confirmation of the foregoing by Paul's direct testimony. *Much labour;* confirms and strengthens the most conspicuous point in *v.* 12, viz. that the prayers of Epaphras involved intense effort.

Laodicea and *Hierapolis*: other cities of the valley of the Lycus : see Introd. iv. This statement suggests that in these cities also the Gospel was first preached by Epaphras. And the nearness of the cities, and the main road passing through all three, would make it easy to carry the good news of salvation from one to the others.

14. A third greeting. *Luke*: mentioned by name only here, and Philem. 24 where he and *Demas* are called Paul's fellow-workers, and 2 Tim. iv. 11. Probably he wrote the Third Gospel: see my *Corinthians* p. 493. Now *v.* 11 implies that he was a Gentile. Perhaps he was the only Gentile N. T. writer. Notice that, of the four Evangelists, Mark and Luke were with Paul at Rome. Only here do we learn that Luke was a *physician*. Possibly this term was added merely for definiteness, or more likely in remembrance of medical help kindly rendered by Luke to Paul. Luke was with Paul on his second and third missionary journeys and on his voyage to Rome, as we learn from the first person 'we' and 'us' in Acts xvi. 10—17, xx. 5—xxi. 18, xxvii. 1—xxviii. 16. That they are together now at Rome, and again (2 Tim. iv. 11) during Paul's second imprisonment there, is a coincidence worthy of note. Luke seems to have been his almost inseparable companion. Hence the affection expressed here : *Luke, the physician, the beloved one.*

The absence of any commendation of *Demas* here is an unfortunate, though perhaps undesigned, coincidence with his later desertion of Paul recorded in 2 Tim. iv. 10. There was nothing to move Paul to say anything about him, even when speaking in warm terms of *Luke*. But in Philem. 24 he is counted, with Mark, Aristarchus, Luke, among Paul's fellow-workers.

15. After three greetings to the Christians at Colossæ, now follows a greeting to a neighbouring Church. *Laodicea*: the nearer of the two other Churches for which (*v.* 13) Epaphras prayed so earnestly. *Nymphas*: evidently a member of the Church at Laodicea. For, had he been at Colossæ, in the Church to which this letter was sent, this greeting to him could hardly have been put after that to brethren twelve miles away. Paul's reason for singling him out of the Church at Laodicea, in this special way, is probably to be found in the words following. *The Church in their house*: same words in Rom. xvi. 5, 1 Cor. xvi. 19, where see notes. Cp. Philem. 2. That *Nymphas* opened his *house* for worship, accounts for his special mention here.

The Sinai, Alex., and Ephraim copies read *in their house*. So RV. text. The Vatican MS. reads *her house*. So RV. margin. Some later uncials and most cursives read *his house*. The first reading has best documentary support. If genuine, it might easily have been altered by a copyist who could not understand a plural pronoun after the one name *Nymphas*. And, if so, the substituted pronoun might be of either gender: for the Greek name may be either masculine *Nymphas*, or feminine *Nympha*. Thus the better attested reading *their* would account for both the others. We may therefore accept it as the more likely. Paul wrote *their house* probably because in entertaining the Church others, perhaps his wife and family, were associated with Nymphas. So was Prisca with Aquila: Rom. xvi. 5.

16. This injunction suggests that the same errors were prevalent both at Colossæ and Laodicea. *The Epistle:* that now concluding, as in Rom. xvi. 22, 1 Th. v. 27. *That from Laodicea:* not written from Laodicea. For it was to be read by the Christians at Colossæ as well as by others: *also ye read.* And these others must have been the Christians at Laodicea. It could only be a letter to the Church there; to be sent *from Laodicea* and read at Colossæ. And, if so, this injunction suggests very strongly that it was written by Paul. Doubtless the letter was to be left at Laodicea by Tychicus as he passed through on his way to Colossæ; and if so it would be at Laodicea, when this letter reached Colossæ. Paul bids that each letter be sent to, and read in, the other of the two Churches.

What was this letter of Paul to the Church at Laodicea? Two suppositions are possible. It may have been lost; sharing the fate which, under 1 Cor. v. 9, we saw reason to believe had overtaken an epistle to the Corinthian Church. If we had no epistle meeting the conditions of the case, we might accept this suggestion with some confidence. But another explanation is at hand. We shall see, under Eph. i. 1, that the Epistle to the Ephesians, although sent expressly to the Church at Ephesus, the metropolis of the Roman province of Asia which included Laodicea and Colossæ, was probably designed also for other Churches in the same province. If so, it is quite conceivable that Paul gave orders to Tychicus to leave at Laodicea, for the Church there, a copy of the Epistle to the Ephesians. And this copy would be the letter *from Laodicea* which Paul wished the Colossians to *read.* This wish we can well understand. For the two Epistles, though closely related in thought and phraseology, are yet quite distinct. Each supports the other. The letter to Ephesus deals chiefly with the Church: that to Colossæ expounds the dignity and work of Christ, and rebuts certain special errors. This suggestion is so free from objection, and meets so well all the facts of the case, that with our scanty information we may accept it as probable. It has also an advantage over the former suggestion in not requiring us to believe that Paul wrote at the same time and sent by the same messenger to the same province four epistles.

17. *Archippus:* mentioned elsewhere only Philem. 2, where see note. The word *say-ye* suggests that he was close at hand to hear what was said; and was therefore probably a member of the Church at Colossæ. Indeed it is most unlikely that a warning to a member of another Church would be thus sent. And this agrees with his apparent relation to Philemon, who also seems to have been a Colossian. That this word to Archippus is put after a direction about Laodicea, is very small presumption that he was a Laodicean. For, apart from locality, Paul may have thought fit to reserve this warning to be the last of his injunctions. That Archippus is called in Philem. 2 a fellow-soldier of Paul, suggests that he had shared with the Apostle the peril of Christian work. And this agrees with the work *in* the *Lord* referred to here.

The ministry which thou hast received; may be the office of a deacon, as in Rom. xii. 7, where it is distinguished from prophecy and teaching but is joined with them as requiring each a special gift. Or, it may have been some other permanent position in the Church, as when Paul in ch. i. 23 calls himself a minister of the Gospel. Or, some temporary work committed by the Church to Archippus, like '*the ministry* fulfilled' by Paul and Barnabas (Acts xii. 25) when they took a contribution in money from Antioch to Jerusalem. Between these alternatives we have nothing to guide us. This warning is no presumption of unfaithfulness on the part of Archippus. For it may be that his work was specially important, or had been lately entrusted to him. Indeed this last is rather suggested by the words *which thou hast received.* It is remarkable that this warning was sent to Archippus through the Church as a whole: *say ye to Archippus.* Perhaps Paul thought thus to inspire in him a sense of responsibility to the whole Church. *In* the *Lord:* as in *v.* 7, Ph. ii. 29, etc. This work for the Church was a part of his service of Christ. *Fulfil it:* as in Acts xii. 25: 'fill up by actual and faithful service the outline of work sketched out by this commission.'

18. *The greeting by the hand of me Paul:* word for word as in 1 Cor. xvi. 21, 2 Th. iii. 17. At this point the chained hand of the prisoner takes the pen from the friend who was writing for him, whose name probably we should know, and adds as a mark of genuineness the few words which follow. And the chained hand bids us *remember the bonds* of him who writes. This reference to

himself claims for the warnings he now sends the loving and grateful respect due to the prisoner in the Lord. *Grace:* the undeserved favour of God through Christ. Paul desires that this divine smile be his readers' companion : be *with you.*

The personal details of DIVISION V. link the doctrinal and practical teaching of the Epistle with the actual life of Paul. They remind us that the Gospel is not mere abstract truth but touches the every-day life of actual men. This historic setting of the Gospel, which we find in many casual notices in Paul's Epistles and in the narratives of the Book of Acts, by affording matter for historical criticism, furnishes proof of the historic truth of the statements on which the Gospel rests. It also helps us, by reproducing the surroundings and the inner and outer life of the Apostle, to understand and better appreciate the thought embodied in the doctrinal parts of his Epistles. Time spent in bringing together, and endeavouring to interpret, these scanty notices will bear abundant fruit in a clearer conception of his inner thought and of the Gospel which permeated and moulded and ennobled his entire inner and outer life.

THE ERRORS AT COLOSSÆ. Since this Epistle was professedly (ch. ii. 4) written to guard the readers against error, it can be fully understood only by reproducing in some measure the errors it was designed to counteract. To do this, is no easy task. For the errors combated are not formally stated. Paul endeavours to meet them not so much by direct disproof as by asserting and enforcing positive and contrary truth. This method leaves us in considerable doubt about the nature of the errors refuted. But it has the immense advantage of making exact knowledge of them a matter of secondary importance. For we can understand and appreciate the positive teaching of the Epistle, even while somewhat uncertain about the precise nature of the specific errors against which this positive teaching was adduced. At the same time whatever knowledge we can gain about the error combated will shed light upon the argument and thought of the Apostle. We will therefore gather together all the indications the Epistle affords of the nature of these errors; and then compare them with similar teaching in the rest of the New Testament and in other early literature.

Our thoughts go back at once to another letter written by Paul to counteract serious and definite error, the Epistle to the Galatians. The points of comparison and contrast in the two Epistles will help us to understand, after our study in a previous volume of the errors in Galatia, those with which Paul is now dealing.

We notice at once the entirely different tone of the two Epistles. The news from Galatia was altogether bad. Paul's one thought about the Christians there was wonder at their early desertion of the truth. But the news about Colossæ evokes gratitude to God. And with this gratitude no sorrow is mingled. This does not prove that the errors at Colossæ were in themselves less deadly than those in Galatia. But it proves clearly that the peril was not so near. In Galatia the defection was (Gal. i. 6) already going on : in Colossæ Paul hopes to ward off what at present is only a danger. Moreover the stronger language of the earlier letter may have been prompted by Paul's closer relation to the Churches addressed, and to the fact that his authority as an Apostle had been directly attacked by the false teachers. On the other hand, whereas the Churches of Galatia had been founded by Paul himself and the news of their defection reached him years afterwards, the news of the danger among the Colossians was brought by the man who first told him the story of their conversion. This would naturally soften the language of the Epistle before us.

Both in Galatia and at Colossæ one element of error was observance of the sacred seasons of the Law of Moses: Gal. iv. 10, Col. ii. 16. With this were associated at Colossæ, and doubtless in Galatia, restrictions of food. And at Colossæ as at Rome (Rom. xiv. 3) some were ready to 'judge' others according as they observed or neglected these restrictions. The false teachers in Galatia strenuously asserted the abiding obligation of circumcision : ch. v. 3, vi. 12. And the references to circumcision in Col. ii. 11 leave little or no doubt that the rite was insisted upon by the false teachers at Colossæ. Here then we have an element common to the two cases, viz. the continued validity of the ancient law. In other words, both errors were of Jewish origin. But the whole tone of both Epistles proves that the false teachers were members of the Church. Jews who rejected Christ would have no common ground of approach to the Gentile Christians of Asia Minor. We must therefore suppose that in both cases the false teachers were Jewish converts who maintained that all Christians were bound to keep the whole Law of Moses. Possibly, the false teachers here referred to were not members of the Church at Colossæ but Jewish Christians moving about in Asia Minor and exerting an evil influence.

Amid these errors already familiar to us there appears at Colossæ, as disproved by Paul, other teaching of which we find no trace in the Epistle to the Galatians.

Except to Nazarites and priests ministering at the altar, the Law of Moses laid no restrictions on drink. But in Col. ii. 16 we find men who made both eating and drinking a standard of judgment about their fellow-Christians. Similar persons seem to be referred to in Rom. xiv. 21. The words of the false teachers quoted in Col. ii. 21 prove that these prohibitions of food and drink were very stringent. And from v. 22 we learn that they were of merely human origin. All this proves that the teachers in question added to the Divinely commanded restrictions of the Law of Moses other restrictions of their own. With the refusal to eat certain kinds of food stands in close connection the general description in Col. ii. 23 of such needless and useless abstinence as *hard treatment* of *the body*. We may safely say that in the error feared at Colossæ an ascetic element, going far beyond the Mosaic prohibitions, occupied a conspicuous place.

It is also worthy of note that, whereas to the Galatians Paul speaks of the advocates of circumcision as seeking to be justified by works of law and rebuts their error by proclaiming justification through a faith like that of Abraham, his disproof of the errors at Colossæ makes no reference to justification, but is prefaced by a profound exposition of the dignity of the Son of God and of His relation to the created universe, to the Church, and to the work of salvation. This different method of reply suggests that the error at Colossæ differed from that in Galatia as being specially derogatory to the unique dignity of the Son of God as the Creator and Ruler of the universe and as the one sufficient Saviour of men. We notice also that the restrictions referred to in Col. ii. 21 are overturned by reference to the original purpose of the food needlessly forbidden.

Other elements are easily detected. With asceticism is ever associated professed *humility*. And in the warnings to the Church at Colossæ *worship of the angels* is a marked feature. This accounts probably for the mention in ch. i. 16 of the different ranks of angels as created by the Son, and in ch. ii. 15 as being led in triumph by Him. Now angels have their place of honour in the Old Testament; and are mentioned by Paul and by Christ. But nothing in the Bible affords ground for offering them worship. Such worship therefore implies fuller information: and this could be obtained only by visions of the unseen world and its mysterious and glorious inhabitants. We therefore are not surprised to find that the false teacher claimed to have had such visions, and pretended (ch. ii. 18) to *investigate what he had seen*.

Such were some of the outward forms of the religion practised

AT COLOSSÆ.

by the teachers in question. We may conceive them asserting the abiding validity of the Law of Moses, going beyond its restrictions by ascetic prohibitions of merely human origin which refused to the body its rightful nourishment, performing a ritual of angel-worship, and doing all this on the ground of supposed revelations of the unseen world.

Under these outward forms of religion lay other elements. The worshippers claimed to be philosophers. Their philosophy must have been, like that of Greece, an attempt to reach the realities underlying the phenomena around. That the attempt was complete failure, Paul declares by calling their philosophy *empty error*. Like the prohibitions of food and drink, this teaching consisted, as did much ancient philosophy, of unproved assertions, true or false, passed on from one to another. It had therefore for its source and standard only *the tradition of men*. And since these purely human additions to the Divine revelations of the Old Testament could not rise above their source, they were shaped by the *rudiments of teaching common to the whole world*. It cannot be doubted that this theoretical teaching was the foundation both of the ascetic restriction of food and drink and of the worship of angels. For philosophy without visible embodiment would have little attraction for the comparatively uneducated Christians at Colossæ; and we are told by Paul that self-imposed worship and neglect of the body had *repute of wisdom*.

The absence throughout the Epistle of any mention of righteousness or justification—a very marked contrast to the Epistle to the Galatians—suggests that these prohibitions of certain kinds of food, this worship of angels, and philosophy, were not proposed as a means of obtaining the favour of God. And that they were proposed as a means of attaining a higher Christian life, is suggested by Paul's frequently expressed desire that his readers attain true knowledge and wisdom, and by his assertion that all such knowledge dwells in Christ, and that *in Him* His people *are complete:* chs. i. 9, 28, ii. 2, 3, iii. 10, 16, iv. 5. We may conceive these teachers admitting that confessed faith in Christ is the one means of obtaining the favour of God, and yet professing a deeper philosophy and practising a stricter regimen of life and additional modes of worship as means of attaining a spiritual elevation beyond that of the Church in general. In other words, the teaching which Paul opposes was a counsel of perfection for a select few.

Traces of similar error, further developed, are found in Paul's later Epistles. In another letter to the province of Asia (1 Tim. iv. 3) we notice a prohibition of certain kinds of food, a prohibition set aside by a development of the argument in Col. ii. 21. With this is coupled prohibition of marriage: and the whole is said to be a teaching of demons. Of empty Jewish error under the guise of philosophy, we find abundant traces in the Pastoral Epistles; and of the disputes to which naturally it gave rise. So, in Tit. i. 14, we have 'Jewish myths and commands of men.' And that these commands were connected with needless prohibitions, probably of food, we learn from *v.* 15: 'All things are pure to the pure; but to the polluted and unbelieving nothing is pure.' In 1 Tim. i. 4, 8 we read of 'myths and endless genealogies' connected with unlawful use of the Law. Other similar references in ch. vi. 4, 2 Tim. ii. 23, Tit. iii. 9. The darker description in these Epistles as compared with that to the Colossians suggests that during the interval the evil seed had taken root and borne hurtful fruit.

From all this we infer that at Colossæ were professed Christians who not only taught the abiding validity of the Law but added to it further prohibitions of merely human origin, professing thus to point out a way to loftier purity; that with this ascetic element was associated theoretical teaching vainly attempting to explain the phenomena around, teaching based upon supposed visions of the unseen world; that the would-be philosophers practised a ritual in honour of the heavenly beings whom they professed to have seen; and that all this was prompted, not by humility, as was pretended, but by an inflated self-estimate which was in reality a form of self-indulgence. The argument of the Epistle before us proves plainly that this teaching was derogatory to the unique dignity of Christ and inconsistent with the full salvation to be obtained by union with Him.

THE GNOSTICS. The above-noted scanty indications of the errors combated in this Epistle recall at once a very conspicuous feature of Church life in the second century, the chaos of beliefs and sects known as Gnosticism. These later beliefs will help us to understand both the meaning and the importance of Paul's argument in the Epistle before us.

This strange medley of opinions is well known to us from early Christian writings, the sole records of beliefs which otherwise would long ago have been forgotten. The great work of Irenæus quoted in my *Romans* (Introd. ii.) contains a full account of the various forms of Gnostic teaching, with elaborate disproof. Clement of Alexandria refers to the same frequently and by name. The longest work of Tertullian is *Against Marcion*, a conspicuous Gnostic. We have another account of Gnosticism, anonymous but probably by Hippolytus, a later contemporary of Tertullian. The earnestness of these refutations proves how wide-spread and how serious in the eyes of conspicuous members of the early Church were the errors refuted.

The name *Gnostic*, or knowing-one, a curious contrast to the modern name *Agnostic*, i.e. one who does not know, marks out the Gnostics as claiming superior knowledge. And that they adopted this as their name, suggests that they looked upon knowledge as man's highest good. This recalls the warning in 1 Tim. vi. 20. Indeed this warning is embodied in the title of Irenæus' great work: *Refutation of the knowledge falsely so called*.

The rise of this intellectual movement is not difficult to understand. Before Christ came, even outside the sacred nation, men had sought to grasp the realities underlying the phenomena around them, and thus to explain the origin of these phenomena. In their search, two great questions had claimed their attention: Whence came the world? Whence came evil? The first of these questions was discussed by the early Greek philosophers. Their answers are clearly embodied in abundant writings which have come down to us. Of these, the *Timæus* of Plato is a good representative. A favourite belief was that the world was made by subordinate but superhuman beings created by the Supreme God and acting more or less under His direction. The second question received from the Greeks, who carefully discussed morals from a practical point of view, only scanty and indefinite answers. But the answers given to it in Persia and in India reveal the large place it occupied in the thought of those nations. In Persia, the followers of Zoroaster, a somewhat mythical person who lived possibly in the days of the early Persian kings, taught that good and evil are alike eternal, and have their source in two eternal persons, from whom respectively come all things good and bad. This teaching is embodied in the sacred books of Persia, of which the oldest, the *Avesta*, dates perhaps from the third century after Christ, and certainly preserves still earlier traditions. The Indian answer is that matter is essentially evil, and unreal, and opposed to mind; that the world has come into being by successive emanations from the Supreme, each lower and worse with increasing distance from its origin.

An important element common to the Persian and Indian answers is the all-pervading sense of duality and opposition, viz. of good and bad, and of spirit and matter.

The above answers to these great questions were widely disseminated far beyond the limits of the nations which seem to have given them birth. Especially were the philosophies of Greece stimulated and moulded by the speculations of the East.

At the time of Christ Jewish thought was greatly influenced by the Gentile thought around. The influence of Greek writers is very conspicuous in the writings of Philo, an Egyptian Jew contemporary with Christ, who under the form of an allegorical interpretation of the Old Testament introduces very much of the teaching of Plato. On the other hand, the Essenes, a brotherhood said by Philo to be in his day 4,000 strong and described by Josephus as one of the three sects or 'philosophies' of the Jews, (the others being the Pharisees and the Sadducees,) taught that pleasure is evil, and that sin must be overcome by ascetic refusal of pleasure; ideas conspicuously Oriental. In agreement with this belief, they not only obeyed most rigorously the prescriptions of the Law but added to them prescriptions of merely human origin. They despised wealth; and lived together with a common purse and common table in the utmost simplicity. They forbade or discountenanced marriage, recruiting their numbers from the children of others. They believed firmly in an immortal life beyond death; but did not expect a resurrection of the body, looking upon material clothing as a bondage to the spirit. The Essenes had secret doctrines and sacred books of their own: and they paid a certain adoration to the sun; and had secret teaching about, and reverence for, the angels. They gained respect by their strict morality, their simplicity of life, and mutual concord. Many of them were reputed to have the gift of predicting future events: a gift implying special intercourse with the unseen world. All this we learn from contemporary descriptions of them by Philo, especially (vol. ii. 457—459) *The good man always free* §§ 12, 13; and by Josephus, especially *Jewish War* bk. ii. 8. 2—13.

These two forms of Jewish belief present, as the reader will notice, many points of contact with the errors at Colossæ. And we can easily believe that, even where there were no Essenes and no one familiar with the writings of Philo, these modes of thought would exert an influence co-extensive with Jewish nationality.

Into the Jewish nation thus influenced by Gentile thought, Christ was born; and from Jerusalem, carried by Jews, went forth the good news of salvation for all mankind. The Gospel must needs come into contact with, and take up a definite relation to, the religious thought then prevalent. And inasmuch as the Gospel itself professed to explain in some measure the mystery of being and of the world around, it must necessarily, according to the disposition of each who felt its influence, either supplement or correct or displace this earlier teaching, or be itself moulded by it. Gnosticism was a reaction of the existing religious thought of the world, in part Greek but chiefly Oriental, upon the new truth proclaimed by Christ.

The Gnostics were divided into many sects known by various names, for the more part those of their leaders, and each presenting a distinct type of teaching. The sects grouped themselves according to their affinities. But all had conspicuous elements in common. All Gnostic schools agree to give honour to Christ as the Teacher and Saviour of men. But along with this great truth, all teach two great errors, viz. that matter is essentially or practically evil; and that the Creator of the world, who is also the Lawgiver of Sinai, is distinct from, and inferior to, the Supreme God who sent His Son to save the world. The Gnostics favourable to Judaism represent the God of Israel as a deity subordinate to the Supreme, and the Old Testament as imperfect only because preparatory to the New. On the other hand, the anti-Jewish Gnostics represented the God of Sinai as essentially hostile to the God who revealed Himself in Christ.

Of the Jewish Gnostics, Cerinthus is a good example. His date is fixed by a statement of Irenæus (bk. iii. 3. 4) that in his own day there were some who had heard Polycarp say that once the Apostle John, going to a bath, saw Cerinthus within, and fled from the bath in fear lest it should fall. Whatever this story be worth, it is complete proof that Cerinthus lived long before Irenæus, and affords a fair presumption that he was a contemporary of the Apostle John. In his teaching therefore we have a form of Gnosticism almost or quite as early as the days of the Apostles. It is thus described by Irenæus, bk. i. 26. 1 : "A certain Cerinthus in Asia taught that the world was made, not by the Supreme (literally, the First) God, but by a certain power altogether separated and distinct from that Supreme Power which is over the universe, and ignorant of Him who is God over all things. He represented Jesus, not as born from a maiden—for this seemed to him impossible—but as a son of Joseph and Mary like all other men, and as being much greater than others in justice and prudence and wisdom. He taught that after Baptism Christ descended into him, from that Supreme Power which is over all things, in the figure of a dove; and that then he announced the unknown Father, and wrought miracles; and that at last Christ flew back from Jesus, that Jesus suffered and rose but that Christ continued without suffering, a spiritual being."

Epiphanius (*Against Heresies* xxviii.) says that "Cerinthus taught that the Law and the Prophets were inspired by angels, and that the giver of the Law was one of the angels who made the world."

An extreme example of Anti-Jewish Gnostics is found in the Ophites, or followers of the serpent; who taught that the Creator of the world was evil, and that therefore the so-called fall of man was really emancipation from the rule of evil, and the tempter a benefactor of mankind.

Another Gnostic, Saturninus, from Antioch in Syria, taught (Irenæus bk. i. 24. 1, 2) that there is "one Father unknown to all, who made angels, archangels, powers, authorities; that the world and all things in it were made by certain seven angels; that man is a work of angels. . . . He taught that the Saviour was without birth and without body and without form, a man only in appearance. He said that the God of the Jews was one of the angels; and that, because the Father wished to destroy all His princes, Christ came for destruction of the God of the Jews and for the salvation of those who believe him. . . . He said that there are two races of men formed by angels, one bad and the other good; and that because the demons helped the bad, the Saviour came for destruction of bad men and demons and for salvation of the good. They say that marriage and procreation are from Satan. Hence also the more part of them abstain from animal food; by this assumed self-control leading away some into their own error."

More fully developed Gnostic systems, and somewhat later than the above, were those of Basilides, Valentinus, and Marcion. All these flourished in the former half of the second century.

The moral influence of Gnosticism took two opposite directions. On the ground that matter is evil, many Gnostics taught that all pleasure derived from matter is also evil, and that only by refusing such pleasure can men rise above bondage to evil. Of this ascetic side of Gnosticism, the Encratites are an example: Irenæus bk. i. 28. 1. Others, looking upon matter as worthless, taught that man's relation to it is of no moment, and that the spirit within, as being essentially superior to matter, is not soiled by any bodily sin. In this way Gnosticism gave rise to wildest immorality. Of this immoral direction, the Carpocratians are an example: Irenæus bk. i. 25.

Another practical outworking of Gnosticism was that inasmuch as matter was in their view essentially evil, the Son of God could not have entered into any real relation to a material body. All Gnostics therefore taught either, with Saturninus and the Docetæ, that His body was a mere appearance; or, with Cerinthus as quoted above, that the Son of God was united only for a time to the personality of the man Jesus.

The above extracts and descriptions may give some slight conception of the infinite chaos of strange beliefs, held by countless sects, which began to assume definite form at the close of the first century and reached its full development about the middle of the second.

It is at once evident that these strange perversions of the Gospel stand in some real relation to the Epistle to the Colossians. The points of contact are too many and too close to be accidental. Evidently the Epistle is a foregoing protest against the teaching common to all the Gnostics and especially against the early form of Gnosticism which was favourable to Judaism. The statement in Div. ii. that the universe, including the successive ranks of angels, was created by the agency of the Son meets beforehand the Gnostic teaching that creation and salvation had different, and in some measure antagonistic, sources. And the warnings in Div. iii. against mere human prohibitions, and against empty forms of worship based on fancied revelations of the unseen world, might have been written to guard against the practical and ritual sides of Gnosticism. Indeed the warning in Col. ii. 8 is a correct description of the Gnostic teaching of the second century.

All this has been made an argument against the genuineness of the Epistle. Some have said that the letter itself implies the existence of Gnosticism in a form which did not exist till the second century. But we have seen that Cerinthus, whose teaching comes nearest to that of the errors rebuked here, was probably a contemporary of the Apostle John. It is also worthy of note that the Fathers with one consent trace Gnosticism to Simon Magus whom Peter rebuked in Samaria apparently before the conversion of Paul: so Irenæus bk. i. 22. 1, 2. This tradition proves the very early date of the errors in question. Moreover, a system of belief so widespread and so various as Gnosticism reveals a deep-seated cause, one existing long before its various known manifestations. In the speculative teaching of Philo and in the asceticism of the Essenes we have already found, in the time of Christ, a soil ready for such a growth as the errors combated in this Epistle. All this makes very precarious any argument based on the unlikelihood of these opinions existing during the lifetime of Paul; and makes such argument utterly worthless when opposed to the abundant evidence internal and external (see Introd. § ii.) that the Epistle is genuine. Moreover, the references to Gnosticism, sufficient as they are for identification, are far from definite. Had this letter been written in the second century, the references would almost certainly have been more precise.

It is not difficult to suggest an explanation of the indisputable connection between this letter written by Paul in the first century and the errors so prevalent a few years later. We can easily conceive that, soon after the first preaching of the Gospel, as men began to ponder the new teaching and to compare it with their previous beliefs, these last would tend unconsciously to appropriate, or rather to modify so as to harmonize with earlier teaching, the new truth learnt from Christ. Specially would this be the case with those who boasted more profound knowledge, and were therefore not satisfied with teaching given even to the most ignorant. This innate tendency of human nature was the real source of Gnosticism, and may easily even in the days of Paul have revealed itself in early forms sadly prophetic of a fuller subsequent development. These germs of evil so serious would naturally attract the attention of the weary Apostle. It is not unlikely that they were specially prominent at Colossæ. For Phrygia, to which in the popular geography Colossæ belonged, is spoken of by Hippolytus (bk. v. 7-9) as a cradle of Gnostic teaching. The quotations above from the Pastoral Epistles show that the incipient peril was, a few years later, present to the Apostle's anxious thought. The simplest explanation of the whole case is that when the Gospel was first preached there were in the minds of many, Jews and Gentiles, elements of thought which must either be transformed by the Gospel or must themselves mould and pervert it; that this latter possibility soon became in some cases actuality; and that this defection and the peril of further similar defection evoked the warnings contained in the Epistle before us.

REVIEW OF THE EPISTLE TO THE COLOSSIANS.

The occasion and purpose of the Epistle were somewhat as follows. Epaphras, a member of the Church at Colossæ, came to Rome. That he remained at Rome after this letter was sent to Colossæ, suggests that he had other business there besides the conveyance of news to Paul. He tells the imprisoned Apostle the story of the success of the Gospel in the valley of the Lycus. That Gospel had been first preached at Colossæ by Epaphras himself. This implies that he had heard and embraced it elsewhere. Success had followed the preached word ; and in the heart of Asia Minor a new Church had sprung into life. There was then probably no

Church at Laodicea or Hierapolis. For, had there been such, one man would hardly have been the channel through which the Gospel would reach a place so near as Colossæ. And the great interest of Epaphras in the Churches of those two cities suggests that he had had a share in founding them. This good news filled Paul with delight.

Other information was less pleasant. In the valley of the Lycus were Jewish Christians who not only asserted the abiding obligation of the many prescriptions of the Law but added to them prohibitions of merely human origin which branded as evil things which God has created for man's nourishment and pleasure. As a basis of these prohibitions, the same teachers propounded a philosophy professing to explain the origin of the universe, claiming to be derived from revelations of the unseen world, and accompanied by a worship invented by man and directed to the honour of the supposed angelic authors of the vaunted revelations. They promised that this more recondite teaching and stricter rule of life and extra ritual would lead their disciples to a higher development of the Christian life.

The chief features of this false teaching were familiar to Paul. Already in his own nation a very conspicuous place in the creation of the world had been given to angels. And a well-known Jewish brotherhood had claimed fuller knowledge about the angelic powers, and had sought, by strict regimen of life, for nearer approach to God. But he saw in it at once incipient and great peril. The angelic powers to whom these would-be teachers ascribed the creation of the universe obscured the unique dignity of the Son of God as Himself the Creator and Ruler of whatever exists. And, by prescribing abstinence from good things made by God, as a means of attaining a richer spiritual life, they were misrepresenting the nature and aim of material good and were leading men away from the full salvation proclaimed by Christ for all who believe. Such teaching would rob those who accepted it of the prize offered to them in the Gospel.

Epaphras was, for reasons unknown to us, remaining at Rome. But one of his companions, Tychicus, was going to the province of Asia and to Colossæ. And Paul resolves to write a letter to the young converts whose early Christian history was in some respects so hopeful and yet so full of danger.

The first words from the prisoner at Rome were gratitude for the faith and love of the Christians at Colossæ, revealing as these did a blessed future awaiting them. He reminds them that similar results had followed the Gospel wherever preached throughout the world; thus raising their thoughts above their own narrow surroundings to the universal Church. He prays that they may obtain, in abundant measure, the highest knowledge, a knowledge bearing fruit in their whole life. In view of false teaching derogatory to the honour of Christ as the one Creator and Saviour, Paul writes his greatest exposition of the dignity of the Son of God, of His relation to God, to the universe, to the Church universal, and finally to the Church at Colossæ. This leads him to speak of his own relation to the Church and of his deep interest in the Churches of the Lycus. This doctrinal exposition he concludes by again pointing to Christ as Himself the treasure-house of all wisdom.

After erecting the best possible bulwark against error by plain statement of opposite truth, Paul comes in Div. III. to the specific danger at Colossæ. He first says generally that such danger exists, and begs his readers to make Christ whom they have received the pervading element of their whole life. He then describes somewhat more definitely the errors he fears, and shows them to be inconsistent with their Christian profession and with the aim of the death of Christ. Lastly, he states in plain words the specific outward forms in which these errors assail his readers, and concludes his reference to them by pointing them to the Risen Saviour, and to the new life flowing from spiritual contact with Him.

Having thus dealt with the specific occasion of the letter, Paul uses his reference to the Risen Lord as a starting point for moral teaching, first in general terms negative and positive, and then in special reference to the various classes of his readers.

News about himself, he leaves to Tychicus and his companion Onesimus. He then adds greetings from friends at Rome, including Epaphras; and concludes his letter with the usual Apostolic autograph.

The statement in Col. i. 16 that all things were created by the agency of the Son, conspicuous for its emphatic repetition and as being the only place in the Epistles of Paul where this statement is made, has a remarkable counterpart in the emphatic and repeated assertion of Jno. i. 3, the only passage in the Gospels where similar teaching is found. It is thus a link between the two great theologians of the New Testament. Moreover, the prominent place in the Gnostic systems held by the creation of the world, this being attributed to angels or to a subordinate deity, and the evidence that this teaching was prevalent before the death of John, suggests strongly that Jno. i. 3 was prompted by incipient Gnosticism. And it is worthy of note that a unanimous tradition connects the last years of the Apostle John with Ephesus, in the same Roman province as Colossæ. Similar teaching is found in Heb. i. 2, in an Epistle bearing abundant traces of the theological and theosophic speculation so prevalent among the Jews of Alexandria. That the language of Paul resembles so closely language prompted either by Gnostic error or by the modes of thought from which it sprang, somewhat confirms our inference that similar teaching at Colossæ suggested parts of the Epistle before us.

As we now close the Epistle, we are conscious that, in spite of much we cannot understand, it has, even as compared with the earlier Epistles of Paul, greatly widened our vision of things Divine. At the beginning of it, he reminded his readers that the Gospel which saved them had saved others throughout the world, thus suggesting that it must be looked upon in its relation, not to one city, but to the whole human race. Lower down he brought into our view successive ranks of intelligent beings beyond the range of the human eye. Reviewing these and the entire universe seen and unseen, he took us back to the time when it had not yet begun to be; and linked together the whole as created by, and for, the Son of God. The Creator of the universe is also the Head of the Church. And the blood shed on His cross is designed to produce results as wide as the universe. Throughout DIV. I. and DIV. II. this wider view is kept before us. And the clearer light thus derived is focused on the Son of God, to whom Paul points as Himself the mystery in which lies hid, or rather lies open to the eyes of those who believe in Him, all that which is best worth knowing.

Thus within the narrow limits of the damp walls of the dungeon at Rome there opened to the prisoner's eye a vision of the eternal and infinite realities and of the Son of God, Himself the centre and circumference of all reality, wider and deeper and more glorious than had been possible in the years of his unfettered activity. The Epistle we now close is a mirror in which this glorious vision is reflected to the ends of the world that in all ages it may be a light and joy to all who love our Lord Jesus Christ. Thus the things which happened to Paul 'have come to be for the advance of the Gospel.'

EXPOSITION OF THE EPISTLE TO PHILEMON.

SECTION I.
PAUL'S GREETING TO PHILEMON.
VERSES 1—3.

Paul, a prisoner of Christ Jesus, and Timothy, our brother, to Philemon, our beloved one and fellow-worker, ² and to Apphia our sister, and to Archippus our fellow-soldier, and to the Church in thy house; ³ grace to you and peace, from God our Father and the Lord Jesus Christ.

1. *Prisoner:* same word in Eph. iii. 1, iv. 1, 2 Tim. i. 8, Mt. xxvii. 15, 16, Acts xvi. 25, 27. *Of Christ:* not necessarily that He has put Paul in prison, but that in his captivity, and as a captive, the prisoner at Rome stands in special relation to Christ and belongs to Him. Writing a private letter to a friend and asking a favour, Paul refrains from all mention of his apostolic authority. And, while begging mercy for a bondman, he points to his own bonds. This silent plea is urged again in *vv.* 9, 10, 13. That Timothy is, as in Col. i. 1, joint-author of the letter, gives weight to it as touching a matter in which another besides Paul feels interest.

PHILEMON: a not uncommon Greek name. Of this Philemon we know nothing except from this Epistle. He was certainly a Christian and almost certainly (cp. *v.* 19) converted by Paul. That Onesimus was (cp. Col. iv. 9) a native or former inhabitant of Colossæ and was also Philemon's slave, and that, when this letter was written, he was going back to Philemon and also (Col. iv. 9) about to visit Colossæ, suggests that Philemon was an inhabitant of that city. But although he was a *fellow-worker* of Paul and Timothy, he is not mentioned in Col. i. 7 as taking part with Epaphras in founding the Church there. He must therefore have been converted elsewhere: for Paul had never visited Colossæ. Possibly he came to live there already a Christian, or was converted by Paul elsewhere, after the Church had been founded by Epaphras. That Philemon had a slave and had apparently (*v.* 18) been robbed by him, suggests that he was a man of social position; one of the few implied in 1 Cor. i. 26. *Our fellow-worker;* suggests that Philemon had joined with both Paul and Timothy in Christian toil and thus gained their special *love*. Contrast Rom. xvi. 9, where the same terms *beloved* and *fellow-worker* are used, but to different men; and the pronoun is changed from plural to singular.

2. *Apphia:* a woman's name found on several inscriptions in the country around Colossæ, and therefore probably of native origin. There is no reason to identify it with the Roman name Appia. The connection suggests strongly that she was Philemon's wife. And this is the more likely because the letter deals with a domestic matter. On behalf of a runaway slave Paul appeals both to master and mistress. Thus both the Phrygian name and Apphia's mention here are notes of genuineness. Our *sister:* implies that she was a Christian and therefore under Christian obligations.

If Apphia be Philemon's wife, the immediate mention of *Archippus* in a letter touching only a domestic matter suggests that he also was a member of the same family, and probably Philemon's son. This agrees with Col. iv. 17, which seems to imply that he was an officer of the Church at Colossæ. If Archippus was son of Philemon, the latter must have been elderly, not much if any younger than Paul. *Fellow-soldier:* as in Ph. ii. 25. It is perhaps not safe to infer from this title that Archippus had in some special conflict stood bravely by Paul. For the whole Christian life, especially in those days of storm, was a conflict. And if, as we inferred from Col. iv. 17, Archippus held official rank in the Church, this description would be the more appropriate. Paul recognises both Philemon and Archippus as comrades, the one in toil, the other in the ranks of battle. Doubtless, for reasons unknown to us, this distribution of titles was appropriate.

The Church in thy house: a smaller gathering within the Church at Colossæ, like that at Laodicea (Col. iv. 15) in the house of Nymphas. The singular number, *thy*, pays honour to Philemon in his own family as head of the household. This greeting seeks to interest in the case of Onesimus the company accustomed to gather for worship in the house of Philemon. The greeting of *grace and peace* (see under Ph. i. 2) is sent to each member of the family and to the Church meeting in their home.

SECTION II.
PAUL'S JOY AT PHILEMON'S CHRISTIAN LOVE.
VERSES 4—7.

I thank my God always, making mention of thee in my prayers, ⁵ *hearing of thy love and the faith which thou hast towards the Lord and for all the saints,* ⁶ *in order that the fellowship of thy faith may become effectual, in knowledge of every good thing that is in you, for Christ.* ⁷ *For I had much joy and encouragement at thy love; because the hearts of the saints have been refreshed through thee, brother.*

4. As in Ph. i. 3, Rom. i. 8, Paul's first words after a Christian greeting are his own personal thanks to his own God. And, as in 1 Cor. i. 4, Eph. i. 16, these thanks are ceaseless: *I thank my God always. Making mention of you in my prayers:* as in Rom. i. 9. These constant thanks for Philemon are offered in the course of Paul's regular devotions.

5. *Hearing:* day by day, perhaps from frequent references to Philemon by Epaphras and Onesimus. This continual *hearing* prompted continual *thanks*. Contrast 'having heard' in Col. i. 4, referring to one definite recital. *The faith which thou hast:* parallel to *thy love:* so Col. i. 4. Nowhere else do we read of *faith . . . towards all the saints;* except probably in Eph. i. 15. And there is, before *the Lord Jesus*, probably (for the reading is doubtful) a preposition not elsewhere used in this connection. That *love* is put before *faith*, is also remarkable. It has been suggested that the order of words is inverted, and that Paul really meant 'love towards all the saints and faith towards the Lord Jesus.' But such inversion is not elsewhere found in the Bible. [And it seems to be forbidden by the relative singular *which thou hast*, which connects with *faith* all the words following.] Another suggestion is that whereas *the Lord Jesus* is the immediate object of faith, *the saints* are in some way a more distant object in the sense that Philemon's faith took practical form in kindness towards them. But such use of [εἰς πάντας τοὺς ἁγίους] the words rendered *towards all the saints* is altogether without example. Open to least objection is the exposition of the great grammarians Meyer and Winer, viz. that the word *faith* has here the sense of *faithfulness*, as undoubtedly in Rom. iii. 3, 'the faith (or faithfulness) of God,' in Gal. v. 22, where it is placed among

Christian virtues, in Tit. ii. 10, Mt. xxiii. 23, and frequently in classic Greek. The corresponding Greek adjective has frequently this sense: Col. i. 7, iv. 7. The English word *faith* has both senses. The sense suggested here by Meyer has given us the common adjective 'faithful.' Although unusual in the N. T. but common in profane Greek, it seems to be demanded by the impossibility of giving to the word its ordinary sense. And it would explain the position of *love* before *faith* and the unusual preposition following it. It is also the easiest explanation of Eph. i. 15. This less usual sense is closely connected with the more common one. They who believe firmly the promises of God are themselves objects of confidence to others, both in their relation to God and to man. Paul has heard of Philemon's Christian love; and of his trustworthiness in things pertaining to the great Master and in his relations to all Christians. Of all this, he hears frequently from the Colossians with him: and it moves him to constant praise to God.

6. Purpose of the prayer which in Paul's mind is always associated with thanks to God. So, very clearly, in Eph. i. 17. For good things already received do but reveal the need for further blessings. *Fellowship:* see under Ph. i. 5: the spirit of brotherhood, that which prompts us to share with others our joys and their burdens. *Of thy faith,* or *faithfulness:* brotherliness springing from, and thus belonging to, his loyalty to Christ and to all Christians. Paul prays that Philemon's good-fellowship *may become effective,* i.e. may produce results. *In the knowledge:* or rather 'full perception and recognition.' *Every good thing:* every form of Christian excellence or spiritual enrichment: cp. Heb. ix. 11, x. 1. *In you,* or *in us:* (the reading is quite uncertain:) in Philemon and the Christians around, or in Christians generally including Paul. *For Christ:* to advance His purpose and kingdom. Paul desires that the spirit of brotherhood which belongs to Philemon's faithfulness may produce results, and these so abundant and various as to evoke, as their surrounding element, a recognition by others of every excellence which dwells in Christians, and thus tend to the glory of Christ; or, in other words, that Philemon's loyalty to Christ may assume form in a manifestation of Christian brotherhood, and thus secure recognition of all the excellences with which Christ has enriched His people. The special form of brotherliness here in view, we shall learn in § 3. If Paul's request be not granted, one form of Christian excellence will not be recognised. And the closing words of this verse remind us that in this full recognition the honour of Christ is involved.

7. Reason, primarily for Paul's thanks, and then for the prayer naturally following those thanks. His gratitude is prompted by *joy . . . and encouragement* (as in Ph. ii. 1) caused by Philemon's action. *I had:* when Paul heard about Philemon's *love.* Then follow proofs of it. *Hearts:* same word in Ph. i. 8, ii. 1, Col. iii. 12. It denotes always the seat of the emotions, where influences from without evoke feelings within. Here the emotion was that of being *refreshed:* same word in 1 Cor. xvi. 18, 2 Cor. vii. 13, Mt. xi. 28. [The Greek perfect denotes the abiding result of this act of kindness.] Paul refers to matters of fact, viz. acts of kindness by Philemon to Christians. These facts were narrated to him doubtless by Epaphras and Onesimus. They moved him to thanksgiving, and to prayer that the disposition thus manifested might reveal itself still further and thus secure recognition of the excellence of Christianity. This remembrance of Philemon's brotherliness elicits the endearing title, *brother.*

SECTION III.
THE REQUEST ABOUT ONESIMUS.
VERSES 8—21.

For which cause, having much boldness in Christ to command thee that which is fitting, ⁹ *because of* this *love I rather exhort, being such a one as Paul, an old man, and now also a prisoner of Christ Jesus;* ¹⁰ *I exhort thee about my child, whom I have begotten in* my *bonds, Onesimus,* ¹¹ *who formerly* was *to thee unprofitable but now profitable to thee and to me,* ¹² *whom I have sent back to thee himself, that is, my own heart,* ¹³ *whom I was minded to keep with me that on thy behalf he might minister to me in the bonds of the Gospel.* ¹⁴ *But without thy mind I was not willing to do anything, that thy good thing may be, not of necessity, but of free will.* ¹⁵ *For perhaps because of this he was separated for a time that for ever thou mightest hold him;* ¹⁶ *no longer as a servant but more than a servant, a brother beloved, specially so to me, but how much more to thee, both in* the *flesh and in* the *Lord.* ¹⁷ *If then thou hast me as a partner, receive him as me.* ¹⁸ *Moreover, if any injustice he has done thee, or is in debt, reckon this to me.* ¹⁹ *I Paul have written with my own hand, I will repay; in order that I may not say to thee that also thyself to me thou owest besides.* ²⁰ *Yes, brother, I would have help of thee in the Lord. Refresh my heart in Christ.* ²¹ *Trusting to thy obedience I have written to thee knowing that also beyond the things which I write thou wilt do.*

Special matter of this letter. We have an appeal, *vv.* 8, 9: a request, *vv.* 10—17: a detail pertaining to it, *vv.* 18, 19: a further appeal, *vv.* 20, 21.

8, 9a. *For-which-cause:* because of thy kindness to the saints. *Boldness in Christ:* confidence of unrestrained speech arising from Paul's relation to Christ. *To command:* as if by superior authority: same word in Lk. iv. 36, viii. 25. *That which is fitting:* action agreeing with the position and circumstances of the actor. Same word in Eph. v. 4, Col. iii. 18. It suggests slightly that the request following is what Philemon ought to do. *Because of* thy *love*, or *for love's sake:* literally *because of the love.* The definite article refers either to Philemon's love mentioned in *v.* 7 or to the well-known Christian virtue of love. In view of the express mention (*v.* 5) of 'thy love,' and of the introductory particle *for-which-cause*, of which these words seem to be an exposition, the former reference seems the more likely. The two expositions are closely allied. By allowing himself to be influenced by Philemon's love, Paul was paying deference to the central Christian virtue of which this was a concrete example. *Exhort:* as in Ph. iv. 2. Instead of speaking to Philemon with authority as from above, Paul speaks to him as a brother by his side using language calculated to encourage to action.

9b. Two points about Paul, his age and his bonds, strengthening the request which he makes when he might have used words of command. Since this Epistle was probably (see Introd. v.) written about A.D. 64 and Paul's conversion took place apparently (see my *Galatians* p. 193) about A.D. 35, it is quite possible that a man who in Acts vii. 58 is spoken of as young at the stoning of Stephen may here have spoken of himself as *old.* For life is reckoned by deeds rather than by years. After thirty years of hardship and toil for Christ, and this preceded by hard work of another kind, a man of sixty might well seem to himself to have already lived a long life. And the weakness of advancing years gave him a claim upon Philemon, his son in Christ. *Prisoner of Christ Jesus:* as in *v.* 1. It is here added to old age as a second plea. Paul stands in special relation to Christ, his relation to Him is that of one who for His sake has been put in prison, and the prisoner is old. Such is the man who now forbears to use his indisputable authority and merely makes a request.

[Some commentators separate *such-a-one* from the words following and make it refer to v. 8, where Paul suggests his right to command. But this back-reference is not grammatically necessary: and it is unlikely that Paul would lay stress upon his authority by thus referring to it twice. It is best to take together *such a one as*, these words introducing and picturing old men as a class to which the writer belongs. And the mention of Paul's old age at once recalls his hard surroundings.]

10. The matter of the Epistle, viz. Onesimus: see note under v. 21. *I exhort;* takes up the same word in v. 9 *a*, and adds the object of Paul's exhortations. *My own child:* close harmony with Ph. ii. 22, 1 Cor. iv. 17, where Timothy is so called. These words are at once expounded and amplified by those following, *whom I have begotten etc.:* a close parallel to 1 Cor. iv. 15. They prove that Onesimus was converted by Paul. So apparently was Timothy. *In my bonds*, or *in* these *bonds:* the dark surroundings of a father's joy. Thus for the third time Philemon is made to hear the clanking of the prisoner's chain. And it pleads irresistibly for Paul and for Onesimus.

11. Details about Onesimus. Note the double contrast: *formerly ... profitless ... to thee; but now ... profitable ... to thee and to me.* There is here probably a play upon the name Onesimus, which is a not uncommon Greek word meaning useful or helpful, and which, though different in form, has practically the same sense as the word here rendered *profitable*. Formerly the character of Onesimus contradicted his name: *but now*, in reference both to Philemon and to Paul, the name describes the man. The words *profitless to thee* are explained by v. 18 which suggests or implies that Onesimus had robbed Philemon. And in any case a runaway slave would be, from his master's point of view, *profitless*. *Profitable to thee and to me:* explained by vv. 10, 16. In Onesimus Philemon had gained a brother in Christ: and Paul another son in the Gospel. Therefore, to each of them he was an enrichment.

12. Another detail about Onesimus. *Whom I have sent back:* evidently as bearer of this letter. Thus the runaway but now returning slave comes to Philemon with a character certified by Paul. *Himself:* laying stress upon the personal return of Onesimus. So strongly did Paul's affection cling to him that to send him away was to tear out and send to Philemon his *own heart:* same word as in v. 7.

13. Another detail. *Was-minded:* mere inclination. Paul's contrary resolution and action are stated in v. 14. *I:* emphatic,

giving prominence to the personal inclination which Paul refused to gratify. *To keep with me:* literally 'to hold fast by myself.' These words emphasise still further Paul's personal feeling in this matter. *On thy behalf:* assuming that assistance rendered by Onesimus to Paul would be looked upon by Philemon as service done for himself. Paul thus delicately recognises Philemon's great care for him. [This simple exposition of the preposition ὑπέρ removes all need to give to it the sense of 'instead of,' which it never has in N. T. or in classic Greek.] *Minister:* render friendly service of any kind: see under Rom. xv. 25. This wish of Paul suggests that Onesimus had already shown kindness to him in prison. Possibly such kindness explains the epithet 'beloved brother' applied to Onesimus in *v.* 16 and Col. iv. 9. Then follows a fourth mention of Paul's imprisonment. His *bonds* made more needful to him the help of Onesimus. And they were caused by his endeavour to maintain and spread *the Gospel*. Indeed his arrest at Jerusalem was occasioned by his outspoken proclamation at all hazards of the unalloyed Gospel of salvation through faith. That Paul's captivity stood in this close relation to the Gospel, gave him a special claim to the help of Onesimus, even though his help to Paul might occasion some inconvenience to Philemon. And his bonds explain and justify his wish to retain Onesimus.

14. In contrast to his inclination, Paul now states his actual resolve; and a reason for it, this last in the form of a purpose. *Without thy mind:* same word in 1 Cor. vii. 25, 40. Not having Philemon's judgment about his retaining Onesimus, Paul resolved not to retain him. For, had he done so, the service rendered to Paul by Philemon's slave would have been, so far as he was concerned, done *by way of necessity*. *Thy good thing:* any act of kindness by Philemon, including the help to Paul in prison. Rendered by Philemon's slave, this help would have been a *good thing* from Philemon to Paul: but it would have been done *by way of necessity*, Philemon having no choice in it. Paul desired that it should be *by way of freewill*, i.e. of his own free choice.

15, 16. A reason for this refusal to act without Philemon's consent, viz. that *perhaps* God had another purpose about Onesimus. And Paul wishes to act in harmony with this Divine plan. *Perhaps:* introduces this reason timidly, by way of suggestion. *For this cause:* explained by *in order that for ever etc. He was separated:* a gentle way of describing the flight of Onesimus. *For a time:* literally *for an hour.* It does not imply that Onesimus had left Philemon very lately. For, contrasted with an *eternal* possession, a separation otherwise long would seem short. *Thou mightest have,* or *hold for thy own:* explained in *v.* 16.

No longer as a servant, or *slave:* according to the common use of the word; see under Rom. i. 1. This implies clearly that Onesimus had been a slave of Philemon. Not as such does God intend him to be *for ever,* but as something much more than or *beyond a slave,* viz. *a beloved brother* in Christ. Paul suggests that *perhaps* God permitted Philemon, through the flight of Onesimus, to lose a slave in order that, through his conversion at Rome, the runaway slave might become to him a beloved brother in Christ and thus an *eternal* possession. So would a small and temporary loss become a great and abiding enrichment. *Especially to me:* added by Paul because already, as his child in the Gospel, Onesimus was dearer to him than to any one else. Yet Paul foresees and suggests an endearment stronger even than this superlative endearment: *how much more to thee?* Philemon's closer relation in days gone by to Onesimus should make so much the greater his joy now at the conversion of his once worthless slave. And this in two relations: *in flesh and in* the *Lord.* Paul assumes that the returning runaway will remain with Philemon, and thus be his in outward bodily life; and be his also as a fellow-servant of the one *Lord.* Therefore in this double relation Onesimus will be dear to Philemon; and through this closer relation dearer to him than even to Paul, to whom he is so specially dear.

That both here and in Col. iv. 9 Onesimus is described by the same word *beloved,* and the warm affection expressed in *v.* 12, suggest that he was specially amiable. This may have shown itself in the kind attention (*v.* 13) which Paul would like to have retained.

17. A final appeal, summing up all that precedes; followed by a full and definite request about Onesimus which has been delayed till now that it may come with the accumulated force of the foregoing appeals. *A partner:* companion in the service of Christ and in the blessings of the New Covenant. Same word and sense in 2 Cor. i. 7, viii. 23. A similar appeal in Ph. ii. 1, 'if any partnership of the Spirit.' *Receive him;* implies that Onesimus was returning to Philemon in order to seek his favour, and apparently to remain with him. But the words *him as me* show that Paul is not asking him to receive back Onesimus as a slave. Rather Paul begs for him a Christian welcome, leaving undetermined all future relationships. 'If you look upon me as a comrade, welcome Onesimus whom I love so much as you would welcome me. For whatever you do to him you do to me.'

18, 19. Another matter about Onesimus which might seem to stand in the way of the welcome just asked for. *Done thee any injustice:* same word in the same sense in Col. iii. 25, Gal. iv. 12. The kind of *injustice* is indicated by the words following: *or is-in-debt.* This makes almost certain that Onesimus had been dishonest, either by direct robbery or by unfaithful use of money committed to his charge. For, had not Paul had strong reason to suspect this, he could not have used these words. Probably the hypothetical form of the sentence was only a slight veil thrown over what Paul knew to be fact. If so, he could not ask Philemon to receive back the runaway without referring to this worst feature of the case. The words *reckon this to me* suggest that Onesimus was unable to pay back the stolen money. For, had he been able, Paul would certainly have required him to do so.

I Paul: see under Col. i. 23. *I have written with my own hand:* same words in Gal. vi. 11; cp. 1 Cor. xvi. 21, 2 Th. iii. 17. Whether the whole Epistle was thus written, or at this point Paul took up the pen, we do not know. He binds himself by his own hand to *pay back* what Onesimus owes to Philemon. *Thou owest me besides:* another debt owing in addition to that which Paul promises to pay back. In other words, even if Philemon remits the debt, he will still owe himself to Paul. But this Paul does not wish to *say* to Philemon, and to avoid saying it prefers to bind himself to pay what Onesimus owes. *Owe thyself:* cp. Lk. ix. 25. This can only mean that Paul led Philemon to Christ. Thus while binding himself to pay, he reminds Philemon of a debt on the other side which cannot be paid.

20, 21. Concluding appeals. *Yes, brother:* expression of brotherly confidence. *Would-have-help*, or *let-me-have-help:* a verb cognate to the adjective 'Onesimus' or 'helpful:' see under *v.* 10. It is common in classic Greek in the sense of *receive-help* or *pleasure;* but is not found elsewhere in the New Testament. This suggests that Paul selected it as a play upon the name Onesimus; as though he said to Philemon, be thou an Onesimus to me. *I . . . of thee:* both words emphatic. Paul makes the case of Onesimus his own; and begs pleasure or help for himself from Philemon by his acquiescence in the request of this letter. *In the Lord:* the joy for which Paul begged would be an outflow of Christian life, and therefore to him a means of spiritual good. Cp. Ph. i. 14, where confidence evoked by Paul's bonds is called 'confidence in the Lord.' *Refresh my heart:* same words as in *v.* 7, with emphasis on the word *my*. Paul begs for himself what Philemon has already done for 'the saints.' The word *heart* is added to suggest that Onesimus was so near to the heart of Paul that forgiveness to the slave will be relief and refreshment to the Apostle. This second request, which is a repetition of the first, receiving emphasis from the repetition, belongs as does the first request to the Christian life: it is *in Christ*.

Trusting to thy obedience; silently assumes Paul's right to command, a right already suggested in v. 10 and one which Philemon could not but recognise. Similar obedience to an apostolic command in 2 Cor. vii. 15. *Beyond the things which I say:* viz. the request to receive Onesimus, in spite of his fraud. Paul is sure that Philemon will do more than this. How much more, he is left himself to judge. To us these words suggest, as probably they did to Philemon, the manumission of the converted slave, who though still beyond his master's reach was about to return to him. But for this Paul does not ask. It was left for Philemon's generosity.

That *ONESIMUS* had been a slave of Philemon, is made quite certain by v. 16: 'no longer a slave.' Since he is said in Col. iv. 9 to belong in some sense to Colossæ, and to be then going back there, we infer that the home of Philemon in which Onesimus formerly lived as a slave was at Colossæ. Evidently the slave had first defrauded, and then run away from, his master. Probably, like many fugitives from many lands, he had found his way to the great metropolis in order to hide there among others like himself. At Rome he came under the influence of the imprisoned Apostle, heard the Gospel from his lips, and found in it a liberty which mere escape from earthly bondage cannot give. A complete change took place. The dishonest runaway is now a 'faithful brother:' Col. iv. 9. And he is now, possibly through some special amiability of character, an object of Paul's marked affection. This amiability he seems to have shown by attentive help rendered to Paul in prison. This kind attention of the slave recalls to the prisoner pleasant memories of his master's kindness to many Christians and kindly feeling towards himself. He would like to have had this help still longer: but other considerations determine otherwise. Onesimus has not only run away from Philemon but has robbed him. It would seem that he was so poor as to be unable to repay what he had taken. But the debt must be recognised. Paul bids the fugitive, whom he would much like to retain, to return to his master at Colossæ. A favourable opportunity of doing so presents itself. Tychicus is going there with a letter of congratulation and warning to the Church prompted by the varied news brought by Epaphras.

It is decided that Onesimus shall go with Tychicus. Going thus at Paul's bidding, in company with a well-known and trusted helper of the Apostle, he will receive a better welcome from those who perhaps knew him as a runaway thief. And he takes with him a recommendation even better than this, the letter before us.

Paul reminds Philemon that as an apostle of Christ (cp. 1 Th. ii. 6) he might give commands as a superior. But Christian love moves him to make request as an equal. His age and chain must plead for him. He is writing about a child in the Gospel whose conversation has gladdened the hardships of his prison, for a man whose name is now, from the point of view both of Philemon and of Paul, as appropriate as it was once from Philemon's point of view inappropriate. So great is Paul's love for his convert that to send him back is to rend his own heart. But this he has done; not wishing to take from the hands of Philemon, by retaining his slave, a kindness he has not opportunity to refuse. There must be a Divine purpose in the flight of Onesimus. God designs the master and slave to be united in bonds which will survive all human relationships. In harmony with this Divine purpose Paul has sent back the fugitive, whom he begs Philemon to receive as he would receive the Apostle himself.

Another point demands mention. Probably the runaway had told Paul that he had in some way robbed his master. This debt, moreover, the slave cannot repay. But Paul promises himself to repay it; and reminds Philemon of a debt on the other side which cannot be paid. Again, the prisoner begs acquiescence; and concludes the matter of Onesimus with confidence that Philemon will not only grant his request but will go beyond it.

This story of Onesimus is wonderfully characteristic of Christianity. No other religion can reach and save and raise the dregs of society. A less hopeful case than a runaway thief hiding himself among the outcasts at Rome, there could not be. But the Gospel both found and transformed him; and made one proved to be untrustworthy into a beloved and trusted brother. The rescue and complete restoration of Onesimus, as attested by this letter, reveals the power of the Gospel and thus gives hope for the outcasts around us. Like Paul (1 Tim. i. 16) the fugitive from Colossæ is a pattern of what Christ will do for all who receive Him. As a pedestal on which stands, within sight of all men, this monument of the mercy and power of God, this Epistle is of priceless worth.

SECTION IV.
CONCLUSION.

VERSES 22—25.

At the same time also prepare me a lodging: for I hope that through your prayers I shall be granted to you.
[23] *Epaphras, my fellow-prisoner in Christ Jesus, greets thee:* [24] as do *Mark, Aristarchus, Demas, Luke, my fellow-workers.*
[25] *The grace of our Lord Jesus Christ be with your spirit.*

22. *At the same time;* suggests that Paul may be expected soon after the arrival of Onesimus. *A lodging:* either at an inn or in a private house. All details are left to Philemon's hospitality. This intimation adds force to the main request of the letter. For if Paul comes to Colossæ he will see for himself whether it has been complied with. *For I hope etc.:* to be released from prison, as implied in the foregoing request. *Through your prayers:* a close and important coincidence with Rom. xv. 30, 2 Cor. i. 11, Eph. vi. 19, Col. iv. 3, 2 Th. iii. 1. This confidence in his readers' prayers, even for bodily preservation, is a marked feature of Paul's thought. *Granted,* or *given-as-a-mark-of-favour:* same word as in Ph. i. 29, Rom. viii. 32; a favourite with Paul. *Granted to you:* if, through the favour of God he is set free, this will be a joy and enrichment to those who have prayed for him.

This purpose to visit Philemon is in harmony with the deep interest in the Churches at Colossæ and Laodicea expressed in Col. ii. 1. On what rested Paul's hope of speedy liberation, we do not know. No trace of it is found in the companion Epistles to the Colossians and the Ephesians. On the other hand, Col. iv. 3 and Eph. vi. 19 suggest very strongly that he had then no fear that his imprisonment would end in death.

23, 24. *Epaphras, my fellow-prisoner:* see under Col. iv. 10. The significant addition, *in Christ Jesus,* keeps before us the truth, ever present to the mind of Paul, that this imprisonment stood in special relation to Christ. *Mark, Aristarchus, Demas, Luke:* as in Col. iv. 10, 14. All these joined in the greeting to the Church at Colossæ. The only name found there and, for reasons unknown to us, absent here, is Jesus Justus. And all these, like Aristarchus, Mark, and Jesus Justus in Col. iv. 10, 11, are here called *fellow-workers.*

25. Almost word for word as in Ph. iv. 23, Gal. vi. 18.

CHRISTIANITY AND SLAVERY. It is worthy of note that in this Epistle Paul does not require or ask Philemon to liberate Onesimus. Moreover, while Onesimus was still a slave in the house of Philemon, the latter was apparently a recognised Christian and a beloved friend of Paul. This, together with the silence of the rest of the New Testament, implies that the Apostles did not forbid their converts to hold slaves. Yet, not only has the Gospel put an end to slavery wherever throughout the world it has gained power, but it is the only religious system which has done anything effective in this direction.

The reason of this apparent tolerance of slavery is not far to seek. By asserting the fatherhood of God, the Gospel proclaims the brotherhood of man; and thus asserts a principle utterly inconsistent with one man treating another as his property. On the other hand, had Christ and His Apostles forbidden the holding of slaves, they would have arrayed against the Gospel all those interested in maintaining the existing order of society, and thus have needlessly placed in its way most serious obstacles. And, worse still, by raising a standard of revolt against a social injustice, they would have rallied around themselves multitudes anxious only for relief from a social grievance. An appeal to such classes would have utterly misrepresented Christianity. And their help would have ruined it. Christ therefore offered to men only a spiritual liberation. But this carried with it the living germ of every kind of freedom.

For these reasons the Apostles tolerated slavery. We have no trace of fault found for holding Onesimus as a slave. It does not even lessen Paul's warm recognition of Philemon's excellence. And, even if Onesimus resume his former position, Paul will gladly be Philemon's guest. Yet, while refusing to claim for the slaves a liberty for which they were not yet prepared, and which would have loosened the very framework of society, Paul taught that in Christ the distinction of bond and free no longer exists, and that a believing slave is already virtually free: Gal. iii. 28, 1 Cor. vii. 21. And in Col. iv. 1 he teaches that slaves have just claims upon their masters, claims recognised by a Master in heaven. Such teaching at once improved the lot of the slave, and prepared gradually a way for the emancipation which our day has seen.

From the example of the Apostles in the matter of slavery we may learn an important lesson. There are many things contrary to the spirit of the Gospel which it is inexpedient at once to forbid by civil or ecclesiastical law. In some few cases such prohibition would appeal to unworthy motives. And verbal prohibition can be effective only when supported by the public conscience. The Gospel works always from within, shedding light upon broad principles of right and wrong, light which ultimately reaches and illumines all the details of practical life. But, for this inner illumination, time is often needful. Legislation is effective only when it registers an inward growth of the moral sentiment.

The result of this letter is unknown. But from 1 Tim. i. 3 we infer that after his imprisonment at Rome Paul again visited Ephesus; though perhaps, as his directions to Timothy suggest, only for a short time. If so, it is not unlikely that Paul's wish to visit Colossæ was gratified; and that, under the roof of Philemon, the master, the liberated slave, and the Apostle enjoyed sweet fellowship in Christ.

EXPOSITION OF THE EPISTLE TO THE EPHESIANS.

SECTION I.

THE GREETING.

CH. I. 1, 2.

Paul an apostle of Christ Jesus through the *will of God, to the saints which are at Ephesus and* the *believing ones in Christ Jesus;* ²*grace to you and peace from God our Father and* the *Lord Jesus Christ.*

1. To the Churches *at Ephesus* and at Rome, and to these only *Paul* writes simply in his own name. In all his other letters, for special reasons, he joins others with himself as approving what he is about to say. But there are no such reasons now. It is true that Timothy was (Acts xix. 22) with Paul at Ephesus. But we have no proof that he took any prominent part in the work there. Consequently, the special interest in him which led, apparently, to his association with Paul in the Epistle to the Philippians was not present in this case. *An apostle of Christ Jesus through* the *will of God:* word for word as in Col. i. 1. *The saints:* as in Rom. xv. 25, 26. See under Rom. i. 7. *Which are* or *exist:* calling attention to the existence of saints *at Ephesus. Believing:* same Greek word as in Col. i. 2, uniting the senses of *faithful* and *believing*. Nothing here suggests the meaning *faithful* or *trustworthy*. And, as the exposition *believers in Christ Jesus* would give good sense as a specially Christian designation, this is perhaps the sense intended. *In Christ Jesus:* as in *v.* 15; see under Col. i. 4. *Grace etc.:* word for word as in Rom. i. 7.

The words *in Ephesus* are, in the two oldest and best copies, which very seldom agree in error, found only inserted by a much later hand. Basil says (*Against Eunomius* bk. ii. 19) that they were absent from the earliest copies he had seen. Origen, followed by Jerome, gives an exposition of this verse which suggests that the words were not in the copies used. Tertullian, who holds firmly that the Epistle was written to the Ephesians, charges Marcion (*Against Marcion* bk. v. 11, 17) with interpolating the words 'to the Laodiceans;' and appeals against him to the 'truth of the Church,' but not expressly to the wording of the superscription. This suggests that in the copies he had seen these words were not actually found in the text of the Epistle, but as we may suppose only in the title. All this proves that at a very early date the words were absent from some copies of the Epistle. They are, however, found in all later copies, and in all versions. And, as by Tertullian so by all writers, the Epistle is universally quoted without a shadow of doubt as written to the Ephesians.

Of these remarkable facts, two explanations have been given. (1) That the words are genuine, and were omitted by some copyists because it seemed unlikely that to a Church in which he had lived three years Paul would write a letter without any personal references. But that in the infancy of literary criticism this was detected, that a scribe would dare to omit words for this reason, and that the omission spread so far as the above facts testify, is most unlikely. (2) That copies of this Epistle were sent to other Churches in the province of Asia, each bearing the name of the Church to which it was sent; that the copies bearing the names of other towns have without exception vanished; but that the observed difference between the copies led some early scribes, in uncertainty about the Church intended, to omit altogether the name of any specific town. This would agree with our explanation of 'the letter from Laodicea' in Col. iv. 16. That all copies with names other than Ephesus should vanish completely, seems unlikely. But copies in the metropolis would be more likely to survive than those directed to small towns in the interior such as Laodicea. This view is not discredited by the unanimity with which the Epistle is designated as that to the Ephesians. For it would naturally become known, and take its name, chiefly from the capital of the province: cp. Tertullian quoted in Introd. ii. of my *Romans*. On the whole, this latter seems the easiest explanation of the facts of the case.

This latter suggestion will also account for a letter so general being written to a Church so well known to Paul. In a letter designed also for other Churches in Asia Paul may well have written only words suitable for all, leaving personal matters (ch. vi. 21) to be conveyed by Tychicus.

DIVISION I.

DOCTRINE.

CHAPTERS I. 3—III.

SECTION II.

PRAISE FOR GOD'S ETERNAL PURPOSE OF MERCY TO JEWS AND GENTILES.

CH. I. 3—14.

Blessed be God, the Father of our Lord Jesus Christ, who has blessed us with every spiritual blessing in the heavenly places *in Christ,* [4] *according as He chose us in Him before* the *foundation of* the *world that we should be holy and blameless before Him, in love* [5] *having foreordained us to adoption through Jesus Christ for Him, according to the good pleasure of His will,* [6] *for praise of* the *glory of His grace, which grace He gave to us in the Beloved One.*

[7] *In whom we have redemption through His blood, the forgiveness of our trespasses, according to the riches of His grace,* [8] *which He made to abound toward us in all wisdom and prudence,* [9] *having made known to us the mystery of His will, according to the good pleasure which He purposed in Him,* [10] *for* the *dispensation of the fulness of the seasons, to gather up together all things in Christ, those in the heavens and those on the earth; in Him,* [11] *in whom also we were made a heritage, having been predestined according to* the *purpose of Him who works all things according to the counsel of His will,* [12] *that we should be for praise of His glory who had before hoped in the Christ.*

[13] *In whom also ye, having heard the word of the truth, the Gospel of your salvation—in whom also having believed ye were sealed with the Spirit of promise, the Holy* Spirit, [14] *which is an earnest of our inheritance for redemption of the possession, for praise of His glory.*

Section 2 contains three clearly marked divisions, each closing with a solemn refrain : *vv.* 3—6 ; *vv.* 7—12 ; *vv.* 13, 14.

3. An outburst of praise, beginning word for word as in 2 Cor. i. 3. *God,* the *Father :* or more literally *God and* the *Father of our*

Lord Jesus Christ. The Object of Paul's praise unites in Himself two titles: He is *God* and He is *also* the *Father of Christ.* See under Rom. xv. 6. Christ, our Master, spoke constantly of *God* as His *Father;* and thus gave to men a new conception of God, and to God a new name among men. *Blessed:* literally *spoken-good-of:* see under Rom. i. 25. Paul desires that the goodness of God be recognized by the praises of His creatures. The word *blessed* introduces a song of praise.

We bless God because He first *has blessed us.* The meaning of blessing from God to man may be learnt from the O. T. where the phrase is frequent; a good example in Dt. xxviii. 3—6. It there denotes enrichment with the highest good, especially with such good as only God can give. The form of the Greek word *bless* reminds us that these benefits are conveyed to us by the speaking voice of *God. Spiritual:* pertaining to the Spirit of God; the usual meaning of the word. See under Rom. i. 11. *Spiritual blessing;* enrichment wrought by the Holy Spirit and therefore pertaining to the realm of spiritual things. *Every spiritual blessing;* suggests variety of such benefits, and asserts that no kind of spiritual enrichment is wanting to us. *Heavenly*-places or *heavenly*-things, literally *the heavenlies:* same word in 1 Cor. xv. 40, 48, 49 where evidently it denotes things pertaining to heaven. So Ph. ii. 10. *In the heavenly places:* Eph. i. 20, ii. 6, iii. 10, vi. 12, denoting in each case the supramundane world, and in all but the last the world of heavenly blessedness. And this gives good sense here. The good things with which God has enriched us belong to heaven, and will be there enjoyed. And since already (Ph. iii. 20) our citizenship and (Mt. vi. 20) our treasure are in heaven, Paul could say that *God has* already *blessed us in the heavenly* places. By forming the purpose expounded in *vv.* 4, 5, He has already enriched us: and the riches thus given are laid up for us amid the good things in heaven, where neither accident nor decay can destroy or lessen them.

To the locality of this blessing, viz. in heaven, Paul adds its personal element: *in Christ.* Our spiritual enrichment is a result of events which took place *in* the personality of *Christ,* His birth, death, resurrection, and ascension, a result conditioned by inward spiritual contact with Him. Cp. 2 Cor. v. 19, 'God was, *in Christ,* reconciling the world to Himself.'

It is needless to ask whether Paul refers here to blessing given to men once for all when God gave Christ to die, or given when each one appropriates by faith the various blessings resulting from the events of His human life. For both personal faith and the historic facts are essential links of the chain of blessing : and therefore in Paul's thought they were indissolubly joined.

4. *According as He chose us etc.;* traces up this blessing, given by God to men in time, to its eternal source and counterpart, viz. a corresponding purpose of God before time began. *Chose us,* or more fully, *selected-for-Himself:* He took a smaller out of a larger number. See note under Rom. ix. 13. *Us:* further defined in the fundamental Gospel of Paul, Rom. i. 16, 17, iii. 21, 22, as those who believe the Gospel. Not that their foreseen faith in any way moved God to save them ; but that, moved only by pity for lost man, God resolved to save men by means of the good news announced by Christ, and to save those who should believe it. *In Him;* expounds and justifies 'in Christ' in *v.* 3. *Before* the *foundation of* the *world:* same words in Jno. xvii. 24, 1 Pet. i. 20; instructive parallels. Before God began to make the great platform on which have lived the successive generations of men, all future ages were present to His thought : and in view of the sin and ruin which He foresaw, He resolved to save men ; not all men indiscriminately, but those who should believe the Gospel ; and to place these in special relation to Himself as His own. An interesting parallel in 2 Tim. i. 9. Of that eternal purpose, the salvation of each man is a corresponding realization in time : *according as etc.* And, inasmuch as this purpose could be accomplished only through the agency and the death of Christ and by spiritual contact with Him, it has special reference to Him. In this sense, *God chose us for Himself in Christ. Holy :* subjectively holy, as in 1 Cor. vii. 34 ; see note under Rom. i. 7. For it describes here God's purpose touching what we are to be, viz. unreservedly loyal to Himself ; not, as in *v.* 1, a character already possessed, viz. that of men whom God has claimed for His own and who, by that claim, whatever their actual conduct may be, are placed in a new relation to God. Cp. ch. v. 27, Col. i. 22, 1 Pet. i. 15, 16 ; 1 Th. v. 23. In each case, whether used objectively or subjectively, the word *holy* denotes a special and sacred relation to God. *And blameless :* same word and connection and meaning as in Col. i. 22. It is the negative side of holiness. For all sin opposes God ; and is therefore inconsistent with unreserved devotion to God. *Before Him : i.e.* God, who chose us for Himself, formed for us this purpose of holiness and purity, and watches its accomplishment. Same words in Col. i. 22.

In love; may belong either to *v.* 4, asserting that love to our fellows is the surrounding element of the holiness which God designs for His chosen ones, or to *v.* 5, asserting that God's love to man is the element and source of his predestination of believers to sonship. The latter exposition is the more likely. For there is nothing in the context suggesting, or seeming to require mention of, Christian love. Whereas, in praise to God for blessing received, mention of His love as the ultimate source of all blessing is specially appropriate. By placing these words first, Paul throws into great prominence the *love* which prompted the predestination to sonship.

5. A participial clause, describing in further detail the foregoing statement, 'He chose us.' A similar participial clause in *v*. 9. *Forcordained*, or *predestined:* marked out beforehand a path along which, and a goal to which, He would have the chosen ones go. See under Rom. viii. 29. The syllable *fore-* denotes a destination *before* the time when it can be accomplished. So '*before-*hoped' in *v*. 12. *For adoption :* the marked out goal, viz. reception into the family of God as His sons. See under Rom. viii. 15. *Through Jesus Christ:* expounded in Gal. iv. 4, 5. Through the agency of the Eternal Son we become sons. *For Him:* probably, for God. It denotes the intimate relation to God, the Father of the whole family of heaven, in which as His sons, God designs the predestined ones to stand. Notice that adoption is the immediate aim of this divine purpose, holiness is its ultimate aim: *He chose us to be holy, having forcordained us to adoption.* And the Agent of holiness is the Spirit of adoption.

We have here in close connection election and predestination. The former marks out the objects of salvation ; the latter, the goal to which God purposes to bring them.

Good-pleasure : same word in Ph. i. 15, ii. 13, where see notes. In the case of God, the two senses of benevolence and free choice coalesce. Perhaps here the latter is more conspicuous. *Of His will ;* represents God contemplating and approving His own resolve. *According-to :* a favourite word of Paul to describe a correspondence between action and some underlying principle. This clause traces up to the divinely-approved will of God the foregoing predestination to adoption. Paul remembers with gratitude that this purpose of mercy seemed good in His sight.

6. Further and final aim of the predestination : viz. in order that the *splendour* which belongs to the free undeserved *favour* of God may evoke recognition and *praise*. *Glory :* as in Ph. i. 11. *Grace :* see under Rom. i. 5. *Which grace He gave,* or *which He graciously-gave ;* lays stress by repetition on the undeserved favour of God. *In the Beloved* One : parallel with 'chosen in Him' in *v*. 4. Cp. Col. i. 13, 'Son of His love.'

Paul here represents Christ as a special object of the eternal love of God, and ourselves as united to Christ and therefore sharers of the love with which God regards Him. Thus the love of God to Christ becomes undeserved favour towards those who are united to Christ. God purposed that the grandeur or *glory* of this *grace* should appear, and thus evoke *praise*. To this end, acting in harmony with a divine resolve approved by Him, and in infinite love, God marked out for us, to be appropriated by faith, an entrance into His family as His sons. In this way He chose us for Himself, that we may stand before Him as sacred and spotless men.

7. Second part of § 2. It is a further exposition of the 'grace given in the Beloved One.' *We have:* actual incipient accomplishment of God's purpose of mercy. *In whom . . . redemption:* as in Col. i. 14. *Through His blood:* as in Col. i. 20, 'through the blood of His cross:' practically the same as Rom. v. 9, 'justified in His blood.' These words assert in the clearest manner that our liberation from the penalty and bondage of sin comes through Christ's death upon the cross. The need for this costly means of redemption, Paul expounds in Rom. iii. 26. Notice that liberation was wrought out for us *in* the personality of Christ, and is ours by inward union with Him; and that His violent death is the channel *through* which it comes forth from God to us. *Forgiveness of sins:* as in Col. i. 14. It is in harmony with, and must be measured by, the abundance which characterizes God's favour towards us: *according to the riches* etc. Cp. Col. i. 27, ii. 2, Rom. xi. 33, 2 Cor. viii. 2: favourite phraseology of Paul. Thus God has made us (*v.* 6) objects of His *grace*. Notice the emphatic repetition of this last word, after its use twice in *v.* 6. It is the source of all blessing from God to us.

8. Further elucidation of the grace of God, showing the specific form it took. *Which* grace *'He made to abound towards us:* i.e. gave to us in abundant measure, or so as to work in us abundant results. Same phrase in 2 Cor. ix. 8: cp. Rom. v. 15. It expounds 'the riches of His grace' in *v.* 7. *All wisdom:* every kind of wisdom: see under Col. i. 9. *Prudence:* a practical faculty enabling men to select, in the various details and emergencies of life, the most profitable line of action. The connection of the two words reminds us that in Christ acquaintance with the eternal realities has practical worth as a guide in the details of life; and that among these details we can choose our steps aright only in the light of the eternal realities. Evidently this *wisdom and prudence* are God's gift, making us wise and prudent, as we learn from *v.* 9 where the

knowledge imparted is specified. Paul here asserts that the undeserved favour of God given to us so abundantly has been clothed with every kind of *wisdom and discretion*. These are the forms in which the grace of God was manifested. Cp. Col. i. 9: 'all wisdom and spiritual understanding.'

9. A participial clause explaining the assertion in *v.* 8. By making known to us the mystery, God gave to us in abundant measure His undeserved favour clothed in wisdom and prudence. *Mystery*: as in Col. i. 26. *Of His Will*: the contents of this mystery. It is further described in *v.* 10. This will of God was kept secret during long ages, and is known now only by those to whom God reveals it. It is therefore the mystery of His will. Cp. Rom. xvi. 25. *To us*: to Christians generally: Col. i. 26. Another aspect of the same revelation is given in Eph. iii. 3. It was made known to Paul and through him to his hearers and readers. *According to His good pleasure*: as in *v.* 5. It is not clear whether this refers to *the mystery* or to the *making-known* of it. But, since both are included in the same divine purpose, possibly in Paul's thought they were not distinguished. *He purposed*: as in Rom. viii. 28, ix. 11; important parallels. That which was well-pleasing to God He deliberately purposed to effect. *In Him*: either in Christ or in God. In the former case it would be rendered (RV.) *in Him*: in the latter (AV.) *in Himself*. Although the foregoing possessive pronouns refer to the Father, a comparison with *v.* 4, 'chosen in Him,' suggests that Paul refers here to Christ. Moreover, to say that God's purpose was formed in God, is tautology: to say that it was formed in Christ, adds an important thought kept before us in *v.* 10, viz. the relation of this divine purpose to the Son of God.

10. Exposition of the foregoing. *With-a-view-to etc.*: in forming this purpose God was looking forward to the time of Christ. *Dispensation*: same word as *stewardship* in Col. i. 25, 1 Cor. ix. 17. It denotes the management of a house. And, since this was frequently committed to a superior servant, or steward, it denotes frequently the office of a steward. So always elsewhere in the N.T. It cannot be so here. For, evidently, God is represented as administering His own household. The word falls back therefore on its original meaning of house management. It is the government of God represented as a householder managing his property and servants. *Seasons*: portions of time, looked upon not as periods passing by but as opportunities for action. Same word in ch. v. 16: also 1 Th. v. 1, 1 Tim. iv. 1, 2 Tim. iii. 1, etc. The plural suggests that in the Gospel age several ages had their consummation. *Ful-*

ness: see under Col. i. 19. *The fulness of the seasons:* the time in which the various ages of the kingdom of God find their end and goal, and the accomplishment of the purpose which underlays them. And this can be no other than the Gospel age, and the glorious ages to follow it. Consequently, *the dispensation of etc.* is the mode of divine government which belongs to that age. All this God had in view in forming His purpose of salvation.

To-sum-up-again (same word in Rom. xiii. 9). *all things in Christ:* God's purpose touching the final administration of His kingdom. *All things:* men and things, as in Col. i. 20. God resolved to unite together *in Christ* the dissevered elements of His universe, thus making Him the centre and circumference of all. *Sum-up-again;* suggests an original harmony. This, God purposes to restore. [The middle voice suggests that God will do this to work out His own pleasure.] *All things* include *the things upon the heavens and those upon the earth.* So 1 Col. i. 20; a close parallel. In the one passage Christ is an instrument of universal reconciliation; in the other, a centre of universal harmony.

This verse teaches that the eternal purpose which prompted, as the means of its accomplishment, the mission of the Son of God embraced both earth and heaven; that God has resolved to unite into one whole the various elements in these realms of His empire; and to make Christ the surrounding element and the centre of this all-embracing union. In other words, God's purpose to save man is part of a purpose earlier in time, and wider in extent, than the human race. *In Him:* emphatic repetition of *in Christ*, as a transition to the relative sentence following in which the same idea is again prominent.

11. A new thought: in Christ *we have also been-made-heirs*. This last word is the passive form of a verb denoting to allot something to some one, and especially to allot as an inheritance. In Greek, such a passive may mean either 'to be allotted as an inheritance,' or 'to receive such an allotment.' The latter sense is the more likely here. For, that believers are themselves an inheritance is not taught elsewhere in the N. T. In *v.* 14 they are represented as God's own possession, but not as an inherited possession. But, that they are heirs, is plainly asserted in *v.* 14, Rom. viii. 17, Gal. iii. 29: and some are said in Col. i. 12 to have been made partakers of the allotted portion of the saints. And this allotment of inherited blessing has been made to us in Christ. For, only through His agency and by inward union with Him is the inheritance ours.

The participial clause following traces this allotment of an inheritance to a definite and eternal purpose of God. *Having-been-foreordained:* passive form of the word used in v. 5. We have been made heirs in time because before time began we were in the mind of God marked out for heirship. *According to purpose:* same words in same sense in Rom. viii. 28. They give prominence to the chief element in the foreordination, viz. purpose, and tell us that it was a purpose of Him whose deliberate resolve controls and moulds *all things. Works:* as in Ph. ii. 13. *Works all things:* same words in 1 Cor. xii. 6. *Counsel:* a deliberate purpose taking into account ways and means. This deliberate purpose has its source in *the will* of God. The idea of deliberation distinguishes this phrase from the similar phrase in v. 5 where God's satisfaction with His own purpose is more prominent.

12. A refrain marking the close of the second part of § 2, similar to that in v. 6 at the close of the first part. This fuller refrain tells us that God intended us to be a means of evoking praise of His splendour; and that this praise is an aim of the purpose described in v. 11. God resolved so to bless us that in us others should see and acknowledge His grandeur.

Up to this point Paul's words have been true alike of Jews and Gentiles. He now mentions the two great divisions of mankind which were ever present to his thought. In v. 12 the Jews, and in vv. 13, 14 the Gentiles, are specified. *Before-hoped:* i.e. before *the Christ* came. This hope of a coming deliverer was a distinguishing feature of the Jews: Acts xxvi. 6, 7, xxviii. 20, Lk. ii. 25, 38. It was a bond uniting together the scattered members of the nation; and an inspiration moulding the piety of the more devout. The Gentiles had no such hope: Eph. ii. 12. The word *Christ* is both a designation of the hoped-for Deliverer (Dan. ix. 25, Jno. i. 20, iv. 25) and a proper name of the Incarnate Son. The latter is naturally the usual use of the word. But here the mention of a hope earlier than the incarnation suggests the former use. The Messiah, who was the great object of Jewish hopes, is represented as the ground of their hope: so 1 Cor. xv. 19, Ph. ii. 19. For, long before He appeared, the Jews clung to the hoped-for Deliverer and built upon Him their expectations.

13, 14. Third part of § 2. *In whom:* parallel with the same words in v. 7 at the beginning of the second part. *Also ye:* the Gentile Christians at Ephesus, as well as the Jews referred to specially in v. 12. *Having heard etc.:* means by which salvation had reached the Ephesian Christians, viz. *the word* spoken and heard. *The word of the truth:* as in Col. i. 5. It is a verbal expression corresponding to the eternal realities. *The Gospel of your salvation:* 'the good news which has been and is the means of your salvation.' So 1 Cor. xv. 2. The word preached was an assertion *of the truth:* it was also *the good news* which had been the means of rescuing the Ephesian Christians from the penalty and power of sin.

After the participial clause we expect a finite word. But instead of this we have another participial clause: *in whom also having believed.* Apparently the construction of the sentence is broken off. The relative, *in whom* or *in which,* is repeated, disturbing the orderly course of the sentence. But the irregularity throws into prominence the truth that the sealing afterwards mentioned was in Christ. Paul wishes to say that in Christ the Gentile Christians, *having heard the Gospel,* and *having also believed* it, *were sealed* etc. This surrender of grammar to emphasis is a conspicuous feature in Paul: so ch. ii. 1—5, Rom. v. 12, Gal. ii. 6. *The Spirit of promise:* the gift of the Spirit foretold by the prophets, e.g. Joel ii. 28, 29, Ezek. xxxvi. 26, 27. The Spirit of promise is then identified as *the Holy* Spirit. With this Spirit as an instrument the Gentile Christians had been *sealed:* close parallel to 2 Cor. i. 21, 22. Paul asserts that his readers, whom he distinguishes from the Jews, had *heard the Gospel and* had *believed* it; that through faith they had received *the Holy Spirit* as foretold by the ancient prophets; and that the Spirit thus received was a *seal,* i.e. a divine attestation of the word believed. And he declares with emphatic repetition that this sealing had taken place in virtue of their inward union with Christ. He thus joins the believing Gentiles to those who when Christ came were waiting for His appearance. Notice that the gift of the Spirit proves that the Gentiles are sharers of the blessings brought by Christ: Acts xi. 17, 18. This proof is strengthened by the word *promise,* which reminds us that the Holy Spirit given to the Gentiles was a fulfilment of ancient Jewish prophecy.

This verse is in close harmony with the constant teaching of Paul that they who believe the Gospel are justified, and adopted into the family of God, and receive the Holy Spirit: e.g. Gal. ii. 16, iii. 2, 26.

14. Further teaching about the Holy Spirit, and about God's purpose in sealing us. *Earnest:* a part of the price paid at the time of purchase as a pledge of the whole. See under 2 Cor. i. 22, v. 5: close and important parallels. *Our inheritance:* the benefits of the New Covenant looked upon as coming to us in virtue of our relation to God our Father. Close parallels in Rom. viii. 17, Gal. iii. 29, Col. iii. 24. Of these benefits, the gift of the Spirit is a part given to us when we are received into the family of God. And inasmuch as this gift is a proof that we are children of God, it is also a pledge that the entire inheritance will some day be ours. The word rendered *possession* denotes in 1 Th. v. 9, 2 Th. ii. 14 the *obtaining* of salvation and of the glory of Christ; and in Heb. x. 39 the *preserving* of the soul. But in Mal. ii. 17 and in a quotation in 1 Pet. ii. 9 from Ex. xix. 5 it represents a Hebrew word denoting a peculiar possession or treasure. God declared that Israel, if faithful, should be His own peculiar treasure. And such are they who believe in Christ. They will be God's own for ever. *Redemption;* includes the ideas of liberation and price, and is therefore not complete till actual liberation is effected. Cp. ch. iv. 30, 'the day of redemption;' Lk. xxi. 28, Rom. viii. 23: see under Rom. iii. 24. An aim of the gift of the Spirit is the liberation in the great day from the bondage of death of those whom God has chosen to be specially His own.

For praise of His glory: nearly word for word as in *v.* 12. It is a third refrain closing the third part of § 2. Each refrain represents, as the final purpose of man's salvation in its various parts, an admiring recognition by God's creatures of His essential grandeur. Cp. 1 Pet. ii. 9. The threefold refrain makes this final purpose very conspicuous.

REVIEW. Section 2 is throughout a song of praise for blessings given by God to Paul and his readers, a song rising in each of its three parts till it seems to lose itself in the eternal song of earth and heaven. In the first part we have blessing from man to God for blessing given by God to man in fulfilment of an eternal purpose that men should be sons of God. In the second part we are reminded that the objects of this purpose are sinners. Consequently, God's favour towards them took the form of rescue, through the death of Christ, from the penalty and bondage of sin. Moreover, His favour came to them clothed in a gift of wisdom revealing God's long-hidden purpose to bring men into His family and to make them His heirs, this being part of a wider purpose to unite the creatures of God in heaven and earth into one great whole of which Christ is to be the Head and Centre and Circumference, a purpose of Him whose counsels rule and mould the universe.

Up to this point, in the light of a divine purpose wide as the universe and earlier than time, all human distinctions have been forgotten. But at the close of the second part of the section, we meet the all-important distinction of Jew and Gentile so deeply interwoven into the thought of Paul. The above purpose of God embraces the Jews, who before Messiah came had built their hopes on His expected appearance. And it embraces the Gentiles: for they have not only heard and believed the Gospel but have received the seal of the Holy Spirit promised to ancient Israel, who is Himself a pledge that they will share the inheritance of the sons of Abraham and the deliverance which awaits those who are the peculiar treasure of God. This specific mention of the Gentiles as sharers of the heritage of Israel forms the third and last division of the section. Each division concludes by pointing to the eternal recognition of the greatness of God as the ultimate aim of the blessing and favour so richly poured upon man.

In this section we have a restatement of Paul's teaching in Rom. viii. 28, 29, ix. 11 that salvation is an accomplishment of a divine purpose and choice and predestination. The restatement has the emphasis of conspicuous repetition. The purpose to save man is traced back to eternity; is shown to be part of a purpose embracing both earth and heaven; and is placed in closest relation to Christ. In other words, Paul's earlier teaching has received rich and harmonious development. We have again his favourite thought that the Gospel contains a secret known only to the initiated; as in Rom. xvi. 25, 1 Cor. ii. 7, Col. i. 26. The gift of the Spirit is again appealed to as a proof of the favour of God and as a pledge of a share in the inheritance awaiting the sons of God; in close harmony with Rom. viii. 16, 17, Gal. iii. 29, iv. 6, and with Acts xi. 17, 18. A marked feature of this section is the occurrence in it ten times of the phrase *in Christ* or its equivalents, noting an inward union with Him as the all-embracing and all-pervading element both of salvation and of the eternal purpose to save. This we have already noticed as a conspicuous feature of the writings of Paul, a feature not found elsewhere in the N. T. except, in a peculiar form, in the Gospel and First Epistle of John. Its presence here in so great frequency, but never without meaning, is a clear indication of genuineness: as are the coincidences noted above. We notice the word *redemption* used to describe the deliverance wrought through the death of Christ, as in Rom. iii. 24; and with special reference to the final deliverance, as in Rom. viii. 23. Also the word *wealth*, as in Rom. ii. 4, ix. 23, xi. 33, Col. i. 27; and the word *earnest*, as in 2 Cor. i. 22, v. 5.

As we rise from the study of this section we are conscious that we have heard the tones of a familiar voice, and have learnt from the lips of a revered teacher new lessons equal to the most valuable we had learnt before.

SECTION III.

PRAYER THAT THE READERS MAY RECOGNISE IN THEMSELVES THE GREAT POWER WHICH RAISED CHRIST FROM THE DEAD.

CH. I. 15—23.

For which cause also I, having heard the faith among you in the Lord Jesus, and the faithfulness *towards all the saints,* [16] *do not cease giving thanks on your behalf, making mention* of you *in my prayers;* [17] *that the God of our Lord Jesus Christ, the Father of glory, may give to you* the *Spirit of wisdom and revelation, in the knowledge of Him* [18] *having the eyes of your hearts enlightened, in order that ye may know what is the hope of your calling, what the riches of the glory of His inheritance among the saints,* [19] *and what the surpassing greatness of His power towards us who believe, according to the working of the might of His strength* [20] *which He wrought in Christ when He raised Him from the dead and set* Him *at His right hand in the heavenly* places [21] *beyond and above all principality and authority and power and lordship and every name named not only in this age but also in that which is to be.* [22] *And He subjected all things under His feet; and gave Him,* as *Head above all things, to the Church,* [23] *which is His body, the fulness of Him who fills all things in all.*

Paul began his Epistles to the Philippians and Colossians, after a few words of greeting, with thanks to God for his readers' Christian life. The Epistle before us, he begins with a glorious psalm of praise for blessings given to the whole people of God, which he expounds at some length, followed by specific mention of Jewish and Gentile Christians. The mention of these last suggests now definite thanks to God on his readers' behalf, thanks which pass easily into a wonderful prayer for their further progress. His thanks and prayer occupy this section.

15. *For which cause :* because you have been sealed by the Spirit as heirs of the inheritance of God. *Also I:* Paul placing himself alongside these Gentiles, as interested in their welfare. *Having-heard:* cp. Col. i. 4, to a Church Paul has never visited; and contrast Ph. i. 3, where the absence of this word suggests that he writes from personal knowledge. That Paul speaks only of *having heard* about people among whom (Acts xx. 31) he laboured three years, is certainly remarkable. It can hardly be explained by tidings received since he left Ephesus four or five years before. For it was nearly as long since he was at Philippi; and after leaving Philippi he met the Ephesian elders at Miletus. More likely is the suggestion (see under v. 1) that this letter was written to other Churches besides that at Ephesus, Churches which Paul had never visited; and that chiefly to tidings about these last, together with later tidings about the Ephesians, the word *have-heard* refers. This word therefore supports the suggestion just mentioned. *The faith among you;* differs very slightly from 'your faith,' by making *faith* and the believer distinct objects of thought. *Faith in the Lord Jesus:* similar phrase in 1 Tim. iii. 13, 2 Tim. iii. 15. It represents Christ, the personal object and ground of our faith, as also its surrounding element.

The word *love*, omitted from the text of the RV., is not found in any Greek copy earlier than the Clermont Ms. in the sixth century, and in a correction of the Sinai Ms. made perhaps in the seventh century. It is absent entirely from the Vat. and Alex. Mss. and from the Sinai Ms. as originally written; and seems to have been unknown to the early Biblical scholars, Origen and Jerome. But it is found in the Latin, Syriac, and Coptic Versions. If spurious, the insertion of the word is easily accounted for as a reminiscence of Col. i. 4. But, if genuine, its omission is very difficult to explain. This likelihood of insertion and unlikeliness of omission, together with the united testimony of the ancient Greek Mss., our best witnesses for the text of the N. T., testify strongly that the word was not written by Paul. And that without it the sentence gives a good meaning, I shall endeavour to show.

In the sense in which Paul writes *faith in the Lord Jesus*, we cannot possibly have *faith . . . in all the saints*. Certainly these last cannot be the object or element of Christian faith. But the common classic meaning which I have given to the same word in Philem. 4, and which is found in a few places in the N. T., viz. *faithfulness*, would give a good meaning here. That one word would then be used in the same sentence in two senses, need not surprise us. For each use of the word was common, the first in the N. T. and the other in the Greek spoken everywhere in Paul's day. And the context makes quite clear that the word cannot have in the second clause the meaning which it undoubtedly has in the first. In such cases the mind passes almost unconsciously from one sense of the word to another. Moreover, faith and faithfulness have much in common. They who rest with confidence upon the word and character of God become themselves a rock on which others rest. Hence, in Greek, the same words, substantive and adjective, denote *faith* and *faithfulness*, 'believing' and 'trustworthy.' Between these meanings it is frequently difficult to decide: e.g. Col. i. 2, iv. 9. An example of transition from one to the other, we have in Rom. iii. 3 'What if some did not believe? Shall their want of faith make of no effect the *faith* (or *faithfulness*) of God?' We may therefore accept this meaning as not unlikely. And it enables us to accept also the reading so strongly supported by the best ancient copies. But since no English word combines the two meanings of the Greek word, we can reproduce Paul's full sense only by using two words. The passage may fairly be reproduced, *faith in the Lord Jesus and faithfulness towards all the saints*. The assurance of which Christ was the personal Object and Ground and Sphere produced as its natural result trustworthiness *towards all the saints*. These last words as in Col. i. 4.

16. *Do not cease giving thanks:* cp. Ph. i. 3, Col. i. 3, 9, Rom. i. 8, 9. Paul's constant attitude of mind, since he heard about his readers, has been thankfulness to God for them. For he knew that their faithfulness was God's work and gift.

17. As ever, Paul's thoughts pass imperceptibly into prayer for further blessing. The good he hears prompts him, while giving thanks, to ask for more. *In order that etc.:* matter of the prayer, given as its aim and purpose. So frequently: cp. Philem. 6. For Paul's prayer is a means to a definite end. Knowing that God answers prayer, he prays *in order that God . . . may give*.

The God of our Lord Jesus Christ: who on earth addressed Him as 'My God,' Jno. xx. 17, Mt. xxvii. 46. The word *God* here notes a relation of the Father, not only to men, but to Christ. And the entire teaching of Paul and John assures us that this relation extends, not only to the Incarnate, but to the Eternal, Son. As supreme in the Godhead, the Father occupies, even to the Eternal Son, a relation suitably described by the word *God*. Hence this word is the frequent title of the Father even as distinguished from the Son: see under 1 Cor. iii. 23, viii. 6. For to Him, as *God*, the Son is and ever will be subject: 1 Cor. xv. 28. A genitive following the word *father* usually describes his children. But the abstract term *glory* cannot do this. It is evidently a characterizing quality of *the Father* of Christ and of us. So 2 Cor. i. 3, 'Father of compassions;' Acts vii. 2, 'God of glory,' 1 Cor. ii. 8, 'Lord of glory.' Paul prays to Him to whom the divine Head of the Church bows as *God, to the Father*, clothed in infinite grandeur, of Christ and of us.

Spirit of wisdom: the Holy *Spirit*, as an animating principle possessing and imparting *wisdom*. See under 1 Cor. iv. 21, 'Spirit of meekness;' 2 Cor. iv. 13, Rom. viii. 2, 15. For the word cannot denote here a human spirit: nor does it ever, apparently, denote mere disposition of mind. [The absence of the Greek article is frequent even when the one Holy Spirit is indisputably referred to: e.g. Rom. viii. 9—11, 14, 15. For where a word is in itself sufficiently definite, the Greeks frequently omitted the article, in order to direct attention to the qualities implied in the anarthrous word; in this case, to the Holy Spirit as an animating principle characterized by wisdom.] *Wisdom and revelation:* see under 1 Cor. ii. 5, Rom. i. 17. It is a characterizing prerogative of the Spirit of God to impart a knowledge of eternal realities; and, more definitely, to lift a veil which no hand but that of God can lift and which hides from us the unseen things of God. The former term is general: the latter specific. Paul prays that the Father who is characterized by infinite grandeur, who has already (*v.* 13) sealed his readers with the Spirit of promise, may give to them the same Spirit as an inward source of wisdom and as One who reveals the things unseen. His prayer reminds us that each new influence and work of the Spirit is a fresh gift from God.

Knowledge: literally, *full-knowledge;* as in Col. i. 9, 10, ii. 2, iii. 10. *Of Him:* of God, to whom here Paul prays. The Spirit of wisdom comes to us clothed *in* a deep and real *knowledge* of God; and makes Himself known to us by imparting such knowledge. For God is Himself the great Reality, and the great Object which appears when the veil is lifted.

18. *Enlightened:* as in Heb. vi. 4, x. 32. *The heart:* the inmost centre of human life, and the source of action: see under Rom. i. 21. *The eyes of the heart:* the faculty by which knowledge enters into and illumines this inmost chamber. *Having the eyes of your heart enlightened:* connecting link between the gift of the Spirit and the personal knowledge which Paul desires for his readers. [The accusative case puts these words in apposition, not as we might have expected to the preceding words 'give to you,' but to those following *that ye may know;* in order, apparently, to suggest that only by enlightenment of the heart can we receive this desired knowledge. This use of the accusative is made somewhat the more easy by the occasional use of the accusative absolute, as in Rom. viii. 3.] Before expounding the ultimate aim of his prayer, viz.

knowledge of three things pertaining to the Christian life, Paul states conspicuously a condition on which alone this aim can be attained, viz. the entrance of light, ever the condition of knowledge, into the inmost chamber of our nature. This light he hopes for as a result of the gift of the Spirit of God whose special work is to impart wisdom and to unveil mysteries. For He is the one principle of spiritual life. And, always, life is an essential condition of sight.

That ye may know etc.: ultimate aim of the gift of the Spirit, and of inward enlightenment. So Ph. i. 9, Col. i. 9. This earnest prayer reveals the infinite importance of knowledge as a condition of Christian life. Three matters, Paul desires his readers to know: two in v. 18, and a third in v. 19. *His calling:* a favourite word of Paul, Rom. i. 6, viii. 28, 30, 1 Cor. i. 9, 26, vii. 18, 20, 21, 22, etc; 'the high calling of God,' Ph. iii. 14. It is the Gospel summons to salvation, to the service of God, and to eternal glory. To this *calling* belongs *hope:* for it gives to those who hear and obey it an expectation of infinite blessing to come. Paul desires that his readers may know how great these blessings are. And to this end he has already prayed that they may receive the Spirit of wisdom. For only the Spirit of God can reveal the greatness of the blessings awaiting the sons of God: cp. 1 Cor. ii. 10, 12.

And what etc.: second matter which Paul desires His readers to *know.* It is also the object of the *hope* just mentioned. *His inheritance:* the good things of God which will pass to *the saints* as His children. For they are 'heirs of God,' Rom. viii. 17. Of these good things the Spirit of Adoption is the first: cp. v. 14. This inheritance has an abundance of splendour which will make truly rich all who receive it. Paul desires his readers to know how great is the abundance of this splendour. *Among* or *in the saints:* cp. Col. i. 27, 'among the Gentiles.' *The saints* are represented as standing round their own inheritance. Heirship to the wealth of God is located by God in and among the sacred people of the New Covenant.

19a. A third ultimate aim of Paul's prayer. *Surpassing:* chs. ii. 7, iii. 19: a similar form of the same word, in 2 Cor. iii. 10, ix. 14; the corresponding substantive in Rom. vii. 13, 1 Cor. xii. 31, 2 Cor. i. 8, iv. 7, 17, xii. 7, Gal. i. 13, and a corresponding adverb in 2 Cor. xi. 23. This family of words is peculiar to this Epistle and to the undisputed Epistles of Paul. It embodies a thought evidently familiar to him; and is thus a note of genuineness. *Us that believe:* cp. v. 13: another important harmony with Paul's doctrine of salvation through faith. It tells us the aim and direction of this mighty power. Paul desires his readers to know what, in its operation in the hearts of believers, the greatness of that power is.

19b, 20. *According to* etc.: a standard by which they may measure it. *Working:* or *energy:* see under Ph. iii. 21. Notice the accumulation of synonyms representing different sides of one conception. The word rendered *power* denotes ability to produce results. That rendered *might* is the last part of the words autocrat, democrat; and suggests a controlling influence. The word rendered *strength* is frequently used of muscular force. It suggests the inherent capacity of God for breaking down obstacles and working out His will. *The energy of the might of His strength* is the activity of the all-controlling and inherent capacity for action which dwells in God. Same words together in ch. vi. 10.

Which He wrought: specific activity of the power of God to which Paul has just referred as a measure of the power at work in us. *Wrought* or *energized:* cognate to *working* in v. 19. It is used in Gal. iii. 5, Mt. xiv. 2 for the putting forth of miraculous power. *In Christ:* objectively and historically, in the personality of the God-Man. Similarly, Rom. iii. 24; cp. 1 Cor. xv. 22, 'in Adam all die.' *When He raised Him* etc.: specific manifestation of the energy of God. Close parallel in Ph. iii. 10, 'the power of His resurrection.' Notice that, as ever, Christ is said to have been raised by the power of the Father: so Col. ii. 12, Gal. i. 1, Rom. iv. 21, viii. 11, x. 9. *At His right hand:* see under Col. iii. 1. Christ's session in glory is here represented as being, like His resurrection, a work of God. *In the heavenly places:* word for word as in v. 3. It depicts further the surroundings of the Risen Lord.

21. Further delineation of the position of the Risen One. *Beyond-and above:* movement upwards going beyond even the most exalted. *All principality and authority:* word for word as in Col. ii. 10. Same words in the plural in Col. i. 16; where see note. They evidently describe successive ranks of angels. *Power:* same word as in v. 19. In 1 Pet. iii. 22 we have 'angels and authorities and powers,' made subject to the Risen Saviour. *Lordship:* same word in Col. i. 16, but there placed immediately before 'principalities or authorities.' This change of order makes it impossible to determine whether the order here given is ascending or descending. All that we can infer with certainty is that Paul's faith saw the Risen and Rising One passing through and beyond and above successive ranks of angelic powers until there was in heaven no grandeur which He had not left behind. Then, after naming heavenly powers known to him, he uses a universal phrase covering *not only* those known by men living on earth *in the* present *age, but also* those names which will be needed and used to describe men and angels throughout the eternal future. Whatever may be thus designated, Christ has already passed. *Every name named:* a close parallel in Ph. ii. 9. It includes every kind of character and position as recognised by intelligent persons. *Not only etc.;* emphasises the universal expression by specifying two component parts of it. So Col. i. 16. Same division of time in Mt. xii. 32. *This age:* same words in Rom. xii. 2, 1 Cor. ii. 6, Gal. i. 4; where see notes. It is the present course of things. *That which is to come:* the new course of things to be introduced by the coming of Christ, this looked upon as one definite whole.

22a. Further delineation of the exaltation of Christ. For greater emphasis, it is added as an independent sentence. *All-things;* keeps up the idea of universality already expressed by the words 'all' and 'every.' *All things He subjected under His feet:* word for word as in 1 Cor. xv. 27, which is almost word for word from (Lxx.) Ps. viii. 6. What the Psalmist asserts of man, in poetic ideal, Paul claims in each passage to have been fulfilled in Christ. And rightly. For, as Son of man, He is heir of whatever belongs to man.

22b. The exalted Saviour's relation to the Church. Notice also a fuller statement of His relation to the universe, this including evidently the angelic powers just mentioned. Christ is not only above the angels, but above all created things as their *Head,* i.e. as the seat of supreme authority: see under Col. i. 18. *Above* or rather *beyond all things:* recalling *v.* 21, 'above and beyond all principality etc.' We have here the historic exaltation of the human body and nature of the Son, and His original relation to the universe: see Col. i. 16-18. In this supreme dignity, raised above and controlling all things, God *gave Him to the Church;* evidently in order that the Head of the universe may be also Head of the Church, thus making the universe an ally of the Church.

23. Two important relations of the Church to Christ. *Which is,* or, more fully, *inasmuch as it is:* a reason why God gave Christ to the Church. *His body:* as in Col. i. 18. See note under 1 Cor. xii. 30. In *vv.* 20—22 we saw the mighty power of God raising Christ from the grave in which He lay dead and raising Him through the successive ranks of angels until He sits in glory at the right hand of God. We now learn that the Risen and Enthroned One is God's gift to the Church, to be its Head, i.e. to be Himself a part of

the Church and occupying in it a unique and supreme place as that part which directs the whole and is essential to the vitality of the whole. In other words, He who is above everything created is in closest union with the Church.

The fulness etc.: further description of the Church. It is *the body* of Christ, an outward and visible form consisting of various and variously endowed members all animated by the one Spirit of Christ, of which body He is Himself the Head, the supreme and controlling member. It is also His *fulness:* see under Col. i. 19. *Him who fills all things with all things:* Christ, who gives to the universe in its various parts the fulness with which every part is full. *Fills,* or more accurately *fills for Himself* or *from Himself:* Christ being enriched by the fulness with which He makes the universe full. This keeps before us the similar relation of Christ to the universe and to the Church. In what sense are these words true? The Church can hardly be the fulness with which Christ is Himself full; as in the ordinary use and construction of the word. Rather it is that which Christ makes full; according to a less common classic use in which a fully manned ship is sometimes called a fulness, as though in its full equipment the idea of a ship found its full realisation. He who fills the universe and by its abundant contents reveals Himself as one *who fills all things with all things,* fills also the Church, making it a receptacle of every blessing which proceeds from Him. Somewhat similar is the common use of the same word by the Gnostics, as quoted frequently by Irenæus, in a local sense to describe the abode of blessedness, which they called *the fulness* in contrast to 'the void' or abode of darkness. Also closely akin to the word before us is the verb in Col. ii. 10, 'in Him dwells all the fulness of the Godhead bodily, and ye are *made-full* in Him.' He who has so joined to Himself the Church as to make it His body, the visible organ of His self-manifestation, and Himself its Head, has also made it His *fulness,* the receptacle and embodiment of His own abundance, of the infinite blessings He is able to bestow.

REVIEW. That his readers have been sealed by the Holy Spirit and that He is an earnest of the inheritance awaiting them, moves Paul, on hearing of their faith in Christ and their faithfulness towards all Christians, to give ceaseless thanks on their behalf in his approaches to God in prayer. His thanks pass imperceptibly into prayer that God would give to them that Spirit who is the Bearer of the wisdom of God and the Agent of His revelations to men, this gift assuming the form of imparted knowledge of God, in order that they, receiving light where the heart sees things unseen, may know what blessings await those who have heard and obeyed the Gospel summons, how abundant is the splendour of the inheritance which already belongs to the saints, and how surpassingly mighty is the power which is already at work upon them and will ultimately realise their hopes. Paul gives them a measure by which they may estimate the greatness of this power, viz. the power which raised Christ from the dead to the throne of God, far beyond the shining ranks of heaven and beyond whatever dignity is known in the age now passing or will be known in the ages to come. The exaltation of Christ rivets the Apostle's wondering gaze. He remembers that not only is Christ raised above all angelic powers, but that all things good and bad, personal and impersonal, are put under His control; that the humanity of Christ, itself a part of the created universe, holds in it a place of unique dignity as the supreme part which controls all else; that this supreme Ruler of the universe has been given to the Church to be a part of it, viz. the one supreme and controlling member without which the others cannot live; and that the Church is both His body, the visible organ of His self-manifestation, and His fulness, the receptacle of the effulgence and wealth which ever flow from Him.

Notice carefully that, in consequence of the close relation between Christ and His people, the splendour given to Him and the power which rescued Him from death and gave Him that splendour are a measure of the splendour awaiting His people; and that the power which raised Christ is already at work in those who believe, and will ultimately raise them to the throne of their Risen Lord. A similar argument in Ph. iii. 21. This exaltation above even the highest created beings assures us that no created power will prevent or lessen the glory awaiting us. Notice also the appropriateness here of Paul's favourite metaphor of the Church as the body of Christ. If we are members of His body, where the Head is we must some day be. Therefore, since the Head cannot descend, the exaltation of Christ is a pledge that we shall reign with Him. The Church is also the self-development of Him who fills the universe with His own life; as though apart from the Church our conception of Christ would be incomplete.

SECTION IV.

PAUL AND HIS READERS WERE ONCE DEAD BY REASON OF THEIR SINS.

CH. II. 1—3.

And you, being dead through your trespasses and sins, ² *in which formerly ye walked according to the course of this world, according to the prince of the authority of the air, of the spirit which now works in the sons of disobedience;* ³ *among whom also we all lived formerly in the desires of our flesh, doing the resolves of the flesh and the thoughts: and we were by nature children of anger as also the rest.*

In § 3 Paul prayed that his readers might know the great power of God at work towards those who believe; and, as a measure of it, pointed to Christ raised from the dead and enthroned with God. He sees Christ not only raised above all but the Head of all, and given to the Church to be its Head and the Church His body and His fulness. The original purpose of this reference to Christ's resurrection and ascension, viz. as a measure of the power at work in us, now reappears. In ch. ii. 1, (§ 4,) Paul turns suddenly to his readers and declares that, like Christ, they once were dead: in *vv.* 2, 3 he proves this. In § 5 he goes on to say that in Christ they also have been raised and enthroned.

1. *And you :* the Christians at Ephesus and elsewhere, in contrast to the Risen Saviour. *Being :* as in Col. i. 21. *Dead through trespasses :* as in Col. ii. 13, where see note. *Trespasses* are moral falls: *sins* are moral failures. This twofold description of the same actions emphasizes the cause of spiritual death. Their former position was analogous to that of Christ in the grave. For they *also* were *dead;* and their death, like His, was caused by human sins. These sins had robbed them of the only true life; and had given them up, unless rescued by Him who raises the dead, to eternal corruption. Such was their awful state, utterly beyond reach of human help.

The words in italics (AV. and RV.) are an anticipation of *v.* 5, inserted to complete the English sentence. The verb governing the accusative *you* in *v.* 1 is pushed back to make way for the relative sentences in *vv.* 2, 3, which describe further the sad condition of the persons referred to, until in *v.* 4 its place is supplied by a new sentence. All this is characteristic of Paul: a close parallel in Rom. v. 12. Paul keeps us under the shadow of death that the darkness of the shadow may throw into greater prominence the splendour of the light of life.

2. *In which* sins: as the surrounding element of their life and movement. Cp. 1 Cor. xv. 17. *Ye walked:* see under Col. iii. 7. *Of this world:* the whole realm of men and things around, looked upon as existing in space and as hostile to Christ. *The course,* or *age:* the whole stream and tendency of things around, looked upon as moving forward in time. *According to the course etc.:* carried along by the moving current of men and things around, all belonging to *this world.* The two words *course* and *world* represent the same idea in its reference to time and space respectively. And each word recalls the vast complexity of things and movements around. The combination presents this idea with a completeness not found elsewhere.

Ruler, or *prince:* same word in Rom. xiii. 3, 1 Cor. ii. 6, 8, of earthly rulers; in Rev. i. 5, of Christ as 'the Ruler of the kingdoms of the earth;' and in Jno. xii. 31, xiv. 30, xvi. 11, of Satan. *According to the ruler etc.:* parallel with *according to the course etc.,* and another view of the same truth. Steps guided by the current of things around are guided by the unseen *ruler* of that current. For the visible stream is animated and directed by an unseen spirit. *Authority:* a controlling influence, as in Col. i. 13. A genitive after this word usually denotes either the person exercising authority or those under authority. But we cannot conceive *the air,* the imponderable element around and above us, as either ruling or being ruled over. It must therefore be the locality of this controlling influence. The authority which directs the course of those who float down the stream of things around must be that of evil spirits. That these were conceived, both by Jews and by others in the ancient world, as having their abode in the air, we have in Rabbinical literature and elsewhere, e.g. Diogenes Laertius bk. viii. 32, abundant proof. And this agrees with their comparative power, greater than men and less than the powers of heaven. Apparently, Paul accepted and used this common conception as sufficiently embodying a truth he wished to teach. His words remind us that all around are spiritual enemies, as near as the air we breathe. Over these reigns a tremendous potentate. Along a path marked out by him, led by unseen powers who do his bidding and by the current of things around, once walked the Christians to whom Paul now writes.

The spirit which now works etc.: parallel with *the authority of the air*, and further describing the agency which does the bidding of *the prince* of darkness, as an animating principle moving men from within in contrast to *the course of this world* which carries them along as an influence from without. With *the spirit*, contrast 'the spirits' in 1 Jno. iv. 1. This latter passage looks at the infinite variety, the former at the essential oneness, of these evil influences. A variety of spiritual foes is also portrayed in Eph. vi. 12. *Works*, or *inworks*: as in ch. i. 11, 20, Ph. ii. 13. This interior working is a characteristic of *spirit*. To the Christians at Ephesus this inward influence is past: to others it *now works*. *Sons of disobedience*: ch. v. 6. See note under Col. iii. 6. As a description of the unsaved, it prepares the way for the fuller description in *v*. 3.

After asserting that his readers were once dead through their sins, Paul further describes their former state of death. The sins which had been the means of their destruction were also an element in which they moved. And their path was guided by the current around them, a current belonging to the present material world. It was guided, not by a blind force or unconscious influence, but by a personal ruler, under whose sway was a controlling power as pervasive as the air. This power Paul speaks of as an active animating principle, prompting disobedience to God and making those who yield to it personal embodiments of the principle of disobedience.

3a. To the foregoing description of the former state of the Gentile Christians, Paul now adds an equivalent description including himself and the Jewish Christians: *also we all*. He thus completes his picture of unsaved mankind. By now including *all* men, he brings the Jews specially before us. *Among whom*: as belonging to their number. Paul thus asserts that all men, Jews and Gentiles, were once 'sons of disobedience.' *Lived*: same word as *behaved-ourselves* or *had our manner of life in* 2 Cor. i. 12; also 1 Tim. iii. 15, 1 Pet. i. 17. It denotes life not as an inward principle, but as an outward activity and movement; and is thus parallel and similar to the word 'walk' in *v*. 2. *Formerly*: parallel to the same word in *v*. 2. *In the desires*: same words in Rom. i. 24. *The desires of our flesh*: see under Gal. v. 16, 24; cp. 1 Jno. ii. 16. The plural number recalls the variety of tendencies inherent to the constitution of our bodies and going out after objects pleasant to the senses. These tendencies are the world in which the unsaved move.

Doing the resolves etc.: further description of the *manner of life in the desires of the flesh*, asserting the fulfilment of these desires in action. *The resolves*: Acts xiii. 22: the plural form of the word rendered *will* in ch. 1, 5, 9, 11. It denotes a deliberate wish. The plural number corresponds with the foregoing plural *desires*. *The resolves* differ from *the desires* of the flesh as a definite wish differs from the general liking from which it springs. The repetition of the word *flesh* is emphatic. *The minds:* same word in the singular in Col. i. 21, where see note, and in Mt. xxii. 37. The plural number reminds us that, whereas all men have one *flesh*, they have many *minds*. Moreover, our *minds*, like our flesh, have *wills* of their own. The condemnation implied in this verse teaches that these *wills* do not bow to the will of God; and that, consequently, they who *do* them come under the anger of God. On *the flesh*, see note under Rom. viii. 11.

3b. The last detail in Paul's description of the unsaved. In order to show its importance as in itself claiming attention, Paul adds it as an independent statement: *and we were etc.* He declares that in former days his readers *were children, by nature, of anger*, i.e. exposed to the anger of God. Cp. Jno. xvii. 12, 'the son of destruction:' close Hebrew parallels in Dt. xxv. 2, 'a son of stripes;' 1 Sam. xx. 31, xxvi. 16, 2 Sam. xii. 5, 'a son of death,' i.e. doomed to death. So terrible was the position of those about whom Paul writes that to his vivid thought they seemed to be an offspring of the anger of God. And they were this *by-nature:* i.e. their exposure to the anger of God was an outworking of forces born in them. Same word in Rom. ii. 14, where see note; Gal. ii. 15, iv. 8. *As also the rest:* i.e. of men. Paul solemnly concludes his description of the former state of his readers and himself by saying that the description is or has been true of all men.

These last words must be read in the light of the statement in *v.* 1 that the Ephesian Christians were formerly dead by reason of their own personal sins. All is explained if we assume that men are born in such position that, apart from the salvation wrought out for them in Christ, none can avoid committing actual sin, and that in Christ salvation is offered to all men. If so, the universality of actual sin is a result of the lost state into which we were born. But, to those who have heard the Gospel, present condemnation is a result of rejection of offered salvation, and of actual sins from which Christ would have saved us. This evil nature is easily explained by Paul's teaching in Rom. v. 12. By his first trespass Adam sold himself into bondage to sin and death. This double bondage his children inherit. No power of theirs can save them from actual sin and from the grave. But in Christ God offers to men deliverance now from the bondage of sin and ultimately from the grave. They

SEC. 4.]   EPHESIANS II. 1—3.   297

who continue in sin do so because they reject the offered salvation. The word *by-nature* inserted at the close of Paul's picture of lost humanity increases the darkness of the picture. For it tells us that not only are all men sinners but they are so in consequence of the position in which they were born. None can save them except one who can change their inborn *nature*.

Notice that, without professing to do so, Paul has virtually in vv. 2, 3 explained and justified v. 1, 'dead through your trespasses.' For he has asserted that his readers went once with the mass of mankind along a path marked out by the prince of evil, and were animated by an evil influence under his direction. The lower side of human nature was the element in which they lived : all men are or were numbered among the sons of disobedience, and were under the anger of God. If so, all men are guilty of actual sin ; and all are dead except those whom God has raised from the dead. For the anger of God involves exclusion from the only real life, and leads inevitably to eternal corruption. Consequently, they who thus live are dead through their own sins.

This section is Paul's fullest description of unsaved mankind. And it is a picture of utter and universal ruin. He assumes in v. 1 that all men have committed *trespasses and sins;* and in v. 3 that all were once numbered among *the sons of disobedience* and were under the *anger* of God. We have here universal sin and universal condemnation. This moral ruin Paul traces to a cause common to all men, viz. their *flesh*, the material and lower side of their nature, this being to the unsaved the encompassing and determining element of their life and activity. In harmony with this, the anger of God resting upon all men is traced to the constitution received at birth. This inherited evil is further traced to a personal source mightier than man, viz. to a ruler from beneath who leads men along from within by an animating principle under his direction. Naturally, this inward force of evil operates on man through the lower and material side of his being, giving to it power to control his entire activity. It thus impresses its will on man's own nature, and forces him along a path on which God frowns.

A further analysis of sin is given in ch. iv. 17-19.

SECTION V.

GOD HAS MADE US SHARERS OF THE RESURRECTION LIFE OF CHRIST.

CH. II. 4—10.

But God, being rich in mercy, because of His much love with *which He loved us,* ⁵ *and* we *being dead through our trespasses, has made us alive together with Christ—by grace ye are saved—*⁶ *and raised us with* Him *and made us sit with* Him *in the heavenly places in Christ Jesus;* ⁷ *that He may show in the ages coming on the surpassing riches of His grace in kindness to us in Christ Jesus.* ⁸ *For by grace ye are saved, through faith: and that not of yourselves; the gift is God's;* ⁹ *not of works, that no man may glory.* ¹⁰ *For His workmanship we are, created in Christ Jesus for good works, which God before prepared in order that we may walk in them.*

4, 5. *But God:* in conspicuous contrast to lost and sinful mankind. This new sentence supplies the place of the grammatical conclusion of the foregoing sentence, which was postponed to make way for the further delineation of those dead in sins, and not afterwards added. Similarly, the sentence broken off in Rom. v. 12 has its virtual completion in *v.* 18. This delineation is a dark background for the glory which suddenly and majestically now bursts upon us.

Mercy: compassion for the helpless. It recalls the helplessness of those under the anger of God, and thus completes the picture given in § 4. *Rich in mercy:* cp. ch. i. 7, 18. *Because of His much love;* traces this mercy to its source in the central attribute of God. Upon this unique attribute Paul lingers: *His much love* with *which He loved us.* The past tense refers to the love manifested in the salvation of Paul and his readers. *And we being dead etc.:* a repetition of *v.* 1, for vivid contrast with the foregoing description of God and His love. A close parallel with Rom. iii. 23, where for a similar contrast we have a similar summary of foregoing teaching. This love of contrast, especially of contrast between past and present, is an almost certain mark of Pauline authorship. *Has-made-alive-with-Christ:* as in Col. ii. 13, where the same word is explained by 'having forgiven you all the trespasses.' It reverses all that is implied in the words *dead through trespasses.* We were once, in consequence of our sins, a spiritual corpse given up to corruption utter and helpless, from which nothing could save us except the lifegiving power of God. But God has pardoned our sins and given back to us the eternal life for which we were created. This eternal life is already our assured possession: and the witness of it is the Holy Spirit, the Breath of immortality, already moving our hearts with the pulse of divine life and prompting all Christian activities. *With Christ:* as in Col. ii. 13. Our new immortal life is an outflow of the life breathed on the first Easter morning into His sacred corpse. For, had He not risen, there had been no saving faith, no Gospel, and no life eternal.

By-grace (cp. Rom. iii. 24) *ye-are saved:* each word emphatic. Salvation is by the undeserved favour of God: it is already actual: and this is emphatically asserted. Contrast Rom. v. 10, xiii. 11. We are already saved from the sinking wreck into a lifeboat which cannot sink: but we are not finally safe until the perilous voyage of life is past. Hence Paul can say as here we *are saved;* or as in I Cor. i. 18 we 'are being saved;' or as above we 'shall be saved.'

6. *Raised with* Him: as in Col. ii. 12, iii. 1. It further pictures the new life as a participation in the act of God which raised Christ from the grave and brought Him back to the land of the living. *Made-to-sit-with* Him: only here and Lk. xxii. 55. A new feature of the Christian life. We are not only made alive, and raised from the surroundings of death, but are also sharers of the throne of Christ. Cp. ch. i. 20: 'raised Him from the dead and made Him sit.' Notice the close connection between the Christian's life on earth and the life of his risen and glorified Lord. See under Col. ii. 12. *In the heavenly* places: same words as in ch. i. 3, which they expound. They give further definiteness to the picture of Christ's enthronement in heaven, and declare that already we share even its glorious environment. This resurrection and enthronement are *with* Christ and *in Christ.* For He will be both the companion and the encompassing element of our future glory. And whatever we shall be, to Paul's faith, believers already are. Thus (ch. i. 3) has God 'blessed us with every spiritual blessing in the heavenly places.'

7. Aim of God in raising and enthroning us. Close harmony with ch. i. 6, 12, 14. *That He-may-show:* more fully *show* something *in Himself,* i.e. reveal His own inner nature. Same word in Rom. ii. 15, ix. 17, 22, 1 Tim. i. 16. *The ages coming on:* beginning with the coming of Christ. For only then will God's kindness to men be worthily manifested. To the prophetic eye of Paul, successive ages of future glory are already approaching, like successive

waves of blessing; an endless vista of splendour. That this manifestation is to take place during the ages of glory, suggests that it will be for angels as well as men: cp. ch. iii. 10. *The surpassing riches of His grace:* a superlative term embracing and surpassing ch. i. 7, 19. *Kindness:* so Rom. ii. 4, 'riches of His kindness;' also ch. xi. 22. It is 'mercy' and 'grace' represented as gentleness. *In Christ Jesus:* objectively, through His death and. resurrection, as in ch. i. 20, Rom. iii. 24; and subjectively through inward contact with Him, as in 2 Cor. v. 17. This aim of God in raising us together with Christ proves the infinite greatness of the blessing thus conferred on men. For the means must be sufficient for the end in view. God resolved to manifest the surpassing abundance of His grace; and, to this end, loaded us with kindness. A similar, but further, purpose in ch. iii. 10.

8, 9. In order to justify and expound 'the riches of His grace,' Paul now repeats and amplifies a few words which, in *v.* 4, burst through the grammatical order of the sentence. *By-grace:* by the grace of God; referring definitely to the grace mentioned in *v.* 7. *Through faith:* added in order to give a more complete account of salvation. It embodies a thought ever present to Paul, and ever ready to find expression: compare the casual mention of faith in Rom. iii. 25, 26. *The favour* of God is the divine source, and *faith* is the human channel, of salvation. *This* or *this thing;* refers almost certainly to the salvation just mentioned. For it is neuter, whereas *faith* and *grace* are feminine. Moreover, *not from works,* which must refer to *ye are saved,* is evidently parallel to *not from yourselves,* and thus gives to these words the same reference. They are added as an emphatic exposition, negative and then positive, of the words *by grace.* 'You are not the source of your own salvation: it is a gift: and *the gift* is *God's.* It is *not from* human *works.*' *Not from works, that no one may glory:* marked characteristics of Paul: Rom. iv. 2, 6, ix. 11, xi. 6; iii. 27, 1 Cor. i. 29, Gal. vi. 14. From every side, Paul shuts out, as his wont is, all self-salvation.

10. Proof and amplification of the statement that our salvation is not from ourselves or from works, but from God; viz. that we are ourselves God's *workmanship. Having-been-created etc.:* proof of the foregoing. Paul refers evidently, in words taken from the old creation, to the new creation of the spiritual life. Cp. 2 Cor. v. 17, Gal. vi. 15. Another trace of the hand of Paul. *Created:* a word predicated only of God, and thus denoting a putting forth of power possessed only by God. Even when creating out of existing materials, as in Gen. i. 21, God breathed into them new life; which

man cannot do. The word here teaches that the Christian life is not only a *workmanship* of God but is a new putting forth of creative power. *In Christ:* as in vv. 6, 7. Notice the emphatic and characteristic repetition. *Good works:* as in Rom. ii. 7, xiii. 3, 2 Cor. ix. 8: a phrase found only with Paul. The word *good* includes beneficence and intrinsic worth: another word, noting only excellence, in Mt. v. 16. Just as God created certain animals for certain activities which were a part of His creative purpose, so He designs the new life in Christ to reveal itself in good works. The words following lay further stress on this definite purpose of God. *Beforeprepared:* in eternity, when the new life was only a thought in the mind of God. He then designed that *good works* should be its environment and outward expression. Same word in Rom. ix. 23, '*before-prepared* for glory.' *That we should walk in them:* God's purpose touching these good works. He designs them to be the surrounding element of our movements; in absolute contrast to v. 2, 'in which sins ye walked.'

It is now quite clear that salvation is in no way from ourselves or from works. For even our own good works are a part of God's eternal purpose to give spiritual life to those who believe in Christ. And if they are an outworking of His purpose of mercy, they cannot be a ground of merit, or a source of salvation.

Notice here another reference to the eternal purpose of salvation, already mentioned in ch. i. 4, 5, 9, 11; also in ch. iii. 11. It is a conspicuous feature of this Epistle, and a fuller development of teaching already found in Rom. viii. 28, 29, ix. 11, 23.

The chief significance of § 5 is derived from its relation to § 3. Paul there prayed that God would reveal to his readers the glory awaiting them and the great power of God which some day will realise their hopes and which already is at work in them. As a measure of that power and of that hope, he pointed to the power which raised Christ from the grave and set Him at the right hand of God. In order to make practical use of this comparison, Paul showed in § 4 that all the unsaved are in a position analogous to that of the body of Jesus as it lay *dead* in the grave. For, through their sins, they were separated from the only real life and were doomed to corruption. This state of ruin Paul further described. Although dead, they were capable of movement: but it was a mere floating down a stream, in a channel marked out by the great enemy, under influences directed by him; a mere surrender to the promptings of the lower side of their nature. That the prince of darkness and their own nature led them along the same path, proved that their nature is corrupt, and that they who follow it are under the anger of God. Now the anger of God is death in its worst form.

At the beginning of § 5 we see God looking down with compassion and infinite love upon the lost human race. Paul asserts that He who gave life to the lifeless body of Christ has made alive those who once were dead through their sins. This can only mean that He has rescued them from the corruption which was their inevitable doom and has given back to them spiritual activity and growth. This life is an outflow of that which entered into the silent body of Christ. And, as with Christ so with them, life has been accompanied by removal from the surroundings of death and by exaltation to heaven. All this God did in order to reveal His infinite favour to men. The same truth Paul repeats for emphasis in another form. Since his readers have been made alive, he can rightly say that they have been saved. And, since their resurrection with Christ is an outflow of the mercy and love of God, they are saved by grace. To make this the more conspicuous, Paul adds that salvation is not from themselves or their works, but is the gift of God; and that it has come in this way in order that no one may boast. And he cannot forbear to remind his readers that it is through faith. To complete his proof that salvation is altogether from God and not at all from man, he says that the new life is a work of the creative power of God and an accomplishment of an eternal purpose.

Thus Paul, after raising his readers to the throne of God and setting them beside their risen Lord, leads their thoughts back to the eternal purpose of which the actual salvation of men is an historic realisation. This tracing of the phenomena of time to their source in the eternal thought of God is a conspicuous feature of Paul, a feature nowhere so conspicuous as in this Epistle.

SECTION VI.

THROUGH CHRIST, BOTH JEWS AND GENTILES HAVE BEEN BROUGHT NEAR TO GOD.

CH. II. 11—22.

For this cause remember that formerly ye, the Gentiles in flesh, those called uncircumcision by that which *is called circumcision in flesh, made by hands—*[12] *that ye were at that time separate from Christ, alienated from the commonwealth of Israel, and strangers to the covenants of the promise, having no hope, and without God in the world.* ¹³ *But now, in Christ Jesus, ye who formerly were far off have become near in the blood of Christ.* ¹⁴ *For He Himself is our peace, who has made both one and has broken down the middle wall of partition,* ¹⁵ *having made of no effect the enmity, in His flesh, even the law of commandments in dogmas; in order that He may create in Himself the two into one new man, making peace;* ¹⁶ *and that He may reconcile both in one body to God through the cross, having slain the enmity thereby.* ¹⁷ *And He came and announced peace, as good news, to those far off and to those near;* ¹⁸ *because through Him we both have access in one Spirit to the Father.* ¹⁹ *Therefore no longer are ye strangers and sojourners but fellow-citizens of the saints and members of the household of God,* ²⁰ *having been built up on the foundation of the apostles and prophets,* the *chief corner stone being Christ Jesus Himself,* ²¹ *in whom every building, being fitly framed together, is growing into a holy temple in* the *Lord,* ²² *in whom also ye are being built together for a dwelling-place of God in* the *Spirit.*

Like §§ 4 and 5, § 6 depicts the contrast of past and present. This is indicated by the word 'formerly' in *vv.* 2, 3 and in *vv.* 11, 13. But the earlier contrast was that of men once dead through their sins but now reigning in life. The contrast here is of the same men once far off from the people of God but now united with them in the one rising temple. The first contrast was personal and spiritual: this one is social and in a sense ecclesiastical. Paul comes now to look at salvation in its bearing on the great distinction of Jew and Gentile, a distinction ever present to his thought and already faintly indicated by the change from 'we' to 'you' and 'you' to 'we' in chs. i. 13, ii. 3. This distinction, and the equal importance here given to Jew and Gentile are indications both of early date and of Pauline authorship. For no such conspicuous distinction is found in sub-apostolic writings; nor can we conceive it coming from a writer of the second century: and even in the N. T. it is peculiar to Paul.

As containing respectively the dark and bright sides of the contrast, *vv.* 11, 12 correspond to § 4, *vv.* 13-22 to § 5.

11. *For which cause:* 'because God has so wonderfully saved you, *remember* what you once were.' *Formerly:* placed for emphasis at the beginning of the clause. It recalls the same word in *v.* 2, and resumes conspicuously the contrast of past and present. *The Gentiles:* the well-known class to which they belonged. Its

distinguishing mark, viz. absence of circumcision, is in the perishing body: *in flesh*. These added words give definiteness to the distinction. *Who are called;* further depicts the readers as they were looked upon by those who with some right claimed to be the people of God. Cp. 1 Cor. viii. 5. *Uncircumcision . . . circumcision:* abstract terms put for the persons in whom the abstract quality is found: close parallel in Rom. ii. 26, 27. They who, with evident contempt, *called* the Gentiles *uncircumcision called* themselves *circumcision*. That the distinction is said to be, on both sides, a matter of a name, suggests that it was now practically only a name. *In flesh, made by hands:* not governed by the word *called:* for Jews would not so speak of circumcision. It is rather Paul's own reflection, confirming the above suggestion. He remembers that circumcision was, in the case of those who spoke of the Gentiles as uncircumcised, a mere cutting of the flesh by the hand of man. Yet such was once his readers' position that men who had nothing better than this could speak of them as lower than themselves: for the absence even of this external rite marked them out as destitute of the many advantages of the ancient people of God. The repetition of the words *in flesh* and the added word *made-by-hands* keep vividly before us that the vaunted rite was in the lower side of man's nature and was only a work of man.

12. The grammatical order is broken by a repetition of the word *that*, added for the sake of greater clearness after a rather long description of 'the Gentiles.' *At that season;* corresponds to 'formerly' in *v.* 11, referring to the readers' heathen life. Contrast Rom. iii. 26, xi. 5, 'in the present *season*.' *Separate from Christ:* destitute of all the spiritual blessings which flow from inward union with Him. This full sense is required by the very conspicuous contrast in *v.* 13, 'but now in Christ Jesus;' and by the contrast maintained throughout this chapter between the past and the present. But the words following show that this spiritual destitution is here looked upon in the light of the separation of the Gentiles from the nation to which the ancient promises were given. In those days they had not so much as heard the name of the promised Messiah.

Now follow four further descriptions of those Gentiles, arranged in two pairs. The relation of these items to the main assertion, *ye were separate from Christ*, is left to the readers. *Commonwealth:* either a community of citizens looked upon as definitely constituted, or the rights of its members. Same word in this last sense in Acts xxii. 28. The former sense here, and, with a cognate word, in

Ph. iii. 20: but in these two passages the difference is not great. *The commonwealth of Israel:* the nation looked upon as a community in which each citizen had personal rights. The whole tone of the verse reminds us that Israel possessed the highest spiritual advantages on earth. Cp. Rom. iii. 1, ix. 4. *Israel:* a name of honour, as in Rom. ix. 4, 2 Cor. xi. 22, etc. Before Christ came there was a privileged community: but its members looked upon the Gentiles as aliens. *Alienated:* same word and form in ch. iv. 18, Col. i. 21. [The perfect participle does not imply that they had once been citizens; but simply calls attention to the process of alienation, thus depicting more vividly the sad state of those alienated.] *The Covenants:* the mutual engagements into which God entered with Abraham, and through Moses with Israel. From these covenants came all the spiritual advantages of the Jews. Same word in same connection in Rom. ix. 4: a close coincidence of thought. A conspicuous feature common to these covenants, and the source of their value, was *the promise.* It is here spoken of as one because all the promises looked forward to one glorious consummation. Otherwise in Rom. ix. 9, which recalls the many 'promises.' To these *covenants* and to this *promise,* the Gentile readers of this Epistle were once *strangers:* same word in Heb. xi. 13.

Now follows an awful result of the foregoing. The only hope on earth worthy of the name rests upon *the* great *promise* given in outline to Israel. Consequently, they who have not this hope *have no hope.* To them the roughness of the present life is not cheered by any reasonable and assured prospect of good things to come. *Without-God:* literally *atheists,* i.e. destitute of all the help and peace and joy which comes through knowledge of God and faith in God. This subjective absence of God is quite consistent with the objective truth (Acts xvii. 28) that 'in Him we live and move and are.' The lack of conscious intercourse with a personal God is a marked feature of the best classic writings as compared with the Old Testament. The heathen have no Father in heaven on whose bosom they can rest. *In the world:* the locality of this destitution. In the seething mass of sinful humanity, dominated by the god of this world, away from the brightness of the smile of the God of heaven and from the joy of hope, these Gentiles were: for they had no part in the covenants which God made with Israel nor place in the sacred nation.

13. *But now:* a conspicuous and favourite phrase of Paul recalling the contrast, ever present to his mind, of the past and the present. Same words in same sense in Col. i. 22, 26, iii. 8; Rom: iii. 21,

vi. 22, vii. 6, xi. 30, etc. They are another note of authorship. *In Christ Jesus:* objectively, in the actual and historic person born at Bethlehem, whom Paul acknowledges to be the hoped-for Messiah. Hence the fuller title. Same words and sense in Rom. iii. 24. They are more fully expounded at the end of the verse. *Ye who formerly were far off;* sums up the description in *v.* 12. This summing up of the lower side of a contrast is, as in *v.* 5, an indisputable trace of the hand of Paul. *Become near:* to God and to the people of God. For distance from Israel and from God are the chief points of the description in *v.* 12. And in *vv.* 14, 15 we have peace between Jews and Gentiles given as an explanation of this verse, and in *vv.* 16, 18 reconciliation and approach to God through Christ. *In the blood of Christ:* more specific than *in Christ.* It suggests (cp. ch. i. 7) the continued validity of the violent death of Christ as the means of salvation.

14, 15. Explanation and justification of the triumphant assertion in *v.* 13, and especially of its last words. *He is:* each word very emphatic, pointing conspicuously to Him in whose blood the Gentiles have been brought near. *Our peace;* implies that the distance involves hostility. The words following prove that Paul's first thought is peace between Jews and Gentiles. But the words ' reconciled to God' in *v.* 16 followed by 'access to the Father' in *v.* 18 prove that this involves peace between men and God. In both references, Christ *is our peace.* For where *He is,* and there only, is *peace.* Cp. Jno. xi. 25, 'I am the Resurrection and the Life.'

The plain statement *He is our peace,* which explains and justifies *v.* 13, is itself expounded and supported in *vv.* 14*b*—18. The result of the whole is stated triumphantly in *vv.* 19—22.

Made or *has-made:* simple statement of fact without reference to any definite time. *Both one:* literally *the both things* into *one thing.* As in Col. i. 16, etc., the neuter looks upon persons merely as objects of thought without reference to personality. *And has broken down etc.:* additional detail explaining the general assertion. *Middle-wall:* between houses or courts. Found elsewhere only once : but the meaning is clear. It is further defined by the addition, *of the partition* or *fence.* Same word in Mt. xxi. 33. It denotes something designed to keep away intruders. Here the *fence* is represented as a *wall* between the men to be kept apart. The whole phrase unites the ideas of separation and solidity. This barrier, Christ has broken down. He has thus made the two hostile divisions into one whole.

At the Temple of Jerusalem, between the court of the Gentiles and that of the women, the latter being a part of the sacred enclosure, was a dividing wall on which were inscriptions in different languages warning foreigners, on pain of death, not to pass : Josephus, *Wars* bk. v. 5. 2. This was a visible embodiment of the barrier which Paul here depicts in the metaphor of a *wall;* and helps us to realise the spiritual separation of Jews and Gentiles. But his words do not betray any direct reference to it.

Having-made-of-no-effect (as in Rom. iii. 3) *the enmity:* means by which Christ has broken down the barrier. Consequently, the enmity is that between Jew and Gentile ; especially as the aim of its removal is to *create the two into one new man*. *In His flesh :* evidently our Lord's crucified flesh and blood: so *v.* 16. *The law of commands in dogmas:* in apposition to *the enmity*. By rendering invalid *the Law*, Christ brought to nothing *the enmity*. *The commandments* or *commands :* definite prescriptions of the Law. An example is quoted in Rom. vii. 8-13. These were a characteristic feature of the Law. And they took the form of *dogmas*, i.e. decrees by a superior authority: same word in Col. ii. 14, where see note. This *Law* can be no other than that of Moses. In what sense Christ has made it invalid, we learn from Gal. iii. 25, 26. As first given, obedience to the prescriptions of the Law was a condition of the favour of God : Lev. xviii. 5. This condition made the favour of God impossible. For none can keep the Law, as it claims to be kept. By proclaiming righteousness through faith, Christ set aside, as a condition and means of the favour of God, the ancient Law. Paul says here that by doing so He removed also the hostility between Jew and Gentile. This we can understand. For the Law of Sinai, given only to a part of mankind, became a separation between those who had, and those who had not, received it. And this separation was followed by mutual hatred and hostility. This hatred and its occasion, Christ removed. In Him, both Jew and Gentile, the Law now powerless to condemn or to separate them, become brethren.

That He may create etc. : purpose for which Christ has set aside the Law and its decrees, viz. to unite by creative power into one new unity the two parts into which the Law divided mankind. In *v.* 14 this unity is represented as already attained : *who made both one*. For it will infallibly result from what Christ has already done. It is here represented as a purpose: for its full realisation is still future, dependent on each one's faith. *Create;* recalls the same word in *v.* 10, Col. i. 16. It implies that this unity is wrought by the creative power of God, breathing *new* life and order into hitherto discordant elements. Creation always produces something *new*. Same thought in 2 Cor. v. 17, Gal. vi. 15: an important coincidence. *The two* persons *into one new man:* the masculine form calling attention to the personality of the reconciled ones. So, but less conspicuously, in Gal. iii. 28. *In Himself:* Christ being the surrounding element in which the new creation takes place, and in which the resulting unity abides. While cherishing and working out this purpose, Christ is *making peace*. These words, which describe the entire process of salvation from its conception in the heart of God to its full accomplishment, link the new creation to the *peace* mentioned in v. 14, thus keeping it before us.

16. *And that He may reconcile etc.:* a second purpose of Christ, parallel with 'that He may create etc.' He designed not only to unite together the two hostile divisions of mankind but to *reconcile* the united race *to God*. This implies that behind the hostility of man against man there was also hostility between man and God. Each kind of hostility Christ resolved to remove. The two reconciliations are so closely related that either may be placed before the other, according to the point of view chosen. In this section and Epistle Paul's chief thought is unity of Jew and Gentile. He therefore mentions first peace between man and man. But he remembers that this can be only by peace between man and God. Hence these words. *Reconcile to God:* cp. Col. i. 22, where see note. Another mark of Pauline authorship: Rom. v. 10, 2 Cor. v. 18, 19, 20. *Both* persons, or *the two* persons: a mode of thought different from v. 14, 'the two things into one thing,' and keeping before us the personality of those to be reconciled. *In one body:* viz. the Church, which is the body of Christ. It is thus parallel to 'one new man' in v. 15; and keeps up the dominant thought, viz. the unity of Jews and Gentiles. This exposition agrees better with the tenor of the context than to interpret the *one body* as that nailed to the cross. Moreover, nowhere in the N. T. is attention directed to the oneness of the human body of Christ. *Through the cross:* as the instrument of reconciliation: so 'through His death' in Col. i. 22, Rom. v. 10. *Having-slain etc.:* mode by which Christ purposed to reconcile men to God. It thus expounds *through the cross. The enmity:* probably, of Jews and Gentiles. For this is at once suggested by the same word in v. 15; and is the chief thought of this section. And the removal of this ancient enmity, itself a result of man's sin, comes through the death of Christ. For, had He not died, its removal would have been impossible. While writing about Christ's purpose to break down the barrier between

Jew and Gentile, Paul remembers that this can be done only by breaking down another barrier, that between man and God. Now man can be reconciled to God (see my *Galatians* Diss. vii.) only through the death of Christ. Consequently, *thereby* or *therein*, i.e. in the cross on which He died, Christ slew not only the enmity between man and God but that between man and man, in order to bring in universal harmony. For had He not died, this unity would have been impossible: now it is certain.

17. Another detail in this reconciliation, added as an independent assertion. *And He came:* at His incarnation. *And announced-good-tidings-of-peace:* on earth before His death. Cp. Lk. iv. 21. For the words then spoken were a proclamation of peace for all mankind, and, in view of their subsequent announcement throughout the world by the Apostles, may be said to have been spoken to all mankind. This is better than to understand these words as referring to the preaching of the Gospel on the Day of Pentecost under the influence of the Holy Spirit whose descent is in Jno. xiv. 18 spoken of as a coming of Christ. For the preaching of the Apostles was but a re-echo of the words spoken by Christ on earth, who not only obtained for us peace through His death but *announced* through His own lips the *good-tidings-of-peace.* To this end He *came* from heaven to earth. *Good-tidings:* see under Rom. i. 1; cp. 1 Th. iii. 6. *Peace:* between man and man, as throughout the section. This implies peace with God. But to this last we have no need to assume any direct reference here.

Those far off: put first, although the Gospel came first to the Jews, because the entrance of the Gentiles into the one fold of Christ is the chief matter of this section. This order shows that Paul is thinking of Christ's words, not as spoken to those who heard them on earth, but as spoken virtually to the whole world. *Far off:* as in *v.* 13. *Those near:* the Jews who from childhood had heard of the coming Messiah and of the blessings He would bring. They were 'the sons of the Covenant:' Acts iii. 25.

18. A fact, later in date, yet virtually underlying the assertion of *v.* 17. It is practically a re-statement of *v.* 13. *Through Him:* the emphatic words of the verse. *Access:* same word and almost the same phrase in Rom. v. 2, 'through whom we have obtained access;' a very close parallel. A cognate verb in 1 Pet. iii. 18. Christ took us by the hand and led us *to the Father.* Similarly *v.* 13: 'made near in the blood of Christ.' It includes the whole work of salvation. *We both:* Jews and Gentiles, whose union in Christ is the dominant thought of this section. *In one Spirit:* the divine Agent of all

abiding harmony of man with man. So ch. iv. 4, Ph. i. 27, 1 Cor. xii. 13 : important coincidences.

Notice here the relation of each Person of the Trinity to the work of salvation. Both Jews and Gentiles were far away from God; and consequently each far from the other. Through the agency of the Son, and in the Holy Spirit dwelling in the hearts of all His people, they have been led into the presence and smile of God, and into the harmony of spiritual brotherhood. And to this end the Son Himself came into the world and proclaimed peace to men. Notice also that of this salvation the death of Christ is conspicuously pointed to as the means. In His blood we have been made near. And Christ's aim is to reconcile us to God through the cross, and in that cross to kill the previously-existing enmity.

19. Argumentative summing up of § 6. *Therefore:* two Greek words, a collocation favourite with, and peculiar to, Paul. It sums up the foregoing and draws from it an inference. A close parallel in Rom. v. 18. *Strangers:* as in *v.* 12. *Sojourners:* foreign residents without civic rights. Same word in Acts vii. 6, 29, 1 Pet. ii. 11. Even in this summing up Paul states, as his wont is, the full contrast of past and present. *But ye are:* solemn repetition of the verb, stating not only what they have ceased to be but what they actually are. *Fellow-citizens:* sharing all municipal rights. It represents the Church as a city. *The saints,* or *holy ones:* the sacred people of God. Israel at Sinai was called 'a holy nation:' Ex. xix. 6. The priests were specially holy: Num. xvi. 3, 5. In the New Covenant, they who believe the Gospel become the peculiar people of God, and receive as their usual designation the name *saints:* see under Rom. i. 7; cp. Acts ix. 13, 32, 41. Of this sacred company, the earliest members were Jews. Then Samaritans were added to it; and now these far off Asiatic Greeks. *Members-of-the-household:* same word in Gal. vi. 10, where see note. In the great *household of God,* all are both sons and servants. And to this house and home belong now these far off Gentiles.

20. Process by which these aliens were received into the city and house of God. It further describes their present position. 'The household of God' suggests easily a favourite metaphor, viz. the Church as a building, and more specifically as the temple of God. In this splendid metaphor culminates Paul's teaching here about the union in Christ of Jews and Gentiles. Cp. Mt. xvi. 18 from the lips of Christ; 1 Cor. iii. 9—17, vi. 19, 2 Cor. vi 16, Rom. xv. 20; 1 Pet. ii. 5. It underlies the word rendered *edify* or *build.* The composite word here used is found also in 1 Cor. iii. 10, 12, 14, Col.

ii. 7; and denotes to carry up a building already begun. *The foundation of the Apostles:* that laid by them. So 1 Cor. iii. 10, where Paul stated his own relation to this foundation. And nothing more is suggested now. Another conception in Mt. xvi. 18. But of this there is no hint here. Upon Christ rests firmly, and rises, the Church. By preaching Christ and leading men to Him, the Apostles laid this foundation in actual human life. See under 1 Cor. iii. 11. Now the Apostles, in laying this foundation, were building the house and city of God. To it therefore belong those who were being built into the rising walls. *Prophets:* conspicuously mentioned in 1 Cor. xii. 28 as holding the second rank in the Church. And this is indisputably the meaning of the same word in Eph. iii. 5, iv. 11. As in O. T., they were men who spoke under special inspiration: see note under 1 Cor. xiv. 40. Had the reference here been to the O. T. prophets, the order would have been inverted, 'prophets and apostles.'

Corner-stone: 1 Pet. ii. 6, quoted from Isa. xxviii. 16; but not found elsewhere. Same idea in Ps. cxviii. 22, quoted in Mt. xxi. 42. Christ is both the foundation underlying the entire building and a conspicuous corner stone uniting its walls and thus giving solidity to the whole. This word, which recalls an ancient prophecy touching the Church of Christ, is very appropriate here in a summary of Paul's teaching that in Christ Jews and Gentiles are united into one whole. *Christ Jesus Himself:* cp. v. 14, 'He is our peace.'

21. Further account of this building and of its relation to Christ. *Every building:* various parts of the one great structure. Such were the various Churches, Jewish or Gentile. So Mt. xxiv. 1, 'the buildings of the Temple:' i.e. the various parts of the Temple at Jerusalem. Frequently a great building is begun at different points; and in the earlier stages its parts seem to be independent erections: but as it advances all are united into one whole. So there were in Paul's day, as now, various Churches. But, to his eye, they were parts of, and were advancing towards, one great temple. The separation was apparent and passing: the unity was real and abiding. *Being-fitly-joined-together:* as a living body is united by its joints. Same word in ch. iv. 16. [The present participle describes the process of union as now going on. So does the next word.] *Is-growing:* for the progress of the building is a development of its own inner life. This word supplements the metaphor of a building by that of a tree. Similar metaphor in 1 Cor. iii. 6—9, Rom. xi. 16—24, Jno. xv. 1—8. *A holy temple:* a conception familiar to Paul: see 1 Cor. iii. 16, 17, and my note. The various buildings, separate as they are during erection, are designed to become one great temple. And the temple is essentially *holy:* for it belongs to God. Consequently, they who are built upon the one foundation are numbered among (*v.* 19) the citizen 'saints.' *A holy temple in* the *Lord* or *a temple holy in* the *Lord:* Christ Himself being the surrounding element of this holiness. It notes a closer relation than the O. T. phrase, 'holy to the Lord.' In virtue of their inward union with the one Master, the Jewish and Gentile Churches are growing into one holy temple.

22. *In whom:* as in v. 21. It keeps before us Christ as the element of growth. *Also ye:* as in *v.* 3, i. 13. It brings the Christians at Ephesus conspicuously under the foregoing general assertion; a thought present throughout the Epistle. *Are-being-built-together:* as stones in a rising building. It is, under another metaphor, practically the same as 'fitly joined together,' in *v.* 21, which suggests the union of bones and members in a living body. *Dwelling-place* (same word in Rev. xviii. 2) *of God:* parallel with 'holy temple' in *v.* 21. For this is the central idea of a temple: 1 Cor. iii. 16, where see note. *In* the *Spirit:* the Agent of this indwelling of God in man. They in whom the Spirit dwells are also *in* the *Spirit:* Rom. viii. 9. For the Spirit within raises them into a new element of life. Thus these last words connect Paul's teaching about the holy temple with His frequent teaching about the Holy Spirit. Cp. 1 Cor. iii. 16, vi. 19. They are also parallel to 'in one Spirit' in *v.* 18. For the Spirit is the surrounding element both of man's approach to God and of God's presence in man. Same words also in ch. iii. 5.

In view of the great work wrought in them by God, Paul reminds his readers of their former heathen state. Even before Christ came there was an organized community on earth in special covenant with God, holding special promises and cherishing glorious hopes. By its members, the readers of this Epistle were looked down upon as aliens. And, having no share in its hopes and in its covenant with God, they were without hope and without God. Through the death of Christ, all this is changed. The barrier between Jew and Gentile, which separated both Jews and Gentiles from God, Christ has through His own death broken down; in order that, by creative power, He may make out of two enemies one new man reconciled to God. Of this peace, He is not only the Author but the Herald. And of this approach to God the Holy Spirit is the Agent and Element. Then all is changed. The aliens have become members of the sacred commonwealth and of the family of God. That city and family are a temple whose foundations have been laid by men divinely sent and inspired, and whose conspicuous corner stone is Christ Himself. On this foundation day by day living stones are being laid and fitted together. And thus, in virtue of its own inherent life, the temple is growing. It seems to consist of various separate buildings. But, as it rises, these various parts are becoming, through the one indwelling Spirit, one holy temple of God.

Very conspicuous in this section is the death of Christ as the means by which (v. 13) the far off ones have been brought near, the barrier between Jew and Gentile broken down, and both Jew and Gentile reconciled to God. The barrier thus broken down is the Law with its prescriptions. Similarly in ch. i. 7 the violent death of Christ is the means of the forgiveness of sins. All this is in close harmony with Paul's constant and varied teaching that salvation comes through the death of Christ upon the cross. It can be explained only on the principle asserted in Rom. iii. 26, viz. that God gave Christ to die in order to harmonize with His own justice the justification of believers, or in other words that the need for this costly means of salvation lay in man's sin viewed in the light of the justice of God.

The union of Jews and Gentiles suggests the unity of the Church, a thought already implied in the universal purpose asserted in ch. i. 10 and further developed in ch. iv. 3—6. This unity is a conspicuous feature of the Epistle.

SECTION VII.

THE GOSPEL OF PEACE BETWEEN JEWS AND GENTILES HAS BEEN COMMITTED TO PAUL.

CH. III. 1—13.

For this cause I Paul, the prisoner of Christ Jesus on behalf of you the Gentiles—² if, at least, ye have heard the stewardship of the grace of God given to me for you, ³ that by way of revelation was made known to me the mystery, according as I wrote before in short space, ⁴ whereby ye can, as ye read, perceive my understanding in the mystery of Christ; ⁵ which in other generations was not made known to the sons of men, as now it has been revealed to His holy apostles and prophets in the Spirit: ⁶ that the Gentiles are fellow-heirs and fellow-members of the body and fellow-partakers of the promise in Christ Jesus through the Gospel, ⁷ of which I was made a minister, according to the gift of the grace of God, the grace *given to me according to the working of His power.* ⁸ *To me, the less than least of all saints, was this grace given, to announce to the Gentiles as good news the unsearchable riches of Christ,* ⁹ *and to enlighten all what is the stewardship of the mystery hidden from the ages, in God who created all things,* ¹⁰ *in order that there may be made known now to the principalities and the authorities in the heavenly* places *through the Church the manifold wisdom of God,* ¹¹ *according to a purpose of the ages which He made in Christ Jesus our Lord,* ¹² *in whom we have boldness and access with confidence through* our *faith in Him.* ¹³ *For which cause I ask that ye faint not at my tribulations on your behalf, which is your glory.*

1. *For this cause:* because, on the foundation laid by the Apostles, Paul's readers had been built into the rising walls of the temple of God. Same words in *v.* 14, Tit. i. 5; not elsewhere in the N. T. As in ch. i. 15, so now, a recital of blessings already given moves Paul to pray for more. *I Paul:* as in Col. i. 23. *Prisoner* of *Christ Jesus:* as in Philem. 1, 9. The definite article suggests that he looked upon his imprisonment as placing him in a unique position among the servants of Christ. And this is easily explained. He was a *prisoner* . . . *on behalf of the Gentiles:* for his loyalty to their spiritual rights as fellow-heirs of the Kingdom of God had aroused the hostility of the Jews and thus brought about, after many earlier troubles, his arrest at Jerusalem. He had pursued his path in full view of the peril to which it exposed him, knowing that this loyalty was demanded by the highest interests both of Jews and Gentiles. Same thought in *v.* 13, 'afflictions on your behalf,' and in Col. i. 24, where see note.

At this point the grammatical construction is broken off, as in ch. ii. 1, by a long parenthesis explaining these last words by an account of the Gospel committed to Paul. The close of the parenthesis is marked by a return in *v.* 13 to the thought now before us; and by a repetition in *v.* 14 of the first words of *v.* 1, *for which cause.* But, instead of completing the broken-off sentence, Paul begins in *v.* 14 as in ch. ii. 5 a new sentence.

2. In *vv.* 2—12 Paul expounds at length the relation implied in *v.* 1, 'on your behalf.' *If at least:* not suggesting uncertainty, but asserting that if, as is the fact, the readers have heard about Paul's commission, they cannot doubt that his imprisonment is on their behalf. *Have-heard:* either from Paul's lips when at Ephesus or by report from others. *The grace given to me:* the undeserved

favour with which God had smiled on Paul; as in Rom. xii. 3, 6, xv. 15, 1 Cor. iii. 10. Cp. 1 Cor. xv. 10. This favour prompted Christ's appearance to Paul and the commission then given to him. And Paul never forgot the responsibility to God and to the Gentiles thus laid upon him. The spiritual wealth thus entrusted to him for their good was a *stewardship of the grace of God . . . for you.* Similar thought in Col. i. 25. But here stress is laid upon the undeserved favour to Paul involved in his commission to the Gentiles. So are all tasks given by God to man marks of His favour. For they bring great reward. This sense of responsibility finds expression in Gal. i. 16, Acts xxvi. 16—18.

3. Further account of the stewardship committed to Paul. *The mystery made known* (as in ch. i. 9) to Paul was spiritual wealth entrusted to him for distribution to others. It was therefore a stewardship. *By way of revelation:* mode in which it *was made known* to Paul, viz. by spiritual enlightenment. See under Rom. i. 17. *Mystery* and *revelation* are constant correlatives: Rom. xvi. 25, 1 Cor. ii. 7, 10. For the secrets of God are known only by those for whom God lifts the veil which hides them from unaided human vision. *I have before written:* apparently in this Epistle. For *v.* 6 which gives the contents of this mystery is a summing up of ch. ii. 13—22. Moreover, the present tense, 'reading,' in *v.* 4 suggests that Paul refers to something new. To the same teaching refer also the similar words in ch. i. 9, 'having made known the mystery.' For the union of Jews and Gentiles is part of God's larger purpose (*v.* 10) to unite in Christ the whole universe. *In short* space: viz. in ch. ii. 13—22, words very few for the truths so great, and to Jews so astounding, therein set forth.

4. *Whereby:* more accurately, *to which referring as a standard of comparison. Understanding:* ability to interpret the significance of things observed: see under Col. i. '9. *The mystery of Christ:* expounded in Col. i. 27. The presence of Christ in His people, as a pledge of the splendour awaiting them, is a secret known only to those specially taught by God. This secret, which is the matter understood, is here represented as the surrounding element of the spiritual insight which Paul's readers would recognise in his teaching about the union in Christ of Jews and Gentiles.

5. *Generations:* the successive courses of men living at one time. So Ph. ii. 15, Col. i. 26. *Other:* more correctly *different.* It calls attention to the different and less favoured position of those who lived before the Gospel age. The words are here a note of time. *The sons of men:* men looked upon in the light of their human

origin: so Gen. xi. 5, Ps. viii. 4, xi. 4. 'While the successive *generations* of the past, so *different* in their lower privileges from the men of Paul's day, followed each other from the cradle to the grave, the great secret now revealed was not made known to the offspring of human parents.' *Revealed;* takes up 'made known by way of revelation' in *v.* 3, and asserts that others shared with Paul the truth supernaturally communicated to him. *Apostles and prophets:* as in ch. ii. 20. These were *holy* because in virtue of their office they stood in special relation to God. Cp. Lk. i. 70. *In* the *Spirit:* same words and sense as in ch. ii. 22. Close parallel in Mt. xxii. 43: for David was (Acts ii. 30) a prophet. Both *Apostles and Prophets* were specially inspired by the Holy Spirit, who made known to them truths till then not known to men. They held respectively (ch. iv. 11, 1 Cor. xii. 28) the first and second ranks in the universal Church; differing in the supreme authority exercised by the Apostles.

6. Statement of the mystery now revealed. *That the Gentiles are etc.:* objectively in Christ, subjectively through each one's faith. *Fellow-heirs:* same word and sense in Rom. viii. 17, Heb. xi. 9, 1 Peter iii. 7. To Gentiles, as to Jews, belongs, in virtue of their filial relation to God, the wealth of heaven. *Fellow-members-of-the-body:* a word not found elsewhere and probably coined by Paul. It presents the union of Jews and Gentiles under Paul's favourite metaphor of the Body of Christ. *Fellow-partakers:* same word in ch. v. 7. These three words, beginning with the same syllable, proclaim very clearly the equal rights of Jews and Gentiles. *The promise:* as in ch. ii. 12. It was designed for, and will be fulfilled in, Jews and Gentiles alike; and therefore belongs to both. *In Christ Jesus:* as in ch. ii. 13, which is explained in *vv.* 14, 15. The above was God's purpose from eternity: ch. i. 4. Therefore in His eternal purpose, which is more real than any creature, already Jews and Gentiles are, in virtue of their relation to Christ, sharers of the one inheritance, members of the one body, and sharers of the one promise. *Through the Gospel:* means by which this objective right is subjectively and personally appropriated, and this purpose of eternity accomplished in time. As Abraham, in the day when he believed the promise, stood before God as already father of many nations, so before time began the believing Gentiles stood before God, as, by means of the good news announced by Christ and His servants, sharers with the believing Israelites of the blessings promised to Abraham.

The union of Jews and Gentiles in the one Church may seem to some unworthy to be called 'the mystery of Christ.' But this union is a logical result of the central doctrine of the Gospel, viz. that God accepts into His favour all who believe. Consequently, in the extension to the Gentiles of the rights of the New Covenant, was involved the essence of the Gospel. Hence the strong language of Gal. v. 2, iv. 10, 11. Moreover to Paul, a zealous Jew, it was the most conspicuous feature of the Gospel, and at one time the most serious objection to it. And, in all ages, the universality of the Gospel, embracing on the same terms men of all kinds, is one of the clearest proofs that it comes from the common Parent of all. This universal destiny of the Kingdom of God was in great part veiled under the Old Covenant. But to Paul and his colleagues, through the agency of the Holy Spirit, it had been revealed. A remembrance of these long ages of silence, of his superior privilege, and of the special honour put upon him as an Apostle filled him with wonder and gratitude. See further in *vv.* 8-11.

This verse is another plain note of genuineness. For it gives to the union of Jews and Gentiles an importance in complete harmony with Paul's position, history, and mode of thought; but inconceivable in the second century, when the Gentiles had obtained a secure and predominant position in the Church.

7. *Of which I became a minister:* as in Col. i. 23; stating in each case Paul's relation to a foregoing general statement. *According to the gift etc.:* close parallel to Col. i. 25. The appointment of Paul as a minister of the Gospel is traced to its source in the favour with which God smiled on him. And this *grace* was in harmony with *the working* or activity *of His power.* Otherwise the grace would have been ineffective. As in Gal. ii. 8, 9, Paul felt that in his labours the might of God was at work.

8—12. A new sentence, reasserting and amplifying the statements in *vv.* 2-7. *The less-than-least:* a combination, not found elsewhere, of superlative and comparative: close parallels in 1 Cor. xv. 9, 1 Tim. i. 13. These two passages explain Paul's self-depreciation here; and they reveal his profound sense of the awful sin of lifting a hand against the Church of God. Not merely below the Apostles, as in 1 Cor. xv. 9, but far below *all saints,* i.e. Christians, Paul places himself. *Was given etc.:* a remarkable re-echo of *vv.* 2, 7, revealing Paul's deep sense of the undeserved favour of God which committed to him so glorious a commission. *This grace* is further expounded by the words *to announce to the Gentiles as good tidings etc. Unsearchable:* whose footsteps cannot be traced. So in Rom. xi. 33. The *riches of Christ* extend, in their abundance, farther than the mind of man can follow. When the Gospel went forth to enrich the Gentiles, it passed the thought of Israel. And, to announce as good news this infinite wealth for all that believe, was the mission given to Paul by the undeserved favour of God.

9. *And to enlighten etc.*: another item of the grace given to Paul, or rather another view of the grace just described. *Enlighten*, or *shed light upon:* as in ch. i. 18, 2 Tim. i. 10, Heb. vi. 4, Jno. i. 9. The light may be conceived as cast, either upon the person seeing, who finds himself surrounded by light, or upon the object seen. A cognate word in 2 Cor. iv. 4, 6. *All:* probably not more than our phrase 'all of them,' viz. the Gentiles. For its position is not emphatic; nor have we here the universal phrase found in Rom. v. 12, 18, etc. *Stewardship of the mystery:* as in 1 Cor. iv. 1, 'stewards of the mysteries of God.' It combines the ideas separately expressed in *vv.* 2 and 3. The great secret revealed to Paul was, in reality, spiritual wealth entrusted to him for distribution to others. To make this secret known to the Gentiles, was to give them light. T do this by announcing the unsearchable riches of Christ, was Paul's joyful task. *Hidden from the ages:* from the beginning of time, as in Col. i. 26. *In God:* whose all-knowing mind is the treasury in which this wealth lay hidden. This suggests, as is clearly implied in *v.* 10, that the mystery was not known even to angels. *Who created all things;* links together the purpose kept secret for ages with the creation of the universe: so ch. i. 4, Col. i. 16, 17. And this suggests that the world was created with a view to the realisation of this purpose.

10. Purpose, not of the creation of all things nor of the concealment of the mystery during long ages, but of the chief matter of the sentence, viz. the commission to Paul to proclaim the mystery. For the mention of creation is only passing: and the revelation, which is itself a part of the original purpose, can hardly be said to be the aim of the concealment. Whereas, as expounded above, this ultimate aim increases immensely the grandeur of Paul's commission. The Gospel he preaches is designed to *make-known* even to angels something about God not known before. Cp. 1 Pet. i. 10. *Now:* in contrast to the ages of silence. *The principalities and the authorities:* as in ch. i. 21. The mention of two ranks of angels throws into bolder relief the greatness of this revelation. *In the heavenly* places: as in ch. i. 3. *Through the Church:* as a visible embodiment of God's eternal purpose. *Wisdom of God:* as in Rom. xi. 33, 1 Cor. ii. 7, i. 24. It is God's perfect knowledge of whatever is and can be, enabling Him to select the best ends and means. *Manifold* or *many-coloured;* suggests an extreme variety of means used.

As the various ranks of angels contemplated the Church on earth, consisting of Jews and Gentiles, of every nationality, rank, degree of culture, and previous character, yet now saved from their sins by the one Gospel of Christ united into one living body with Christ as its Head, and as they observed the combination of various means by which this great consummation has been accomplished, they see, as even angels never saw before, the infinite wisdom with which God selects ends worthy of Himself and the most fitting means. Thus the Church becomes a mirror in which the bright ones of heaven see the glory of God. And, in order to show them this glory, God committed the Gospel to Paul. This teaches that heaven and earth are one great whole; and that good done on earth extends to heaven.

11. *According to purpose:* same words and sense as in ch. i. 11, Rom. viii. 28, 2 Tim. i. 9. A cognate word in ch. i. 9. *Of the ages;* keeps conspicuously before us the idea of a long-cherished purpose. Paul here asserts that the ultimate aim described in *v.* 10 was in harmony with, i.e. was a part of, the one eternal purpose. Grammatically, the words which follow may mean either that God *made*, or *accomplished*, in Christ His great purpose. As matter of fact, both are true. But, inasmuch as the full title *Jesus Christ our Lord* calls very marked attention to the historic Saviour and as *v.* 12 speaks of actual access to God through Christ, it is perhaps better to understand Paul to refer here to the virtual accomplishment in Jesus of Nazareth of the eternal purpose.

12. A new statement proving from spiritual matter of fact the statement in *v.* 11. *In whom we have:* as in ch. i. 7. *Boldness:* or rather *the boldness*, i.e. the well-known confidence which does not fear to speak the whole truth. Same word and sense in Ph. i. 20. *Access:* as in ch. ii. 18, Rom. v. 2. *In confidence:* our state of mind in approaching God. Same word in Ph. iii. 4. *Through faith:* as in ch. ii. 8, Rom. iii. 22, etc. A favourite phrase of Paul. *Faith in Him:* literally, *the faith of Him;* i.e. the faith of which He is the personal object. ' *Through* our assurance that the words of Christ are true and will come true, and *in* virtue of our relation to Him, we have a confidence which enables us to speak unreservedly to man and to approach God without fear.' By giving to us this. confidence, God has, in the historic Christ, accomplished a purpose formed before time began.

13. In *v.* 12 Paul completed his account, begun in *v.* 2, of the stewardship committed to him. This prompts a request bearing upon *v.* 1, a reference indicated by the words *on your behalf* which

recall the same words in *v.* 1. They mark the close of the long parenthesis, *vv.* 2-13. Paul then takes up the thought interrupted by the parenthesis, noting the resumption by the words 'for this cause' carried on from *v.* 1 to *v.* 14.

For which cause: because of this boldness towards men and God which Christians have in Christ and through faith. *I ask:* more fully, *ask as a favour to myself:* so Col. i. 9. It is a courteous request suggesting the pleasure and profit which the Christian courage of his readers will give to Paul. *My afflictions on your behalf:* cp. Col. i. 24, 'my sufferings on your behalf;' and see note. *Not to faint:* same word and sense in 2 Cor. iv. 1, 16, Gal. vi. 9. Paul begs his readers, as a personal favour to himself, not to lose courage in the great fight through the hardships which he endures in order to preach the Gospel to them. This request, his own confidence in Christ emboldens him to make. For he is sure that Christ is able to make them also brave. Then follows a reason for not losing heart: *which are your glory.* Paul declares, conscious that his own brave perseverance is a manifestation of the grace of God, that his sufferings are an ornament to his readers. They can point to his unfaltering courage under great hardships as a confirmation of the Gospel which he preaches and they believe. Surely, their hearts need not sink because of afflictions which bring honour to the whole Church. *Glory:* as in 1 Cor. xi. 7, 2 Cor. viii. 23.

REVIEW. Paul's recital in § 2 of blessings conferred, in accomplishment of an eternal purpose, upon Jews and Gentiles, prompts him in § 3 to pray that God may reveal to the Ephesian Christians His own great power already at work in those who believe. As a measure of this power, he points them to Christ raised from the dead and seated at God's right hand. And, that his readers may apply to themselves this standard of measurement, Paul teaches in § 4 that they once were dead, and in § 5 that Christ has breathed into them new life, thus saving them through faith. This salvation he further describes in § 6 as bringing near those who once were far off not only from God but from the ancient people of God, and as reconciling to God Jews and Gentiles united into one body. The various parts of the Church, however separate they may now seem to be, are destined to become one temple, one dwelling-place of God. All this moves Paul to pray for his readers' further development. But, while preparing to pray, the prisoner remembers his bonds, and that they were caused by his loyalty to the truth which brought salvation to the Gentiles. He delays for a moment his prayer that he may set forth his relation to the Gospel which has

SEC. 8.] *EPHESIANS* III. 14—21. 321

brought this unexpected salvation. And this delay interrupts the grammatical sequence of his letter. In undeserved favour, God has made Paul a steward of good things for the Gentiles, by revealing to him a secret kept in silence while successive generations of men passed to the grave. But the secret has now been revealed to certain men whom God has made the mouth-piece of His Spirit. The secret is that through the Gospel the Gentiles are to share all the spiritual privileges of the people of God. Of this Gospel, Paul is a servant. With profound gratitude for God's kindness to one so unworthy, he repeats what he has just said. It is his happy lot to announce as good news the wealth entrusted to him for others, viz. the secret so long hidden in the mind of God. The ultimate aim of the trust reposed in Paul reaches even to the bright ones of heaven, to whom God has purposed to reveal through His united people on earth His own many-sided wisdom. This purpose God has carried into effect in Christ. Its effect is seen in the confidence towards man and God already enjoyed by those who believe. In view of all this, Paul begs his readers, as though half apologizing for mention of his imprisonment, not to be discouraged by his hardships but rather to rejoice in the divinely-given endurance they evoke.

SECTION VIII.

PAUL PRAYS THAT HIS READERS MAY KNOW CHRIST AND THUS ATTAIN THE CONSUMMATION DESIGNED BY GOD.

CH. III. 14—21.

For this cause I bow my knees to the Father [15] *from whom every family in heaven and upon earth is named,* [16] *in order that He may give to you, according to the riches of His glory, to be strengthened with power through His Spirit to the inward man,* [17] *that Christ may dwell through faith in your hearts;* [18] *in order that, being rooted and foundationed in love, ye may be strong to apprehend, with all the saints, what is the breadth, and length, and height and depth,* [19] *and to know the love of Christ which surpasses knowledge; in order that ye may be filled to all the fulness of God.*

[20] *To Him that is able to do beyond all things abundantly beyond the things which we ask or think, according to the power that works*

in us, ²¹ *to Him* be *the glory in the Church and in Christ Jesus, to all the generations of the age of the ages. Amen.*

This section contains in *vv.* 14—19 a sublime prayer for the readers, consisting of three petitions, viz. *vv.* 16, 17 and *vv.* 18, 19*a* and *v.* 19*b*, each leading up to the petition following; and in *vv.* 20, 21 a doxology of praise to Him who is able to surpass in fulfilment our loftiest prayer or thought.

14, 15. *For which cause;* takes up the same words in *v.* 1, after the digression prompted by the latter part of *v.* 1, and continues the line of thought there broken off. That the Christians at Ephesus who were once far off, are now (ch. ii. 21, 22) stones built into the rising walls of the temple of God, was prompting Paul in *v.* 1, while in prison through his loyalty to their spiritual interests, to pray for them. But his prayer was delayed to make way for an account of his Apostolic commission for the Gentiles. This account he closes by an assertion that in Christ his readers and himself have confident access to God. He begs them not to lose heart through his persecutions; and declares that these, by revealing the grandeur of the grace of God, cover them with splendour. And now comes the postponed prayer, introduced by a repetition of the words of the broken-off sentence, *for this cause:* i.e. because of his readers' confident access to God by faith and the glory which is theirs through the sufferings of Paul. Thus both § 7 and § 8 were prompted by the actual spiritual life of those to whom he writes.

Bow . . . knee: same phrase in Rom. xi. 4, xiv. 11, Ph. ii. 10: slightly different from Acts vii. 60, ix. 40, xx. 36, xxi. 5. So intensely real, so deliberate and solemn, is Paul's approach to God for his readers that even while writing he forgets his actual posture and says *I bow my knees.* He turns in prayer *to the Father from whom etc. Family:* same word in Ex. vi. 15, 'These are the families of the sons of Simeon;' and in Num. i. 16, 'leaders of the tribes according to their families,' etc. *Every family in heaven:* the various classes of angels, e.g. those mentioned in ch. i. 21. So in Job i. 6, ii. 1 the 'sons of God' can be no other than angels: and the word is so rendered by the LXX. They are sons of God as sharing, by derivation from Him, His moral and intellectual nature; not by adoption, which is always the reception of a stranger's child, but by creation and continuance in the image of God. *Every amily . . . on earth:* Jews and Gentiles, or any other classes into which the race is divided. Not all men indiscriminately, but the adopted sons, according to Paul's constant teaching: see under

Rom. viii. 17. With the various families of heaven are associated, as children of one divine Father, families of adopted sons on earth And, from the one Father, all these bear the same *name:* cp. ch. i. 21.

Notice that, in harmony with the exalted standpoint of the whole Epistle, when Paul approaches God in prayer his eye passes the limits of earth and sees other races sharing with himself a name which enables them to call God their Father. Thus the cry, My Father God, unites earth to heaven.

16—19. Contents of Paul's prayer. It consists of three parts, *vv.* 16, 17; *vv.* 18, 19*a*; *v.* 19*b*; each under the same conjunction, which represents the contents of the prayer as also its aim ; *in order that God may give . . . in order that ye may be strong . . . in order that ye may be filled.*

16. *In order that He may give to you:* same words and sense in ch. i. 17. *The riches of His glory:* the abundance of the splendour of God. Same words in Rom. ix. 23. Similarly ch. i. 7, Ph. iv. 19. Conscious that the answer to his prayer will reveal the grandeur of God and thus evoke the admiration of men, and that there is in God an infinity of grandeur ready to reveal itself, Paul asks that this infinite grandeur may be the measure of the answer to his prayer.

Strengthened: fitted for the intellectual and moral effort and work and battle of the Christian life. Same word and sense in 1 Cor. xvi. 13, Lk. i. 80, ii. 40. It is practically the same as the similar word in Col. i. 11, Ph. iv. 13. This strengthening is to come by contact *with* divine *power*, which enters into us and makes us strong. Similar connection of thought in Col. i. 11. *Through* (or *by means of*) *His Spirit:* the Bearer of the presence and power of God. Same or similar words and same sense in Rom. v. 5, 1 Cor. xii. 8, 2 Tim. i. 14. *The inward man:* that in man which is furthest removed from the outer world and its influence, the secret chamber in which man's personality dwells alone. Same words and sense in Rom. vii. 22, 2 Cor. iv. 16. Paul prays that, by contact with the might of God and by the agency of the Holy Spirit, the inward Bearer to man's spirit of all divine influences, divine strength may reach and fill this inmost chamber, making his readers strong indeed.

17. A clause exactly parallel to that preceding it. *Dwell:* or *make* His *home:* same word in Col. i. 19, ii. 9; Heb. xi. 9, Mt. ii. 23, iv. 13. In Rom. viii. 9, 11 and 1 Cor. iii. 16 cognate words describe the indwelling of the Spirit of God: cp. also 2 Cor. vi. 16 and Col. iii. 16. *In your hearts:* the locality of spiritual life: same words and sense in Col. iii. 15, 16, Rom. v. 5; cp. Eph. i. 18, iv. 18, vi. 5,

Gal. iv. 6. The heart is the inmost chamber of our nature, whence come our thoughts, words, and actions: see under Rom. i. 21. It is, therefore, practically identical with 'the inner man.' Moreover, the Holy Spirit is the divine person through whose agency Christ dwells in man. For the coming of the 'other Helper' is the coming of Christ to His disciples: Jno. xiv. 18. Hence the indwelling of the Spirit is practically the indwelling of Christ: Rom. viii. 9—11; cp. Gal. ii. 20. Now Christ has all power. Therefore, for Him to make His home in our heart, is for God to give us, by the agency of the Holy Spirit, the Bearer of the presence of Christ, a strength reaching to the inmost chamber of our being. Moreover, faith is the constant condition of the gift of the Spirit: ch. i. 13, Gal. iii. 2, 14. Consequently, it is *through faith* that *Christ* makes His home *in* our *hearts*. Thus each of these parallel clauses explains the other. This unexpected reference to faith is in complete accord with ch. ii. 8, and with the importance everywhere given to faith in the theology of Paul as the means of salvation.

The above exposition is better than to take the indwelling of Christ as a result of the strengthening wrought by the Spirit; a connection of thought not found elsewhere. The presence of Christ in us is not a result, but a means, of the spiritual strength for which Paul prays.

18, 19a. Second petition of Paul's prayer. *Love:* to our fellows, as always when not otherwise defined: see under 1 Cor. xiii. 1. It is a reflection in man of God's love to man. *Rooted:* same word and sense in Col. ii. 7. *Foundationed*, i.e. 'placed upon a solid foundation:' same word in Col. i. 23, Heb. i. 10, Mt. vii. 25. Notice the double metaphor: a similar combination in Col. ii. 7. A man animated by Christian love has therein good soil in which his spiritual life may take firm hold and raise its head securely, and from which it may derive nourishment and growth. He has also a firm rock on which may rest and rise a solid structure of immoveable perseverance. Cp. 1 Jno. ii. 10. Where love does not reign, the Christian life is always unstable.

The above words may grammatically be joined either to those preceding or to those following. In the former case, they would further describe the state of those in whom Christ dwells: in the latter, they would state a condition needful in order *to comprehend the love of Christ*. The latter seems the more likely: so AV. and RV. For the strength implied in this *root* and *foundation* seems to ead up to the strength needful *to comprehend etc.* [This would also more easily explain the nominative participles, *rooted and founda-*

tioned. For the construction, cp. 2 Cor. ii. 4, Gal. ii. 10.] But the difference is slight. For Paul's first petition, in *vv.* 16, 17, leads up to the second as a means to an end; so that in any case the firmness developed by Christian love is a condition of the spiritual strength needful to comprehend the love of Christ.

That ye may etc.: immediate object of the second petition. *May-be-strong:* an emphatic Greek word, found in the Greek Bible only here and Sirach vii. 6, denoting strength to carry us through and out of difficulty. It suggests the difficulty of comprehending the love of Christ. *Comprehend:* same word and sense in Acts iv. 13, x. 34, xxv. 25. It denotes firm mental grasp. And what Paul desires for his readers he desires for *all the saints.* This desire is prompted by remembrance that it is designed equally for all. *What is the breadth etc.:* an indirect question suggesting wonder and adoring curiosity. *Breadth and length etc.:* as though Paul attempted to measure *the love of Christ* in each direction, e.g. how wide is its compass, how far it will carry us, how high it will raise, and from what depth it will rescue. But these must not be taken as the intended distinction of the four dimensions. They are altogether indefinite, simply noting measurement in every direction. Cp. Job xi. 7—9. What Paul desires his readers to *comprehend,* he does not in *v.* 18 say, but interrupts his sentence to suggest its manysidedness and vastness. The matter to be grasped is stated in *v.* 19*a.*

To know: already implied in *comprehend,* but inserted for marked contrast to the words which follow. *The love* of *Christ:* to us, revealed (2 Cor. v. 15) in His death for all, and well known to Paul as a constraining power and as the ground (Gal. ii. 20) of his faith in Christ. *Surpassing:* as in ch. i. 19, ii. 7: passing all limits and all measurement; and doing this, as implied in *v.* 18, in every direction. This *love surpassing knowledge,* Paul desires his readers *to comprehend and to know.* Nor was this an empty wish. For, though human knowledge cannot fathom it, a determined effort to fathom it ever leads to blessed result by revealing its immeasurable depth. Thus in a very real sense men may know that which in its fulness surpasses knowledge. The greatness and difficulty of this attempt to fathom the unfathomable prompted the emphatic word rendered *may-be-strong.* And, since this strength is possible only to those whose Christian life is made firm by, and draws nourishment from, love to their brethren, and rests upon this love as on a solid foundation, Paul prefaces this second petition by the words *rooted and foundationed in love.*

19b. Third and culminating petition. Paul desires his readers (1) to be strengthened by the indwelling of Christ, in order that thus (2) they may know the love of Christ, and in order that thus finally (3) they may be filled etc.

Filled: made full or fully developed so as to attain the goal of their being. *Fulness:* result of being *filled* or *fulfilled:* see under Col. i. 19. *The fulness of God:* either that with which God is Himself full or the fulness which He gives, filling others or working in them a realisation of the possibilities of their being. These senses are closely allied. For all good in man is an outflow of the eternal excellence of God. And only by being filled with blessing from God can we attain our own complete development. This divinely-given and full development is the measure and aim of the fulness with which Paul prays that his readers *may be filled: to all the fulness of God.* [The preposition *εἰς* has the same sense of a goal to be reached in ch. iv. 13.] Such fulness leaves in man no aching void and no defect. It is God's gift and is an impartation to man, according as he is able to contain it, of that infinite abundance in which every desire of the nature of God finds ever complete satisfaction.

Such is Paul's prayer. It begins and ends with an appeal to the infinite wealth of God. This is, as he approaches the one Father of angels and men, the measure of his desire and his faith. For, to answer his prayer, will reveal the abundance of the splendour of God. His first petition is that his readers be strengthened by the agency of the Holy Spirit, even to the inmost chamber of their being : or, what is practically the same, that Christ may make His home in their hearts. He remembers that this inward presence of Christ is, like all Gospel blessings, through faith. This first petition is but a stepping stone to others greater. Paul desires that Christ may dwell in his readers' hearts in order that by personal and inward contact with Him they may know the infinite greatness of His love. To form any worthy conception of this love, passes so completely all human intellectual power that before asking for this knowledge Paul prays that his readers may receive from the Spirit of God divine strength for this arduous spiritual task. And he reminds them that this strength needs the nourishment and support found in Christian love. He wishes them to measure in every direction the love of Christ, that the failure of their measurement may reveal a vastness which leaves behind the utmost limits of human and created thought. Yet even this is not the ultimate aim of Paul's prayer. Knowledge, even of God, is but a means to a further end. Paul desires his readers to know in order that thus they may be made full, or rather that thus they may attain the goal of their being. And this goal is God Himself. He prays that, by the impartation of that fulness in which are realised the possibilities of God's own nature, his readers may attain the satisfaction of every spiritual instinct and the aim of their being.

20. Rising by three successive stages, Paul has now reached the summit of his mighty prayer. Conscious of the greatness and difficulty of that for which he has asked, he remembers that the omnipotence of God passes infinitely all human word or thought. In this surpassing power of God his faith now takes refuge.

To Him that is able: cp. Rom. xvi. 25, Jude 24. Paul has prayed that his readers be strengthened by the power of God so as to have strength to comprehend the surpassing love of Christ. He now appeals to the only source of this strength, the infinite power of God. *Beyond all things*: passing all limits. This is further expounded by the parallel phrase, *exceedingly beyond etc. The things which we ask or think:* specific details included in all things. God's power *to do* goes not only beyond these but *exceedingly beyond* them. *Think:* as in Rom. i. 20: a looking through things around to the realities underlying them. Of such mental sight, Paul is conscious: *we think*. His thoughts go beyond his prayers. But God's ability to perform goes infinitely beyond both prayers and thoughts.

This appeal to the power of God to perform this great petition is in harmony with the truth that already His power is at work in His people's hearts: *according to the power which is at work in us.* Close parallel of thought and expression in ch. i. 19, 20. The power already at work in them, a power surpassing all word and thought of man, stimulates Paul's faith that the great prayer just offered will be answered.

Glory: manifested grandeur evoking admiration. See under Rom. i. 21. The infinite power of God assures Paul that his great prayer will be answered. He knows that the answer will be an outshining of the grandeur of God and will evoke the adoring admiration of His creatures. And this is his heartfelt desire: *to Him be the glory. In the Church:* the human locality of this admiration. Only in the company of the saved is the grandeur of God recognised. To the outer and human sphere of this praise is now added its inner and divine sphere: *and in Christ Jesus.* A somewhat similar combination in ch. i. 3. Only through the historic facts of Christ and so far as we are inwardly united to Him do we recognise the grandeur of God.

The age of the ages: Hebrew superlative, like 'song of songs.'

Eternity is here represented as one superlative *age;* the one age in which all ages culminate. Slightly different in Gal. i. 5. *Generations:* as in *v.* 5. Since the men living together on earth are ever changing by death, this word receives sometimes a temporal sense. And Paul here projects into eternity the most conspicuous feature of our conception of time, viz. the passing by of successive generations. Even where generations cannot pass away, and where we cannot easily conceive fresh generations rising, Paul uses a term derived from human life on earth in order to describe in the clearest colours possible the endlessness of the song of praise which the manifested power of God will evoke: *to all the generations of the age of the ages.*

The mention of *the Church* in this endless song implies that it will itself endure for ever. This is also clearly implied in ch. v. 27. For the bride of the eternal King can never die. We may therefore conceive the glorified human race to continue for ever as a definite and glorious part of the Kingdom of God.

This doxology is the climax of the Epistle. Taking up his pen to write, the prisoner's first thought is praise to God for blessings already given to his readers. All these he traces to their ultimate source in an eternal purpose of God, a purpose embracing the universe. In the spiritual life of the servants of Christ, the realisation of this purpose has already begun. This moves Paul to pray that his readers may know the infinite greatness of the power already at work in them. As a measure of it, he points to the power which raised Christ from the grave to the throne of God; and declares that spiritually they are already raised from the dead and seated with Christ in heaven. Having thus described their salvation from beneath upwards, Paul further describes it laterally as a bringing near those who were once far away from the people of God, and as a building together of Jews and Gentiles upon one foundation into one glorious temple.

All this moves Paul again to pray for his readers. But he delays his prayer, in view of the just-described union of Jews and Gentiles, to expound his own commission to the Gentiles. Like the blessings for which Paul gave thanks in his first outburst of praise, this commission also has its source in an eternal purpose; and is wider in its scope than the human race, embracing even angels in their successive ranks. The Apostle then, deliberately and solemnly, betakes himself to prayer. He prays to the Father of angels and of men; and appeals to the wealth of splendour ever waiting to reveal itself in Him. He prays that, by the agency of the Spirit and by the indwelling of Christ, his readers may receive, in the inmost chamber of their being, strength to grasp the immeasurable love of Christ, that thus by knowing that which passes knowledge they may themselves be made full to an extent measured by the fulness which God waits to give. The vastness of his prayer compels Paul to appeal to the all-surpassing power of God : and this power evokes from him a song of adoring praise. Thus from praise to prayer and prayer to praise, in the light of the eternal past and the eternal future and in view of a universe to be united under the sway of Christ, in stately and increasing grandeur, rolls forward this glorious anthem, till it culminates in a song of praise begun in the Church on earth but destined to continue through the successive periods of the age of ages.

Notice that each of the two prayers is dominated by thought of the power of God (ch. i. 19, iii. 20) already working in Christians and able to work in them blessings beyond their utmost thought.

DIVISION II.

MORAL TEACHING.

CHS. IV.—VI.

SECTION IX.

UNITY AND GROWTH OF THE CHURCH.

CH. IV. 1-16.

I, therefore, the prisoner in the *Lord, exhort you to walk worthily of the calling with which ye were called,* ² *with all lowliness of mind and meekness, with longsuffering, forbearing one another in love,* ³ *giving diligence to keep the unity of the Spirit in the bond of peace.*

⁴ *One body* there is *and one Spirit, according as also ye were called in one hope of your calling ;* ⁵ *one Lord, one faith, one Baptism,* ⁶ *one. God and Father of all, who is over all and through all and in all.*

⁷ *But to each one of us has been given grace according to the measure of the gift of Christ.* ⁸ *For which cause* one *says, "W h e n*

He went up on high, He led captive a captivity and gave gifts to men." (Ps. lxviii. 18.) ⁹ *Now this, "He went up," what is it but that He also went down into the lower parts of the earth?* ¹⁰ *He that went down is Himself also He that went up beyond and above all the heavens, that He might fill all things.* ¹¹ *And Himself gave some to be apostles, some prophets, some evangelists, some pastors and teachers,* ¹² *with a view to the full equipment of the saints, for the work of ministry, for building up of the body of Christ;* ¹³ *until we all attain to the oneness of the faith and of the knowledge of the Son of God, to a full-grown man, to the measure of the stature of the fulness of Christ;* ¹⁴ *that we may no longer be babes, wafted about and carried about by every wind of doctrine, by the trickery of men, in craftiness, after the wiles of error;* ¹⁵ *but speaking the truth in love may grow up into Him in all things, who is the Head, even Christ,* ¹⁶ *from whom all the body, being jointed together and knit together through every joint of supply, according to* the *working in measure of each one part, makes the increase of the body for the building up of itself in love.*

Since only upon revealed truth can morals rest securely, the moral teaching of this Epistle is not only preceded by the profound doctrines of DIV. I., but is also in this section, after an introductory exhortation in *vv.* 1-3, intertwined with more specific teaching about (*vv.* 4-6) the unity of the Church arising from the unity of God, and about (*vv.* 7-11) the variety of gifts with which the Risen Saviour has endowed it, in order (*vv.* 12-16) to further the harmonious development of all the members of the Church.

1. *I exhort you, then;* introduces, as do the same words in Rom. xii. 1, a practical application of the foregoing teaching. The great truth that God is working in us beyond our thought ought to mould our conduct. *Prisoner in the Lord:* Christ the Master being the element in which Paul lives, and so living finds himself in prison at Rome. For all that he is and does is *in* the *Lord.* Similar thought in Ph. i. 13: a slightly different conception in Eph. iii. 1. *I, the prisoner:* Paul's own personality and circumstances appealing to his readers: so ch. iii. 1, Gal. v. 2, 2 Cor. x. 1. *Walk worthily:* same words and sense in Col. i. 10; similar words in Ph. i. 27. *Calling:* as in ch. i. 18. The grandeur of the Gospel call lays upon us an obligation to choose such steps in life as are in harmony with the prospect of blessing which that call opens to our view.

2. *Lowliness-of-mind, meekness, long-suffering:* same three words together in Col. iii. 12, where see note. The first two are joined

under one preposition and strengthened by the word *all*. Our 'walk' in life must be accompanied by a correct estimate of our utter powerlessness for good and by a consequent absence of self-assertion; and this at all times and in all circumstances. And with this must be a disposition slow to give way to unfavourable influences from without. *Forbearing one another:* same words in same connection in Col. iii. 13; see note. This participial clause both continues Paul's account of the disposition he desires in his readers and describes the practical working, and the source, of *longsuffering*, the point last mentioned. If Christian *love* be the element of our life, we shall refrain from anything which would injure or grieve our brethren, whatever provocation they may give.

3. A second participial clause giving a motive for the forbearance just described, viz. that want of it may endanger Christian unity. *Giving-diligence:* same word and sense in Gal. ii. 10; a cognate word in 2 Cor. vii. 11, 12, viii. 7, 8, 16. It suggests difficulty, and a resolute effort to overcome it. *The Spirit:* of God; see v. 4. *The unity of the Spirit:* harmony wrought by the Spirit among the members of the one Body of Christ. Similarly, the spirit of life produces harmony in the variously endowed members of the human body, making each member helpful to all the others. In a dead body this harmony is lost; and each member pursues its own way along the path of corruption. Since this *unity* is a work *of the Spirit* of God, but is conditional on man's self-surrender to the Spirit, we are bidden *to keep* it. And, since this is sometimes difficult, inasmuch as everything which needs forbearance tends to destroy unity in the Church, Paul bids us *to give diligence to keep etc. Peace:* harmony with those around us: so ch. ii. 14, 15, 17, Rom. xiv. 19, 1 Cor. xiv. 33, Acts vii. 26. It is represented as a silken cord binding into one the members of the Church: *in the bond of peace*. Contrast Acts viii. 23, 'bond of injustice.' This mutual peace, which is the encompassing element of the unity of the Spirit, has the same source as the peace of God which fills the breast of each believer: Col. iii. 15, Ph. iv. 7.

4—6. Seven objective unities, underlying the subjective unity which Paul desires his readers to maintain. *One body:* the Church, which occupies a unique relation to Christ as His Body. So ch. ii. 16, Rom. xii. 5, 1 Cor. xii. 12, 13. *One Spirit:* the Holy Spirit, the one animating principle of the Church, giving to it life and unity as the one Body of Christ. Thus every living human body is a pattern of the Church. And this unity is in harmony with the truth that the good news of salvation opens, to all who receive it, the same prospect of good things to come : *according as ye were called in one hope*. Cp. ch. i. 18. This *one hope* animates all the members of the *one body*, and has its source in the *one Spirit*. Cp. Col. iii. 5. So in secular matters the uniting power of a common hope often binds together a company of men, and makes it a living unity.

One Lord, or *Master :* whom all obey. So 1 Cor. viii. 6, cp. 1 Tim. ii. 5. Each of His servants relies upon the same Gospel promise : *one faith*. And each has entered the company of His professed followers by the *one* gate of *Baptism*.

One God : final and supreme unity. So 1 Cor. viii. 6, 1 Tim. ii. 5. Since the word *God* does not need a defining genitive in order to give a complete sense, it is perhaps better to understand it absolutely : there is *one God* who is *also Father of all*. Grammatically, the word *all*, three times repeated, may denote all things, or men, or believers. Probably here the last. For Paul is evidently thinking about members of the one body. Throughout § 9 we have no reference to the outside world. *Above all :* reigning supreme over all His people : so Rom. ix. 5. *Through all :* using them as instruments to work out His purposes : cp. Rom. xi. 36 ; an important parallel. *In all :* dwelling in, and filling, their hearts.

Notice here seven unities, arranged in two groups of three and surmounted by one supreme unity presented in a threefold relation to us. Among these unities are the three Persons of the Trinity, each possessing a unity of His own and Himself a centre of unity to the servants of God : *One Spirit . . . One Lord . . . One God*. Same order in 1 Cor. xii. 4—6, a close parallel. As ever, Paul rises from the Son to the Father : and in the presence of the Father he lingers. For all unity in the creature has its source in this Supreme Unity.

7. After the unity of the Church, based upon the eternal unities of the Godhead, now follow the manifold gifts to the various members of the Church. *To each one of us :* no member left without an endowment. *Was given grace :* the undeserved favour of God revealed in the gift of capacities for usefulness: a thought frequent with Paul, e.g. Rom. xii. 6, 1 Cor. xii. 4, also 1 Pet. iv. 10. The kind and degree of *the grace given to each one* is determined by *the measure of the free gift of Christ*, i.e. by His wisdom and love : a close parallel in Rom. xii. 3, 6. We may therefore cheerfully acquiesce in the absence of some gifts which others have, knowing that other gifts have been chosen for us by the unerring wisdom of Christ.

8—10. A parenthesis, in thought though not in form. It links the spiritual endowments given by Christ to all His servants with the historic facts of His life on earth; a connection ever present to the thought of Paul. This is introduced by a quotation connecting the deliverance wrought by Christ with deliverances wrought by God for ancient Israel and celebrated in their ancient songs. The speaker of the words here quoted is not mentioned: and, since no one is suggested by the context and God is addressed in the second person, it is best to understand the speaker to be the Psalmist. Cp. 1 Cor. vi. 16, Heb. ii. 6. The introductory formula, *For which cause one says*, occurs again in ch. v. 14, Jas. iv. 6, and not elsewhere in the N. T. It asserts that the words quoted were in some sense prompted by the gifts of Christ to the Church. This demands explanation.

Psalm lxviii. is evidently a song of triumphant praise to God for a great deliverance from enemies of Israel and of God: cp. *vv.* 1, 12, 20, 21. The Psalmist compared it to that wrought by God when He led Israel through the wilderness and revealed Himself in majesty on Sinai. He accosts the conqueror as, after complete victory, returning in triumph to heaven, whence He came in power to save His people: 'Thou hast gone up on high.' The triumphal procession is, as usual, accompanied by captives, these attesting the greatness of the victory: 'Thou hast led captive a captivity.' As usual, there are also 'gifts' which the conqueror has 'received,' either from the gratitude of those whom He has rescued or from others who seek His favour. And we are told that these gifts were received by Him 'among men;' who are represented as standing round and observing the triumph of God. Among these astonished observers are 'the rebellious ones,' who had vainly refused to bow to His yoke but now witness His complete victory. Of this victory, a purpose is that God may reign securely, undisturbed upon His throne, as King among men. The truth underlying this poetic imagery is that, by conspicuously rescuing His people, God has manifested His power in a way which even His enemies cannot fail to recognise; and that, the victory being now complete, His power is again hidden from the eyes of men. This truth, the Psalmist has represented under the figure of a conqueror's return from the field of victory.

Now Paul saw that all such earlier deliverances culminated in the deliverance wrought by Christ, through His life and death and resurrection among men on earth, for those who believe the Gospel. In Him, God had come conspicuously forth from His unseen dwelling place in heaven; and had wrought for His people complete salvation by victory over their spiritual enemies. The ascension of Christ marked the completion of this victory; and was thus the triumphant return of the Conqueror to His home on high. Whatever therefore the Psalmist said about an earlier deliverance was true in still greater measure of the ascension of Christ. Moreover, whatever God did for ancient Israel was made possible only by the death of Christ on the cross, which reconciled mercy to sinful man with the justice of God. Consequently, the deliverance celebrated by the Psalmist was due, and is here attributed by Paul, to the incarnate Son of God. Hence the introductory formula: *for which cause* one *says*.

Among many songs of praise for deliverances wrought by God, Paul chose one containing a poetic figure which has an exact and literal counterpart in the ascension of Christ from earth to heaven. And since, through the victory over the powers of darkness gained by Christ on the cross, multitudes of His enemies had been brought to bow to Him in cheerful submission, Paul was able appropriately to retain in his quotation the word *captivity*, which belongs only to the drapery of the Psalm. Moreover, the practical gain to men of Christ's victory, of which gain the gifts mentioned in *v.* 7 were a part, suggested retention of the word *gifts*, which also belongs to the drapery of the Psalm. And, in order to make clear the relation of Christ's victory to the spiritual gifts about which he is here speaking, Paul does not hesitate to change the form of the quotation and to write *He gave gifts to men*. For the word altered is only a part of the dramatic picturing of the passage quoted. And the alteration makes at once evident the connection between the quotation and the matter which in this section Paul has in hand. The 'gifts received' by the Conqueror revealed the completeness of His victory: the *gifts* which the ascended Saviour *gave* to His servants on earth revealed the completion of His work for them. The essential point of connection between the quoted Psalm and the gifts bestowed by Christ is that, just as in ancient days God sometimes came forth from the unseen world and manifested Himself to men by working for His servants unexpected deliverance, and then again retired from their view, so still more conspicuously in Paul's day He had wrought deliverance by the incarnation and death and ascension of Christ.

A Targum reads in Ps. lxviii. 18 'Thou hast given to them gifts;' as does the Syriac Version. If this reading was known to Paul, it may have suggested the change here adopted. But this is not needful to explain the change. It was justified by the fact that the alteration pertains only to the drapery of the Psalm. And it was needful in order to show the bearing of the quotation upon Christ's gifts to the Church. [In the Lxx., the Sinai Ms. reads ανθρώποις. If this reading was in Paul's mind, it might possibly have made easier to him the change from the singular number in the Psalm to the plural in the quotation.]

This quotation is the first we have met with in the four Epistles now before us; a marked contrast to the Epistles of his third missionary journey, already annotated. Or rather, in its abundance of quotations from the O. T., the second group of Paul's Epistles differs greatly from all his other Epistles. This difference, we cannot explain. For reasons unknown to us, the O. T. was, during his third missionary journey specially near to the Apostle's thought.

9. *Now this, He went up:* viz. Christ. For Paul has asserted, and now assumes, that in His ascension Ps. lxviii. finds its most complete fulfilment. Inasmuch as the original dwelling place of God and of the Son of God is the highest heaven, Paul justly points out that the ascent of Christ implies that He had already come down from heaven to save His people. This is asserted by God in Ex. iii. 8; and by Christ in Jno. iii. 13, vi. 62. Certainly Christ's return in triumph to the skies implies His previous incarnation. Moreover, all this reminds us at once that Christ's ascent was preceded by a still deeper descent, that before He *went up* to heaven He *went down* into the realms of the dead. And Paul taught that He died in order to make mercy to the guilty consistent with the justice of God, and therefore possible. Consequently, had He not gone down into the grave, there had been no triumphant ascent of Christ as (Acts v. 31) a Prince and Saviour. And so closely was this thought interwoven into the whole teaching of Paul that we cannot doubt that he here refers to it. The descent of Christ into the abode of the dead is also the simplest explanation of the words *into the lower parts of the earth*. For this can hardly mean that *earth* is *lower* than heaven, which is self-evident. It recalls rather the constant conception of the ancient world that just as the bodies of the dead are beneath the earth so even their souls are in the under-world. So in Ph. ii. 10 dead persons capable of worship are described as 'under the earth.' The same thought underlies the O. T. conception of Hades. If this exposition be correct, we have here an express assertion that Christ went down into the world of the dead. And this agrees with Jno. xx. 17 where Christ risen from the dead says that He had not yet ascended to God, thus implying that His spirit did not go from the cross to the throne. But, apparently, the chief significance of these words is not so much the descent of Christ into

the realms of the dead as a tremendous fact involved in this descent viz. that He who ascended in triumph had previously died. The readers of the Epistle knew well that He died for their sins and to save them from sin. Had He not died, there had been no spiritual gifts for men. For these were the purchase of His blood. The descent of Christ into Hades is mentioned here, apparently, as a strong pictorial contrast to His triumphant ascent to heaven.

The connection between His death and triumph is also plainly stated in Col. ii. 14, 15.

The words before us do not imply that Christ went to the abode of the lost awaiting their final doom. For even the righteous dead are in the under-world: so Acts ii. 34.

10. Lingering upon the contrast between the death and ascension of Christ, Paul asserts the identity of the dead and the risen Saviour; and further describes the grandeur and the aim of His ascension. *Beyond-and-above all the heavens:* until the loftiest seat on high became lower than the ascended Lord. Same word and same thought in ch. i. 21. Similar thought in Heb. iv. 14. It depicts an extreme contrast to 'the lower parts of the earth.' *All the heavens:* suggesting a variety of abodes in heaven. Cp. Jno. xiv. 2. This variety is closely related to the various ranks in Eph. i. 21. *May fill all things:* primarily the palaces of heaven. These the Son, at His incarnation, left. At His ascension He returned to claim His own again. He now fills all things, not only as the Eternal Son but as the God-Man, the slain Lamb. His return to heaven marked the completion of the work for which He came to earth. And we can easily conceive that for this completion it was needful that His spirit, driven through man's sin into exile from its body, should descend to the lowest depth reached by His servants, in order that from that depth He might raise them to be sharers of His throne. To this end He must needs claim for His own, by entering its gloomy chambers, even the realms of the dead. Therefore, in order that the whole universe might become 'the fulness of Him who fills all in all,' He both descended and rose.

Verses 8—10 teach the important truth that the inward experiences of Christians rest upon the outward historic facts of the human life of Christ. His descent into the grave has for us the deepest persona interest: His triumphant ascent to heaven was our spiritual enrichment. That this truth is embodied in an O. T. quotation, reminds us that the greatest deliverances in the sacred songs of Israel have been surpassed by the mightier work wrought by Christ. Led from step to step by this quotation, we have followed the Saviour into the dark regions of the dead; and from afar have witnessed His exaltation until the brightest abodes of heaven have been left behind in His triumphal progress. A close parallel in Ph. ii. 9—11.

11. *And HE gave:* emphatic addition to 'is Himself also etc.' in v. 9. It also takes up the thought in v. 7 which was interrupted by the reference to the ascension and descent of Christ, 'to each one has been given grace.' *Apostles* . . . *Prophets:* close parallel in 1 Cor. xii. 28, 'first apostles, secondly prophets.' *Apostles:* see under 1 Cor. xv. 7, Rom. i. 1 : the highest rank in the Church. *Prophets:* the second rank. See under 1 Cor. xiv. 40. *Evangelists* or *gospellers:* see under Rom. i. 1. Only found in 2 Tim. iv. 5, Acts xxi. 8. Its position here after *apostles* and *prophets* suggests a definite order of men : its form suggests an order of preachers. That they are called a gift of Christ, implies that they were endowed with special capacity for usefulness, as were the apostles and prophets. *Shepherds,* or *pastors:* same word in Lk. ii. 8. A frequent and appropriate metaphor for those who have charge of others in the Church. So Ezek. xxxiv. 2, 9, 10, 23, Jno. x. 16, 1 Pet. ii. 25, Heb. xiii. 20: cognate verb in Jno. xxi. 16, Acts xx. 28, 1 Pet. v. 2. It denotes evidently a class of men whose work is to find food for, to protect, and to guide, the members of the Church. *Teachers:* men whose work is to impart Gospel truth. Close parallel in 1 Cor. xii. 28, 'thirdly teachers.' Cp. Acts xiii. 1, 'prophets and teachers.' The *pastors and teachers* are grammatically closely joined as describing either the same office or offices closely allied. Since the food of the flock of Christ is Gospel truth, these two words describe probably the same office. Now in Acts xx. 28 the elders or bishops are exhorted to shepherd the flock of God. And in 1 Tim. iii. 2 Paul requires that a bishop be 'apt to teach.' We may therefore take these titles as describing the elders, not however as filling an office but as endowed by Christ with capacity fitting them for it. Such capable officers are indeed Christ's best gifts to His Church. Moreover, if outside the circle of the elders there were others possessing in a marked degree the gift of teaching, these would come under the assertion of this verse. For all capacities for Chris tian work are gifts of the Risen Lord.

Notice here not only gifts for each member but special gifts fitting certain members for special offices. Such gifts are an enrichment to the whole Church, which needs for its various officers divinely-given capacities corresponding to the work of each.

12—16. Aim of the gifts just mentioned, viz. the full development of the Church in every part; with an exposition in detail of this development.

Full-equipment: for the work and battle of the Christian life. Cognate words in 1 Cor. i. 10, 2 Cor. xiii. 9, 11: see notes. *Of the saints:* a title noting the sacred relation to God of all Church-members. This first clause states the general aim of Christ's gift of officers to His Church. Then follow subordinate aims needful for its attainment. *Ministry:* see under Rom. xii. 8. The absence of any reference here to the specific office of a deacon, the mention above of various Church-officers, and the frequency of this word in the general sense of any office, suggest that it is here used in this more general sense. So 1 Cor. xii. 5, 'varieties of ministries.' *Work of ministry:* result to be attained by this official ministration. For this practical end, Christ endowed certain Church-members with special capacities. *For building up etc.:* further aim, parallel with and defining that just mentioned. It reproduces the metaphor of ch. ii. 20—22. As in English, so in Greek the same word, *building*, denotes both the structure erected and the act of erection. *The body of Christ:* Paul's favourite metaphor, found already in ch. i. 23. This combination of two metaphors links with the idea of the progress of a rising building that of the growth of a living body and the vital relation of the Church to Christ. Similar combination in *v.* 16. This *work of ministry* and *building of the body of Christ,* we may perhaps understand as means leading to *the full equipment of the saints.* [The prepositions πρός and εἰς are used here together, as in Rom. xv. 2, apparently for the further and nearer objects in view.] God designs that, through the agency of the officers of the Church and through the consequent progress of the Church as a whole, each individual Christian, standing as he does in special relation to God, may attain his full development.

13. Further aim of Christ's gift of Church-officers; represented here as the length of time during which the gift will continue in the Church: *until we attain.* Not that the gift will then cease: for in Rom. v. 14 the reign of death, which was *until* Moses, continues still. *We all:* i.e. Church-members in contrast to office-bearers. *Attain:* to overtake an object aimed at: same word and sense in 1 Cor. x. 11, xiv. 36. *The unity of the faith:* complete harmony of the members of the one body of Christ arising from their faith in *the Son of God.* Cp. *v.* 5: 'one faith.' It is practically the same as 'the unity of the Spirit' in *v.* 3. For the uniting Spirit is obtained through faith. Paul means probably *the faith and the knowledge of the Son of God.* For the phrase *faith of the Son of God,* though strange to

English ears, is good Greek. So ch. iii. 12, twice in Gal. ii. 16, 20, iii. 22, Ph. iii. 9, etc. It denotes the mental act in which we accept and lean upon the words of Christ. Our *faith* has for its personal object, *and* our *knowledge* for its object matter, *the Son of God.* To believe His words, is to know Him.

Full-grown: as in Ph. iii. 15, Col. i. 28, iv. 12, 1 Cor. ii. 6, xiv. 20. *Man*, not 'men:' for Paul thinks of the ideal oneness of Christian manhood. These words are parallel with *to the unity of the faith.* By attaining this unity we attain the full stature of men in Christ. *To the measure of etc.*: in apposition to, and expounding, the foregoing. *The fulness of Christ*: the abundant blessing and full development, these being practically the same, which Christ has and gives. It is 'the fulness of God' in ch. iii. 19. This fulness raises those who receive it to the stature of Christian manhood. And this is the *measure* to which Paul would have his readers attain. The word rendered *stature* denotes bodily height in Mt. vi. 27, Lk. ii. 52, xii. 25, xix. 3. In Jno. ix. 21, 23, Heb. xi. 11, it denotes length of life. The former sense is suggested here by *full-grown man*, and by 'growth' in *vv*. 15, 16. Christ gave to His Church various personal endowments that, through exercise of these by those to whom they were given, its members might attain their full development, even the standard erected for them by the wealth of Christ.

This verse suggests that all disunion is a mark, not only of ignorance and want of faith, but of spiritual childishness and diminutive Christian life.

14—16. In *v*. 13 Paul stated that the gifts of Christ to the Church were designed to continue till all His servants attain full development. This was really a statement of Christ's purpose in bestowing these gifts. Grammatically, *vv*. 14-16 announce a further purpose to be attained by the purpose implied in *v*. 13 or by the purpose asserted in *v*. 12. Practically, they expound in detail these purposes; negatively in *v*. 14, positively in *vv*. 15, 16.

14. A state from which Christ designs to save His people. The word *no-longer* implies that it was actual and frequent among the Christians of Paul's day. *Babes;* keeps up by contrast the metaphor of 'full-grown' in *v*. 13. So 1 Cor. iii. 1 in contrast to ch. ii. 6, where we have the same words. Then follows a picture of spiritual babyhood. *Wafted-about*: like a wave of the sea. Same metaphor in Jas. i. 6, 'he who doubts is like a wave of the sea carried by wind:' a close parallel. Instability under external pressure is a mark both of weak faith and of spiritual childishness. *Carried-about* or *around;* emphasises an idea already present in *wafted-about*, viz.

useless movement hither and thither. *Every wind of teaching:* the changing cause of this ceaseless and useless motion. On *babes, teaching* operates like *wind* on water. *Every wind:* recalling the infinite variety of such influences. The immature Christian is carried along by what he hears, good or bad. He is therefore at the mercy of every influence brought to bear upon him, and is borne hither and thither in ceaseless and useless movement.

In the trickery of men: the source of this teaching, represented as the surrounding element and atmosphere of this vain movement. *Trickery:* literally *dice-playing,* the gamester's art. *In craftiness etc.:* parallel with, and expounding, the foregoing. *Craftiness:* as in 2 Cor. iv. 2: a disposition to do anything to gain one's ends. *The wiles,* or *deliberate-system,* literally *the method,* of *error:* a way of working peculiar to those who are away from the truth. This is the path and goal of those by whom the immature ones are led.

This verse opens a dark picture of the Churches in Paul's day: for this teaching of error must be that of professed Christians. But the picture is no darker than that in 2 Cor. xii. 21. We have here men wandering in, and dominated by, error. While professing to teach Divine truth, they do anything to gain their ends, using even the trickery of a dice-player. By such teachers, some immature Christians are carried about from one belief to another like the tossing waves of the sea. Against their craft nothing can stand firmly except robust Christian manhood. To guard His servants from this peril, by raising them to men in Christ, the Risen Lord has enriched His Church with abundant and various spiritual gifts.

15, 16. Positive side of Christ's purpose for His people. *Speaking-truth:* either statements corresponding with fact, as in Gal. iv. 16; or teaching or belief corresponding with reality. This latter sense is at once suggested here by the contrast with 'error' in *v.* 14, and by the whole context. [The participle preceding a finite verb recalls the same construction in ch. iii. 18.] Paul teaches that knowledge of the truth is a necessary condition of Christian growth. Consequently, it matters little whether the words *in love* be joined to the words preceding them or to those following, i.e. whether *love* be the surrounding element of the *truth* we speak or of our *growth.* In either case Paul teaches that for growth there must be both love and knowledge of the truth. Cp. ch. iii. 18. *We-may-grow;* keeps before us the idea of progress. So *v.* 13, 'come to a fullgrown man.' *Into Him:* our spiritual development bringing us into closer inward contact with Christ. *In all things:* every part of our nature being, by this development, united more closely to Christ.

Who is etc.: Christ into whom we are to grow is related to the Church as is *the head* to a living body. Same favourite metaphor in ch. i. 22, Col. i. 18. And He it is *from whom* the Church, His *body*, derives unity and growth. *All the body :* parallel with 'we all' in v. 13. Same words in same connection in Col. ii. 19. They represent the entire Church as one whole. *Being-fitted-together:* same word and same present participle in ch. ii. 21. It suggests harmonious and close union like the various parts of a living body. *Knit-together:* same word in Col. ii. 19; a close parallel to this verse. It adds to the idea of adaptation that of actual coming together. *Joint:* same word and sense as in Col. ii. 19, 'through the joints and bands receiving supply and being brought together.' The similarity of these verses seems to compel us to understand *through every joint* as the means by which this close union of the various members is brought about; rather than as the means of the growth afterwards mentioned. The added words *of the supply* teach that the manifold contact of member with member in the Church, which binds these members into one compact body, is also a means of supplying the spiritual needs of the Church and thus helping its spiritual growth. Same thought in Col. ii. 19. *The working in measure of each one part:* each member of the Church being active for the general good, according to the spiritual endowment of each. Cp. Rom. xii. 3. Just so, in a healthy body, each member is active, and the activity of each contributes to the general good. And in proportion to this activity of the several parts is the health of the whole : *according to the working etc. Makes the increase* (or *growth*) *of the body :* chief assertion of v. 16, corresponding to *may-grow* in v. 15. This growth is derived from Christ, and is conditioned by compact union of the members and by the normal activity of each. *For the building-up of itself:* the metaphor of a rising building added, as in v. 12, to that of a living and growing body. *In love:* the encompassing element of Christian progress. Same words in v. 15, iii. 18.

In § 9 Paul enters upon the moral teaching of this Epistle. After praise and prayer on his readers' behalf in chs. i—iii., interwoven with loftiest doctrinal teaching, he now exhorts them to action worthy of the Gospel call. Of such worthy conduct, the first point emphasised is Christian unity. Paul suggests that the preservation of unity requires effort, and a mutual forbearance possible only to the lowly in heart. Then follows a statement of the objective and eternal unities which underlie all Christian unity. From these he passes to Christ's various gifts to the members of the Church. He reminds us that these gifts were from the ascended Saviour; and that His ascension was a triumph grander than the many triumphs of God celebrated in the ancient songs of Israel. After this passing reference to Christ's ascension and to His previous descent into the grave, Paul specifies further His gifts to the Church, mentioning specially the various grades of Church officers. These were given for the full development of the Church, which is the body of Christ. It can rise above the vacillations of childhood only by spiritual growth derived from Christ its Head, a growth uniting it more closely to Him, and nourished by the active co-operation of each member in compact union with his fellows.

That in this Epistle the spiritual union of believers with Christ and with each other is treated of before morality, reveals Paul's estimate of its importance. The new life in Christ ever draws together those united to Him; and is therefore hindered by all disunion. Therefore, since the mind of Christ moulding human conduct is the one source of the highest morality, whatever separates Christians is hostile to morality.

SECTION X.

A TOTAL CHANGE OF LIFE NEEDED.

CH. IV. 17—24.

This then I say and testify in the *Lord, that ye no longer walk according as the Gentiles walk in vanity of their mind,* [18] *being darkened in the understanding, alienated from the life of God because of the ignorance which is in them because of the hardening of their hearts;* [19] *men who, being past feeling, have given up themselves to wantonness for* the *working of all uncleanness with greediness.* [20] *But not so have ye learnt Christ;* [21] *if indeed ye have heard Him and have been taught in Him, according as it is truth in Jesus* [22] *that ye must needs put away, as concerns your former manner of life, the old man which is corrupting according to the desires of deceit;* [23] *and be renewed by the Spirit of your mind,* [24] *and put on the new man, which, after God, has been created in righteousness and holiness of truth.*

After emphasising the need of unity and mutual help among Christians, Paul now asserts the need of a total change of life, a complete renunciation of the sins of heathenism. This he prefaces in *v*. 17 by a solemn protestation; and then in *vv*. 18, 19 depicts, as a warning, the moral and spiritual state of the heathen. He then says that Christ (*vv*. 20, 21) requires a complete surrender (*v*. 22) of the old life and (*vv*. 23, 24) a life altogether new.

17. *This then I say;* resumes the exhortation interrupted by the assertion in *v*. 4 of the great unities underlying the unity which in *v*. 3 Paul bids his readers endeavourto maintain. *Protest:* as in Gal. v. 3. He calls God to witness the truth of what he is about to say. *In* the *Lord:* like 'in Christ' in Rom. ix. 1. This protest is an outflow of Paul's union with Christ. *That ye no longer walk;* recalls their earlier contrary life. Along the same path *also the Gentiles now walk.* This path Paul bids his readers henceforth avoid.

Now follows as a warning, a description of the forbidden path. *Vanity:* cp. 1 Cor. iii. 20, 'the reasonings of the wise . . . are vain.' *Their mind* is at work, but with no good result. And this useless activity is the mental element of their action: *in the vanity of their mind.*

18. In two parallel participial clauses this useless mental effort is traced to its source. *The understanding:* the mental eye which looks through objects around to their underlying significance. Same word in Col. i. 21. Upon this mental eye falls no light : therefore the heathen are in this all-important faculty *darkened.* This statement, the rest of *v.* 18 further develops. *Alienated:* same word in ch. ii. 12. *The life of God:* the immortal life which God Himself lives and which He gives to His servants. Cp. 'the peace of God,' in Ph. iv. 7. To this, the only real life, the heathen are strangers. So terrible is their position. *The ignorance which is in them:* stronger than their ignorance. In their hearts dwells an absence of knowledge of all that is best worth knowing. And, |since knowledge of God is the channel of life, ignorance results in separation from life: *alienated from the life . . . . because of the ignorance.* Cp. Jno. xvii. 3: 'this is the eternal life, that they may know Thee.' A keen rebuke to the vaunted knowledge of the Greeks. Then follows the cause of their ignorance. *Hardening:* as in Rom. xi. 8. Same phrase in Mk. vi. 52, viii. 17, Jno. xii. 40. *The heart* is *hardened* when it becomes less sensible to influences from without; in this case, influences from God. These are designed to fill and mould and raise the whole life. But the heart of the heathen is unmoved by these good influences. And, since they are the one source of the only real knowledge, hardening produces *ignorance.* Moreover, since knowledge is the avenue of spiritual life, the hardened and

ignorant ones are destitute of that *life*. Thus the two clauses, each introduced by the word *because-of*, are successive links of causation.

Such is the inward state of the heathen. Their heart is insensible to things divine; therefore ignorance reigns in them, and the true life is far off. No wonder that in these darkened ones the mind works to no purpose, and that their path in life is wrong.

19. Further description of the same men, setting forth the immoral result of this 'hardening.' *Past-feeling:* literally *having-become-insensible-to-pain*, i.e. sin no longer painful to them. *Gave-up:* surrender to a hostile power. Same word and sense in Rom. i. 24, 26, 28: an important parallel and complement to this passage. By willingly embracing sin they *gave up themselves* to its power: and by decreeing that sinners fall victims to the power of their own sin 'God gave them up.' *Themselves:* the most tremendous sacrifice ever laid on the altar of sin. *Wantonness:* insolent casting aside of all restraint. *Uncleanness:* anything inconsistent with personal purity. Same words together in 2 Cor. xii. 21, Gal. v. 19. *Wantonness* is almost personified as a power to which these men surrendered themselves in order to work out everything which defiles men. *Insolence* is their master: and *every* kind of *impurity* is their aim. *Covetousness:* desire of having more, an inordinate longing for the good things of earth. See under Col. iii. 5. As a conspicuous form of selfishness, it stands in close relation to bodily self-indulgence. So here and ch. v. 3, Col. iii. 5. This close relation makes it needless to give to the word here any other than its ordinary meaning.

Such is the state of the heathen. The darkening of their minds has made them in some measure insensible to the evil of sin. They have therefore given themselves up to gross and defiling sin and to the worship of material good.

20, 21a. *Ye not so:* conspicuous and double contrast to the Gentiles. *Christ:* Himself the matter of the knowledge they have acquired. So in Gal. i. 16, 1 Cor. i. 23. He is the matter revealed and preached. *If at least etc.;* strengthens the foregoing assertion by adding a condition within which it is undoubtedly true. *If* they have *heard* Christ etc., then certainly they *have not so learnt Him*. *Heard Him:* by hearing they received not merely His words but Christ Himself. So in v. 20 they *learnt Christ*. And He is not only the matter heard but the personal encompassing element of the teaching received: *taught in Him*. They first *heard* the truth of Christ and thus received Him; and then, abiding in Him, received further instruction.

21b. A statement in harmony with the foregoing. This *truth* can be no other than that stated in *v.* 22, viz. that God requires us to put away the old man. This is *a truth in Jesus:* for in Him who was born in Bethlehem a command has gone forth to all men everywhere to repent. The teaching received by the Asiatic Christians was in agreement with the moral truth of this command: *according as etc.* Notice the Saviour's names. They 'learnt Christ,' i.e. they embraced the meaning of His official title. There *is truth in Jesus:* for in that historic Person God spoke to man.

22. The moral 'truth,' now plainly stated. *Put-away:* as clothes are laid aside. Same word and idea in Col. iii. 8, Rom. xiii. 12. *That ye put away:* this moral truth brought to bear on the Christians at Ephesus. *Manner-of-life:* same word and sense in Gal. i. 13, 'my manner of life formerly.' *In-view-of the former manner-of-life:* aspect of their case which makes it needful to *put away etc.* The *old man:* same words and sense in Col. iii. 9, where we have the same metaphor of laying aside clothing: see note. *Which is corrupting:* moral deterioration and destruction going on day by day. Of this, eternal death is the awful consummation. So is the corruption of a corpse a consummation of mortification before death. The abstract principle of *deceit* with its tendencies is represented almost as a person cherishing *desires.* In the unsaved, these are a ruling power. And the corruption now going on is what we should expect when such a principle guides the steps of men: *according to the desires of deceit.* These last words keep before us the teaching in *v.* 18 that ignorance and error are the treacherous basis of human life without Christ. A building erected on such a foundation is doomed to fall.

23. Positive side of the moral 'truth in Jesus.' *And be renewed:* from day to day, in contrast to the 'advancing corruption of the old man. Similar word, and same idea of progressive renovation, in Col. iii. 10, Rom. xii. 2. *The Spirit of your mind:* the Holy Spirit looked upon as enlightening the mind. Similarly, in Rom. vii. 23 the law of God is called 'the law of my mind.' Nowhere else in the Bible is the Holy Spirit spoken of as belonging to man or to man's mind. But the phrase is intelligible and appropriate. Whereas, to understand it as describing the human spirit, is to make the collocation of *spirit* and *mind* unmeaning. The Holy Spirit is the Agent of the renewal: Tit. iii. 5. And He renews men by enlightening their intelligence. Paul could therefore say, *be renewed by the Spirit of your mind,* and 'the Gentiles walk in the vanity of their mind.'

24. *And put on:* once for al, lin contrast both to 'put off' in *v.* 22

and to the gradual renewal in *v.* 23. Same word in Col. iii. 10, where we have also a term equivalent to *the new man.* *After God:* Himself the pattern, as He is also the Author, of this new creation. Cp. Col. iii. 10, 'according to the image of Him that created Him.' The new man has already *been created,* and is therefore waiting to be put on. *In righteousness:* right doing, the surrounding element of this new creation. *Holiness:* not the very common word usually so rendered, but a rare word found, in conjunction with *righteousness,* in Lk. i. 75. Cognate words in Acts ii. 27, xiii. 34, 35, 1 Tim. ii. 8, Tit. i. 8, 1 Th. ii. 10. It denotes agreement with the eternal sanctities of right. This *righteousness and holiness* belong to the truth, just as 'the desires' which lead to moral corruption belong to 'deceit.' The moral teaching which found utterance in Jesus, and which because it corresponds with the eternal realities is *truth,* finds its outward expression in conduct agreeable to the Law and to the eternal principle of right. Such conduct is the surrounding element of *the new man which has been created* in the likeness of *God* and which Paul bids his readers *put on.*

[Notice carefully the tenses in *vv.* 22—24. The old man is day by day corrupting: we are therefore bidden to lay it once for all aside. The new man has already been created: we are therefore bidden once for all to put it on. But the renewal wrought by the Holy Spirit operating on our mind progresses day by day.]

Such is the broad platform which Paul lays for his subsequent moral teaching. He points·to the heathen, to their moral insensibility and to the consequent darkness which has clouded their minds and reduced to worthlessness their mental efforts, and to their reckless self-abandonment to every kind of sin ; and silently reminds his readers that this was once a picture of themselves. But the truth which spoke in Jesus has changed all this. The old corrupting life, Paul bids them lay aside ; and bids them put on the new life breathed into man by the creative power of God, in the likeness of God, and receiving daily progressive renewal by the mental illumination of the Holy Spirit.

SECTION XI.
SUNDRY PRECEPTS.
CH. IV. 25—V. 21.

For which cause, having put away falsehood, speak ye truth each with his neighbour. For we are members one of another. ²⁶ *Be angry and sin not: let not the sun go down on your provocation;* ²⁷ *neither give place to the devil.* ²⁸ *He that steals, let him steal no longer; but rather let him labour, working with his hands that which is good, that he may have to impart to him who has need.* ²⁹ *Let no corrupt speech go forth from your mouth, but if anything is good for edifying as the need may be, that it may give grace to those that hear.* ³⁰ *And grieve not the Holy Spirit of God in whom ye have been sealed for* the *day of redemption.* ³¹ *Let all bitterness and fury and anger and clamour and railing be put away from you, with all badness.* ³² *And become kind one to another, compassionate, forgiving each other, according as God in Christ forgave you.*

¹ *Become then imitators of God as beloved children:* ² *and walk in love according as Christ loved you and gave up Himself on our behalf an offering and sacrifice to God for an odour of perfume.*

³ *But fornication and all uncleanness or covetousness, let them not be named among you, as becomes saints:* ⁴ *and shamefulness and foolish talking and jesting, which are not fitting, but rather thanksgiving.* ⁵ *For this ye know being aware that no fornicator or unclean person or covetous one, which is an idolater, has inheritance in the kingdom of Christ and of God.* ⁶ *Let no one deceive you with empty words. For because of these things comes the anger of God upon the sons of disobedience.* ⁷ *Become not then partakers with them.*

⁸ *For ye were once darkness, but are now light in* the *Lord. As children of light walk,* ⁹ *(for the fruit of the light is in all goodness and righteousness and truth,)* ¹⁰ *proving what is well-pleasing to the Lord.* ¹¹ *And be not sharers with others in the unfruitful works of darkness, but rather reprove them.* ¹² *For the things secretly done by them, it is a shame even to speak of.* ¹³ *But all things when reproved are made manifest by the light. For everything which is made manifest is light.* ¹⁴ *For which cause* he *says, "Rise up, sleeper, and arise from the dead, and Christ shall give light to thee."*

¹⁵ *Look then carefully how ye walk, not as unwise but as wise,* ¹⁶ *buying up the opportunity, because the days are bad.* ¹⁷ *For this cause be not senseless, but understand what is the will of the Lord.* ¹⁸ *And be not drunk with wine, in which is riot, but be filled with the Spirit;* ¹⁹ *speaking one to another with psalms and hymns and spiritual songs, singing and chanting in your heart to the Lord;* ²⁰ *giving thanks always for all things, in the name of our Lord Jesus Christ, to God even the Father;* ²¹ *subjecting yourselves one to another in the fear of Christ.*

After asserting in § 10 the broad underlying principles of Christian morality, Paul comes in § 11 to apply them in detail to various specific vices and virtues. Without any formal divisions, his discourse flows on with orderly sequence, shedding light on each point it touches. In *vv.* 25—31 we have a series of prohibitions; and in *vv.* 32—v. 2 positive injunctions supported by the example of God and of Christ. Then follow in *vv.* 3—7 other prohibitions, supported by threatenings. These are further supported in *vv.* 8—14 by a comparison of the past and present under the aspects of darkness and light. In *vv.* 15—21 we have sundry exhortations culminating in an exhortation to spiritual song and praise. A word about mutual subordination closes § 11, and becomes the key-note of § 12.

25. *For which cause:* a desired practical result of the foregoing general moral principles. *Falsehood:* in all its forms. [The Greek article looks upon it as a definite and well-known object of thought.] *Having-put-away:* once for all. [The participle does not imply that this had already taken place, but merely makes it a necessary preliminary to the truth-speaking to which Paul here exhorts his readers. See under Rom. v. 1.] *Speak ye truth each with his neighbour:* almost word for word from Zech. viii. 16, the prophet's word correctly expressing Paul's thought. That this exhortation comes first, was probably suggested by the last word of § 10. *Members one of another:* same words in same sense in Rom. xii. 5. They bring Paul's favourite metaphor of the Church as the body of Christ, asserted in ch. i. 23 and further expounded in ch. iv. 12, 16, to bear upon this detail of practical morality. If we are members of one body, we have one interest. And, where this is recognised, falsehood is impossible. For it is only a cloak to hide our selfish disregard of the interests of others.

To limit the word *neighbour* to fellow-Christians, would contradict both the broad compass of the word itself and the plain teaching of Lk. x. 29. And the same width must be given to the words following which support this exhortation. If so, all men are here said to be members of one body. And, in a very real sense, this is true. The whole human race, like a human body, is so joined together that benefit or injury to any one member is done to the whole, and thus indirectly done in some measure to each other member. They who know this have nothing to hide ; and will therefore speak the truth. Notice here an application of Paul's favourite metaphor wider than is found elsewhere in his Epistles.

26, 27. *Be angry and sin not:* word for word from Ps. iv. 4. Grammatically each word conveys an exhortation. But practically the whole force of the exhortation falls upon the second verb. The first exhortation implies that anger may sometimes be right ; and is therefore practically permissive. Paul bids us see that our anger be ever joined to sinlessness. Then follow two warnings against dangers which always attend anger. It is always wrong when it becomes an abiding state of mind : and in all danger Satan is near, seeking for entrance. *The sun go down:* the solemn close of the day. Even nature, by dividing life into short portions, suggests retrospection as each portion passes. And such retrospection is a safeguard against sinful anger. *Your provocation,* or *any provocation of yours:* cognate word in Rom. x. 19. It is therefore not necessarily sinful. It denotes a rousing of the emotion of anger. *Give place:* as in Rom. xii. 19. Paul suggests that when anger continues Satan is near ; and warns that we be careful not to afford him an opportunity of doing us spiritual harm. *The devil:* see under ch. vi. 11.

28. *He that steals etc.* : a general precept which all Paul's readers must obey. For Christ bids every sinner to put away his sin. *But rather let him labour. . . . that he may have to impart etc.:* exact opposite to stealing. To avoid *labour,* a thief impoverishes others. He must now work *that* by possessing *he may* be able *to impart,* i.e. to give a portion of his own possession, *to him that has need. Working with his hands:* vivid picture of actual toil. *That which is good:* in contrast to the evil of theft.

29. *Every corrupt* (or *bitter*) *word:* put conspicuously first as the serious matter of this prohibition. *Out of your mouth :* graphic delineation of speech, revealing the inappropriateness of such talk from the lips of Christians. Then the prohibition : *let it not go forth. But if any* discourse be *good* etc.: the contrasted positive exhortation. *For edification :* i.e. tending to *build-up* the spiritual life, and thus to supply *the need* (same word as above) of men. A further purpose, explaining the foregoing words, is *that it may give* *grace to the hearers,* i.e. convey to them the favour of God and its consequent benefits. In Jas. iv. 6, 1 Pet. v. 5, Ps. lxxxiv. 11, Ex. iii. 21, God *gives grace.* This last passage denotes the favour towards Israel wrought by God in the hearts of the Egyptians. The others refer to His own favour with which God enriches the lowly: a meaning practically the same as here.

30. A fifth prohibition. *The Holy Spirit of God:* full and solemn title. *Grieve:* literally *cause-sorrow-to:* same word several times in 2 Cor. ii. 2—5, vii. 8, 9. It is here a strong anthropomorphism. They who resist the Spirit and thus provoke His displeasure are here said to cause Him sorrow. Only thus can we conceive the influence of man's sin upon the mind of God. If it stood alone, this phrase would not in itself necessarily imply that the Spirit of God is a Person distinct from the Father. For it might be understood as a mere circumlocution for Him. But when we have learnt this doctrine from Jno. xvi. 13, Mt. xxviii. 19, (see under 1 Cor. xii. 11,) it sheds new light upon, and thus receives confirmation from, these words. *Ye were sealed:* same phrase in same connection and sense in ch. i. 13. *Redemption:* as in ch. i. 14, Rom. viii. 23. The great day will be a final and complete deliverance of the servants of Christ, and in this sense a *day of redemption.* And the gift of the Spirit has that day in view: *sealed for the day etc.* God has given to believers *the Holy Spirit* that in their hearts He may be a divine testimony that in the day of days they will be rescued from death and the grave. Now all sin tends to deface that seal and thus to destroy this divine attestation. Consequently, this last prohibition contains a strong motive for obedience to those foregoing.

31. A compact group of prohibitions. Notice its comprehensiveness: *all . . . all. Bitterness:* cognate to a word in Col. iii. 19; see note. *Fury and anger:* see under the same words in Col. iii. 8. *Clamour:* a loud or earnest cry. Same word in Acts xxiii. 9, Mt. xxv. 6, Heb. v. 7. Both anger and clamour so easily pass the bounds of right that the words are, as here, often used in a bad sense. *Railing . . . badness:* as in Col. iii. 8, in the same connection. This last term is separated from the others as generic and inclusive.

32— V. 2. A group of closely allied positive exhortations, inserted as a conspicuous contrast among these warnings against sin. *Become:* in contrast to 'put away from you.' It implies that the readers are not yet what Paul desires them to be. *Compassionate:* literally, *good-hearted. Forgiving each other:* as in Col. iii. 13, where the same motive is given. *God forgave you:* (cp. Col. ii. 13:) as the ultimate source of the grace of pardon. But it reaches us *in Christ,* i.e. through the facts of His human life and through inward union with Him. Outside of Christ there is no forgiveness from God.

1, 2. On this divine pattern Paul lingers. We must be *imitators of God.* And this because we are His *children*, objects of His tender *love.* For children are expected to bear their father's likeness: and loved ones are influenced by those who love them. *And* love is to be the encompassing element and directive principle of their steps in life: *walk in love.* Similar phrase in Rom. xiv. 15. To the example of the Father, Paul adds that of the Son: *according as also Christ etc. Gave up Himself on your behalf*: as in Rom. viii. 32, Gal. ii. 20, Eph. v. 25. Grammatically, these words mean simply self-surrender for our benefit. But the following word *sacrifice* and Paul's constant teaching about the purpose of the death of Christ prove abundantly that he refers here to Christ's self-surrender to death for our salvation: an infinite contrast to the self-surrender in ch. iv. 19. *Offering:* a general term for everything given to God. *Sacrifice:* a more specific term for the gifts laid upon the altar. It is a frequent translation of the ordinary Hebrew word for bloody sacrifices; but is sometimes used in the LXX. (e.g. Lev. ii. 1, 3) for unbloody offerings. Wherever used in the N. T., it has reference to the ritual of the altar: e.g. Rom. xii. 1, Ph. ii. 17, iv. 18. The two words are together, in reversed order, in Ps. xl. 6, quoted in Heb. x. 5, 8. The psalmist's thought there passes from the specific to the general, denying that either one or other is desired by God. *To God:* most easily joined to the words immediately foregoing. For the mention of sacrifice recalls at once the deity to whom it is offered. *An odour of perfume:* as in Ph. iv. 18, where the gift from Philippi is said to be a sacrifice pleasant to God as perfume is fragrant to man.

3, 4. Another group of warnings against sin. *Fornication, uncleanness:* as in Gal. v. 19. Paul passes from the specific to the general, to which last he gives the widest latitude: *all uncleanness. Covetousness:* as in ch. iv. 19. By the conjunction *or* it is separated, as belonging to a different class, from the two foregoing sins. *As becomes saints:* their relation to God making it unfitting that the sins of heathenism should be *even named among* them. *Shamefulness:* a wide term including (Col. iii. 8) 'shameful speaking.' *Jesting:* literally quick versatility of speech which easily degenerates into evil. Since the last two prohibitions seem to relate only to trifles, Paul pauses to say that *foolish-speaking* and *jesting are not fitting.* Instead of such inappropriate mirth he proposes the gladness of *thanksgiving.* So Ph. iv. 6, Col. ii. 7, iv. 2.

5. A solemn assertion supporting the three prohibitions in v. 3. The word I have rendered *being-aware* denotes the process of *coming to know*, and is almost equal to *perceiving*. *Ye know this* that I am going to say, *perceiving that every fornicator etc.* The three sins are in the same order as in v. 3. On the last sin Paul lingers to assert again, as already in Col. iii. 5, that the *covetous* man is an *idolater*. *Has no inheritance in the kingdom :* close parallels in 1 Cor. vi. 9, 10, Gal. v. 21. *Of Christ and God :* climax, rising as ever with Paul from the Son to the Father. These last are here placed in closest relation. But we have no proof that they denote the same divine Person.

6. Further support of the above prohibitions. Paul warns his readers against some who will say that sin is a trifle : *let no one deceive you*. In a heathen city, and to converts from heathenism, persuasion to sin would most frequently come from heathens. And to such probably Paul chiefly refers. But his words are quite general. *Empty words :* mere sounds destitute of truth. Cp. '*empty* deception' in Col. ii. 8. A similar compound word in 1 Tim. vi. 20, 2 Tim. ii. 16. *For because etc. :* solemn confirmation of the foregoing, and proof that the *words* are *empty*. *Comes the anger of God :* word for word as in Col. iii. 6. *The sons of disobedience :* as in ch. ii. 2, and Col. iii. 6 where see note.

7. *Become not ;* courteously suggests that they were not such already. *Partakers-with them :* joined with them as sharers of their sin and of the anger of God which falls upon sinners. Same word in contrasted surroundings in ch. iii. 6.

8—10. *For ye were etc. :* an appeal to the readers' former life, supporting the foregoing dissuasive. This contrast of past and present is a genuine trait of Paul : cp. Rom. iii. 21, xi. 30, xvi. 26. 'Darkened in mind (ch. iv. 18) *ye were* yourselves *formerly* an embodiment of *darkness*.' Cp. 2 Cor. vi. 14. '*But now* the *light* which has illumined your path has transformed you into its own nature.' *In* the *Lord :* the change has come in virtue of their inward union with the Master. *Children of light.* Cp. 1 Th. v. 5, 'sons of light and sons of day ;' Lk. vii. 35, 'children of wisdom.' Contrast Eph. ii. 3, 'children of anger.' *Light* is a condition of sight and therefore of knowledge. In darkness we know not where we are going : 1 Jno. ii. 11. The Gospel gives light : for it reveals to us our own nature and our environment. And, to those who believe, it becomes the mother of a new nature : *children of light*. Moreover, since the light enters into them and becomes in some sense a part of themselves, they are themselves *light*. This lays upon them an obligation to choose such steps as are in harmony with the light which has transformed them. Similar thought in Rom. xiii. 13.

9. A parenthesis explaining and thus justifying the foregoing metaphorical exhortation. The Gospel, which to those who believe it is a ray of light, bears fruit, i.e. produces by the outworking of its own life good results: *fruit of the light.* See under Rom. i. 13. Cp. 'fruit of the Spirit' in Gal. v. 22. *Goodness :* practical beneficence, as in Gal. v. 22. *Righteousness :* conduct in agreement with the Law, as in Rom. xiv. 17. *Truth :* moral agreement with the eternal realities. In each of these directions and in every form of them, the light bears fruit. That the light works these good results is a reason why we should 'walk as children of the light.'

10. A participial clause collateral to, and supplementing, the exhortation of *v.* 8. 'Children of light' ought, in virtue of the new life they have received, ever to put to the proof, and thus find out, *what is well-pleasing to the Lord,* i.e. to their Master Christ. *Well-pleasing :* same word and thought in Col. iii. 20, Ph. iv. 18, 2 Cor. v. 9, Rom. xii. 1, 2, xiv. 18. *Proving :* same word and thought in Rom. xii. 2, Ph. i. 10. This putting to the proof will unmask the deception of empty words : *v.* 6.

11. Another exhortation, added to that in *v.* 8. *Partakers-with* others : same word in Ph. iv. 14; a cognate word in Ph. i. 7, Rom. xi. 17, 1 Cor. ix. 23. *The works . . . of darkness:* as in Rom. xiii. 12. These are *fruitless;* in marked contrast to 'the fruit of the light.' They produce no good result. Cp. Rom. vi. 21. *But rather even reprove :* something more than mere refusal to participate. *Reprove :* or *convict,* i.e. prove to be wrong. Same word in 1 Cor. xiv. 24, 1 Tim. v. 20, Tit. i. 9, 13, Lk. iii. 19, and especially Jno. iii. 20.

12. Justifies the foregoing by pointing to the need for reproof. *Secretly :* in conspicuous prominence. The secrecy of these sins makes more needful their public reproof. *Done:* more fully *being-done,* i.e. from time to time. These are sins so bad that *even to speak* of them is polluting, and therefore *shameful.* Paul suggests that, bad as is the outward conduct of the heathen, under the surface lie still worse sins which in their vileness pass description.

13. Another reason for reproving sin. Not only are there sins needing reproof but to reprove them is an appointed work of Christians. *All things :* all sorts of sin, as is proved by the word following, *when-they-are-reproved. Manifested :* set conspicuously before the eyes of others, in contrast to things 'done secretly : see under Rom. i. 19. Whenever a sin is proved to be such, the

reproof is caused by *the light* falling upon it and thus making its true character conspicuous. *For all that is* from day to day *manifested etc.:* proof of the foregoing. Every conspicuous object is in a true sense luminous. For it partakes the brightness which makes it conspicuous. And that conspicuous objects shine, proves that to reveal the nature of whatever is illumined is the specific work of light: *by the light* it *is manifested.* Now Christians are 'children of light.' Therefore the presence of a Christian among sinners ought to reveal to them their sin.

14. *For which cause* he (or some one) *says:* same form of quotation as in ch. iv. 8, Jas. iv. 6. That these two passages are express quotations from the O. T., suggests very strongly that the quotation before us was so intended. But no such passage is found. Nor is there anything in the O. T. which these words recall. On the other hand they give a complete and harmonious sense. In an ordinary document we should guess that in a moment of forgetfulness a passage from some other work was quoted as Holy Scripture. And perhaps this is the best explanation here. We may reverently suppose that the Spirit of inspiration, which even in this quotation guarded the Apostle from doctrinal error, did not think fit to protect him against this trifling oversight. See under Gal. iii. 18. Or possibly, without thinking of the author, Paul merely quotes a familiar passage from some author unknown to us.

For which cause: because to bring to light things hidden in darkness is a specific work of Christians. *Up, sleeper:* the sinner, who needs arousing from his deep sleep. A frequent metaphor, suggested by the metaphor of darkness: cp. Rom. xiii. 11, 1 Th. v. 6, 1 Pet. ii. 9. *Arise from the dead:* a still stronger metaphor. Notice the climax: *up, sleeper. . . . arise from the dead. Christ shall-give-light to-thee:* a motive for rising from the sleep of sin, viz. that light is waiting for the sleeper. And this is also, since Christians are a medium through which the light shines, a reason why (*v.* 11) they should reprove the sin which (*v.* 12) exists all around them.

15, 16. Further exhortations; after the parenthesis in *vv.* 12—14, which supports the concluding exhortation of *v.* 11. *Look then:* practical application of the teaching in *vv.* 12—14. *Carefully* or *accurately:* same word in 1 Th. v. 2, 'ye know accurately.' It suggests the need of extreme care in choosing our steps in life. *How ye walk;* recalls *v.* 8, '*walk* as children of light.' It is further expounded by *not as unwise but as wise.* This implies that Christian wisdom, which is a knowledge of that which is most worth knowing, is a practical guide in life. See under 1 Cor. ii 5. *Buying up the opportunity:* as in Col. iv. 5, in a very similar connection. It is parallel to *not as unwise etc.* as a further description of *how* Paul would have his readers *walk.* A reason for this last injunction is added: *because the days are evil.* Cp. Gen. xlvii. 9. *Evil* is in power. It is therefore important to seize every opportunity for good. In ch. vi. 13, 'the *evil* day' is a definite time of special peril,

17. *Because of this:* because evil around makes it needful to 'walk as wise men.' In view of his readers' peril, Paul points to a means of wisdom: *understanding what is the will of the Lord.* Not to use this means of divine guidance, would be *senseless. Do not become:* as in *v.* 7; cp. *v.* 1, iv. 32. Perhaps it was suggested, instead of the simpler words 'be not,' by a half-conscious remembrance that human character is ever developing, for good or bad. *Senseless:* a man without brains; a worse term than 'unwise.' *What is the will of the Lord:* close parallel to *v.* 10; cp. Acts xxi. 14. That the will of God must ever be the directive principle of human life, was ever present to the thought of Paul: Rom. xii. 2, Eph. i. 1, 5, 9, 11, Col. i. 9. The same honour he here gives to *the will of the Lord* Jesus Christ. He thus recognises the Crucified One as still his Master.

18. To the foregoing general precept Paul now adds a prohibition of a definite sin specially inconsistent with it. He thus illustrates the general principle, and looks at this sin in the light of it. *In which:* in being drunk with wine, the sin here prohibited. *Dissoluteness:* a reckless waste of money and of life itself. A typical example is the prodigal son, touching whom a cognate word is used in Lk. xv. 13, 'living dissolutely.' Paul says that in drunkenness is reckless waste of all we have and are.

Filled with the *Spirit:* every thought, purpose, word, act, prompted and controlled by the Holy Spirit. [The present imperative describes this all-pervading influence as ever going forth from the Spirit. The aorist in Acts ii. 4, iv. 8, 31, ix. 17, xiii. 9 describes a sudden and all-controlling impulse.] This salutary influence from above filling and raising man is an absolute antithesis to the destructive inspiration of strong drink. That both influences operate on man from within, justifies the somewhat strange contrast here. *With* the *Spirit:* literally *in* the *Spirit:* a form of speech chosen possibly because they whom the Holy Spirit fills live and move in Him as their life-giving environment. We obey this command when we claim by faith the influences of the Holy Spirit and surrender ourselves to His guidance.

19—21. Four participial clauses containing exhortations collateral to the foregoing exhortation, 'be filled with the Spirit,' and thus completing the contrast to 'be not drunk with wine.' *Speaking to yourselves etc.*: very close parallel to Col. iii. 16, where see note. With *psalms* and *songs* correspond respectively the cognate verbs *chanting* and *singing*. The second participial clause is parallel to the first. Paul first bids his readers speak in their songs *one to another;* and then bids them sing *to the Lord*. To Him they can and must sing in their *heart*, both in vocal praise and when their song is silent. *Giving thanks etc.*: a third co-ordinate participial clause still further defining what Paul desires in his readers. *Thanks always for all things*: a constant thought of Paul: so Col. iii. 17, a close parallel, i. 12, ii. 7, iv. 2, Eph. v. 4, i. 16. It specifies the contents of these songs *to the Lord*. And our *thanks* are *given in the name of Christ*, in acknowledgment that only through Him comes all real good; to *God* our *Father*, the ultimate source of blessing.

Grammatically, the three foregoing participial clauses describe accompaniments of being 'filled with the Spirit.' Actually, they describe its results. Instead of riotous songs stimulated by the wine cup, Paul desires the vocal and silent praise to God which the Holy Spirit ever prompts.

The last participial clause is the key-note of §§ 12-14. *Submitting*: as in Col. iii. 18. *One to another*: according to their various relations, as Paul now proceeds to expound. *Fear of Christ*: cp. 'the will of the Lord' in *v*. 17. It is another note of the majesty of Christ, and in no small degree a proof of His divinity.

REVIEW OF § 11. Without any marked order, but each thought suggesting that which follows, compactly yet clearly, Paul touches and illumines, in the light of the essential principles of the Gospel, many practical duties of life. He warns his readers against falsehood by reminding them that all men are members of one body and therefore have one interest, and that therefore nothing is to be gained but much lost by one man deceiving another. He gives a safe and easy guard and limit to anger: it must not continue to the morrow. The man who, in order to live in idleness, robs others must now work in order to help others who are in need. All evil talking is shut out by a precept that we are so to speak as to edify those who hear us. And all this is strengthened by reference to the Holy Spirit, the seal of our future deliverance, who observes all we say or do and is grieved by evil. All bitterness of temper or word must be laid aside: kindness and forbearance must take their place. For we are beloved children of God, and must therefore imitate our

Father and walk in the steps of Christ who so loved us as to give up Himself for our salvation.

All impurity and covetousness must be banished even from the lips of the sacred people: foolish talking must be superseded by thanksgiving. For, whatever men may say, sensuality, and covetousness which is a form of idolatry, will exclude their votaries from the kingdom of God. With those guilty of such sins, we must have no part. For, our life is altogether changed. Once darkness we are now children of light : and spiritual light produces, by the outworking of its own nature, moral excellence. Our only relation to the works of darkness must be reproof. For the hidden sins of heathenism need it. And light reveals, by its own nature, in their true colours objects otherwise hidden. We must therefore carefully and wisely choose our steps. Because the times are bad, we must embrace every opportunity of doing and saying good. This, i.e. to learn the will of Christ, will need all our intelligence. Paul warns against drunkenness, which ever leads to ruin. We need to be filled and stimulated not with wine but by the Spirit of God. His inspiration prompts, not the loud voice of revelry, but sacred song, sometimes inaudible but always heart-felt, and ever assuming the form of thanks to Christ. This will be accompanied by mutual subordination, a duty to be further discussed.

SECTION XII.

DIRECTIONS TO WIVES AND HUSBANDS.

CH. V. 22—33.

Wives, be subject *to your own husbands as to the Lord.* [23] *Because man is head of the woman, as also Christ* is *Head of the Church. He* is *Saviour of the Body.* [24] *Nevertheless, as the Church submits to Christ, so also the wives to the husbands in everything.*

[25] *Husbands, love your wives, as also Christ loved the Church and gave up Himself on its behalf,* [26] *that He might sanctify it, having cleansed it by the bath of water, with* the *word,* [27] *that He may Himself present to Himself the Church glorious not having spot or wrinkle or any of the suchlike things, but that it may be holy and blameless.* [28] *So ought the men to love their own wives as their own bodies. He that loves his own wife loves himself.* [29] *For no one ever hated his own flesh, but nourishes and cherishes it as also Christ*

does *the Church*. ³⁰ *Because we are members of His Body*. ³¹ "*For this cause, a man will leave father and mother and will be joined to his wife; and the two will become one flesh.*" (Gen. ii. 24.) ³² *This mystery is great. But I speak in regard to Christ and in regard to the Church.* ³³ *Nevertheless, also ye severally, let each one thus love his own wife, as himself; and the wife that she fear the husband.*

The implied general exhortation at the end of § 11, 'submitting yourselves one to another,' is now specialised in reference to the three most conspicuous relations of social life; in § 12 to wives and husbands, in § 13 to children and parents, in § 14 to slaves and masters. The same three relations are discussed in the same order in Col. iii. 18—iv. 1. But the discussion here is much more full and valuable; especially that of the first pair, which is developed under the influence of the dominant thought of this Epistle.

22—24. *The wives to their own husbands:* similar injunction to Col. iii. 18. Their *own* husbands: noting a peculiar and intimate relation. The words in italics, 'be subject' are supplied from the close of the foregoing sentence. *As to the Lord:* slightly different from 'as is fitting in the Lord' in Col. iii. 18. The wife must recognise that her position of subordination is ordained by Christ and that in bowing to her husband she does but submit to her Master in heaven. Thus the Gospel lays upon her a new obligation. But, as we shall see, by laying upon the husband a like obligation it gives to the wife new rights. *Because man is etc.:* a fact containing a reason for the foregoing injunction. *Head of the woman:* as in 1 Cor. xi. 3, a close parallel. The head and body are vitally united, and share the same nature. But the one is placed above the other to direct its action. Paul asserts that this is the relation of *man* to *the woman*. To this metaphor is added another similar metaphor which still further expounds the subjection of the woman to the man: *as also Christ* is *Head of the Church*. Same favourite metaphor in ch. i. 22, iv. 12, 16. Its frequency is explained by the ideal aspect of the Church which is the dominant thought of this Epistle.

He is *Saviour of the Body:* an important assertion thrown in, which practically limits the foregoing comparison. From the *head of the woman* the *Head of the Church* differs in that *HE* (very emphatic) is *Saviour of the Body*. This completes the foregoing metaphor by calling the Church *the Body* of Christ; and makes conspicuous a difference between the metaphors by an assertion about Christ and the Church quite inapplicable to the relation of man and woman. *The Body* of which *Christ* is Head, He has *Himself* rescued from bondage and death.

Nevertheless etc.; reasserts, in spite of the difference just mentioned, the primary injunction of *v.* 22. *In everything:* a subjection universal within the limit fixed by its aim, viz. *as to the Lord.* She must do nothing even in obedience to the husband which she cannot do for Christ.

25. *Husbands, love the wives:* word for word as in Col. iii. 19. *According as also etc.:* ground of this exhortation. If the woman's relation to the man resembles that of the Church to Christ, the love with which *Christ loved the Church* must be a model of man's love to his wife. This comparison is the more natural in Greek because the word *Church* is feminine. *And gave-up Himself on its* (or *her*) *behalf:* historic manifestation and proof of this pattern love. *Gave-up on-behalf-of:* same words in ch. v. 2, Gal. ii. 20. It is Christ's self-surrender to death.

In this verse and in Jno. iii. 16 we have two aspects, each supplementing the other, of the love which prompted the death of Christ. Since the purpose of salvation embraced the world, and since God brings to bear on every man an influence which unless resisted will lead him to salvation, Christ said to Nicodemus, in a general statement about the Gospel, that 'God so loved the world that He gave etc." But the eternal love of God foresaw all who would accept the Gospel and be finally saved. Consequently, this foreseen result of the gift of Christ may be spoken of as the aim of His self-surrender, and therefore as the object of the love which prompted it. Each of the saved can say He 'loved me and gave up Himself for me.' And the lost will know that their destruction was due, not to a limitation of God's love, but to their own rejection of His offered mercy.

26, 27. A digression expounding the moral aim of Christ's self-surrender. Cp. Tit. ii. 14. It is very appropriate in this exposition of Christian morality. *May-sanctify it:* subjective holiness, i.e. the actual and unreserved devotion and loyalty of the Church to Christ. For this is clearly implied in the words following. So the word *holy* in *v.* 27. This is here represented as an aim of the death of Christ. And rightly so: for without it there can be no full blessedness. And an intelligent purpose includes all means necessary to the end in view. In 1 Cor. i. 2, the same word denotes the objective holiness of all the people of God, i.e. His claim that they live only for Him. In this sense even the carnal Corinthian Christians were already 'sanctified.' Wherever sanctification means more than this, viz. the actual devotion which God claims, it is represented, not as attained, but as a divine purpose. So 1 Th. v. 23, Jno. xvii. 17 : cp. 1 Cor. vii. 34, 2 Cor. vii. 1. Since loyalty to God is ever the work of the Holy Spirit, since the gift of the Spirit implies pardon of sin, and since Christ died in order to harmonize the justification of believers with the justice of God and thus make it possible, Paul here asserts that ' Christ . . . gave up Himself *in order that He may sanctify*' the Church. See a close and important parallel in 2 Cor. v. 15, where we are taught that Christ died in order that we may live a life of devotion to Him.

Having-cleansed it *by the bath of water:* a necessary preliminary to the actual devotion to God which Christ purposes to work in His people. For all impurity is opposed to unreserved devotion to God, and must therefore be removed before subjective holiness can be realised. So Rom. vi. 11, 'dead to sin, but living for God.' Similarly, in symbolic ritual, the priests in the Temple washed themselves at the brazen laver before they approached the altar : Ex. xxx. 18—21. *Cleanse :* same word in 2 Cor. vii. 1, Tit. ii. 14, Heb. ix. 14, 1 Jno. i. 7, 9, Acts xv. 9 ; important parallels. It denotes removal of the stain which mars the moral beauty of sinners. *Bath :* same word in Tit. iii. 5, ' bath of the new birth ; ' and Sirach xxxi. 30, ' one who is baptized from a dead body and again touches it, what has he been profited by his bath ? ' in reference to ceremonial purification. It denotes, as does the English word *bath*, both the act of washing and the vessel in which we wash. In view of these two other passages and of Acts xxii. 16, we can hardly doubt that Paul refers here to Baptism. And such reference presents no difficulty. As commanded by Christ, Baptism was binding on all who had not received it and who sought deliverance from the stain of sin ; and was therefore in this sense a condition and instrument of spiritual purification. This does not imply any magical efficacy in the outward rite, but only its divine obligation in all ordinary cases. In Paul's day, the peril frequently involved in outwardly confessing Christ made this obligation a most serious element in the way of salvation. Hence the language of these three passages.

This reference to Baptism was probably suggested by the metaphor in *v.* 27. Paul silently reminds his readers that Baptism, which to many of them had been so perilous, was but the bride's bath on the eve of marriage, in their case a necessary precursor of the joy of eternal union with the great King.

With the *word:* joined most naturally to *that He may sanctify it.* For the intervening words give a complete sense, and describe a necessary preliminary to the sanctification which Christ designs. Having noted this preliminary, Paul adds the instrument of sanctification, viz. the *word* of the Gospel, God's chosen instrument of salvation. Cp. Jno. xvii. 17, 'sanctify them in the truth. Thy word is truth.' Same word, in the singular number as here, and referring to the Gospel, in ch. vi. 17, Rom. x. 8, 17, Heb. vi. 5, 1 Pet. i. 25. In eternity the Son of God purposed to draw men, *by a* spoken *word*, viz. the Gospel, to bow to God with unreserved and joyous devotion. Similarly, by a '*word* of God' the world was made: Heb. xi. 3.

27. Further and ultimate aim of the purpose described in v. 26. It is clothed in a not unfrequent metaphor: 2 Cor. xi. 2, Rev. xix. 7, 9, xxi. 9, Jno. iii. 29, Mt. xxv. 1. *Present:* same word in Col. i. 22, 28, Rom. vi. 13, 16, 19, xii. 1; and, in the same connection as here, 2 Cor. xi. 2. *Himself to Himself:* emphatic assertion that the Giver and Receiver are the same. For the Bride has been rescued and purified by the self-surrender of the Bridegroom. *Glorious:* clothed in splendour exciting universal admiration; cp. Rev. xxi. 11, 'having the glory of God.' Christ designs *the Church* to be *glorious*, and as such to be His own for ever. *Spot:* any blemish. *Wrinkle:* a mark of decay. Maintaining his metaphor, Paul describes moral imperfections as bodily blemishes. *But that it may be etc.;* completes the description of the glorious Church. *Holy:* subjectively: for, objectively, as claimed by God, Paul's readers were (ch. i. 1) already holy. This word keeps before us the subjective sanctification of v. 26. Instead of *having spot or wrinkle*, Christ designs *the Church* to be *holy and blameless:* same words together in the same connection in ch. i. 4. They are added in the form of a purpose in order to throw emphasis on the holiness and blamelessness of the Church as specially designed by Christ.

Notice that *present to Himself* corresponds to *sanctify* and *holy:* for that is holy which is devoted to God. *Not having spot or wrinkle* corresponds, as a negative element implied in holiness, to *cleanse* and *blameless*.

28a. Application of the foregoing metaphor to the matter in hand, viz. the duty of husbands to love their wives. *In this way:* 'according as Christ loved the Church.' *As their own bodies:* i.e. looking upon their wives as being their own flesh and blood. These words link together two closely related metaphors, viz. the Church as the Body (v. 23) and as the Bride (v. 27) of Christ; and brings them to bear, thus linked together, upon the relation of husband and wife.

28b—30. These verses develop an argument lying in 'as their own bodies.' Husband and wife have one interest. Therefore, affection towards the wife brings proportionate gain to the husband. In this sense, *he that loves his own wife, loves himself.* This argument, v. 29 further supports. Paul asserted in v. 25 that a man's relation to his wife is like that of Christ to the Church. And he has frequently taught that the Church is the Body of Christ. If so, Christ's love to the Church is like a man's love to his own body. This latter love Paul declares to be universal, and further describes. *His own flesh :* his body, in view of its material constitution, which has special needs and demands special care. *Nourishes :* finds the food needful for its health and development. *Cherishes :* 1 Th. ii. 8: keeps warm, as a hen her chickens. Every one feeds his own body and protects it from cold. And as every one acts towards his own body so *Christ* acts towards *the Church.* This treatment of us by Christ is illustrated by a restatement of the fact that *we are members of His Body.*

31, 32. The words of Gen. ii. 24 (almost word for word from the LXX.) taken up by Paul and woven into his argument about the relation of Christ to the Church as a pattern to husbands and wives. Same quotation in Mt. xix. 5, Mk. x. 7, 8. Adam asserts that because woman is derived from man the relation of husband and wife is the closest of human relationships. By appropriating these words, Paul brings them to bear on the argument before him. And they prove clearly that (v. 28) to love one's wife is to love oneself. For they assert that husband and wife are one flesh. This plain reference of the quotation makes it needless to seek in it an assertion about Christ. And certainly the Son of Mary did not *leave His mother* in order to be united to the Church. *Because of this :* because woman was taken out of man, as stated in Gen. ii. 23. It is a part of the quotation. We therefore need not assume a special reference to v. 30. *A man will leave :* whenever in all generations a man marries. *The two shall become one flesh :* the chief point in the quotation. So close is the marriage relation that it seems in some sense to suspend the distinction of personality. Now, whatever is done to one part of a living body affects the whole. Consequently, kindness to one's wife is kindness to oneself.

This quotation casts light upon the assertion in v. 23 that 'man is head of the woman.' The head and body are one flesh, so closely and vitally united that injury or benefit done to one is done to the other. Yet the head directs and the body obeys. All this is true both of man and woman and of Christ and the Church. Of each of these relationships the human body is a metaphor. Even Christ and the Church are *one flesh:* for both are human. But Christ directs; and the Church obeys. The human body is thus a pattern of two important relations, viz. of husband and wife and of Christ and the Church. It is therefore a link uniting these relations, and making each a pattern of the other. This double metaphor is not found elsewhere. And it greatly strengthens the obligations here enforced. The wife is bound to obey her husband, as the Church, of which she is a member, obeys Christ. The husband is bound to love his wife, as Christ loved the Church. To fail in this is, as this quotation proves, to act as a man would who did not care for his own body. We have thus a double motive for marital love, the example of Christ and the instinct of self-preservation.

32. *This mystery:* (same word in Rom. xi. 25:) the marriage relation described in the foregoing quotation. See note under 1 Cor. iii. 4. Under the marriage relation lies secret teaching known only to those taught by God. *But I speak:* Paul's own use here of this quotation as distinguished from the hidden truth underlying marriage. *With reference to Christ and with reference to the Church:* these represented as distinct objects of thought. While quoting Genesis, Paul is thinking not so much of man and woman as of Christ and the Church. In other words, under the specific matter in hand lie broader truths. Even marriage, so important in itself, receives greater importance from being a visible setting forth of the relation of Christ to the Church.

It is needless to discuss here whether marriage is a sacrament: for this would involve a definition of the term. Certainly, marriage cannot be put on a level with the two rites ordained by Christ for all His servants. But Paul's teaching here implies clearly its unchangeable sacredness. And this felt sacredness has ever found expression in acts of worship accompanying the marriage ceremony. Callous must they be who can enter the solemn obligations of wedlock without recognising its divine sanction and sacred duties.

33. *Nevertheless:* or, more fully, 'I say nothing *except* this one thing.' It breaks off the discourse to insist on the one thing needful. *Ye severally:* transition from a mystery touching Christ and the Church to readers of this Epistle, taken *one by one. Thus love:* i.e. in the manner, and for the reasons, just expounded. *As himself:* 'as their own bodies' in *v.* 28. *And the wife* must remember that *the husband* has been set over her by Christ, and that therefore insubordination to him is disobedience to Christ. An obligation so solemn may well evoke her *fear.* So careful is Paul to balance the duty of the husband by that of the wife.

REVIEW. At the close of § 11 Paul bids his readers to submit one to another. He then discusses in order three very special kinds of submission. Of these, the first and noblest and most significant is that of the wife to her husband. The Apostle bids her render to him a reverence similar to that which she pays to her Master in heaven; and supports this by asserting a similarity between the marriage relation and that of the Church to Christ. This similarity he describes by comparing each of these relations to that of the head and members of a human body; but points out the limits of his comparison by reminding us that the Head of the Church is also its Saviour. He concludes his injunction to the wife by urging her to take as her pattern the submission of the Church to Christ.

If Paul speaks first of the duties of the wife, he finds it needful to linger longer over those of the husband. Just as the wife must look on the Church's submission to Christ as a pattern of her own submission to her husband, so the husband is bound to take Christ's love to the Church, manifested in His death, as a pattern for his own love to his wife. Paul then leaves for a moment the duty of husbands to describe, in language borrowed from the metaphor he is here using, the purpose of Christ's self-sacrifice for the Church, viz. to present to Himself the Church as His loyal and spotless bride. The purity needed in the bride of Christ recalls the baptismal water through which these Asiatic Christians had passed, and which was designed to be the entrance into a spotless life. Going back to the subject specially in hand, Paul bids husbands to love their wives like Christ loved the Church, to love them even as they love their own bodies. These last words introduce another motive for love to the wife, a motive which is at once more fully developed. To love one's wife, is to love himself: and all are careful to feed and protect their own bodies. Since we are members of the Body of Christ, this care for our own body has a divine counterpart in Christ's kindness to the Church. The double analogy involved in this argument, viz. that the human body consisting of head and members has one counterpart in the relation of husband and wife and another spiritual counterpart in the relation of Christ to the Church, Paul supports by a quotation from Genesis which asserts that husband and wife are one flesh as though parts of one living body. He adds that in this quotation he is referring to Christ and the Church. He thus finds in the Bible strong support for his second motive for love to the wife, viz. that in loving her the husband is loving himself. The Apostle concludes by repeating, and placing side by side, the mutual duties of husband and wife.

SEC. 13.] *EPHESIANS* VI. 1—4. 365

This section is throughout characteristic of Paul. As in his earlier Epistles the duties of to-day are enforced by reference to broad and abiding principles. Thus, as ever with him, little details of common life are raised into dignity. And these details are made an occasion of expounding broad principles, which thus receive important practical illustration. The O. T. quotation finds for the relation of the Church to Christ an important and most instructive counterpart in the original constitution of our race. We notice also, as before, Paul's fairness. While defending the rights of the weaker, he does not forget the obligations involved in those rights.

SECTION XIII.
DIRECTIONS TO CHILDREN AND PARENTS.
CH. VI. 1—4.

Children, obey your parents in the *Lord. For this is just.* "² *Honour thy father and mother;"* (*which is the first commandment with promise;*) "³ *that it may be well with thee, and that thou mayest be long-living upon the earth."*

⁴ *And, ye fathers, provoke not your children, but nurture them in* the *discipline and admonition of the Lord.*

1. *Children, obey your parents:* nearly word for word as in Col. iii. 20. *In* the *Lord:* as in Col. iii. 20. *Just:* in harmony with the eternal principles of right which found embodiment in the Law of God. Same word in same sense in Col. iv. 1, Ph. i. 7, iv. 8, etc.

The phrase *in* the *Lord* affords no proof or presumption, especially in the absence of other reliable indications, that infant children were baptized in Paul's day. For doubtless many who might fairly be called *children* had by their own faith and confession entered the Church. It was therefore suitable that to them directions should be given. Moreover the close and peculiar relation of children to their parents places all children of Christian parents, from the earliest days of opening consciousness, in a peculiar and close relation to the Church of which their parents are members. Paul therefore writes to them. His words prove that he looked upon them as part of the flock for which he had to care. This intimate relation found, in the early Church, legitimate and suitable expression in the administration of Baptism to infants. That this formal recognition of the relation of infants to the New Covenant dates from the early morning of the Church, is made certain by the literature of a later day. But we have no sure proof that it was as early as this Epistle. Certainly this passage is easily explained without assuming it.

With his usual careful study of the O. T. Paul notices that in the Decalogue the fifth commandment differs from the rest in being supported by a definite promise. So were several later commands: e.g. Dt. xxiv. 19, xxv. 15. But of the many and various commands given to Moses this is the *first commandment* which has attached to it a definite *promise*. At the close of the second commandment there is a virtual and implied promise. But it is only general, and is not specially attached to this one command. The definite promise in the fifth commandment raises it into conspicuous prominence. To this prominence Paul points when enforcing upon children the duty of obedience.

After this digression, which explains the significance of what follows, Paul goes on to quote the exact words of the ancient promise. *That it may be well with thee etc.:* almost word for word from Ex. xx. 12, except that the concluding words 'which the Lord thy God gives thee' are omitted. This promise is very frequent in Deuteronomy, referring indisputably to the gift of the land of Canaan: ch. iv. 40, v. 33, vi. 2, 3, xi. 8—12, etc. This reference is quite inapplicable to Paul's Gentile readers at Ephesus. By omitting these words he makes the promise applicable to all persons in all lands. And this is the simplest explanation of the omission. The Greek word rendered *earth* denotes both a particular country, viz. in Ex. xx. 12 Canaan, or the whole world consisting of many countries. This latter more general meaning is given to it here by the omission of the defining words 'which the Lord gives thee.' The original promise may refer either to the long life of individuals or to the long continuance of the nation. As quoted by Paul, it can refer only to individuals. But this ancient promise cannot be appealed to as absolute now to all children who honour parents. For the New Covenant promises blessing for this life only indirectly, and under various conditions and limitations. The promise is here quoted chiefly to remind the readers of the special honour given to this command by the promise attached to it. This honour marks the abiding importance of this universal precept.

4. *And, ye fathers:* to the duty of the weaker, Paul adds as before the obligation of the stronger. So Col. iii. 21. *Provoke:* move to anger by word or act. *Nurture:* same word as in ch. v. 29. It denotes here, as the following words prove, not material food, but

the care needful for moral and spiritual growth. *Discipline:* derived from the word *boy,* and denotes all that pertains to the training of a boy: a cognate word in Acts vii. 22, xxii. 3. The same cognate word is found in Lk. xxiii. 16, 22 in the simpler sense of punishment. This suggests that the idea of punishment was often associated with the word : so does the same or cognate word in 1 Cor. xi. 32, 2 Cor. vi. 9, 1 Tim. i. 20, Rev. iii. 19, Heb. xii. 5—10. We may understand it here to mean a training which includes punishment when needful. *Admonition:* same word in 1 Cor. x. 11, Tit. iii. 10: a cognate word in Col. i. 28, iii. 16, and 1 Cor. iv. 14 where see note. Perhaps *discipline* refers rather to the father's firm hand ; *admonition* to his faithful voice.

SECTION XIV.

DIRECTIONS TO SERVANTS AND MASTERS.

CH. VI. 5—9.

Servants, obey them that are masters according to flesh, with fear and trembling, in singleness of heart as to Christ; ⁶ *not by way of eye-service as men-pleasers, but as servants of Christ, doing the will of God from the heart;* ⁷ *with good-will doing service, as for the Lord and not for men;* ⁸ *knowing that, whatever good thing each one does, this he will receive from the Lord, whether he be a servant or a free man.*

⁹ *And, ye masters, do the same things to them, forbearing threatening, knowing that the Lord both of them and of you is in heaven ; and there is no respect of persons with Him.*

Verse 5 contains a general precept for slaves. This is further expounded in *vv.* 6, 7 ; and is supported in *v.* 8 by a broad principle pertaining alike to slaves and freemen.

Servants, (or *slaves,*) *obey your lords according to flesh:* word for word as in Col. iii. 22 except that 'in all things' is omitted here. *Fear and trembling:* as in Ph. ii. 12. It is a counterpart of 'fearing the Lord' in Col. iii. 22; and describes in strong language an anxious desire to do right and a consciousness of the spiritual peril of disobedience. *In singleness of your heart:* almost word for word as in Col. iii. 22. There may be an apparent fear arising from duplicity of heart. *As for Christ:* in conspicuous contrast to *the lords according to flesh.* The slave must look upon obedience to his earthly master *as* obedience rendered *to Christ.*

6, 7. Exposition, negative and positive, of what is involved in 'as to Christ.' *By-way-of eye-service:* taking as their principle of action a *service* aiming only at the *eye* of a human lord. Slightly different in form from 'with *eye-service*' in Col. iii. 22. *As servants of Christ:* positive exposition, after the negative exposition just given, of the words ' as to Christ' in *v.* 5. *As servants of Christ,* they are *doing the will of God:* for every command and purpose of Christ is from God and for God. *From the heart:* as in Col. iii. 23. *With good-will :* parallel with *from* the *heart,* adding to it the idea of gladness. While *serving* earthly masters, they do so gladly : for they look upon their service *as for the Lord* Jesus Christ, *and not for men.* They do the bidding of men, but their real aim is to please a Master in heaven.

8. A great and broad truth underlying and supporting the specific direction just given and expounded. A close parallel in Col. iii. 24. From Christ, the real Master, there will be reward corresponding exactly to the work done, whether by a Christian *slave* or a Christian *freeman.*

9. *And ye masters* or *lords :* like 'and ye fathers' in *v.* 4. To the precepts for slaves is now added a precept for masters. So Col. iv. 1. *The same things do ye to them:* 'treat the slave on the principle just expounded for his treatment of you.' *Threatening,* or literally *the threatening :* a common fault of masters. For it is easier to threaten than to punish. *Threatening* is often an empty and irritating assertion of authority. *Knowing that etc. :* as in Col. iv. 1. The action, as of the slave, so of the master, must be guided by knowledge. *Both of them and of you :* emphatic. Master and slave are put side by side as servants of *the* one *Master in* the *heavens.* So Col. iv. 1. *Respect-of-persons :* as in Col. iv. 25. *With Him :* literally *in His presence.* Before the judgment seat of Christ in heaven respect of appearances has no place. Close parallel in Rom. ii. 11.

Speaking to slaves, Paul reminds them that their masters are such only in reference to the outward and bodily life. He nevertheless bids the slave to obey his lord, with anxious care to do right, and with a pure motive, looking upon his obedience as really paid to Christ Such service will not be designed merely to catch the eye or to please men. It will be a service of Christ, doing God's will heartily and gladly, as work done for Christ and not for men. This exhortation Paul supports by the universal principle that every good thing, by whomever done, will be rewarded by Christ.

Masters have their duties as well as slaves, duties based on the

SEC. 15.] EPHESIANS VI. 10—17.   369

same broad principles. Especially must they avoid threatening, a common fault of the stronger party. This will be easily avoided by those who believe that both Master and servant stand before an impartial Master in heaven.

SECTION XV.
THE CHRISTIAN WARFARE.
CH. VI. 10—17.

Henceforth, be powerful in the *Lord, and in the might of His strength.* ¹¹ *Put on the panoply of God, that ye may be able to stand against the wiles of the devil.* ¹² *Because to us the wrestling is not with blood and flesh, but with the principalities, with the authorities, with the world-rulers of this darkness, with the spiritual things of wickedness in the heavenly places.* ¹³ *Because of this take up the panoply of God, in order that ye may be able to withstand in the evil day, and having accomplished all things to stand.* ¹⁴ *Stand then, having girded your loins with truth, and having put on the breastplate of righteousness,* ¹⁵ *and having shod your feet with a preparation of the Gospel of peace;* ¹⁶ *amid all taking up the shield of faith, with which ye will be able to quench all the burning darts of the wicked one:* ¹⁷ *and take the helmet of salvation; and the sword of the Spirit, which is God's word.*

10. *Henceforth* or *the rest,* i.e. all that remains to be said. Same words, in another case, in Gal. vi. 17, introducing as here a final exhortation. *Be-made-powerful:* i.e. day by day, for each day's work and fight. Same word in Ph. iv. 13, a close parallel. *In* the *Lord:* in Christ our Master, the encompassing element from which we daily draw power. Apart from Him we can do nothing : Jno. xv. 5. Paul bids his readers accept the power which dwells in Christ and is obtained by inward union with Him. *The might of His strength:* same words in ch. i. 19, (where see note,) describing the might of God. While bidding his readers receive power in Christ, Paul remembers the infinite strength of Christ, capable of controlling and crushing all hostile power ; and points to this omnipotence as the source of the needed power. Cp. ch. iii. 16, 'be strengthened with power.' Both the personality of Christ and His infinite might are the surrounding element of Christian strength. Cp. 1 Jno. iv. 16, 'He that dwells in love dwells in God.'

24

11. A second exhortation, pointing to a means of strength and giving a motive for using it. *Put-on:* same word and sense in Rom. xiii. 14, in the same sense of putting on weapons. *Panoply:* an English form of the Greek word here used, which denotes an entire and full suit of armour and weapons. Same word in Wisdom v. 18, 'He shall take His zeal as a panoply;' Judith xiv. 3, 'having taken up their panoplies;' 2 Macc. iii. 25, 'a golden panoply.' This *panoply* is described in detail in *vv.* 14—17. It is the entire provision *of God* to protect His servants and to arm them for the battle of life. All this, Paul bids his readers appropriate to themselves.

That ye may etc.: purpose of, and motive for, *putting on the panoply of God. Stand:* maintain your Christian position. It is the opposite of falling or fleeing. Same word and sense in Rom. v. 2, xi. 20, 1 Cor. x. 12, xv. 1, 2 Cor. i. 24. *Able to stand;* suggests the difficulty of holding our own in the Christian fight. *Wiles:* same word and sense in ch. iv. 14, 'wiles of error.' *The devil:* an English form of a Greek word meaning slanderer, and so used in 1 Tim. iii. 11, 2 Tim. iii. 3, Tit. ii. 3. The same word is used by the LXX., e.g. 1 Chr. xxi. 1, Job i. 6, 7, 9, 12, as a rendering of *Satan,* a Hebrew word meaning 'opponent.' In other places, the LXX. merely reproduces the Hebrew word Satan, as in 1 Kgs. xi. 14, 23, where it is simply a human opponent. The Hebrew form is found in Rom. xvi. 20, 1 Cor. v. 5, vii. 5, 2 Cor. ii. 11, xi. 14. In the N. T. the two words are practically equivalent as a proper name of the great enemy of God and man. His weapon is deception; and with this he seeks to overthrow and put to flight the soldiers of the cross. In order that we may maintain our ground, Paul bids us *put on the panoply of God.*

12. A tremendous fact supporting the motive just given. As usual with Paul, the fact is stated, first negatively, then positively: *not with . . . but with. Wrestling:* a technical term of the Greek athletic contests. So Homer *Iliad* bk. xxiii. 635. It was probably suggested here by the word 'stand.' For the wrestler's work is to maintain his position and to throw down his adversary. And it is a most graphic picture of the Christian life. For, unlike military conflict, in wrestling each one contends alone against a personal antagonist, and can gain the victory only by intense personal effort and watchfulness. This suitability of the word led Paul to forsake for a moment the military metaphor involved in the word 'panoply,' to which he returns in *v.* 13, and to borrow another metaphor from the Greek athletic festivals. *With blood and flesh:* so 'flesh and blood' in 1 Cor. xv. 50, Gal. i. 16. It denotes mankind as limited by the

constitution of the human body. The Christian struggle is not against persons so limited. This is true even when we have resolute human opponents. For these are but instruments of unseen and more tremendous foes.

But with . . . with . . . with . . . with: graphic description of the real enemies. *The principalities . . . the authorities:* same words in same order in ch. i. 21, iii. 10, Col. i. 16, ii. 10, 15, denoting in each case ranks of superhuman beings. Here the context implies various ranks of fallen angels. Possibly, as suggested under Col. i. 16, *the principalities* were the highest rank; and *the authorities* an order exercising sway over men or angels or natural forces. This last is also suggested by the term *world-rulers* which describes the realm over which they rule. Throughout the world they reign supreme. And they belong to *this darkness,* to the present state of ignorance, the moral and intellectual night which hides from the view of the children of this world their impurity and their peril. The *spiritual-things* or powers: the Greek neuter including persons and things, as in Col. i. 16 and elsewhere frequently. *Of evil* or *wickedness:* a characterizing quality of these spiritual enemies.

In the heavenly places: same words in ch. i. 3, 20, ii. 6, iii. 10; in each case in a local sense, denoting superhuman abodes. And so probably here. It describes the superhuman abode of the fallen angels, already described in ch. ii. 2 as 'the air.' This locality agrees with their nature. They are above men and below the throne of God. It forms a climax in Paul's description of his readers' enemies. They have to struggle not against men like themselves limited by the weakness of bodily life, but against the various ranks of angels, against the lords who rule over the darkness which envelops the present world, against spiritual beings whose nature is bad and whose home is in realms far above the abodes of men. The frequent use of the first two terms of this series and in the order here given suggests that they denote definite classes of angels. All else is uncertain. Possibly the term *world-rulers* is a fuller description of *the principalities and authorities.* And the last term is evidently a description of all the spiritual foes with which the Christian has to contend. If therefore we take the first two terms as describing two classes, the third and fourth terms are probably further descriptions of the same superhuman antagonists.

Although Paul often speaks of the Christian life as a conflict, only here does he name the opponent. In 1 Jno. v. 4, 5, the enemy to be conquered is called 'the world.' This calls attention to the outward and visible form, and the multiplicity, of the foes arrayed against us. In 1 Jno. iv. 4, the power of this multiform antagonist is traced to one animating and personal principle. In 2 Cor. iv. 4, 'the God of this age' proves his hostility by blinding 'those who believe not.' And the passage before us speaks of various superhuman powers acting under direction of one supreme foe.

13. After the reason given in *v.* 12, Paul repeats the exhortation of *v.* 11. He then adds, in the form of a purpose, a motive : *that ye may be able etc.* It is parallel to a similar purpose in *v.* 11. The repetition emphasises our need for weapons and armour in order to maintain our position. *Withstand:* to hold one's own against another : same word in Gal. ii. 11, Jas. iv. 7, 1 Pet. v. 9. *Evil:* as in ch. v. 16, 'because the days are evil.' But here *the evil day* is spoken of as future. Yet there is nothing to suggest the revelation of 'the lawless one' mentioned in 2 Th. ii. 8. Probably Paul thinks of the day of severe trial which comes sooner or later to every soldier of Christ. So certain is this trial that to his thought it becomes definite as *the evil day*. These words correspond to 'against the wiles of the devil' in *v.* 11. But here Paul mentions the day of battle; there, the enemy with whom we fight. *Having-accomplished* or *worked-out:* same word in Ph. ii. 12, Rom. vii. 18, xv. 18. *All things:* i.e. needful for victory.

14—17. Specification of armour and weapons included in 'the panoply of God.' *Stand then:* an exhortation summing up the foregoing. It keeps before us an idea prominent in *v.* 11, and still more so in *v.* 13, viz. the need for immoveable firmness in face of foes who would put us to flight or trample us under foot. Notice that the word *stand* at the end of *v.* 13 notes a position still held when the battle is over. It is therefore represented as a goal kept in view. The same word here refers to a position to be maintained now. We must stand now in order that we may stand then.

The Christian armament. *Having-girded . . . having-put-on . . . having-shod:* preliminaries needful in order to maintain our position. Cp. Isa. xi. 5, 'having girded his loins with righteousness.' To gird himself, was the soldier's first preparation for battle. Only then could he put on his weapons. The Christian's girdle is *truth:* i.e. a subjective conception corresponding with the eternal realities. See under Rom. i. 18. It is the absolute opposite of the error of heathenism. Without such hold of eternal truth, the Christian lacks all compactness of character and is like a soldier going into battle with ungirt loins. *Breastplate:* covering the vital parts of the body. *Righteousness:* as in ch. iv. 24, v. 9. Same words in Isa. lix. 17 'He put on *righteousness* as a *breastplate*.' Without strict uprightness, the Christian is like a soldier whose breast is unprotected. His conceptions must agree with the eternal realities, and his conduct with the eternal law of right. *The Gospel of peace:* cp. Isa. lii. 7 'How beautiful . . . the feet of him that brings good tidings, that publishes peace.' *Readiness:* ever prepared for the Christian fight. This readiness comes from *the Gospel of peace,* i.e. from the announcement as good news that to us in midst of conflict there is peace. Just as the *shod foot* is ready at once to meet the enemy, so they who have heard and grasped *the Gospel of peace* are *in readiness* for any conflict which may await them. That they are ready and eager to proclaim the Gospel, is only a part of the more general readiness mentioned here.

16. Another participial clause somewhat separated from those foregoing and noting a fourth preliminary needful for Christian stability. *Having-taken-up:* parallel with 'having-girded etc.' Same word in *v.* 13. *Shield:* large Roman shield some four feet by two and a half, used by heavily armed troops. It was usually of wood covered with leather. *Faith:* belief of the Gospel, the unique condition of salvation. It saves us from both the guilt and power of sin, as being the one condition of union with Christ. *Burning darts:* arrows with affixed torches, used to set fire to ships or towns. So Octavius used against the ships of Antony ' fire-bearing darts;' Dio Cassius bk. l. 34. *The evil one:* same word as in *vv.* 12, 13. Close parallels in 2 Th. iii. 3, Mt. xiii. 19, 1 Jno. ii. 13f, v. 18f. It is equivalent here to 'the devil' in *v.* 11. The evil thoughts which he suggests are like *burning darts:* for they tend to kindle strange fire in the hearts of men. But they cannot injure those 'guarded in the power of God through *faith:*' 1 Pet. i. 5. Since faith is thus a complete protection, it is here called a *shield able to quench all the burning darts* cast against it. Paul thus teaches the absolute safety of those who believe. *Ye shall be able:* in every future attack.

17. Two more details of the Christian armour. But, instead of participles as before, these are added in the imperative mood as separate exhortations. *Helmet of salvation :* same words in Isa. lix. 17. [This accounts probably for the peculiar form of the word *salvation,* a form not used elsewhere by Paul but found in Lk. ii. 30, iii. 6.] *Salvation:* in its widest sense, viz. present deliverance from sin to be consummated in eternity by complete deliverance from every kind of evil. Such *salvation* is a *helmet* covering our heads from what would otherwise be fatal blows. Cp. 1 Th. v. 8, 'put on . . . as a helmet, hope of salvation.'

Sword: as in Rom. viii. 35, xiii. 4, Acts xvi. 27. The one weapon of attack here mentioned. *Of the Spirit:* either as given by the Spirit, like 'panoply of God;' or used by the Spirit. These senses here almost coincide. *Word of God:* same words in Heb. xi. 3. Cp. '*word of* Christ' in Rom. x. 17. It can be no other than the Gospel, the mighty voice of God raising into new life those who were spiritually dead. The word preached is a *sword:* for, armed with it, the servants of Christ attack and overturn the kingdom of darkness and set free its captives. It is put into their hands by *the Spirit* of God. For, under His influence were spoken (Acts i. 2) even the words of Jesus. And He is with the preacher, making His word to be a sharp sword in the hearts of those who hear.

Such is Paul's description of the enemy with whom the Christian has to fight and of the armament needed for victory. Our foes are both one and many; and our real foes are unseen and superhuman. They consist of successive ranks of evil angels ruling from their lofty abode the material world around us, and acting under direction of one guileful chief. Well may the time of their most severe attack be called 'the evil day.' Paul bids his readers hold their own in face of these tremendous foes. And, that they may do this, he bids them appropriate the whole equipment provided for them by God. First of all, the soldier must gird himself, for attack or defence; then put on his breastplate covering the chief part of his body, and his sandals so as to be ready at a moment's notice to march against the enemy. For still further protection, he must take up and carry the great shield; and with his right hand put on the helmet and grasp his sword.

Paul mentions only one weapon of attack but several pieces of defensive armour, because his chief thought is to encourage his readers to maintain their position against the onslaught of tremendous foes. To this end they need knowledge of the eternal realities, strict integrity, a readiness for every emergency prompted by the glad tidings of peace, firm faith, actual experience of salvation borne triumphantly aloft, and in their lips the recorded words of God to man.

SECTION XVI.
A REQUEST FOR PRAYER.

CH. VI. 18—20.

With all prayer and supplication praying at every season in the *Spirit, and watching for this with all perseverance and supplication for all the saints;* [19]*and on my behalf, in order that to me may be given utterance, in opening my mouth, with boldness to make known the mystery of the Gospel,* [20]*for which I am an ambassador in a chain, that in it I may speak boldly, as I must needs speak.*

Now come participial clauses containing virtually another exhortation, a collateral addition to those foregoing. In *v.* 14 Paul bade his readers stand firm, and that they might do this bade them put on the armament provided by God. The details are added, at first in the form of past participles, 'having girded' etc. But, as Paul enumerates them he passes unconsciously to direct exhortation in the imperative mood. Now follow two present participles noting, not preliminaries, but accompaniments of the original exhortation. It is best to join these participles to the dominant exhortation of § 15, 'stand then,' rather than to the subordinate exhortation, 'take the helmet,' which is a mere detail. Paul bids his readers to maintain their position in face of all their foes; and while doing this to pray for all the saints (*v.* 18) and (*vv.* 19, 20) for himself.

18. *With* or *by-means-of:* using prayer as a means of obtaining blessing. *Prayer and supplication:* as in Ph. iv. 6. In *every* way they must approach God in *prayer,* and must make *petition* for definite benefits. *In every season:* same words in similar connection in Lk. xxi. 36. *In* the *Spirit:* prayers prompted by Him. So Rom. viii. 15, 'in whom we cry, Abba, Father.'

And watching for etc.: a second participial clause, adding further details. *Watching:* as in Col. iv. 2, 1 Cor. xvi. 13. For successful prayer, we must keep wide awake, i.e. with our faculties in full exercise. And this must be accompanied by unlimited *perseverance:* cognate to a word in Col. iv. 2, Rom. xii. 12. This suggests that for a continual exercise of our faculties in prayer every kind of sustained effort is needful, and bids us make the effort. *Petition:* as above. Our watchfulness must be accompanied both by sustained effort and by definite request for definite blessing. ' *Touching all the saints:* cp. ch. v. 3. It is best to understand the first participial clause in this verse as referring to prayer in general; and the second as going on to speak specifically of prayer for our fellow-Christians.

19. *And on my behalf:* a particular request for prayer, added to the foregoing more general request. *That to me may be given etc.:* purpose and contents of the desired prayer. It expounds *on my behalf*. *Utterance*, or *word:* as in 1 Cor. i. 5. *In opening my mouth*, or *when I open my mouth:* same phrase in 2 Cor. vi. 11. *Boldness:* unreserved speech, as in 2 Cor. iii. 12. Paul asks his readers to pray that whenever he begins to speak God will give him something to say, in order that with unreserved speech he may *make known the Gospel*. *The mystery of the Gospel:* the secret, known only by those to whom God reveals it, which belongs to the good news announced by Christ. See under 1 Cor. iii. 4. Cp. Col. iv. 3, 'to speak the mystery of Christ.'

20. *On behalf of which* mystery of the Gospel: i.e. in order to 'make it known.' *I am an ambassador:* same word and sense in 2 Cor. v. 20. It expresses Paul's sense of the dignity of his apostolic office. *In a chain:* strange paradox; (for by all nations ambassadors were held to be inviolate;) and a graphic picture of Paul's present position. The hand which writes or signs this letter is bound by a chain. But since this chain was borne for Christ's sake and by Christ's providential arrangement, it was to Paul an honourable badge of office. Moreover, that Paul was bound, made it more needful that God should give him unrestrained speech. Cp. 2 Tim. ii. 9. *In order that etc.:* ultimate aim of the prayer which Paul requests, supplementing and expounding the purpose given in *v.* 19. *In it:* in 'the mystery of the Gospel.' *I-may-speak-boldly:* cognate to 'boldness' in *v.* 19, keeping before and emphasising the idea of unrestrained speech. *As I must needs speak:* same words in same connection in Col. iv. 3. The imperative need for unrestrained proclamation of the Gospel, together with his own solemn and official relation to it, prompt Paul to ask his readers' prayers that God may give him fit utterance.

This section reveals unmistakeably the hand and thought of Paul. The man who himself prays for every Church to which he writes may well ask his readers' prayer 'for all the saints.' And this request for prayer on his own behalf, attesting as it does his deep sense of the efficacy of prayer, is in close harmony with similar requests in Rom. xv. 30, 2 Cor. i. 11, Col. iv. 3, 1 Th. v. 25, 2 Th. iii. 1; and with Ph. i. 19. The word *ambassador* is one of many proofs of his consciousness of the grandeur of his office: cp. ch. iii. 2, Rom. xv. 15, 16, 2 Cor. iii. 6, xi. 2, xiii. 10.

SECTION XVII.
ABOUT TYCHICUS. FAREWELL.
CH. VI. 21—24.

*But that ye may know the matters touching me, how I am doing, Tychicus, the beloved brother and faithful minister in the Lord, will make known to you all things; *²² whom I have sent to you for this very thing that ye may know the things about us and that he may encourage your hearts.*

²³ Peace to the brethren, and love with faith, from God the Father and the Lord Jesus Christ. ²⁴ Grace be with all who love our Lord Jesus Christ with incorruptness.

21, 22. A close and verbal parallel with Col. iv. 7, 8. *Also ye:* as well as others who are to receive like information. It is a note of genuineness. For from Col. iv. 7 we learn that *Tychicus* was commissioned to carry intelligence and encouragement to others besides those to whom this letter was written. So slight an indication is not like the work of a personator. And such a one would probably have mentioned Onesimus. *Encourage your hearts:* as in Col. iv. 8.

23, 24. *Peace:* inward rest prompting outward harmony, as in ch. i. 2. At the end of an Epistle, only here and Gal. vi. 16. *To the brethren:* noting their close relation to each other and to Paul. This suggests the addition *and love:* i.e. one to another, its usual sense when not otherwise defined. See under 1 Cor. xiii. 1. *With faith:* more fully Gal. v. 6, 'faith working by means of love.' *From God etc.:* source of this inward rest, and of this mutual love associated with faith. For the former compare ch. i. 2; and for the latter 1 Jno. iv. 19, 'we love because He first loved us.' Both *peace* and *love with faith* are a work and gift of *God* and of *Christ*. *Grace with all who love etc.:* a contrast to 1 Cor. xvi. 22. *In incorruptness:* same words in 1 Cor. xv. 42. The absence of decay (so Rom. ii. 7, 2 Tim. i. 10) which will characterize our resurrection bodies must characterize our present love to Christ.

REVIEW OF THE EPISTLE. As usual, Paul's first words, after a Christian greeting, are praise to God. But, in what seems to have been a circular letter to several Churches, his thanks are not for special blessings to his readers but for the blessings conferred on all the people of God. These he traces to their source in a purpose of God in Christ older than the world but now made known to men, viz. His purpose to unite under the rule of Christ both earth and heaven. This purpose embraces not only those who were long waiting for the appearance of Christ but also the Gentile readers of this Epistle who have already received as a seal of their acceptance the Spirit of God promised of old to Israel.

All this, and what he has heard about their faith and faithfulness, move Paul to constant thanks on his readers' behalf. His praise turns imperceptibly into prayer. He prays that God may give to them the Holy Spirit to reveal the things of God and specially to teach how great are the blessings to which He has called them, how rich is the inheritance belonging to the people of God, and how mighty the power at work in those that believe. Of this last Paul gives a measure in the power which raised Christ from the grave and to heaven, above the highest ranks of angels. He adds that God gave Christ, thus exalted, to the Church to be its Head, and the Church to be His body and His fulness.

The assertion that the power which raised Christ from the grave is at work in believers, Paul goes on to prove by saying that, in consequence of their sins which brought them under the anger of God, both his readers and himself were once dead; and that, by saving them through faith, God had raised them from the dead and made them sharers of the throne of Christ. He did this in order to reveal throughout eternity, in His kindness to them, the abundance of His favour to men. This salvation was wrought by the creative power of God, not prompted by any good in man, but designed by God to lead to good works.

Having described salvation as an inward and spiritual change from death to life, Paul goes on to describe it as a changed relation to the covenant-people of God. They who were once far off aliens have, through the death of Christ, been brought near and built into the rising walls of the living temple of God.

In view of all this the Apostle seemed to be approaching God in prayer. But he pauses for a moment to say that to himself and others had been revealed a secret hidden during long ages, viz. God's purpose, mentioned above, to unite Jews and Gentiles into one body, in order thus to reveal to the various ranks of heaven, by this wonderful accomplishment of a divine purpose, His own manifold wisdom. In view of all this, Paul turns solemnly to God in prayer that He may give to his readers spiritual strength, by the indwelling presence of Christ, that thus they may be able to comprehend the incomprehensible love of God, and that thus they may be made full to an extent limited only by the fulness of God. And, while offering this great prayer he remembers that God is able to surpass in fulfilment all prayers and thoughts of men.

From this mount of transfiguration Paul comes down to discuss, in the light of the glory there revealed, matters of practical life. He begs his readers to walk worthy of their divine call ; and specially urges them to do all they can to preserve Christian unity. This last exhortation he supports by pointing to the great spiritual unities on which rest the Christian Church. From unity he passes to the various spiritual gifts with which the triumphant Saviour has enriched His Church in order that it may lay aside the vacillation of childhood and grow into Christian manhood, into a compact and healthy body in which each part helps the well-being and development of the whole. He reminds his readers of the darkness and sin around them, and of the better lesson they have learnt, viz. that in Christ the old life of sin has been laid aside and a new life put on. What is involved in this change, is then expounded in an informal but appropriate series of general precepts. Falsehood, inordinate anger, theft, evil-speaking, and such things must be laid aside : and Christian kindness must take their place. For all sin excludes from the kingdom of God and brings the sinner under the anger of God. His servants must not only avoid, but rebuke, the shameful practices of the heathen. For they are children of the light: and light ever reveals the hidden things of darkness. All this needs wisdom. Instead of the drunken songs of the godless there must be songs of praise to God. And each must loyally accept his place in the social order.

These last words are a stepping-stone to directions about the three most conspicuous social relations. Wives must view their husbands as set over them by Christ, and thus in some sense sharing His authority. And husbands must remember that this authority lays upon them an obligation to imitate Christ's love to, and self-sacrifice for, the Church. Just as the Church is united to Christ as the body to the head, so the ancient record of creation says that husband and wife are one flesh. Consequently, the husband's kindness or unkindness to his wife is kindness or unkindness to himself. In view of this mysterious relation, the husband must love his wife, and the wife reverence her husband. Similar mutual duties, resting upon their relation to Christ, rest upon children and parents, servants and masters.

All that remains is an exhortation to maintain, armed by the might of Christ, an unbroken front in face of the tremendous spiritual enemies arrayed against the Christian. In this inevitable and deadly conflict, God has provided for His servants a complete armament. The truth is their girdle, righteousness their breastplate : and the good news of salvation will fit their feet for the path before them. Faith will preserve them from the darts of the enemy, salvation will enable them to lift up their heads in triumph ; and the word which God has put into their lips will be an effective weapon of attack. The Apostle begs their prayers for all Christians, and for himself that he may be able to proclaim the Gospel as the necessities of the case demand.

All personal matters are left to Tychicus, the bearer of the letter.

The width of view already noted as characterizing the Epistles to the Colossians characterizes also that to the Ephesians. But the one Epistle is by no means a duplicate of the other. The same keen eye looks now, with independent gaze, in a somewhat different direction. And the tone of the letters is different. Forceful argument and appeal against perilous error have given place to the serenity of victory. Again the Apostle's thought ascends the stream of time to its source in eternity ; not as before to search out the origin of the material universe, but to contemplate the salvation of man when salvation was only a deliberate thought in the eternal mind of God. Even the historic distinction of Jew and Gentile, separated for a time that they may be united for ever, is viewed in the light of this eternal purpose. The various ranks of angels are still in sight. They bow to their ascending Lord ; and they will learn from saved and united humanity the many-sided wisdom of God. The conception of the Church receives a marked development. Throughout the Epistle the ideal Church is ever before us, one and manifold, in its relation to the one Spirit and Lord and God, as the permanent realization of the eternal purpose of God, and as the chosen Bride of Christ, purified by Him that she may be His for ever.

Already in other Epistles we have witnessed Paul's approach to God in prayer. But in the Epistle we now close his prayer takes a more sustained and loftier flight. With strong wing he follows, in spiritual elevation, his rising Lord, and with mighty effort endeavours to grasp the infinite love of Christ and to make his own the infinite fulness of God. And on the summit of his lofty flight, raised by the power of God working in him, he seems to join the chorus of the glorified Church in its eternal song.

DISSERTATION I.

THE EPISTLES BEFORE US COMPARED WITH THOSE TO THE ROMANS, CORINTHIANS, AND GALATIANS.

1. In my earlier volumes I have endeavoured to show that the Epistles there annotated were written within a year, amid the active evangelistic toil of Paul's third missionary journey. In Introd. ii. and v. of this volume I have tried to prove that the Epistles just expounded were written by Paul, probably during his first imprisonment at Rome. If these inferences be correct, the two groups of Epistles were separated by a lapse of some years and by a total change of circumstances. We come now to compare the groups, in order to trace in them the effect on the Apostle of this lapse of time and these altered circumstances. Our investigation will also test in some measure the conclusions we have reached about the authorship of the Epistles; thus supplementing the argument of Introd. ii. And it will embody some of the practical gains we have derived from our study of these Epistles.

2. In Ph. i. 1, for the first time in the Epistles of Paul we find definite mention of Church officers; in two orders, *bishops and deacons*. The former title appears in Acts xx. 28 as a description of 'the elders of the Church' at Ephesus, summoned by Paul to Miletus, whom he bids to act as shepherds of the Church. Still earlier, in Acts xv. 2, 4, 6, 22, 23, we find at Jerusalem a body of elders associated with the Apostles in discussing a most important matter of doctrine. And from ch. xiv. 23 we learn that Paul appointed elders in the Churches founded during his first missionary journey. With these passages, Ph. i. 1 is an important coincidence. That in the letters to Corinth which deal specifically with Church matters the bishops are not mentioned, but are mentioned in this later letter, reminds us that as times rolled by the officers of the Church would gain an importance they could not have when officers and members were alike new converts. The word *deacons* reveals a second order

of Church-officers. And in Rom. xvi. 1 a lady is called a deacon of the Church at Kenchæa.

In 2 Cor. i. 8—11, iv. 8—11 we traced the deep impression made upon the heart of the Apostle by a recent and deadly peril. With this we now contrast the serene calm with which in Ph. i. 20—26 he contemplates the uncertain issue of his approaching trial before Nero. In active work, Paul clung to life. But in his dungeon at Rome the prisoner had become familiar with the King of Terrors and had learnt to look upon his face without emotion. The secret of this serene calm we learn in ch. iv. 6, 7, and in *vv.* 11—13. The profound peace which reigns in these passages and throughout this Epistle, brightening here and there into a joy which even the gloom of a prison and the shadow of the gallows cannot dim, belongs to the autumn maturity of the Apostle's inner life. These words of peace are gems of priceless worth.

As in 2 Cor. viii. 9 so in Ph. ii. 5—11, the incarnation of Christ is appealed to as an example for us; as an example in the former case, of generosity, in the latter of unselfishness. But the second exposition of the example of Christ is far richer than the first. We have the pre-incarnate Son *existing in* the *form of God* and *equal to God*, contemplating this equality and refusing to use it for His own gratification. We see Him as *He emptied Himself*, then treading a path of humiliation till it led Him to the *cross;* and raised by God, as a recompense for His obedient self-sacrifice, till the loftiest in heaven bow the knee in worship and proclaim His majesty. This passage, full of dramatic grandeur, is the most complete exposition in the N. T. of the Incarnation of Christ.

The word rendered *I-have-learnt-the-mystery* in ch. iv. 12 links the cognate word *mystery* already used by Paul in 1 Cor. ii. 7, iv. 1, Rom. xvi. 25 with the Greek mysteries; and thus gives to the word as used by him a definite reference which sheds important light upon his conception of the Gospel.

The references to Epaphroditus in Ph. ii. 25-30 and to the gift from Philippi in ch. iv. 10, 18 rescue from oblivion a most beautiful Christian character and a most interesting incident of Christian life in an apostolic Church.

3. In Col. i. 9, 10, more emphasis is put on the value of *knowledge* of God as an element of the Christian life than in the similar prayer in Ph. i. 9, 10. The same thought is prominent in Col. ii. 2, 3, iii. 10, 16. It is a feature of the group of Epistles now before us. As compared with 2 Cor. iv. 4, the fuller term in Col. i. 15, *of the invisible God*, reminds us that an *image* is a presentation of that

which would otherwise be unseen. The accurate term *Firstborn before every creature* is an important addition to the teaching of the N. T. about the Son of God. In Col. i. 16 for the first time Paul traces to the Son the creation of the universe: *through Him and in Him and for Him were all things in heaven and earth created; Himself before all things, and all things held together in Him.* Once stated, this teaching carries conviction by its close harmony with Paul's earlier teaching about the relation of Christ to the work of God. But the explicit statement of what would otherwise be only an inference is of infinite value.

In Col. i. 18, ii. 19 Christ is called *the Head of the Body*, i.e. *of the Church:* a new and most important development of Paul's favourite metaphor. So far was it from his thought at an earlier time that he wrote, in 1 Cor. xii. 21, 'the head cannot say to the feet I have no need of you:' a statement utterly inapplicable to Christ. But it is in complete harmony with the original metaphor; of which indeed it is a logical development. As dwelling in each member, Christ is the lifegiving Spirit of the Body. But as human and corporeal He is also the highest part of it, the supreme and directive part, essential to the life of the whole. This important development of the metaphor was probably suggested to Paul by his study, embodied in this Epistle, of the grandeur of the Son of God and of His relation to the universe and to the Church.

In Col. ii. 13 we have a new and important conception of the state of the unsaved as not merely dying but already *dead by reason of* their *trespasses*, and therefore beyond reach of salvation except by Him who raises the dead. The same thought in germ is found in Rom. vii. 9, 'the Law came to life, but I died;' and in Jno. v. 24, 25. It is completed by the teaching in Col. ii. 13 that forgiveness of trespasses is life to whose who were spiritually dead. The Law as a *handwriting nailed to the cross* of Christ and thus made invalid is in complete accord with Paul's teaching in Rom. vii. 4, 'dead to the Law through the body of Christ.' But the figure is new, and valuable. Already in Rom. viii. 38 Paul has mentioned angels of superior rank. But in Col. i. 16, and in ii. 15, successive ranks of angels come conspicuously into view. And in ch. i. 20 we learn that the purpose of salvation embraces in some sense even the inhabitants of heaven. The references to Epaphras in Col. i. 7, iv. 12 preserve for us the memory of a worthy member of an apostolic Church. The statements in Col. i. 6 and more emphatically in *v.* 23 that the Gospel preached at Colossæ is preached also throughout the world is more suitable to the later, than to the earlier, part of Paul's life.

4. An important gain in the Epistle to the Ephesians is that Paul's teaching about the purpose of predestination in Rom. viii. 28, 29, the purpose of election in ch. ix. 11, and about adoption in ch. viii. 15, Gal. iv. 5 is combined in Eph. i. 4—12 into one profound exposition of a purpose earlier than the world and embracing the universe, a purpose of Him who works all things according to the counsel of His will. This combination gives unity and vast extension to what was before somewhat fragmentary and limited. Very conspicuous is the threefold refrain of praise in Eph. i. 6, 12, 14: a remarkable development of a germ found in Ph. i. 11. Already in Ph. i. 9—11, Col. i. 9—12 Paul has led his readers in prayer to God. But these prayers are left far behind by the mighty intercessions of Eph. i. 16—23, iii. 14—21, in which, pleading for his readers, the Apostle rises step by step to the very throne of God until in the second intercession prayer is lost in a shout of praise. In all ages these great liturgies have been ladders by which the holiest of men have found nearer access to God. A development in the Epistle to the Colossians of an earlier metaphor, viz. Christ *the Head* of His body the Church, receives now a still richer development. In Eph. i. 22, Christ, already Head of the universe, is said to be God's gift to the Church to be its Head. In ch. iv. 15, 16, the Head is the source of the Church's compactness and development, and the goal of its growth: all development uniting the members each to the others and all to Christ. And in ch. v. 23—31 His relation to the Church as its Head is made a pattern for the relation of husband and wife, and the union of the Church with Christ is represented as a vital union of a living body with its head. The metaphor of the Church as the bride of Christ, so richly expounded in this passage, is but an expansion of a germ already found in 2 Cor. xi. 2. Indeed, throughout the Epistle we have valuable developments not only of the teaching of the earlier group, but of that of the Epistle to the Colossians. For example, we have fuller teaching about the superhuman powers of the unseen world. We read in Eph. iii. 10 that God designs even the bright ones of heaven in their various ranks to learn through the Church the manifold wisdom of God. And in chs. ii. 2, vi. 12 we find in conflict with men superhuman and evil powers, acting under direction of one supreme leader. Eph. ii. 3 is in subtle harmony with Rom. v. 12—14. Paul there taught us that through Adam's sin we were born under the dominion of bodily death, i.e. we were by nature doomed to the grave. He now tells his readers that they *were by nature children of wrath, even as the rest*, i.e. as all men. This implies that the actual sins through which (Eph. v. 6) comes the

anger of God are done *by nature*, i.e. in virtue of a condition received at birth. This evil inheritance must have had an evil origin. And this can be no other than the sin of him through whom 'death passed through to all men.' Eph. ii. 3 is thus a most valuable addition to the teaching of the N. T. about the unsaved.

5. Comparing the eight Epistles I have annotated we notice the vivacity and earnestness of the earlier group, and the profound calm, the wider mental vision, and the deeper insight into the nature and purpose of God, of the later group. Each group supplements the other. The orderly exposition of the Gospel in the Epistle to the Romans and the keen defence of its central doctrine, Justification through Faith, in that to the Galatians explain the casual references to faith and to salvation through faith, and to Jews and Gentiles, in the later group. Without this explanation the later Epistles would lack their doctrinal foundation. The glorious ideal of the Church given in the Epistle to the Ephesians rises immensely above anything in the letters to Corinth. But it would not supply the place of the vivid pictures there drawn of actual Church life in the Apostolic Age. All the letters correspond—and the correspondence grows as we examine them—with the circumstances of the writer. In the midst of active evangelical toil Paul gives us in the Epistle to the Romans an account of the Gospel he preached and in that to the Galatians a sample of the arguments with which he defended it to his countrymen. The letters to the Corinthians reflect the actual condition of Churches in which he laboured. The later Epistles give us the mature thought nurtured in the solitude of his imprisonment at Rome. In the letter to Philippi we have an outburst of Christian affection to the purest of the Churches founded by Paul, revealing his inmost spiritual life. That to Colossæ embodies his loftiest thought about the nature and work of his Master. The letter to Ephesus depicts the Church as in the eternal past it presented itself to the loving thought and purpose of Christ; and as it will stand, when the toil and conflict and sorrow of the present life are but a fading dream of the past, in glorious reality before the satisfied eye of Him who loved it and gave Himself for it, the spotless bride of the Eternal Son.

The great and independent worth of each of these Epistles is a complete confirmation of the confident belief of all Churches throughout the world in the second century that they are all from the pen of the greatest of the Apostles.

DISSERTATION II.

PAUL'S CONCEPTION OF THE CHURCH.

1. Already in a note under 1 Cor. i. 9 I have endeavoured to show that in the N. T. the word *church* denotes usually the company of the professed servants of Christ living in one city: e.g. 1 Cor. i. 2, 'the Church of God which is at Corinth;' ch. iv. 17, 'as I teach in every Church;' ch. vii. 17, 'as I give charge in all the Churches.'

We notice also that Paul always assumes that they to whom he writes have already personal spiritual life. Even to the Galatians who were (Gal. i. 6, iv. 9) 'turning away to another Gospel.... to the weak and poor rudiments,' he writes, in ch. iii. 26, 'ye are all sons of God through faith.' And, as sons, they had received (ch. iv. 6) the Spirit of His Son crying in their hearts, Abba, Father. In ch. iii. 2 Paul bases an argument on their inward spiritual experience: 'was it through works of law that ye received the Spirit or through hearing of faith?' The Corinthian Christians, of whom some had once been guilty of gross sin, were now 'justified:' 1 Cor. vi. 11. In them dwells the Spirit of God: ch. iii. 16, vi. 19. This implies real spiritual life; although it was only the infantile life of babes in Christ. The Roman Christians had already been 'justified in His blood ... reconciled to God through the death of His Son;' and this experience was to them the ground of a confident hope that they 'will be saved in His life:' Rom. v. 9, 10. Already they had been grafted into the good olive tree: ch. xi. 17. The only question now is about (*vv.* 20, 22) their continuance in faith. Similarly, the Colossian Christians had been 'rescued from the authority of darkness and translated into the kingdom of the Son of His love:' Col. i. 13. So ch. ii. 13: 'He has made you alive together with Him, having forgiven you all your trespasses.' And Eph. ii. 8, 'By grace ye are saved through faith.' Paul never tries to lead his readers to Christ, but always assumes that already by faith they are united to Him.

Similarly 1 Jno. ii. 12, 'I write to you, little children, because your sins are forgiven you.' In 1 Pet. i. 3 the readers are said to be 'born again ... guarded in the power of God through faith.'

All this does not imply that there were in the Apostolic Churches no false brethren. Any such, Paul leaves charitably out of sight. Nor does it imply that all had attained a lofty spiritual standard

The Corinthian Christians were only babes in Christ. But even babes have life. Paul assumes that his readers are what they profess to be, sincere followers of Christ. And his words imply that it is the privilege of all such to enjoy forgiveness of sins and the indwelling presence of the Spirit of God.

Paul assumes also that all his readers have been baptized. So in Gal. iii. 27 his argument implies that they who are 'sons of God through faith' have been 'baptized for Christ.' An appeal in Rom. vi. 1 is based in *v.* 3 upon the assumed Baptism of the Christians at Rome. Similarly Col. ii. 12. By Baptism the Christians at Corinth had been united to the visible fellowship of the Church of Christ: so 1 Cor. xii. 13, 'all were baptized into one body.' 'To the Church of God at Corinth' the Epistle was written: ch. i. 2. The letters of Paul pourtray throughout men joined to Christ by inward spiritual life and joined to each other in a visible community.

2. Although even in the largest towns the Christian community is always spoken of as one Church, the Christian community in a province is never so called. We read of 'the Church at Corinth' and of 'the Churches of Galatia.' Cp. Rev. i. 4, 'the seven Churches in Asia.' The one apparent exception in the N. T. is Acts ix. 31, 'the Church throughout all Judæa and Galilee and Samaria.' But in 1 Cor. xii. 28 we read that 'God put in the Church first Apostles, secondly prophets, etc.' The word *Church* here can mean only the Church universal. This loftier use of the word receives in the Epistles before us a most important development.

In Col. i. 18, 24 *the Church* is called the body of Christ, the body of which He is Head. In Eph. i. 22, 23, the Risen and Exalted Saviour, who is Head above all things, is said to be God's gift to *the Church.* God designs (ch. iii. 10) that through *the Church* may be known to the successive ranks of angels the manifold wisdom of God. In *the Church* and in Christ Jesus (*v.* 21) throughout all ages will glory be given to God. In ch. v. 23—32 *the Church* is spoken of as the bride of Christ, object of His special love, and united to Him as a living body is united to its head.

This phraseology and the conception of the Church therein embodied are a conspicuous feature of the Epistles now before us and especially of that to the Ephesians. In his busy apostolic toil Paul's thought was occupied chiefly by the actual Churches he had planted and their pressing needs. But in his prison at Rome these Churches are far away. And his mind is at leisure to contemplate the ideal Church as in His eternal purpose it stood before the Eye of God, and as in glorious reality and perfection it will stand for ever before the eyes of God and of angels and of men. Already once to the Corinthians he has spoken about the universal Church. That universal Church is now to him the one great and engrossing object of thought.

Paul's conception of the Church is embodied chiefly in five important metaphors. The Church is the temple of God, the body of Christ, and the bride of Christ. The Kingdom of God is once spoken of as an olive tree. And in a reported address of Paul the Church is called a flock. These metaphors claim now our best attention.

3. In Eph. iv. 11 we read that Christ gave to the Church 'shepherds.' And in Acts xx. 28 Paul bids the elders of the Church at Ephesus to 'shepherd the Church;' and speaks of coming wolves who will not 'spare the flock.' Similarly in Heb. xiii. 20 Christ is 'the great Shepherd of the sheep.' So 1 Pet. ii. 25; and v. 2—4 where elders are bidden to 'shepherd the flock of God' and Christ is called the Chief Shepherd. All this recalls the teaching of Christ in Jno. x. 1—16 about Himself as 'the Good Shepherd' and about the 'one flock and One Shepherd.'

This metaphor reminds us that Christians are living individuals, and teaches that they need the protection of one greater than themselves, and that for protection and well-being God designs them to be associated together. To leave the flock is to leave the Shepherd.

4. In 1 Cor. iii. 19, 16, vi. 19, 2 Cor. vi. 16, Paul calls his readers a building and temple of God, and justifies this title by saying that in them dwells the Spirit of God. Of that temple Christ i the one Foundation. By preaching Christ Paul laid that Foundation in the hearts of the men at Corinth: 1 Cor. iii. 10, 11. Similarly, in Eph. ii. 19—22 we have a foundation laid by the Apostles and Prophets, of which Christ Himself is the Corner-stone, and upon which many buildings are rising into one holy temple, destined to be a dwelling-place of God in the Spirit. A similar metaphor is found in 1 Pet. ii. 4—7, where Christians are called living stones of a spiritual house and Christ the chief Corner-stone. This metaphor may be traced to the lips of Christ in Mt. xvi. 18, 'I will build My Church.' Cp. Mt. xxi. 42, Isa. xxviii. 16, Ps. cxviii. 22.

In a building many stones are united into one immoveable whole, each stone made firm by union with other stones. This metaphor implies that Christ designs His people to be united together in firm and mutually helpful fellowship. Of that temple Christ is the Builder: Mt. xvi. 18. And, as Himself in His humanity a part of His own Church, He is its Foundation and its Corner-stone. Moreover, this building is the dwelling-place of God. So, emphatically,

1 Cor. iii. 16, vi. 19, Eph. ii. 22. Indeed the Hebrew and Aramaic word rendered *temple* denotes a palace, the residence of a king: see under 1 Cor. iii. 16. So, after giving directions about the erection of the tabernacle, God says in Ex. xxix. 45, 'I will dwell among the children of Israel, and will be their God.' The chief thought of every Israelite about the tabernacle was that it was the royal tent of the God of Israel. So, but in an infinitely higher degree, Christ spoke in Jno. ii. 21 'about the temple of His body.' For that sacred human form was in a unique sense the dwelling-place of God in which He manifested Himself to men. And from that temple went up to God the incense of ceaseless devotion. In the same sense but in a lower degree the Church is the temple of God. Of this temple the body born at Bethlehem and now glorified is the Holy of holies. The whole temple will stand for ever, purified and completed, revealing even amid the glories of heaven the infinite grandeur and love of God.

5. In Rom. xi. 16—24 we have an olive tree into which Gentiles have been grafted and from which unbelieving Jews have been broken off. This suggests the continuity of the Kingdom of God in the Old and New Covenants. For the Gentiles were grafted into a tree already growing. And it recalls a similar but more fully developed metaphor from the lips of Christ in Jno. xv. 1—7: 'I am the true Vine . . . ye are the branches.' Cp. Ps. lxxx. 8, Isa. v. 1—7, Jer. ii. 21.

A tree differs from a building in that its progress is an outworking of its own inner life according to the laws of that life. The Church is not a mere structure rising only by additions from without, but a living tree growing and bearing fruit by its own inherent vitality, each twig growing out of an earlier branch and drawing nourishment and growth through other branches from the root. Of this tree, Christ is Himself the Root and Stem.

6. The metaphor of the Church as the body of Christ, so conspicuous in the teaching of Paul, and in the N. T. peculiar to him, has been already expounded, as used in Paul's earlier Epistles, in a note under 1 Cor. xii. 30. It receives in the Epistles before us a new and important development. We find the metaphor in 1 Cor. xii. 12—27, Rom. xii. 4, 5; and in its richer development in Col. i. 18, 24, ii. 19, Eph. i. 23, ii. 16, iv. 12, 16, 25, v. 23, 30.

An animal body differs from a tree in possessing a far greater variety of organs, each endowed with peculiar faculties and all needed for the general good. The use of these faculties gives rise to a varied activity without parallel in plant life. The condition and source of this activity is the inward presence of the mysterious spirit of life, the unseen bond of union and source of harmony to the many members of the body. So in the Church we have a multitude of members, each endowed with capacities peculiar to itself but needful for the good of the whole, and all animated and moved and controlled by the one Spirit of God.

Of this complex living body Christ is, through His Spirit, the life-giving and directing principle. The Church is therefore His Body. Of old He dwelt on earth in a complex human body with its various and variously-endowed members, in order that through human lips He might speak to dying men words of life and might reach out to men sinking into ruin a human hand able to save. So now He dwells on earth in the Church with its various members possessing various capacities all needful for the life and health and growth of the whole, in order that through human lips and hands He may speak to and save the fallen race of man. The Church is thus in some sense a continuation or repetition of the Incarnation.

To this metaphor, so applied, the Epistles before us add an important development. We now learn that Christ is not only the animating Spirit, but also the Head, of the Church. The head is part of the body, consisting as does the rest of flesh and bone. But it is the highest, and immeasurably the noblest, part. As human, Christ is Himself a part of His Church, the Corner-stone of the Temple He is building, and a member of His own Body.

This metaphor is the fullest and richest picture of the Church in the New Testament. And it affords the noblest ideal of the Christian life. In a healthy body every member is active, moved and controlled by one spirit, each member putting forth its powers in harmony with all the others, for the good of the whole. Everything in us contrary to this ideal is spiritual disease tending to death.

7. The metaphor of the body of Christ suggests that the Church is dear to Christ as is a man's own body to himself. This thought is developed in the metaphor of the Bride of Christ. Already, as recorded in Mt. xxii. 2, Christ had spoken of 'a king who made a marriage feast for his son.' In Rev. xix. 9 we read of 'the marriage supper of the Lamb.' And in ch. xxi. 9 the New Jerusalem, the eternal home of redeemed humanity, is called the Lamb's Bride. Similarly in 2 Cor. xi. 2, Paul wishes to present the Church as a pure maiden to Christ. In Eph. v. 22—33 this metaphor is further developed, in conjunction with that of the Body of Christ, and is made a basis of important teaching.

This last metaphor reminds us that the Church is an object of

Christ's tender love and great delight, and that as Queen she will share His throne. When the Bridegroom found her, she was enslaved and polluted. But He loved her, rescued her from bondage, washed her in His own blood, and will clothe her in royal raiment. And it warns us that injury or insult to the Church is done, in the presence of the Bridegroom, to His affianced and much-loved Bride.

8. In Mt. xvi. 18 Christ is recorded to have said in words most solemn at a most important turning point (cp. v. 19) of His teaching: I WILL BUILD MY CHURCH. This implies that to erect a Church, i.e. to gather together a community which should be specially His own, was an essential part of the work He came to do. And this is confirmed by the foregoing metaphors, and by the entire teaching of Paul. For each of these metaphors embodies conspicuously the idea of the union of many members into one organized body, a union needful not only for growth and well-being but for life. From them we learn that Christ designs His servants to be not only inwardly and individually united to Himself but united to each other in outward and visible fellowship; in order that the company of His professed followers may be the earthly home of the people of God, in which by mutual help their spiritual life may be sheltered and nourished and developed, and in order that by their mutual co-operation the Gospel may be carried to the ends of the earth. The Church thus embodies in itself the main results already attained by Christ through the Gospel, and is the living organ for the attainment of further results.

This aim has been to a large degree achieved. In the Churches to which Paul wrote, the Christian life found the home it needed, and found suitable embodiment before the eyes of men. And the forces thus embodied overthrew classic paganism. Even in the darkest ages, the Churches were a visible monument, often fearfully defaced but always recognisable, of the Kingdom of God. They have ever directly or indirectly afforded shelter, often rude and unworthy though valuable, to a vast number of sincere followers of Christ. And to-day, with spiritual power ever increasing, the Churches of Christ, i.e. the people of God associated in visible communities, are the chief agency for carrying out in the world Christ's purpose of mercy to men. They are the Light and the Life of the world. The pulsations of that life are felt everywhere even to heathen lands: and that light is spreading to the ends of the earth.

9. The Epistles I have annotated say very little about the officers

and organization of the Apostolic Churches. This comparative silence reminds us that in a living body every member is endowed with faculties for usefulness. In proportion to the vitality of the whole, the peculiar work of the officers of the Church is less conspicuous. And this would be specially so where all members were alike recent converts.

In 1 Cor. xii. 28, Rom. xii. 6, Eph. iv. 11 we find not only various special endowments but official rank: *apostles, prophets, teachers*. And in Ph. i. 1 a greeting is sent to *bishops and deacons*.

In agreement with these passages, great prominence is given in Mt. x. 2, Mk. iii. 14, Lk. vi. 13 to the Apostles as holding the first rank among the servants of Christ. In the presence of them only Christ ordained the Lord's Supper, and afterwards gave the command to baptize: Mt. xxvi. 20, 26, xxviii. 16—20. In Acts i. 1—13 we find them in close relation to the risen Saviour: and they seem to have been with Him at His ascension. At once they occupy in the infant Church a place of supreme authority: Acts i. 26, ii. 14, 42, vi. 2, 6.

A pressing need suggested, as recorded in Acts vi. 6, the appointment of men to take charge of certain financial matters. They were chosen by the church-members, but were appointed to their work by laying on of the Apostles' hands. That they were not appointed till the need arose, and that no directions about their appointment are recorded as having been given by Christ, marks a conspicuous difference between the New and Old Covenants. It teaches that Christianity is primarily not an organization but a life, and that Christ designed the necessary organization to arise not by verbal prescription but from a felt need under the guidance of His ever-present Spirit.

In Acts xi. 30 we find in authority at Jerusalem a body of *elders*. To them, in association with the Apostles, was submitted by the Church at Antioch an important doctrinal question: ch. xv. 2. The delegates from Antioch were received in open session by the whole Church, in which however the Apostles and elders were conspicuous: *v.* 4. But the doctrinal question was discussed only by the Apostles and elders: *v.* 6. And although their decision was accepted by (*v.* 22) the whole Church, the formal decree came only (*v.* 23) from the Apostles and elders. This proves that in the Church of Jerusalem was a definite order of men to whom, in conjunction with the Apostles, were committed the highest interests of the Church.

From Acts xiv. 23 we learn that Paul appointed *elders* in each of the Churches founded on his first missionary journey. And in ch. xx. 17 we read of the elders of the Church at Ephesus. Of these Paul speaks in *v.* 28 as *bishops*, as shepherds of the Church, and as appointed bishops by the Holy Spirit. In Ph. i. 1 we have two definite orders of officers: *bishops and deacons*. Comparison with Acts xx. 23, 28 assures us that the former is only another title for elders.

In close harmony with Acts xiv. 23, to a Church just founded, from which he had been suddenly torn away, Paul writes (1 Th. v. 12) about those who labour among, and rule over, and admonish, his readers. This implies that, on the founding of the Church, officers were appointed for its spiritual oversight.

Still further light is cast upon the officers of the Apostolic Churches by the Pastoral Epistles. Each of these was accepted with complete confidence as a genuine work of Paul by Irenæus, Clement of Alexandria, and Tertullian, in the latter part of the second century. And the absence of any reference in them to bishops as superior to elders, in conspicuous contrast to the Epistles attributed to Ignatius, is complete proof of their very early date, and is a strong presumption of their genuineness.

In 1 Tim. iii. 1—13 we find stated the qualifications needed by *bishops* and by *deacons*: a close coincidence with Ph. i. 1. Light is cast upon the work of a bishop by Paul's remark in 1 Tim. iii. 5: 'If any one knows not how to rule his own house, how will he care for the Church of God?' In ch. v. 17 we read of elders who 'rule well' and of some 'who labour in word and teaching.' Titus is bidden (Tit. i. 5) to 'appoint elders in every city.' In *v.* 7 the elder is called 'a steward of God,' and must be able to exhort with healthy teaching and to disprove the words of those who contradict.

That there were elders in the various Churches, is assumed in 1 Pet. v. 1—4. They are also called shepherds of the flock of God. Similarly in Heb. xiii. 17 we find 'rulers' who will give account, and whom Christians are bidden to obey.

All this proves beyond doubt that in the Apostolic Churches were men called *elders* or *bishops* who exercised an authority for which they were responsible to God. At Philippi, at Ephesus, and at Jerusalem we find a plurality of men sharing this authority. On the other hand, in the Church at Jerusalem James seems to have held a place of unique honour: see note on *James* under Gal. ii. 21. This slight indication is the only trace in the N. T. of authority in any Church exercised only by one man.

In the Churches thus constituted we find Paul exercising Apostolic authority. Writing to a Church in which discipline had become lax, he asks (1 Cor. iv. 21) whether he is to come 'with a rod,' a conspicuous badge of authority. Touching one notorious offender in the same Church he has already (ch. v. 3) pronounced judgment; and gives what is practically a command to the Church to carry out his decision. In 2 Cor. xiii. 2 he threatens further punishment unless the unfaithful ones repent; and speaks in v. 10 of severe action in accord with the authority given to him by Christ. He forbids (1 Cor. xiv. 34) women to speak in the Churches; and gives (vv. 27—30) directions about the conduct of joint worship. About public contribution (ch. xvi. 1) he gave directions to the Churches of Galatia and to that at Corinth. Other matters needing regulation, he leaves (ch. xi. 34) till his own arrival.

All this proves that Paul did not look on the Churches he founded as independent of external control. He never forgets that in them Christ dwells as the Supreme Lord. But this spiritual presence of Christ by no means makes the Church infallible; and therefore does not render superfluous the guidance and authority of superior human wisdom.

Such then were the Churches founded by Paul; organized communities of professed and real servants of Christ, each governed by its own officers, and all under the direction of the great Apostle. About the other Churches of the Apostolic age, we have no information.

10. Very little is said in the N. T. about the mode of appointment of these church-officers. In Acts xiv. 23 we read that Paul and Barnabas appointed elders in the Churches founded on their first missionary journey. Timothy is said in 1 Tim. iv. 14 to have received a gift by laying on of the hands of the presbytery; and in 2 Tim. i. 6, by the hands of Paul.

In Tit. i. 5, we learn that Paul had charged Titus to appoint elders in each Church in Crete. But the complete silence of the N. T. until this late Epistle about any Church there suggests that Paul is writing to Titus, to whom (e.g. 2 Cor. viii. 6) he had already entrusted other important missions, about the organization of new Churches, committing to him a work which he had himself done (e.g. Acts xiv. 23) in other newly-founded Churches but was unable through lack of time to do in Crete. We have no hint whatever that Titus possessed any abiding prerogative of ordaining elders. To Timothy at Ephesus similar authority seems to have been delegated, as we infer from 1 Tim. i. 3, iii. 14, 15, v. 9—11, 19. But these directions by no means imply that he held a permanent position in the Church there. He and Titus seem rather to have been sent as special commissioners to various Churches. So 1 Cor. iv. 17, 2 Cor. viii. 6, Ellicott speaks of Timothy as "overseer and bishop of the important Church of Ephesus;" but without adducing any proof except the passages noted above. Lightfoot says (*Philippians* p. 197) that "it is the conception of a later age which represents Timothy as bishop of Ephesus and Titus as bishop of Crete. St. Paul's own language implies that the position which they held was temporary."

Still less have we any hint that the elders of the various Churches were unable to appoint others to fill up vacancies or if needful to increase the number of their elders. Of an order of men possessing an exclusive right to ordain elders we find throughout the N. T. no trace. The direction to Timothy in 1 Tim. v. 22, 'Lay hands quickly on no one,' refers probably to reception of new church-members; and therefore has no bearing on the ordination of church-officers. In short, the N. T., while revealing plainly the existence of an order of men to whom were entrusted the most sacred interests of the Church, gives no specific directions about the mode of their appointment.

11. As in the Epistles of Paul so in that of Clement of Rome and in the lately discovered *Teaching of the Apostles* we find only two orders of ordinary church-officers. In marked contrast to all these, the letters attributed to Ignatius reserve the title *bishop* for one man exercising supreme authority in his own Church, with whom are associated a lower order of elders. So *Ep. to Ephesians* ch. iv.: "the presbyter is joined to the bishop as the strings to the harp." This use of the word *bishop* reveals the firm establishment of a higher order in the Churches, one not mentioned in the New Testament. And apparently, as we infer from the large number of bishops in the early Church, there was a bishop in each congregation.

The origin of these congregational bishops is easily explained. The needs and the dangers of the Churches made needful in each Church a single head. Perhaps imperceptibly in each presbytery the ablest man became its virtual leader. The manifest advantage of having a leader would suggest the appointment of a successor when he was removed. And thus the practice would become universal. This explanation is given by Jerome in his commentary on Tit. i. 5, vol. vii. p. 562, ed. Migne. "The Churches were governed by a common council of elders. But after that each one reckoned that those whom he had baptized were his own, not Christ's, throughout the whole world it was decreed that one elected from the elders should be put over the others, to whom should belong the care of the Church." Possibly this monarchical and congregational episcopacy was suggested or stimulated by the removal of the Apostles by death. They were, while they lived, a bond of union to the various Churches under their charge. Their departure would create a new need. And, guided by what to me seems to have been a divine instinct, the various Churches endeavoured to strengthen themselves by concentration of authority in each Church in the hands of one man. Diocesan episcopacy was a further and later development in the same direction.

12. The Churches founded by the Apostles were united by common faith, by loyalty to one Master in heaven, and by common perils. This inward unity naturally expressed itself, with increasing definiteness, in one outward organization. The lineal descendants of the Churches founded by the Apostles held together and held in the main the same doctrines, which last were in substantial agreement with the teaching of the Apostles. Around them grew up in the second century the chaos of Gnostic sects, contradicting each other and rejecting the teaching of the Apostles. The discord outside gave emphasis to the unity within. Thus arose the conception of the Catholic Church, the one lineal descendant of the many Churches founded by the Apostles. This conception found conspicuous and appropriate embodiment in the Ecumenical Councils which after the conversion of Constantine assembled from time to time to formulate the belief, and regulate the discipline, of the universal Church.

This outward and organic unity exists no longer. Instead of One Catholic and Apostolic Church we see to-day many Churches bearing various names and with distinct organizations. The complete difference between past and present is illustrated by the difference between modern Councils and Synods and that which assembled at Nicæa. However some may try to conceal it, the old order has given place to new, the Church of Christ has entered a new stage of its development.

These divisions are an outworking of forces which none could hinder. The German reformers could not and dared not refrain from proclaiming the Gospel which had made them free. And they who accepted it could do no other than unite in Christian fellowship in order to nourish and develop the new life they had found. In so doing they were imitating the example of the early Christians. Their fellowship was necessarily outside the historic Church of Germany. For the officers of that Church with all the ecclesiastical and secular authority at their disposal rejected the teaching of the Reformers and persecuted the teachers. Luther had no thought, at the beginning of his work, of founding a new Church. But the pressing spiritual need of those whom his word, re-echoed from many lips, had saved gave him no alternative. The necessities of the case compelled him and his companions to organize the Christian life springing up around them. Thus arose the Protestant Churches of Germany. And, when once the Christian life had begun to organize itself outside the historic Church, return was impossible. For that Church was unable to supply the spiritual need of the Protestants; and required as a condition of return an assertion as true of that which they believed to be false. Thus in Germany, through influences bad and good which none could hinder, the followers of Christ have been divided into different Christian communions. And this revolt against spiritual despotism has been, I cannot doubt, an immense gain to the nation.

In England political causes gave another direction to the development of the Church. For immoral reasons the monarch thought fit to set aside the spiritual authority of the pope, which for ages the Church in England had recognised; and appointed bishops who supported him in this rejection. Elizabeth at her accession swept clear the bench of bishops, except one bishop who bowed to her will, and appointed others ready to obey her. Under thi violent compulsion the national Church, retaining in some part its ancient forms, was forced along a new path. The result is a Church possessing a sort of lineal continuity with the historic Church of England, yet broken off, under lay compulsion, from the historic Church of the West, with which previously it had been closely connected. And I cannot doubt that this great separation has been an immense gain to England and to th world.

Other inevitable divisions followed. The Act of Uniformity left to a large body of Christian pastors no alternative except to abandon their pastorate or take a solemn oath which they believed to be false. To their lasting honour they refused to be false to the truth and to themselves. We wonder not that multitudes to whom their word had been the word of life still gathered around them begging for spiritual food. That cry they could not refuse. Nor could they refuse to build folds for the sheep of Christ left without shelter. Thus arose the Nonconformist Churches of England.

Similarly, in time of great spiritual torpor, the Wesleys and their companions could not but proclaim the Gospel which had given them peace. Nor could they refuse to the many souls saved by their preaching the spiritual oversight they so greatly needed. Thus arose the Methodist Societies. Wesley had no thought of founding a community outside the Anglican Church; and strongly urged his followers to remain in the ancient fold. But to that Church their spiritual life owed nothing directly: to his ministry they owed everything. In the Anglican Church they could not find the spiritual nourishment they needed. And the spiritual life of many thousands to-day, throughout the world, proves that their separation from the historic Church of England has not separated them from Christ; just as the spiritual life of the Anglican Church proves that separation from the historic Church of the West has not placed it outside the Covenant of God.

Thus an irresistible course of events has led the outward forms of modern Christianity away from the Apostolic ideal.

13. We have various recommendations for restoring to the Church visible and organic unity.

Some would sweep away the historic Christianity of nearly nineteen centuries and begin to re-erect the Church, taking the New Testament as a ground-plan and endeavouring to reproduce exactly the forms of life there pourtrayed. But the growth and experience of the centuries are far too precious to be thus set aside. To the Christian life existing at our birth and before we were born we owe our knowledge of God and our spiritual life. And the outward forms of the Apostolic Churches are as unfit for present needs as are the clothes of childhood to a full-grown man. The Gospel is not a written prescription but a life: and life ever reveals itself in the development of new forms. To ignore the developments of the past, is to throw away the hope of healthy development in the future.

14. Others suggest, as a means of restoring visible unity, that all Christians should join their own communion; that the members of all other Churches should forsake the home in which they have found spiritual life and nourishment and enter the speakers' own Church. Of those who advocate this suggestion, most or all assert that there is and can be only one legitimate visible Church, the lineal descendant of the Churches founded by the Apostles, that to this alone belongs the Covenant of God, and that to this one Church we are bound at all costs to return.

Let us trace this suggestion to its logical and practical results. In Germany, if there is only one legitimate Church, that must be the Roman Catholic Church, the only existing communion there older than the Reformation. Consequently, the assertion before us would compel every German to join that Church. But the Roman Church requires, as a condition of admission, a profession of faith (set forth in the bull of Pius IV., *Injunctum nobis*) which almost all Protestants believe to contain serious error. This belief they cannot surrender till it is disproved. Therefore, in the absence of such disproof, they are compelled to remain outside the one historic Church of Germany. And, if so, their spiritual needs require a church-organization. Even in our own day, inability to accept a new dogma of the Roman Church has compelled many of its most scholarly members to forsake their spiritual birthplace and to organize outside it another communion. If the Old Catholics and Protestants of Germany were right in so doing, there may be in one country more than one legitimate Church.

Not a few Anglicans claim that in England their own is the one and only legitimate Church, on the ground that it is the lineal descendant of the pre-Reformation Church. But, on this ground, it is difficult to deny the legitimacy, even in England, of the Roman Church, which is certainly the lineal descendant in the West of the Churches founded by the Apostles. Nor is it easy to prove that the helpless submission of the Church in England to the violence of Henry and Elizabeth was anything less than a surrender of all ecclesiastical prerogative and monopoly. Strange to say, many who claim that the Anglican Church is the only legitimate Church in England fraternise with the Old Catholics, who have set up and now maintain another organization alongside the historic Church of Germany.

Look where we will, similar perplexity surrounds all claims to ecclesiastical monopoly. No one, making such claims, can say which is the one legitimate Church in Scotland, or Ireland, or America, or Madagascar. All claims to be the one, visible, legitimate Church are disproved by the facts of modern Christendom.

The above claim is sometimes stated in another form, viz. that Christ ordained in His Church a priesthood to be handed down by episcopal ordination to all generations, and that the assured possession of the blessings of the New Covenant is conditioned by the ministration of this priesthood. So Gore, *The Church and the Ministry* p. 71: "But their authority to minister in whatever capacity, their qualifying consecration, was to come from above, in such sense that no ministerial act could be regarded as *valid*—that is, as having the security of the divine covenant about it—unless it was performed under the shelter of a commission, received by the transmission of the original pastoral authority which had been delegated by Christ Himself to His Apostles." The writer is prepared for the logical results of this assertion. So on p. 345 he says: "It follows then—

not that God's grace has not worked, and worked largely, through many an irregular ministry where it was exercised or used in good faith—but that a ministry not episcopally received is invalid, that is to say, falls outside the conditions of covenanted security and cannot justify its existence in terms of the covenant."

For this limitation of the New Covenant we may fairly demand proof. We expect to find it in the Book of the Covenant, i.e. in the New Testament, our only reliable authority for the actual teaching of Christ and His Apostles. Instead of such proof we have in the book just quoted a very scanty and unsatisfactory argument on pp. 70, 71, three proofs on pp. 76—82 "that the existence of an Apostolic succession serves several important ends;" and on pp. 83—111 answers to five objections. But throughout the New Testament, as already seen, we have no reliable trace of anything like Anglican episcopacy. In the many statements of the conditions of salvation, the ministration of an episcopally ordained order of men is never suggested. Faith is the unique condition of salvation: ' He that believes has everlasting life.' As commanded by Christ, Baptism and the Lord's Supper are obligatory. But we have no hint that their validity depends on the episcopal ordination of the ministrant. An Apostle reminds (Gal. iii. 15) some who were leading his converts astray that even to a man's confirmed covenant no one adds further conditions. Who is it that dares to add conditions to the Covenant of God?

It is worthy of note that the limitation just combated would not, if maintained, restore unity to the Church. For in many countries, e.g. England and America, are two or more Churches, each claiming Apostolic succession.

Many practical difficulties forbid the sudden removal of the distinguishing and separating features of our modern Churches. For these are forms in which spiritual life has clothed itself. Now life has needs: and these needs determine its outward forms. Roughly to remove the outward forms would greatly endanger the inward life. In all attempts at union the needs of the spiritual life must be carefully kept in view.

15. Another method of reunion, involving no danger, and fruitful of blessing, is open to us. Let us have ever in view Paul's ideal of One Church and One Lord; and let us work towards it in all practical ways. To do this, is not difficult. For, in spite of its many divisions, the Church is in a very real sense One; and has one interest as it has one life and One Lord. Let us then in the interior working of each denominational Church keep ever in view the

interests of the Church Universal. Let no one try to advance his own Church at the cost of another; and let us embrace every opportunity of asserting the universal brotherhood of the people of God and of helping other Churches. Such co-operation will reveal the essential unity underlying the variety of modern Church life. And it is the best possible way to organic unity. Only through One Spirit can the Churches grow into One Body.

The above suggestion will forbid, as contrary to the ideal, the needless multiplication of separate Churches, or the division of existing Churches except in the very rare cases in which such division is necessary to avoid some greater evil. Such an emergency arose not long ago in Scotland. And I cannot doubt that the Disruption of the Established Church and the formation of the Free Church were an outflow of spiritual life and a great gain to the highest interests of the Kingdom of God. Another emergency was caused by the result of the Vatican Council. But such are very rare. It is our happiness to see Christian thought everywhere tending towards reunion of separated Churches.

It is often said that the divisions of the Church are a great hindrance to Christian work and progress. Certainly the rivalry of contending Churches has done much harm. But, as suggested above, there may be plurality and variety without contention. And the needless multiplication of Churches is undesirable. But the main divisions of the Church have been an immense gain to the Church as a whole. This is well shown in reference to the great separation in England caused by the Act of Uniformity, on p. 610 of Green's *Short History of the English People*. No Church in modern times has prospered spiritually with undivided sway. Again and again rivalry has provoked spiritual activity. Different Churches embody different types of Christian life: and the types thus embodied are a lesson and an enrichment to the whole. This manifest gain reveals the hand of God even in the divisions of the one Church of Christ. These divisions, caused or made needful by man's imperfection and sin, are God's own mode of purifying and perfecting His Church and thus leading it to a higher unity.

The sectional Churches may be compared to the chapels of a great cathedral. If at night we examine one of these by candlelight, it may seem to be an independent structure yet a fit and beautiful place in which to worship God. But when daylight floods the sanctuary, the little chapel is seen to be but a part of a more glorious whole. Its distinctive beauty remains and is more clearly seen. But our chief wonder is evoked by the grandeur of the vast structure of which it forms a part. In the rising Church of God, at present the scaffolding obscures to some eyes the work of others. But already from the workers goes up to God a grand harmony of praise and Christian life. Let us maintain it. Soon the building will be complete, the scaffolding removed, and the one great Temple will appear, the realised conception of the eternal thought of God, radiant in His light, the everlasting and glorious home of the one family of God.

DISSERTATION III.

PAUL'S CONCEPTION OF CHRIST.

1. From the Church we now pass to its Head and Lord. I shall endeavour to reproduce in scanty outline Paul's conception of Christ as portrayed in his Epistles, and then compare it with that of the other writers of the New Testament, in order thus to reproduce the impression actually made by Christ on the most intelligent of His early followers. This will supplement the short sketch given in Diss. i. of my *Romans*.

2. We notice that Paul never compares Christ with other men, even as superior to them. Throughout his letters we have no trace of that sense of human equality which no difference of rank or worth can ever altogether efface. To be Christ's servant or slave, is to Paul a title of honour; and frees him from the need of seeking the favour of men: Rom. i. 1, Ph. i. 1, 1 Cor. vii. 22, Gal. i. 10. Every mention of Christ breathes profound reverence as for one infinitely greater than man and infinitely near to God.

In Rom. i. 3, 4, 9, v. 10, viii. 3, 29, 32, 1 Cor. i. 9, xv. 28, 2 Cor. i. 19, Gal. i. 16, ii. 20, iv. 4, 6, Eph. iv. 13, Col. i. 13, 1 Th. i. 10, Christ is called the Son of God, evidently in a sense implying a unique relation to God. That He who died for us is God's own Son, is appealed to in Rom. viii. 32 as a proof of God's love to man. This suggests the case of a man who gives up his own son to save others, and thus confirms our inference that this title notes a relation different in kind from man's relation to God. The same title is found, in an Epistle closely related to those of Paul, in Heb. i. 2, 5, 8, iii. 6, iv. 14, v. 5, 8, vi. 6, vii. 3, 28, x. 29. And in Heb. iii. 6 Christ as the Son is contrasted with Moses who was but a faithful servant. In Rom. viii. 3 we read that God sent

'His own Son in the likeness of the flesh of sin.' This can refer only to the incarnation of Christ. And it implies that before His birth He was already Son of God; or in other words that before His incarnation He occupied a unique relation to God. Similarly, 2 Cor. viii. 9 and Ph. ii. 6 imply the pre-existence of Him who 'emptied Himself' and 'became poor.'

Col. i. 15—17 asserts that the Son was earlier than the angels and the universe, and Himself created them; that whereas they were created He is 'Earliest-Born;' and that even the angels and the universe were created not only by His agency but for Him.

In Rom. v. 12—19 (cp. 1 Cor. xv. 22) Christ is compared with Adam in his relation to the race. Now Adam's relation is unique. Not only was he the first man but from him sprang all others. That the later-born Son of man holds a relation to the race superior to that of its one human father, reveals His unique and superhuman dignity.

Christ, who made the world, will judge it: 2 Cor. v. 10. And He will at the great day change the bodies of His dead servants into the likeness of His own glorious body.

3. A similar but more definite conception of Christ is embodied in the Gospel and First Epistle of John. In Jno. iii. 31 the Baptist says that whereas he is from the earth Christ is from above, thus asserting a radical difference. Christ calls conspicuous attention to Himself as the Bread of life, the Light of the world, the Good Shepherd, the one Way by which men may come to God, as the Resurrection and the Life: Jno. vi. 35, viii. 12, x. 11, xiv. 6, xi. 25. And, while ever distinguishing Himself from His disciples, He unites Himself with the Father under one personal pronoun: ch. xvii. 21, 22.

Christ calls Himself and is called by John 'the Son of God.' And this title was understood by His enemies to imply equality with God: Jno. v. 18, x. 33. Yet no hint is added suggesting that the inference was incorrect. In Jno. iii. 16, 1 Jno. iv. 9 (cp. Jno. i. 14, 18) we read of 'the Only-begotten Son,' a term asserting conspicuously a relation to God shared by none else. All judgment has been committed to the Son; and at His voice the dead will leave their graves and go forth to just retribution: Jno. v. 22, 29, 30, vi. 39, 40, 44, 54. Christ claims to be earlier than Abraham and the world: Jno. viii. 58, xvii. 5. By His agency was made whatever has been made: ch. i. 3. His own existence is traced to the beginning, without any hint, where we most expect it, that He then began to be: v. 1. In Jno. xx. 28 He accepts from Thomas with evident approval the august title 'My Lord and my God.' In ch. i. 1 we have an explicit assertion that 'the Word was God.' Verse 14 leaves no doubt that 'the Word' is the Person afterwards known to John as his beloved Master. And the usage of the entire New Testament, confirmed by the assertion in v. 3, assures us that the predicate 'God' denotes that in which the Creator differs from His creatures.

In the three Synoptist Gospels we have a type of teaching differing widely from the teaching both of Paul and of John. But this difference only emphasises the one conception of Christ common to all these documents. In Mt. xi. 27 Christ claims that He alone and those taught by Him know God. Again we have the title 'Son of God' as an assertion of unique dignity: Mt. iii. 17, iv. 3, 6, viii. 29, xiv. 33, xvi. 16, xvii. 5. In a parable recorded by all three Synoptists Christ represents Himself as the 'Son' in contrast to all His predecessors who were only 'servants:' especially Mk. xii. 6, 'one beloved son.' Again and again Christ announces Himself as the Judge of the world, with angels as His attendants, thus asserting His superiority to them: e.g. Mt. xiii. 30, 41, xvi. 27, xxv. 31, 32.

To sum up. All the various writers of the New Testament agree to claim for Christ, or to represent Him as claiming for Himself, a relation to God as much above the greatest men of the Old Covenant as the position of the king's son is above that of the noblest and highest of the king's servants. They teach that in the great day, when the best of men will stand guilty before God, Christ will sit on the throne of God and pronounce judgment on all. Even the angels are His servants. Paul and John assert that the carpenter of Nazareth existed before the earliest archangel, the Creator of angels and of the universe. And John gives to Him, and records His acceptance of, the jealously-guarded title, 'God.' Such honour to a contemporary is unique in the history and literature of the world.

4. The above quotations imply a Person distinct from the Father yet sharing with Him those infinite attributes which mark off the Creator from even the greatest of His creatures. For the solemn assertion in Col. i. 16 that the universe was created by the agency of the Son cannot mean that it was created by the Father, or by some special attribute of the Father. Moreover, He who created is immediately afterwards described as the Head of the Church and the Firstborn from the dead, terms evidently revealing a Person distinct from the Father. Nor can Jno. i. 3. For the Word is said in v. 14 to have 'become flesh' and to have dwelt visibly among men. These passages thus differ from Prov. viii. 22—31 where we have no indication of anything beyond a bold personification. The same

personal and eternal distinction is implied in Jno. xvii. 5, 'the glory which I had with Thee before the world was;' and in v. 24, 'Thou lovedst Me before the foundation of the world.' This agreement of writers so different as Paul and John is complete proof that the ablest of the early Christians believed in an eternal Person distinct from the Father.

We notice that the titles 'God' and 'the only God' are often given by Paul to the Father even to distinguish Him from the Son. This is explained by the subordinate relation to the Father which with Paul the Son ever occupies. So 1 Cor. iii. 23, ' Ye are Christ's: and Christ is God's ;' ch. xi. 3, 'Of every man Christ is Head . . . the Head of Christ is God ;' ch. xv. 28, ' Then shall the Son Himself be made subject to Him that subjected all things to Him, that God may be All in all.' Thus even in relation to the Eternal Son the Father is supreme.

This teaching of Paul receives explanation and supplement in other teaching attributed to Christ in the Fourth Gospel, and especially in Jno. v. 19—30, vi. 38, 39. Christ here asserts most plainly that His being is derived from, and His action guided by, the Father; and that His entire activity is unreserved devotion to the Father. And the context forbids us to limit this teaching to the human nature of the Son. Rather the whole picture suggests that, whatever the Son became in time and in visible human form, He already was in His eternal relation to the Father.

While asserting the existence of a divine Person other than the Father, Paul and John speak ever of one God. And this one God is distinctively the Father. So 1 Cor. viii. 6 'One God, the Father ... and one Lord:' and ch. xi. 3, xii. 5, 6. Similarly Jno. xvii. 3, ' The only true God and Jesus Christ whom Thou hast sent.' Yet in Jno. x. 30, xvii. 11, 22 the Father and Son are said to be 'one thing.' [The Greek neuter suggests very clearly unity of nature and relation, not of person. It may be illustrated by 1 Cor. iii. 8, ' He that plants and he that waters are "one thing."'] And this unity of the Father and Son is held up as a pattern for the mutual unity of believers. This suggests that the unity of Father and Son manifests itself in absolute harmony of character and aim. But this harmony is no mere agreement of two persons. It is manifestly an outflow of an essential relation of the Father and Son; especially of the Son's eternal derivation from, and devotion to, the Father. We may conceive each Person of the Godhead as being alone in His own sphere : not three supreme Persons, but One, viz. the Father; not three Lords in the Church, but One, our Lord Jesus Christ; not three animating principles guiding men from within, but One, viz. the Holy Spirit, Himself a divine Person distinct from the Father and the Son, bearer of the presence and activity of the Father and the Son. Consequently, in our dealings with these three divine Persons we have to do with only One God.

The above conception of God, although profoundly mysterious, is yet intelligible. And it is involved in the actual words of Paul and John and in Mat. xxviii. 19. To the thought and faith of the writers of the N. T. were present three distinct Persons existing from eternity in closest relation and in mutual intercourse and love: the Father supreme, existing and being what He is because He wills so to be and for no other reason, eternal and underived; the Son sharing to the full all that the Father has and is except only His Fatherhood i.e. His underived and absolute supremacy, being such as He is because the Father wills Him so to be; and the Spirit possessing all the attributes derived by the Son from the Father and going forth from the Father and the Son to be in the servants of God the divine source of a life of unreserved devotion to God. That this conception of God was actually held by the foremost of the immediate followers of Christ and was by them attributed to Christ, the Christian documents compel us to believe.

5. Not very much is said by Paul about the incarnation of the Son of God. But it is plainly referred to in 2 Cor. viii. 9, 'Because of you He became poor, though He was rich, that ye by His poverty might become rich.' For only in reference to the abundance of His divine prerogatives could the Son be spoken of as rich. And this divine wealth is the only counterpart of the wealth with which Christ will enrich His people. This passage, therefore, asserts that at His incarnation the Son laid aside something which He previously possessed. The same is asserted in Ph. ii. 7, ' He emptied Himself,' under which passage I have ventured to suggest that for a time and for our salvation the Eternal Son, by a definite act, gave up the full exercise of His divine powers. This suggestion is in harmony with the above passages; and with the teaching that the miracles of Christ were wrought in the strength of the Spirit of God, that He knew not the day of His return, and that the Word not only put on flesh but ' became flesh.'

6. Paul's teaching about the death of Christ has been expounded on pages 224—228 of my *Galatians*. But very remarkable teaching, peculiar to Paul, about the relation of Christ to our salvation now demands careful attention.

Christ is constantly said to be the means or Agent, as of creation, so of our salvation. We are 'justified *through* the redemption which is in Christ,' and 'reconciled to God through the death of His Son:' Rom. iii. 24, v. 10. And our salvation is *in* Him, and He dwells *in* us. So Eph. i. 3, 4, 'who has blessed us with all spiritual blessing in Christ, according as He has chosen us in Him;' and ch. ii. 13, 'In Christ Jesus ye . . . have been made near,' and elsewhere frequently. In ch. iii. 17 we read, 'that Christ may dwell in your hearts;' in Gal. ii. 20, 'Christ lives in me.' This language implies that Christ is both the encompassing element in which His people live and move and are safe and an animating principle moving them from within. The new life is also a sharing *with* Christ all that He has and is. So Rom. viii. 17, 'fellow-heirs with Christ;' and Eph. ii. 5, 'risen and enthroned with Him.' This being so, Christ is the pattern of the new life and of our future glory. So Rom. vi. 11, 'in *like* manner (as Christ died to sin) reckon yourselves also to be dead to sin and living for God;' ch. viii. 29, 'predestined to be conformed to the image of His Son;' Ph. iii. 21, 'conformed to the body of His glory.' Lastly, Christ is the aim and goal, as of creation, so of the new life. So 2 Cor. v. 15, 'He died that they who live may live *for* Him.' And Col. i. 16, 'all things have been created through Him and *for* Him.' In short, the new life is through Him, and in Him, and with Him, and like Him, and for Him. This remarkable teaching runs through the Epistles of Paul.

That the new life is *in* Christ, is almost as conspicuous with John as with Paul; but in the peculiar phrase 'abide in Him.' And this phrase is traced to the lips of Christ. So Jno. vi. 56, xv. 1—7, xvii. 21, 23, 1 Jno. ii. 5, 6, etc. This remarkable expression and the teaching underlying it are a conspicuous element in the two chief writers of the New Testament.

Equally conspicuous, and peculiar to Paul, is his teaching that the great closing events of the life of Christ are reproduced in His people. And this in two ways. In Rom. vi. 2—11, Gal. ii. 19, 20, vi. 14, Col. ii. 12, 20, iii. 1, 3 believers are said to be dead with Christ to sin, to the Law, to the world; buried with Him, and risen with Him. This can only mean that through the death of Christ they have escaped from the penalty and bondage of sin, from the curse pronounced by the Law, and from the despotism of the present world; and that their new life is a result of His resurrection. On the other hand, in Col. ii. 13 and Eph. ii. 1—6 they are said to have been at one time dead by reason of their sins but now made alive and risen and enthroned with Christ. This phraseology teaches the utter and hopeless ruin of sinners; and teaches that through the life which entered into the dead body of Christ a new life has entered into those who believe in Him.

This conspicuous and peculiar teaching of Paul has no parallel in the literature of the world. And it reveals the deep impression made upon him by the death and resurrection of Christ. Evidently, he believed that in some special sense our salvation comes through Christ's death upon the cross, that He who died had in very truth risen from the dead, that of His resurrection our new life is a result, and that our life is a sharing of His life and is conditioned by inward union with Him. No one could speak thus in reference to a man. Every line of Paul's teaching about Christ assumes His divinity.

The foregoing exposition of doctrine has historic worth. For the Christian documents prove that the early followers of Christ, the men who gained for Him the homage of all succeeding ages, agreed in a belief that their Master occupies a relation to God different in kind from, and higher than, that of even the loftiest and earliest creatures. And, as we have seen, this conception of Christ involves a new conception of God, a conception unknown to the speculations of heathen philosophy and to the definite teaching of the Old Testament. This new conception survived the chaos of Gnostic teaching so prevalent in the second century: it was formulated in the fourth century in the Nicene Creed, the great historic creed of the Church of Christ: and in all ages it has been held firmly by an overwhelming majority of the followers of Christ. With scarcely an exception those who during the last eighteen centuries have done most for the highest welfare of men have held firmly the remarkable belief about Christ which we have now traced to the unanimous agreement of His earliest followers.

Whence came this new and strange and persistent belief about Christ and about God? Certainly not from contemporary thought, Jewish or Gentile. For contemporary literature, even the writings of Philo, contains nothing which has more than a slight outward resemblance to it. Its source must be sought elsewhere.

We have only one alternative. Either the conception before us came actually from the lips of Christ, or we are compelled to believe that His earliest disciples, the chief agents of a spiritual revolution which has changed and saved the world, made for Him a claim which He would Himself have rejected with horror as awful blasphemy, and set forth most serious error about the nature of God. This latter suggestion is absurd. We are therefore compelled to believe that Christ actually claimed to be the Eternal Son of God. Thus the Christian documents contain, apart from any special authority of Holy Scripture, complete historical proof that Christ actually claimed the august dignity given to Him by the writers of the New Testament. And the moral grandeur of the picture of Christ therein pourtrayed, together with the effect of Christianity upon the world, forbid the thought that the Great Teacher was Himself in serious error, or knowingly taught error, touching His own relation to God.

Decisive as is this argument, it is by no means the whole historical proof of the divinity of Christ. For the homage paid to Him by Paul and his companions can be traced to their confident belief that their Master had risen from the dead. If this belief was false, His disciples were in error not only about His nature but about a matter of fact said to have taken place in their own day and in the city in which the Gospel gained its first great victories. The unlikeliness of this supposition, I have already in my *Credentials of the Gospel* endeavoured to show. Our only alternative is to believe either that a complicated tissue of delusions without parallel among the errors of mankind has saved the world or to believe that with God in eternity is One who shares to the full, by derivation from Him, and with unreserved devotion to Him, whatever He has and is, the Eternal Son of an Eternal Father. Difficult as is this latter belief, it is much less difficult than the historic impossibilities involved in its denial. We therefore accept it with confidence and with adoring gratitude as an assured result of our study of the writings of Paul compared with the rest of the New Testament and read in the light of the present state and the past history of the world.

DISSERTATION IV.

THE GOSPEL OF PAUL.

1. In Diss. i. of my *Commentary on Romans* I endeavoured to show that that Epistle was a systematic exposition of the Gospel as Paul understood it, comprising five great doctrines, viz. (1) That God accepts as righteous all who believe the Gospel, this doctrine being put prominently forward as the foundation-stone of the teaching of Paul; and (2) That this salvation comes to us through the death of the Son of God: also (3) That God designed us to be, by union with Christ, sharers of the life of Christ, a life devoted to God;

and (4) That this design is realised in each one through faith and in proportion to his faith, (5) Through the agency of the Holy Spirit. In other words, we have here Justification through faith, and through the death of Christ; Sanctification in Christ, through faith, and through the Holy Spirit. I also tried to show that the confidence with which Paul asserted these doctrines, taken in connection with the deep underlying harmony between them and the teaching of the other very dissimilar documents of the New Testament, affords complete historical proof that each of these doctrines was actually taught by Christ. We will now look at them again for a moment in the light cast upon them by the Epistles annotated in this volume; and thus supplement the notes on these several doctrines under Rom. iii. 22, 26, vi. 10, 11, viii. 4, 39.

2. A remarkable re-echo of Rom. i. 17, iii. 21, 22 is found in Ph. iii. 9, 'not having a righteousness of my own, that which is from law, but that which is through faith of Christ, the righteousness from God on the condition of faith.' We have here Paul's foundation doctrine of Justification through Faith expressed in his favourite phraseology. That faith is a condition of salvation, is implied in Ph. i. 27, 'contend together for the faith of the Gospel;' and in v. 29, 'to you it is given not only to believe in Him but also to suffer on His behalf.' Paul had heard of the 'faith' of the Colossian Christians: Col. i. 4. A present and conscious salvation, which is involved in the doctrine of Justification through Faith, is implied in Col. i. 13, 14: 'who rescued us out of the authority of darkness and translated us into the Kingdom of the Son of His love, in whom we have redemption, the forgiveness of our sins.' Similarly, v. 21, 'you who were formerly alienated and enemies in your mind in wicked works, now He has reconciled.' Salvation through Faith is plainly stated in ch. ii. 12, 'in whom ye were also raised through faith in the working of God who raised Him from the dead;' and a present salvation in v. 13, 'having forgiven us all our trespasses.' Assured salvation speaks again in Eph. i. 7, 'in whom we have redemption through His blood, the forgiveness of our trespasses;' and in ch. ii. 8, 'by grace ye are saved through faith.' Faith as a condition of salvation is implied also in ch. i. 13, 'having believed, ye were sealed with the Holy Spirit;' and in v. 19, 'the exceeding greatness of His power towards you that believe.' These incidental and unexpected references to faith as a condition and means of salvation are in remarkable agreement with the unique place given to faith in the Epistles to the Romans and Galatians. And the mention of forgiveness of sins in Col. i. 14, ii. 13, Eph. i. 7 is a close coincidence with

Acts xiii. 38, 39, where in a recorded address of Paul the same words are used as an equivalent to Justification through Faith.

Under Rom. iii. 22 and in Dissertations iv.—vi. of my *Galatians* I have shown that this last doctrine, expressed however in phraseology very different from that of Paul, underlies or is in close agreement with all the various types of teaching found in the New Testament, in a manner which affords complete historical proof that it came from the lips of Christ.

3. The second great doctrine of Paul, viz. that salvation comes to us through the death of Christ, that for this end He died, and that the need for this costly means of salvation lay in our sins looked upon in the light of the justice of God, finds abundant expression in the Epistles now before us. It explains Ph. iii. 10, 'fellowship of His suffering, being conformed to His death.' It is plainly stated in Col. i. 22, 'now He has reconciled us in the body of His flesh through death;' and is suggested by *v.* 24, 'the sufferings of Christ . . . on behalf of His body, the Church.' The same doctrine finds conspicuous and remarkable expression in Col. ii. 14, 'having blotted out the handwriting against us by the decrees; and He took it out of the way, having nailed it to the cross.' These words imply clearly that the death of Christ removed an obstacle to salvation which had its root in the Law. Still more clear is Eph. i. 7, 'in whom we have redemption through His blood, the forgiveness of our trespasses;' also ch. ii. 13, 'ye who formerly were far off became near in the blood of Christ;' and *v.* 16, 'that He might reconcile both in one body to God through the cross, having slain the enmity thereby.'

These quotations may supplement my note under Rom. iii. 26, and Diss. vii. of my *Galatians*, where I have shown that the same doctrine in almost the same words runs through the New Testament. And from the Apostles' days to our own day it has been firmly believed by almost all Christians. This remarkable agreement in so remarkable a doctrine points to a common source. And this can be no other than the Great Teacher whom all Christians worship.

4. That God designs all who are justified through faith to live a new life of unreserved loyalty to Himself like the loyalty of Christ, is plainly taught in Ph. i. 20, 21, ii. 5—8, Col. i. 22, ii. 6, 7, iii. 10—15, Eph. i. 4, ii. 10, iv. 20—24, v. 1, 2, 27; and is implied throughout these Epistles. That this new life is conditioned by faith, we read in Ph. i. 25, 29, Col. ii. 7, Eph. i. 19, iii. 17; and that the Spirit of God is its immediate superhuman source, in Ph. iii. 3, Col. i. 8, Eph. i. 13, 17, ii. 22, iii. 16, iv. 30. These three doctrines I have further expounded under Rom. vi. 10, 11, viii. 4.

5. We have now, by consecutive study of most of his Epistles, reproduced in outline the Gospel as Paul understood and preached it. And so clearly marked are its main features that we cannot doubt the substantial correctness of the picture. This Gospel, thus reproduced, we have at various points compared with the teaching of other documents of the New Testament. And our comparison, scanty though it has been, has revealed to us a substantial harmony underlying these various types of teaching. This harmony is an historical fact of the utmost importance; and demands explanation. Its importance is increased by the universal reception of these doctrines, almost unknown as they were before the time of Christ, wherever there are Christians; and by the effect of Christianity upon the world, as attested by comparison of Christian and non-Christian nations.

The facts just adduced greatly strengthen the argument at the close of Diss. iii. For this Gospel and the unique and superhuman dignity of Christ must stand or fall together. Practically, all who accept or reject the one accept or reject the other. Consequently, either these doctrines are true and Christ is the Eternal Son of God or all His early followers whose writings have come down to us have utterly misrepresented both the Teacher and His teaching and have buried them under a thick tissue of most serious error. Yet these men have rescued their Master's name from comparative oblivion, have gained for Him the homage of the world, and have initiated a movement which has turned back from the ruin to which it was hastening the entire current of human history and has saved the world. Results so glorious are not born of error. And if not, the Gospel preached and expounded by Paul is indeed good news from God.

Such are the results, up to this point, of our study of the Epistles of Paul. We have found in them a full and harmonious account of his teaching, and of his conception of the dignity of the Great Master from whom he learnt it. This religious teaching and this conception of Christ we have compared with the other documents preserved for us in the New Testament. And this comparison, viewed in the light of the effect of Christianity upon the world, has convinced us that Paul rightly interpreted the teaching and the claims of Christ, and has convinced us that His teaching is true and His claims just. Thus Paul has led us to Christ; and in Christ we have found Eternal Life.

The only Epistles of Paul not yet annotated by me are two short letters, the earliest extant, written on his second missionary journey to the lately founded Church at Thessalonica, and three short letters to two of his most valued companions, written apparently after liberation from his first imprisonment at Rome. Of these, the former group contains the fullest account we have of Paul's teaching about the Second Coming of Christ, and the latter our most complete picture of the organization of the Churches founded by the Apostles. But they do not in any way modify the results we have derived from the Epistles already annotated.

Printed by Hazell, Watson, & Viney, Ld., London and Aylesbury.

www.ingramcontent.com/pod-product-compliance
Lightning Source LLC
Chambersburg PA
CBHW030546300426
44111CB00009B/874